D1616381

Register Your Book

at www.phptr.com/ibmregister/

Upon registration, we will send you electronic sample chapters from two of our popular IBM Press books. In addition, you will be automatically entered into a monthly drawing for a free IBM Press book.

Registration also entitles you to:

- Notices and reminders about author appearances, conferences, and online chats with special guests

- Access to supplemental material that may be available

- Advance notice of forthcoming editions

- Related book recommendations

- Information about special contests and promotions throughout the year

- Chapter excerpts and supplements of forthcoming books

Contact us

If you are interested in writing a book or reviewing manuscripts prior to publication, please write to us at:

Editorial Director, IBM Press
c/o Pearson Education
One Lake Street
Upper Saddle River, New Jersey 07458

e-mail: IBMPress@pearsoned.com

Visit us on the Web: www.phptr.com/ibmpress/

Performance Tuning for Linux® Servers

ON DEMAND COMPUTING BOOKS

Business Intelligence for the Enterprise
Biere

On Demand Computing
Fellenstein

Grid Computing
Joseph and Fellenstein

Autonomic Computing
Murch

RATIONAL

*Software Configuration Management Strategies
and IBM Rational ClearCase®, Second Edition*
Bellagio and Milligan

WEBSPHERE BOOKS

IBM® WebSphere®
Barcia, Hines, Alcott, and Botzum

*IBM® WebSphere® Application Server for
Distributed Platforms and z/OS®*
Black, Everett, Draeger, Miller, Iyer, McGuinnes,
Patel, Herescu, Gissel, Betancourt, Casile, Tang,
and Beaubien

*Enterprise Java™ Programming with IBM®
WebSphere®, Second Edition*
Brown, Craig, Hester, Pitt, Stinehour, Weitzel,
Amsden, Jakab, and Berg

IBM® WebSphere® and Lotus
Lamb, Laskey, and Indurkhya

IBM® WebSphere® System Administration
Williamson, Chan, Cundiff, Lauzon, and Mitchell

*Enterprise Messaging Using JMS and IBM®
WebSphere®*
Yusuf

MORE BOOKS FROM IBM PRESS

*Developing Quality Technical Information,
Second Edition*
Hargis, Carey, Hernandez, Hughes, Longo,
Rouiller, and Wilde

AS/400, Second Edition
Lin and Gayla

*Building Applications with the Linux Standard
Base*
Linux Standard Base Team

An Introduction to IMS™
Meltz, Long, Harrington, Hain, and Nicholls

Search Engine Marketing, Inc.
Moran and Hunt

Inescapable Data
Stakutis and Webster

DB2® BOOKS

*DB2® Universal Database V8 for Linux, UNIX,
and Windows Database Administration
Certification Guide, Fifth Edition*
Baklarz and Wong

Understanding DB2®
Chong, Liu, Qi, and Snow

Integrated Solutions with DB2®
Cutlip and Medicke

High Availability Guide for DB2®
Eaton and Cialini

*DB2® Universal Database V8 Handbook for
Windows, UNIX, and Linux*
Gunning

DB2® SQL PL, Second Edition
Janmohamed, Liu, Bradstock, Chong, Gao,
McArthur, and Yip

*DB2® Universal Database for OS/390 V7.1
Application Certification Guide*
Lawson

*DB2® for z/OS® Version 8 DBA Certification
Guide*
Lawson

*DB2® Universal Database V8 Application
Development Certification Guide, Second
Edition*
Martineau, Sanyal, Gashyna, and Kyprianou

*DB2® Universal Database V8.1 Certification
Exam 700 Study Guide*
Sanders

*DB2® Universal Database V8.1 Certification
Exam 703 Study Guide*
Sanders

*DB2® Universal Database V8.1 Certification
Exams 701 and 706 Study Guide*
Sanders

DB2® Universal Database for OS/390
Sloan and Hernandez

*The Official Introduction to DB2® for z/OS®,
Second Edition*
Sloan

*Advanced DBA Certification Guide and
Reference for DB2® Universal Database v8 for
Linux, UNIX, and Windows*
Snow and Phan

DB2® Express
Yip, Cheung, Gartner, Liu, and O'Connell

*DB2® SQL Procedure Language for Linux,
UNIX and Windows*
Yip

DB2® Version 8
Zikopoulos, Baklarz, deRoos, and Melnyk

Performance Tuning
for Linux® Servers

Linux

Edited by Sandra K. Johnson, Ph.D,

Gerrit Huizenga, and Badari Pulavarty

IBM Press
Pearson plc
Upper Saddle River, NJ • Boston • Indianapolis • San Francisco
New York • Toronto • Montreal • London • Munich • Paris • Madrid
Capetown • Sydney • Tokyo • Singapore • Mexico City
www.phptr.com/ibmpress

Note to U. S. Government Users: Documentation related to restricted right. Use, duplication, or disclosure is subject to restrictions set forth in GSA ADP Schedule Contract with IBM Corporation.
IBM Press Program Manager: Tara Woodman, Ellice Uffer
IBM Press Consulting Editor: Rich Ferri

Cover design: IBM Corporation
Published by Pearson plc
Publishing as IBM Press

Library of Congress Catalog Number: 2005920043

IBM Press offers excellent discounts on this book when ordered in quantity for bulk purchases or special sales, which may include electronic versions and/or custom covers and content particular to your business, training goals, marketing focus, and branding interests. For more information, please contact:

U. S. Corporate and Government Sales
1-800-382-3419
corpsales@pearsontechgroup.com.

For sales outside the U. S., please contact:
International Sales
international@pearsoned.com.

ISBN 0-13-144753-X
Text printed in the United States on recycled paper at RR Donnelley in Crawfordsville, IN.
First printing, May 2005

Contents

CHAPTER 6   BENCHMARKS AS AN AID TO UNDERSTANDING WORKLOAD PERFORMANCE   131

Part III: System Tuning   171

CHAPTER 7   SYSTEM PERFORMANCE PRINCIPLES AND STRATEGY: A BENCHMARKING METHODOLOGY CASE STUDY   173

CHAPTER 8   SCHEDULER TUNING   187

CHAPTER 12   **NETWORK TUNING   277**

CHAPTER 13   **INTERPROCESS COMMUNICATION   289**

CHAPTER 14   **CODE TUNING   301**

Part IV: Performance Characterization of Linux Server Applications   329

CHAPTER 15   WEB SERVERS   331

CHAPTER 16   FILE AND PRINT SERVERS   343

CHAPTER 17   DATABASE SERVERS   361

Preface

The Linux (open source) operating system has benefited from a foundation of less expensive hardware, stability, and technical developments. The most popular use of Linux is as a web server. Today, it is doing a host of corporate services such as email, firewall, proxy, gateway, database, applications, file server, printing, and more. Linux is now poised to become a competitive operating system on the higher-end servers of the enterprise world. Major Wall Street firms, movie production companies, and many other businesses are now turning to Linux for their enterprise server needs.

As more servers are being deployed, their performance becomes a critical factor in the efficiency of the overall system and affects all users. Although replacing the entire server with a newer and faster one may be an alternative, it is often more appropriate to only replace or add to those components that need it, leaving the rest alone. Often, poor performance is due to bottlenecks in individual hardware subsystems, an incorrectly configured operating system, or a poorly tuned application.

The keys to improving performance are to understand what hardware and software configuration options are available, understand the performance tools and how to use them, and then analyze the results obtained from the tools so suitable changes can be made to positively affect the server.

This book provides the basic knowledge and skills needed to understand and improve the performance of Linux servers. It consists of several chapters written by Linux practitioners and, based upon their collective practical experience, describes the Linux performance monitoring, evaluation and measurement, analysis, and tuning of Linux servers. Also included is a discussion of the methodologies for improving and maximizing the performance of business server applications running on an Intel-based hardware platform and the Linux operating system.

The book uses the simple and progressive approach to performance tuning. It starts with a discussion on the Linux kernel followed by Linux servers, performance tools, and tuning techniques. It then takes the reader into the performance characterization of

Linux servers followed by tuning examples that can be adapted for use in various situations.

The book focuses on two Linux distributions for illustration purpose: Red Hat Enterprise Linux and Novel SUSE Linux Enterprise Server. In addition, the Intel-based platform is assumed as the base server hardware. This is mainly the result of its popularity in the Linux community. The performance tuning of Linux servers on other platforms can be easily adapted. The server applications include web server, file and print server, database server, network management server, and web application server. The discussions and examples used in this book are based upon the Linux 2.4, 2.5, and 2.6 kernels.

The book consists of five parts: "Linux Overview," "Performance Analysis Tools," "System Tuning," "Performance Characterization of Linux Server Applications," and "Tuning Case Studies."

- Part 1, "Linux Overview," provides an overview of Linux installation, and the Linux kernel and server architectures.

- Part 2, "Performance Analysis Tools," provides a detailed review of performance tools in three areas: system performance and monitoring, system trace, and benchmarking.

- Part 3, "System Tuning," discusses performance tuning principles and strategy, as well as scheduler, memory, I/O, file system, and network and code tuning.

- Part 4, "Performance Characterization of Linux Server Applications," describes the performance characteristics of server applications, including factors that might affect their performance. It includes discussions on web, file, database, and application servers.

- Part 5, "Tuning Case Studies," provides several examples of how to integrate all the work in the previous sections to undertake a tuning project with different scenarios. Included are case studies on scheduling, I/O, file system, and network and commercial workload tuning.

- The book also includes an appendix which discusses many of the kernel tunable parameters and explains how to use the sysctl, /proc, and sysfs interfaces to tune the Linux kernel.

Acknowledgments

This book is dedicated to the many developers, system administrators, and others who have spent countless hours addressing Linux performance analysis and tuning issues on a regular basis.

The book has been a work in progress for several months, and I am indebted to many people for helping to make it happen. It started with a visionary idea of writing a book on Linux performance in fall 2002 with Bill Hartner, Duc Vianney, Peter Wong, and I brainstorming various "what-if" scenarios regarding various Linux performance publications. This idea quickly turned into a reality a couple of weeks later when Bill was contacted by Mark Taub at Prentice Hall with the suggestion of writing a book on Linux performance. Special thanks to Bill, Duc, and Peter for their brainstorming suggestions during that initial meeting. Thanks also to Mark Taub for the initial contact, which transformed our ideas into a working reality.

It has been an eventful journey in getting authors, additional authors, and editors working on this effort. I am indebted to all of the chapter authors for their dedication and perseverance in working on this project. Special thanks to the associate editors, Gerrit Huizenga and Badari Pulavarty, for their tireless efforts in working on this project through its many changes. I am forever indebted to Christine Lorenz, our technical writer, for going above and beyond the call of duty in working on the edits, interacting regularly with the authors, editors, and publisher, and practicing overall project management for this work. Through all of the challenges of working with many different individuals, Chris has exhibited the epitome of fortitude. Finally, many thanks to my mentor, Joan Mitchell, for sharing with me her words of wisdom and experience as I labored through this process.

Dr. Sandra K. Johnson

About the Editors

Dr. Sandra K. Johnson is a senior technical staff member with more than 16 years of experience. She has worked in several areas including workload characterization and the performance analysis of cache coherence protocols, memory subsystems, parallel I/O subsystems, Java servers, and Linux. She was the Linux Performance Architect in the IBM Linux Technology Center, and is currently the Chief Technology Officer for Global Small and Medium Businesses for IBM's Systems and Technology Group.

Gerrit Huizenga is a software engineer and architect for Linux Base Technologies in IBM's Linux Technology Center in Beaverton, Oregon. Gerrit has been architecting, designing, and implementing operating system capabilities with a focus on performance, scalability, standards, and security for 20 years. Prior to his work at the IBM Linux Technology Center, Gerrit was the Chief Technologist for Operating Systems at Sequent Computer Systems, Inc.

Badari Pulavarty is a senior engineer at IBM in Beaverton, Oregon. Badari has 15 years of experience developing UNIX operating systems. His main interests are Linux performance issues on VM, I/O, file systems, and storage subsystems.

About the Contributors

Vaijayanthimala Anand is a senior software engineer with several years of network protocol/driver development and architecture experience. She has been working on Linux kernel performance for the past three years. She holds an MS in Computer Science from the University of Houston.

Steve Best works at the IBM Linux Technology Center in Austin, Texas. He is currently working on the Journaled File System (JFS) for Linux project. Steve has done extensive work in operating system development, with a focus in the areas of file systems, internationalization, and security.

Dr. Edward G. Bradford is a senior engineer. Ed has more than 15 years of experience developing and managing the development of UNIX operating systems. He now works on Linux performance issues in comparison to other platforms.

Mark Brown has more than 20 years of UNIX and Linux experience, including service on the GNU C Library Steering Committee. He specializes in operating system API and ABI specification, and C runtime library issues.

Mingming Cao is a Linux kernel developer at the IBM Linux Technology Center in Beaverton, Oregon. Her areas of interest include interprocess communication, file systems, and I/O.

Ruth Forester is a performance engineer at the IBM Linux Technology Center in Beaverton, Oregon. She has been involved in UNIX and database performance for 15 years for both end users and systems design. She participated in the development of the TPCD and served on the TPC for seven years. She has done work in applications performance as well as performance impacts on L1-L2-L3 caches.

Steven French is a senior engineer at the IBM Linux Technology Center responsible for Linux files system design and has more than 15 years of experience designing and implementing network software. He is the author of the CIFS file system in the Linux kernel, a member of the Samba team, and chair of the CIFS working group within the Storage Networking Industry Association.

Dominique Heger focuses on operating systems performance, performance modeling, algorithms and data structures, and I/O scalability. He has worked for IBM, Hewlett-Packard, and Unisys. He holds a Ph.D. in Information Systems.

Michael Hohnbaum is a software engineer at the IBM Linux Technology Center in Beaverton, Oregon. He has worked on operating systems for large SMP systems for the past 20 years. Currently Michael is involved with an open source server virtualization project.

Dr. Khoa Huynh is a senior software engineer at the IBM Linux Technology Center in Austin, Texas. He has worked in various areas of the operating system for more than 15 years, from performance modeling/evaluation, kernel development, and network computing, to service and support. His interests are in the areas of system architectures, performance evaluation, and software quality.

Dr. Wilfred C. Jamison is a software engineer currently working on SOA and On Demand Solutions for IBM. He is an expert on WebSphere performance and has published several articles on performance engineering, best practices for Java performance, and improving performance from a memory usage perspective. He has led a group called WebSphere Performance for the Linux Platform that studied the performance characteristics of WebSphere Application Server on different platforms (IA32, S390, POWER4) using Linux.

Hanna Linder is a software engineer for IBM at the Linux Technology Center in Beaverton, Oregon. She has worked with UNIX/Linux for 10 years. Hanna has spoken at international and local Linux kernel conferences and meetings. She is currently working on supporting Linux on IBM xSeries systems.

Chris McDermott is a software engineer at the IBM Linux Technology Center in Beaverton, Oregon. He has 15 years of experience with Linux/UNIX operating systems. He is currently responsible for bringing up the kernel and other enabling features on IBM xSeries hardware.

Erich Nahum has been a research staff member at IBM Research since 1996. He has a Ph.D. in Computer Science from the University of Massachusetts and has worked on server performance issues for 14 years.

Steven Pratt has been employed by IBM for 15 years. He has a BS in Computer Science from Worcester Polytechnic Institute. Steven has worked in the area of volume management and file systems since 1994 and has been developing on Linux since 1998. He has worked on the HPFS and JFS filesystems for OS/2 and was one of the lead designers for the OS/2 LVM and the Linux Enterprise Volume Management System (EVMS). For the past three years, Steven has worked on file and disk I/O performance in Linux.

Chandra Seetharaman is an operating systems engineer and has worked on UNIX/Linux operating systems for more than a decade. He is currently working on Class Based Kernel Resource Management (CKRM) for Linux. He works for IBM in Beaverton, Oregon.

Narasimha Sharoff is a software engineer at IBM in Beaverton, Oregon. He is currently working on Linux System Management Projects in the Linux Technology Center. He holds a BE from Mysore University, India, and an MS in Computer Science and Engineering from OGI/OHSU.

Nivedita Singhvi is a software engineer at the IBM Linux Technology Center in Beaverton, Oregon. Her interests include Linux networking and I/O development. She is currently working on virtualization technologies.

John Tran has been a software developer for IBM in the Toronto Laboratory since 2000. His primary focus has been DB2 performance on Linux.

Dr. Duc J. Vianney is a senior software engineer with more than 25 years of experience in computer performance evaluation and measurement. He worked at Harris Computer Systems and Gould Computer Systems before joining IBM in 1989 to work on DOS, OS/2, Win-OS/2, and Linux. He currently works on performance issues involving Linux on Power.

Peter Wai Yee Wong is a senior software engineer at the IBM Linux Technology Center in Austin, Texas. He has 10 years of experience on performance analysis in the areas of database and graphics. Peter holds a Ph.D. in Computer Science from Ohio State University.

## PART I

Linux Overview

## CHAPTER ONE

Linux Installation Issues

By Khoa Huynh

INTRODUCTION

You've made the decision, and you're ready to begin. However, you may have to slow down a little and make some crucial decisions before beginning your Linux installation. This chapter can help! It is important to discuss several installation issues that pertain to overall system performance. The decisions you make about these areas can help optimize the performance of the Linux operating system as well as the applications that will eventually run on it. You'll also need to review key configurable kernel features that are available in the 2.6 kernel that can impact performance for some applications. These features can be set or selected during installation or bootup time. It's also important to review the simple but powerful Linux logging facility. And last, this chapter helps you examine Linux system initialization and the two different initialization styles that have been adopted by various Linux distributions.

So, you have some planning to do. Certain areas of the installation need some thought before you proceed.

PREINSTALLATION PLANNING

Before installing Linux on the system, there are several things worth considering that might help optimize the performance of the operating system and the applications that run on it later. These areas include the following:

- Placing partitions
- Using multiple hard drives
- Selecting file systems
- Converting file systems
- Configuring RAID

Ready? Let's examine each in further detail.

Partition Placement

At a minimum, Linux requires a root and a swap partition. Where these and other frequently accessed partitions reside on disks ultimately impacts system performance. Following are some of the recommendations for placement of the root, swap, and other frequently accessed partitions that take advantage of the disk geometry:

- Use separate partitions for root, swap, /var, /usr, and /home.
- Most drives today pack more sectors on the outer tracks of the hard drive platter than on the inner tracks, so it's much faster to read and write data from the outer tracks. Lower-numbered partitions are usually allocated at the outer tracks (for example, /dev/hda1 is closer to the drive's outer edge than /dev/hda3), so place partitions that require frequent access first.

- The first partition should be the swap partition (to optimize memory swap operations).
- The next partition should be /var because log entries are frequently written to /var/log.
- The next partition should be /usr, because base system utilities and commands are placed in /usr.
- The root and /home partitions can reside near the end of the drive.

Now that we have considered how best to place the most frequently used partitions on a hard drive, we will look at how to take advantage of your multiple hard drives—if you have more than one in your system.

Using Multiple Hard Drives

Most systems today have more than one hard drive. If your system has only one drive, and if performance is really important to you (which is why you are reading this book in the first place!), you may need to seriously consider adding more drives to your system to improve performance. To take full advantage of multiple drives, you'll need to do the following:

- Place frequently accessed partitions on the faster drives.
- If the drives are relatively equal in performance, place frequently used partitions on alternate drives. For example, place /var on one drive and /usr on another drive. The swap partition should be on its own drive.
- Consider using RAID if you have multiple drives with relatively equal performance. (This will be discussed in more detail later.)

• Place each drive as the master device on its own I/O channel (for example, IDE) to maximize bus throughput. You will need to modify the file system table (/etc/fstab) after moving drives across I/O channels because the device name will change. If the drive contains the root or /boot partition, you need to edit the grub /boot/grub/menu.lst file as well.

When using multiple hard drives, you need to make some decisions in modifying the file system table. In the next section, we'll discuss selecting file systems.

Selecting File Systems

In addition to the original ext2 file system, new enterprise Linux distributions, such as RHEL 3, RHEL 4, and SLES 9, also support journaled file system technology, such as ext3 and ReiserFS. XFS is also included in several Linux distributions but may not be fully supported. Table 1.1 shows the general advantages and disadvantages of each type of file system.

Table 1.1   File System Types

File System Type	*Comment*
ext3	Easy to upgrade from existing ext2 file system
ReiserFS	Best performance with small files; fully supported by major enterprise distributions
XFS	Best performance, especially with large files

Some Linux distributions, such as Red Hat and SUSE, also include the IBM JFS (Journaled File System), which is designed for high-performance e-commerce file servers and is used on many IBM enterprise servers supporting high-speed corporate intranets. The selection of file system(s) ultimately depends on the role and the expected workload the system is supposed to handle. Careful planning before installation is highly recommended. Making the right decisions during installation can save you headaches later on.

Several mkfs and mount options might yield file system performance improvements under specific circumstances. See Chapter 11, "File System Tuning," for a complete discussion of tuning file systems for improved performance on Linux.

Converting File Systems

If the existing file system is ext2, converting it to ext3 can be done using the `tune2fs` command. For example, if you want to convert the existing ext2 partition /dev/hda1 to ext3, issue the following command:

```
tune2fs -j /dev/hda1
```

Converting to a file system type other than ext3 is more time-consuming. For example, to convert /usr, which is on /dev/hdb2, to ReiserFS, do the following:

1. Choose an empty partition that is larger than /dev/hdb2—say, /dev/hdb3—as a temporary partition.

2. Format the temporary partition:

   ```
   mkreiserfs /dev/hdb3
   ```

3. Create a temporary directory:

   ```
   mkdir /mnt/tempfs
   ```

4. Copy the contents of /usr to a temporary directory:

   ```
   cp -preserver=all -R /usr/mnt/tempfs
   ```

5. Unmount /usr:

   ```
   umount /usr
   ```

6. Unmount /mnt/tempfs:

   ```
   umount /mnt/tempfs
   ```

7. Mount /usr on /dev/hdb3:

   ```
   mount /dev/hdb3 /usr
   ```

8. Reformat the old /usr partition:

   ```
   mkreiserfs /dev/hdb2     mount /dev/hdb2 /mnt/tempfs
   ```

9. Copy the contents of /usr back to its original partition:

   ```
   cp -preserve=all -R /usr /mnt/tempfs
   ```

10. Unmount /usr:

    ```
    umount /usr
    ```

11. Unmount /mnt/tempfs:

    ```
    umount /mnt/tempfs
    ```

12. Remount /usr on its original partition:

```
mount /dev/hdb2 /usr
```

Repeat this process for other directories you want to convert.

The final step for preinstallation planning for optimization is configuring RAID.

Configuring RAID

RAID (Redundant Array of Inexpensive Disks) lets you configure multiple physical disks into a single virtual disk, thereby taking advantage of multiple disks and I/O channels working in parallel on a disk I/O operation. Many Linux distributions, especially enterprise versions, now provide RAID support. The easiest way to configure RAID is during installation. However, RAID can be configured on a preinstalled system as well. Here's how:

1. If new partitions are created, modify /etc/fstab appropriately. If the root and /boot partitions are on these new partitions, modify the /boot/grub/menu.lst file accordingly.

2. If existing partitions are combined to create a new RAID partition:

   • Verify that the raidtools package is present:

   ```
   mkraid -V
   ```

   • Verify that RAID support is compiled into the kernel:

   ```
   cat /proc/mdstat
   ```

   • Create or modify /etc/raidtab. Create the following entry for each of the RAID devices:

   ```
   /* Create RAID device md0 */
   raiddev /dev/md         0      /* New RAID device */
   raid-level              0      /* RAID 0 as example here */
   nr-raid-disk            2      /* Assume two disks */
   /* Automatically detect RAID devices on boot */
   persistent-superblock   1
   chunk-size              32     /* Writes 32 KB of data to each disk */
   device                         /dev/hda1
   raid-disk               0
   device                         /dev/hdc1
   raid-disk               1
   ```

Large chunk sizes are better when working with larger files; smaller chunk sizes are more suitable for working with smaller files.

3. Create the RAID device:

```
mkraid /dev/md0
```

4. View the status of the RAID devices:

```
cat /proc/mdstat
```

5. Format the RAID device with the ReiserFS file system, for example:

```
mkreiserfs /dev/md0
```

6. Modify /etc/fstab to indicate which partition(s) are on the RAID device. For example, to have /usr on the RAID device /dev/md0, make sure that the /usr line in /etc/fstab points to /dev/md0.

To squeeze the most performance out of the disk I/O subsystem, make sure that DMA and 32-bit transfers are enabled. This can be done via the hdparm utility, as follows (all commands are examples only):

1. Verify that DMA is enabled:

```
hdparm -d /dev/hda
```

2. If DMS is not enabled, enable it by issuing the following command:

```
hdparm -d1 /dev/hda
```

3. Verify that 32-bit transfers are enabled:

```
hdparm -c /dev/hda
```

4. If 32-bit transfers are not enabled, enable them by issuing the following command:

```
hdparm -c1 /dev/hda
```

5. Verify the effectiveness of the options by running simple disk read tests as follows:

```
hdparm -Tt/dev/had
```

So far, we have discussed how best to set up the disk I/O subsystem for optimal performance. Now we need to look at two key configurable kernel features that are available on the 2.6 kernel. These 2.6 kernel features can impact performance for some application workloads.

CONFIGURABLE 2.6 KERNEL FEATURES

Two new features available in the 2.6 kernel merit serious consideration because they can impact Linux system performance for some workloads: I/O elevators and huge TLB (Translation Look-aside Buffer) page support. These features must be explicitly enabled (for example, in the kernel configuration file or the boot kernel command line).

I/O Elevators

An elevator is a queue where I/O requests are ordered by the function of their sector on disk. Two I/O elevators are now available in the 2.6 kernel: *anticipatory* and *deadline*. The default mode is anticipatory. Using anticipatory mode, synchronous read operations are scheduled together with a delay of a few milliseconds, anticipating the "next" read operation. This mode should help read performance for commands that require multiple synchronous reads, especially during streamed writes. However, several workloads that seek all over the disk, performing reads and synchronous writes, such as database operations, can actually suffer with anticipatory I/O. For these workloads, the deadline I/O scheduler is better and can deliver up to a 10% performance improvement over the anticipatory scheduler. Select the deadline I/O scheduler by booting with `elevator = deadline` on the kernel command line.

Huge TLB Page Support

Huge TLB page support is now present in the 2.6 kernel as well as in the latest 2.4 kernel-based Linux distributions, such as RHEL 3. The TLB is the processor's cache of virtual-to-physical memory address translations. As such, the number of TLB entries is very limited, and a TLB miss is very costly in terms of processor cycles. With huge TLB page support, each dedicated, large TLB entry can map a 2MB or 4MB page, thus reducing the number of TLB misses, and could increase performance by a few percent for database operations. This is even more critical as more and more systems with gigabytes of physical memory are now available. Huge pages are reserved inside the kernel, are mapped by dedicated, large TLB entries, and are not pageable, making it very attractive for large database applications. A user application can use these pages either via the *mmap* system calls or shared memory system calls. Huge pages must be preallocated by the superuser (for example, the system administrator), preferably during system initialization when huge contiguous memory blocks are still available, before they can be used. More specifically, to use this huge TLB page support on the 2.6 kernel, you need to consider the following:

- The kernel must be built with CONFIG_HUGETLB_PAGE (under the Processor types and features section of the kernel configuration file) and CONFIG_HUGETLBFS (under the File system section) configuration options.

- /proc/meminfo should be able to show the huge page size supported, the total number of huge pages in the system, and the number of huge pages that are still available.
- /proc/filesystem should also show a file system of type hugetlbfs configured in the kernel.
- /proc/sys/vm/nr_hugepages indicates the current number of configured huge pages in the system.
- Huge pages can be preallocated by using the following command:

```
echo x >/proc/sys/vm/nr_hugepages
```

where x is the number of huge pages to be preallocated. This command can be inserted into one of the local *rc* initialization files so it can be executed during system initialization. (On RHEL 3 systems that are based on the 2.4 kernel technology, this can be done by echoing the value in megabytes into /proc/sys/vm/hugetlb_pool or by putting the value in the /etc/sysctl.conf file.)

- To use huge pages via mmap system calls, the superuser must first mount a file system of type hugetlbfs on the directory /mnt/huge. Any files created on /mnt/huge will use huge pages. User applications can use mmap system calls to request huge pages.
- To use huge pages via shared memory system calls (shmat / shmget), there is no need to mount hugetlbfs. However, it is possible for the same user application to use any combination of mmap and shared memory system calls to use huge pages.

It should be noted that the use of huge pages is most effective on large memory systems. Using huge pages on systems with limited physical memory can adversely affect system performance because huge pages, if they can be allocated, must be physically contiguous and are not pageable, thus making memory swapping ineffective.

In the event of any problems with your system, Linux can log the event. This allows better system management.

LINUX LOGGING FACILITY

One of the key requirements of enterprise systems is to log pertinent events that happen on the system to aid in system management and post failure system debugging. Fortunately, Linux provides an excellent, fully configurable, and simple logging facility.

All Linux logs are in plain text, so any text tool can be used to view them, such as vi, tail, more, or less. A browser, such as Mozilla, can be used to display a log file and provide search capability. Scripts can also be written to scan through logs and perform automatic functions based on the contents.

The main location for Linux logs is in the /var/log directory. This directory contains several log files that are maintained by the system, but other services and programs can put their log files here as well. Most log files require root privilege, but this can be overcome by simply changing the access rights to these files.

/var/log/messages

The /var/log/messages log is the core system log file. It contains the boot messages when the system comes up as well as other status messages as the system runs. Errors with I/O subsystem, networking, and other general system errors are logged in this file. Messages from system services, such as DHCP servers, are also logged in this file. Messages indicating simple actions on the system, such as when someone becomes root, are also listed here.

/var/log/XFree86.0.log

The /var/log/XFree86.0.log shows the results of the last execution of the XFree86 X Window server. If there are problems getting the graphical mode to come up, this file usually provides an answer as to what is failing.

In addition to these two log files, there might be other log files in the /var/log directory that are maintained by other services and applications running on the system. For example, there might be log files associated with running a mail server, resource sharing, or automatic tasks.

Log Rotation

Log files can become large and cumbersome, especially on systems that have been running for long periods of time. To solve this problem, Linux provides a tool, logrotate, to rotate the logs so that the current log information does not get mixed up with older messages. The logrotate command can be run manually as needed, or it can be run automatically on a periodic basis. When executed, logrotate takes the current version of the log files and adds a sequence number to the end of the log filename. The larger the sequence number after the log filename, the older that file is. For example, messages.2 is older than messages.1, which is older than the current messages file. The automatic behavior for logrotate can be configured using the /etc/logrotate.conf file. More details are available on the logrotate man page.

In addition to /var/log/messages, dmesg provides a quick view of the kernel messages, which can be helpful when you want to know what happened during the last system boot.

Logger

The logger facility generates system log messages out of your own scripts and programs that are recognized and processed by the syslogd daemon. This lets you send messages to the log files without worrying about the format of the log files or whether the logging facility has been customized.

Customized Logging

The Linux logging facility consists of two daemons: klogd for kernel messages and syslogd for user-space messages. These daemons can be configured through the /etc/syslog.conf and /etc/sysconfig/syslog files. You can edit the /etc/syslog.conf file to specify what you want to do with a particular type of message. For example, you can specify that critical kernel messages should be put on a remote host for security reasons.

Here is an example of customized logging taken from the /etc/syslog.conf man page:

```
kern.*                    /var/adm/kernel
kern.crit                 @finlandia
kern.crit                 /dev/console
kern.info;kern.!err       /var/adm/kernel-info
```

The first statement directs any message from the kernel to the file /var/adm/kernel.

The second statement directs all kernel messages of the priority crit and higher to the remote host finlandia. Sending critical log messages to the remote host can help prevent malicious users from modifying the message log files on the local system to cover their tracks. It can also be useful in the event the local system crashes and the disks get irreparable errors.

The third statement directs these messages to the actual console, so the person who works on the console will see them.

The fourth line tells the syslogd to save all kernel messages that come with priorities from info up to warning in the /var/adm/kernel-info file. Everything from err and higher priority is excluded.

The ability to customize logging like this provides a great deal of flexibility and control over the Linux environment.

SYSTEM INITIALIZATION: BSD VERSUS SYSTEM V INITIALIZATION

System initialization starts where the kernel bootup ends. The first program that the kernel runs is the init process. The init process reads the system initialization table (/etc/inittab) to see how various daemons need to be initialized and started. This section examines how system initialization works in Linux.

The various Linux distributions have adopted two system initialization styles. Red Hat and Debian use the System V initialization type. Others, such as Slackware, use the BSD style.

The Filesystem Hierarchy Standard (FHS) v2.0 for Linux states that either BSD- or System V-style initialization is acceptable. The standard stopped short, however, of outlining exactly where the rc scripts would go, except to say that they would be below /etc. Future revisions to the standard might provide further guidance.

Under system initialization, the biggest difference between BSD and System V is the init scripts. With BSD style, all daemons are started essentially by only a few scripts. For example, the init process in Slackware, which adopts the BSD style, runs the system script (/etc/rc.d/rc.S) to prepare the system. The rc.S file enables the system's virtual memory, mounts necessary file systems, cleans up certain log directories, initializes Plug and Play devices, loads kernel modules, configures PCMCIA devices, and sets up serial ports. The local script (rc.local) is available for system administrators to tailor to the specific system on which it is running. The system and local scripts can, in turn, call other scripts to accomplish their objectives, but they are called by the init process sequentially.

Many other Linux distributions make use of System V style instead of the BSD style. Unlike the BSD style, the System V scripts are independent, stand-alone initialization scripts. They make use of runlevels that correspond to different groups of processes or tasks to be executed. The scripts are run from runlevels 0 to 6 by default, even though several runlevels are not used. In other words, each runlevel is given a subdirectory for init scripts that allows for maximum flexibility in initializing the system and necessary daemons. The BSD style, by having only a few scripts to start everything, does not allow for the kind of flexibility System V brings. It does, however, make things easier to find.

It should be noted that, even though Slackware adopts the BSD-style system initialization, it does provide System V initialization compatibility. In fact, many Linux distributions use the same init binary, so the difference is not that great between various Linux distributions when it comes to system initialization.

Initialization Table (/etc/inittab)

As mentioned earlier, the system initialization table (/etc/inittab) specifies to the init process how to initialize and start various daemons during system bootup. Comments in /etc/inittab are preceded by # and are skipped over by the init process. Non-comment lines in /etc/inittab have the following format:

```
id:runlevel:action:process
```

- `id` is a unique identifier for the rest of the line. It is typically limited to two characters.

- `runlevel` can be null or contain a valid runlevel, which defines the state that the system will be running in. Runlevels are essentially groups of processes or actions to be executed during system initialization. They can be used as follows:
  - Runlevel 0: System halt
  - Runlevel 1: Maintenance mode (single-user mode)
  - Runlevel 6: System reboot
  - Runlevels 2–5: Can be customized
- `action` can be several different commands, the most common being `respawn`, but it can also be any one of the following: `once`, `sysinit`, `boot`, `bootwait`, `wait`, `off`, `ondemand`, `initdefault`, `powerwait`, `powerfail`, `powerokwait`, `ctrlaltdel`, or `kbrequest`.
- `process` is the specific process or program to be run.

Now let's see how the system initialization table (/etc/inittab) works in BSD and System V flavors. We'll use Slackware Linux as an example for BSD style and Red Hat for System V style.

BSD inittab (Slackware)

Slackware Linux uses the BSD-style file layout for its system initialization files. All of the system initialization files are stored in the /etc/rc.d directory. Remember, the /etc/rc.d/rc.S script is called by the init process to enable the system's virtual memory, mount necessary file systems, clean up certain log directories, initialize Plug and Play devices, and then call other scripts in the /etc/rc.d directory to complete other work. This includes loading kernel modules (/etc/rc.d/rc.modules), configuring PCMCIA devices (/etc/rc.d/rc.pcmcia), and setting up serial ports (/etc/rc.d/rc.serial).

After system initialization is complete, init moves on to runlevel initialization. As described previously, a runlevel describes the state in which your machine will be running. The files listed in Table 1.2 define the different runlevels in Slackware Linux.

Table 1.2   Runlevels in Slackware Linux

rc.0	Halt the system (runlevel 0). By default, this is symlinked to rc.6.
rc.4	Multiuser startup (runlevel 4), but in X11 with KDM, GDM, or XDM as the login manager.
rc.6	Reboot the system (runlevel 6).
rc.K	Start up in single-user mode (runlevel 1).
rc.M	Multiuser mode (runlevels 2 and 3), but with the standard text-based login. This is the default runlevel in Slackware.

Runlevels 2, 3, and 4 start up the network services if enabled. The files listed in Table 1.3 are responsible for the network initialization.

Table 1.3 Network Initialization

rc.inet1	Created by netconfig, this file is responsible for configuring the actual network interface.
rc.inet2	Runs after rc.inet1 and starts up basic network services.
rc.atalk	Starts up AppleTalk services.
rc.httpd	Starts up the Apache web server.
rc.samba	Starts up Windows file- and print-sharing services.
rc.news	Starts up the news server.
rc.sysvinit	The rc.sysvinit script searches for any System V init scripts in /etc/rc.d and runs them if the runlevel is appropriate. This is useful for certain commercial software packages that install System V init scripts and scripts for BSD-style init.

In addition to the rc scripts listed here, rc.local contains specific startup commands for a system. rc.local is empty after a fresh install because it is reserved for local administrators. This script is run after all other initialization has taken place.

Sys V inittab (Red Hat)

Under Red Hat, all the system initialization scripts are located in /etc/rc.d. Because Red Hat uses the System V style, the /etc/rc.d subdirectory has even more subdirectories, one for each runlevel: rc0.d to rc6.d and init.d. Within the /etc/rc.d/rc#.d subdirectories (where # is replaced by a single-digit number) are links to the master scripts stored in /etc/rc.d/init.d. The scripts in init.d take an argument of start, stop, reload, or restart.

The links in the /etc/rc.d/rc#.d directories all begin with either an S or a K for start or kill, respectively, a number that indicates a relative order for the scripts, and the script name (generally, the same name as the master script found in init.d to which it is linked). For example, S20lpd runs the script lpd in init.d with the argument start, which starts up the line-printer daemon.

The nice part about System V initialization is that it is easy for root to start, stop, restart, or reload a daemon or process subsystem from the command line, simply by calling the appropriate script in init.d with the argument start, stop, reload, or restart. For example, the script lpd can be called from the command line, as follows:

```
/etc/rc.d/init.d/lpd start
```

Red Hat defines the runlevels as follows (the default runlevel is 3):

- Runlevel 0: System halt
- Runlevel 1: Single-user mode
- Runlevel 2: Multiuser mode (the same as runlevel 3, but without networking)
- Runlevel 3: Full multiuser mode
- Runlevel 4: Unused
- Runlevel 5: X11
- Runlevel 6: System reboot

When not called from a command line with an argument, the rc script parses the command line. For example, if it is running K20lpd, it runs the lpd init script with a `stop` argument. When init has followed the link in /etc/inittab to rc.d/rc3.d, it begins by running all scripts that start with a K in numerical order from lowest to highest, then likewise for the S scripts. This ensures that the correct daemons are running in each runlevel and are stopped and started in the correct order. For example, the sendmail or bind/named (Berkeley DNS or Domain Name Service daemon) cannot be started before networking is started. In contrast, the BSD-style Slackware starts networking early in the rc.M script. As a result, you must always be cognizant of the order of the entries when modifying Slackware startup scripts.

All of the initialization scripts are simple ASCII text files that can be easily modified with vi or any text editor. As noted earlier, many Linux distributions use the same init binary, so the difference is not that great between various Linux distributions when it comes to system initialization. In fact, symbolic links can be added to make a BSD-style initialization look like a System V-style initialization, and vice versa.

SUMMARY

We have discussed in this chapter several important considerations prior to installing Linux on your system. Among these considerations are partition placement, RAID support, and file system selection. We then looked at two key configurable kernel features that are now available in the 2.6 kernel: I/O elevators and huge TLB page support. These features can be set or selected during installation or bootup time and may impact some large I/O-intensive applications. We also discussed the powerful, yet simple, Linux logging facility. Finally, we took a look at Linux system initialization and the two different initialization styles that have been adopted by various Linux distributions.

REFERENCES

[1] Denton, Chad. "Making Penguins Fly: Boost Performance in Your Linux System," *Computer Power User*, October 2003, pp. 53-55.

[2] Tallinn. "The New Linux Kernel 2.6 for Users and Developers," *Training Course Material*, Linux Summit 2004.

[3] Walden, C. "Windows to Linux RoadMap: Working with Logs," *developerWorks*, November 2003.

[4] Bandel, D. "Linux System Initialization," *Linux Journal*, Issue 56, December 1998.

[5] Web resource: `http://gus-br.linuxmag.com.br/pt/config/init.html`, Slackware User Group, Brasil.

## CHAPTER TWO

Kernel Overview

By Badari Pulavarti

INTRODUCTION

Now that you've made important decisions about how to install Linux on your system, you need to learn more about the Linux kernel to make important tuning decisions. We'll discuss how Linux evolved and then delve into its architecture. We'll include information on how the kernel is organized, what its responsibilities are, and how memory management is handled. We'll discuss process management and interprocess communication, followed by an overview of the Linux Symmetrical Multiprocessing Model. Finally, we'll examine the Linux file systems.

THE EVOLUTION OF LINUX

Linux is an operating system for personal computers developed by Linus Torvalds in 1991. Initially, Linux supported only the Intel 80x86 processor. Over the years, support has been added so that Linux can run on various other processors. Currently, Linux is one of very few operating systems that run on a wide range of processors, including Intel IA-32, Intel IA-64, AMD, DEC, PowerPC, Motorola, SPARC, and IBM S/390.

Linux is similar to UNIX in that it borrows many ideas from UNIX and implements the UNIX API. However, Linux is not a direct derivative of any particular UNIX distribution.

Linux is undoubtedly the fastest-growing operating system today. It is used in areas such as embedded devices all the way to mainframes. One of the interesting and most important facts about Linux is that it is open-sourced. The Linux kernel is licensed under the GNU General Public License (GPL); the kernel source code is freely available and can be modified to suit the needs of your machine.

As we move on to the next section, we'll take a more comprehensive look at the architecture of the Linux kernel.

LINUX KERNEL ARCHITECTURE

Let's begin this section by discussing the architecture of the Linux kernel, including responsibilities of the kernel, its organization and modules, services of the kernel, and process management.

Kernel Responsibilities

The kernel (also called the operating system) has two major responsibilities:

- To interact with and control the system's hardware components
- To provide an environment in which applications can run

Some operating systems allow applications to directly access hardware components, although this capability is very uncommon nowadays. UNIX-like operating systems hide all the low-level hardware details from an application. If an application wants to make use of a hardware resource, it must make a request to the operating system. The operating system then evaluates the request and interacts with the hardware component on behalf of the application, but only if it's valid. To enforce this kind of scheme, the operating system needs to depend on hardware capabilities that forbid applications to directly interact with them.

Organization and Modules

Like many other UNIX-like operating systems, the Linux kernel is *monolithic*. This means that even though Linux is divided into subsystems that control various components of the system (such as memory management and process management), all of these subsystems are tightly integrated to form the whole kernel. In contrast, *microkernel* operating systems provide bare, minimal functionality, and all other operating system layers are performed on top of microkernels as processes. Microkernel operating systems are generally slower due to message passing between the various layers. However, microkernel operating systems can be extended very easily.

Linux kernels can be extended by *modules*. A module is a kernel feature that provides the benefits of a microkernel without a penalty. A module is an object that can be linked to the kernel at runtime.

Using Kernel Services

The kernel provides a set of interfaces for applications running in user mode to interact with the system. These interfaces, also known as system calls, give applications access to hardware and other kernel resources. System calls not only provide applications with abstracted hardware, but also ensure security and stability.

Most applications do not use system calls directly. Instead, they are programmed to an application programming interface (API). It is important to note that there is no relation between the API and system calls. APIs are provided as part of libraries for applications to make use of. These APIs are generally implemented through the use of one or more system calls.

/proc File System—External Performance View

The /proc file system provides the user with a view of internal kernel data structures. It also lets you look at and change some of the kernel internal data structures, thereby changing the kernal's behavior. The /proc file system provides an easy way to fine-tune system resources to improve the performance not only of applications but of the overall system.

/proc is a virtual file system that is created dynamically by the kernel to provide data. It is organized into various directories. Each of these directories corresponds to tunables for a given subsystem. Appendix A explains in detail how to use the /proc file system to fine-tune your system.

Another essential of the Linux system is memory management. In the next section, we'll cover five aspects of how Linux handles this management.

Memory Management

The various aspects of memory management in Linux include address space, physical memory, memory mapping, paging, and swapping.

Address Space

One of the advantages of virtual memory is that each process thinks it has all the address space it needs. The virtual memory can be many times larger than the physical memory in the system. Each process in the system has its own virtual address space. These virtual address spaces are completely separate from each other. A process running one application cannot affect another, and the applications are protected from each other. The virtual address space is mapped to physical memory by the operating system. From an application point of view, this address space is a flat linear address space. The kernel, however, treats the user virtual address space very differently.

The linear address space is divided into two parts: user address space and kernel address space. The user address space cannot change every time a context switch occurs and the kernel address space remains constant. How much space is allocated for user space and kernel space depends mainly on whether the system is a 32-bit or 64-bit architecture. For example, x86 is a 32-bit architecture and supports only a 4GB address space. Out of this 4GB, 3GB is reserved for user space and 1GB is reserved for the kernel. The location of the split is determined by the PAGE_OFFSET kernel configuration variable.

Physical Memory

Linux uses an architecture-independent way of describing physical memory in order to support various architectures.

Physical memory can be arranged into banks, with each bank being a particular distance from the processor. This type of memory arrangement is becoming very common, with more machines employing NUMA (Nonuniform Memory Access) technology. Linux VM represents this arrangement as a *node*. Each node is divided into a number of blocks called *zones* that represent ranges within memory. There are three different zones: *ZONE_DMA*, *ZONE_NORMAL*, and *ZONE_HIGHMEM*. For example, x86 has the following zones:

ZONE_ DMA	First 16MB of memory
ZONE_ NORMAL	16MB – 896MB
ZONE_ HIGHMEM	896MB – end

Each zone has its own use. Some of the legacy ISA devices have restrictions on where they can perform I/O from and to. ZONE_DMA addresses those requirements.

ZONE_NORMAL is used for all kernel operations and allocations. It is extremely crucial for system performance.

ZONE_ HIGHMEM is the rest of the memory in the system. It's important to note that ZONE_HIGHMEM cannot be used for kernel allocations and data structures—it can only be used for user data.

Memory Mapping

While looking at how kernel memory is mapped, we will use x86 as an example for better understanding. As mentioned earlier, the kernel has only 1GB of virtual address space for its use. The other 3GB is reserved for the kernel. The kernel maps the physical memory in ZONE_DMA and ZONE_NORMAL directly to its address space. This means that the first 896MB of physical memory in the system is mapped to the kernel's virtual address space, which leaves only 128MB of virtual address space. This 128MB of virtual space is used for operations such as vmalloc and kmap.

This mapping scheme works well as long as physical memory sizes are small (less than 1GB). However, these days, all servers support tens of gigabytes of memory. Intel has added PAE (Physical Address Extension) to its Pentium processors to support up to 64GB of physical memory. Because of the preceding memory mapping, handling physical memories in tens of gigabytes is a major source of problems for x86 Linux. The Linux kernel handles high memory (all memory about 896MB) as follows: When the Linux kernel needs to address a page in high memory, it maps that page into a small virtual address space (kmap) window, operates on that page, and unmaps the page. The 64-bit architectures do not have this problem because their address space is huge.

Paging

Virtual memory is implemented in many ways, but the most effective way is hardware-based. Virtual address space is divided into fixed-size chunks called *pages*. Virtual memory references are translated into addresses in physical memory using page tables. To support various architectures and page sizes, Linux uses a three-level paging mechanism. The three types of page tables are as follows:

- Page Global Directory (PGD)
- Page Middle Directory (PMD)
- Page Table (PTE)

Address translation provides a way to separate the virtual address space of a process from the physical address space. Each page of virtual memory can be marked "present" or "not present" in the main memory. If a process references an address in virtual memory that is not present, hardware generates a page fault, which is handled by the kernel. The kernel handles the fault and brings the page into main memory. In this process, the system might have to replace an existing page to make room for the new one.

The replacement policy is one of the most critical aspects of the paging system. Linux 2.6 fixed various problems surrounding the page selection and replacement that were present in previous versions of Linux.

Swapping

Swapping is the moving of an entire process to and from secondary storage when the main memory is low. Many modern operating systems, including Linux, do not use this approach, mainly because context switches are very expensive. Instead, they use paging. In Linux, swapping is performed at the page level rather than at the process level. The main advantage of swapping is that it expands the process address space that is usable by a process. As the kernel needs to free up memory to make room for new pages, it may need to discard some of the less frequently used or unused pages. Some of the pages cannot be freed up easily because they are not backed by disks. Instead, they have to be copied to a backing store (swap area) and need to be read back from the backing store when needed. One major disadvantage of swapping is speed. Generally, disks are very slow, so swapping should be eliminated whenever possible.

PROCESS MANAGEMENT

This section discusses process management in Linux, including processes, tasks, kernel threads, scheduling, and context switching.

Processes, Tasks, and Kernel Threads

A *task* is simply a generic "description of work that needs to be done," whether it is a lightweight thread or a full process.

A *thread* is the most lightweight instance of a task. Creating a thread in the kernel can be expensive or relatively cheap, depending on the characteristics the thread needs to possess. In the simplest case, a thread shares everything with its parent including text, data, and many internal data structures, possessing only the minimum differences necessary to distinguish the thread from another thread.

A *process* is a "heavier" data structure in Linux. Several threads can operate within (and share some resources of) a single process, if desired. In Linux, a process is simply a thread with all of its heavyweight characteristics. Threads and processes are scheduled identically by the scheduler.

A *kernel thread* is a thread that always operates in kernel mode and has no user context. Kernel threads are usually present for a specific function and are most easily handled from within the kernel. They often have the desirable side effect of being schedulable like any other process and of giving other processes a target (by sending a signal) when they need that function to take effect.

Scheduling and Context Switching

Process scheduling is the science (some would say art) of making sure that each process gets a fair share of the CPU. There is always an element of disagreement over the definition of "fair" because the choices the scheduler must make often depend on information that is not apparent.

Process scheduling is covered more thoroughly in later chapters in this book, but it is important to note that it is deemed by many Linux users to be more important to have a scheduler that gets it mostly right all of the time than completely right most of the time—that is, slow-running processes are better than processes that stop dead in their tracks either due to deliberate choices in scheduling policies or outright bugs. The current Linux scheduler code adheres to this principle.

When one process stops running and another replaces it, this is known as a *context switch*. Generally, the overhead for this is high, and kernel programmers and application programmers try to minimize the number of context switches performed by the system. Processes can stop running voluntarily because they are waiting for some event or resource, or involuntarily if the system decides it is time to give the CPU to another process. In the first case, the CPU may actually become idle if no other process is waiting to run. In the second case, either the process is replaced with another that has been waiting, or the process is given a new *timeslice*, or period of time in which to run, and is allowed to continue.

Even when processes are being scheduled and run in an orderly fashion, they can be interrupted for other, higher-priority tasks. If a disk has data ready from a disk read, it signals the CPU and expects to have the information taken from it. The kernel must handle this situation in a timely fashion, or it will slow down the disk's transfer rates. Signals, interrupts, and exceptions are asynchronous events that are distinct but similar in many ways, and all must be dealt with quickly, even when the CPU is already busy.

For instance, a disk with data ready causes an *interrupt*. The kernel calls the interrupt handler for that particular device, interrupting the process that is currently running, and utilizing many of its resources. When the interrupt handler is done, the currently running process resumes. This in effect *steals* time from the currently running process, because current versions of the kernel measure only the time that has passed since the process was placed on the CPU, ignoring the fact that interrupts can use up precious milliseconds for that process.

Interrupt handlers are usually very fast and compact and thereby handle and clear interrupts quickly so that the next bit of data can come in. At times, however, an interrupt can require more work than is prudent in the short time desired in an interrupt handler. An interrupt can also require a well-defined environment to complete its work (remember, an interrupt utilizes a random process's resources). In this case, enough information is collected to defer the work to what is called a *bottom half handler*. The bottom half handler is scheduled to run every so often. Although the use of bottom halves was common in earlier versions of Linux, their use is discouraged in current versions of Linux.

INTERPROCESS COMMUNICATIONS

Linux supports a number of Interprocess Communication (IPC) mechanisms to allow processes to communicate with each other. Signals and pipes are the basic mechanisms, but Linux also supports System V IPC mechanisms.

Signals

Signals notify events to one or more processes and can be used as a primitive way of communication and synchronization between user processes. Signals can also be used for job control.

The kernel can generate a set of defined signals, or they can be generated by other processes in the system, provided that they have the correct privileges.

Processes can choose to ignore most of the signals that are generated, with two exceptions: SIGSTOP and SIGKILL. The SIGSTOP signal causes a process to halt its execution. The SIGKILL signal causes a process to exit and be ignored. With the exception of the SIGSTOP and SIGKILL signals, a process can choose how it wants to handle the various signals. Processes can block the signals, or they can either choose to handle the signals themselves or allow the kernel to handle the signals. If the kernel handles the signals, it performs the default actions required for the signal. Linux also holds information about how each process handles every possible signal.

Signals are not delivered to the process as soon as they are generated, but instead are delivered when the process resumes running. Every time a process exits a system call, if there are any unblocked signals, the signals are then delivered.

Linux is POSIX-compatible so the process can specify which signals are blocked when a particular signal-handling routine is called.

Pipes

A *pipe* is a unidirectional, first-in first-out (FIFO), unstructured stream of data. Writers add data to one end of the pipe, and readers get the data from other end of the pipe. After the data is read, it is removed from the pipe. Pipes provide simple flow control.

For example, the following command pipes output from the `ls` command, which lists the directory's files, into the standard input of the `less` command, which paginates the files:

```
$ ls | less
```

Linux also supports *named pipes*. Unlike pipes, named pipes are not temporary objects; they are entities in the file system and can be created using the `mkfifo` command.

System V IPC Mechanisms

Linux supports three types of interprocess communication mechanisms that first appeared in UNIX System V (1983). These mechanisms are message queues, semaphores, and shared memory. The mechanisms all share common authentication methods. Processes can access these resources only by passing a unique reference identifier to the kernel via system calls. Access to these System V IPC objects is checked using access permissions much like accesses to files are checked. The access rights to a System V IPC object are set by the creator of the object via system calls.

Message Queues

Message queues allow one or more processes to write messages, which will be read by one or more reading processes. In terms of functionality, message queues are equivalent to pipes, but message queues are more versatile than pipes and have several advantages over pipes. Message queues pass data in messages rather than as an unformatted stream of bytes, allowing data to be processed easily. The messages can be associated with a type, so the receiver can check for urgent messages before processing non-urgent messages. The type field can also be used to designate a recipient in case multiple processes share the same message queue.

Semaphores

Semaphores are objects that support two atomic operations: set and test. Semaphores can be used to implement various synchronization protocols. Semaphores can best be described as counters that control access to shared resources by multiple processes. Semaphores are most often used as a locking mechanism to prevent processes from accessing a particular resource while another process is performing operations on the resource.

A problem with semaphores, called *deadlocking*, occurs when one process has altered a semaphore's value as it enters a critical region but then fails to leave the critical region because it crashed or was killed. Linux protects against this by maintaining lists of adjustments to the semaphore arrays. The idea is that when these adjustments are applied, the semaphore will be returned to the state it was in before the process's set of semaphore operations were applied.

Shared Memory

Shared memory allows one or more processes to communicate via memory that appears in all of their virtual address spaces. Access to shared memory areas is controlled through keys and access rights checking. When the memory is being shared, there are no checks on how the processes are using the memory. Each process that wishes to share the memory must attach to that virtual memory via a system call. The process can choose where in its virtual address space the shared memory goes, or it can let Linux choose a free area large enough. The first time that a process accesses one of the pages of the shared virtual memory, a page fault occurs. When Linux fixes that page fault, it allocates a physical page and creates a page table entry for it. Thereafter, access by the other processes causes that page to be added to their virtual address spaces.

When processes no longer wish to share the virtual memory, they detach from it. So long as other processes are still using the memory, the detach operation affects only the current process. When the last process sharing the memory detaches from it, the pages of the shared memory currently in physical memory are freed.

Further complications arise when shared virtual memory is not locked into physical memory. In this case, the pages of the shared memory may be swapped out to the system's swap disk during periods of high memory usage.

THE LINUX SYMMETRICAL MULTIPROCESSING (SMP) MODEL

Types of Multiprocessing

A multiprocessing system consists of a number of processors communicating via a bus or a network. There are two types of multiprocessing systems: loosely coupled and tightly coupled.

Loosely coupled systems consist of processors that operate stand-alone. Each processor has its own bus, memory, and I/O subsystem, and communicates with other processors through the network medium. Loosely coupled systems can be either homogeneous or heterogeneous.

Tightly coupled systems consist of processors that share the memory, bus, devices, and sometimes cache. Tightly coupled systems run a single instance of the operating system. Tightly coupled systems can be classified into symmetric and asymmetric systems. Asymmetric systems are configured so that each processor is assigned a specific task. Asymmetric systems have a single "master" processor that controls all others. Symmetric systems treat all processors the same way—processes have equal access to all system resources. In the symmetric model, all tasks are spread equally across all processors.

Symmetric systems are subdivided into further classes consisting of dedicated and shared cache systems. Symmetrical Multiprocessing (SMP) systems have become very popular and have become the default choice for many large servers.

Concurrency and Data Serialization

In an ideal world, an SMP system with n processors would perform n times better than a uniprocessor system. In reality, this is not the case. The main reason that no SMP system is 100% scalable is because of the overhead involved in maintaining additional processors.

Locks, Lock Granularity, and Locking Overhead

Locks basically protect multiple threads from accessing or modifying a piece of critical information at the same time. Locks are especially used on SMP systems where multiple processors execute multiple threads at the same time. The problem with locking is that if two or more processors are competing for the same lock at the same time, only one is granted the lock, and the other waits, spinning, for the lock to be released. In other words, the other processors are not really doing any useful work. Locking, therefore, must be limited to the smallest amount of time possible.

Another common technique used to address this problem is to employ finer-grain locking. With finer-grain locking, instead of using a single lock to protect 100 things, 100 locks are used instead. Although the concept seems very simple, most of the time, it is hard to implement because of various interactions, dependencies, and deadlock. You need to program methodically to prevent deadlock situations, compared to having a single lock.

Another important area to consider is locking overhead. All locking techniques come with a price. Operating system designers need to choose the right kind of locking primitive to address a rights issue. In Linux 2.6, most global locks are removed and most of the locking primitives are optimized for extremely low overhead.

Cache Coherency

Cache coherency is a problem that occurs in multiprocessors, because each processor has an individual cache, and multiple copies of certain data exist in the system. When the data is changed, only one processor's cache has the new value. All other processors' cache has old values.

Processor Affinity

Processor affinity is one of the most important things that can improve system performance. As processes access various resources in the system, lots of information about the resources will be in processor caches, so it's better for a processor to run on the same processor due to the cache warmth. In some architectures, especially with NUMA, some resources are closer to the processor compared to others in the same system. In these systems, processor affinity is extremely important for system performance.

The file system is one of the most important parts of an operating system. In the following sections, the Linux alternative in file systems explains how well Linux has you covered.

FILE SYSTEMS

This section provides an overview of file systems on Linux and discusses the virtual file system, the ext2 file system, LVM and RAID, volume groups, device special files, and devfs.

Virtual File System (VFS)

One of the most important features of Linux is its support for many different file systems. This makes it very flexible and well able to coexist with many other operating systems. Virtual file system (VFS) allows Linux to support many, often very different, file systems, each presenting a common software interface to the VFS. All of the details of the Linux file systems are translated by software so that all file systems appear identical to the rest of the Linux kernel and to programs running in the system. The Linux Virtual File System layer allows you to transparently mount many different file systems at the same time.

The Linux virtual file system is implemented so that access to its files is as fast and efficient as possible. It must also make sure that the files and their data are maintained correctly.

ext2fs

The first file system that was implemented on Linux was ext2fs. This file system is the most widely used and the most popular. It is highly robust compared to other file systems and supports all the normal features a typical file system supports, such as the capability to create, modify, and delete file system objects such as files, directories, hard links, soft links, device special files, sockets, and pipes. However, a system crash can leave an ext2 file system in an inconsistent state. The entire file system has to be validated and corrected for inconsistencies before it is remounted. This long delay is sometimes unacceptable in production environments and can be irritating to the impatient user. This problem is solved with the support of journaling. A newer variant of ext2, called the ext3 file system, supports journaling. The basic idea behind journaling is that every file system operation is logged before the operation is executed. Therefore, if the machine dies between operations, only the log needs to be replayed to bring the file system back to consistency.

LVM and RAID

Volume managers provide a logical abstraction of a computer's physical storage devices and can be implemented for several reasons. On systems with a large number of disks, volume managers can combine several disks into a single logical unit to provide increased total storage space as well as data redundancy. On systems with a single disk, volume managers can divide that space into multiple logical units, each for a different purpose. In general, a volume manager is used to hide the physical storage characteristics from the file systems and higher-level applications.

Redundant Array of Inexpensive Disks (RAID) is a type of volume management that is used to combine multiple physical disks for the purpose of providing increased I/O throughput or improved data redundancy. There are several RAID levels, each providing a different combination of the physical disks and a different set of performance and redundancy characteristics. Linux provides four different RAID levels:

- *RAID-Linear* is a simple concatenation of the disks that comprise the volume. The size of this type of volume is the sum of the sizes of all the underlying disks. This RAID level provides no data redundancy. If one disk in the volume fails, the data stored on that disk is lost.

- *RAID-0* is simple striping. Striping means that as data is written to the volume, it is interleaved in equal-sized "chunks" across all disks in the volume. In other words, the first chunk of the volume is written to the first disk, the second chunk of the volume is written to the second disk, and so on. After the last disk in the volume is written to, it cycles back to the first disk and continues the pattern. This RAID level provides improved I/O throughput.

- *RAID-1* is mirroring. In a mirrored volume, all data is replicated on all disks in the volume. This means that a RAID-1 volume created from n disks can survive the failure of n–1 of those disks. In addition, because all disks in the volume contain the same data, reads to the volume can be distributed among the disks, increasing read throughput. On the other hand, a single write to the volume generates a write to each of the disks, causing a decrease in write throughput. Another downside to RAID-1 is the cost. A RAID-1 volume with n disks costs n times as much as a single disk but only provides the storage space of a single disk.

- *RAID-5* is striping with parity. This is similar to RAID-0, but one chunk in each stripe contains parity information instead of data. Using this parity information, a RAID-5 volume can survive the failure of any single disk in the volume. Like RAID-0, RAID-5 can provide increased read throughput by splitting large I/O requests across multiple disks. However, write throughput can be degraded, because each write request also needs to update the parity information for that stripe.

Volume Groups

The concept of volume-groups (VGs) is used in many different volume managers.

A volume-group is a collection of disks, also called physical-volumes (PVs). The storage space provided by these disks is then used to create logical-volumes (LVs).

The main benefit of volume-groups is the abstraction between the logical- and physical-volumes. The VG takes the storage space from the PVs and divides it into fixed-size chunks called physical-extents (PEs). An LV is then created by assigning one or more PEs to the LV. This assignment can be done in any arbitrary order—there is no dependency on the underlying order of the PVs, or on the order of the PEs on a particular PV.

This allows LVs to be easily resized. If an LV needs to be expanded, any unused PE in the group can be assigned to the end of that LV. If an LV needs to be shrunk, the PEs assigned to the end of that LV are simply freed.

The volume-group itself is also easily resizeable. A new physical-volume can be added to the VG, and the storage space on that PV becomes new, unassigned physical-extents. These new PEs can then be used to expand existing LVs or to create new LVs. Also, a PV can be removed from the VG if none of its PEs are assigned to any LVs.

In addition to expanding and shrinking the LVs, data on the LVs can be "moved" around within the volume-group. This is done by reassigning an extent in the LV to a different, unused PE somewhere else in the VG. When this reassignment takes place, the data from the old PE is copied to the new PE, and the old PE is freed.

The PVs in a volume-group do not need to be individual disks. They can also be RAID volumes. This allows a user to get the benefit of both types of volume management. For instance, a user might create multiple RAID-5 volumes to provide data redundancy, and then use each of these RAID-5 volumes as a PV for a volume-group. Logical-volumes can then be created that span multiple RAID-5 volumes.

Device Special Files

A typical Linux system has at least one hard disk, a keyboard, and a console. These devices are handled by their corresponding device drivers. However, how would a user-level application access the hardware device? Device special files are an interface provided by the operating system to applications to access the devices. These files are also called device nodes that reside in the /dev directory. The files contain a major and minor number pair that identifies the device they support. Device special files are like normal files with a name, ownership, and access permissions.

There are two kinds of device special files: block devices and character devices. Block devices allow block-level access to the data residing on the device, and character devices allow character-level access to the device. When you issue the `ls -l` command on a device, if the returned permission string starts with a b, it is a block device; if it starts with a c, it is a character device.

devfs

The virtual file system, devfs, manages the names of all the devices. devfs is an alternative to the special block and character device node that resides on the root file system. devfs reduces the system administrative task of creating device nodes for each device in the system. This job is automatically handled by devfs. Device drivers can register devices to devfs through device names instead of through the traditional major-minor number scheme. As a result, the device namespace is not limited by the number of major and minor numbers.

A system administrator can mount the devfs file system many times at different mount points, but changes to a device node are reflected on all the device nodes on all the mount points. Also, the devfs namespace exists in the kernel even before it is mounted. Essentially, this makes the availability of device nodes independent of the availability of the root file system.

With the traditional solution, a device node is created in the /dev directory for each and every conceivable device in the system, irrespective of the existence of the device. However, in devfs, only the necessary and sufficient device entries are maintained.

NEW FEATURES IN LINUX 2.6

Linux is getting better! New features are constantly being added to ensure its integrity and increase its functionality. The following is a list of key new features in Linux 2.6. Note that some of these features have been backported to various 2.4-based distribution releases:

- New architecture support (x86-64)
- Hyperthreading/SMT support
- (O)1 scheduler
- Preemption support
- NUMA
- NPTL
- I/O scheduler support
- Block layer rewrite
- AIO
- New file systems
- ACL
- Sysfs
- Udev
- Networking improvements
- Linux security module
- Processor affinity
- Module rewrite
- Unified driver model
- LVM

SUMMARY

In this chapter, we've explained the key components of the Linux kernel to help you understand how the kernel is architected and organized. In the next chapter, we'll go a step further and discuss some of the servers that Linux runs on.

REFERENCES

[1] Gorman, Mel. *Understanding the Linux Virtual Memory Manager*, Prentice Hall, 2004.

[2] Love, Robert. "Linux Kernel Development," *Developer's Library*, 2004.

[3] Vahalia, Uresh. *UNIX Internals: The New Frontiers*, Prentice Hall, 1996.

[4] Linux kernel mailing lists.

[5] Linux kernel sources and documentation.

## CHAPTER THREE

Overview of Server Architectures

By Michael Hohnbaum, Hanna Linder, and Chris McDermott

INTRODUCTION

Now that we've covered Linux kernel fundamentals, it's time to define the typical server processing model most common in the Linux Server market. We'll describe some of the basic building blocks and standard features that comprise today's server platforms. The focus in this chapter is on computers with multiple CPUs and large memory, and those that support large disks. We'll also focus on the architecture of the server more than the software algorithms designed to utilize the various capabilities of large computers. By the end of the chapter, you will have a better understanding of some of the main architectures and topologies available. You will understand the difference between SMP, NUMA, and clustered systems.

LINUX SERVERS

A *computer* consists of one or more processors, memory, and I/O devices. I/O devices are connected to the computer through I/O buses such as PCI. Additionally, some computers have service processors to assist in system control (booting, error handling) and monitoring (power, cooling).

A *server* is a computer that provides services to other computers. For example, a DNS server is a computer that provides the domain name lookup service to other computers connected to it via a network. A computer functioning as a server is not limited to providing only one service, although for simplicity and security reasons, it is common to restrict a server to a single service.

One of the most appealing features of the Linux kernel is its modular design. This design has made it relatively easy to port the Linux kernel to new architectures or enhance and extend existing architecture ports to support new features. It is also one of the fundamental reasons why Linux has become so popular. Today, Linux runs in computing environments that range from embedded systems to desktops to entry-level and enterprise-level servers to proprietary mainframe systems. Linux has probably made its biggest impact in the small- to mid-range server market. Linux runs well on servers with two to four CPUs, although current stable kernels support up to 32 CPUs. Two to four CPU servers are currently considered the Linux "sweet spot" from a performance point of view.

In the following section, you will learn about systems and processors. We will discuss how a computer is configured to run as a server, as well as mixing processors within the same system.

PROCESSORS AND MULTIPROCESSING

Most server-class systems are designed to support more than one processor. The most common type of multiprocessor systems supported by Linux are the tightly coupled Symmetrical Multiprocessing or Shared Memory Multiprocessing architectures (SMP). These tightly coupled architectures are called SMP because each processor shares the same system bus, and therefore, each processor is symmetrical to or equidistant from system memory and I/O resources. In other words, memory access and I/O access times from any processor in the system are uniform.

The advantage of SMP systems is that they provide more computing power, because there are more processors with which to schedule work. In a perfect world, an SMP system provides linear scalability as more processors are added to the system. To explain further, a workload on an *n*-processor system could perform *n* times faster than the same workload on a one-processor system. Realistically, because processors in an SMP server share system resources (the memory bus, the I/O bus, and so on), linear scalability is difficult to achieve. Achieving acceptable scalability in an SMP environment involves both optimized hardware and software. The hardware must be designed to exploit the system's parallel characteristics. System software must be written to take full advantage of the parallelism built into the hardware. On the other hand, the fact that processors share certain system resources places limitations on the amount of parallelism that can be achieved. Both system hardware and software must implement complicated locking logic and algorithms to provide *mutual exclusion* of shared system resources. The system must prevent concurrent access to any shared resource to preserve data consistency and correct program operation. Mutual exclusion is one of the primary factors that limit the scalability of any SMP operating system. SMP support in the Linux kernel has evolved from a model that completely serialized access to the entire kernel to a design that now supports multiple layers and types of locks within kernel components at every level of the kernel. The 2.6 Linux kernel continues to improve SMP scalability over previous kernel versions by implementing features that further exploit parallelism in SMP environments.

Server Topologies

Any size of computer can be configured to run as a server. Some services can be provided by a single processor computer, whereas other services, such as large databases, require more substantial computer hardware. Because the typical single-processor system with memory and a few disk drives should be common to anyone attempting to tune Linux on a server, this chapter focuses on larger server configurations with multiple processors and potentially large amounts of disk storage.

Linux can support servers effectively with up to 16 processors on 2.4-based kernels and 32 processors on 2.6-based kernels (and up to 512 processors on some architectures). As the processor count scales up, a similar scaling up of memory and I/O capacity must occur. A 16-processor server with only 1GB of memory would most likely suffer performance problems from a lack of memory for the processors to make use of. Similarly, a server with a large memory would be hampered if only one disk drive were attached, or only one path to get to disk storage. An important consideration is the balance of a server's elements so that adequate resources exist for the work being performed.

An important characteristic of multiprocessor configurations is the manner in which the processors are connected—the server's topology. The basic multiprocessor system employs a large system bus that all processors connect to and that also connects the processors to memory and I/O buses, as depicted in Figure 3-1. Multiprocessor systems like these are referred to as Symmetric Multiprocessors (SMPs) because all processors are equal and have similar access to system resources.

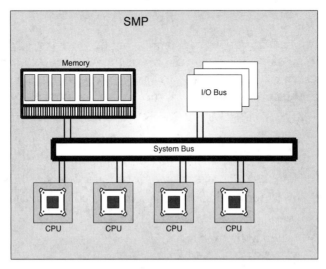

Figure 3-1   The basic multiprocessor system.

How many processors a server needs is determined by the workload. More processors provide more processing power and can provide additional throughput on CPU-bound jobs. If a workload is CPU-bound—processes are waiting excessively for a turn on a processor—additional processor capacity might be warranted.

SMP systems are fairly common and can be found with two to four processors as a commodity product. Larger configurations are possible, but as the processor count goes up, more memory is attached, and more I/O devices are used, the common system bus becomes a bottleneck. There is not enough capacity on the shared system bus to accommodate all the data movement associated with the quantity of processors, memory, and I/O devices. Scaling to larger systems then requires approaches other than SMP.

Various approaches for larger scaling have been employed. The two most common approaches are clusters and Non-Uniform Memory Architecture (NUMA). Both of these approaches have a common basis in that they eliminate a shared system bus. A cluster is constructed of a collection of self-contained systems that are interconnected and have a central control point that manages the work that each system (node) within a cluster is performing. Each node within a cluster runs its own operating system (that is, Linux) and only has direct access to its own memory. NUMA systems, on the other hand, are constructed from nodes connected through a high-speed interconnect, but a common address space is shared across all nodes. Only one operating system image is present, and it controls all operations across the nodes. The memory, although local to each node, is accessible to all nodes in one large, cache-coherent physical address space. Clusters and NUMA systems are discussed in more detail in later sections.

Mixing Processors

Many modern server platforms support the mixing of processor speeds and steppings (revisions) within the same system. Special consideration must be taken to ensure optimal operation in such an environment. Usually, the processor vendor publishes specific guidelines that must be met when mixing processors with different speeds and different features or stepping levels. Some of the most common guidelines are as follows:

- The boot processor is selected from the set of processors having the lowest stepping and lowest feature set of all other processors in the system.
- The system software uses a common speed for all processors in the system, determined by the slowest speed of all processors configured in the system.
- All processors use the same cache size, determined by the smallest cache size of all processors configured in the system.

System software must implement and follow similar restrictions or guidelines to ensure correct program operation.

As you have learned from this section, Linux can support servers with multiprocessors. However, you have also learned the memory has to be increased to avoid performance problems. The next section addresses the memory issue.

MEMORY

Servers tend to have large quantities of memory. Amounts of 1GB to 4GB of memory per processor are common. The amount of memory needed for a server varies depending on the type of work the server is doing. If a server is swapping excessively, additional memory should be considered. Some workloads perform substantially better if there is enough memory on the server to keep common, heavily used data locked in memory. Other workloads use small amounts of memory with transient data, so additional memory would not be a benefit.

The maximum amount of memory a process on a server can address is limited by the processor's word size. Server processors have either 32-bit or 64-bit words. Registers on processors are the size of a word and are used to hold memory addresses. The maximum amount of memory that can be addressed by a processor is a function of the word size. 32-bit processors have a 4GB limit on memory addressability (2 raised to the 32nd power). On Linux the user-space process is provided only 3GB of address space, with the last gigabyte of address space reserved for use by the kernel.

On 64-bit processors, the 4GB limit goes away, but most 64-bit implementations put a restriction on the maximum address below the possible maximum (that is, 2 raised to the 64th power).

Some 32-bit processors (for example, Pentium) implement additional address bits for accessing physical addresses greater than 32 bits, but these are accessible only via virtual addressing by use of additional bits in page table entries. x86-based processors currently support up to 64GB of physical memory through this mechanism, but the virtual addressability is still restricted to 4GB.

64-bit processors are appropriate for workloads that have processes that need to address large quantities of data. Large databases, for example, benefit from the additional memory addressability provided by 64-bit processors. 32-bit processors, on the other hand, are better for workloads that do not have large addressability requirements, because code compiled for 32-bit processors is more compact (because addresses used in the code are half the size of 64-bit addresses). The more compact code reduces cache usage.

Processor speeds and memory speeds continue to increase. However, memory speed technology usually lags processor technology. Therefore, most server systems implement smaller high-speed memory subsystems called *caches*. Cache memory subsystems are implemented between the processors and memory subsystems to help bridge the gap between faster processor speeds and the slower memory access times. The advantage of implementing caches is that they can substantially improve system performance by exploiting a property called *locality of reference*. Most programs, at some point, continuously execute the same subset of instructions for extended periods of time. If the subset of instructions and the associated data can fit in the cache memory, expensive memory accesses can generally be eliminated, and overall workload performance can be substantially increased.

Most processors today implement multiple levels of caches. In addition, some servers can also implement multiple cache hierarchies. The processor caches are typically much smaller and faster than caches implemented in the platform. Caches range in size from a few kilobytes to a few megabytes for on-chip caches and up to several megabytes for system caches. Caches are broken into same-sized entries called cache lines. Each cache line represents a number of contiguous words of main memory. Cache line sizes range from a few bytes (in processor caches) to hundreds of bytes (in system caches). Data is inserted into or evicted from caches on cache line boundaries. The Linux kernel exploits this fact by ensuring that data structures or portions of data structures that are accessed frequently are aligned on cache line boundaries. Cache lines are further organized into sets. The number of lines in a set represents the number of lines a hash routine must search to determine whether an address is available in cache. Caches implement different replacement policies to determine when data is evicted from a cache. Caches also implement different cache consistency algorithms to determine when data is written back to main memory and provide the capability to flush the total contents of a cache. Proper operating system management of system caches can have an impact on system performance.

As much as memory is important to keeping things running smoothly, I/O capacity is also important. Along with memory, this is a component that keeps the processors effective.

I/O

One difference between server systems and other mid-range class computers is the I/O subsystem. Server systems support much larger numbers of I/O devices and more complex I/O topologies. Because servers typically host large amounts of data and need to make data available to consumers quickly, I/O throughput and bandwidth can play a key role in system performance.

I/O buses serve as a connection from I/O devices to the system memory. The prevalent I/O bus on modern servers is PCI. Servers have multiple PCI slots that allow PCI cards that interface to SCSI, Fibre Channel, networks, and other I/O devices.

A server configuration can vary from a single disk up to thousands of disks. Although the number of system disks is limited to 256 in the 2.4 kernel series, this limit has been increased for the 2.6 kernel. Servers with only one or two disks might use IDE technology for the disks, but systems with more than a few disks mostly use SCSI technology. Fibre Channel is also used, especially for larger storage networks that might encompass multiple Fibre Channel adaptors, switches, and enterprise-level storage arrays.

Multipath I/O (MPIO) provides more than one path to a storage device. In basic MPIO configurations, the extra path(s) to the storage device is (are) available for failover only—that is, when the system detects an error attempting to reach the storage device over the primary path, it switches over and uses the secondary path to access the storage device. More advanced MPIO configurations use additional paths to increase the bandwidth between the storage device and memory. The operating system attempts to load-balance across the multiple paths to maximize the amount of data throughput between memory and disks.

A server needs at least one network connection, but again, depending on the type of work the server is performing, it might have multiple network connections, either all to the same network (with the multiple connections providing increased network bandwidth) or to multiple networks. Ethernet is the network technology most in use. Although 10Mbps Ethernet is still supported, most Ethernet today operates at the rate of at least 100Mbps, with Gigabit Ethernet becoming the default on modern servers. Other network technologies, such as ATM, exist and are supported by Linux but are not as widespread as Ethernet.

Other I/O devices are also connected to servers. Most servers have a CD-ROM device for loading software onto the system. They might also have a CD-writer. Some type of device to back up system data is also needed. Tape devices are usually used for this, although other backup mechanisms and strategies are possible.

Large servers have some form of service processor that is used for controlling the initial power-on reset sequence, booting the operating system, and monitoring the system (power supply, cooling, and so on) during normal operation. Service processors often participate in machine fault handling and provide other services for the normal functioning of the server.

The multiprocessors, memory, and I/O subsystems are the kernel components that make an enterprise server. The hardware of the Linux Enterprise Server provides the foundation to bring this high-powered functionality to life.

LINUX ENTERPRISE SERVERS

An *enterprise server* is a server intended for use in a data center. The term implies a certain level of functionality above that of a simple PC-class box running a hobbyist version of Linux. An enterprise server supports the computing needs of a larger organization, with needs that are larger and more complex than those of an individual user or department.

Historically, mainframes served enterprises, and smaller systems served departments or users. However, over the past 20 years, there has been a significant change in computer technology. Now, enterprise-class servers are being built from commodity hardware. At this point, an important distinguishing factor in determining if a server is an enterprise server is the software functionality it provides.

The functionality that is expected in an enterprise server includes the following:

- Advanced management capabilities
    Performance monitoring and tuning
    Storage management, usually in the form of a logical volume manager
    Resource management
    Security monitoring
    User account creation

- Performance and scalability
    Capability of the OS to make effective use of the system resources
    Raw system performance capable of doing enterprise-level computing
    Multiple processors
    Capable of supporting GBs of memory
    Large I/O capabilities (disks, networks)

- Reliability, Availability, Serviceability (RAS)
    Five-nine's of availability (99.999% available)
    Problem diagnostics
    Debugging tools
    Error logging

The criteria for calling a server an enterprise server are subjective, but the capabilities listed here are factors to consider.

The enterprise server serves the complex needs of today's businesses. You can add to this complexity by including clusters. Linux cluster technology allows intensive tasks to run on multiple servers, allowing you to pool your resources.

LINUX CLUSTERS

There are two distinct types of clusters: high-performance clusters and high-availability clusters. The commonality between the two cluster types is that they are both made up of a set of independent computers that are interconnected and working on a common task. Each independent computer within a cluster is called a *node*.

The goal of a high-performance cluster is to perform large computational tasks, spreading the work across a large number of nodes. The goal of a high-availability cluster is for an application (typically a database) to be able to continue functioning even through the failure of one or more nodes. A high-performance cluster is not typically considered an enterprise server, but rather is dedicated to specific computationally intensive tasks. A high-availability cluster, on the other hand, usually operates as an enterprise server.

High-performance clusters (HPCs) tend to have a higher node count than high-availability clusters, with 100 node clusters being common. High-availability clusters tend to have smaller node counts, typically not exceeding 16 nodes, and more commonly only two to four nodes.

High-Performance Clusters

High-performance clusters are an inexpensive way of providing large computational power for problems that are divisible into multiple parallel components. The nodes typically are inexpensive single- or dual-processor computers. Because large numbers of nodes are involved, size is an important consideration. Computers that fit into a 1U form factor that allow for stacking large quantities per rack are commonly used for high performance clusters. Most major hardware vendors sell systems capable of being clustered. Nodes are headless—that is, they have no keyboard, monitor, or mouse. Larger clusters might include a separate management LAN and/or a terminal server network to provide console capability to the nodes.

Each node in an HPC has its own local disk storage to maintain the operating system, provide swap space, store programs, and so on. Some clusters have an additional type of node—a storage server—to provide access to common disk storage for shared data. There is also a master node that provides overall control of the cluster, coordinating the work across nodes and providing the interface between the cluster and local networks.

The interconnect for nodes in an HPC can be Ethernet (10, 100, 1000MBps) or it can be a specialty interconnect that delivers higher performance, such as myrinet. The choice of the interconnect technology is a trade-off between price and speed (latency and bandwidth). The type of work a cluster is designed to do influences the choice of interconnect technology.

Certain file systems are designed for use in cluster environments. These file systems provide a global, parallel cluster file system—for example, GPFS from IBM or CXFS from SGI. These file systems provide concurrent read/write access to files located on a shared disk file system.

Communication between HPC nodes often makes use of message-passing libraries such as MPI or PVM. These libraries are based on common standards and allow the easy porting of parallel applications to different cluster environments.

High-Availability Clusters

Some workloads are more sensitive to failure—that is, a failure of the workload can have expensive repercussions for a business. Sample workloads include customer relationship management (CRM), inventory control, messaging servers, databases, and file and print servers. Availability is critical to these workloads; availability requirements are often described as the five-nines of availability (99.999%). Providing that level of availability allows about 5 minutes of outage per year.

One method of preventing downtime caused by failure of a system running these critical workloads is the use of high-availability (HA) clusters. An HA cluster consists minimally of two independent computers with a "heartbeat" monitoring program that monitors the health of the other node(s) in the cluster. If one node fails, another node detects the failure and automatically picks up the work of the failed node.

It is common for HA clusters to be built from larger computers (four or more processors). Typical HA clusters have only a handful of nodes. Ideally, there is enough excess capacity on the nodes in a cluster to absorb the workload from one failed node. Thus, in a two-node cluster, each node should normally run at 50% capacity so that there is headroom to absorb the load of the other node. In a four-node cluster, each node could run at 75% capacity and there would be sufficient excess capacity to absorb the workload of a failed node. Thus, it is more efficient to have larger node counts. However, the efficiency of large node centers comes at the cost of additional complexity and administrative overhead.

For HA clusters, all nodes need to have access to the data being used by the application, which is normally a database. Use of Fibre Channel adapters and switches is usually necessary to connect more than a few nodes to a common disk storage array. This can often be the limiting factor on the number of nodes in an HA cluster.

Within the Linux community is an active group focused on high-availability clusters (see http://linux-ha.org). This site provides details on the design and configuration of Linux high-availability clusters and provides links to papers that describe various implementations and deployments of Linux HA clusters.

Clusters are a way of consolidating resources. In the following section, see what consolidation means in terms of the mainframe.

EXAMPLES OF SERVER SYSTEMS

Several server systems are available. The performance of these servers is critical to the success of the evolving information infrastructure. Here, we'll discuss a few examples of what is available.

IBM Mainframes—zSeries

Mainframe servers are the ideal platform for some Linux server consolidation efforts. Mainframe servers are large, extremely reliable platforms. These platforms have high memory and I/O bandwidth, low memory latencies, shared large L2 caches, dedicated I/O processors, and very advanced RAS capabilities. IBM zSeries platforms are the mainstay of this technology.

Mainframes support logical partitioning, which is the capability to carve up the machine memory, processor, and I/O resources into multiple machine images, each capable of running an independent operating system. The memory allocated to a partition is dedicated physical memory, whereas the processors can be dedicated or shared, and the I/O channels can also be either dedicated or shared among partitions. When I/O or processor resources are shared among partitions, this sharing is handled by firmware controlling the partitioning and is invisible to the operating systems running in the partitions.

Although Linux can run in a partition on a mainframe, the real advantage is to run large numbers of Linux server images in virtual machines under z/VM. z/VM is an operating system that provides virtual machine environments to its "guests," thus giving each guest the view of an entire machine. This virtual machine implementation allows for supporting a large number of Linux images limited only by system resources. Real deployments have provided thousands of Linux servers running as guests in virtual machines hosted by z/VM on a single mainframe.

Resources can be shared among the Linux images, and high-speed virtual networks are possible. These virtual networks essentially run at memory speed, because there is no need to send packets onto a wire to reach other Linux guests.

New instances of Linux virtual machines are created completely through software control and can be readily scripted. This simplifies system management and allows deployment of a new Linux server (as a guest to z/VM) in a matter of minutes, rather than the hours it would take to install a new physical server. Physical resources do not have to be reserved and dedicated for each guest; rather, under control of z/VM, all the system resources are shared.

z/VM understands the hardware and can exploit the advanced RAS capabilities on behalf of the guest servers. A robust workload monitoring and control facility is provided that supplies an advanced resource management capability. z/VM also provides many debugging tools to assist in diagnosing software problems with a Linux guest, and it also aids in testing new servers. For details on the IBM mainframe technology circa 2000, see `http://www.research.ibm.com/journal/rd43-56.html`.

These machines are optimal for server consolidation. They can support hundreds to thousands of discrete Linux images. Workload types suited to run in this environment exhibit the following characteristics:

- I/O-intensive operations (for example, serving web pages)
- Lightly loaded servers

Computation-intensive, graphic-oriented workloads are not good matches for mainframe servers—nor are workloads that check the system clock often. Heavily loaded servers also are not good candidates for consolidation on a mainframe server.

Older mainframes did not support IEEE-format floating-point operations. Thus, all floating-point operations under Linux had to be converted to the IBM proprietary format, executed, and then converted back to IEEE format. Newer mainframes support IEEE format and do not pay this performance penalty.

Advanced mainframe system management and programming skills are needed for planning and installing a Linux deployment under z/VM. However, after the system is installed and configured, adding new virtual servers is fairly simple.

Hardware Design Overview

The IBM zSeries architecture implements either 12 or 20 processors on a processor module. There are multiple types of processors, which are determined by the microcode that is loaded that controls the processor. The principal types of processors are the processor units, which are equivalent to CPUs on most servers, and the System Assist Processor (SAP), which handles control of the I/O operations. Each machine has at least two SAPs, and could have more depending on the I/O capacity needs.

The modules have two large L2 caches, with each L2 cache shared among half the processors on the module. This differs from standard servers that have an L2 cache associated with each processor. The shared L2 cache allows a process to migrate between processors without losing its cache warmth.

Memory bandwidth is 1.5GBps per processor with an aggregate system bandwidth of 24GBps. The very large memory bandwidth design favors applications that do not have cache-friendly working sets or behavior.

Normal Linux servers usually run at no more than 50% average utilization to provide headroom for workload spikes. The design of the mainframes allows systems to run at 80% to 90% utilization.

Reliability

A significant feature of the mainframe servers is their extremely high reliability. Reliability on these systems is measured in terms of the overall availability. Five-nines of reliability—that is, 99.999% availability—is a common target that is achievable at the hardware level. This amounts to less than 5 minutes of downtime per year. This level of reliability is achieved through advanced hardware design techniques referred to as Continuous Reliable Operation (CRO).

The goal of continuous reliable operation is to keep a customer's workload running without interruptions for error conditions, maintenance, or system change. While remaining available, the machine must also provide reliable results (data integrity) and stable performance. These requirements are met through constant error checking, hot-swap capabilities, and other advanced methods.

IBM Mainframe I/O Design

Each system has two or more processors dedicated to performing I/O operations. SAPs run specialized microcode and manage I/O operations, removing the work of managing I/O operations from the main processors. I/O cards supported are as follows:

- ESCON-16 channel cards
- FICON channel cards
- Open Systems Adapter (OSA) Express
- Gigabit Ethernet (GbE)
- Asynchronous Transfer Mode (ATM)
- Fast Ethernet (FENET)
- PCI-Cryptographic Coprocessor (PCI-CC) cards

ESCON is a zSeries technology that supports 20MBps half-duplex serial bit transmission over fiber-optic cables.

FICON is a newer zSeries technology capable of supporting 100MBps full-duplex serial interface over fiber. It supports multiple outstanding I/O operations at the same time to different channel control units. FICON provides the same I/O concurrency as up to eight ESCON channels.

Open Systems Adapter cards (Ethernet, token ring, or ATM) provide network connectivity. The OSA-Express card implements Queued Direct I/O (QDIO), which uses shared memory queues and a signaling protocol to exchange data directly with the TCP/IP stack.

Disk storage is connected via ESCON or FICON. The recommended storage device is the Enterprise Storage Server (ESS), commonly known as Shark. Shark is a full-featured disk-storage array that supports up to nearly 14 terabytes of disk storage. The ESS has large internal caches and multiple RISC processors to provide high-performance disk storage. Multiple servers can be connected to a single ESS using Fibre Channel, ESCON, FICON, or UltraSCSI technology. More information about the ESS is available at http://www.storage.ibm.com/hardsoft/products/ess/ess.htm.

Blades

Blades are computers implemented in a small form factor, usually an entire computer, including one or two disk drives, on a single card. Multiple cards (blades) reside in a common chassis that provides power, cooling, and cabling to support network and system management connectivity. This packaging allows significant computing power to be provided in dense packaging, thus saving space. Blades are used heavily in data centers that need large quantities of relatively small independent computers, such as large web server environments. Blades are also candidates for use in clusters.

Because size is a significant factor for blade designs, most blades are limited to single processors, although blades with dual processors are available. As processor technology and packaging continue to advance, it is likely that blades with high processor counts will become available. However, the practicality of large processor count blades is somewhat hampered by the amount of I/O connectivity available.

NUMA

Demand for greater computing capacity has led to the increased use of multiprocessor computers. Most multiprocessor computers are considered Symmetric Multiprocessors (SMPs) because each processor is equal and has equal access to all system resources (such as memory and I/O buses). SMP systems generally are built around a system bus that all system components are connected to and which is used to communicate between the components. As SMP systems have increased their processor count, the system bus has increasingly become a bottleneck. One solution that is gaining use by hardware designers is Non-Uniform Memory Architecture (NUMA).

NUMA systems colocate a subset of the system's overall processors and memory into nodes and provide a high-speed, high-bandwidth interconnect between the nodes, as shown in Figure 3-2. Thus, there are multiple physical regions of memory, but all memory is tied together into a single cache-coherent physical address space. In the resulting system, some processors are closer to a given region of physical memory than are other processors. Conversely, for any processor, some memory is considered local (that is, it is close to the processor) and other memory is remote. Similar characteristics can also apply to the I/O buses—that is, I/O buses can be associated with nodes.

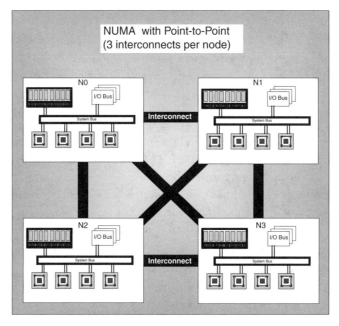

Figure 3-2   NUMA's high-bandwidth interconnect.

Although the key characteristic of NUMA systems is the variable distance of portions of memory from other system components, there are numerous NUMA system designs. At one end of the spectrum are designs where all nodes are symmetrical—they all contain memory, CPUs, and I/O buses. At the other end of the spectrum are systems where there are different types of nodes—the extreme case being separate CPU nodes, memory nodes, and I/O nodes. All NUMA hardware designs are characterized by regions of memory being at varying distances from other resources, thus having different access speeds.

To maximize performance on a NUMA platform, Linux takes into account the way the system resources are physically laid out. This includes information such as which CPUs are on which node, which range of physical memory is on each node, and what node an I/O bus is connected to. This type of information describes the system's topology.

Linux running on a NUMA system obtains optimal performance by keeping memory accesses to the closest physical memory. For example, processors benefit by accessing memory on the same node (or closest memory node), and I/O throughput gains by using memory on the same (or closest) node to the bus the I/O is going through. At the process level, it is optimal to allocate all of a process's memory from the node containing the CPU(s) the process is executing on. However, this also requires keeping the process on the same node.

Hardware Implementations

Many design and implementation choices result in a wide variety of NUMA platforms. This section discusses hardware implementations and provides examples and descriptions of NUMA hardware implementations.

Types of Nodes

The most common implementation of NUMA systems consists of interconnecting symmetrical nodes. In this case, the node itself is an SMP system that has some form of high-speed and high-bandwidth interconnect linking it to other nodes. Each node contains some number of processors, physical memory, and I/O buses. Typically, there is a node-level cache. This type of NUMA system is depicted in Figure 3-3.

A variant on this design is to put only the processors and memory on the main node, and then have the I/O buses be separate. Another design option is to have separate nodes for processors, memory, and I/O buses, which are all interconnected.

It is also possible to have nodes that contain nodes, resulting in a hierarchical NUMA design. This is depicted in Figure 3-3.

Types of Interconnects

There is no standardization of interconnect technology. More relevant to Linux, however, is the topology of the interconnect. NUMA machines can use the following interconnect topologies:

- *Ring topology*, in which each node is connected to the node on either side of it. Memory access latencies can be nonsymmetric—that is, accesses from node A to node B might take longer than accesses from node B to node A.
- *Crossbar interconnect*, where all nodes connect to a common crossbar.
- *Point-to-point*, where each node has a number of ports to connect to other nodes. The number of nodes in the system is limited to the number of connection ports plus one, and each node is directly connected to each other node. This type of configuration is depicted in Figure 3-3.

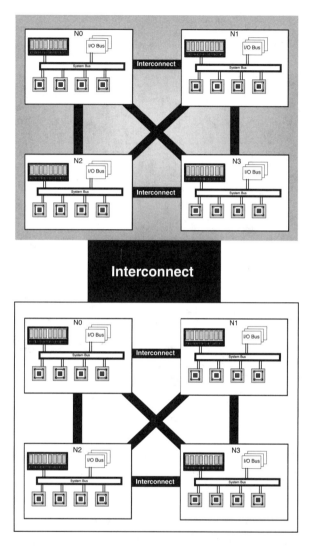

Figure 3-3 Hierarchical NUMA design.

- *Mesh topologies*, which are more complex topologies that, like point-to-point topologies, are built on each node having a number of connection ports. Unlike point-to-point topologies, however, there is no direct connection between each node. Figure 3-4 depicts a mesh topology for an 8-node NUMA system with each node having three interconnects. This allows direct connections to three "close" nodes. Access to other nodes requires an additional "hop," passing through a close node.

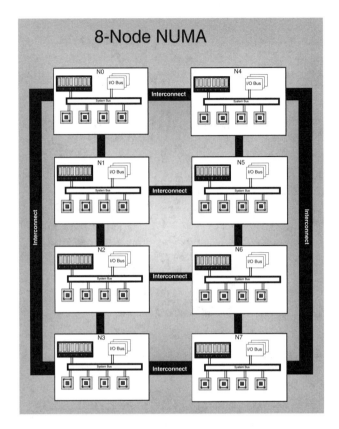

Figure 3-4   8-node NUMA configuration.

The topology provided by the interconnect affects the distance between nodes. This distance affects the access times for memory between the nodes.

Latency Ratios

An important measurement for determining a system's "NUMA-ness" is the latency ratio. This is the ratio of memory latency for on-node memory access to off-node memory access. Depending on the topology of the interconnect, there might be multiple off-node latencies. This latency is used to analyze the cost of memory references to different parts of the physical address space and thus influences decisions affecting memory usage.

Specific NUMA Implementations

Several hardware vendors are building NUMA machines that run the Linux operating system. This section briefly describes some of these machines, but it is not an all-inclusive survey of the existing implementations.

One of the earlier commercial NUMA machines is the IBM NUMA-Q. This machine is based on nodes that contain four processors (i386), memory, and PCI buses. Each node also contains a management module to coordinate booting, monitor environmentals, and communicate with the system console. The nodes are interconnected using a ring topology. Up to 16 nodes can be connected for a maximum of 64 processors and 64GB of memory. Remote-to-local memory latency ratios range from 10:1 to 20:1. Each node has a large remote cache that helps compensate for the large remote memory latencies. Much of the Linux NUMA development has been on these systems because of their availability.

NEC builds NUMA systems using the Intel Itanium processor. The most recent system in this line is the NEC TX7. The TX7 supports up to 32 Itanium2 processors in nodes of four processors each. The nodes are connected by a crossbar and grouped in two supernodes of four nodes each. The crossbar provides fast access to nonlocal memory with low latency and high bandwidth (12.8GBps per node). The memory latency ratio for remote-to-local memory in the same supernode is 1.6:1. The remote-to-local memory latency ratio for outside the supernode is 2.1:1. There is no node-level cache. I/O devices are connected through PCI-X buses to the crossbar interconnect and thus are all the same distance to any CPU/node.

The large IBM xSeries boxes use Intel processors and the IBM XA-32 chipset. This chipset provides an architecture that supports four processors, memory, PCI buses, and three interconnect ports. These interconnect ports allow point-to-point connection of up to four nodes for a 16-processor system. The system depicted in Figure 3-2 approximates the configuration of a four-node x440. Also supported is a connection to an external system with additional PCI slots to increase the system's I/O capacity. The IBM eServer xSeries 440 is built on this architecture with Intel Xeon processors.

MPIO on NUMA Systems

Multipath I/O, as mentioned earlier in this chapter, can provide additional I/O bandwidth for servers. However, on NUMA platforms, it can provide even larger benefits. MPIO involves using multiple I/O adaptors (SCSI cards, network cards) to gain multiple paths to the underlying resource (hard disks, the network), thus increasing overall bandwidth. On SMP platforms, potential speedups due to MPIO are limited by the fact that all CPUs and memory typically share a bus, which has a maximum bandwidth. On NUMA platforms, however, different groups of CPUs, memory, and I/O buses have their own distinct interconnects. Because these distinct interconnects allow each node to independently reach its maximum bandwidth, larger I/O aggregate throughput is likely.

An ideal MPIO on NUMA setup consists of an I/O card (SCSI, network, and so on) on each node connected to every I/O device, so that no matter where the requesting process runs, or where the memory is, there is always a local route to the I/O device. With this hardware configuration, it is possible to saturate several PCI buses with data. This is even further assisted by the fact that many machines of this size use RAID or other MD devices, thus increasing the potential bandwidth by using multiple disks.

Timers

On uniprocessor systems, the processor has a time source that is easily and quickly accessible, typically implemented as a register. On SMP systems, the processors' time source is usually synchronized because all the processors are clocked at the same rate. Therefore, synchronization of the time register between processors is a straightforward task.

On NUMA systems, synchronization of the processors' time source is not practical because not only does each node have its own crystal providing the clock frequency, but there tends to be minute differences in the frequencies that the processors are driven at, which thus leads to time skew.

On multiprocessor systems, it is imperative that there be a consistent system time. Otherwise, time stamps provided by different processors cannot be relied on for ordering. If a process is dispatched on a different processor, it is possible that there can be unexpected jumps (backward or forward) in time.

Ideally, the hardware provides one global time source with quick access times. Unfortunately, global time sources tend to require off-chip access and often off-node access, which tend to be slow. Clock implementations are very architecture-specific, with no clear leading implementation among the NUMA platforms. On the IBM eServer xSeries 440, for example, the global time source is provided by node 0, and all other nodes must go off-node to get the time.

In Linux 2.6, the i386 timer subsystem has an abstraction layer that simplifies the addition of a different time source provided by specific machine architecture. For standard i386 architecture machines, the timestamp counter (TSC) is used, which provides a very quick time reference. For NUMA machines, a global time source is used (for example, on the IBM eServer xSeries 440, the global chipset timer is used).

SUMMARY

This chapter has shown you that Linux has a lot to offer! While familiarizing you with all Linux has to offer as far as server architecture, the point here is the enhanced design of the Linux kernel. This design helps you shape your system to your needs.

Each feature works together to form a powerhouse of software technology. From the power of the processors and multiprocessors, to the technique of configuration, to the versatility of the memory, Linux has your server!

## PART II

Performance Analysis Tools

## CHAPTER FOUR

System Performance Monitoring

By Gerrit Huizenga, Peter Wai Yee Wong, and Vaijayanthimala Anand

INTRODUCTION

This chapter focuses on tools that initially help monitor the overall performance of the system. After the overall system performance characteristics of a workload are understood, the same tools can be useful in identifying which particular processes are bottlenecks to the overall workload. In many cases, the system monitoring tools can help drive system tuning such that the key bottlenecks can be substantially reduced or eliminated. In other cases, these tools simply pinpoint applications or processes that need tuning, reconfiguration, or, in the most extreme case, algorithmic changes to improve overall workload performance and throughput.

In particular, this chapter examines tools that provide insights into the following:

- Overall system CPU utilization
- Memory utilization
- Disk I/O utilization and latency
- Network utilization

Several of the tools provide information about different aspects of system utilization; however, to simplify the organization of this chapter, tools are discussed in the section that is most appropriate to the majority of their monitoring capabilities. These tools are often the first, and sometimes the only, means used for understanding and improving the performance of a given workload. However, there are cases where these high-level tools point to a single application or set of tasks that are a bottleneck that cannot be resolved by global system tuning. In those cases, future chapters discuss tools that allow a performance analyst to zoom in on a problem application to better understand the operation of the application and its interaction with the underlying operating system.

BACKGROUND ON LINUX AND PERFORMANCE ANALYSIS

Linux entered the marketplace primarily through grassroots efforts that recognized the price/performance benefits of Linux on small servers. Linux has been very effective in that market space and has become an increasingly popular operating system for use in the wider enterprise market. This popularity has encouraged hardware vendors to port Linux to platforms with more processors, more processor types, more physical memory, and larger I/O configurations. Software vendors have seen the benefits of porting more complex software to Linux, and end users are putting together more complex configurations. As these workloads increase in complexity, end users are beginning to expect the same or higher levels of performance as they had with proprietary systems. These increased expectations of performance translate into performance analysis and improvements in scalability of the operating system's scheduler, memory management, disk, and network I/O subsystems.

Historically, systems vendors provided a proprietary operating system and performed the analysis of core subsystems internally and with a relatively small set of critical applications that were key to the core of their businesses. Those vendors were able to use advanced and often proprietary performance analysis tools, including sophisticated bus monitors, proprietary chip counters, simulations tools, native performance monitoring packages, and tools to analyze the performance of complex software and hardware configurations. Many of these complex tools were made available to selected customers or used through service contracts to allow customers to analyze their workload's performance characteristics and to assess the results of complex tuning changes. The intent of part of this book is to explore some of the tools and the best practices that can be more universally applied today to improve the overall performance of Linux and the applications that run on Linux.

Linux provides some new challenges in performance analysis but also offers some unique advantages. Specifically, Linux runs on a much wider range of hardware platforms than most proprietary operating systems, including RISC and CISC architectures, 32-bit and 64-bit systems, uniprocessor systems, embedded systems, small (two to four CPUs) and large (eight to 128) symmetrical multiprocessing systems. The workloads on these Linux-based systems and the underlying processor combinations tend to be more varied than any other single operating system has addressed, including desktops, laptops, embedded systems, mail servers, file servers, application servers, database servers, and content servers. Although many workloads have been used at various times in tuning Linux, Linux has not been tuned for a specific, single workload. Moreover, the same core Linux kernel and base libraries are expected to run reasonably well on all of these workloads. Because of these trade-offs and the widespread expectations that Linux works reasonably well on all workloads, there is a good chance that your unique workload will not run optimally on Linux without the benefit of system analysis, performance monitoring, and (potentially) system and application tuning.

Performance in these increasingly complex workloads is influenced by many factors. Obviously, processor speed, memory size, number of network or disk I/O controllers, and size and speed of disks are significant components of all workload performance characteristics. Other major components include the application's own performance characteristics, the nature of the workload, the communications between applications, the access patterns for data on disk or on the network, and, of course, the usage models of the end users using the applications.

Tuning a particular workload often starts with the assumption that many of the physical characteristics of the environment will remain unchanged, such as the number of processors, the processor type, number of disks, and so on. The primary goals in performance analysis are to identify what components of the workload are the current bottlenecks to increased performance and overall throughput and, when the workload has saturated the capacity of the available hardware, to understand what hardware configuration improvements would increase the workload's throughput and performance.

Many Linux performance tools are available today in the open-source community in addition to a few commercial tools. Many of the examples in this chapter are drawn from a common distribution running a Linux 2.4 kernel, although in general the same tools should exist and have the same capabilities in any distribution based on the Linux 2.6 kernel. In some cases, the data collected by the kernel is provided through different interfaces or based on different in-kernel accounting mechanisms. In any case, the information provided by the tool should be similar or identical. If your distribution does not have a particular tool installed or you believe that a particular tool is not sufficiently current, you may want to consult the distribution media for the tool or pick up the latest version from the tool's maintainer. See, for instance, `http://linuxperf.nl.linux.org/general/tools/tools.html` for a pointer to some of the currently available tools.

CPU UTILIZATION

One of the primary indicators of system performance is the responsiveness of the system to its users. Although most user reports of performance tend to be very subjective, there are several more quantitative measures than can be applied to end-user perceptions. For instance, humans tend to generally perceive any response within 50 milliseconds as virtually instantaneous. Interactive applications, especially those that involve text entry, appear slow when that 50-millisecond threshold is exceeded. Users of complex systems may have been acclimated to system response times of several seconds or, for occasional highly complex activities, possibly even minutes. Each workload has its own response times, often established with the user through days, weeks, months, or even years of interaction with the system. When the user's expectations are no longer satisfied, the user tends to call the support desk to indicate that response times have degraded, possibly catastrophically, to the point where the user can no longer complete his task in a reasonable amount of time.

These calls to the support desk serve as an unplanned opportunity to employ performance analysis tools of various types. Unfortunately, reactive applications of these tools without known baselines can present quite a challenge to the uninitiated. Having an opportunity to monitor the application before a crisis, as well as creating and archiving various performance statistics, typically helps expedite a resolution to any complaints to the support desk. Also, some general experience with how to recognize certain signs of system performance problems is invaluable in understanding performance problems with a workload. Systematic and methodic application of the tools described here, typically coupled with general knowledge of the workload, should make it possible to narrow down any performance bottlenecks. And with a knowledge of the bottleneck from a system perspective, a system administrator or performance analyst should be able to employ system tuning, system reconfiguration, workload reconfiguration, or detailed analysis of specific workload components to further identify and ultimately resolve any performance bottleneck.

In a methodical analysis of the system, often one of the first and most basic tools is a simple measure of the system's CPU utilization. In particular, Linux and most UNIX-based operating systems provide a command that displays the system's load average:

```
$ uptime
 17:37:30 up 3 days, 17:06,   7 users,   load average: 1.13, 1.23, 1.15
```

In particular, the load average represents the average number of tasks that could be run over a period of 1, 5, and 15 minutes. Runnable tasks are those that either are currently running or those that can run but are waiting for a processor to be available. In this case, the system had only one CPU, which can be determined by looking at the contents of /proc/cpu:

```
$ cat /proc/cpu
processor      : 0
vendor_id      : GenuineIntel
cpu family     : 6
model          : 8
model name     : Pentium III (Coppermine)
stepping       : 6
cpu MHz        : 647.195
```

```
cache size       : 256 KB
fdiv_bug         : no
hlt_bug          : no
f00f_bug         : no
coma_bug         : no
fpu              : yes
fpu_exception    : yes
cpuid level      : 2
wp               : yes
flags            : fpu vme de pse tsc msr pae mce cx8 sep mtrr pge mca
   cmov pat pse36 mmx fxsr sse
bogomips         : 1291.05
```

In this case, there is only an entry for a single processor, so on average there was slightly more work for the processor to do than it could keep up with. At a high level, this implies that the machine has more work to do than it can keep up with. Note: If uptime showed a load average of something less than 2.00 on a two-CPU machine, that would indicate that the processors still have additional free cycles. The same would be true on a four-CPU machine with a load average less than 4.00, and so on. However, the load average alone does not tell the entire story.

In this case, the machine in question was a laptop. The workload included an email client, word processors, web browsers, some custom applications, chat clients, and so on, all running simultaneously. However, the response time to the various workloads was deemed to be acceptable by the user.

This implies that the operating system scheduler was appropriately prioritizing tasks that needed to be run based on those that were most interactive. No significant server aspects were running on the machine, so there was no impact from the high load average on other clients or machines.

So, although the tool indicates that the CPU was fully utilized, it does not indicate what the system was doing or why it was so busy. And, if the response time for the users of the system was acceptable, there may not be any reason to probe more deeply into the system's operation.

However, this chapter would be uninteresting if we stopped there. Quite often, simple tools like uptime are a user's quick way to attempt to account for any perceived slowness in an application's response time. If the load average for the system indicates that the response time may be caused by an overloaded processor (or processors), a variety of other tools can be used to narrow down the cause of the load.

To drill down a bit further into how the processors are being used, we'll look at three tools that provide us with a variety of different insights about the CPU utilization: vmstat, iostat, and top. Each of these commands has a different focus on system monitoring, but each can be used to get a different perspective on how the processor is being utilized. In particular, the next step would be to understand if the processor is primarily spending time in the operating system (often referred to as kernel space) or in the application (often referred to as user space) or if the processor is idle. Further, if the processor is idle, understanding why it is idle is key to any further performance analysis. A processor can be idle for a number of reasons. For instance, the most obvious reason is that a process cannot run. This may sound too obvious, but if a component of the workload, such as a particular process or task, is not running, performance may be impacted. In some cases, caching components or fallback mechanisms allow some applications to continue to run, although with degraded throughput. As an example, the Internet domain name service is often configured to consult a daemon called *named* or to consult a service off-host. If one name service provider, such as the first one listed with a name-server line in /etc/resolv.conf, is not running, there may be a timeout period before another information provider is consulted. To the user, this may appear as sporadic delays in the application. To someone monitoring the system with uptime, the load average may not appear very high. However, in this case, the output from vmstat may help narrow the problem. In particular, many of the tools that we will look at in this chapter and the next two will help you understand what the machine's CPU is doing, from which a performance analyst can create hypotheses about the system performance and then attempt to validate those hypotheses.

vmstat

vmstat is a real-time performance monitoring tool. The vmstat command provides data that can be used to help find unusual system activity, such as high page faults or excessive context switches, which can degrade system performance. The frequency of data display is a user-specified parameter. A sample of the vmstat output is as follows:

```
procs -----------memory---------- ---swap-- -----io---- --system-- ----cpu---
       -
 r   b   swpd   free   buff  cache   si   so    bi    bo   in    cs  us sy id wa
18   8     0 5626196   3008 122788    0    0 330403   454 2575  4090 91  8  1  0
18  15     0 5625132   3008 122828    0    0 328767   322 2544  4264 91  8  0  0
17  12     0 5622004   3008 122828    0    0 327956   130 2406  3998 92  8  0  0
22   2     0 5621644   3008 122828    0    0 327892   689 2445  4077 92  8  0  0
23   5     0 5621616   3008 122868    0    0 323171   407 2339  4037 92  8  1  0
21  14     0 5621868   3008 122868    0    0 323663    23 2418  4160 91  9  0  0
22  10     0 5625216   3008 122868    0    0 328828   153 2934  4518 90  9  1  0
```

vmstat produces the following information:

- The procs section reports the number of running processes (r) and blocked processes (b) at the time of reporting. You can use the information in this section to check whether the number of running and blocked processes is similar to what you expected. If it isn't, you can check a number of things: the parameters of the applications and kernel, system scheduler and I/O scheduler, the distribution of processes among available processors, and so on.
- The memory section reports the amount of memory being swapped out (swpd), free memory (free), buffer cache for I/O data structures (buff), and cached memory for files read from the disk (cache) in kilobytes. The value of swpd reflects kswapd activities.
- The swap section returns the amount of memory swapped in (si) from disk and swapped out (so) to disk, in kilobytes per second. Note that so reflects the kswapd activity as data is swapped out to the swap area. However, si reflects page fault activities as pages are swapped back to the physical memory.
- The io section reports the number of blocks read in (bi) from the devices and blocks written out (bo) to the devices in kilobytes per second. Pay particular attention to these two fields when running I/O-intensive applications.
- The system section reports the number of interrupts (in) and context switches (cs) per second.
- The cpu section reports the percentage of total CPU time in terms of user (us), system (sy), true idleness (id), and waiting for I/O completion (wa). Perhaps the most common metric is CPU utilization. If wa is large, examine the I/O subsystem—you may conclude, for example, that more I/O controllers and disks are needed to reduce the I/O wait time.

For I/O-intensive workloads, you can monitor bi and bo for the transfer rate and in for the interrupt rate. You can monitor swpd, si, and so to see whether the system is swapping. If so, you can check on the swapping rate. Perhaps the most common metric is CPU utilization and the monitoring of us, sy, id, and wa. If wa is large, you need to examine the I/O subsystem. You might come to the conclusion that more I/O controllers and disks are needed to reduce the I/O wait time.

Like uptime, when vmstat is run without options, it reports a single snapshot of the system. If you run uptime, followed by vmstat, you can get a quick snapshot of how busy the system is and some indication of what the processor is doing with the percentage breakdown of user, system, idle, and waiting on I/O times. In addition, vmstat provides an instantaneous count of the number of runnable processes. Note that uptime provides another view of the number of runnable processes across three time periods: 1 minute, 5 minutes, and 15 minutes. So, if the load average from `uptime` remains above 1 for any period of time, the number of runnable tasks reported by `vmstat` should also be near 1.

Because `vmstat` can also provide information at regular, repeated intervals, you can get a more dynamic view of the system with the following command:

```
$ vmstat 5 10
```

This command outputs `vmstat` information every 5 seconds for 10 iterations. Again, the output should generally show about one runnable task in each line of output if the load average has been 1 for the past 1/5/10 minutes per the output of `uptime`. Do not be surprised to see peaks of 5, 7, or even 20 in the output of `vmstat`! Remember that the load average is a calculated average as opposed to an instantaneous snapshot. Both views have their benefits to system performance analysis.

`vmstat` also provides a rough view of how much time the processor is spending in the operating system, how much time is spent in user application space (including libraries provided as part of the application or operating system), how much time is idle, and how much time the operating system is blocked waiting on I/O. Various workloads have different utilization patterns, so there are no definite rules as to what values are good or bad. In these cases, it is good to have developed a baseline for your workload to help you recognize how the workload has changed as the response time or system load increases. `vmstat` helps identify which tools can help drill down into any workload degradations or provide clues as to where tuning or reconfiguration can improve workload performance.

The remainder of this section explores a few examples. Imagine a scenario where users are reporting poor response times with a workload. Examining the load average via `uptime` shows the load average to be very low, possibly even well below the baseline times. Further, `vmstat` shows that the number of runnable jobs was very low and that the system was relatively idle from the percentage of CPU idle time. An analyst might be interpret these results as a sign that some key process had exited or was blocking waiting on some event that wasn't completing. For instance, some applications use a form of semaphore technique to dispatch work and wait for completion. Perhaps the work was dispatched to a back-end server or other application and that application has for some reason stopped processing all activity. As a result, the application closest to the user is blocked, not runnable, waiting on some semaphore to notify it of completion before it can return information to the user. This might cause the administrator to focus attention on the server application to see why it is unable to complete the requests being queued for it.

In another scenario, suppose that the load average is showing a load in excess of 1, possibly even a full point higher on average than established baselines. In addition, vmstat shows one or two processes always runnable, but the percentage of user time is nearly 100% over an extended period of time. Another tool might be necessary to find out what process or processes are using up 100% of the CPU time—for instance, ps(1) or top(1). ps(1) provides a listing of all processes that currently exist, or some selected subset of processes based on its options. top(1) (or gtop(1)) provides a constantly updating view of the most active processes, where *most active* can be defined as those processes that are using the most processor time. This data might help identify a runaway process that is doing nothing useful on the system. If vmstat(1) had reported that the processes were mostly running in user space, the administrator might want to connect a debugger such as gdb(1) to the process and use breakpoints, tracing, or other debugging means to understand what the application was doing. If vmstat had reported that most of the time was being consumed as "system" time, other tools such as strace(1) might be used to find out what system calls were being made. If vmstat(1) had reported that a large percentage of time was being spent waiting for I/O completion, tools such as sar(1) could be used to see what devices were being used and also provide some possible insights into which applications or file systems were in use, whether the system was swapping or paging, and so on.

vmstat(1) provides some simple insights into the current state of the system. In this section, we looked at the areas that primarily interact with the CPU utilization. However, vmstat(1) also provides some insight into memory utilization, basic swapping activity, and I/O activity. Later sections in this chapter look at more of these areas in detail.

top and gtop

top and gtop are very useful tools for understanding the tasks and processes that contribute to the high-level information provided by vmstat or uptime. They can show which processes are active and which ones over time are consuming the most processing time or memory.

The top command provides an updating overview of all running processes and the system load. top provides information on CPU load, memory usage, and usage per process, as detailed in the snapshot that follows. Note that it also provides load average snapshots much like uptime(1) does; however, top also provides a breakout of the number of processes that have been created but that are currently sleeping, and the number of processes that are running. "Sleeping" tasks are those that are blocked waiting on some activity, such as a key press from a user at a keyboard, data from a pipe or socket, requests from another host (such as a web server waiting for someone to request content), and so on. `top(1)` also shows load average for each processor independently, which can help identify any imbalances in scheduling tasks. By default, the output of `top` is refreshed frequently, and tasks are sorted by percentage of CPU consumption. Other sorting options are possible, such as cumulative CPU consumption or percentage of memory consumption.

```
4:52pm  up  5:08,   3 users,   load average: 2.77, 5.81, 3.15
37 processes: 36 sleeping, 1 running, 0 zombie, 0 stopped
CPU0 states:   5.1% user, 53.1% system,   0.0% nice, 41.1% idle
CPU1 states:   5.0% user, 52.4% system,   0.0% nice, 41.4% idle
Mem:    511480K av,    43036K used,   468444K free,       0K shrd,    2196K
Swap:  263992K av,       0K used,   263992K free                     21432K

  PID USER    PRI  NI  SIZE  RSS SHARE STAT %CPU %MEM  TIME COMMAND
 1026 root      2   0   488  488   372 S     1.1  0.0  0:00 chat_s
 7490 root     11   0  1012 1012   816 R     0.5  0.1  0:00 top
    3 root     19  19     0    0     0 SWN   0.3  0.0  0:00 ksoftirqd_C
    4 root     19  19     0    0     0 SWN   0.1  0.0  0:00 ksoftirqd_C
    1 root      9   0   536  536   468 S     0.0  0.1  0:04 init
    2 root      9   0     0    0     0 SW    0.0  0.0  0:00 keventd
    5 root      9   0     0    0     0 SW    0.0  0.0  0:00 kswapd
    6 root      9   0     0    0     0 SW    0.0  0.0  0:00 bdflush
    7 root      9   0     0    0     0 SW    0.0  0.0  0:00 kupdated
    9 root      9   0     0    0     0 SW    0.0  0.0  0:00 scsi_eh_0
   10 root      9   0     0    0     0 SW    0.0  0.0  0:00 khubd
  331 root      9   0   844  844   712 S     0.0  0.1  0:00 syslogd
  341 root      9   0  1236 1236   464 S     0.0  0.2  0:00 klogd
  356 rpc       9   0   628  628   536 S     0.0  0.1  0:00 portmap
```

`top` includes the following information in its output:

- Line 1 shows the system uptime, including the current time, how long the system has been up since the last reboot, the current number of users, and three load average numbers. The load average numbers represent the average number of processors ready to run during the previous 1, 5, and 15 minutes.

- Line 2 includes the process statistics, including the total number of processes running at the time of the last `top` screen update. This line also includes the number of sleeping, running, zombie, and stopped processes.

- Lines 3 and 4 display CPU statistics for individual CPUs, including the percentage of CPU time used by the user, system, `niced`, and idle processes.

- Line 5 provides memory statistics, including total memory available, used memory, free memory, shared memory by different processes, and memory used for buffers.

- Line 6 shows virtual memory or swap statistics, including total available swap space, used swap space, free swap space, and cached swap space.
- The remaining lines show statistics on the individual processes. Some of the more useful top parameters are as follows:

d　Delay between updates to the data.

p　Display only the processes specified. Up to 20 processes can be specified.

s　Display a summary of time being spent by the process and its children. Also displays dead time.

I　Do not report idle processes.

H　Show all threads by process.

N　Number of times to produce the reports.

top also has a dynamic mode to change report information. Activate dynamic mode by pressing the f key. By further pressing the j key, you can add a new column to show the CPU last used by an executing process. This additional information is particularly useful for understanding the process behavior in an SMP system.

This section barely scratches the surface of the types of information that top or gtop provide. For more information on top, see the corresponding man page; for more information on gtop, see the built-in help command.

sar

sar is part of the sysstat package. sar collects and reports a wide range of system activity in the operating system, including CPU utilization, the rate of context switches and interrupts, the rate of paging in and paging out, the shared memory usage, the buffer usage, and network usage. sar(1) is useful because it constantly collects and logs system activity information in a set of log files, which makes it possible to evaluate performance problems both prior to the reporting of a performance regression event as well as after the event. sar can often be used to pinpoint the time of the event and can also be used to identify specific changes in the system's behavior. sar can also output information with a shorter interval or a fixed number of intervals, much like vmstat. Based on the values in the count and interval parameters, the sar tool writes information the specified number of times spaced at the specified intervals in seconds. In addition, sar can provide averages for a number of data points that it collects. The following example provides statistics on a four-way SMP system by collecting data every 5 seconds:

CPU Utilization

```
11:09:13   CPU   %user   %nice   %system  %iowait   %idle
11:09:18   all    0.00    0.00     4.70    52.45    42.85
11:09:18    0     0.00    0.00     5.80    57.00    37.20
```

```
11:09:18     1    0.00    0.00    4.80    49.40   45.80
11:09:18     2    0.00    0.00    6.00    62.20   31.80
11:09:18     3    0.00    0.00    2.40    41.12   56.49
11:09:23   all    0.00    0.00    3.75    47.30   48.95
11:09:23     0    0.00    0.00    5.39    37.33   57.29
11:09:23     1    0.00    0.00    2.80    41.80   55.40
11:09:23     2    0.00    0.00    5.40    41.60   53.00
11:09:23     3    0.00    0.00    1.40    68.60   30.00
. . .
Average:   all    0.00    0.00    4.22    16.40   79.38
Average:     0    0.00    0.00    8.32    24.33   67.35
Average:     1    0.00    0.00    2.12    14.35   83.53
Average:     2    0.01    0.00    4.16    12.07   83.76
Average:     3    0.00    0.00    2.29    14.85   82.86
```

One component of CPU consumption by the system is the networking and disk servicing routines. As the operating system generates I/O, the corresponding device subsystems respond by signaling the completion of those I/O requests with hardware interrupts. The operating system counts each of these interrupts; the output can help you visualize the rate of networking and disk I/O activity. sar(1) provides this input. With baselines, it is possible to track the rate of system interrupts, which can be another source of system overhead or an indicator of possible changes to system performance. The -I SUM option can generate the following information, including the total number of interrupts per second. The -I ALL option can provide similar information for each interrupt source (not shown).

Interrupt Rate

```
10:53:53          INTR    intr/s
10:53:58           sum    4477.60
10:54:03           sum    6422.80
10:54:08           sum    6407.20
10:54:13           sum    6111.40
10:54:18           sum    6095.40
10:54:23           sum    6104.81
10:54:28           sum    6149.80
. . .
Average:           sum    4416.53
```

A per-CPU view of the interrupt distribution on an SMP machine is available through the sar -A command (the following example is an excerpt from the full output). Note that the IRQ values of the system are 0, 1, 2, 9, 12, 14, 17, 18, 21, 23, 24, and 25. Due to the limited width of the page, interrupts for 9, 12, 14, and 17 have been clipped away.

Interrupt Distribution

```
10:53:53  CPU  i000/s i001/s i002/s … i018/s  i021/s i023/s i024/s  i025/s
10:53:58    0 1000.20   0.00   0.00 …   0.40    0.00   0.00   3.00    0.00
10:53:58    1    0.00   0.00   0.00 …   0.00    0.00   0.00   0.00 2320.00
10:53:58    2    0.00   0.00   0.00 …   0.00 1156.00   0.00   0.00    0.00
10:53:58    3    0.00   0.00   0.00 …   0.00    0.00   0.00   0.00    0.00
Average:    0  999.94   0.00   0.00 …   1.20  590.99   0.00   3.73    0.00
Average:    1    0.00   0.00   0.00 …   0.00    0.00   0.00   0.00  926.61
Average:    2    0.00   0.00   0.00 …   0.00  466.51   0.00   0.00 1427.48
Average:    3    0.00   0.00   0.00 …   0.00    0.00   0.00   0.00    0.00
```

The study of interrupt distribution might reveal an imbalance in interrupt processing. The next step should be an examination of the scheduler. One way to tackle the problem is to bind IRQ processing to a specific processor or a number of processors by setting up an affinity for a particular device's interrupt (or IRQ) to a particular CPU or set of CPUs. For example, if 0x0001 is echoed to /proc/irq/ID, where ID corresponds to a device, only CPU 0 will process IRQ for this device. If 0x000f is echoed to /proc/irq/ID, CPU 0 through CPU 3 will be used to process IRQ for this device. For some workloads, this technique can reduce contention on certain heavily used processors. This technique allows I/O interrupts to be processed more efficiently; the I/O performance should increase accordingly.

MEMORY UTILIZATION

Workloads have a tendency to consume all available memory. Linux provides reasonably efficient access to physical memory and provides access to potentially huge amounts of "virtual" memory. Virtual memory is usually little more than a capability of an operating system to offload less frequently used data to disk storage while presenting the illusion that the system has an enormous amount of physical memory. Unfortunately, the price for offloading memory can be ten or a hundred times more expensive in terms of application latency. Those high latencies can impact application response times dramatically if the memory that is paged out to disk is the wrong memory, or if the application's active memory footprint is larger than the size of physical memory.

Many performance problems are caused by insufficient memory, which triggers system swapping. Thus, it is useful to have tools that monitor memory utilization—for example, how the kernel memory is consumed per process or per thread, and how the memory is consumed by the kernel data structures along with their counts and sizes. As with CPU utilization, understanding how both the system and individual processes are behaving is key to tracking down any performance problems caused by memory shortages.

/proc/meminfo and /proc/slabinfo

Linux provides facilities to monitor the utilization of overall system memory resources under the /proc file system—namely, /proc/meminfo and /proc/slabinfo. These two files capture the state of the physical memory. A partial display of /proc/meminfo is as follows:

```
MemTotal:        8282420 kB
MemFree:         7942396 kB
Buffers:           46992 kB
Cached:           191936 kB
SwapCached:            0 kB
HighTotal:       7470784 kB
HighFree:        7232384 kB
LowTotal:         811636 kB
LowFree:          710012 kB
SwapTotal:        618492 kB
SwapFree:         618492 kB
Mapped:            36008 kB
Slab:              36652 kB
```

MemTotal gives the total amount of physical memory of the system, whereas MemFree gives the total amount of unused memory.

Buffers corresponds to the buffer cache for I/O operations. Cached corresponds to the memory for reading files from the disk.

SwapCached represents the amount of cache memory that has been swapped out in the swap space.

SwapTotal represents the amount of disk memory for swapping purposes. If an IA32-based system has more than 1GB of physical memory, HighTotal is nonzero.

HighTotal corresponds to memory greater than ~860MB of the physical memory.

LowTotal is the memory used by the kernel. Mapped corresponds to the files that are memory-mapped.

Slab corresponds to the memory used for the kernel data structures. By capturing /proc/meminfo periodically, you can establish a pattern of memory utilization. With the aid of simple scripts and graphics tools, the pattern can be also summarized visually.

To understand kernel memory consumption, examine /proc/slabinfo. A partial display of /proc/slabinfo is as follows:

```
tcp_bind_bucket        56    224    32    2    2    1
tcp_open_request       16     58    64    1    1    1
inet_peer_cache         0      0    64    0    0    1
secpath_cache           0      0    32    0    0    1
flow_cache              0      0    64    0    0    1
```

The first column lists the names of the kernel data structures. To further describe tcp_bind_bucket, there is a total of 224 tcp_bind_bucket objects, 56 of which are active. Each data structure takes up 32 bytes. There are two pages that have at least one active object, and there is a total of two allocated pages. Moreover, one page is allocated for each slab. This information highlights certain data structures that merit more focus, such as those with larger counts or sizes. Thus, by capturing meminfo and slabinfo together, you can begin to understand what elements of the operating system are consuming the most memory. If the values of LowFree or HighFree are relatively small (or smaller than usual), that might indicate that the system is running with more requests for memory than usual, which may lead to a reduction in overall performance or application response times.

ps

To find out how the memory is used within a particular process, use ps for an overview of memory used per process:

```
$ ps aux
```

```
USER  PID %CPU %MEM   VSZ  RSS TTY STAT START TIME COMMAND
root    1  0.0  0.0  1528  528 ?   S     15:24 0:00 init [2]
root    2  0.0  0.0     0    0 ?   SN    15:24 0:00 [ksoftirqd/0]
root    3  0.0  0.0     0    0 ?   S<    15:24 0:00 [events/0]
root    4  0.0  0.0     0    0 ?   S<    15:24 0:00 [khelper]
root    5  0.0  0.0     0    0 ?   S<    15:24 0:00 [kacpid]
root   48  0.0  0.0     0    0 ?   S<    15:24 0:00 [kblockd/0]
root   63  0.0  0.0     0    0 ?   S     15:24 0:00 [pdflush]
root   64  0.0  0.0     0    0 ?   S     15:24 0:00 [pdflush]
```

The output of the ps aux command shows the total percentage of system memory that each process consumes, as well as its virtual memory footprint (VSZ) and the amount of physical memory that the process is currently using (RSS). You can also use top(1) to sort the process listing interactively to see which processes are consuming the most memory and how that consumption changes as the system runs.

After you have identified a few processes of interest, you can look into the specific allocations of memory that the process is using by looking at the layout of the processes' virtual address space. /proc/pid/maps, where *pid* is the process ID of a particular process as found through ps(1) or top(1), contains all mappings of the processes' address spaces and their sizes. Each map shows the address range that is allocated, the permissions on the page, and the location of the backing store associated with that address range (if any). /proc/pid/maps is not a performance tool per se; however, it provides insight into how memory is allocated. For example, for performance purposes, you can confirm whether a certain amount of shared memory is allocated between 1GB and 2GB in the virtual address space. The preceding map can be used to examine its utilization.

The following output is for process ID 3162:

```
$ cat /proc/3162/maps

08048000-08056000 r-xp 00000000 03:05 33015     /usr/lib/gnome-applets/battstat-applet-2
08056000-08058000 rw-p 0000d000 03:05 33015     /usr/lib/gnome-applets/battstat-applet-2
08058000-08163000 rw-p 08058000 00:00 0
40000000-40016000 r-xp 00000000 03:02 40006     /lib/ld-2.3.2.so
40016000-40017000 rw-p 00015000 03:02 40006     /lib/ld-2.3.2.so
40017000-40018000 rw-p 40017000 00:00 0
40018000-4001a000 r-xp 00000000 03:05 578493    /usr/X11R6/lib/X11/locale/lib/common/
    xlcDef.so.2
4001a000-4001b000 rw-p 00001000 03:05 578493    /usr/X11R6/lib/X11/locale/lib/common/
    xlcDef.so.2
4001b000-4001d000 r-xp 00000000 03:05 128867    /usr/lib/gconv/ISO8859-1.so
4001d000-4001e000 rw-p 00001000 03:05 128867    /usr/lib/gconv/ISO8859-1.so
4001f000-40023000 r-xp 00000000 03:05 514375    /usr/lib/gtk-2.0/2.4.0/loaders/
    libpixbufloader-png.so
40023000-40024000 rw-p 00003000 03:05 514375    /usr/lib/gtk-2.0/2.4.0/loaders/
    libpixbufloader-png.so
40025000-40031000 r-xp 00000000 03:05 337881    /usr/lib/libpanel-applet-2.so.0.0.19
40031000-40032000 rw-p 0000c000 03:05 337881    /usr/lib/libpanel-applet-2.so.0.0.19
40032000-400d2000 r-xp 00000000 03:05 337625    /usr/lib/libgnomeui-2.so.0.600.1
400d2000-400d6000 rw-p 0009f000 03:05 337625    /usr/lib/libgnomeui-2.so.0.600.1
400d6000-400d7000 rw-p 400d6000 00:00 0
400d7000-400df000 r-xp 00000000 03:05 53        /usr/X11R6/lib/libSM.so.6.0
400df000-400e0000 rw-p 00007000 03:05 53        /usr/X11R6/lib/libSM.so.6.0
400e0000-400f4000 r-xp 00000000 03:05 51        /usr/X11R6/lib/libICE.so.6.3
400f4000-400f5000 rw-p 00013000 03:05 51        /usr/X11R6/lib/libICE.so.6.3
```

vmstat

vmstat was introduced in the section on CPU utilization. However, its primary purpose is to monitor memory availability and swapping activity, and it provides an overview of I/O activity. vmstat can be used to help find unusual system activity, such as high page faults or excessive context switches, that can lead to a degradation in system performance. A sample of the vmstat output is as follows:

```
procs -----------memory---------- ---swap-- -----io---- --system-- ----cpu---

r  b   swpd   free   buff  cache   si   so    bi    bo    in    cs us sy id wa
18  8      0 5626196  3008 122788   0    0   330403  454 2575  4090 91  8  1  0
18 15      0 5625132  3008 122828   0    0   328767  322 2544  4264 91  8  0  0
17 12      0 5622004  3008 122828   0    0   327956  130 2406  3998 92  8  0  0
22  2      0 5621644  3008 122828   0    0   327892  689 2445  4077 92  8  0  0
```

23	5	0	5621616	3008	122868	0	0	323171	407	2339	4037	92	8	1	0
21	14	0	5621868	3008	122868	0	0	323663	23	2418	4160	91	9	0	0
22	10	0	5625216	3008	122868	0	0	328828	153	2934	4518	90	9	1	0

The memory-related data reported by vmstat includes the following:

- memory reports the amount of memory being swapped out (swpd), free memory (free), buffer cache for I/O data structures (buff), and cached memory for files read from the disk (cache) in kilobytes.
- swap, in kilobytes per second, is the amount of memory swapped in (si) from disk and swapped out (so) to disk.
- io reports the number of blocks read in (bi) from the devices and blocks written out (bo) to the devices in kilobytes per second.

For I/O-intensive workloads, you can monitor bi and bo for the transfer rate, and in for the interrupt rate. You can monitor swpd, si, and so to see whether the system is swapping. If so, you can check on the swapping rate. Perhaps the most common metric is CPU utilization and the monitoring of us, sy, id, and wa. If wa is large, you need to examine the I/O subsystem. You might come to the conclusion that more I/O controllers and disks are needed to reduce the I/O wait time.

I/O UTILIZATION

Although the overall processor speeds, memory sizes, and I/O speeds continue to increase, I/O throughput and latency are still orders of magnitude slower than equivalent memory access. Additionally, because many workloads have a substantial I/O component, I/O can easily become a significant bottleneck to overall throughput and overall application response times. For I/O-intensive applications, the performance analyst must be able to access tools that help provide insights into the operations of the I/O subsystem.

This section initially looks at disk I/O. A future section looks at networking I/O because the tools to measure throughput and latency for each are different.

For disk I/O, performance is often evaluated in terms of throughput and latency. Disk drives tend to be able to handle large sequential transfers much better than small random transfers. Large sequential transfers allow optimizations such as read ahead or write behind, allow the storage system to reduce head movement and perform full track writes when possible. However, many applications rely on the capability to access data in disparate, often unpredictable locations on the media. As a result, the I/O patterns of various workloads are often a mix of sequential and random I/O, with varying sizes of block transfers.

When evaluating I/O performance on a system, the performance analyst needs to keep in mind several things. The first, and perhaps most obvious (although it is often forgotten), is that I/O performance cannot exceed the performance of the underlying hardware. Although we will not go into much detail on this aspect, it is very helpful when analyzing I/O throughput and latency to understand the system's underlying limitations. For instance, the performance aspects of the storage device, the I/O buses connecting the storage devices (for example, SCSI and Fibre Channel), any limitations imposed by the storage fabric (such as a Fibre Channel Switch), the host bus adapters, the systems interconnect bus (for example, PCI, PCI-X, and Infiniband), and in some cases the system's architecture (such as how host bus adapters perform DMA, how memory is interleaved, and NUMA connectivity) all contribute to the overall performance analysis of the I/O subsystem. In more complex system configurations, it may be helpful to maintain a list of "speeds and feeds" for the system to help distinguish between hardware bottlenecks and software bottlenecks.

To understand software bottlenecks and related performance impacts, the two major considerations are overall I/O throughput and latency of any individual I/O requests. Ideally, a system wants to optimize the data transfer rate to and from the media. However, because the latency of an individual request can be extremely long compared to the speed of the processor, applications can effectively stall waiting for I/O. Take, for example, an application that reads a block of data that provides information on how to access the next block of data, and so on. If the system or application is unable to optimize this pattern, performance is limited to the combined latencies of the I/O subsystem. One common solution to this problem is to perform many similar operations like this simultaneously. Multitasking—the capability of many tasks to run in parallel—allows an application or operating system to schedule many long latency I/O requests simultaneously, even when each application might spend a large portion of the time blocked on an individual request. As a result, the overall efficiency of the I/O subsystem, or the total I/O throughput, might approach the capacity of the underlying I/O subsystem. And, although it is always a goal of the operating system and the individual applications to optimize for overall system throughput, doing so at the expense of end-user response times is not usually an acceptable trade-off.

The underlying I/O subsystem latencies can be severely impacted by the incoming pattern of data transfer requests. For instance, if disk I/O requests alternately ask for a block of I/O at the "beginning" and "end" of the disk media, the physical disk arm may need to make relatively slow adjustments to position the disk head over the selected disk block. This type of access would obviously slow down all accesses to a given device, thereby reducing the number of I/O operations that could be completed over a period of time. Further, such a bizarre access pattern would likely reduce not just the number of devices per logical drive, but also the overall I/O transfer rate.

Another solution to multitasking is to ensure that the data requests from the applications and operating system are well distributed among the disks connected to the system. Distributing the I/O requests to multiple disks effects a level of parallelism that further reduces the performance impacts of the individual latencies of disk drives. Redistributing the application data among a number of disk devices often requires a solid understanding of the workload as well as an understanding of the data access patterns of that workload.

Although system monitoring tools do not provide the capability to track each I/O that a particular application issues, there are tools that allow a performance analyst to monitor the total number of I/Os processed by the system, the number of I/O operations per logical disk drive, and the overall I/O transfer rate. The two primary tools discussed in the next sections are iostat(1) and sar(1). You can use these tools to understand what the I/O bottlenecks are, what disks or interconnects are underutilized, and what the latencies are from a system perspective (as opposed to an application perspective).

Before exploring the specific tools, keep in mind that there are many techniques for increasing I/O performance. These techniques include purely hardware-related solutions (such as using disk drives that have higher revolutions per minute, thereby providing lower I/O latencies, larger disk cache sizes, or I/O controller cache sizes). They also include improved data transfer rates for both reads and writes, and/ increases in I/O bus speeds or I/O fabric speeds, which both increase data transfer rates and reduce I/O latencies. Also, some disk drives and disk storage subsystems provide multiported logical or physical disks, allowing parallel I/O from a single disk, which again increases potential I/O throughput. Additionally, hardware and software RAID (Redundant Array of Independent Disks) were designed to increase access parallelism by striping data across multiple disk drives.

The tools discussed in the following sections provide data that can be useful in considering hardware and software solutions as well as improvements in data layout.

iostat

The iostat command monitors system I/O activities by observing how long the physical disks are active in relation to their average transfer rates. The iostat command generates reports that can be used to change system configuration to better balance the I/O load among physical disks. iostat(1) also provides CPU utilization that can sometimes be useful in comparing directly against the I/O activities. If no display interval is given, iostat gives out I/O information since the system was last booted. If a display interval is given, the first set of output represents total activity since boot time, and subsequent displays only show the delta activities. The following display corresponds to copying files from /dev/sdo7 to /dev/sds7, /dev/sdp7 to /dev/sdt7, and /dev/sdr7 to /dev/sdu7:

```
avg-cpu:  %user   %nice    %sys %iowait   %idle
           0.21    0.00    0.80    2.07   96.92


Device:    tps Blk_read/s Blk_wrtn/s   Blk_read    Blk_wrtn
sdx       0.00       0.00       0.00         32           0
sdw       0.00       0.00       0.00         32           0
sdv       0.00       0.00       0.00         32           0
sdu       2.49       0.05    1443.46       2778    79552392
sdt       4.94       0.10    2871.73       5322   158268008
sds       4.95       0.10    2860.91       5330   157671720
sdr      30.20    1518.55       0.42   83690898       23288
sdq      60.25    2902.76       0.92  159978258       50896
sdp       0.00       0.01       0.00        378          24
sdo      59.49    2883.87       0.90  158937034       49520
```

`iostat` reports CPU utilization similar to how it is provided by the `top` tool. It splits the CPU time into user, nice, system, I/O wait, and system idle. It is followed by the disk utilization report. The disk header is followed by lines of disk statistics, where each line reports the activities of one logical disk that is configured. The `tps` column represents the number of I/O requests that are issued to the logical disk. However, the size of the I/O requests is not given. `Blk_read/s` and `Blk_wrtn/s` represent the amount of data read from and written to the logical drive in a number of blocks per second. Again, the block size is not given. Finally, `Blk_read` and `Blk_wrtn` correspond to the amount of data read from and written to the logical drive in a number of blocks per second, without specifying the block's size.

The -k option displays statistics in kilobytes, the -p option gets per-partition statistics, and the -x option gets information such as average wait time and average service time. In the data, the count on `Blk_read` of `sdo` is very close to the count of `Blk_wrtn` of `sds`, as data is copied from `sdo7` to `sds7`. In addition, the rate of reads is slightly higher than the rate of writes. This report can highlight disk I/O bottlenecks, if any, and helps database designers lay out data to achieve higher access parallelism.

sar

`sar` is included in the `sysstat` package. `sar` collects and reports a wide range of system activities in the operating system. Activities include I/O operations, CPU utilization, the rate of context switches and interrupts, the rate of paging in and paging out, and the use of shared memory, buffer, and network. Based on the values in the count and interval parameters, `sar` writes information the specified number of times spaced at the specified intervals in seconds. For example, the command `sar -b 3 12` reports disk usage every 3 seconds for a total of 12 seconds. In addition, at the end of data collection, average statistics are given. sar is a very option-rich tool. The remainder of this section discusses a few features of the tool:

- sar displays I/O statistics similar to iostat. sar provides the total number of I/O operations (tps), which is further split into read operations (rtps) and write operations (wtps). sar also provides the rates of read and write operations under bread/s and bwrtn/s. The following data is collected every 2 seconds for a total of 18 seconds. At the end of the data collection, the averages of five fields are given. However, operations for individual logical drives are not given.

	tps	rtps	wtps	bread/s	bwrtn/s
12:59:15					
12:59:17	37.50	37.50	0.00	396.00	0.00
12:59:19	66.50	66.50	0.00	16140.00	0.00
12:59:21	268.50	268.50	0.00	66560.00	0.00
12:59:23	333.50	261.50	72.00	64548.00	9620.00
12:59:25	153.50	40.50	113.00	9728.00	27984.00
12:59:27	133.00	5.00	128.00	1024.00	31744.00
12:59:29	119.50	7.50	112.00	1536.00	27776.00
12:59:31	133.00	5.00	128.00	1024.00	31744.00
Average:	155.63	86.50	69.13	20119.50	16108.50

- sar provides data on CPU utilization for individual processors as well as for the whole system. This particular feature is especially useful in multiprocessor environments. If some processors do more work than others, the display clearly shows. You can then check whether the imbalanced use of processors is from, for example, the applications or the scheduler of the kernel. The following data is collected from a four-way SMP system every 5 seconds:

	CPU	%user	%nice	%system	%iowait	%idle
11:09:13						
11:09:18	all	0.00	0.00	4.70	52.45	42.85
11:09:18	0	0.00	0.00	5.80	57.00	37.20
11:09:18	1	0.00	0.00	4.80	49.40	45.80
11:09:18	2	0.00	0.00	6.00	62.20	31.80
11:09:18	3	0.00	0.00	2.40	41.12	56.49
11:09:23	all	0.00	0.00	3.75	47.30	48.95
11:09:23	0	0.00	0.00	5.39	37.33	57.29
11:09:23	1	0.00	0.00	2.80	41.80	55.40
11:09:23	2	0.00	0.00	5.40	41.60	53.00
11:09:23	3	0.00	0.00	1.40	68.60	30.00
. . .						
Average:	all	0.00	0.00	4.22	16.40	79.38
Average:	0	0.00	0.00	8.32	24.33	67.35
Average:	1	0.00	0.00	2.12	14.35	83.53
Average:	2	0.01	0.00	4.16	12.07	83.76
Average:	3	0.00	0.00	2.29	14.85	82.86

- `sar` also provides interrupt information among the processors:

```
10:53:53  CPU   i000/s  i001/s  i002/s  i003/s  i004/s  i005/s  i006/s  i007/s
10:53:58    0  1000.20    0.00    0.00    0.40    0.00    0.00    3.00    0.00
10:53:58    1     0.00    0.00    0.00    0.00    0.00    0.00    0.00 2320.00
10:53:58    2     0.00    0.00    0.00    0.00 1156.00    0.00    0.00    0.00
10:53:58    3     0.00    0.00    0.00    0.00    0.00    0.00    0.00    0.00
Average:    0   999.94    0.00    0.00    1.20  590.99    0.00    3.73    0.00
Average:    1     0.00    0.00    0.00    0.00    0.00    0.00    0.00  926.61
Average:    2     0.00    0.00    0.00    0.00  466.51    0.00    0.00 1427.48
Average:    3     0.00    0.00    0.00    0.00    0.00    0.00    0.00    0.00
```

The study of interrupt distribution reveals an imbalance of interrupt processing. One method to tackle this imbalance is to affinitize IRQ processing to a specific processor or to a number of processors. For example, if 0x0001 is echoed to /proc/irq/ID, where ID corresponds to a device, only CPU 0 will process IRQ for this device. If 0x000f is echoed to /proc/irq/ID, CPU 0 through CPU 3 will be used to process IRQ for this device. For some workloads, this technique can reduce contention on certain heavily used processors. This technique allows I/O interrupts to be processed more efficiently, causing the I/O performance to increase accordingly.

NETWORK UTILIZATION

Computer networking is a major computer discipline by itself as it has become ubiquitous. The government, private companies, and the mass media heavily rely on the Internet to function. The World Wide Web, e-mail, instant messaging, and so on have made the world much smaller, putting dispersed countries much closer than ever before. Search engines are very popular in getting information to your fingertips in a fraction of a second. eBusiness has taken business to the next level, where people, without leaving the place of their comfort, can shop, bank, trade stocks, play games with remote partners, collaborate on work, and so on. All these are made possible through advances in computer networking such as high-speed and high-bandwidth networks. Moreover, these advances facilitate new computer infrastructures such as cluster networks, storage networks, and multitiered setups. Tanenbaum has very good coverage of major topics in this field, such as the TCP/IP protocol suite, circuit and packet switching, wireless communications, security, and voice and data transmission.

Linux not only offers many of the powerful network capabilities that other major operating systems provide, but it also surpasses them through additional features such as masquerading. The Linux kernel supports several networking protocols such as TCP/IP, IPX (Internetwork Packet Exchange), and AppleTalk DDP, and it supports features such as packet forwarding, firewall operations, proxy, masquerading, tunneling, and aliasing.

Many network monitoring tools available in Linux help you evaluate the performance of any Linux network. Some of these tools can also be used to troubleshoot network problems along with monitoring performance. The Linux kernel makes a large amount of networking system information available to the user, helping you monitor the health of the network and detect problems in configuration, runtime, and performance.

This section explores only some of the tools that are readily available in most major Linux distributions. In this section, we look at the network tools `netstat`, `nfsstat`, `tcpdump`, `ethtool`, `snmp`, `ifport`, `ifconfig`, `route`, `arp`, `ping`, `traceroute`, `host`, and `nslookup`.

System and network administrators use some of these tools every day. Tools such as `ping`, `route`, `arp`, `traceroute`, `ethtool`, and `tcpdump` are used to determine network problems. These tools can be described as follows:

- The command `ping ipaddress/hostname` shows if a computer is operating and if network connections are intact. `ping` uses the Internet Control Message Protocol (ICMP) Echo function. A small packet is sent through the network for a given IP address. If a reply to the packet is received, the computer network connection is alive. It also tells how many hops lie between the source computer and the destination computer.

- The `route` command can be used to display the route table, add a route, delete a route to the table, and flush all the routes.

- The `arp` command is useful if `ping` does not work—that is, if the network connection is not alive—to determine the root cause of the problem. The `arp -a` command can be used to make sure that the hardware address is correctly associated with the right system. The other options available with this command include flushing the arp cache, adding to the cache.

- The IRRT Toolset (Internet Routing Register Toolset) makes routing information more convenient and useful for network engineers by providing tools for automated router configuration, routing policies analysis, and maintenance.

- `ifconfig` determines a host's media access control address. If another host with a duplicate IP address exists on the network, the arp cache may have had the media access control address for the other computer placed in it, in which case, the `arp` command can be used to delete the saved address in the cache and add the correct address to the arp cache.

- `traceroute` tracks one of the possible routing pathways. It can measure the time taken to travel between each hop (router) and identify the hop's address as the packet travels through the network.

- `ethtool` queries and changes the settings of an Ethernet device. The devices are assigned a number for identification, such as eth0, eth1... eth*n* for *n* Ethernet devices in the system. This tool uses this device name to query/change the settings.

- `tcpdump` sniffs network packets. It captures all the packets that are seen at the computer. It can be used for network monitoring, protocol debugging, and data acquisition. `tcpdump` puts the NIC into promiscuous mode in order to capture all the packets going through the wire. Numerous options exist to filter the output down to only those packets of interest. The drawback with `tcpdump` is that the buffer can overflow and wrap around. `tcpdump` on high-bandwidth networks tends to drop packets—that is, `tcpdump` cannot keep up with the rate of the packets.

- `ethereal` is another network sniffing tool similar to `tcpdump`. `ethereal` can read capture files from `tcpdump`.

- `host` is a tool used to retrieve the host name for a given IP address from the Domain Name System. This tool is much more flexible than `nslookup` and is suited for use in shell scripts.

- Some of the network security tools that are available on Linux include tools such as `snort` (a network intrusion detection system), `dsniff` (a suite of powerful network auditing and penetrating-testing tools), and `SAINT` (Security Administrator's Integrated Network Tool).

Network Statistics

The `netstat` utility, available in the net-tools package, displays a large amount of information related to the networking subsystem.

`netstat` is one of the most frequently used tools for monitoring network connections on a Linux server. `netstat` displays a list of active sockets for each network protocol, such as TCP and UDP. It also provides information about network routes and cumulative statistics for network interfaces, including the number of incoming and outgoing packets and the number of packet collisions. The `netstat` output that follows shows a number of network protocol statistics and routing information, such as Internet protocol (IP), transport control protocol (TCP), and user datagram protocol (UDP). From the statistics, you can tell whether the number of packets received is higher or lower than expected. This tool can easily be used to investigate performance degradation between kernels.

Without any arguments, `netstat` displays a list of the existing network sockets and their connection information. All protocol families are displayed, including UNIX domain sockets. The following are typical lines from sample output:

```
$ netstat
Active Internet connections (servers and established)
Proto Recv-Q Send-Q Local Address        Foreign Address        State
tcp        0       0 *:32768              *:*                    LISTEN
tcp        0       0 *:smux               *:*                    LISTEN
tcp        0       0 *:9099               *:*                    LISTEN
tcp        0       0 *:sunrpc             *:*                    LISTEN
tcp        0       0 *:x11                *:*                    LISTEN
tcp        0       0 *:http               *:*                    LISTEN
tcp        0       0 *:ftp                *:*                    LISTEN
tcp        0       0 *:ssh                *:*                    LISTEN
tcp        0       0 *:telnet             *:*                    LISTEN
tcp        0       0 nethostA:smtp        *:*                    LISTEN
tcp        0       0 nethostA:32974       nethostB:ssh           ESTABLISHED
tcp        0       0 nethostA:32996       nethostB:ssh           ESTABLISHED
tcp        0       0 nethostA:33002       64.233.161.99:http     ESTABLISHED
tcp        0       0 nethostA:33005       nethostB:ftp           ESTABLISHED
udp        0       0 *:32768              *:*
udp        0       0 *:snmp               *:*
udp        0       0 *:sunrpc             *:*
Active UNIX domain sockets (servers and established)
Proto RefCnt Flags       Type       State       I-Node Path
unix  2      [ ACC ]     STREAM     LISTENING   2012   /dev/gpmctl
unix  2      [ ACC ]     STREAM     LISTENING   159792 /tmp/ksocket-
   nivedita/kdeinit-:0
unix  2      [ ACC ]     STREAM     LISTENING   2210   /tmp/.X11-unix/X0
unix  2      [ ACC ]     STREAM     LISTENING   79840  /tmp/.ICE-
   unix/dcop15789-1077867386
```

The first column indicates the protocol family of the socket, which is commonly either `tcp` (transport control protocol), `udp` (user datagram protocol), or `unix` (UNIX domain socket). The second and third columns indicate the amount of data, in bytes, that is currently present in receive and send socket queues. The next columns list the local and remote address and port information. The last column displays the protocol state that the socket is currently in.

The IP addresses are normally translated into host names (nethostA, nethostB) unless the `-n` flag is provided to `netstat`.

To display only select address families, their corresponding flags can be provided. For example, `netstat --tcp` or `-t` displays only the TCP sockets present. A full listing of the flags for the individual families is available in the `netstat` man page.

The asterisk (*) indicates a wildcard. For the local address, this is typical of listener processes, which listen on all the local interfaces. Remote host address and port information is displayed when the socket has made a connection to a remote host and is in *established* state. You see ssh, http, and ftp connections in progress in the preceding display.

Displaying Interface Information

This information is identical to that displayed by the `ifconfig` command. It is a listing of the statistics provided by the interface. These include the MTU (maximum transmission unit) and counts of packets received and sent that were successful, erroneous in some way, dropped, or overflowed.

```
$ netstat -i
```

```
Kernel Interface table
Iface    MTU Met    RX-OK RX-ERR RX-DRP RX-OVR    TX-OK TX-ERR TX-DRP TX-OVR Flg
eth0    1500 0      21941      0      0      0    11998      0      0      0 BMRU
lo     16436 0        795      0      0      0      795      0      0      0 LRU
```

TCP/IP Protocol Statistics

The Linux kernel supports the statistics counters specified in RFC 2012 as part of the Simple Network Management Protocol (SNMP) Management Information Base (MIB). It also implements a large number of counters that are Linux-specific and capture network protocol events, primarily TCP.

The `netstat` utility displays most, but not all, of the counters present in the kernel. To see the full list of the events being counted, view the content of the /proc/net/snmp and /proc/net/netstat files. The former contains the RFC 2012 counters, and the latter contains the extended Linux-specific MIB. The following is a sample listing of SNMP counters produced by the `netstat -s` command:

```
netstat -s
Ip:
    662968 total packets received
    0 forwarded
    0 incoming packets discarded
    659592 incoming packets delivered
    162297 requests sent out
Tcp:
    5721 active connections openings
    39 passive connection openings
    0 failed connection attempts
    0 connection resets received
    1 connections established
```

```
    136759 segments received
    152791 segments send out
    20660 segments retransmited
    3 bad segments received.
    1165 resets sent
Udp:
    14031 packets received
    15 packets to unknown port received.
    0 packet receive errors
    7519 packets sent
```

Moreover, network communication involves heavy interrupt processing. Thus, in conjunction with `netstat`, `vmstat` can be used to capture the number of interrupts, and `sar` can be used to determine the spread of interrupt processing.

nfsstat

Network File System (NFS) is a technique to incorporate a file system from a remote machine into the local file system—that is, NFS uses the same read and write interface to access data remotely as the one used locally. `nfsstat` is a simple tool that prints NFS kernel statistics. `nfsstat` prints the counts of NFS API calls during a workload. In the following example, the server is running an I/O workload. Output from `nfsstat` shows the counts of reads and writes, which can be used for debugging purposes. The counts of reads and writes can also be used to understand performance issues.

```
Server nfs v3:
null         getattr      setattr      lookup       access       readlink
0       0%   8       0%   0       0%   6       0%   43      0%   0          0%
read         write        create       mkdir        symlink      mknod
262242 44%   328004 55%   2       0%   0       0%   0       0%   0          0%
remove       rmdir        rename       link         readdir      readdirplus
3       0%   0       0%   0       0%   0       0%   0       0%   0          0%
fsstat       fsinfo       pathconf     commit
1       0%   1       0%   0       0%   2586    0%
```

SUMMARY

This chapter provided information about a number of Linux performance tools currently available—namely, CPU tools, memory tools, I/O tools, and network tools. This set of tools provides information for understanding the utilization of system resources under a certain workload. Some of the tools can also reveal the system activities in user space. This chapter described the data provided by the tools and how they can be used in performance analysis.

Most of the basic tool features needed for performance analysis are available through existing tools. However, there is a need for additional tools to provide a better understanding of traffic, including process migration and remote memory access among nodes in NUMA systems. In addition, there is a need for tools that can store and display performance data in a variety of views to help developers understand, navigate, and tune the kernel or user applications. One such tool is gnuplot. The displayed data should have various levels of compactness to support different levels of data density, especially those involved with multithreaded or SMP machines where data tends to be complex and multidimensional. Performance tools are crucial for helping advance Linux into the enterprise system market.

REFERENCES

[1] gnuplot: http://www.gnuplot.org/.

[2] gprof: http://sources.redhat.com/binutils/docs-2.12/gprof.info/index.html.

[3] Hinton, Glenn, et al. "The Microarchitecture of the Pentium 4 Processor," http://www.intel.com/technology/itj/q12001/pdf/art_2.pdf.

[4] Luo, Yue, et al. "Benchmarking Internet Servers on SuperScalar Machines," *Computer*, February 2003, pp. 34-40.

[5] Kernprof: http://oss.sgi.com/projects/kernprof.

[6] netstat: http://www.ussg.iu.edu/usail/man/linux/netstat.8.html.

[7] nfsstat: http://www.die.net/doc/linux/man/man8/nfsstat.8.html.

[8] oprofile: http://oprofile.sourceforge.net/doc.

[9] Performance Inspector: http://www-124.ibm.com/developerworks/opensource/pi/.

[10] Readprofile: http://nodevice.com/sections/ManIndex/man1303.html.

[11] sysstat: http://perso.wanadoo.fr/sebastien/godard/.

[12] strace: http://sourceforge.net/projects/strace.

[13] Stallings, William. *Computer Organization and Architecture—Designing for Performance, Sixth Edition*. Prentice Hall, 2003.

[14] tcpdump: http://www.die.net/doc/linux/man/man8/tcpdump.8.html.

[15] top: http://nodevice.com/sections/ManIndex/man1818.html.

[16] Intel VTune: `http://www.intel.com/software/products/vtune/`.

[17] vmstat: `http://nakula.rvs.uni-bielefeld.de/cgi-bin/man.sh?man=8+` `vmstat`.

[18] Web resource: `http://www.ping127001.com/pingpage.htm`.

[19] Web resource: `http://www.ethereal.com/docs/man-pages/tcpdump.8.html`.

[20] Web resource: `http://csrc.nist.gov/tools/tools.htm`.

[21] Web resource: `http://www.ripe.net/ripencc/pub-services/db/irrtoolset/`.

[22] Web resource: `http://www.insecure.org/tools.html`.

[23] Tanenbaum, Andrew. *Computer Networks, Third Edition*. Prentice Hall, 1996.

## CHAPTER FIVE

System Trace Tools

By Ron Cadima, Gerrit Huizenga, Duc J. Vianney, and Peter Wai Yee Wong

INTRODUCTION

When a performance bottleneck or problem occurs, system tracing tools can help you identify the source of the problem. When tracing a system, you need to know not only which tools to use, but when and where to use them.

Generally, system tracing involves multiple steps: With each step, you delve deeper into the problem to ultimately create a solution or optimize the system or the appropriate application. By taking a system-wide view of the problem first, and then zeroing in on a specific application or series of events, you can more reliably determine the true cause of the performance problem. For example, just because the system slows down after a particular application is started does not necessarily mean the application is the cause of the slowdown. The application might be a catalyst that exposes a problem within another application on the system.

A number of Linux tracing tools are available in the open-source community. This chapter discusses several of the most common:

- `top`, which gives an overall picture of what processes are using the system and the system resources they are using
- `strace`, which traces all the system calls from an application
- Oprofile, which provides the profile of a running system based on system timer or performance counter support, including the amount of time the system spends within an application
- Performance Inspector, which is a suite of tools for identifying performance problems and characteristics

This chapter also discusses requirements that need to be met before you begin tracing a system.

Note that given the dynamic nature of Linux, new system tracing tools are likely to be developed, and existing tools, including the ones discussed in this chapter, will continue to be updated.

REQUIREMENTS FOR SYSTEM TRACING

To capture useful information for troubleshooting a performance problem, follow these guidelines before you begin to trace a system:

- Use the right tool for the right step of your analysis. If the data that the tool you use is not reliable because it is the wrong tool for the job, your time is wasted analyzing the wrong data or application.
- Ensure that the system that is being traced has enough memory and storage. For example, if there is not enough memory, swapping occurs, which can distort the results.
- Know the overhead of the tool you are using. If the tool is very intrusive into your system, the performance analysis might be inaccurate.
- Use a defined test scenario to make your measurements. It is imperative that you use a consistent set of steps for the measurements and that the results are repeatable. Measure the same functions in the same order during each step of the analysis.
- Use a controlled environment. Do not allow other processes or functions to be performed during the measurements and traces unless they are part of the measurement scenario. After you have applied fixes based on the results of the measurements and traces, you can begin a new round of testing with new applications added to the mix. The best rule of thumb is to keep the scenario simple and know what is running when.

THE *TOP* UTILITY

The `top` utility is shipped on most platforms and with most releases of Linux. `top` reports on processor activity in real time and is most useful for obtaining an overall picture of the processes that are using the system and the resources they are using. `top` lets you specify the delay between measurements and the number of measurements to take. `top` also allows a batch mode of operation that writes the data in a normal text format. Another option to `top` lets you specify that the only processes that are displayed are those that are actually running.

   `top` reports the approximate amount of memory a process is using. You can configure `top` to show a process hierarchy.

Use `top` as a first step in your analysis to see which processes are running in the system and how much of the system time they are consuming. By running `top` over a period of time and directing the output to a file, you can see which processes are running when. You can also approximate when a process stops, when large amounts of memory are consumed, and when one or two processes start to consume large amounts of processor time. For example, if `top` output indicates that a particular process is consuming most of the processing time, you can use other tools to identify the location within the application where the time is being consumed. The same holds true for memory usage. If a large amount of memory is suddenly being consumed or a gradual buildup in memory consumption has occurred, use a lower-level trace tool to identify where the increase in memory usage is occurring.

The following is a sample of the `top` report. The display is updated by default every 5 seconds.

```
# top

 8:24 am  up 4 days, 19:31,  1 user,  load average: 0.16, 0.06, 0.09
 57 processes: 55 sleeping, 2 running, 0 zombie, 0 stopped
 CPU states:  2.1% user,  0.6% system,  0.0% nice,  4.3% idle
  Mem:    252976K av,  211516K used,   41460K free,       0K shrd,   29820K buff
  Swap:   522072K av,   27060K used,  495012K free                  76836K cached

PID    USER     PRI  NI  SIZE  RSS SHARE STAT %CPU  %MEM   TIME  COMMAND
20269  root      16   0   224  224   188   R   98.4  0.0   0:09  pi_watch
20270  root      10   0  1040 1040   828   R    1.9  0.4   0:00  top
1      root       9   0   464  428   412   S    0.0  0.1   0:08  init
2      root       9   0     0    0     0  SW    0.0  0.0   0:00  keventd
3      root      19  19     0    0     0 SWN    0.0  0.0   0:00  ksoftirqd_CPU0
4      root       9   0     0    0     0  SW    0.0  0.0   0:09  kswapd
5      root       9   0     0    0     0  SW    0.0  0.0   0:00  bdflush
6      root       9   0     0    0     0  SW    0.0  0.0   0:02  kupdated
8      root       9   0     0    0     0  SW    0.0  0.0   0:00  khubd
10     root      -1 -20     0    0     0  SW    0.0  0.0   0:00  mdrecoveryd
14     root       9   0     0    0     0  SW    0.0  0.0   0:14  kjournald
127    root       9   0     0    0     0  SW    0.0  0.0   0:00  kjournald
128    root       9   0     0    0     0  SW    0.0  0.0   0:00  kjournald
129    root       9   0     0    0     0  SW    0.0  0.0   0:00  kjournald
428    root       9   0   536  528   456   S    0.0  0.2   0:00  syslogd
432    root       9   0   428  412   376   S    0.0  0.1   0:00  klogd
449    rpc        9   0   560  556   484   S    0.0  0.2   0:00  portmap
468    rpcuser    9   0   660  576   576   S    0.0  0.2   0:00  rpc.statd
581    root       9   0   972  732   732   S    0.0  0.2   0:00  sshd
594    root       9   0   716  588   588   S    0.0  0.2   0:00  xinetd
615    root       9   0  1644 1260  1068   S    0.0  0.4   0:14  sendmail
624    smmsp      8   0  1176  772   688   S    0.0  0.3   0:00  sendmail
```

634	root	9	0	400	368	352	S	0.0	0.1	0:14	gpm
643	root	9	0	604	564	528	S	0.0	0.2	0:00	crond
674	xfs	9	0	6136 4	552	1032	S	0.0	1.7	0:06	xfs
692	daemon	9	0	512	492	456	S	0.0	0.1	0:00	atd
701	root	9	0	816	612	612	S	0.0	0.2	0:00	login
702	root	9	0	388	344	344	S	0.0	0.1	0:00	mingetty
703	root	9	0	388	344	344	S	0.0	0.1	0:00	mingetty
704	root	9	0	388	344	344	S	0.0	0.1	0:00	mingetty
705	root	9	0	388	344	344	S	0.0	0.1	0:00	mingetty
706	root	9	0	388	344	344	S	0.0	0.1	0:00	mingetty
709	root	9	0	1384	1028	1028	S	0.0	0.4	0:00	bash
826	root	9	0	484	460	420	S	0.0	0.1	0:09	pam_timestamp_c
16054	root	9	0	8624	8192	5476	S	0.0	3.2	4:02	gnome-terminal
16055	root	9	0	1528	1528	1164	S	0.0	0.6	0:01	bash
19021	root	9	0	1856	1752	900	S	0.0	0.6	0:02	oprofiled
20175	root	9	0	1512	1512	1152	S	0.0	0.5	0:00	bash

When active processes are displayed, only the actual process that is running is shown—no information about memory or CPU is displayed.

While `top` is running, you can add or modify some options to change what is being reported. The program accepts options from the keyboard. You can also create a configuration file to define what to measure and how to measure it. Use the `info top` command to obtain online documentation on these capabilities.

Some of the more useful `top` parameters are as follows:

d   Delay between updates to the data.

p   Displays only the processes specified. Up to 20 processes can be specified.

S   Displays a summary of time being spent by the process and its children. Also displays dead time.

I   Does not report idle processes.

H   Shows all threads by process.

N   Number of times to produce the reports.

If `top` does not work on a system, ensure that the /proc file support is active on the system. Active /proc file support is required for `top` to run.

STRACE

`strace` ships with all versions of Linux. `strace` traces all of the system calls from an application and is useful for seeing how a particular application is using the system. Use `strace` to determine if an application is performing a large number of a particular type of system call, such as reads or writes to a file, memory allocations and frees, task forks and clones, or other system calls. With `strace` verbose mode enabled, the actual parameters being passed to `strace` and the results are displayed. You can use verbose mode to verify that the correct parameters are being passed and that the results being passed back are expected. This type of information is useful for debugging a new application or to see what is going on in an application that has been identified as having a problem by a higher-level trace tool.

Some typical uses of `strace` are to determine if the blocking factor for disk I/O is correct and optimal. You can see if memory is constantly being allocated and freed as opposed to the allocation of a buffer pool and the reuse of buffers. For example, if threads are constantly being forked or cloned and then freed, you can investigate a method of reusing existing threads to reduce the overhead of the thread creates and frees. You can also use threads to validate that the parameters (such as addresses or buffer sizes) that are being passed on system calls are correct.

The only drawback of the `strace` tool is that you must measure the application from its startup until the time the application terminates or you kill it. You cannot start tracing in the middle of the application and end tracing without ending the application.

See the `info strace` command for more information.

The following is a sample `strace` report.

```
# strace

execve("/piperf/bin/pi_watch", ["pi_watch", "100"], [/* 32 vars */]) = 0
uname({sys="Linux", node="tpcw.ltc.austin.ibm.com", ...}) = 0
brk(0)                                = 0x804a000
old_mmap(NULL, 4096, PROT_READ|PROT_WRITE, MAP_PRIVATE|MAP_ANONYMOUS, -1, 0) =
    0x40016000
open("/etc/ld.so.preload", O_RDONLY)   = -1 ENOENT (No such file or directory)
open("tls/i686/mmx/libc.so.6", O_RDONLY) = -1 ENOENT (No such file or directory)
open("tls/i686/libc.so.6", O_RDONLY)   = -1 ENOENT (No such file or directory)
open("tls/mmx/libc.so.6", O_RDONLY)    = -1 ENOENT (No such file or directory)
open("tls/libc.so.6", O_RDONLY)        = -1 ENOENT (No such file or directory)
open("i686/mmx/libc.so.6", O_RDONLY)   = -1 ENOENT (No such file or directory)
open("i686/libc.so.6", O_RDONLY)       = -1 ENOENT (No such file or directory)
open("mmx/libc.so.6", O_RDONLY)        = -1 ENOENT (No such file or directory)
open("libc.so.6", O_RDONLY)            = -1 ENOENT (No such file or directory)
open("/piperf/bin/tls/i686/mmx/libc.so.6", O_RDONLY) = -1 ENOENT (No such file or
    directory)
stat64("/piperf/bin/tls/i686/mmx", 0xbfffefb0) = -1 ENOENT (No such file or
    directory)open("/piperf/bin/tls/i686/libc.so.6", O_RDONLY) = -1 ENOENT (No such
    file or directory)
stat64("/piperf/bin/tls/i686", 0xbfffefb0) = -1 ENOENT (No such file or directory)
open("/piperf/bin/tls/mmx/libc.so.6", O_RDONLY) = -1 ENOENT (No such file or
    directory)
stat64("/piperf/bin/tls/mmx", 0xbfffefb0) = -1 ENOENT (No such file or directory)
```

```
open("/piperf/bin/tls/libc.so.6", O_RDONLY) = -1 ENOENT (No such file or directory)
stat64("/piperf/bin/tls", 0xbfffefb0)   = -1 ENOENT (No such file or directory)
open("/piperf/bin/i686/mmx/libc.so.6", O_RDONLY) = -1 ENOENT (No such file or
    directory)
stat64("/piperf/bin/i686/mmx", 0xbfffefb0) = -1 ENOENT (No such file or directory)
open("/piperf/bin/i686/libc.so.6", O_RDONLY) = -1 ENOENT (No such file or directory)
stat64("/piperf/bin/i686", 0xbfffefb0)  = -1 ENOENT (No such file or directory)
open("/piperf/bin/mmx/libc.so.6", O_RDONLY) = -1 ENOENT (No such file or directory)
stat64("/piperf/bin/mmx", 0xbfffefb0)   = -1 ENOENT (No such file or directory)
open("/piperf/bin/libc.so.6", O_RDONLY) = -1 ENOENT (No such file or directory)
stat64("/piperf/bin", {st_mode=S_IFDIR|0777, st_size=4096, ...}) = 0
open("/etc/ld.so.cache", O_RDONLY)      = 3
fstat64(3, {st_mode=S_IFREG|0644, st_size=43183, ...}) = 0
old_mmap(NULL, 43183, PROT_READ, MAP_PRIVATE, 3, 0) = 0x40017000
close(3)                                = 0
open("/lib/tls/libc.so.6", O_RDONLY)    = 3
read(3, "\177ELF\1\1\1\0\0\0\0\0\0\0\0\0\3\0\3\0\1\0\0\0`V\1B4\0"..., 512) = 512
fstat64(3, {st_mode=S_IFREG|0755, st_size=1531064, ...}) = 0
old_mmap(0x42000000, 1257224, PROT_READ|PROT_EXEC, MAP_PRIVATE, 3, 0) = 0x42000000
old_mmap(0x4212e000, 12288, PROT_READ|PROT_WRITE, MAP_PRIVATE|MAP_FIXED, 3,
    0x12e000) = 0x4212e000
old_mmap(0x42131000, 7944, PROT_READ|PROT_WRITE,
    MAP_PRIVATE|MAP_FIXED|MAP_ANONYMOUS, -1, 0) = 0x42131000
close(3)                                = 0
set_thread_area({entry_number:-1 -> 6, base_addr:0x40016a80, limit:1048575,
    seg_32bit:1, contents:0, read_exec_only:0, limit_in_pages:1, seg_not_present:0,
    useable:1}) = 0
munmap(0x40017000, 43183)               = 0
write(2, " val = 1724500000\n", 18 val = 1724500000
)       = 18
exit_group(0)                           = ?
```

The -c option produces a call count report and produces output similar to the following.

```
# strace -c

execve("/piperf/bin/pi_watch", ["pi_watch", "100"], [/* 32 vars */]) = 0
 val = 1724500000
% time     seconds  usecs/call     calls    errors syscall
------ ----------- ----------- --------- --------- ----------------
 44.77    0.000124           7        19        17 open
 18.77    0.000052           7         8         7 stat64
 15.52    0.000043           9         5           old_mmap
  4.33    0.000012          12         1           munmap
  2.89    0.000008           8         1           read
  2.89    0.000008           8         1           write
  2.89    0.000008           4         2           fstat64
```

```
2.89     0.000008          8           1              set_thread_area
2.17     0.000006          6           1              uname
1.81     0.000005          3           2              close
1.08     0.000003          3           1              brk
------  -----------   -----------   ---------   ---------  -----------------
100.00   0.000277                     42          24 total
```

A summary report generated by the -c option gives you an idea of what system calls are being made and which system calls are consuming all of the resources. You can then use a more detailed profiler to investigate from where these calls are being made.

You can use an additional parameter to add the timestamp to each call. The timestamp gives a good indication of the relative time when each call took place and whether there is a certain time frame when groups of calls are being made. This information could help narrow down the problem to a specific time frame and set of functions.

OPROFILE

OProfile is a system-wide tracing tool that is available for the Intel, Power PC, AMD, sparc64, and PA-RISC platforms.

The OProfile tool works off of the system timer support or the performance counter support, if available. OProfile is a useful tool for obtaining a profile of a running system. This profile shows the amount of time being spent in an application and the number of times an application was running when OProfile made its measurement. It also gives information by application and library symbols.

The most unique function of OProfile is that it provides a report that shows the source code for an application with the number of measurements made for each line of code in the application. This function applies to C code and is very useful to determine where in an application to concentrate the tuning efforts.

OProfile is now shipped as part of some Red Hat distributions and is available from other Linux operating system providers. Note that the OProfile web site contains a disclaimer that they are not responsible for the version that ships with Red Hat. Some versions of Red Hat require that SMP support be enabled in the kernel configuration and that the OProfile driver must be built as a loadable module and not built into the kernel. If it's built into the kernel, duplicate function name errors occur.

One other item to note is that on the version that is downloaded from the OProfile development web site, you must run the autosetup.sh command as the first step. This is not always clear in the documentation.

It is best to use the OProfile patch on kernel source that is obtained from the www.kernel.org web site. This patch ensures that all the required support is included in the kernel source. If you use a specific vendor version of the kernel source, you might not have the latest patches. As vendors upgrade their kernel source to newer versions of the Linux kernel, the patches will be included.

Refer to the OProfile web site at `http://oprofile.sourceforge.net/` for detailed information on the tool and to download a copy.

The next sections examine the various parts of OProfile, including `opcontrol`, `oprof_start`, `oprofpp`, `op_time`, `op_to_source`, and `op_merge`.

opcontrol

`opcontrol` initializes the OProfile tool and starts and stops the data collection. The specific command options available with `opcontrol` are as follows:

- `--init`. Causes the OProfile driver to be loaded if it isn't already active and makes the driver interface available.
- `--setup`. Defines the specific setup parameters to be used by OProfile. You can bypass this option by accepting the defaults or by using one of the `setup` options directly. Some of the more useful `setup` options are buffer size, performance counter mask to use, number of events between samples, and filters for looking at a specific PID or PID group.
- `--start-daemon`. Starts the profiling daemon without starting the profiler. Use the `--start` option to start profiling.
- `--start`. Starts the profile measurement.
- `--dump`. Causes the collected profiling data to be dumped to the oprofile daemon.
- `--stop`. Stops the profiling data collection.
- `--shutdown`. Stops data collection and removes the daemon.
- `--reset`. Clears current session data but not saved session data.

Refer to the OProfile documentation for further information.

The following examples show the initialization and starting of the OProfile functions for counter support, creating separate profiles for libraries and the kernel, and saving session data.

Using the Counter Support

The following command initializes OProfile to start counter 0 to use the CPU clock not-halted event and to make the measurement after every 400,000 counter events. Performance counter 1 is set to data memory references, and the measurement is made after every 10,000 events. The Linux kernel executable file is located at /usr/src/Linux and is called vmlinux. After the initialization, the measurement is started.

```
opcontrol --ctr0-event=CPU_CLK_UNHALTED --ctr0-count=400000
opcontrol --ctr1-event=DATA_MEM_REFS --ctr1-count=10000
opcontrol --vmlinux=/usr/src/Linux/vmlinux
opcontrol --start
```

When using performance counters, ensure that the count values are large enough to prevent all the time from being spent in processing the performance counter handler. If the counter count value is too low, it is possible that the system will stop functioning and require a reboot. The performance counters are set up to interrupt when a counter overflow occurs. Therefore, if the count is too low, the time will be spent processing the counter overflow interrupt and nothing else.

Separate Profiles for Libraries and the Kernel

```
opcontrol --separate=kernel --vmlinux=/usr/src/Linux/vmlinux
opcontrol --start
  my_test --run
  pprofpp -kl -p /lib/modules/Linux/kernel /usr/local/bin/oprofiled
```

These commands profile the OProfile daemon itself, including when the daemon was running inside the kernel driver and the libraries it is using.

Saving Session Data

The following command saves the profiling data that has been collected in a file called /var/lib/oprofile/samples/run1. This name can then be passed on to the reporting functions to be processed.

```
opcontrol --save=run1
```

oprof_start

oprof_start is a GUI interface for opcontrol. oprof_start contains window sections where you can select counter events and a sampling rate, configuration options, and the status of the profiling.

Data Profiling Tools

The following sections describe the tools that profile the sample data OProfile collects. These tools are oprofpp, op_time, op_to_source, and op_merge.

oprofpp

oprofpp produces the following types of reports:

- *List symbol mode.* Provides a sorted histogram report of sample counts against functions, as shown in a system data walkthrough.
- *Detailed symbol mode.* Provides individual sample counts for instructions inside a function.
- grprof *mode,* which produces a flat grprof-style report.

Some of the more interesting options that can be used to control the report output are as follows:

- Symbol processing: -l is a histogram of counts by symbol name; -s is a detailed listing of the position of the address and the number of samples by symbol; -L is a detailed listing of all symbols.
- -g dumps the report to a file in gprof format.
- -o reports the function and line number for all samples.
- -k reports on shared libraries and kernel entries with respect to the application.
- -d and -D are used to detangle the C++ symbols. -D is a more simplified style of reporting.

The following sample listing shows the counts and time by kernel symbols.

```
# oprofpp -l
Cpu type: PIII
Cpu speed was (MHz estimation) : 863.886
Counter 0 counted CPU_CLK_UNHALTED events (clocks processor is not halted) with a
    unit mask of 0x00 (No unit mask) count 431500
vma       samples  %            symbol name          image name
c0123290 24        0.0182187    do_timer             /usr/src/linux/vmlinux
c0138810 24        0.0182187    sys_fchdir           /usr/src/linux/vmlinux

. . .

c0122950 100       0.0759111    ptrace_readdata      /usr/src/linux/vmlinux
c0122a10 103       0.0781885    ptrace_writedata     /usr/src/linux/vmlinux
c024b690 103       0.0781885    tcp_rfree            /usr/src/linux/vmlinux
c0107df0 107       0.0812249    copy_siginfo_to_user  /usr/src/linux/vmlinux
c011eb40 108       0.081984     sys_setitimer        /usr/src/linux/vmlinux
c0157240 108       0.081984     proc_file_lseek      /usr/src/linux/vmlinux
c0142e30 109       0.0827431    pipe_write           /usr/src/linux/vmlinux
c0123900 111       0.0842613    alloc_uid            /usr/src/linux/vmlinux
c0122af0 112       0.0850205    init_timervecs       /usr/src/linux/vmlinux

. . .

c011f8c0 406       0.308199     do_softirq           /usr/src/linux/vmlinux
c010d464 411       0.311995     IRQ0x77_interrupt    /usr/src/linux/vmlinux
```

c0133ad0	416	0.31579	swap_out_pmd	/usr/src/linux/vmlinux
c01073f0	437	0.331732	release_segments	/usr/src/linux/vmlinux
c024b6b0	454	0.344636	tcp_poll	/usr/src/linux/vmlinux
c0131e50	463	0.351469	alloc_area_pmd	/usr/src/linux/vmlinux
c01483e0	463	0.351469	dcache_dir_close	/usr/src/linux/vmlinux
c014c6b0	465	0.352987	move_lock_status	/usr/src/linux/vmlinux
c014c440	479	0.363614	lock_get_status	/usr/src/linux/vmlinux
c010c850	522	0.396256	sys_ptrace	/usr/src/linux/vmlinux
c0134250	528	0.400811	rmqueue	/usr/src/linux/vmlinux
c024b480	541	0.410679	tcp_mem_schedule	/usr/src/linux/vmlinux
c0122c70	555	0.421307	second_overflow	/usr/src/linux/vmlinux
c01c9b70	564	0.428139	config_chipset_for_pio	/usr/src/linux/vmlinux
c011f2b0	571	0.433453	do_adjtimex	/usr/src/linux/vmlinux
c0148a00	572	0.434212	filldir64	/usr/src/linux/vmlinux
c01b3150	603	0.457744	figure_loop_size	/usr/src/linux/vmlinux
c0114920	613	0.465335	mtrr_ioctl	/usr/src/linux/vmlinux
c01b30d0	630	0.47824	compute_loop_size	/usr/src/linux/vmlinux
c0208bb0	649	0.492663	qla1280_initialize_adapter	/usr/src/linux/vmlinux
c018aea0	676	0.513159	sys_semop	/usr/src/linux/vmlinux
c01b1e10	723	0.548837	floppy_release_irq_and_dma	/usr/src/linux/vmlinux
c0247ed0	725	0.550356	ip_build_and_send_pkt	/usr/src/linux/vmlinux
c0133bf0	726	0.551115	try_to_swap_out	/usr/src/linux/vmlinux
c0118a60	728	0.552633	sys_sched_getparam	/usr/src/linux/vmlinux
c01325e0	757	0.574647	kmem_cache_grow	/usr/src/linux/vmlinuxc0129f80
	959	0.727988	do_swap_page	/usr/src/linux/vmlinux
c02484b0	1011	0.767461	ip_build_xmit_slow	/usr/src/linux/vmlinux
c01c9180	1417	1.07566	hpt34x_dmaproc	/usr/src/linux/vmlinux
c0148400	1540	1.16903	dcache_dir_lseek	/usr/src/linux/vmlinux
c01069c0	1828	1.38766	gunzip	/usr/src/linux/vmlinux
c0208fd0	1890	1.43472	qla1280_pci_config	/usr/src/linux/vmlinux
c0108b60	1950	1.48027	handle_signal	/usr/src/linux/vmlinux
c0148150	2193	1.66473	sys_ioctl	/usr/src/linux/vmlinux
c010e5f0	2414	1.83249	__constant_c_and_count_memset	/usr/src/linux/vmlinux
c013a1a0	2482	1.88411	sys_writev	/usr/src/linux/vmlinux
c01174c0	2813	2.13538	do_page_fault	/usr/src/linux/vmlinux
c0118cb0	3646	2.76772	show_task	/usr/src/linux/vmlinux
c02489f0	3718	2.82238	ip_build_xmit	/usr/src/linux/vmlinux
c013a230	6183	4.69358	sys_pread	/usr/src/linux/vmlinux
c010e4e0	8802	6.6817	__constant_memcpy	/usr/src/linux/vmlinux
c013ae60	42015	31.8941	write_locked_buffers	/usr/src/linux/vmlinux

op_time

op_time produces summary reports relative to the binaries that are running on the system. Use this report to find out where time is being spent when your test case is running.

You can then use other reports to narrow your focus to specific functions and code segments within the application to see where the problem may exist.

Many of the same options that are available for `oprofpp` are also available for `op_time`.

The following sample report uses the `-D` option.

```
# op_time -D
1           0.0043   0.0000  /lib/libhistory.so.4.3
1           0.0043   0.0000  /opt/kde3/lib/kwin.so
1           0.0043   0.0000  /opt/kde3/lib/libartsflow.so.1.0.0
1           0.0043   0.0000  /usr/X11R6/lib/X11/locale/lib/common/ximcp.so.2
1           0.0043   0.0000  /usr/lib/vslick/bin/vs
2           0.0087   0.0000  /bin/gawk
2           0.0087   0.0000  /lib/modules/2.4.19-4GB/kernel/drivers/usb/usb-uhci.o
2           0.0087   0.0000  /opt/kde3/lib/libartsmidi.so.0.0.0
3           0.0130   0.0000  /bin/ps
3           0.0130   0.0000  /lib/modules/2.4.19-4GB/oprofile/oprofile.o
4           0.0173   0.0000  /lib/libreadline.so.4.3
4           0.0173   0.0000  /opt/kde3/lib/libkdecore.so.4.0.0
5           0.0216   0.0000  /opt/kde3/lib/libmcop.so.1.0.0
5           0.0216   0.0000  /usr/local/bin/op_help
16          0.0692   0.0000  /usr/X11R6/lib/libX11.so.6.2
16          0.0692   0.0000  /usr/lib/gconv/ISO8859-1.so
19          0.0822   0.0000  /lib/libpthread.so.0
20          0.0865   0.0000  /opt/kde3/lib/libkio.so.4.0.0
25          0.1082   0.0000  /usr/lib/libstdc++.so.5.0.0
26          0.1125   0.0000  /usr/X11R6/bin/XFree86
33          0.1428   0.0000  /opt/kde3/lib/libkonsolepart.so
45          0.1947   0.0000  /bin/bash
59          0.2553   0.0000  /sbin/insmod
68          0.2942   0.0000  /lib/ld-2.2.5.so
163         0.7052   0.0000  /lib/modules/2.4.19-4GB/kernel/fs/reiserfs/reiserfs.o
297         1.2849   0.0000  /lib/libc.so.6
308         1.3325   0.0000  /usr/lib/qt-3.0.5/lib/libqt-mt.so.3.0.5
661         2.8597   0.0000  /usr/src/Linux/vmlinux
3950        17.0892  0.0000  /usr/local/bin/oprofiled
17373       75.1622  0.0000  /piperf/bin/pi_watch
```

op_to_source

The `op_to_source` tool generates annotated source for assembly listings. If the profiled application is built with debug information, a report contains the actual source code with the profiled counts interleaved. If the application is built without the debug information, `op_to_source` can produce the assembler report. Use the `--assembly` (`-a`) option to produce this type of report.

The `op_to_source` level of reporting is one step above an application debugger that allows you to step through your application to check the execution logic. `op_to_source` provides you with the information necessary to determine where in the application you need to focus the debugging effort.

The following is sample output from `op_to_source` for a sample program.

```
# op_to_source

:/*
 *   IBM Performance Inspector
 *   Copyright (c) International Business Machines Corp., 2003
 *
 *   This library is free software; you can redistribute it and/or modify
 *   it under the terms of the GNU General Public License as published
 *   by the Free Software Foundation; either version 2.1 of the License, or
 *   (at your option) any later version.
 *
 *   This library is distributed in the hope that it will be useful,
 *   but WITHOUT ANY WARRANTY; without even the implied warranty of
 *   MERCHANTABILITY or FITNESS FOR A PARTICULAR PURPOSE.  See
 *   the GNU General Public License for more details.
 *
 *   You should have received a copy of the GNU General Public License
 *   along with this library; if not, write to the Free Software
 *   Foundation, Inc., 59 Temple Place, Suite 330, Boston, MA 02111-1307 USA
 */
                                  :
#include <stdio.h>
#include <stdlib.h>
#include <unistd.h>
int One(unsigned long long cps);
int Two(unsigned long long cps);
int Four(unsigned long long cps);
int Eight(unsigned long long cps);
int Sixteen(unsigned long long cps);
int ThirtyTwo(unsigned long long cps);
int SixtyFour(unsigned long long cps);

int val = 0;
/*********************************/
    10 0.003%     580 0.000% :void pc50() { /* pc50 total:  153902 52.31%
40667094 52.46% */
                              :     int i;
                              :
119226 40.52% 29583773 38.16% :     for(i = 0; i < 5000; i++) {
34613 11.76% 11071427 14.28% :         val = val + i;
                              :     }
```

```
    53 0.018%    11314 0.014% :}
                      :
:/**********************************/
     8 0.002%       290 0.000% :void pc25() { /* pc25 total:    70463 23.95%
18765427 24.20% */
                      :    int i;
                      :
60711 20.63% 16897936 21.79% :   for(i = 0; i < 2500; i++) {
 9693 3.295% 1851007 2.387% :      val = val + i;
                      :    }
    51 0.017%    16194 0.020% :}
                      :
                      :/**********************************/
    13 0.004%     5455 0.007% :void pc15() { /* pc15 total:    43572 14.81%
11245713 14.50% */
                      :    int i;
                      :
39415 13.39% 11069245 14.27% :   for(i = 0; i < 1500; i++) {
 4046 1.375%  136253 0.175% :      val = val + i;
                      :    }
    98 0.033%    34760 0.044% :}
                      :
                      :/**********************************/
     9 0.003%       116 0.000% :void pc10() { /* pc10 total:    26148 8.888%
6818423 8.795% */
                      :    int i;
                      :
20936 7.116% 5433262 7.008% :   for(i = 0; i < 1000; i++) {
 5154 1.752% 1365913 1.762% :      val = val + i;
                      :    }
    49 0.016%    19132 0.024% :}
                      :
                      :/**********************************/
                      :int main(int argc, char *argv[]) { /* main total:
84 0.028%    22107 0.028% */
                      :    int i;
                      :    int iter;
                      :
                      :    if(argc == 2) {
                      :        iter = atoi(argv[1]);
                      :    }
                      :    else {
                      :        fprintf(stderr, " Usage: watch iter\n");
                      :        fflush(stderr);
                      :        exit(0);
                      :    }
                      :
```

```
                                :    val = 0;
    47 0.015%    10143 0.013% :    for(i = 0; i < iter; i++) {
     5 0.001%     1011 0.001% :       pc50();
    11 0.003%     6072 0.007% :       pc25();
     9 0.003%     1313 0.001% :       pc15();
    12 0.004%     3568 0.004% :       pc10();
                                :    }
                                :
                                :
                                :    fprintf(stderr, " val = %d\n", val);
                                :    return(0);
                               :}
                                :
                                :
/*   * Total samples for file : "/piperf/src/pi_watch.c"
 *
 *   294169 100.0% 77518764 100.0%
 */


/*
 * Command line: op_to_source --source-dir=/piperf/src --output-dir=/temp
   /piperf/bin/pi_watch
 *
 * Interpretation of command line:
 * Output annotated source file with samples
 * Output all files
 *
 * Cpu type: PIII
 * Cpu speed (MHz estimation) : 662.229
 *
 *
 Counter 0 counted CPU_CLK_UNHALTED events (clock's processor is not halted)
     with a unit mask of 0x00 (No unit mask) count 400000
 * Total samples : 294169
 *
 Counter 1 counted DATA_MEM_REFS events (all memory references, cacheable and
     non) with a unit mask of 0x00 (No unit mask) count 1000
 * Total samples : 77518764
 */
```

op_merge

op_merge merges profiling samples created with the --separate option when applied to the same binary. op_merge can produce reports for separate shared libraries and then merge the reports for a complete system view. You can also produce reports on a combination of a subset of profiled applications.

Performance Inspector

The Performance Inspector (PI) is a suite of tools that identifies performance problems and characteristics. PI is distributed with a kernel patch and the source to build the device driver and tools. Procedures are also included to automate the install process and build for installing the tools. Support is provided for Intel 32- and 64-bit platforms, Power PC 32- and 64-bit systems, S390 32- and 64-bit systems, and the AMD Hammer processor.

The tools included in all versions of Performance Inspector include the following:

- *Above Idle*. Shows how idle, process, and interrupt times are distributed over the processor(s) on the running system. Above Idle is a phase 1 tool that identifies hot spots with respect to processor time and interrupt time spent in the system. This tool can also be used on SMP systems to see how well the multiple active processes are being spread over multiple CPUs.
- *Per-Thread Time*. Hooks into the process dispatch and interrupt code to maintain information on the total amount of time spent within a process, the time spent handling interrupts, and the amount of idle time. Summary information is provided on a per-CPU basis and for the system as a whole. APIs are provided to allow a developer to include calls within this application to measure functions and code snippets.
- *System Trace Data Collection*. Trace hooks are added to the kernel to collect data on what is happening within the system. Hooks are provided for process dispatches, process timeslices, interrupt entry and exits, process forks and clones, process startup execution, system timer interrupts, and memory mapping of code segments. It is also possible for an application to write its own trace records.

  Command files, libraries, and post processors are included to allow automatic tracing functions and reports. The most significant of these functions allow the measurement and reporting of jitted methods within Java applications. This function is very useful in identifying what methods are running and how much time they are using.
- *JPROF*. Performs Java execution profiling. This tool includes the capability to obtain detailed information on jitted methods. To use this tool, use a version of the Java SDK that includes JVMPI support.
- *Java Lock Monitor (JLM)*. Reports hold-time accounting and contention statistics with Java applications. The IBM Java 1.4 SDK is required to use this tool.

In addition to these common measurement functions, an additional set of functionality is provided on Intel 32-bit systems. This functionality includes the following:

- *Performance counter support.* Supports starting and stopping the counter, reporting counter contents, and displaying counter settings. The Trace Data Collection and Per-Thread Time functions base their measurements on the performance counters instead of the system clock. Instead of seeing how much time is spent within a process, you see how many instructions are executed, or how many branches or jumps are performed.
- *Instruction tracing.* Instruction tracing records all the branches taken while the measurement is active. Branches include calls, jumps, and any other execution path change. A post-processor tool is provided to report an instruction trace, including the number of instructions executed and where in the code the execution occurs. This reporting can also be done for Java jitted methods.
- *Dynamic kernel patch.* For certain releases of Red Hat and SUSE distributions, a version of the tools is provided that does not require a patch to the Linux kernel. Instead, the device driver dynamically patches the required hooks into the running system and runs the Performance Inspector tool suite.

The Performance Inspector installation requires you to apply a kernel patch and rebuild the kernel. After that step is complete, the various tools are built. Because some of the tools are sensitive to the version of Java that is being used, the tool build process must be redone when a new version of the Java support is used. However, this requirement does not affect the kernel. The kernel needs to be patched and built only once.

An exception to the installation procedure is provided for the Intel 32-bit support. A special version of the Performance Inspector is provided that does not require the kernel to be patched as long as the kernel being used is the default kernel shipped with supported versions of Red Hat and SUSE. The kernel source needs to be installed and the tools built as before, but the kernel does not have to be rebuilt. The PI driver dynamically patches the kernel at the appropriate places. The kernel patches are removed when the driver is uninstalled.

When none of the PI performance probes in the kernel are active, there is minimal impact on system performance. At most, a compare and short branch instruction are added to the code path where the probes are located. For the dynamic version of the IA32 PI, no extra overhead is added when the driver is not loaded.

When performing a trace, there is usually a 2% to 3% overhead on the system. Instruction tracing obviously adds more overhead, but it is for use in a debug environment. N tracing is done in a working production environment without any major impacts to performance or throughput.

Most of the PI functions can be controlled from APIs issued from the user's program as well as from the PI's own command files. When using the API interface, either from C code or Java, you can fine-tune when, where, and what information is collected. All of the source is provided and can be used as a coding sample.

Refer to `http://www-124.ibm.com/developerworks/oss/pi/index.html` for more information and to obtain a copy of the Performance Inspector.

The remainder of this chapter examines in detail the various features of the Performance Inspector.

Above Idle

Above Idle works by hooking into the process timeslice logic and interrupt handler within the kernel. Above Idle keeps track of the amount of time that is spent while a processor is busy, idle, or handling interrupts. It is useful for identifying processor over-load, high interrupt activity, and poor distribution of work within a multiprocessor sys-tem. When active, Above Idle gathers information over a user-specified measurement period. The default is 1 second. When using the default, Above Idle determines the amount of time the system spent while idle, active, and processing interrupts. The per-centage of processor idle, active, and interrupt processing time is then calculated and displayed by the processor when running on a multiprocessor system. Parameters are used to define how many measurements to make and the time interval between measurements.

To start the Above Idle measurement, enter **swtrace ai,** which uses the defaults to report system usage every second until the measurement is manually stopped.

The following example shows a sample Above Idle output.

```
# swtrace ai

Above Idle instrumentation enabled

    CPU 0   IDLE= 48.83, BUSY= 49.74, INTR=  1.44
    CPU 1   IDLE=  0.00, BUSY= 99.81, INTR=  0.19
    CPU 2   IDLE= 96.10, BUSY=  3.70, INTR=  0.20
    CPU 3   IDLE= 22.10, BUSY= 77.71, INTR=  0.19
    CPU 4   IDLE= 16.50, BUSY= 83.30, INTR=  0.20
    CPU 5   IDLE= 16.66, BUSY= 83.10, INTR=  0.25
    CPU 6   IDLE= 16.83, BUSY= 82.96, INTR=  0.21
    CPU 7   IDLE= 60.72, BUSY= 39.08, INTR=  0.20

    CPU 0   IDLE= 98.54, BUSY=  0.00, INTR=  1.46
    CPU 1   IDLE= 86.35, BUSY= 13.48, INTR=  0.17
    CPU 2   IDLE= 99.78, BUSY=  0.00, INTR=  0.22
    CPU 3   IDLE= 99.77, BUSY=  0.00, INTR=  0.23
    CPU 4   IDLE= 18.91, BUSY= 80.87, INTR=  0.22
    CPU 5   IDLE= 10.75, BUSY= 89.05, INTR=  0.20
    CPU 6   IDLE= 99.77, BUSY=  0.00, INTR=  0.23
    CPU 7   IDLE= 99.73, BUSY=  0.00, INTR=  0.27
```

```
CPU 0  IDLE= 98.59, BUSY=  0.00, INTR=  1.41
CPU 1  IDLE= 99.80, BUSY=  0.00, INTR=  0.20
CPU 2  IDLE= 99.81, BUSY=  0.00, INTR=  0.19
CPU 3  IDLE= 99.79, BUSY=  0.00, INTR=  0.21
CPU 4  IDLE=  1.19, BUSY= 98.65, INTR=  0.16
CPU 5  IDLE=  0.00, BUSY= 99.77, INTR=  0.23
CPU 6  IDLE= 99.78, BUSY=  0.00, INTR=  0.22
CPU 7  IDLE= 99.85, BUSY=  0.00, INTR=  0.15
```

The example was run on an eight-way SMP machine and shows data collected over 3 seconds.

Per-Thread Time

When active, per-thread time (PTT) accumulates the amount of time spent by each process within the system, as well as idle time and interrupt time. If you are processing on an Intel IA 32-bit system, you can use a performance event counter instead of using the real-time clock. For example, a measurement can be made that identifies the number of instructions executed by each process, the idle process, and the interrupts. The totals for process time, IRQ time, and idle time are provided for each processor in the system, as well as a system total of all processors.

PTT is activated via an API call, PTTInit, or an external program called ptt. In both cases, you specify the measurement medium as system timer or performance counter. After it is activated, you can run a program called pttstats to display the current values for idle, process, and interrupt times. You can run the pttstats program any number of times. A terminate command stops the measurement. The last counts before the terminate command is issued remain stored in the buffers until another init command is received. The following shows a sample PTT report:

```
Tools version 2040024
PTT_STATISTICS_SIZE = 263096
IBM_NR_CPUS = 16

Per Thread Time Summary

Total Dispatches:      3763
Total IRQs:            334
Total Thread Time:     151469140
Total IRQ Time:        721564
Total Idle Time:       2158895609
Total tool time:       81755
Total Measurement:     2311086313
Total Period:          0
```

Per Thread Time Detail

Details by CPU

```
              IRQ      Dispatch
  CPU         Count    Count        Times
-----------------------------------------------------
   1          334      3763
Thread Time:                        151469140
IRQ Time:                           721564
Idle Time:                          2158895609
Tool Time:                          81755
Total Time:                         5311168068
```

Details by Process

PID	Dispatch Count	IRQ Count	Process Time
0	708	303	2158895609
1	5	0	34407
2	83	0	139154
3	1	0	7162
7	15	0	168819
11	5	0	3466
324	1	0	6799
409	11	0	30641
671	1281	24	113156655
722	3	0	30128
723	2	0	8944
727	12	0	35688
728	2	0	11927
834	23	0	62077
869	11	0	170978
963	98	3	15182854
971	148	1	971766
992	137	1	1821399
995	48	0	2676763
999	393	0	3993366
11580	3	0	135687
11581	53	0	1156413
12281	544	1	6954629
12282	36	0	1006592
12297	140	1	3702826

```
Total Process Time:          2310364749
```

End of reports

APIs are provided to allow applications to start this measurement and to obtain the total amount of time spent in the process being measured. APIs allow an application to be instrumented to measure the amount of time spent between specific operations or positions within the application. On Intel 32-bit applications, measurements such as instructions retired can be used as a performance counter measurement.

Trace Profiling

Trace profiling works by hooking the kernel timer interrupt. When the timer interrupt is processed, the profiling code creates a trace record that contains the address where the processor was executing when the timer interrupt occurred. This trace record is then written into a trace buffer. When the profiling is complete, these trace records can be dumped out to a file where a post-processing program produces various reports.

You can run a trace profile to identify hot spots within the system by identifying the applications that consume the most time and which functions within those applications are causing them to use all that time. This includes jitted methods with Java applications.

Use the run.tprof command to perform the trace and produce the default reports.

By looking at the run.tprof command file, you can see the specific steps you need to follow to take a profile trace and produce the reports.

The following example shows a sample trace report for a small C application.

```
# run.tprof
ProcessorSpeed 398000000
TraceCycles 25382010763
  TraceTime 63.774(sec)

TOTAL TICKS 25383
(Clipping Level : 0.1 % 25 Ticks)


==================================
TPROF Report Summary

)) Process
)) Process_Module
)) Process_Module_Symbol
)) Process_Thread
)) Process_Thread_Module
)) Process_Thread_Module_Symbol
)) Module
)) Module_Symbol
==================================


==================================
```

```
)) Process
===============================

LAB TKS %%% NAMES

PID 19094 75.22 SystemProcess_0000
 PID 6284 24.76 /space/piperf/bin/WatchedPot_057c


===============================
)) Process_Module
===============================

LAB TKS %%% NAMES

 PID 19094 75.22 SystemProcess_0000
MOD 19094 75.22 vmlinux

PID 6284 24.76 /space/piperf/bin/WatchedPot_057c
MOD 6284 24.76 /space/piperf/bin/WatchedPot


===============================
)) Process_Module_Symbol
===============================

LAB TKS %%% NAMES

PID 19094 75.22 SystemProcess_0000
MOD 19094 75.22 vmlinux
SYM 19094 75.22 default_idle

PID 6284 24.76 /space/piperf/bin/WatchedPot_057c
MOD 6284 24.76 /space/piperf/bin/WatchedPot
SYM 3154 12.43 ThirtyTwo
SYM 1615 6.36 Sixteen
SYM 808 3.18 Eight
SYM 404 1.59 Four
SYM 202 0.80 Two
SYM 101 0.40 One


===============================
)) Process_Thread
===============================

LAB TKS %%% NAMES

PID 19094 75.22 SystemProcess_0000
TID 19094 75.22 tid_0000
```

```
  PID 6284 24.76 /space/piperf/bin/WatchedPot_057c
TID 6284 24.76 tid_057c


===============================
)) Process_Thread_Module
===============================

LAB TKS %%% NAMES

PID 19094 75.22 SystemProcess_0000
TID 19094 75.22 tid_0000
MOD 19094 75.22 vmlinux

PID 6284 24.76 /space/piperf/bin/WatchedPot_057c
TID 6284 24.76 tid_057c
MOD 6284 24.76 /space/piperf/bin/WatchedPot


===============================
)) Process_Thread_Module_Symbol
===============================

LAB TKS %%% NAMES

PID 19094 75.22 SystemProcess_0000
TID 19094 75.22 tid_0000
MOD 19094 75.22 vmlinux
SYM 19094 75.22 default_idle

PID 6284 24.76 /space/piperf/bin/WatchedPot_057c
TID 6284 24.76 tid_057c
MOD 6284 24.76 /space/piperf/bin/WatchedPot
SYM 3154 12.43 ThirtyTwo
SYM 1615 6.36 Sixteen
 SYM 808 3.18 Eight
SYM 404 1.59 Four
SYM 202 0.80 Two
 SYM 101 0.40 One


===============================
)) Module
===============================

LAB TKS %%% NAMES

MOD 19096 75.23 vmlinux
MOD 6284 24.76 /space/piperf/bin/WatchedPot
```

```
=================================
)) Module_Symbol
=================================

  LAB TKS %%% NAMES

MOD 19096 75.23 vmlinux
SYM 19094 75.22 default_idle

MOD 6284 24.76 /space/piperf/bin/WatchedPot
SYM 3154 12.43 ThirtyTwo
SYM 1615 6.36 Sixteen
SYM 808 3.18 Eight
SYM 404 1.59 Four
SYM 202 0.80 Two
SYM 101 0.40 One
```

When profiling applications, the level of optimization used when the application is compiling can have an effect on the trace output. With optimization on, functions that execute the same base code are all rolled up into the application instead of reported on separately by symbol name. Therefore, it is a good idea to make the first few profiling runs on applications that have not been compiled with optimization turned on.

Instruction Tracing

A special version of trace profiling that sets up the system to use the hardware's instruction trace capabilities is available on Intel IA32 systems. Instruction tracing starts from the branch instruction signal and then creates trace records every time a code branch, jump, or call is performed. Instruction profiling provides a detailed trace of the execution path in the system without the need to have a debugger installed or code compiled with the debug option enabled.

Use instruction tracing only for very short, controlled measurement periods, because it can produce a significant number of tracing records. Instruction tracing is primarily useful for determining the exact execution path through the entire system for the function being executed.

A small command file, run.itrace, is provided to simplify the taking of an instruction trace profile.

The following example shows a small output of run.itrace.

```
# run.itrace
- - - - - - - - - - - - - - - - - - - - - - - - - - -
ss: 0x8049a5c 1 push ebp
ss: 0x8049a5d 2 mov ebp, esp
ss: 0x8049a5f 3 sub esp, 0x8
```

```
ss: 0x8049a62 5 call 0x420628d8
0 1 1 4 @ 0 func1:/piperf/bin/itracec 8a1_0_/piperf/bin/itracec_ CALL
ss: 0x8049a6a 1 push ebp
 ss: 0x8049a6b 2 mov ebp, esp
ss: 0x8049a6d 3 sub esp, 0x8
ss: 0x8049a70 5 call 0x420628d8
0 1 1 4 @ 0 func2:/piperf/bin/itracec 8a1_0_/piperf/bin/itracec_ CALL
ss: 0x8049a78 1 push ebp
ss: 0x8049a79 2 mov ebp, esp
ss: 0x8049a7b 3 sub esp, 0x8
ss: 0x8049a7e 5 call 0x420628d8
0 1 1 4 @ 0 func3:/piperf/bin/itracec 8a1_0_/piperf/bin/itracec_ CALL
ss: 0x8049a86 1 push ebp
ss: 0x8049a87 2 mov ebp, esp
ss: 0x8049a89 3 sub esp, 0x8
ss: 0x8049a8c 5 call 0x420628d8
0 1 1 4 @ 0 func4:/piperf/bin/itracec 8a1_0_/piperf/bin/itracec_ CALL
ss: 0x8049a94 1 push ebp
ss: 0x8049a95 2 mov ebp, esp
ss: 0x8049a97 3 sub esp, 0x8
ss: 0x8049a9a 5 call 0x420628d8
0 1 1 4 @ 0 func5:/piperf/bin/itracec 8a1_0_/piperf/bin/itracec_ CALL
---------------------------------
```

This report shows the assembler instructions that were executed between the entry and the branch instruction. The report provides a detailed view of what is going on in the system. To relate this back to the actual C code, you would have to compile the C code with the assembler option and calculate the offsets to the assembler instructions to find them in the listing.

If you add the -c option to the post-processing report generator, the output would look similar to the following.

```
# run.itrace -c
cpu ring instruction_count offset symbolname_modulename pid_tid_pidname
  To_instruction
0 1 2 4 @ 32 printf:/lib/i686/libc-2.2.93.so 8a1_0_/piperf/bin/itracec_ RETURN
0 1 1 5 @ 54 main:/piperf/bin/itracec 8a1_0_/piperf/bin/itracec_ CALL
0 1 1 4 @ 0 func1:/piperf/bin/itracec 8a1_0_/piperf/bin/itracec_ CALL
0 1 1 4 @ 0 func2:/piperf/bin/itracec 8a1_0_/piperf/bin/itracec_ CALL
0 1 1 4 @ 0 func3:/piperf/bin/itracec 8a1_0_/piperf/bin/itracec_ CALL
0 1 1 4 @ 0 func4:/piperf/bin/itracec 8a1_0_/piperf/bin/itracec_ CALL
0 1 1 4 @ 0 func5:/piperf/bin/itracec 8a1_0_/piperf/bin/itracec_ CALL
0 1 1 6 @ 0 func6:/piperf/bin/itracec 8a1_0_/piperf/bin/itracec_ CALL
0 1 3 1 @ 50 <plt>:/piperf/bin/itracec 8a1_0_/piperf/bin/itracec_ JUMP
0 1 1 6 @ 0 printf:/lib/i686/libc-2.2.93.so 8a1_0_/piperf/bin/itracec_ CALL
0 1 2 2 @ 0 __i686.get_pc_thunk.bx:/lib/i686/libc-2.2.93.so
8a1_0_/piperf/bin/itracec_ RETURN
```

```
0 1 1 8 @ 11 printf:/lib/i686/libc-2.2.93.so 8a1_0_/piperf/bin/itracec_ CALL
0 1 1 7 @ 0 _IO_vfprintf_internal:/lib/i686/libc-2.2.93.so
8a1_0_/piperf/bin/itracec_ CALL
0 1 2 2 @ 0 __i686.get_pc_thunk.bx:/lib/i686/libc-2.2.93.so
8a1_0_/piperf/bin/itracec_ RETURN
0 1 1 6 @ d _IO_vfprintf_internal:/lib/i686/libc-2.2.93.so
8a1_0_/piperf/bin/itracec_ CALL
0 1 3 1 @ 470 <plt>:/lib/i686/libc-2.2.93.so 8a1_0_/piperf/bin/itracec_ JUMP
0 1 1 4 @ 0 __errno_location:/lib/i686/libc-2.2.93.so
8a1_0_/piperf/bin/itracec_ CALL
0 1 2 2 @ 0 __i686.get_pc_thunk.bx:/lib/i686/libc-2.2.93.so
8a1_0_/piperf/bin/itracec_ RETURN
0 1 2 5 @ 9 __errno_location:/lib/i686/libc-2.2.93.so
8a1_0_/piperf/bin/itracec_ RETURN
-----------------------------------
```

Java Profiler

JPROF is a Java profiling agent that dynamically responds to JVMPI events based on options passed at Java invocation. The profiler is generally referred to as JPROF but uses an executable library called libjprof.so. JPROF provides JIT address-to-name resolution to support tprof and ITtrace data reduction. Other functions include Java Lock Monitor and Java HeapDump. The profiler has been implemented for IBM JDK 1.2.2 and later and is based on the support in the JDK for the JVMPI interface.

The following example shows a report generated by the trace profiler on a Java application.

```
Tprof Reports

           ProcessorSpeed        688000000
             TraceCycles       10949059046
               TraceTime        15.914(sec)



 TOTAL TICKS          125160
 (Clipping Level :    0.1 %   125 Ticks)


    ================================
       TPROF Report Summary

    )) Process
    )) Process_Module
    )) Process_Module_Symbol
    )) Process_Thread
```

```
)) Process_Thread_Module
)) Process_Thread_Module_Symbol
)) Module
)) Module_Symbol
================================

================================
)) Process
================================

LAB    TKS    %%%      NAMES

PID  15645 12.50      SystemProcess_7
PID  15645 12.50      SystemProcess_1
PID  15645 12.50      SystemProcess_0
PID  14388 11.50      SystemProcess_2
PID  14074 11.24      SystemProcess_4
PID  12806 10.23      SystemProcess_3
PID  10935  8.74      SystemProcess_6
PID  10462  8.36      SystemProcess_5
PID   4710  3.76      java_6
PID   4302  3.44      sshd_5
PID   2823  2.26      sshd_3
PID   1566  1.25      java_4
PID   1257  1.00      java_2
PID    881  0.70      java_5

================================
)) Process_Module
================================

LAB    TKS    %%%      NAMES

PID  15645 12.50      SystemProcess_7
 MOD  15645 12.50       vmlinux

PID  15645 12.50      SystemProcess_1
 MOD  15645 12.50       vmlinux

PID  15645 12.50      SystemProcess_0
 MOD  15645 12.50       vmlinux

PID  14388 11.50      SystemProcess_2
 MOD  14388 11.50       vmlinux

PID  14074 11.24      SystemProcess_4
```

```
 MOD  14074 11.24     vmlinux

 PID  12806 10.23     SystemProcess_3
 MOD  12806 10.23     vmlinux

 PID  10935  8.74     SystemProcess_6
 MOD  10935  8.74     vmlinux

 PID  10462  8.36     SystemProcess_5
 MOD  10462  8.36     vmlinux

 PID   4710  3.76     java_6
 MOD   2109  1.69     vmlinux
 MOD   1767  1.41     JITCODE
 MOD    268  0.21     /opt/IBMJava2-141/jre/bin/libhpi.so
 MOD    243  0.19     /opt/IBMJava2-141/jre/bin/classic/libjvm.so
 MOD    175  0.14     /lib/tls/libpthread-0.29.so

 PID   4302  3.44     sshd_5
 MOD   1966  1.57     vmlinux
 MOD   1349  1.08     /lib/libcrypto.so.0.9.7a
 MOD    480  0.38     /usr/sbin/sshd
 MOD    462  0.37     /lib/tls/libc-2.3.2.so

 PID   2823  2.26     sshd_3
 MOD   1369  1.09     vmlinux
 MOD    844  0.67     /lib/libcrypto.so.0.9.7a
 MOD    302  0.24     /usr/sbin/sshd
 MOD    280  0.22     /lib/tls/libc-2.3.2.so
 PID   1566  1.25     java_4
 MOD    767  0.61     vmlinux
 MOD    532  0.43     JITCODE

 PID   1257  1.00     java_2
 MOD    601  0.48     vmlinux
 MOD    434  0.35     JITCODE

 PID    881  0.70     java_5
 MOD    444  0.35     vmlinux
 MOD    299  0.24     JITCODE

 ===============================
 )) Process_Module_Symbol
 ===============================
```

```
LAB    TKS    %%%      NAMES

PID  15645 12.50      SystemProcess_7
 MOD  15645 12.50       vmlinux
  SYM  15605 12.47        default_idle

PID  15645 12.50      SystemProcess_1
 MOD  15645 12.50       vmlinux
  SYM  15606 12.47        default_idle

PID  15645 12.50      SystemProcess_0
 MOD  15645 12.50       vmlinux
  SYM  15608 12.47        default_idle

PID  14388 11.50      SystemProcess_2
 MOD  14388 11.50       vmlinux
  SYM  14341 11.46        default_idle

PID  14074 11.24      SystemProcess_4
 MOD  14074 11.24       vmlinux
  SYM  14043 11.22        default_idle

PID  12806 10.23      SystemProcess_3
 MOD  12806 10.23       vmlinux
  SYM  12675 10.13        default_idle

PID  10935  8.74      SystemProcess_6
 MOD  10935  8.74       vmlinux
  SYM  10913  8.72        default_idle

PID  10462  8.36      SystemProcess_5
 MOD  10462  8.36       vmlinux
  SYM  10387  8.30        default_idle

PID   4710  3.76      java_6
 MOD   2109  1.69       vmlinux
  SYM    404  0.32        n_tty_receive_buf
  SYM    144  0.12        opost_block
  SYM    141  0.11        sigprocmask
  SYM    140  0.11        .text.lock.tty_io
  SYM    136  0.11        tty_write
  SYM    130  0.10        n_tty_receive_room

 MOD   1767  1.41       JITCODE
  SYM    621  0.50        hellop.main([Ljava/lang/String;)V
  SYM    143  0.11        java/io/OutputStreamWriter.write([CII)V
```

```
MOD     268  0.21        /opt/IBMJava2-141/jre/bin/libhpi.so

MOD     243  0.19        /opt/IBMJava2-141/jre/bin/classic/libjvm.so

MOD     175  0.14        /lib/tls/libpthread-0.29.so

PID    4302  3.44     sshd_5
MOD    1966  1.57        vmlinux
 SYM     236  0.19          read_chan
 SYM     125  0.10          n_tty_chars_in_buffer

MOD    1349  1.08        /lib/libcrypto.so.0.9.7a
 SYM    1345  1.07          NoSymbols

MOD     480  0.38        /usr/sbin/sshd
 SYM     474  0.38          NoSymbols

MOD     462  0.37        /lib/tls/libc-2.3.2.so

PID    2823  2.26     sshd_3
MOD    1369  1.09        vmlinux
 SYM     175  0.14          read_chan

MOD     844  0.67        /lib/libcrypto.so.0.9.7a
 SYM     842  0.67          NoSymbols

MOD     302  0.24        /usr/sbin/sshd
 SYM     298  0.24          NoSymbols

MOD     280  0.22        /lib/tls/libc-2.3.2.so

PID    1566  1.25     java_4
MOD     767  0.61        vmlinux
 SYM     151  0.12          n_tty_receive_buf

MOD     532  0.43        JITCODE
 SYM     161  0.13          hellop.main([Ljava/lang/String;)V

PID    1257  1.00     java_2
MOD     601  0.48        vmlinux
 SYM     132  0.11          n_tty_receive_buf

MOD     434  0.35        JITCODE
 SYM     126  0.10          hellop.main([Ljava/lang/String;)V

PID     881  0.70     java_
MOD     444  0.35        vmlinux
MOD     299  0.24        JITCODE
```

```
=================================
)) Process_Thread
=================================

LAB    TKS    %%%      NAMES

PID  15645 12.50      SystemProcess_7
 TID  15645 12.50       tid_0000

PID  15645 12.50      SystemProcess_1
 TID  15645 12.50       tid_0000

PID  15645 12.50      SystemProcess_0
 TID  15645 12.50       tid_0000

PID  14388 11.50      SystemProcess_2
 TID  14388 11.50       tid_0000

PID  14074 11.24      SystemProcess_4
 TID  14074 11.24       tid_0000

PID  12806 10.23      SystemProcess_3
 TID  12806 10.23       tid_0000

PID  10935  8.74      SystemProcess_6
 TID  10935  8.74       tid_0000

PID  10462  8.36      SystemProcess_5
 TID  10462  8.36       tid_0000

PID   4710  3.76      java_6
 TID   4668  3.73       tid_main

PID   4302  3.44      sshd_5
 TID   4298  3.43       tid_02c5

PID   2823  2.26      sshd_3
 TID   2823  2.26       tid_02c5

PID   1566  1.25      java_4
 TID   1527  1.22       tid_main

PID   1257  1.00      java_2
 TID   1222  0.98       tid_main

PID    881  0.70      java_5
 TID    832  0.66       tid_main
```

```
=================================
)) Process_Thread_Module
=================================

LAB    TKS    %%%      NAMES

PID  15645 12.50      SystemProcess_7
 TID  15645 12.50       tid_0000
  MOD  15645 12.50        vmlinux

PID  15645 12.50      SystemProcess_1
 TID  15645 12.50       tid_0000
  MOD  15645 12.50        vmlinux

PID  15645 12.50      SystemProcess_0
 TID  15645 12.50       tid_0000
  MOD  15645 12.50        vmlinux

PID  14388 11.50      SystemProcess_2
 TID  14388 11.50       tid_0000
  MOD  14388 11.50        vmlinux

PID  14074 11.24      SystemProcess_4
 TID  14074 11.24       tid_0000
  MOD  14074 11.24        vmlinux

PID  12806 10.23      SystemProcess_3
 TID  12806 10.23       tid_0000
  MOD  12806 10.23        vmlinux

PID  10935  8.74      SystemProcess_6
 TID  10935  8.74       tid_0000
  MOD  10935  8.74        vmlinux

PID  10462  8.36      SystemProcess_5
 TID  10462  8.36       tid_0000
  MOD  10462  8.36        vmlinux

PID   4710  3.76      java_6
 TID   4668  3.73       tid_main
  MOD   2075  1.66        vmlinux
  MOD   1767  1.41        JITCODE
  MOD    268  0.21        /opt/IBMJava2-141/jre/bin/libhpi.so
  MOD    236  0.19        /opt/IBMJava2-141/jre/bin/classic/libjvm.so
  MOD    174  0.14        /lib/tls/libpthread-0.29.so

PID   4302  3.44      sshd_5
 TID   4298  3.43       tid_02c5
```

```
      MOD    1965  1.57      vmlinux
      MOD    1349  1.08      /lib/libcrypto.so.0.9.7a
      MOD     478  0.38      /usr/sbin/sshd
      MOD     461  0.37      /lib/tls/libc-2.3.2.so

  PID   2823  2.26       sshd_3
   TID   2823  2.26       tid_02c5
    MOD   1369  1.09       vmlinux
    MOD    844  0.67       /lib/libcrypto.so.0.9.7a
    MOD    302  0.24       /usr/sbin/sshd
    MOD    280  0.22       /lib/tls/libc-2.3.2.so

PID   1566  1.25      java_4
 TID   1527  1.22      tid_main
  MOD    734  0.59      vmlinux
  MOD    532  0.43      JITCODE

PID   1257  1.00      java_2
 TID   1222  0.98      tid_main
  MOD    580  0.46      vmlinux
  MOD    434  0.35      JITCODE

PID    881  0.70      java_5
 TID    832  0.66      tid_main
  MOD    410  0.33      vmlinux
  MOD    299  0.24      JITCODE


=================================
)) Process_Thread_Module_Symbol
=================================

LAB    TKS    %%%      NAMES

PID  15645 12.50      SystemProcess_7
 TID  15645 12.50       tid_0000
  MOD  15645 12.50       vmlinux
   SYM  15605 12.47        default_idle

PID  15645 12.50      SystemProcess_1
 TID  15645 12.50       tid_0000
  MOD  15645 12.50       vmlinux
   SYM  15606 12.47        default_idle

PID  15645 12.50      SystemProcess_0
 TID  15645 12.50       tid_0000
  MOD  15645 12.50       vmlinux
   SYM  15608 12.47        default_idle
```

```
PID  14388 11.50      SystemProcess_2
 TID  14388 11.50       tid_0000
  MOD  14388 11.50        vmlinux
   SYM  14341 11.46         default_idle

PID  14074 11.24      SystemProcess_4
 TID  14074 11.24       tid_0000
  MOD  14074 11.24        vmlinux
   SYM  14043 11.22         default_idle

PID  12806 10.23      SystemProcess_3
 TID  12806 10.23       tid_0000
  MOD  12806 10.23        vmlinux
   SYM  12675 10.13         default_idle

PID  10935  8.74      SystemProcess_6
 TID  10935  8.74       tid_0000
  MOD  10935  8.74        vmlinux
    SYM  10913  8.72          default_idle

PID  10462  8.36      SystemProcess_5
 TID  10462  8.36       tid_0000
  MOD  10462  8.36        vmlinux
   SYM  10387  8.30         default_idle

PID   4710  3.76      java_6
 TID   4668  3.73       tid_main
  MOD   2075  1.66        vmlinux
   SYM    404  0.32          n_tty_receive_buf
   SYM    144  0.12          opost_block
   SYM    141  0.11          sigprocmask
   SYM    140  0.11          .text.lock.tty_io
   SYM    136  0.11          tty_write
   SYM    130  0.10          n_tty_receive_room

  MOD   1767  1.41        JITCODE
   SYM    621  0.50          hellop.main([Ljava/lang/String;)V
   SYM    143  0.11          java/io/OutputStreamWriter.write([CII)V

  MOD    268  0.21        /opt/IBMJava2-141/jre/bin/libhpi.so

  MOD    236  0.19        /opt/IBMJava2-141/jre/bin/classic/libjvm.so

  MOD    174  0.14        /lib/tls/libpthread-0.29.so

PID   4302  3.44      sshd_5
 TID   4298  3.43       tid_02c5
  MOD   1965  1.57        vmlinux
```

```
       SYM     236   0.19          read_chan
       SYM     125   0.10          n_tty_chars_in_buffer

       MOD    1349   1.08          /lib/libcrypto.so.0.9.7a
       SYM    1345   1.07          NoSymbols

       MOD     478   0.38          /usr/sbin/sshd
       SYM     472   0.38          NoSymbols

       MOD     461   0.37          /lib/tls/libc-2.3.2.so

PID    2823   2.26     sshd_3
 TID   2823   2.26       tid_02c5
  MOD  1369   1.09       vmlinux
   SYM    175   0.14       read_chan

  MOD    844   0.67       /lib/libcrypto.so.0.9.7a
   SYM    842   0.67       NoSymbols

  MOD    302   0.24       /usr/sbin/sshd
   SYM    298   0.24       NoSymbols

  MOD    280   0.22       /lib/tls/libc-2.3.2.so

PID    1566   1.25     java_4
 TID   1527   1.22       tid_main
  MOD    734   0.59       vmlinux
   SYM    151   0.12       n_tty_receive_buf

  MOD    532   0.43       JITCODE
   SYM    161   0.13       hellop.main([Ljava/lang/String;)V

PID    1257   1.00     java_2
 TID   1222   0.98       tid_main
  MOD    580   0.46       vmlinux
   SYM    132   0.11       n_tty_receive_buf

  MOD    434   0.35       JITCODE
   SYM    126   0.10       hellop.main([Ljava/lang/String;)V

PID     881   0.70     java_5
 TID    832   0.66       tid_main
  MOD    410   0.33       vmlinux

  MOD    299   0.24       JITCODE

==================================
)) Module
==================================
```

```
LAB    TKS   %%%      NAMES

MOD 116871 93.38      vmlinux
MOD   3032  2.42      JITCODE
MOD   2193  1.75      /lib/libcrypto.so.0.9.7a
MOD    782  0.62      /usr/sbin/sshd
MOD    743  0.59      /lib/tls/libc-2.3.2.so
MOD    443  0.35      /opt/IBMJava2-141/jre/bin/libhpi.so
MOD    441  0.35      /opt/IBMJava2-141/jre/bin/classic/libjvm.so
MOD    311  0.25      /lib/tls/libpthread-0.29.so
MOD    208  0.17      NoModule
MOD    133  0.11      /opt/IBMJava2-141/jre/bin/libjava.so


===============================
 )) Module_Symbol
===============================

LAB    TKS   %%%      NAMES

MOD 116871 93.38      vmlinux
 SYM 109178 87.23       default_idle
 SYM    783  0.63       n_tty_receive_buf
 SYM    413  0.33       .text.lock.tty_io
 SYM    411  0.33       read_chan
 SYM    378  0.30       sigprocmask
 SYM    331  0.26       __wake_up
 SYM    310  0.25       sysenter_past_esp
 SYM    299  0.24       schedule
 SYM    271  0.22       tty_write
 SYM    256  0.20       opost_block
 SYM    246  0.20       add_wait_queue
 SYM    229  0.18       n_tty_receive_room
 SYM    229  0.18       n_tty_chars_in_buffer
 SYM    197  0.16       __copy_from_user_ll
 SYM    191  0.15       sys_rt_sigprocmask
 SYM    177  0.14       do_select
 SYM    174  0.14       __copy_to_user_ll
 SYM    170  0.14       remove_wait_queue
 SYM    154  0.12       write_chan
 SYM    153  0.12       pty_write
 SYM    139  0.11       sys_select
 SYM    125  0.10       kill_fasync

 MOD   3032  2.42      JITCODE
 SYM   1011  0.81       hellop.main([Ljava/lang/String;)V
 SYM    254  0.20       java/io/OutputStreamWriter.write([CII)V
 SYM    198  0.16       sun/nio/cs/StreamEncoder.flushBuffer()V
 SYM    168  0.13       java/lang/String.<init>(Ljava/lang/String;I)V
```

```
SYM    168   0.13      java/io/PrintStream.write([BII)V
SYM    132   0.11      java/io/PrintStream.write(Ljava/lang/String;)V

MOD   2193   1.75      /lib/libcrypto.so.0.9.7a
SYM   2187   1.75        NoSymbols

MOD    782   0.62      /usr/sbin/sshd
SYM    772   0.62        NoSymbols

MOD    743   0.59      /lib/tls/libc-2.3.2.so
SYM    152   0.12        memset
SYM    125   0.10        __memchr

MOD    443   0.35      /opt/IBMJava2-141/jre/bin/libhpi.so

MOD    441   0.35      /opt/IBMJava2-141/jre/bin/classic/libjvm.so
SYM    141   0.11        jitCacheAlloc

MOD    311   0.25      /lib/tls/libpthread-0.29.so

MOD    208   0.17      NoModule
SYM    208   0.17        NoSymbols

MOD    133   0.11      /opt/IBMJava2-141/jre/bin/libjava.so
```

Offset Report

```
=================================
)) Module_Symbol_Offset
=================================

LAB     TKS    %%%      NAMES

MOD 116871 93.38      vmlinux
SYM 109178 87.23        default_idle
  OFF 109174 87.23        0x2d

SYM    783   0.63      n_tty_receive_buf
  OFF    440   0.35        0x157

SYM    413   0.33      .text.lock.tty_io
  OFF    204   0.16        0xb1

SYM    411   0.33      read_chan

SYM    378   0.30      sigprocmask
  OFF    321   0.26        0x77
```

```
SYM    331  0.26        __wake_up
OFF    326  0.26          0x37

SYM    310  0.25        sysenter_past_esp
OFF    127  0.10          0x3

SYM    299  0.24        schedule
OFF    277  0.22          0x22d

SYM    271  0.22        tty_write

SYM    256  0.20        opost_block

SYM    246  0.20        add_wait_queue
OFF    212  0.17          0x37

SYM    229  0.18        n_tty_receive_room

SYM    229  0.18        n_tty_chars_in_buffer
OFF    212  0.17          0x33

SYM    197  0.16        __copy_from_user_ll

SYM    191  0.15        sys_rt_sigprocmask

SYM    177  0.14        do_select

SYM    174  0.14        __copy_to_user_ll

SYM    170  0.14        remove_wait_queue
OFF    147  0.12          0x1d

SYM    154  0.12        write_chan

SYM    153  0.12        pty_write

SYM    139  0.11        sys_select

SYM    125  0.10        kill_fasync

MOD   3032  2.42        JITCODE
SYM   1011  0.81          hellop.main([Ljava/lang/String;)V
OFF    405  0.32            0x1e0
OFF    257  0.21            0x1e3
OFF    192  0.15            0x1e4

SYM    254  0.20          java/io/OutputStreamWriter.write([CII)V
```

```
SYM      198  0.16      sun/nio/cs/StreamEncoder.flushBuffer()V

SYM      168  0.13      java/lang/String.<init>(Ljava/lang/String;I)V

SYM      168  0.13      java/io/PrintStream.write([BII)V

SYM      132  0.11
java/io/PrintStream.write(Ljava/lang/String;)V

MOD     2193  1.75      /lib/libcrypto.so.0.9.7a
SYM     2187  1.75        NoSymbols
OFF      141  0.11        0x2bcf3

MOD      782  0.62      /usr/sbin/sshd
SYM      772  0.62        NoSymbols

MOD      743  0.59      /lib/tls/libc-2.3.2.so
SYM      152  0.12        memset

SYM      125  0.10        __memchr

MOD      443  0.35      /opt/IBMJava2-141/jre/bin/libhpi.so

MOD      441  0.35      /opt/IBMJava2-141/jre/bin/classic/libjvm.so
SYM      141  0.11        jitCacheAlloc

MOD      311  0.25      /lib/tls/libpthread-0.29.so

MOD      208  0.17      NoModule
SYM      208  0.17        NoSymbols
OFF      134  0.11        0xffffe410

MOD      133  0.11      /opt/IBMJava2-141/jre/bin/libjava.so
</pre>
```

Java Lock Monitor

Java Lock Monitor (JLM) support is provided with version 1.4.0 of the IBM JDK. JLM provides monitor hold time accounting and contention statistics on monitors used in Java applications and the JVM itself. JLM provides support for the following counters.

Counters associated with contended locks:

- *Total* number of successful acquires.
- *Recursive acquires*. Number of times the monitor was requested and was already owned by the requesting thread.

- *Number of times the requesting thread was blocked* waiting on the monitor because the monitor was already owned by another thread.
- *Cumulative time* the monitor was held.

The following statistics are also collected on platforms that support 3-Tier Spin Locking (x86 SMP):

- Number of times the requesting thread went through the *inner (spin) loop* while attempting to acquire the monitor.
- Number of times the requesting thread went through the *outer (thread yield) loop* while attempting acquire the monitor.

Garbage collection (GC) time is removed from hold times for all monitors held across a GC cycle.

A monitor can be acquired either recursively, when the requesting thread already owns it, or nonrecursively, when the requesting thread does not already own it. Nonrecursive acquires can be further divided into fast and slow. Fast is when the requested monitor is not already owned and the requesting thread gains ownership immediately. On platforms that implement 3-Tier Spin Locking, any monitor acquired while spinning is considered a fast acquire, regardless of the number of iterations in each tier. Slow is when the requested monitor is already owned by another thread and the requesting thread is blocked.

The JLM is controlled via a sockets interface, which allows the JLM to be controlled from a remote site. An `rtdriver` program is provided to produce the proper commands: `jlstar` starts the measurement, `jlmdump` writes the current results to a file, and `jlmstop` stops the measurement. You can issue the `jlmdump` command multiple times. Each time `jlmdump` is issued, a new file with the information in it is produced, allowing for the collection of information at critical points in the application execution.

The following example shows a sample Java Lock Monitor report.

```
Java Lock Monitor Report
Version_4.26 (05.01.2002)
  Built : ( Wed May  1 14:44:28 CDT 2002 )


  JLM_Interval_Time 34021158156


System (Registered) Monitors
```

%MISS	GETS	NONREC	SLOW	REC	TIER2	TIER3	%UTIL	AVER-HTM	MON-NAME
87	5273	5273	4572	0	710708	18487	1	95408	ITC Global_Compile lock
9	6870	6869	631	1	113420	2976	0	11807	Heap lock
5	1123	1123	51	0	11098	286	1	248385	Binclass lock
0	1153	1147	5	6	1307	33	0	47974	Monitor Cache lock
0	46149	45877	134	272	36961	877	1	6558	ITC CHA lock
0	33734	23483	19	10251	6544	150	1	17083	Thread queue lock
0	5	5	0	0	0	0	0	9309689	JNI Global Reference lock
0	5	5	0	0	0	0	0	9283000	JNI Pinning lock
0	5	5	0	0	0	0	0	9442968	Sleep lock
0	1	1	0	0	0	0	0	0	Monitor Registry lock
0	0	0	0	0	0	0	0	0	Evacuation Region lock
0	0	0	0	0	0	0	0	0	Method trace lock
0	0	0	0	0	0	0	0	0	Classloader lock
0	0	0	0	0	0	0	0	0	Heap Promotion lock

```
Java (Inflated) Monitors
```

%MISS	GETS	NONREC	SLOW	REC	TIER2	TIER3	%UTIL	AVER-HTM	MON-NAME
15	68	68	10	0	2204	56	2	11936405	
									test.lock.testlock1@A09410/A09418
2	42	42	1	0	186	5	0	300478	
									test.lock.testlock2@D31358/D31360
0	70	70	0	0	41	1	0	7617	
									Java.lang.ref.ReferenceQueue$Lock@920628/920630

```
LEGEND:
                 %MISS : 100 * SLOW / NONREC
                  GETS : Lock Entries
                NONREC : Non Recursive Gets
                  SLOW : Non Recursives that Wait
                   REC : Recursive Gets
                 TIER2 : SMP Wait Hierarchy
                 TIER3 : SMP Wait Hierarchy
                 %UTIL : 100 * Hold-Time / Total-Time
               AVER-HT : Hold-Time / NONREC
```

Descriptions of the report's fields are as follows:

- JLM_Interval_Time. Time interval between the start and end of measurement. Time is expressed in the units appropriate for the hardware platform: cycles for x86, IA64, and S390, and time-based ticks for PPC.

- %MISS. Percentage of the total GETS (acquires) where the requesting thread was blocked waiting on the monitor.

```
%MISS = (SLOW / NONREC) * 100
```

- GETS. Total number of successful acquires.

  ```
  GETS = FAST + SLOW + REC
  ```

- NONREC. Total number of nonrecursive acquires. This number includes **SLOW** gets.
- SLOW. Total number of nonrecursive acquires which caused the requesting thread to block waiting for the monitor to no longer be owned. This number is included in NONREC.

  To calculate the number of nonrecursive acquires in which the requesting thread obtained ownership immediately (FAST), subtract SLOW from NONREC. On platforms that support 3-Tier Spin Locking, monitors acquired while spinning are considered FAST acquires.

- REC. Total number of recursive acquires. A recursive acquire is one where the requesting thread already owns the monitor.
- TIER2. Total number of Tier 2 (inner spin loop) iterations on platforms that support 3-Tier Spin Locking.
- TIER3. Total number of Tier 3 (outer thread yield loop) iterations on platforms that support 3-Tier Spin Locking.
- %UTIL. Monitor hold time divided by JLM_Interval_Time. Hold time accounting must be turned on.
- AVER-HTM. Average amount of time the monitor was held. Recursive acquires are not included because the monitor is already owned when acquired recursively.

  ```
  Total hold time / NONREC
  ```

- MON-NAME. Monitor name or NULL (blank) if the name is not known.

Performance Inspector Executable Tools

The following tools, which are shipped with the Performance Inspector, provide support for the PI functions.

swtrace

swtrace is a software tracing mechanism that runs on Linux. swtrace is normally run from a command prompt by issuing the swtrace command with the appropriate arguments.

swtrace uses software trace hooks to collect data. Trace hooks are identified by both a major code and a minor code. Trace data is collected to a trace buffer that is allocated when swtrace is initialized or turned on. The size of the trace buffer can be set when swtrace is initialized. The `swtrace` command allows the user to select which major codes are traced, when tracing starts, when tracing stops, when data is transferred from the trace buffer to disk, and formatting of the trace data.

The major parameters supported by `swtrace` are as follows:

- `init`. Tells the trace profiler to allocate the trace buffers and initialize the system for tracing. With `init`, the size of the trace buffer to be allocated and the performance counter to use for taking the trace can be optionally specified.
- `enable`. Enables the trace hooks within the Linux kernel. This controls what information is placed in the trace buffer.
- `disable`. Keeps the specified trace hooks from being measured.
- `on`. Starts the trace. The trace information is gathered until the `swtrace off` command is given.
- `get`. Dumps the contents of the trace buffers to a file for processing by the report generator program.
- `it_install`. Initializes the instruction trace facility.
- `it_remove`. Resets the instruction trace functionality.

Other parameters display information about the Performance Inspector and control the rate of profiling. The command file run.tprof is generated when PI is installed in the system. This command file contains all the steps necessary to take a profiling trace and produce a report.

post

`post` produces various reports based on the trace profiling data. When a trace profiling report is produced, it is written to a file called tprof.out. When you install the Performance Inspector, you identify the directory where this file will be saved. If you want to keep the current tprof.out file, you must rename it something else before running another run.tprof command.

One option supported by the `post` command is `-show`. `-show` creates a file called post.show, which is a dump in a readable format of all the trace records. When all the trace hooks are enabled, post.show gives a detailed look at the sequence of events that occurred in the system, from execs to dispatches to interrupts.

pipcntr

`pipcntr` controls and displays the performance counters when PI is running on Intel IA32 platforms. This program can start and stop counters and display the contents of the counter registers and the counter control register settings. You can use this utility to start a performance counter and then run the per-thread time utility using this counter. The same holds true for the trace profiling function.

ptt

`ptt` starts and stops the per-thread time measurement. When starting, you can also specify what metric to use to perform the measurement.

pttstats

`pttstats` displays the per-thread time of every process in the system. On Intel IA32 systems, the measurement metric can be either the real-time clock or a performance monitor counter.

SUMMARY

This chapter has introduced a number of tools to help you identify performance problems and bottlenecks. It is important that you have a controlled test environment as well as a detailed test scenario to follow. The test must be repeatable and reliable. Start with the simplest items and continue to the more complex items as you collect and establish base data points. Trying to analyze everything at once will only lead to more time wasted finding the real problem.

Many other trace tools are currently being produced. Some that are worth exploring are `vtune`, which can be used on Intel platforms; `dprobes`, which is available on multiple platforms for looking at the kernel and load-module debug tracing-type information; `tracer`, which hooks into the kernel and provides tracing information; and many others. The tools covered in this chapter have been in existence for a number of years and provide good documentation and report formatting. They also provide a wide variety of reporting format options. As with most Linux products, they are provided free of charge via open source.

How performance analysis, tracing, and tuning are carried out is an individual preference. Each environment is unique and requires that the person performing the analysis use tools and methods that he is comfortable with and can understand. The golden rule to follow is to keep it simple. As long as the analysis is done in a simple and methodical manner, the chances for success are high.

REFERENCES

[1] Web resource: `http://oprofile.sourceforge.net/about/`

[2] Web resource: `http://www-124.ibm.com/developerworks/oss/pi/`

## CHAPTER SIX

Benchmarks as an Aid to Understanding Workload Performance

By Gerrit Huizenga

INTRODUCTION

In Chapter 4, "System Performance Monitoring," we talked about monitoring the performance aspects of a system as a way to understand some of the characteristics of a workload. We also looked at some tools for monitoring individual applications. These tools typically provide information about the system's performance at a specific point in time. Some tools also monitor the system at regular intervals and log performance statistics, allowing a performance analyst to watch how the system's performance changes over time. Although performance monitoring data can be critical to understanding how a workload operates over time, such data is only a one-dimensional view of overall workload response time. For instance, very few workloads run at a steady state of operation for their entire lifetime. Workloads are primarily responsive to human interaction, although there may be other significant factors that generate workload activity. Because these interactions are so random, periodic monitoring often happens with little insight into the types of requests the users are generating or how representative those requests are of the general load that the workload can handle. Further, although this style of monitoring is useful for identifying performance bottlenecks, it is less effective for understanding how well the workload could or should perform. It is also difficult to evaluate the potential advantages of changes in hardware or configuration or predict what will happen when the system is reconfigured.

In Chapter 4, we mentioned that statistics gathered by most monitoring tools are easiest to understand if they can be put in context based on past workload behaviors. For instance, when a workload has been working well for months, and suddenly the response time increases by an order of magnitude, being able to compare current monitoring data with past monitoring data can help provide insights into the problem area. This technique is useful for problem analysis; however, general system tuning is much simpler with a predictable workload. Also, a workload that depends on tens or hundreds of users generating interactions with the system is difficult to set up and difficult to make repeatable. Again, having a predictable workload that can be automated and that can simulate the interactions of the users allows a performance analyst to run the workload repeatedly, changing selected aspects of the environment and observing the changes in the underlying system statistics.

Repeatability and consistency are the primary indicators of a potential benchmark. With those two factors, you can perform a statistically valid scientific application of a control environment and can analyze the results of changes to the control environment. Using the monitoring methods discussed in this chapter, you can identify system statistics that are constant from run to run, those that change slightly, and those that have dramatic change as various aspects of the configuration are modified. These basic tools allow you to perform "what-if" scenarios for analysis in a basic sense. Exploring these scenarios allows you to tune your workload and your environment to get the best responses out of your system and to decide when portions of your system need to be improved. In some cases, you can also identify bottlenecks within the applications using this process, leading to direct modifications to the applications supporting your workload.

Further enhancements to this benchmark would include the capability to measure those factors of your workload that are critical to its overall throughput. For instance, on a file server, the capability to measure the number of files opened and sent to the end user over a period of time may provide a key measure representing the overall throughput of your file server. A web server may choose to measure the number of network connections created as a useful measure of work being done. Being able to identify a few key measures for a consistent, repeatable workload allows a performance analyst to use simple metrics to compare the results of various changes to the system environment. And this is exactly the point of benchmarking: creating a frame of reference for evaluating and improving the overall performance of your workload in your environment.

BENCHMARKING TO IMPROVE YOUR WORKLOAD

Benchmarking can be as simple as using a watch to measure the elapsed time of a single command or as complex as multitier workloads spanning multiple machines, requiring hard data consistency, multiple measurement points, complex derived metrics, and rigorous evaluations and publication standards. As a result, some benchmarks can be run on your home laptop; others require a highly trained staff with complex multimillion-dollar hardware configurations. If your goal is to use benchmarking to help improve your own workload, you need to decide if it makes sense to create your own benchmark or if it would be appropriate to make use of a standard benchmark.

The best approach to evaluate your workload is to run your own applications on your own system and measure the key metrics for your workload. However, most end-user workloads do not include standardized measurement points for bandwidth, latency, or overall user response times. Ideally, workloads would be designed with these measurement points in place, but that is rarely the case. In some workloads, underlying components may include some measurement points such as a database, which may have some capability to report transactions per second reference rates for various database tables. However, these measurement points may represent only a small subset of the overall workload and may not provide a realistic view of user response times for your end users.

So, if your workload doesn't have great measurement points at hand, what other options are available to measure its throughput? One option is to create a benchmark based on your workload. However, creating your own benchmark is often proportional in difficulty to the general complexity of the workload you want to model. Benchmark creation can be expensive, complex, difficult to validate, and hard to keep up-to-date as your workload changes. It often requires a significant investment to maintain such a benchmark, and such effort is not recommended for the faint of heart.

Another option is to identify an existing benchmark that models a workload similar to your own. Although a number of complex benchmarks model complex but common real-world workloads, not all possible workloads could possibly have a preexisting benchmark. In those cases, a set of benchmarks model common components of various complex workloads, such as file system benchmarks, file serving benchmarks, mail server benchmarks, networking benchmarks, and so on. Some of these benchmarks are available within the open source community; others are available from commercial or independent nonprofit organizations. These benchmarks typically provide standardized baseline measures under a wide variety of operating conditions, including different processor types, different operating systems, different disk configurations, various tuning parameters, and so on. Component benchmarks are often referred to as *microbenchmarks*; larger benchmarks are often referred to as *application benchmarks* or *enterprise benchmarks*, depending on their focus.

Running a benchmark a single time is quite uninteresting. The real value in running a benchmark is the capability to archive the relevant operating parameters such as the hardware configuration, software configuration, tuning variables, and so on and then compare successive runs with past results. Comparing and contrasting machine configurations, cost, and key performance parameters allows you to make intelligent decisions about potential upgrades, tuning possibilities, or additional software that might improve the overall performance and user response times of your workload. Existing benchmarks typically have gone to great pains to ensure great portability, consistent results from run to run, comparable results in similar hardware and system environments, and generally informative metrics about common aspects of traditional workloads. All this effort on standardization and consistency of benchmarks makes them powerful tools to evaluate potential improvements in your workload or even hardware or software solutions in light of your proposed workload.

WHAT TYPES OF BENCHMARKS ARE THERE?

We have already referenced microbenchmarks, application benchmarks, and complex workload benchmarks. In this section, we examine a few benchmarks in each of these classes and give a brief overview of how the benchmarks might be used to help evaluate your own workload characteristics.

MICROBENCHMARKS

This section looks at several types of microbenchmarks, including operating system benchmarks, disk benchmarks, network benchmarks, and application benchmarks.

Operating System Benchmarks

The operating system benchmarks discussed in this section are as follows:

- LMbench
- AIM7
- AIM9
- Reaim
- SPEC SDET

LMbench

(http://www.bitmover.com/lmbench/)
LMbench is a suite of simple benchmarks in the true sense of a microbenchmark. It contains a series of small tests for measuring latency and bandwidth of some of the most fundamental of all UNIX or Linux APIs. The bandwidth measures include a measure of reading from cached files, copy memory completely in user level, measuring the bandwidth of data through a UNIX pipe, and some simple benchmarks for TCP. Usually, these bandwidth measures are done by copying a block of memory or issuing a read() call in a loop, with calls to a system clock before and after the loop. Counting the number of bytes transferred per unit of time provides a measure of the overall bandwidth of the various APIs. The measures selected can then be compared between different operating systems, processor types, hardware memory subsystems, and so on for these basic APIs.

LMbench also measures the rate at which an operating system switches from user level into the operating system's protected mode using a very simple system call. Because events like this happen much faster than the system's timer granularity, a common technique is to run a simple primitive in a loop and measure the number of calls to the primitive per some unit of time. Relatively straightforward math then enables a calculation of the average rate per transaction. Other primitives measured by LMbench include the establishment of TCP connections, creation of pipes, creation of processes, rate at which signals are received, and so on. LMbench is fairly mature and has been careful to take into account some of the more complex side effects that can typically plague benchmarking efforts. For instance, the test for process creation looks at the cost of process creation via `fork()`, as well as the cost of `fork()+exit()` and `fork()+exec()`. On memory tests, the documentation describing how to interpret the results points out the performance impacts of various hardware configurations—most specifically, the impact of various sizes of memory caches. LMbench also takes into account compiler differences by recommending a common compiler that should provide equivalent results for all architectures. It is possible to use different compilers on different architectures, but the performance analyst must take this into account when comparing results. Although all of the tests are fairly simple in concept, the wealth of experience included makes it much cheaper to use an off-the-shelf benchmark for simple comparisons. Also, the publicly available test results—and, in this case, the publicly available source code—allows a performance analyst to easily compare any differences in different environments. In the following results, some information provides simple measures, such as the time for a simple system call such as `read()` or `write()`. Other results show throughputs for a variety of data transfer sizes.

LMbench Sample Output
This first section summarizes the machine being tested, including the kernel version (output of `uname(1)`, memory sizes to be tested, processor speeds, and so on).

```
[lmbench2.0 results for Linux herkimer.ltc.austin.ibm.com 2.6.3

#1 SMP Wed Mar 10 19:51:47 CST 2004 i686 i686 i386 GNU/Linux]
[LMBENCH_VER: Version-2.0.4 20030113111940]
[ALL: 512 1k 2k 4k 8k 16k 32k 64k 128k 256k 512k 1m 2m 4m 8m 16m
32m 64m 128m 256m 512m]
[DISKS: ]
[DISK_DESC: ]
[ENOUGH: 5000]
[FAST: ]
[FASTMEM: NO]
[FILE: /usr/tmp/XXX]
```

```
[FSDIR: /usr/tmp]
[HALF: 512 1k 2k 4k 8k 16k 32k 64k 128k 256k 512k 1m 2m 4m 8m 16m
32m 64m 128m 256m]
[INFO: INFO.herkimer.ltc.austin.ibm.com]
[LOOP_O: 0.00000234]
[MB: 512]
[MHZ: 495 MHz, 2.02 nanosec clock]

[...]

[OS: i686-pc-linux-gnu]
[TIMING_O: 0]
[LMBENCH VERSION: lmbench-2alpha13]
[USER: ]
[HOSTNAME: herkimer.ltc.austin.ibm.com]
[NODENAME: herkimer.ltc.austin.ibm.com]
[SYSNAME: Linux]
[PROCESSOR: i686]
[MACHINE: i686]
[RELEASE: 2.6.3]
[VERSION: #1 SMP Wed Mar 10 19:51:47 CST 2004]

[...]
```

This section provides the output of several system calls run for a short period of time in a loop. It also calculates the average time for the system call based on the amount of time run divided by the number of system calls successfully executed.

```
Simple syscall: 0.4189 microseconds
Simple read: 0.7907 microseconds
Simple write: 0.6517 microseconds
Simple stat: 47.4274 microseconds
Simple fstat: 1.5631 microseconds
Simple open/close: 54.3922 microseconds
Select on 10 fd's: 6.7666 microseconds
Select on 100 fd's: 34.5312 microseconds
Select on 250 fd's: 82.4412 microseconds
Select on 500 fd's: 159.6176 microseconds
Select on 10 tcp fd's: 8.2204 microseconds
Select on 100 tcp fd's: 52.6321 microseconds
Select on 250 tcp fd's: 127.5116 microseconds
Select on 500 tcp fd's: 248.5455 microseconds
Signal handler installation: 1.742 microseconds
Signal handler overhead: 9.899 microseconds
Protection fault: 1.310 microseconds
Pipe latency: 28.2951 microseconds
AF_UNIX sock stream latency: 97.5933 microseconds
Process fork+exit: 806.4286 microseconds
```

```
Process fork+execve: 2265.0000 microseconds
Process fork+/bin/sh -c: 10137.0000 microseconds
File /usr/tmp/XXX write bandwidth: 5923 KB/sec
n=2048, usecs=12993
Pagefaults on /usr/tmp/XXX: 6 usecs
```

This section provides the size of an mmap region and the number of microseconds to complete a mapping of that size.

```
"mappings
0.524288 30
1.048576 43
2.097152 71
4.194304 121
8.388608 219
16.777216 412
33.554432 848
67.108864 1691
134.217728 3326
268.435456 6750
536.870912 14383
```

This section shows how long in microseconds it takes to complete a read from a file system.

```
"File system latency
0k      1000    5307    10741
1k      1000    3835    7716
4k      1000    3770    7717
10k     1000    2602    6395
```

This section provides latency timings for various network connections and a summary of the bandwidth of several local networking calls.

```
UDP latency using localhost: 93.2020 microseconds
TCP latency using localhost: 177.5119 microseconds
RPC/tcp latency using localhost: 239.6613 microseconds
RPC/udp latency using localhost: 140.2291 microseconds
TCP/IP connection cost to localhost: 272.5500 microseconds
Socket bandwidth using localhost: 29.04 MB/sec
Avg xfer: 3.2KB, 41.8KB in 13.5080 millisecs, 3.09 MB/sec
AF_UNIX sock stream bandwidth: 50.00 MB/sec
Pipe bandwidth: 196.79 MB/sec
```

This section provides the rate in MBps of reads of various byte sizes, from 512 bytes to 512MB.

```
"read bandwidth
0.000512 100.16
0.001024 182.24
```

```
0.002048 313.72
0.004096 469.94
0.008192 402.96
0.016384 238.67
0.032768 245.45
0.065536 244.97
0.131072 242.77
0.262144 228.47
0.524288 209.52
1.05 197.06
2.10 198.86
4.19 196.74
8.39 198.87
16.78 197.20
33.55 199.74
67.11 193.44
134.22 199.26
268.44 196.50
536.87 199.57
```

This section provides the bandwidth of a complete open/read/close cycle in MBps (shown in the second column) for various block sizes (shown in the first column).

```
"read open2close bandwidth
0.000512 7.85
0.001024 15.73
0.002048 30.36
0.004096 57.20
0.008192 80.01
0.016384 117.05
0.032768 156.55
0.065536 191.84
0.131072 208.20
0.262144 207.66
0.524288 195.78
1.05 194.32
2.10 192.59
4.19 197.70
8.39 195.38
16.78 198.77
33.55 196.26
67.11 197.06
134.22 197.39
268.44 187.94
536.87 197.56
```

This section provides the throughput in MBps (shown in the second column) of mmap read access of various sizes (shown in the first column) ranging from 512 bytes to

512MB. A read implies that the data is mmap()'d and accessed/touched by the processor, leading to page faults by the operating system. This should provide a fair comparison to similar operations doing a read() system call from a file.

```
"Mmap read bandwidth
0.000512 1589.89
0.001024 1747.58
0.002048 1849.51
0.004096 1876.64
0.008192 1925.34
0.016384 1806.04
0.032768 945.75
0.065536 939.72
0.131072 949.63
0.262144 786.75
0.524288 389.81
1.05 285.60
2.10 280.14
4.19 277.49
8.39 280.36
16.78 277.84
33.55 280.44
67.11 277.87
134.22 280.45
268.44 277.83
536.87 280.41
```

This section provides the same measures as given in the preceding section, with the full open/mmap/close cycle, again where the data is accessed after the mmap(), and before the close().

```
"Mmap read open2close bandwidth
0.000512 6.47
0.001024 12.99
0.002048 25.54
0.004096 49.57
0.008192 88.09
0.016384 142.55
0.032768 222.20
0.065536 303.94
0.131072 382.90
0.262144 373.09
0.524288 255.05
1.05 210.47
2.10 212.69
4.19 213.20
8.39 216.84
16.78 214.64
```

```
33.55 217.02
67.11 215.04
134.22 217.51
268.44 215.38
536.87 216.09
```

This section measures the rate at which the C library's bcopy() function can copy unaligned data. Unaligned data often requires more complex copying algorithms than aligned data. For instance, aligned data may be copied a double word at a time (64 bits at a time), but unaligned data may need to be copied by the library one byte at a time. In particular, the bcopy() routine needs to ensure that it never attempts to read a byte that is not present in the calling process's address space. This often makes an unoptimized bcopy() routine extremely slow. As the size of the data to be copied (in the first column) increases, the rate of data copying of a good bcopy() implementation should directly approach that of the aligned bcopy() measurements that follow. A simplistic solution may iterate through the data one byte at a time and be substantially slower for copying large blocks of data. An incorrectly optimized implementation could manage to generate a segmentation fault via a reference to data that is not mapped into the application's address space.

```
"libc bcopy unaligned
0.000512 870.40
0.001024 1300.36
0.002048 1755.31
0.004096 2095.21
0.008192 2166.23
0.016384 376.98
0.032768 383.18
0.065536 379.35
0.131072 382.55
0.262144 252.74
0.524288 196.17
1.05 183.64
2.10 186.51
4.19 185.17
8.39 187.81
16.78 187.52
33.55 190.23
67.11 188.79
134.22 190.93
268.44 189.05
```

This version is the same as the preceding version, where the first column is the amount of data being copied (512 bytes to 512MB) and the second is the throughput in MBps.

```
"libc bcopy aligned
0.000512 870.49
0.001024 1299.05
0.002048 1755.31
0.004096 2093.22
0.008192 2048.00
0.016384 376.47
0.032768 383.11
0.065536 379.29
0.131072 382.55
0.262144 259.08
0.524288 196.61
1.05 183.96
2.10 186.65
4.19 185.68
8.39 188.25
16.78 187.65
33.55 190.75
67.11 189.32
134.22 191.57
268.44 191.24

"unrolled bcopy unaligned
0.000512 1045.57
0.001024 1033.53
0.002048 1044.55
0.004096 1033.31
0.008192 996.75
0.016384 342.01
0.032768 335.21
0.065536 332.38
0.131072 318.58
0.262144 241.38
0.524288 173.98
1.05 159.09
2.10 160.30
4.19 159.16
8.39 160.63
16.78 159.23
33.55 159.44
67.11 159.55
134.22 161.25
268.44 159.70
```

```
"unrolled partial bcopy unaligned
0.000512 5399.13
0.001024 5122.18
0.002048 5342.10
0.004096 5665.45
0.008192 3491.16
0.016384 386.58
0.032768 387.40
0.065536 387.93
0.131072 388.87
0.262144 245.68
0.524288 180.23
1.05 163.28
2.10 164.81
4.19 164.77
8.39 166.05
16.78 165.24
33.55 167.56
67.11 166.40
134.22 166.58
```

AIM7 and AIM9

AIM Technologies released two commonly used benchmarks in the mid-1980s. Caldera/SCO acquired AIM Technologies and released the AIM7 and AIM9 benchmarks under the GPL license in 1999. (See `http://www.caldera.com/developers/community/contrib/aim.html` for details.) The source can be downloaded from `ftp://ftp.sco.com/pub/opensource/` or `http://sourceforge.net/projects/aimbench`. Although both AIM7 and AIM9 are old enough to be nearly obsolete, they are interesting primarily because they are freely available under the GPL in source form and provide a useful performance perspective in understanding today's Linux systems and the workloads running on those systems.

AIM7

(`http://cvs.sourceforge.net/viewcvs.py/ltp/benchmarks/`)

The AIM7 benchmark is often referred to as the AIM Multiuser Benchmark because it focuses on systems that support multiple interactive users. Although the benchmark is somewhat dated compared to the tasks that multiple users run on a single system today, the test still stresses some of the core subsystems of the underlying operating system in a fairly generic way. For instance, the AIM7 test focuses on running a large number of tasks simultaneously, which stresses the operating system's scheduler, as well as the process creation and process exit capabilities. The test attempts to use a reasonable amount of storage that is scaled to the number of users in this synthetic workload; however, the amount of storage actually used by the benchmark is fairly low for today's storage-hungry workloads. The test minimizes the use of floating-point and complex mathematical operations, making it less useful as a benchmark for the high-performance computing needs of the scientific and technical communities. Other benchmarks focus on more commonly used matrix multiplications, problem partitioning, and computation-intensive workloads. AIM7 spends a fairly high percentage of time sorting and searching through relatively large quantities of data, although the amount of data is probably low by today's standards. Also, today's workload mix tends to offload operations like that to databases rather more standard brute-force search and sort algorithms. AIM7 also attempts to focus more on the system libraries and system calls than some other benchmarks. When used as part of a comprehensive set of benchmarking, AIM7 provides useful input into the comparative performance of various UNIX systems, most of which purport to supply similar capabilities on different implementations of the operating system and on different hardware.

AIM9
(`http://cvs.sourceforge.net/viewcvs.py/ltp/benchmarks/`)
AIM9 is referred to as the AIM Independent Resource Benchmark. It has a more component-oriented focus on benchmarking than AIM7. In many respects, it provides a view that is similar to that of LMbench in that it measures discrete capabilities such as additions per second or sorts per second. This is in contrast to AIM7, which provides a measure of more user-visible operations. AIM9 attempts to avoid measures that are impacted by the operating system's memory subsystem or scheduler; instead it focuses on the processor-bound capabilities. AIM9 measures a slightly different set of underlying operations than LMbench. In particular, AIM9 has a larger focus on integer and floating-point calculations, while also providing another view of disk performance testing, and localhost networking tests such as TCP, UDP, fifos, and pipes. The tests typically run for a short, fixed period of time and measure the number of underlying operations completed during that time. The specific tests, the amount of time for each test to run, and a number of environmental factors, such as locations of various files and which compiler to use, can be easily reconfigured.

The performance of a system is more than the sum of its parts. The complex interactions of system calls, locking, network latency, disk latency, user input, application dependencies, and many other factors combine in ways that are often difficult to predict. Component viewpoints such as those provided by LMbench and AIM9 may be important in understanding raw processor power, general operating system comparisons, and performance impacts of certain critical application operations, but it is rarely possible to extrapolate the performance of a complex workload from such a narrowly focused benchmark. However, understanding the component limitations in terms of performance and throughput helps provide useful background when trying to analyze performance problems in more complex workload scenarios.

Sample AIM9 Output

```
AIM Independent Resource Benchmark - Suite IX v1.1,

January 22, 1996
Copyright (c) 1996 - 2001 Caldera International, Inc.
All Rights Reserved

Machine's name
: Machine's configuration
: Number of seconds to run each test [2 to 1000]
: Path to disk files                                  :

Starting time:      Fri Feb 21 11:41:25 2003
Projected Run Time: 1:00:00
Projected finish:   Fri Feb 21 12:41:25 2003
```

```
---------------------------------------------------------------------------
 Test   Test         Elapsed    Iteration  Iteration   Operation
 Number Name          Time (sec) Count      Rate        Rate
                                            (loops/sec) (ops/sec)
---------------------------------------------------------------------------
 1      add_double  60.06      835         13.90276    250249.75
Thousand Double Precision Additions/second
 2      add_float   60.03      1252        20.85624    250274.86
Thousand Single Precision Additions/second
 3      add_long    60.02      2060        34.32189    2059313.56
Thousand Long Integer Additions/second
 4      add_int     60.01      2060        34.32761    2059656.72
Thousand Integer Additions/second
 5      add_short   60.00      5148        85.80000    2059200.00
Thousand Short Integer Additions/second
 6      creat-clo   60.00      16990       283.16667   283166.67
File Creations and Closes/second
 7      page_test   60.00      12495       208.25000   354025.00
System Allocations & Pages/second
 8      brk_test    60.01      4645        77.40377    1315864.02
System Memory Allocations/second
 9      jmp_test    60.00      372707      6211.78333  6211783.33
Non-local gotos/second
 10     signal_test 60.00      17050       284.16667   284166.67
Signal Traps/second
 11     exec_test   60.00      3499        58.31667    291.58
Program Loads/second
 12     fork_test   60.00      2607        43.45000    4345.00
Task Creations/second
```

```
13      link_test   60.00     97321 1622.01667      102187.05
Link/Unlink Pairs/second
14      disk_rr     60.00      1147   19.11667       97877.33
Random Disk Reads (K)/second
15      disk_rw     60.01       976   16.26396       83271.45
Random Disk Writes (K)/second
16      disk_rd     60.00      3934   65.56667      335701.33
Sequential Disk Reads (K)/second
17      disk_wrt    60.00      1843   30.71667      157269.33
Sequential Disk Writes (K)/second
18      disk_cp     60.01      1296   21.59640      110573.57
Disk Copies (K)/second
19      sync_disk_rw 60.41       14    0.23175         593.28
Sync Random Disk Writes (K)/second
20      sync_disk_wrt 60.61       32    0.52797        1351.59
Sync Sequential Disk Writes (K)/second
21      sync_disk_cp 61.57       33    0.53598        1372.10
Sync Disk Copies (K)/second
22      disk_src    60.00     52799  879.98333       65998.75
Directory Searches/second
23      div_double  60.03      1541   25.67050       77011.49
Thousand Double Precision Divides/second
24      div_float   60.00      1540   25.66667       77000.00
Thousand Single Precision Divides/second
25      div_long    60.00      1854   30.90000       27810.00
Thousand Long Integer Divides/second
26      div_int     60.00      1854   30.90000       27810.00
Thousand Integer Divides/second
27      div_short   60.00      1854   30.90000       27810.00
Thousand Short Integer Divides/second
28      fun_cal     60.00      5082   84.70000    43366400.00
Function Calls (no arguments)/second
29      fun_call    60.00     11919  198.65000   101708800.00
Function Calls (1 argument)/second
30      fun_cal2    60.00      9282  154.70000    79206400.00
Function Calls (2 arguments)/second
31      fun_cal15   60.01      2860   47.65872    24401266.46
Function Calls (15 arguments)/second
32      sieve       60.63        67    1.10506           5.53
Integer Sieves/second
33      mul_double  60.01       975   16.24729      194967.51
Thousand Double Precision Multiplies/second
34      mul_float   60.00       973   16.21667      194600.00
Thousand Single Precision Multiplies/second
35      mul_long    60.00     88643 1477.38333      354572.00
Thousand Long Integer Multiplies/second
36      mul_int     60.00     88643 1477.38333      354572.00
```

```
Thousand Integer Multiplies/second
37      mul_short    60.00      70502 1175.03333      352510.00
Thousand Short Integer Multiplies/second
38      num_rtns_1  60.00      38632  643.86667       64386.67
Numeric Functions/second
39      new_raph    60.00      93107 1551.78333      310356.67
Zeros Found/second
40      trig_rtns   60.01       2523   42.04299      420429.93
Trigonometric Functions/second
41      matrix_rtns 60.00     406791 6779.85000      677985.00
Point Transformations/second
42      array_rtns  60.04       1100   18.32112         366.42
Linear Systems Solved/second
43      string_rtns 60.00        840   14.00000        1400.00
String Manipulations/second
44      mem_rtns_1  60.01       2465   41.07649     1232294.62
Dynamic Memory Operations/second
45      mem_rtns_2  60.00     165114 2751.90000      275190.00
Block Memory Operations/second
46      sort_rtns_1 60.00       2375   39.58333         395.83
Sort Operations/second
47      misc_rtns_1 60.00      80427 1340.45000       13404.50
Auxiliary Loops/second
48      dir_rtns_1  60.00      17727  295.45000     2954500.00
Directory Operations/second
49      shell_rtns_1 60.00      4519   75.31667          75.32
Shell Scripts/second
50      shell_rtns_2 60.01      4516   75.25412          75.25
Shell Scripts/second
51      shell_rtns_3 60.00      4517   75.28333          75.28
Shell Scripts/second
52      series_1     60.00   1701469 28357.81667     2835781.67
Series Evaluations/second
53      shared_memory 60.00    203788 3396.46667      339646.67
Shared Memory Operations/second
54      tcp_test     60.00     59795  996.58333       89692.50
TCP/IP Messages/second
55      udp_test     60.00    113791 1896.51667      189651.67
UDP/IP DataGrams/second
56      fifo_test    60.00    326544 5442.40000      544240.00
FIFO Messages/second
57      stream_pipe  60.00    232668 3877.80000      387780.00
Stream Pipe Messages/second
58      dgram_pipe   60.00    228686 3811.43333      381143.33
DataGram Pipe Messages/second
59      pipe_cpy     60.00    376647 6277.45000      627745.00
Pipe Messages/second
```

```
60      ram_copy    60.00    2262411 37706.85000      943425387.00
Memory to Memory Copy/second
--------------------------------------------------------------------------------
   -----Projected Completion time:  Fri Feb 21 12:41:25 2003
Actual Completion time:      Fri Feb 21 12:41:29 2003
Difference:                  0:00:04

AIM Independent Resource Benchmark - Suite IX
   Testing over
```

Reaim

Reaim is a project that was in development by the Open Source Development Lab (OSDL) at the time this book was written. It is an effort to update AIM7 for today's workloads. Reaim's goal is to provide a mixed application workload with some repeatable, concrete measures for throughput. Its goal is to be self-contained, easy to set up, configure, and run. It also aims to provide quick results that allow operating system developers to measure the benefits of specific changes or allow application performance analysts to quickly understand the benefits of some system configuration changes or modifications of underlying operating system tuning parameters.

SPEC SDET

SPEC SDET is a retired benchmark that is still available to members of the Standard Performance Evaluation Corporation (SPEC) organization. SPEC SDET is another benchmark that measures a mixed workload, although the components of that workload mix are somewhat dated. However, it provides a fairly simple, self-contained environment to measure the throughput of a set of scripts. Each script is run for five iterations by default, with an increasing number of users. The number of times the scripts are run and the number of users are configurable. The output shows both scalability under load and absolute performance at any stress point.

SPEC SDET is the first benchmark covered in this chapter that is a controlled benchmark. Specifically, the SPEC organization has strict rules governing how the test must be run and how the results must be portrayed. In many cases, results may be subject to audit to establish validity. In some cases, there are slightly less-strict rules for research or evaluation purposes and such runs must be clearly identified as specified by the license the end user agreed to when she acquired the benchmark. In our case, the results were run on an internal machine and were not conformant. In particular, the operating system had custom modifications and the lack of controls means that these may not be repeatable and that the specific results should not be compared against any other SPEC SDET results.

Many major benchmarks come with such restrictions on how the tests can be run, how the results should be repeatable, and how the results should be auditable. These restrictions and publication guidelines are intended to protect the integrity of the benchmark, preventing anyone from generating misleading comparisons. The organizations providing the benchmarks strive to ensure that anyone attempting to compare performance or price performance numbers can do so and therefore make informed decisions about technologies, capabilities, and so on of a platform or software offering.

Because these benchmarks become a standard for comparison, the competition to publish the best numbers can be intense. And because the costs of running, tuning, and optimizing these large benchmarks can be so high, typically only large companies purchase licenses to use the benchmarks, procure the complex hardware environment required to run the benchmark, and apply the experience and resources needed to generate publishable numbers. Benchmarks also tend to drive new technologies, which improve the components measured by that benchmark. One constant concern that the major benchmark providers diligently address is the tendency of technologists to optimize specifically for the benchmark. If any component of the benchmark does not reflect actual, common usage of the components being measured, the benchmark could become less useful to real users. Therefore, the benchmarking companies constantly evaluate the results and work to improve the validity and utility of their benchmarks.

With all of that in mind, included in the following are the results from one such test that is less stringently controlled, primarily because it is retired, but also because the test is less complex and easily repeatable by an end user.

SPEC and the benchmark name SPECsdm are registered trademarks of the Standard Performance Evaluation Corporation. This benchmarking was performed for research purposes only. This benchmark run is noncompliant, and the results may not be compared with other results.

```
SDET results 1-20 users, 5 iterations:
1 users: 2553 2011 2553 2553 2307 mean: 2395 stddev: 10.01%
2 users: 4931 4022 4260 4186 4586 mean: 4397 stddev: 8.24%
3 users: 5869 5373 5934 5046 6206 mean: 5685 stddev: 8.22%
4 users: 6666 5830 6000 6233 7422 mean: 6430 stddev: 9.91%
5 users: 6642 7142 7929 7826 7317 mean: 7371 stddev: 7.13%
6 users: 7970 8089 8470 8605 8307 mean: 8288 stddev: 3.16%
7 users: 9403 8936 9264 8456 8344 mean: 8880 stddev: 5.32%
8 users: 9230 10034 9085 9350 9411 mean: 9422 stddev: 3.86%
9 users: 10031 10836 10351 10220 10657 mean: 10419 stddev: 3.13%
10 users: 11320 11764 11842 10843 11726 mean: 11499 stddev: 3.64%
11 users: 10909 12036 12492 12336 11478 mean: 11850 stddev: 5.51%
12 users: 12485 11250 12743 12067 12378 mean: 12184 stddev: 4.73%
```

```
13 users: 13371 13333 12219 11011 11878 mean: 12362 stddev: 8.13%
14 users: 12923 11325 11004 13298 13298 mean: 12369 stddev: 9.03%
15 users: 11297 10588 11739 14285 13953 mean: 12372 stddev:13.34%
16 users: 13395 13150 14117 13457 13333 mean: 13490 stddev: 2.73%
17 users: 13275 12830 14069 14036 13814 mean: 13604 stddev: 3.95%
18 users: 13584 13251 13360 13360 14117 mean: 13534 stddev: 2.57%
19 users: 13680 14279 12930 13790 13902 mean: 13716 stddev: 3.60%
20 users: 13584 13308 13740 13872 13636 mean: 13628 stddev: 1.54%
```

For reference, the metric of interest in the preceding is the number of scripts per hour executed by each of five runs of the test with the indicated number of users. The tests are run five times, and the metric of interest for each run is printed, followed by the mean and standard deviation of those values.

In this particular case, we were looking at how the Linux scheduler performed with a couple of algorithms, attempting to identify whether a new approach would have benefits for multitask workloads. With only the output of a single run here, we cannot compare the results or come to any specific conclusions; however, we can see what the output format shows us. The first two columns indicate the number of users, or the amount of stress that the benchmark was applying to the system, moving upward from simulating a single user to simulating 20 users. The next five columns show the number of tasks completed in each run, followed by the mean and standard deviation of those five runs. In particular, it is interesting to note that this test generates results that are probably less stable than might be ideal. Using the mean value as the primary comparison key and noting the standard deviation between each set of five runs indicates the runs' stability. Some standardized benchmarks provide highly stable results where variations of a single unit of the measurement metric are common on repeated runs. Other benchmarks derive more stable metrics from a mathematical analysis of the underlying raw data. Deriving metrics is best left to the experts in defining and developing benchmarks. Benchmark metrics can be as misleading as any other statistics if results are derived without appropriate context and without a solid understanding of the underlying sources of variance in the raw numbers.

In this particular benchmark, the high standard deviation may actually be a side effect of the operation of the Linux scheduler that was measured at the time, or it may be inherent in the benchmark. Without a wide variety of tests against which to correlate the results, the metrics could easily be taken out of context, and a performance analyst could draw invalid conclusions. On the other hand, such microbenchmarks can be invaluable when measuring the impact of various tuning parameters and hardware or software configurations. And results from the slightly more complex microbenchmarking workload, such as AIM7, Reaim, and SPEC SDET often have a higher correlation with real customer workloads without the added complexity and difficulty in measurement that those real workloads entail.

Disk Benchmarks

This section discusses the following disk benchmarks:

- Bonnie/Bonnie++
- IOzone
- IOmeter
- tiobench
- dbench

We have examined two classes of microbenchmarks: those that focus on the primitive, primary capabilities of the underlying processor and operating system, and those that use simplistic workload simulations that exercise some of the more commonly used operating system components such as the scheduler or IPC mechanisms. Next, we'll look at a few other classes of benchmarks that focus on other components of the system. These include benchmarks for the disk subsystem, various file systems, and the networking subsystem. These components often have a higher correlation with specific aspects of the end-user workload and therefore are quite valuable in isolating and identifying the key performance characteristics of the file systems and disk subsystems underlying the end-user workload. Many of these benchmarks are developed from or related to traces of actual workloads running on specific file systems. Others are simply designed to create a stressful environment in which throughput can be measured in best-case and worst-case scenarios.

Bonnie/Bonnie++

Bonnie is primarily a file system test useful to measure underlying file system performance and identify bottlenecks. Bonnie and Bonnie++ focus on a set of sequential read and write tests and some random read/write testing. Bonnie measures both character-at-a-time reads and writes and block-at-a-time reads and writes. The character-at-a-time tests use the operating system's `getc()` and `putc()` functions to provide some measure of the overhead of the stdio libraries, whereas the block transfers use the `read()` and `write()` system calls to provide a measure of the file system throughput and latency with very little additional overhead. The random tests run a user-specified number of threads, each of which seeks to a random location and performs a `read()`; at a random interval, the block that was read is updated and written back via `write()`.

```
$ ./Bonnie -d bonnie-tmp -m laptop
File 'bonnie-tmp/Bonnie.31541', size: 104857600
Writing with putc()...done
```

```
Rewriting...done
Writing intelligently...done
Reading with getc()...done
Reading intelligently...done
Seeker 1...Seeker 2...Seeker 3...start 'em...done...done...done...
                -------Sequential Output-------- ---Sequential Input-- --Random--
                -Per Char- --Block--- -Rewrite-- -Per Char- --Block--- --Seeks---
Machine    MB K/sec %CPU K/sec %CPU K/sec %CPU K/sec %CPU K/sec %CPU  /sec %CPU
laptop    100  5911 56.2 14987 27.5  3703  4.7  8889 70.7 12414  4.5 981.6  7.6
```

In the preceding run, the default block size was used (100MB). Bonnie did about 100 million (100MB, one character at a time) `putc()` operations at a rate of 5911KBps, utilizing 56% of the CPU. The same I/O done in blocks was about 15KBps using only 27% of the CPU. The overhead for doing a byte at a time was more than three times that of doing block I/O operations, so obviously the resulting reduced CPU utilization indicates that the library interface is fairly CPU-intensive. Application writers may use this same data to decide whether they want the advantages of using buffered I/O with an eye toward the worst case being a byte-at-a-time, or the advantages of doing direct `read()` and `write()` operations with the resulting overhead as quantified in the preceding output for a particular hardware and operating system combination. Note that the comparison may not be completely fair. The block size used by Bonnie is 16K, but the underlying block size for `getc()` and `putc()` is only 4K on the version of Linux and glibc used on the test machine. Also, the random seeks and reads using the strategy of 10% modify and write may not map directly to any particular application, although they do provide an initial basis for comparison.

Bonnie++ is a benchmark derived directly from Bonnie. It begins with the same tests that are in Bonnie but extends the very simple application with support for larger files (more than 2GB on a 32-bit machine), a number of parameters to control block sizes, the capability to set the random number generator seed, the capability to generate data for use in a spreadsheet, and so on.

```
$ ./bonnie++
Writing a byte at a time...done
Writing intelligently...done
Rewriting...done
Reading a byte at a time...done
Reading intelligently...done
start 'em...done...done...done...done...done...
Create files in sequential order...done.
Stat files in sequential order...done.
Delete files in sequential order...done.
Create files in random order...done.
Stat files in random order...done.
Delete files in random order...done.
```

```
Version 1.93c        ------Sequential Output------ --Sequential Input- --Random-
Concurrency   1      -Per Chr- --Block-- -Rewrite- -Per Chr- --Block-- --Seeks--
Machine        Size K/sec %CP K/sec %CP K/sec %CP K/sec %CP K/sec %CP  /sec %CP
laptop          1G   121  88 11920  23  4797   8   452  73 17249  13  71.9   1
Latency             529ms      3201ms      3105ms      127ms      376ms     2487ms
Version 1.93c        ------Sequential Create------ --------Random Create--------
laptop              -Create-- --Read--- -Delete-- -Create-- --Read--- -Delete--
              files /sec %CP  /sec %CP  /sec %CP  /sec %CP  /sec %CP  /sec %CP
               16    294  69 26593  90 11278  72   346  82 27319  90   889  70
Latency             1128ms      3338us      195ms      199ms      3321us     1187ms
1.93c,1.93c,laptop,1,1087268459,1G,,121,88,11920,23,4797,8,452,73,17249,13,71.9,1,16
,,,,,294,69,26593,90,11278,72,346,82,27319,90,889,70,529ms,3201ms,3105ms,127ms,376ms,
2487ms,1128ms,3338us,195ms,199ms,3321us,1187ms
```

Note that Bonnie++ includes measures of I/O latency and shows the rate of file creation and deletion with interspersed reads. This model provides some insight into the sort of operations that a mail server might perform. In fact, Bonnie++ has an option to perform an `fsync()` after each write operation, as many mail servers might do. The last line of the output describes the same results in a format that might be suitable for inclusion in a spreadsheet or for analysis by a Perl script.

IOzone

IOzone is another file system benchmark that can be used to compare a number of different workloads or operating system platforms. In addition to common tests for read and write, IOzone can test such capabilities as reading backward, reading a stride of data (for example, every third or fifth block of data), various block sizes, and random mixes of reads and writes. IOzone also can test reads and writes through stdio—for example, via `fread()`/`fwrite()`. IOzone allows a performance analyst to model different types of workloads with its rich set of configuration parameters, including simulating diverse workloads like primarily sequential decision support database workloads or transaction processing workloads, which consist of read-mostly, highly random I/O patterns. IOzone also can use asynchronous I/O and can model performance differences between primarily synchronous and asynchronous I/O-based workloads. IOzone also can model applications using threaded and nonthreaded workloads and can use `mmap()` as the underlying API for reads and writes of file operations.

IOmeter

IOmeter is another I/O and file system subsystem test that is useful for I/O testing on a single machine but can also be used on clustered systems. The test was originally written by Intel and later released into the public domain. IOmeter is available for download at `http://sourceforge.net/projects/iometer/`. IOmeter is another test that runs on multiple operating systems and can be used to compare operating systems. However, it also can be used on a single system to compare changes in kernel configuration parameters, application tuning, hardware configuration, and so on.

IOmeter provides a slightly different view of performance tuning. Its goal is not to run a task and see how quickly it completes or see how many operations it completes in a period of time. Instead, it provides a steady-state workload and allows you to monitor various aspects of the system under load. You can also vary the workload and see how the underlying system responds. In addition, you can vary the system parameters, configuration, and so on to see how that impacts the workload. In other words, it provides more tuning control points for analyzing changes in workloads than any of the other benchmarks discussed previously. A similar tool that launched before IOmeter was publicly available is pgmeter, also known as Penguinometer. pgmeter is available at `http://pgmeter.sourceforge.net/` (or `http://sourceforge.net/projects/pgmeter`).

tiobench

tiobench is a file system benchmark that is threaded and can generate tests using one or more simultaneous threads of I/O. This allows the simulation of applications that generate I/O in parallel, either independently of each other (truly random) or with some coordination (for example, with some sequential I/O).

```
$ ./tiobench.pl

gerrit@w-gerrit2:/nue/tiobench-0.3.3$ ./tiosum.pl
No size specified, using 1022 MB
Run #1: ./tiotest -t 8 -f 127 -r 500 -b 4096 -d . -TTT

Unit information
================
File size = megabytes
Blk Size  = bytes
Rate      = megabytes per second
CPU%      = percentage of CPU used during the test
Latency   = milliseconds
Lat%      = percent of requests that took longer than X seconds
CPU Eff   = Rate divided by CPU% - throughput per cpu load

File size in megabytes, Blk Size in bytes.
Read, write, and seek rates in MB/sec.
Latency in milliseconds.
Percent of requests that took longer than 2 and 10 seconds.

Sequential Reads
```

Kernel	File Size	Blk Size	Num Thr	Rate	(CPU%)	Avg Latency	Maximum Latency	Lat% >2s	Lat% >10s	CPU Eff
2.6.3	1022	4096	1	12.82	5.645%	0.303	1450.99	0.00000	0.00000	227
2.6.3	1022	4096	2	17.45	7.706%	0.446	1749.80	0.00000	0.00000	226
2.6.3	1022	4096	4	16.77	7.419%	0.901	2100.15	0.00038	0.00000	226
2.6.3	1022	4096	8	18.54	8.404%	1.585	1717.18	0.00000	0.00000	221

Random Reads

Kernel	File Size	Blk Size	Num Thr	Rate	(CPU%)	Avg Latency	Maximum Latency	Lat% >2s	Lat% >10s	CPU Eff
2.6.3	1022	4096	1	0.26	0.637%	15.081	2199.50	0.02500	0.00000	41
2.6.3	1022	4096	2	0.46	0.685%	16.754	293.99	0.00000	0.00000	66
2.6.3	1022	4096	4	0.41	0.717%	37.062	1367.18	0.00000	0.00000	57
2.6.3	1022	4096	8	0.35	0.591%	84.926	3423.89	0.40000	0.00000	59

Sequential Writes

Kernel	File Size	Blk Size	Num Thr	Rate	(CPU%)	Avg Latency	Maximum Latency	Lat% >2s	Lat% >10s	CPU Eff
2.6.3	1022	4096	1	18.68	24.68%	0.194	799.52	0.00000	0.00000	76
2.6.3	1022	4096	2	17.21	22.51%	0.411	3206.45	0.00076	0.00000	76
2.6.3	1022	4096	4	18.78	24.89%	0.684	3277.35	0.00191	0.00000	75
2.6.3	1022	4096	8	18.10	23.86%	1.357	6397.58	0.01615	0.00000	76

Random Writes

Kernel	File Size	Blk Size	Num Thr	Rate	(CPU%)	Avg Latency	Maximum Latency	Lat% >2s	Lat% >10s	CPU Eff
2.6.3	1022	4096	1	0.58	0.698%	0.236	66.66	0.00000	0.00000	83
2.6.3	1022	4096	2	0.73	0.911%	1.106	967.64	0.00000	0.00000	81
2.6.3	1022	4096	4	0.70	0.911%	2.677	1474.37	0.00000	0.00000	77
2.6.3	1022	4096	8	0.78	1.035%	6.960	3392.60	0.05000	0.00000	75

tiobench allows for a variety of patterns, as shown from the help option. A single run can be set up to do a large set of tests with multiple block sizes, multiple numbers of threads, each thread issuing a random set of interspersed I/Os, which can be configured to resemble a number of applications using a single file system.

```
$ tiobench.pl --help
Usage: ./tiobench.pl [<options>]
Available options:
        [--help] (this help text)
        [--identifier IdentString] (use IdentString
as identifier in output)
```

```
[--nofrag] (don't write fragmented files)
[--size SizeInMB]+
[--numruns NumberOfRuns]+
[--dir TestDir]+
[--block BlkSizeInBytes]+
[--random NumberRandOpsPerThread]+
[--threads NumberOfThreads]+
```
```
+ means you can specify this option multiple times to cover
multiplecases, for instance: ./tiobench.pl --block 4096
--block 8192 will first runthrough with a 4KB block size
and then again with a 8KB block size.--numruns specifies
over how many runs each test should be averaged
```

Overall, tiobench is a simple set of code with some fairly flexible configuration capabilities to simulate some multiple application workloads or to simulate very simple database random or sequential style models from a purely file-system-oriented perspective.

dbench

dbench is a workload created to model another benchmark: NetBench. NetBench is the *de facto* industry standard benchmark for measuring Windows file servers. However, as with several benchmarks discussed later in this chapter, NetBench requires access to a large number of clients and a very large server to measure performance. With many benchmarks, the complexity of the benchmark makes it better suited to benchmark teams sponsored by larger vendors to create a run, usually after a product is generally available. NetBench is also poorly suited to help developers analyze code during the development cycle because of the long cycle time for testing and the complex testing environment required.

Many Linux developers prefer to analyze the performance of various aspects of their code as that code is developed. That analysis requires benchmarks that are easy to run, benchmarks that can be easily understood, and benchmarks that require minimal hardware configurations. dbench was written by the developers of the Windows file system support for Linux and achieves those goals. Their goal was to use dbench to analyze their code for compatibility, functionality, performance, and scalability on Linux.

dbench was developed based on a set of network traces captured while running NetBench. The theory was that if you can simulate the traffic pattern on the network from accessing a network file system, you can generate effectively the same load with a program that does nothing except generate those patterns. NetBench used a more brute-force approach where each network client was an individual computer, generating file system accesses at the rate a real user might generate file system accesses. By effectively simulating the file system traffic on the local machine, the server portion of the network file system code should be stressed in much the same way.

dbench effectively eliminates the need for a network in this case, simply simulating locally the traffic that would otherwise come in over the network. This simplifies the overall analysis to a point that allows the developers to focus on a single component of the entire system—the way that the file system code responds to a relatively standardized client load. In fact, with this level of simulation, it is now possible to simulate workloads even larger than those often done in a NetBench configuration, and with only a single machine.

Running dbench is very simple—its only argument is the number of clients to run, so the following output is the result of running dbench while simulating 16 clients.

```
$ dbench 16
16 clients started
    16       637  234.00 MB/sec
    16      3070  285.37 MB/sec
    16      4086  214.91 MB/sec
    16      4909  177.61 MB/sec
    16      7051  177.85 MB/sec
    16      8999  174.34 MB/sec
    16     11030  174.34 MB/sec
    16     13069  173.72 MB/sec
    16     15765  179.60 MB/sec
    16     17505  176.47 MB/sec
    16     20106  180.02 MB/sec
    16     22086  179.87 MB/sec
    16     24246  179.19 MB/sec
    16     26469  179.88 MB/sec
    16     27781  175.42 MB/sec
    16     30133  177.20 MB/sec
    16     32413  177.82 MB/sec
    16     34923  179.28 MB/sec
    16     37410  181.32 MB/sec
    16     39026  179.35 MB/sec
    16     42022  182.70 MB/sec
    16     44060  182.13 MB/sec
    16     46126  181.81 MB/sec
    16     48693  183.46 MB/sec
    16     50478  182.01 MB/sec
    14     53321  183.62 MB/sec
    12     55804  185.15 MB/sec
     7     59312  188.96 MB/sec
     1     62463  191.78 MB/sec
     0     62477  191.49 MB/sec
Throughput 191.494 MB/sec 16 procs
```

The final line indicates the overall throughput of the underlying file system when responding to the rough equivalent of 16 NetBench client systems. The interim lines provide a running summary of the throughput. As with any benchmark, it is important to understand exactly what the workload being measured is. It is also important for the performance analyst to understand how that measurement might relate to his own workload. As an example, NetBench tends to model a workload that is very write intensive—as much as 90% writes. Most real-user situations rarely have a need to write so much data to the server or to write that percentage of data for a long period of time. However, writes tend to be more resource-intensive and harder to optimize than reads. In this case, dbench could be useful for some worst-case analysis of a workload or an environment, but it is unlikely to be directly representative of that workload.

dbench was originally written to model another benchmark. However, dbench is weak in a couple of properties that would make it a much more useful benchmark. In particular, dbench seems to have a very wide variation in the throughput results between runs, even when run repeatedly on identical hardware under what are believed to be identical conditions. This deviation in the average run results means that the test often needs to be run many times and an average and standard deviation for those results needs to be calculated. This means that running dbench from a development and stress perspective can be very useful but that using dbench as a multiplatform or multiconfiguration test requires additional runs and more stringent analysis of the results. Also, absolute results from dbench tend to be nearly meaningless because of these deviations. However, dbench remains a useful tool for generating stress, seeing how the system responds under that stress, and for providing some reasonable guidelines on the benefits of configuration changes, such as comparing different file systems on the same hardware and software stack, or changing some file system or related kernel parameters on a given configuration. As with all benchmarks, a solid understanding of their operation, strengths, and weaknesses, as well as an ability to compare the benchmark's operation to that of the end-user workload to be used on a given machine, critical.

A companion tool to dbench is tbench. Whereas dbench factored out all the networking and real client component of NetBench, tbench factors out all the disk I/O. tbench was constructed from the same NetBench traces and models the related networking traffic in a network file system. Here is the output from a 32-thread (client) run; the output is nearly identical to that of dbench but measures the effective throughput of only the networking component of a NetBench-style workload.

```
32 clients started
   32         735   402.57 MB/sec
   32        1978   395.83 MB/sec
   32        3735   399.99 MB/sec
   32        5781   390.50 MB/sec
   32        7870   382.69 MB/sec
   32       10164   382.61 MB/sec
```

```
32      12356   380.21 MB/sec
32      14491   379.11 MB/sec
32      16614   376.35 MB/sec
32      18638   372.94 MB/sec
32      20838   372.71 MB/sec
31      23087   373.25 MB/sec
31      25178   371.87 MB/sec
31      27435   373.10 MB/sec
31      29571   372.40 MB/sec
30      31702   371.65 MB/sec
29      33870   370.35 MB/sec
28      36058   371.11 MB/sec
26      38345   371.14 MB/sec
22      40935   374.55 MB/sec
20      43394   376.73 MB/sec
20      45815   377.82 MB/sec
18      48291   379.80 MB/sec
17      50970   383.07 MB/sec
15      53593   385.23 MB/sec
13      56601   389.88 MB/sec
 7      59426   393.44 MB/sec
 2      61201   390.04 MB/sec
 2      61966   381.01 MB/sec
 1      62323   370.27 MB/sec
 0      62477   364.31 MB/sec
Throughput 364.306 MB/sec 32 procs
```

By using these two tests independently, it is possible to simulate the conditions under which the untested component is assumed to be infinitely fast. This helps find bottlenecks in individual subsystems without being dependent on bottlenecks or performance constraints in other subsystems. For instance, some of the complex benchmarks discussed later in this chapter provide a single or small set of numbers to represent the overall throughput of a highly complex workload. In these complex workloads, a combination of processing speed, network capacity, disk latency, file system performance, database workload, Java performance, web server response times, and other factors combine to yield a single throughput and/or latency result. But if a single component of the workload is misconfigured or inadequate for the environment being tested, the overall number suffers, often without any direct feedback as to the cause of the deficiency. At that point, an analyst needs to look at the detailed statistics provided by the benchmark, understand what portions are most critical to the workload's throughput, and attempt to tune or otherwise correct that subsystem and rerun. This process can take days for an expert, and for the uninitiated, this process of analysis, retuning, reconfiguration, and so on can take months!

It may appear that tests like dbench, tbench, and other component tests are "the only way to go." The initial answer is: Definitely. However, even detailed analysis of the various components does not provide a comprehensive view of how those components interact. For instance, dbench can indicate that the file system component is working well, and tbench can help tune the networking component to work well. But if there are interactions between the networking component and the underlying file system code, such as locking, scheduling, or latency issues, the overall result of a comparable NetBench may be quite different. If it is different, it is most likely that the more holistic view is the one that will perform the worst. As with software design, integrated circuit design, home building, automobile manufacture, and so on, there is distinct value in doing performance analysis on the various components before integrating them into a greater whole. But they are not a replacement for doing full integration testing and performance analysis on the integrated set of those tools and components. As with automobile design, it is possible to design an engine that performs so well that it could push an automobile to 200 mph. But if the remainder of the automobile's components are not designed and tested to meet those same performance specifications, the end user of that automobile may not be happy with how the vehicle performs and handles under that user's workload.

Network Benchmarks

This section discusses the following network benchmarks:

- Netperf
- SPEC SFS

Netperf

Netperf is a fairly comprehensive set of network subsystem tests, including support for TCP, UDP, DLPI (Data Link Provider Interface), and UNIX Domain Sockets. Netperf is actually two executable programs: a client-side program, Netperf, and an accompanying server-side program, Netserver. Netserver is usually automatically executed out of a system's inetd daemon; all command specification is done via the Netperf command-line interface. Netperf communicates with Netserver over a standard TCP-based socket, using that communication channel to establish the subsequent tests. A secondary control and status connection is opened between the client and server, depending on the test options selected, and performance statistics are returned to the client over this secondary connection. During a test, there should be no traffic (other than potential keepalive packets) on the primary control channel. Therefore, if the performance analyst shuts off all other network traffic to the machine, Netperf can measure the full capability of the network performance of a pair of machines and their corresponding network fabric.

Netperf is primarily useful for measuring TCP throughput, which accounts for the majority of network traffic generated by modern applications. Netperf comes with a couple of scripts that help automatically generate some basic tests covering socket size and send buffer size: `tcp_stream_script` and `tcp_range_script`. The first one runs Netperf with some specific socket sizes (56K, 32K, 8K) and send sizes (4K, 8K, 32K). The second script uses a socket size of 32K by default and iterates over send sizes from 1K to 64K.

Here is some sample output from a run of Netperf.

```
RCV      SND    MSG   TIME    THRUPUT  CPU   CPU   Snd    RCV
                                       sebd  recv  lat    lat
131070 131070 8192 60.00   798.59   9.28 11.34 1.903 2.327
131070 131070 8192 60.00   796.62   9.12 11.48 1.876 2.360
131070 131070 8192 60.00   800.74   9.14 11.78 1.869 2.411
131070 131070 8192 60.00   796.92   9.24 11.90 1.899 2.447
131070 131070 8192 60.00   800.05   9.20 11.48 1.885 2.350
RCV = RCV socket size (bytes)
SND = send socket size (bytes)
MSG = send msg size (bytes)
TIME = elapsed time (seconds)
THRUPUT = throughput (10^6 bits/second)
CPU send = CPU utilization send local (%)
CPU recv =  CPU utilization receive remote (%)
Snd lat = Service Send local (us/KB)
RCV lat = Demand RCV remote (us/KB)
```

See `http://www.netperf.org` for the benchmark and some archived results.

SPEC SFS

SPEC (`http://www.spec.org/`) provides a benchmark for network file systems. It is primarily used today for benchmarking NFS v2 and v3 servers. It allows for benchmarking both the UDP and TCP transports. SPEC SFS also provides a breakdown of all the common network file operations used by NFS, including reading directories, reading files, writing files, checking access rights, removing files, updating access rights, and so on. At the completion of a test run, an indication of the throughput for each operation is generated. The test attempts to simulate a real-world workload with an appropriate mix of the underlying operations so that the results should be relevant to any reasonable NFS workload. A performance analyst may want to monitor the operations of her own workload and compare it to the published breakdown of operations as run by the SPEC SFS benchmark before drawing too many conclusions.

As with other SPEC-based tests, there are strict run rules, configuration requirements, data integrity requirements, and reporting requirements for test results. It is still possible to use the test for internal testing and to use it to compare the results of various configuration changes to an environment.

Application Benchmarks

This section discusses the following benchmarks:

- The Java benchmarks Volanomark, SPECjbb, and SPECjvm
- PostMark
- Database benchmarks

Java Benchmarks

Three commonly used benchmarks for comparing implementations of Java, Java settings, or Java on particular platforms are Volanomark (`http://www.volano.com/benchmarks.html`), SPECjbb, and SPECjvm. Volanomark is a benchmark designed to simulate the VolanoChat application. VolanoChat is a chat room application written entirely in Java and has certain application characteristics that are similar to many Java applications. In particular, Volanomark simulates long-running network connections with lots of threads instantiated on the local operating system. Because chat benchmarks are inherently interactive, latency and response times are very important, and the Volanomark benchmark's goal is to see how many connections to the chat room can be maintained within a specified response time. Obviously, the more connections you can maintain with a reasonable latency, the less overhead the operating system or the Java implementation consumes. Volanomark can be implemented with both the server application and all clients running on the local host. This would be useful for separating the network component from the overall equation and focusing exclusively on the Java implementation and the underlying operating system performance characteristics. However, a more realistic workload involves setting up clients on a network, driving a server. This helps measure end-to-end latency as well as overall Java performance. It also simulates a more reasonable customer deployment of Java in which Java is used as a middleware layer in a multitier client/server configuration.

Java, SPECjvm, and SPECjbb also add a new level of complexity over the benchmarks discussed thus far. Most of the preceding benchmarks may not be affected significantly by system tuning. They are more likely to be affected by hardware configuration changes, total available system memory, I/O configuration, and so on. For these benchmarks, the same operating system configuration options, hardware configuration options, and so on are often secondary to the tuning configuration parameters of the version of Java in use. Java itself has configuration parameters governing the size of the heap it uses, the number of threads, the type of threads, and so on. Each of these configuration parameters interacts with the test and the underlying operating system in ways that are often difficult to predict. As a result, benchmark publication efforts often run waves of tests, changing various configuration parameters at each level with some intelligent guesses as to the potential interactions of the configuration parameters. This technique is fairly common for finding the best results a particular benchmark can provide. However, a benchmark like this can also be used to model the impacts of various configuration changes. The benchmark in this case can provide a scientific control against which to compare various changes.

Using the benchmark as a control allows the performance analyst to try out different versions of Java, different operating systems or kernels, different configuration parameters for Java, and so on. This gives the performance analyst more insights into optimizing similar workloads.

Volanomark provides a high-level metric for indicating throughput, including messages sent, messages received, total messages, elapsed time, and average throughput in messages per second. The following is the output from a sample run.

```
$ volanomark 1024 1024 1000
Running with start heap = 1024 max heap=1024 msg_count=1000
[ JVMST080: verbosegc is enabled ]
[ JVMST082: -verbose:gc output will be written to stderr ]
  <GC[0]: Expanded System Heap by 65536 bytes
java version "1.4.1"
Java(TM) 2 Runtime Environment, Standard Edition (build 1.4.1)
Classic VM (build 1.4.1, J2RE 1.4.1 IBM build
cxia32dev-20030702 (JIT enabled: jitc))

VolanoMark(TM) Benchmark Version 2.1.2
Copyright (C) 1996-1999 Volano LLC.  All rights reserved.
Creating room number 1 ...
20 connections so far.
Creating room number 2 ...
40 connections so far.
Creating room number 3 ...
60 connections so far.
Creating room number 4 ...
80 connections so far.
Creating room number 5 ...
100 connections so far.
Creating room number 6 ...
120 connections so far.
Creating room number 7 ...
140 connections so far.
Creating room number 8 ...
```

```
160 connections so far.
Creating room number 9 ...
180 connections so far.
Creating room number 10 ...
200 connections so far.
Running the test ...
<AF[1]: Allocation Failure. need 528 bytes, 0 ms since last AF>
<AF[1]: managing allocation failure, action=1 (0/1019991016)
  (53683736/53683736)>
  <GC(4): GC cycle started Mon Nov 24 10:13:30 2003
  <GC(4): freed 1018220216 bytes, 99% free
(1071903952/1073674752), in 83 ms>
  <GC(4): mark: 68 ms, sweep: 15 ms, compact: 0 ms>
  <GC(4): refs: soft 0 (age >= 32), weak 0, final 0,
phantom 0>
<AF[1]: completed in 94 ms>
Test complete.

VolanoMark version = 2.1.2
Messages sent       = 200000
Messages received   = 3800000
Total messages      = 4000000
Elapsed time        = 79.49 seconds
Average throughput  = 50321 messages per second
```

SPECjvm is a benchmark controlled by and made available through the Standard Performance Evaluation Corporation (SPEC). SPECjvm is primarily used to measure the client-side performance of JVM, including how well it runs on the underlying operating system. SPECjvm also measures the performance of the just-in-time (JIT) compiler. The underlying operating system and hardware performance also affect the throughput measures of SPECjvm.

SPECjbb measures a more complex application environment, specifically that of an order processing application for a wholesale supplier. Like SPECjvm, SPECjbb also measures the system's underlying hardware and operating system performance. SPECjbb is loosely modeled on the TPC-C benchmark; however, it is written entirely in Java. SPECjbb models a three-tier system (database, application, user interface) with a focus on the Java-based application layer in the middle tier. The middle tier models a typical business application and is the basis for the generated metrics of interest. SPECjbb is conveniently self-contained, which means that it does not need a complex database to be installed (it implements a simple tree-based data structure in JVM for the database tier) and does not need a web server because it provides a randomized simulation of user input on the first tier.

PostMark

PostMark is another type of application test, although a bit different from the preceding Java application tests. PostMark provides a means of testing a specific usage pattern on a file system—specifically, the usage pattern that might be seen on a mail server. In particular, mail servers tend to operate on many small files. Many of the other benchmarks focus specifically on file system throughput in terms of the amount of data sent to or fetched from the file system. PostMark recognizes the pattern used by mail servers (and often news servers, and possibly some web-based e-commerce servers) in which small files are frequently created and written, appended to, and read and deleted. In fact, the access patterns of most mail servers are a subset of all possible file system operations. Therefore an I/O and disk storage subsystem that performs that set of operations well should provide a higher-performance mail server.

PostMark provides statistics at the completion of a run that indicate how many files can be modified in common patterns per second. These common patterns include the overall elapsed time, elapsed time performing actual transactions and the average transaction rate in terms of files per second, total files created and the creation rate, total number of files read and the average rate at which those files were read, and so on for file appends, deletions, and so on. The test also reports on the overall amount and rate of data read and written.

As with many of the more complex benchmarks, many of the parameters for rates of file creation, appends, and so on can be modified to better represent a particular workload. See `http://www.netapp.com/tech_library/3022.html` for more information on PostMark.

Database Benchmarks

Database benchmarks are worthy of an entire book of their own and are mentioned here only briefly. Databases are often the backbone of many enterprises, maintaining customer records, sales records, inventory, marketing patterns, video clips, images, sounds, order fulfillment information, and so on. Although there are several major patterns for databases, two of the most common are online transaction processing (OLTP) and decision support (DS) (sometimes referred to as business intelligence (BI)). These two major models have fairly different operational characteristics, especially as to how they stress the underlying hardware and operating system. OLTP tends to be used more often for recording all aspects of transactions done in a dynamic environment. For instance, an OLTP system can be viewed as a set of point of sale (POS) terminals all doing queries on current inventory, updating sales numbers, looking up prices, and so on, much like a checkout stand at a store or an e-commerce web front end to a company's inventory. These operations tend to use the database's organizational capabilities to generate queries based on selected attributes. They do the smallest number of disk I/Os to locate the specific record or set of records for which an operator is searching. Occasionally when a record is located, some data related to that record is updated, such as the number available when one is sold. In the OLTP model, most disk I/O is done in fairly small chunks (sometimes as small as 2K or 4K), and the processor is used to help run joins on tables or calculate the next offset in the table to look up. The access pattern is typically read-mostly with a small number of writes.

Decision support, on the other hand, is often run on a database generated through an OLTP mode of operation. However, in this case, the entire database is often searched for trends, summary operations, full reports on a day's activities, and so on. In the case of DS workloads, nearly the entire database is read, often in large chunks (more often 64K or 2MB at a time), and a limited amount of processing is done based on the data returned. Occasionally, summary writes are written back to the database.

These two models are sufficiently different in that distinct benchmarks help model these workloads. For the OLTP model, the gold standard for benchmarking is the TPC-C benchmark, published by the Transaction Processing Council (http://www.tpc.org/). The same organization also publishes the TPC-H benchmark, which models the decision support style workload. Both of these benchmarks have evolved over the years to attempt to represent real-life workloads. These tests are also very rigorously controlled, as is the reporting of the results. As with the SPEC tests discussed earlier, the run rules are well established and controlled, various requirements are placed on the coherence of data stored in the database, benchmark runs must be highly controlled, results must be published and auditable, and all publications must be done on hardware and software that is generally available or will soon be generally available. Because these benchmarks are often used by major companies to decide what hardware, operating system, and database to purchase, these benchmarks not only provide throughput and latency measures, but they also calculate performance relative to cost metrics.

The downside of these tests is that they can be very resource-intensive to set up and run. In some cases, the size of the database to be used can be very large, and it can take hours or days to create and load the initial database. After the database is loaded, runs can take anywhere from a few hours to many days to complete. And, in some cases, the cost of the required hardware can be prohibitive, even for large companies. As a result, most benchmark runs on the larger configurations come from large departments of large hardware or software vendor companies that have large budgets dedicated to demonstrating the value of their products in terms of raw performance or significant cost advantage over their competitors.

As an alternative to the expensive, complex, and rigorously controlled databases, the Open Source Development Lab (http://www.osdl.org/) has developed a couple of similar, but vastly simpler, tests for performance analysts to run on a smaller scale. For

OLTP workloads, the OSDL's Database Test #1 (OSDL DBT-1: `http://www.osdl.org/`
`lab_activities/kernel_testing/osdl_database_test_suite/osdl_dbt-1/`)
models an e-commerce site (similar to TPC-W). Database Test #2 (OSDL DBT-2:
`http://www.osdl.org/lab_activities/kernel_testing/osdl_database_test_su`
`ite/osdl_dbt-2/`) attempts to model the TPC-C benchmark, and Database Test #3
(OSDL DBT-3: `http://www.osdl.org/lab_activities/kernel_testing/osdl_`
`database_test_suite/osdl_dbt-3`) attempts to model the TPC-H benchmark.

All three of these tests are freely available and can be used to compare hardware and
software configuration changes, application changes, and different application or operating system stacks. Of course, because the applications and their results are not tightly
controlled like the TPC or SPEC benchmarks, keep in mind that comparing publicly
published numbers may show inconsistencies in results, especially because the results
are not typically audited or validated by anyone other than the individual or company
that publishes the results. However, as a tool for a performance analyst, these test suites
are much more accessible for day-to-day testing than the TPC or SPEC tests.

WEB SERVER BENCHMARKS

This section discusses the following web server benchmarks:

- SPECweb, SPECweb SSL, and TPC-W
- SPECjAppServer and ECPerf

SPECweb, SPECweb SSL, and TPC-W

Web serving is a very common workload today. Everyone is interested in ensuring that
their web server is fast enough to serve up whatever content they have to publish. Of
course, different people publish or make available different information or services via the
web. Three benchmarks worth highlighting are SPECweb, SPECweb SSL, and TPC-W.
Each of these benchmarks covers a somewhat different class of web servers, although
there are some overlaps. Most web serving today has a mix of static content (for example, "publish once-read often" content) and dynamic content (for example, where each
page is created on-the-fly with localized or customized content). Static content is often
items like news stories, PDF documents, results files, source archives, audio or video
files, and so on. These documents vary in size, depending on the goals of the web server,
so sometimes the static content is very small, and sometimes very large, with every possible mix in between. More often, today's coolest sites are those that allow you to log in, set
your preferences, and get content tailored to your interests. This might include customized news stories, targeted advertising, personalized shopping information, and so

on. SPECweb is a test designed to model the access to a web server and benchmark the rate at which the web server can provide static and dynamic content to the user. The rate of static to dynamic content is pre-set by the benchmark rules, although with some tinkering, those numbers can be adjusted to better model your own workload.

SPECweb SSL is built on top of the same SPECweb harness, but its goal is to measure the performance of encrypted data transfers using the standard Secure Sockets Layer (SSL) encryption methods. Because of the overhead of encryption, the computational power required for SSL transfers is higher on the server. Therefore the maximum number of connections that can be simultaneously supported with reasonable latency is typically less than that of non-SSL-based connections.

The third major benchmark in this class is TPC-W, which is a more comprehensive test in that it attempts to model an entire e-commerce site. This includes a mix of SSL and non-SSL accesses, includes the assumption of a database underlying the related web-based queries, and allows for transactions on that database via the web interface. In part, TPC-W is a database benchmark as well as a web-serving benchmark.

This increasing complexity in the benchmark is in some ways a method for determining if transactions are truly the sum of their components (for example, web serving, database access, file system access, processor speed, system call overhead, and so on) or if other factors are at work that increase latency or decrease throughput. In general, these complex workloads are not as fast as the microbenchmarks or more focused subsystem benchmarks might indicate. These complex workloads often have interactions that are hard to predict. In some cases, these complex workloads are run on a single machine (for example, database and web server on the same machine), where the two workloads may interact with each other. For instance, if the database consumes as much memory as the system has to offer, the web server may be constrained in how many pages it can serve up simultaneously. Or, if the database has high latency to fetch content for dynamically generated web pages, the web server may not be able to send complete web pages fast enough to keep a person browsing the web site interested.

This is where the use of a more complex benchmark, possibly in combination with some of the system monitoring tools we discussed earlier, can be extremely helpful in identifying bottlenecks and reconfiguring or optimizing the system to improve overall latencies. One solution sometimes used to improve performance is to isolate the applications that make up the various tiers of this workload, such as running the database on one system and the web server on another system. In this case, the two applications communicate over an internal network, and the results are served to the Internet via the web server. In these multitier configurations, where each tier is run on a distinct platform, the bottlenecks often shift to being network-centric. In that case, some of the networking benchmarks we mentioned earlier can help set some of the expectations for the rate at which the applications can share data on the internal network. In this case, the tuning may be very different from the environment where multiple tiers are run on the same platform.

SPECjAppServer and ECPerf

Continuing the trend in increasing complexity, SPECjAppServer (`http://www.spec.org`) and ECPerf (`http://java.sun.com/j2ee/ecperf/index.jsp`) add Java-based processing to the web serving and database components. This tends to model many of the e-commerce and general web-serving environments available on the Internet today. In these two benchmarks, the web client interacts with the web server. The web server requests content from the database, which is typically preprocessed by Java or J2EE applications before being handed to the web server for submission to the web client. In these environments, we now have a complex balance of a database (heavily I/O-centric, some CPU processing power, with heavy memory consumption) interacting with a Java or J2EE application (primarily CPU-intensive, sometimes higher memory requirements) and a web server (somewhat CPU-intensive, often high memory requirements, and typically network-intensive), all interacting via one or more internal networks. In fact, for security, quite often the database tier interacts with only the Java/J2EE machines on a private network, and the Java/J2EE machines interact with the web servers on another, also internal, network. The web servers then have full Internet access but serve as a level of protection for the more business-critical database server.

SPECjAppServer and ECPerf allow a performance analyst to configure and measure the throughput and latency for these configurations; they also allow two or more tiers to run on the same machine. In some cases, security concerns drive a three-tier configuration to run on three separate machines; in other cases, performance may drive multiple tiers to run on the same machine. In any case, the ability to benchmark the various configurations and test various databases, web servers, Java or J2EE implementations, various file systems, network topologies, CPU types, CPU speeds, memory configurations, operating or application tuning parameters, and so on allows the performance analyst to analyze various "what-if" scenarios and hopefully optimize a workload to get the best possible performance for the end user.

Other Application Benchmarks

Two other common application benchmarks worth mentioning are the Oracle Applications Standard Benchmark (`http://www.oracle.com/apps_benchmark/index.html`) and the SAP Standard Application Benchmark (`http://www50.sap.com/benchmark/`). These two benchmarks are available from the vendors of the respective products (Oracle, SAP) as a way to test their applications on various vendor platforms and operating systems. Many other vendors have benchmarks to help compare their applications against their competitors' as well as to help a performance analyst improve a local deployment of the vendor's applications. Although the performance analyst may use these tools directly, quite often the intent of these benchmarks is to allow vendors to publish numbers, which helps an analyst decide what hardware or software environment to purchase. However, these tools can also be used to analyze an environment for general configuration changes and tuning possibilities.

SUMMARY

This chapter started with microbenchmarks, worked through component benchmarks, looked at some relatively simple application benchmarks, and discussed complex work-load modeling benchmarks. If every performance analyst were expected to use every one of these benchmarks when setting up a workload, no one would ever have time to set up a workload. So how can you use all this knowledge without getting bogged down by all the options available?

First, it is most useful to consult some of the more rigorously maintained bench-marking sources, such as `http://www.tpc.org/` or `http://www.spec.org/`, to identify benchmarks and workloads that compare well with the workload you intend to run. By comparing the various configurations, performance metrics, costs, and applications, you can prescreen and use the benchmarking results to help influence your purchase and initial configuration options.

Next, in those cases where you choose to use some component in your environment that is not directly part of a benchmark, you can use a microbenchmark to see how that component compares to one used in a published benchmark. For instance, suppose you have evaluated web-serving results and chosen a particular configuration and web server for your environment. Further, as a performance analyst who is familiar with your proposed workload, you may realize that the new 2.5 gigabit Ethernet over fiber is the solution you will need to meet your web-serving goals. However, you are curious as to how much benefit that might give you over the published numbers for 100 megabit Ethernet. Because your configuration is otherwise very similar to a published result, you may be able to use a benchmark like NetPerf to compare throughput and latency of 100 megabit and 2.5 gigabit Ethernet. Although the raw numbers might suggest that 2.5 gigabit is 25 times faster, you expect that latency may chew up some of that bandwidth, and it may not be possible for your hardware to achieve maximum throughput. So, using a bench-mark can help you develop a relative comparison that can set an upper bound on what type of performance improvement your environment might achieve from changing the networking interconnect. Of course, this provides some guidance, but as you've seen, the more complex environment may keep you from reaching even that upper bound. So, you may choose to set up the full web-serving test with your hardware configuration with your vendor as part of your acceptance test.

This is a rather simple example, but the intention is that with some knowledge of the underlying constraints, you can use simpler benchmarks to model aspects of more complex workloads or benchmarks. With experience, you should be able to build a repertoire of benchmarks that help you analyze or project the performance of future workloads as well.

One caveat: Even with the published benchmarks, vendors use many advanced techniques that demonstrate the performance and price/performance ratio of their products. A performance analyst should carefully analyze the benchmark configuration of any publication and compare that configuration to his own. Results may not be directly comparable if there are changes in the way database schema are used or hardware is configured, or if a particular software stack is different. The performance analyst may want to develop a relationship with the vendor to help understand how the benchmark results may compare to his local configuration and situation.

## PART III

System Tuning

System Performance Principles and Strategy: A Benchmarking Methodology Case Study

By Sandra K. Johnson

INTRODUCTION

With a focus on platform-independent issues, this chapter presents a strategy and methodology for measuring, analyzing, and improving the performance and scalability of the Linux operating system. In the Linux open-source community, where changes to the code occur at a rapid pace, it is important to obtain accurate information to evaluate the performance of applications or workloads executing on Linux in a timely manner. Let's begin with an overview of the various performance evaluation methodologies used to quantify software performance, with some specifically focusing on Linux-related issues. Included is a detailed case study on quantifying and addressing Linux performance issues using the benchmarking methodology. This case study includes benchmarking analysis methodology, Symmetrical Multiprocessing (SMP) scalability, and specific benchmarks used to evaluate performance, including examples of performance results. We'll begin with the performance evaluation methodologies.

PERFORMANCE EVALUATION METHODOLOGIES

This section presents an overview of several methodologies used to evaulate software performance, particularly the Linux operating system, including tracing, workload characterization, numerical analysis, and simulation. All of these methodologies are useful in evaluating the performance of the Linux operating system. For example, much tracing and profiling occur in improving Linux performance.

Tracing

Tracing involves the instrumentation of executing applications or simulated applications to collect runtime information such as instruction and data addresses, timestamps associated with such addresses, cache misses, memory access times, register contents, and procedure or system calls. Tracing has the advantage of providing detailed runtime information that can be used to identify a performance issue. However, tracing has the disadvantage of requiring a significant amount of memory resources to store the generated trace, and the methodology for generating traces may be time-prohibitive. In addition, trace generation may occur in an obtrusive manner, changing the behavior of the executing application. Some of these disadvantages are addressed by periodically collecting trace samples. There are various methodologies for facilitating this process.

Several tools are available to help you generate traces. Typical trace tools generate log files containing timestamped records, which are post-processed to obtain such performance data as execution profiles, instruction counts, and hot spots. Linux tracing tools include `strace`, OProfile, the Linux Trace Toolkit (LTT), and others. More information on Linux tracing and associated tools is included in Chapter 5, "System Trace Tools."

Workload Characterization

Workload characterization involves the static or dynamic analysis of an application or workload to determine specific behaviors, such as the fraction of shared memory, or read or write accesses. The data to be analyzed may be traces generated from an instrumented application or workload, some hybrid of traces and numerical analysis, or some other source. This information can be used to provide hints regarding potential performance issues. For example, if the footprint of an application fits into the cache, but it exhibits long execution times, it may be the result of a large percentage of shared writes. Workload characterization can provide detailed information about an application or workload, which may be used to improve the design of applications, hardware, and software. However, the time required to generate this information may be significant, especially when detailed information is obtained. In addition, workload characterization for performance tuning is one of several factors used to isolate performance issues.

Numerical Analysis

Numerical analysis involves the creation of mathematical models for hardware or software systems. This methodology has the advantage of quickly obtaining data. Numerical models are useful for determining high-level trends about the behavior of systems that are simple to moderate in levels of complexity. However, the accuracy of numerical models is diminished as the level of complexity of the system modeled is increased. In addition, these models require workload characterization information, statistical random number input parameters, or other information to drive them.

Simulation

Simulation is a programmatic model of a system, and it varies from simple to complex. A simulator is typically driven by traces, events, or some other means. Simulators, specifically those that are detailed models of the system under study, offer the advantage of accuracy of results. However, they are time-consuming to execute, with some simulators executing for days, weeks, or months before producing results. In addition, simulators may also consume an extensive amount of resources. There are mechanisms for mitigating the impact of complex simulators, such as checkpointing interim results as the simulator executes. However, simulators are typically not the methodology used for tuning the performance of systems in a timely manner.

BENCHMARKING METHODOLOGY CASE STUDY

Benchmarks are applications used to model a specific workload or to analyze the behavior of a specific system component. With the use of tools to instrument the executing benchmark, accurate performance information is collected in a timely manner. This benchmark data is then analyzed to isolate any existing performance issues.

It is important that server benchmarks provide coverage for a diverse set of workloads, including web, print, mail serving, file serving, and database, to have the greatest performance impact. In addition, various components of the kernel (for example, scheduler and virtual memory manager) may be stressed by each benchmark. Typically, macrobenchmarks are used to evaluate the overall workload performance on the operating system. Various performance analysis techniques (described later in this chapter) are then used to isolate issues, which may target a specific kernel component. A microbenchmark that stresses this component is then used to facilitate a more detailed analysis to address the issue.

ANALYSIS METHODOLOGY

A strategy for improving Linux performance and scalability includes running several industry-accepted and component-level benchmarks, selecting the appropriate hardware and software, developing benchmark run rules, setting performance and scalability targets, and measuring, analyzing, and improving performance and scalability.

Performance is defined as raw throughput on a uniprocessor (UP) or SMP. A distinction is made between SMP scalability (CPUs) and resource scalability (for example, the number of network connections).

Hardware and Software

The architecture assumed for the majority of this discussion is IA-32 (for example, x86), from one to eight processors. Also examined are the issues associated with nonuniform memory access (NUMA) IA-32 and NUMA IA-64 architectures. The selection of hardware typically aligns with the selection of the benchmark and the associated workload. The selection of software aligns with the evaluator's middleware strategy and/or open-source middleware. The following lists several workloads that are typically targeted for Linux server performance evaluation. Each workload includes a description of sample hardware discussed in this chapter.

- *Database.* You can use a query database or an online transaction processing benchmark. The hardware is an eight-way SMP system with a large disk configuration. IBM DB2 for Linux is the database software used, and the SCSI controllers are IBM ServeRAID 4H. The database is targeted for eight-way SMP.
- *SMB file serving.* A typical benchmark is NetBench. The hardware is a four-way SMP system with as many as 48 clients driving the SMP server. The middleware is Samba (open source). SMB file serving is targeted for four-way SMP.
- *Web serving.* The benchmark is SPECweb99. The hardware is an eight-way SMP with a large memory configuration and as many as 32 clients. For the purposes of this discussion, the benchmarking was conducted for research purposes only and was noncompliant (see this chapter's "Acknowledgments" section for details). The web server is Apache, which is open-source and the most popular web server.
- *Linux kernel version.* The level of the Linux kernel.org kernel (2.4.x, 2.6.x, or 2.7.x) used is benchmark-dependent. It is discussed later in the "Benchmark" section. The Linux distribution selected is Red Hat 7.1 or 7.2 in order to simplify administration. The focus is kernel performance, not the performance of the distribution. The Red Hat kernel is replaced with one from kernel.org and the patches under evaluation.

Run Rules

During benchmark setup, run rules are developed that detail how the benchmark is installed, configured, and run, and how results are to be interpreted. The run rules serve several purposes:

- They define the metric that will be used to measure benchmark performance and scalability (for example, messages/sec).
- They ensure that the benchmark results are suitable for measuring the performance and scalability of the workload and kernel components.
- They provide a documented set of instructions that will allow others to repeat the performance tests.
- They define the set of data that is collected so that performance and scalability of the system under test (SUT) can be analyzed to determine when bottlenecks exist.

These run rules are the foundation of benchmark execution. Setting benchmark targets, which typically occurs after the run rules have been defined, is the next step in the evaluation process.

Setting Targets

Performance and scalability targets for a benchmark are associated with a specific SUT (hardware and software configuration). Setting performance and scalability targets requires the following:

- Baseline measurements to determine the performance of the benchmark on the baseline kernel version. Baseline scalability is then calculated.

- Initial performance analysis to determine a promising direction for performance gains (for example, a profile indicating the scheduler is very busy might suggest trying an $O(1)$ scheduler).

- Comparing baseline results with similar published results (for example, finding SPECweb99 publications on the same web server on a similar eight-way from spec.org). It is also desirable to compare Linux results with the results of other operating systems. Given the competitive data and baseline results, select a performance target for UP and SMP machines.

- Finally, a target may be predicated on making changes to the application. For example, if the methodology the application uses for asynchronous I/O is known to be inefficient, it may be desirable to select the performance target assuming the I/O method will be changed.

Measurement, Analysis, and Tuning

The benchmark executions are initiated according to the run rules in order to measure both performance and scalability in terms of the defined performance metric. When calculating SMP scalability for a given machine, there exists an alternative between computing this metric based on the performance of a UP kernel and computing it based on the performance of an SMP kernel, with the number of processors set to 1 (1P). The important factor here is consistency, so either option is acceptable, as long as the same alternative is used when comparing results.

Before any measurements are made, both the hardware and software configurations are tuned before performance and scalability are analyzed. Tuning is an iterative cycle of tuning and measuring. It involves measuring components of the system such as CPU utilization and memory usage, and possibly adjusting system hardware parameters, system resource parameters, and middleware parameters. Tuning is one of the first steps of performance analysis. Without tuning, scaling results may be misleading. In other words, they might not indicate kernel limitations, but rather some other issue.

The first step required to analyze the SUT's performance and scalability is to understand the benchmark and the workload tested. Initial performance analysis is made against a tuned system. Sometimes analysis uncovers additional modifications to tuning parameters.

Analyzing the SUT's performance and scalability requires a set of performance tools. The use of open-source community (OSC) tools is desirable whenever possible to facilitate posting of analysis data to the OSC in order to illustrate performance and scalability bottlenecks. It also allows those in the OSC to replicate results with the tool or to understand the results after using the tool on another application on which they can experiment. In many instances, ad hoc performance tools are developed to gain a better understanding of a specific performance bottleneck. Ad hoc performance tools are usually simple tools that instrument a specific component of the Linux kernel. It is advantageous to share such tools with the OSC. A sample listing of performance tools available includes the following:

- */proc file system*. meminfo, slabinfo, interrupts, network stats, I/O stats, and so on.
- *SGI's lockmeter*. For SMP lock analysis.
- *SGI's kernel profiler (kernprof)*. Time-based profiling, performance counter-based profiling, annotated call graph (ACG) of kernel space only.
- *IBM Trace Facility*. Single-step (mtrace) and both time-based and performance counter-based profiling for both user and system space.

Ad hoc performance tools help you further understand a specific aspect of the system. Examples are as follows:

- *sstat*. Collects scheduler statistics.
- *schedret*. Determines which kernel functions are blocking for investigation of idle time.
- *acgparse*. Post-processes kernprof ACG.
- *copy in/out instrumentation*. Determines alignment of buffers, size of copy, and CPU utilization of copy in/out algorithm.

Performance analysis data is then used to identify performance and scalability bottlenecks. You need a broad understanding of the SUT and a more specific understanding of certain Linux kernel components that are being stressed by the benchmark to understand where the performance bottlenecks exist. You must also understand the Linux kernel source code that is the cause of the bottleneck. In addition, the Linux OSC can be leveraged to help you isolate performance-related issues and developing patches for their associated resolution.

Exit Strategy

An evaluation of Linux kernel performance may require several cycles of running the benchmarks, analyzing the results to identify performance and scalability bottlenecks, addressing any bottlenecks by integrating patches into the Linux kernel, and running the benchmark again. You can obtain the patches by finding existing patches in the OSC or by developing new ones. There is a set of criteria for determining when Linux is "good enough," which terminates the process.

If the targets have been met and there are no outstanding Linux kernel issues to address for the specific benchmark that would significantly improve its performance, Linux is "good enough." In this instance, it is better to move on to address other issues. Second, if several cycles of performance analysis have occurred, and there are still outstanding bottlenecks, consider the trade-offs between the development costs of continuing the process and the benefits of any additional performance gains. If the development costs are too high relative to any potential performance improvements, discontinue the analysis and articulate the rationale appropriately.

In both cases, when reviewing all the additional outstanding Linux kernel-related issues to address, assess appropriate benchmarks that may be used to address these kernel component issues, examine any existing data on the issues, and decide to analyze the kernel component (or collection of components) based on this collective information.

BENCHMARKS

There are a variety of bottlenecks used and associated kernel components stressed by the specific collection of benchmarks in a suite. Some of these are detailed in Table 7-1. In addition, performance results and analysis are included for some of these benchmarks.

Table 7-1 Linux Kernel Performance Benchmarks

Linux Kernel Component	Database Query	VolanoMark	SPECweb99 Apache2	NetBench	Netperf	LMbench	tiobench IOzone
Scheduler		X	X	X			
Disk I/O	X						X
Block I/O	X						
Raw, Direct, and Asynch I/O	X						
File system (ext2 and journaling)			X	X		X	X
TCP/IP		X	X	X	X	X	
Ethernet driver		X	X	X	X		
Signals		X				X	
Pipes						X	
Sendfile			X	X			
pThreads		X	X		X		
Virtual Memory			X	X		X	
SMP Scalability	X	X	X	X	X		X

The benchmarks discussed are selected based on a number of criteria: *industry benchmarks*, which are reliable indicators of a complex workload, and *component-level benchmarks*, which indicate specific kernel performance problems.

Industry benchmarks are generally accepted by the industry to measure the performance and scalability of a specific workload. These benchmarks often require a complex or expensive setup, which is not available to most of the OSC. However, some of these may be available to the OSC by the Open Source Development Lab (OSDL). Examples include the following:

- *SPECweb99*. Representative of web serving performance.
- *SPECsfs*. Representative of NFS performance.
- *Database query*. Representative of database query performance.
- *NetBench*. Representative of SMB file-serving performance.

Component-level benchmarks measure the performance and scalability of specific Linux kernel components that are deemed critical to a wide spectrum of workloads. Examples include the following:

- *Netperf3*. Measures the performance of the network stack, including TCP, IP, and network device drivers.
- *VolanoMark*. Measures the performance of the scheduler, signals, TCP send/receive, and loopback.
- *Block I/O test*. Measures the performance of VFS, raw and direct I/O, block device layer, SCSI layer, and low-level SCSI/fibre device driver.

Some benchmarks are commonly used by the OSC because the OSC already accepts the importance of the benchmark. Thus, it is easier to convince the OSC of performance and scalability bottlenecks illuminated by the benchmark. In addition, generally no licensing issues prevent the publication of raw data. The OSC can run these benchmarks because they are often simple to set up and the hardware required is minimal. Examples include the following:

- *Lmbench*. Used to measure performance of the Linux APIs.
- *IOzone*. Used to measure native file system throughput.
- *dbench*. Used to measure the file system component of NetBench.
- *SMB Torture*. Used to measure SMB file-serving performance.

Many benchmark options are available for specific workloads. Some important benchmarks are not listed here. For more information on specific benchmarks, see Chapter 6, "Benchmarks as an Aid to Understanding Workload Performance."

Results

It is important to understand various benchmarks, so we have chosen three benchmarks used to quantify Linux kernel performance: database query, VolanoMark, and SPECweb99. For all three benchmarks, an eight-way machine is used, as detailed in Figures 7-1 through 7-3.

Database Query Workload

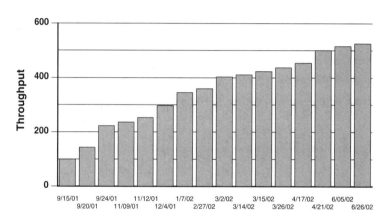

Netfinity 8500R, 8-Way 700 MHz Pentium III with 2MB L2 cache, 8GB RAM, IBM ServeRAID, Red Hat 7.1, Linux kernel 2.4.6 / 2.4.16 / 2.4.17, DB2 7.1 EEE

Figure 7-1   Database query benchmark results.

Figure 7-1 shows the database query benchmark results and describes the hardware and software configurations used. It also shows the progress made over a period of time in achieving the target. Some of the issues addressed have resulted in performance improvements. They include adding bounce buffer avoidance, ips, io_request_lock, readv, kiobuf, and O(1) scheduler kernel patches, as well as several DB2 optimizations.

The VolanoMark benchmark creates 10 chat rooms of 20 clients. Each room echoes the messages from one client to the other 19 clients in the room. This benchmark, not yet an open-source benchmark, consists of the VolanoChat server and a second program that simulates the clients in the chat room. It is used to measure the raw server performance and network scalability performance.

VolanoMark can be run in two modes: loopback and network. Loopback mode tests the raw server performance. Network mode tests the network scalability performance. VolanoMark uses two parameters to control the size and number of chat rooms.

The VolanoMark benchmark creates client connections in groups of 20 and measures how long it takes the server to take turns broadcasting all the clients' messages to the group. At the end of the loopback test, it reports a score as the average number of messages transferred per second. In network mode, the metric is the number of connections between the clients and the server. The Linux kernel components stressed with this benchmark include the scheduler, signals, and TCP/IP.

Figure 7-2 shows the VolanoMark benchmark results for loopback mode. Also included is a description of the hardware and software configurations used and our target for this benchmark. We have established close collaboration with the members of the Linux kernel development team on moving forward to achieve this target. Some of the issues we have addressed that have resulted in improvements include adding the O(1) scheduler, SMP scalable timer, tunable priority preemption, and soft affinity kernel patches. As illustrated, we have exceeded our target for this benchmark; however, we are addressing some outstanding Linux kernel components and Java-related issues that we believe will further improve the performance of this benchmark.

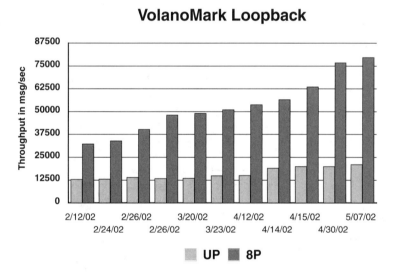

Netfinity 8500R, 8-Way 700 MHz Pentium III with 2MB L2 cache, 4GB RAM
Red Hat 7.1, Linux kernel 2.4.17 + patches + tuning

Figure 7-2   VolanoMark benchmark results; loopback mode.

The SPECweb99 benchmark work was conducted for research purposes only and was noncompliant. (See the "Acknowledgments" section later in this chapter for more information.) This benchmark presents a demanding workload to a web server. This workload requests 70% static pages and 30% simple dynamic pages. Sizes of the web pages range from 102 to 921,000 bytes. The dynamic content models GIF advertisement rotation. There is no SSL content. SPECweb99 is relevant because web serving, especially with Apache, is one of the most common uses of Linux servers. Apache is rich in functionality and is not designed for high performance. However, we chose Apache as the web server for this benchmark because it currently hosts more web sites than any other web server on the Internet. SPECweb99 is the accepted standard benchmark for web serving. SPECweb99 stresses the following kernel components: scheduler, TCP/IP, various threading models, sendfile, zero copy, and network drivers.

Figure 7-3 shows our results for SPECweb99. Also included is a description of the hardware and software configurations used and our benchmark target. We have a close collaboration with the Linux kernel development team and the IBM Apache team as we make progress on the performance of this benchmark. Some of the issues we have addressed that have resulted in the improvements shown include adding O(1) and read copy update (RCU) dcache kernel patches and adding a new dynamic API mod_specweb module to Apache. As shown in Figure 7-3, we have exceeded our target on this benchmark; however, we are addressing several outstanding Linux kernel component-related issues that we believe will significantly improve the performance of this benchmark.

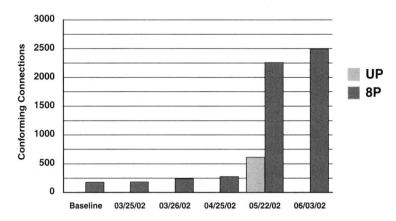

Figure 7-3   SPECweb99 benchmark results using the Apache web server.

SUMMARY

Linux has enjoyed great popularity, specifically with low-end and mid-range systems. In fact, Linux is regarded as a stable, highly reliable operating system to use for web servers for these machines. However, high-end, enterprise-level systems have access to gigabytes, petabytes, and exabytes of data. These systems require a different set of applications and solutions with high memory and bandwidth requirements, in addition to larger numbers of processors. This introduces a unique set of issues that may be orders of magnitude more complex than those present in smaller installations. For Linux to be competitive for the enterprise market, its performance and scalability must improve.

You should now have a sense of the strategy for improving Linux kernel performance, with special emphasis on eight-way SMP scalability. This includes an overview of several performance evaluation methodologies, including tracing, workload characterization, numerical analysis, and simulation. For benchmarking, the strategy includes understanding the hardware and software used, defining the run rules, and setting the benchmark targets. In addition, it includes measurement and analysis to find the performance issues, and proposed solutions to resolve them by creating improvements, through kernel patches to the Linux kernel, focusing on architecture-independent issues. Performance tools and benchmarks, selected to provide coverage for a diverse set of workloads and to address specific kernel components, are used to accomplish this task. Also presented are selected benchmark results, which quantify progress toward making Linux better for eight-way SMP scalability. This methdology is a means of substantiating that the performance of the Linux kernel can be improved by working with the OSC to address degradation issues. This will make Linux better and ready for the enterprise market.

ACKNOWLEDGMENTS

SPEC and the benchmark name SPECweb are registered trademarks of the Standard Performance Evaluation Corporation. The benchmarking was conducted for research purposes only and was noncompliant with the following deviations from the rules:

1. It was run on hardware that does not meet the SPEC availability-to-the-public criteria. The machine was an engineering sample.
2. access_log wasn't kept for full accounting. It was written, but it was deleted every 200 seconds.

For the latest SPECweb99 benchmark results, visit `http://www.spec.org`.

REFERENCES

[1] Linux Scalability Effort: `http://sourceforge.net/projects/lse`.

[2] Linux Technology Center Linux Kernel Performance: `http://www.ibm.com/developerworks/opensource/linuxperf/`.

[3] Next Generation Posix Threads: `http://www.ibm.com/pthreads`.

[4] Kernel Spinlock Metering for Linux: `http://oss.sgi.com/projects/kernprof`.

[5] Kernprof (Kernel Profiling): `http://oss.sgi.com/projects/lockmeter`.

[6] Transaction Processing Council: `http://www.tpc.org`.

[7] VolanoMark: `http://www.volano.com/benchmarks.html`.

[8] SPECweb99 benchmark: `http://www.spec.org/osg/web99`.

## CHAPTER EIGHT

Scheduler Tuning

By Chandra Seetharaman

INTRODUCTION

If computers had a single program and a single processor, there would be no need for a scheduler to implement resource management policies. The program would run until completion, and then the machine would halt. Computers today, however, seldom run a single program and a single processor. More often, the "single program" is an operating system that provides a variety of system services, implements a number of resource management policies, and generally never runs to completion.

Linux is such an operating system. Although it can be used for some very specific purposes, a more typical situation is where Linux is managing multiple tasks, with each utilizing one or more processors. Ensuring that each task gets a fair slice of time on a processor is the job of a scheduler.

Included in this chapter is an examination of the policies and issues that arise in granting a level of fairness to a task, and a discussion of symmetric multiprocessing and NUMA architectures. A discussion of the Linux 2.6 scheduler and an examination of its tunable parts are also included here.

We'll begin our discussion with the less demanding scheduling for the single processor.

SINGLE-PROCESSOR SYSTEMS

When using a single processor, scheduling is simple; all tasks use the same processor. The scheduler algorithm for a single processor centers on fairness; in other words, is every process getting a fair turn at the processor? Optimizations tend to streamline both user and kernel code by minimizing the number of context switches. Ideally, every process gets an executable timeslice, and no process is preempted. The need by most tasks to perform some I/O, and the fact that I/O is traditionally slower than a processor, mean that unless a task is CPU-bound, scheduling becomes necessary.

Tasks might use only a fraction of their timeslice before voluntarily giving up the processor to wait for some other event, such as a signal or an I/O completion. In the context of fairness, the implementation needs to consider whether it makes sense to schedule a task that frequently gives up the processor, as opposed to a process that executes until preempted.

The versatility of the Linux scheduler moves seamlessly from single-processor systems to more complex scheduling. With a load-balancing policy, the scheduler can ensure scheduling on the multiprocessors also.

SYMMETRIC MULTIPROCESSING (SMP)

Symmetric multiprocessing (SMP) enables multiple processors to execute the same kernel-level code concurrently, sharing a single copy of the operating system. Therefore, SMP introduces more complex scheduling. The same single processor scheduling algorithms can be used on SMP machines; however, they do not yield optimal results. For example, all tasks may be scheduled to execute on one processor, leaving other processors idle. This situation can be avoided by implementing a load-balancing policy, which ensures that tasks are spread out as evenly as possible among all the processors.

The concepts of *fair* and *best* make the situation more complicated. What is fair and best depends on the cost involved in moving a task from processor to processor. Processors today have some amount of onboard cache that can reduce the need for frequent memory accesses. Optimizations must try to enforce fairness without sacrificing the capability to utilize a warm cache (that is, a cache already filled with a working set of the current task). If the cache needs to be flushed for each task as it takes its timeslice, system time will be dominated by measurable delays due to memory fetches.

NON-UNIFORM MEMORY ACCESS (NUMA)

In Non-Uniform Memory Access (NUMA) architecture, a machine consists of multiple nodes, with each node consisting of one or more processors and local memory. A single system image of the operating system is typically used by NUMA machines, and all of the memory is accessible to tasks executing on any of the processors on any node. Local memory access times are faster than remote memory access times, and it is desirable for tasks executing on a processor on a given node to have its associated working set on the local memory of that node.

Migration of a task to another processor on the same node might be necessary, but migration of a task to another node should be avoided because of the cost of remote fetches. Some architectures have an onboard cache for remote memory to try to mitigate the cost of remote fetches, which further complicates task placement methodology.

A variant on this situation occurs when memory that is closest or fastest to a processor is dependent on some other condition—for example, electrically by location on the bus, or logically by other components' management of the memory. In all cases, however, the same issue remains: some memory is "better" than others.

Successful scheduling on a NUMA machine is more complex than on a single processor. A policy that frequently migrates tasks from their original processor might still perform well if it can keep those tasks close to the memory they use. Processor speeds have increased over the years, and it can be well worth the extra instruction cycles to determine how best to keep memory references local rather than remote.

As if successful scheduling on a NUMA machine weren't challenging enough, Linux has also provided answers to scheduling on machines with multithread support. This gets even more interesting as you work around the virtual CPU.

SYMMETRIC MULTITHREADING (SMT)

Recently, processors started providing multithread support in a single physical CPU. In Symmetric Multithreading (SMT), a single physical CPU appears as two or more virtual CPUs. These virtual CPUs share the core resources of the physical processor, which include the execution engine and processor cache.

Symmetric multithreading allows two or more tasks to be executed simultaneously in the processor, which results in increased performance of the processor. But it has scheduler implications.

Consider a case where a system has two physical CPUs that support four virtual CPUs. The system's performance will be better if the scheduler is aware of the fact that the four virtual CPUs are not the same. If there are only two tasks in the system, the scheduler should place both of them in two different physical CPUs. Also, when a task that was running on a virtual CPU is ready to run, it should be placed in the same physical CPU to take advantage of the cache warmth.

Whether you run a physical CPU or a virtual one, Linux strives to provide ultimate performance. With the version 2.6 release of the multiqueue scheduler, Linux is working hard to give you what you need!

THE 2.6 LINUX SCHEDULER

Before release 2.4 of the Linux kernel, SMP machines were not seriously considered in terms of performance. As the 2.2 version of the kernel matured, however, it became increasingly evident that good SMP performance was important to Linux users. Although it remains desirable for performance reasons to keep as much of the SMP code as possible under a configuration option, it has also become more important to commercial Linux users that SMP code utilize the processors efficiently and treat applications equitably.

To achieve its scheduling objectives, Linux assigns a static priority to each task that can be modified by the user through the `nice()` system call. Linux has a range of priority classes, varying from 0 to MAX_PRIO, where MAX_PRIO=140. The first MAX_RT_PRIO priorities, where MAX_RT_PRIO=100, are set aside for real-time tasks. The remaining 40 priority classes, [100..140], are set aside for time sharing (that is, normal) jobs, representing the [−20..19] `nice` value of UNIX processes. Lower `nice` values correspond to lower static priority and higher importance. Real-time tasks always have a higher priority than normal tasks.

Each task maintains an effective priority, which is determined by the interactivity of the task. The more interactive a task, the more important it becomes. Temporary effective priority bonuses or penalties are given based on the recent sleep average of a given task. The sleep average is a number in the range of [0..MAX_SLEEP_AVG(=10 seconds)], and it accounts for the number of ticks a task spent voluntarily not using its timeslice and waiting for an I/O completion. A bonus is given for higher sleep averages, and a penalty is given for lower sleep averages.

A task is considered interactive when its effective priority exceeds its static priority by a certain level (which can only be due to its accumulating sleep average). High-priority tasks reach interactivity with a much smaller sleep average than lower-priority tasks.

A timeslice is the maximum time a task can run before yielding to another task. It is simply a linear function of the static priority of normal tasks projected into the range of [MIN_TIMESLICE(=10 milliseconds)..MAX_TIMESLICE(=200 milliseconds)]. The higher the static priority of a task, the longer the timeslice. The timeslice in the kernel is defined as multiples of a system tick. A tick is defined by the fixed delta (1 HZ) of two consecutive timer interrupts. In Linux 2.6, HZ=1000—the timer interrupt routine is called once every millisecond—at which time the currently executing task is charged a tick.

The scheduler needs to decide which task to run next and for how long. Effective priority determines which task to run next; static priority determines for how long.

The Linux scheduler in 2.6 is a multiqueue scheduler that assigns a run queue to each CPU. Each run queue performs per-CPU scheduling. It consists of two arrays of task lists: the active array and the expired array. Each array index represents a list of runnable tasks at their respective effective priority level. A task with the highest effective priority from the active array is chosen to run first. After the allotted timeslice completes, the task is moved from the active list to the expired list after replenishing the timeslice and effective priority to guarantee that all tasks get a chance to execute. When the active array is empty, expired and active arrays are swapped. This makes the scheduler O(1) because it does not have to traverse a potentially large list of tasks, as was needed in the 2.4 scheduler.

Interactive tasks relinquish the CPU before their timeslices expire because they have to wait for I/O completion. When the timeslice of an interactive task expires, the task is put back in the active array instead of in the expired array in order to give it an advantage over the processor hogs. As a result, a situation can arise when the active array continues to have tasks, which in turn may cause the starvation of tasks in the expired array. To avoid this situation, if the first expired task is waiting for more than STARVA-TION_LIMIT(=10seconds) times the number of tasks in the run queue, the interactive task is simply put in the expired array.

The 2.6 scheduler contains support for different CPU topologies like SMT and NUMA through sched domains. The scheduling policy is set in the sched domain data structure by the architecture depending on the system topology. Those scheduling policies are used while scheduling tasks to the CPUs.

Sched domains are created hierarchically as it appears on the system topology.

Although the 2.6 scheduler can work on different CPU configurations, some of the configurations depend on load balancing to assist. Load balancing keeps the system load, especially for multiprocessers, balanced.

LOAD BALANCING

The scheduler attempts to keep the system load as balanced as possible. It does this by running rebalance code when tasks change state or make specific system calls, called *event balancing*, and at specified intervals measure in jiffies, called *active balancing*. Tasks must do something explicit for event balancing to take place, whereas active balancing occurs without any action from any task.

Event balance policy is defined in each sched domain data structure, again depending on the system topology.

When an event balancing occurs, the scheduler searches up the domain hierarchy and performs the load balancing at the highest domain that suggests a load balancing.

Active balancing happens at each tick. The scheduler starts at the lowest domain and works its way up, checking the last time the domain is balanced and the interval the domain specified for rebalancing. This is to determine if the domain should be balanced. The scheduler does balancing, if warranted.

When a run queue of a processor becomes empty, it proactively pulls tasks from other run queues to balance the load.

In addition to keeping the system load balanced, the scheduler also has tunable parameters that can improve response time for those critical tasks.

TUNABLE PARTS OF THE SCHEDULER

The scheduler has a number of tunable parameters that can be used to do different things, such as improve the response of interactive tasks, increase the timeslice for high-priority tasks, and penalize a parent for creating processor hogs.

The remaining sections of this chapter list and describe the tunable parameters of the scheduler and the likely effects when the value of the tunable is increased or decreased.

*CHILD_PENALTY

Description: The value of this parameter is the percentage of the parent's sleep average that a child inherits.

Effect: Increasing the value of this parameter increases the child's effective priority, making it more interactive and giving it higher importance during scheduling. Decreasing the value has the opposite effect. This parameter has no effect on the parent's sleep average.

*CREDIT_LIMIT

Description: This is the number of times a task earns sleep_avg over MAX_SLEEP_AVG and is then considered highly interactive. After that point, the task is penalized less for its sleep_avg, thereby providing much less response time. On the other hand, CPU hogs earn negative credit and are given a limited increase in their priority levels for their sleep.

Effect: Reducing the value of this parameter helps highly interactive tasks by raising them to the highly interactive level, and decreasing has the opposite effect.

The 2.6 version of the kernel has multiple tunable parameters that can be altered to improve the performance of the Linux system as needed by the user.

*EXIT_WEIGHT

Description: This parameter determines whether the parent is penalized for creating children that are processor hogs relative to the parent. The sleep average of the parent is modified depending on the sleep average of the child and the value of this parameter.

Effect: Setting this value to zero causes the parent to inherit the child's sleep average when the child exits. Increasing the value of this parameter reduces the effect of the child's sleep average on the parent.

*INTERACTIVE_DELTA

Description: The value of this parameter determines the offset that is added in determining whether or not a task is considered interactive. A task needs to be considered interactive for it to be put back in the active array when its timeslice has expired.

Effect: If this parameter is increased, a task needs to accumulate a larger sleep average to be considered interactive. Decreasing the value of this parameter has the opposite effect.

*MAX_SLEEP_AVG

Description: The value of this parameter is the maximum sleep average a task can accumulate for the purposes of calculating the scheduling bonus. A task with this sleep average gets the maximum bonus as indicated by PRIO_BONUS_RATIO.

Effect: If the value of this parameter is increased, tasks need to accumulate a larger sleep average to get the same priority bonus. Decreasing the value has the opposite effect.

*MAX_TIMESLICE

Description: The value of this parameter is the timeslice that is allocated to the task with the highest static priority (MAX_RT_PRIO).

Effect: Increasing the value of this parameter gives the highest-priority task more time for execution before it is rescheduled. Decreasing the value of this parameter has the opposite effect.

*MIN_TIMESLICE

Description: The value of this parameter is the timeslice that is allocated to the task with the lowest static priority (MAX_PRIO-1).

Effect: Increasing the value of this parameter gives the lowest-priority task more time for execution before it is rescheduled. Decreasing the value of this parameter has the opposite effect.

*PARENT_PENALTY

Description: This is the percentage of the sleep average that the parent is permitted to keep.

Effect: Decreasing this parameter penalizes the parent for creating more children by reducing its effective priority. This parameter has no effect on the child's sleep average.

*PRIO_BONUS_RATIO

Description: The value of this parameter specifies the percentage of the priority range used to provide a temporary bonus to interactive tasks.

Effect: Increasing the value of this parameter gives interactive tasks more bonuses and processor hogs more penalties. Decreasing the value has the opposite effect. For example, for a PRIO_BONUS_RATIO of 25%[−12.5..12.5%], the priority range would be [−5..4]. Consider a task with 'nice=0'(static priority 120). If the sleep average is 0 for this task, a penalty of 5 is imposed, resulting in an effective priority of 125. On the other hand, if the sleep average of this task is MAX_SLEEP_AVG(=10 seconds), a bonus of 5 is granted, leading to an effective priority of 115. In no case can the effective priority go lower than −20 or exceed 19, even with this temporary bonus applied.

*STARVATION_LIMIT

Description: This is the multiplication factor used to decide whether an interactive task is placed in an active or expired array, to avoid starvation of the tasks in the expired array. If the first expired task is waiting for more than STARVATION_LIMIT(=10seconds) times the number of tasks in the run queue, the interactive task is placed in the expired array.

Effect: Increasing the value of this parameter helps interactive tasks by keeping them in the active array at the expense of starving noninteractive tasks, even if the static priorities of the noninteractive tasks are high. Decreasing the value moves the interactive tasks to the expired array faster and might affect their response.

SUMMARY

Overall, the Linux kernel is designed to give you the best possible performance in which to complete tasks. Because of the complexity of computers today, Linux is always working to improve the technology to ensure tasks reach completion. The 2.6 scheduler is part of that technology. The Linux scheduler can be as simple as scheduling on a single processor, or as involved as ensuring the task needs on a NUMA machine.

REFERENCES

[1] Web resource: http://www.finux.org/Reprints/Reprint-Bligh-OLS2004.pdf

## CHAPTER NINE

The Linux Virtual Memory—Performance Implications

By Dominique Heger

INTRODUCTION

The virtual memory subsystem can be considered the core of any UNIX system. This chapter discusses the implementation of the virtual memory system and the effects and impacts on almost every other subsystem in the operating system. The chapter first elaborates on some of the basic memory management issues; secondly, it outlines a more detailed analysis of how the Linux operating system incorporates virtual memory management tasks. The virtual memory subsystem enables a process (also labeled a task or default thread) to view linear ranges of bytes in the address space. This is allowed regardless of the physical layout or the fragmentation encountered in physical memory. The thread is allowed to execute in a virtual environment that appears as the entire address space of a CPU. This (supporting) execution framework results in providing a process with a large programming model. In such a scenario, a virtual view of memory storage referenced as the address space is presented to an application while the virtual memory subsystem transparently manages the virtual storage infrastructure, therefore incorporating the physical memory subsystem as well as secondary storage (see Figure 9-1).

The kernel image section is also known as the identity mapped segment, whereas the kernel module section is often referred to as the page table mapped segment. See the section "Kernel Address Space" for a detailed discussion. The high reference for the address space (0xFFFF ..) is platform-dependent. On a 32-bit system, the per-process virtual address space equals 4GB, whereas on a 64-bit system, the theoretical per-process virtual address space of 2^{64} is normally not fully utilized. Some systems (the actual processor per se) allow only a per-process virtual address space of 2^{44}.

To help you better understand the concept of memory and address space, let's begin by discussing the subsystems and challenges.

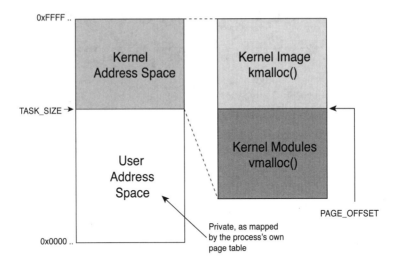

Figure 9-1   Address space structure (generic view).

MEMORY AND ADDRESS SPACE

Because the physical memory subsystem has a lower latency than the disk subsystem, one of the challenges faced by the virtual memory subsystem is to keep the most frequently referenced portions of memory in the faster primary storage. In the event of a physical memory shortage, the virtual memory subsystem is required to surrender some portion of physical memory. This is done by transferring infrequently used memory pages out to the backing store. Therefore, the virtual memory subsystem provides resource virtualization in the sense that a process does not have to manage the details of physical memory allocation. The process also doesn't have to manage information and fault isolation because each process executes in its own address space. In most circumstances, hardware facilities in the memory management unit perform the memory protection functionality by preventing a process from accessing memory outside its legal address space. The exception to this is memory regions that are explicitly shared among processes.

Address Space

A process's virtual address space is defined as the range of memory addresses that are presented to the process as its environment. At any time in a process's life cycle, some addresses are mapped to physical addresses and some are not. The kernel creates the basic skeleton of a process's virtual address space when the `fork()` system call is initiated. The virtual address layout within a process is established by the dynamic linker and may vary from hardware platform to hardware platform. In general, the virtual address space is composed of equal-sized components that are referenced as virtual pages. In an IA-32 environment, the page size is 4KB; in an IA-64 setup the page sizes can be configured as 4, 8, 16, and 64KB. The virtual address space of any Linux process is further divided into two main regions: the user space and the kernel space. The user space resides in the lower portion of the address space, starting at address zero and extending to a platform-specific TASK_SIZE limit as specified in processor.h (see Figure 9-1). The remainder of the address space is reserved for the kernel. The user portion of the address space is marked private, specifying that it is mapped by the process's own page table. On the other hand, the kernel space is shared among all the processes. Depending on the hardware infrastructure, the kernel address space is either mapped into the upper portion of each address space of a process or occupies the top portion of the virtual address space of the CPU. During execution at the user level, only the user address space is accessible, because an attempt to operate on a kernel virtual address would result in a protection violation fault. While executing in kernel mode, both user and kernel address space are accessible.

User Address Space

Each address space is represented in the Linux kernel through an object known as the mm structure. Because multiple tasks may share the same address space, the mm structure is a *reference counted* object that exists as long as the reference count is greater than zero. Each task structure incorporates the mm pointer to the mm structure that defines the address space of the task (process).

Figure 9-2 represents the scenario where a process attempts to read a word at address z. The actual read operation is depicted by number 1. Because the page table is assumed to be empty, the read operation causes a page fault. In response to the page fault, the Linux kernel searches the VM area list of this particular process to locate the VM area that holds the faulting address. After determining which page must be accessed for this particular request, Linux initiates a disk file read, as illustrated by number 2. As the I/O subsystem provides the file, the operating system copies the data into an available page frame, as indicated by number 3. The last step required to finalize the read page fault consists of updating the page table to reflect the mapping of the virtual-to-physical page frame that contains the data. At this point, the system can reinitiate the read request. It will complete successfully this time, because the required data is now available.

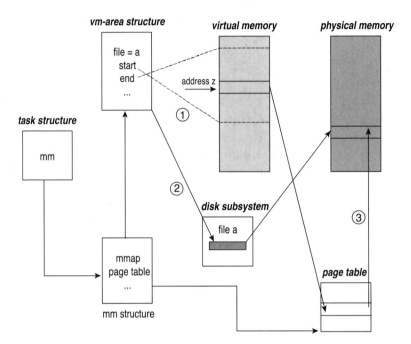

Figure 9-2   VM area structures.

Tasks that access only the kernel address space, such as the kswapd or the pdflush thread, utilize an anonymous address space; therefore, the mm pointer references NULL in these cases. The mm structure is considered the entry point into the core of the virtual memory subsystem, because it contains pointers to the two main data structures that establish the virtual memory environment. The first structure is the page table; the second structure is known as the virtual memory area. From the kernel's perspective, the presence of a system-wide page table is sufficient to implement virtual memory. Some of the more traditional large page tables, including the clustered page table approach, are not efficient when representing large address spaces.

The VM Area Structures

To circumvent the issue of large page tables, Linux does not represent address spaces with page tables per se, but utilizes a set of VM area structure lists instead. The idea behind this approach is to partition an address space into contiguous page ranges that can be handled the same way, where each range can be represented through a single VM area structure. In such a case, where a process accesses a page in which no translation exists in the page table, the VM area responsible for this particular page holds all the information necessary to establish and install the page. As depicted in Figure 9-2, the VM area list lets the Linux kernel create the actual page table entry for any given address that is mapped in the address space of a particular process. The consequence of this scenario is that the per-process page table can be considered a cache subsystem. In other words, if a translation is available, the kernel simply use it; if the translation is missing, the kernel can create it based on the corresponding VM area. Treating the page table as a cache provides significant flexibility because the translations for clean pages can be removed at will. The translations for dirty pages can be removed only if pages are backed up by a file. Prior to removal, these pages have to be cleaned by writing the page content back to the file. This cache-like utilization behavior of page tables in Linux provides the foundation for a rather efficient copy-on-write implementation.

An example of utilizing a VM area-based approach is that if a process maps a significant number of different files into its address space, the process (more specifically, the Linux kernel) may have to maintain a VM area list that consists of hundreds of entries. This results in the system slowing down as the VM area list grows, making it necessary to traverse the list on every page fault. To circumvent the performance implication of traversing the list, the Linux operating system tracks the number of VM areas on the list. In a situation where the size of the list reaches a certain threshold (normally 32 entries), the system creates a secondary data structure that organizes the VM areas in a self-balancing binary search tree. The implication of utilizing a binary tree-based search algorithm is that given a virtual address, the matching VM area structure can be located in a number of steps. These steps reveal a logarithmic relationship to the number of VM areas in the address space. To expedite the scenario where the system has to visit all the VM area structures, the Linux kernel maintains (after reaching the threshold) the linear and binary tree structures.

Kernel Address Space

As illustrated in Figure 9-1, the overall kernel address space can be decomposed into a kernel image section and a kernel module section. (The kernel image is also known as the identity mapped segment, and the kernel module is also referred to as the page table-mapped segment.)

Kernel Module Section

The kernel module section is mapped by the kernel private page table and is primarily utilized to implement the kernel's `vmalloc()` area. This allows the system to allocate large contiguous virtual memory regions. As an example, the memory necessary to load a particular kernel module is allocated in this section of address space. The address range associated with `vmalloc()` is governed by the two platform-specific parameters VMALLOC_START and VMALLOC_ END. The `vmalloc()` section does not necessarily occupy the entire page table mapped segment, therefore leaving open the possibility to utilize portions of the segment for platform-specific purposes and functions.

Kernel Image Section

The kernel image section is unique in the sense that there is a direct correlation or mapping between a virtual address in this segment and the physical address it translates into. The mapping is platform-specific, but the one-to-one identity relationship provides the segment with its name. This segment could be implemented via a page-table-based approach, but more efficient platform-dependent techniques can be utilized. In other words, the system can rely on a simple mapping formula similar to (pfn = (addr – PAGE_OFFSET) / PAGE_SIZE). This formula can be used to minimize the overhead of utilizing a full page table-based implementation. Despite this simple methodology, some Linux systems use a table called the *page frame map* to keep track of the status of the physical page frames in the system. For each page frame, this table contains one page frame descriptor (pfd) that contains various resource-related system maintenance data. The information stores counts or the number of address spaces that are utilizing the page frame, various flags that indicate whether the frame can be paged out to disk, or whether the page is marked as dirty.

In Linux, there is no direct correlation between the actual size of the physical address space and the size of the virtual address space. However, both are limited in size. To better manage your address space, Linux has developed high-memory support.

HIGH-MEMORY SUPPORT

On contemporary systems, the size of the virtual address space normally exceeds the size of the physical address space. However, the size of the physical address space increases roughly in line with Moore's Law, which states that every 18 months, the chip capacity doubles in size. In addition, the size of the virtual address space is platform-dependent and cannot easily be changed. This scenario represents a unique challenge to the Linux system as the size of physical memory approaches the size of the virtual address space; the identity mapped segment may no longer be large enough to map the entire physical address space. As an example, the IA-32 architecture defines an extension that supports a 36-bit physical address space, despite the fact that the virtual address space is limited to 32 bits. The problem is that the total physical address space cannot be directly described by the virtual address space.

The *highmem* Interface

Other operating systems, such as Solaris, face a similar challenge when running on certain platforms. The Linux system addresses this issue via the highmem interface. In Linux, high memory is defined as physical memory that cannot be addressed through the identity mapped segment. The highmem interface provides indirect access to this memory by dynamically mapping high-memory pages into a small portion of the kernel address space that is reserved for this purpose. This portion of the kernel address space is referred to as the kmap() segment. The kmap() interface maps the page frame specified by the argument page into the kmap segment. The argument has to be a pointer to the page frame descriptor of the page to be mapped. The routine returns the virtual address to which the page has been mapped. In the case where the kmap segment is saturated, the routine blocks until space becomes available. As a result, high memory cannot be utilized for code that cannot block execution for an indefinite amount of time, such as interrupt handlers. In summary, supporting high memory on a system results in extra overhead that should be avoided whenever possible. High-memory support is an optional component of the Linux kernel. For example, it is disabled on Linux IA-64 systems.

To use memory more efficiently, Linux provides paging and swapping. The following section discusses another way to protect resources when it comes to memory.

PAGING AND SWAPPING

Each user process in Linux operates on a single, contiguous virtual address space. This virtual address consists of several different types of memory objects, such as the program text (read only) and program data (copy-on-write). When a program is loaded into a process's virtual address space, the area is initially memory mapped and backed by the program binary. This allows the virtual memory system to free and reuse these text pages rather easily. As an example, when a data page is modified, the virtual memory system has to create a private copy of the page and assign it to the process that initiated the update. Private data pages are initially referred to as copy-on-write or zero-fill-on-demand pages. The pages have to be treated differently when a page-out situation arises. Most application programs allocate more virtual memory than they ever use at any given time. For example, the text segment of a program often includes large amounts of error-handling code that is seldom or never executed. To avoid wasting memory on virtual pages that are never accessed, Linux (as well as most other UNIX operating systems) utilizes a method called *demand paging*. When you adopt this method, the virtual address space starts out empty. In other words, all virtual pages are marked in the page table as *not present*. When accessing a virtual page that is not present, the CPU generates a *page fault*. This fault is intercepted by the Linux kernel and triggers the page fault handler. As a result, the kernel can allocate a new page frame, determine the content of the accessed page, load the page, and finally update the page table to mark the page as *present*. At that point, execution returns to the process that caused the page fault. Because the required page is now present and therefore available, the instruction can now execute without causing a page fault.

A physical resource such as memory can experience a resource shortage as multiple threads from different applications compete for the scarce resource. In such a scenario, the Linux system has to choose a page frame that backs a virtual page that has not been accessed recently and has to write the page to a special area on the disk called the *swap space*. Now the system is capable of reusing the page frame to back the new virtual page that is being requested. The exact place where the old page is written depends on the kind of swap space used in the infrastructure. Linux supports multiple swap space areas, where each area can consist of either an entire disk partition or a specially formatted file in an existing file system. Therefore, the page table associated with the old page has to be updated accordingly. The Linux system maintains this update procedure by labeling the page-table entry as *not present*. To keep track of where the old page has been stored, Linux records the page's disk location. To summarize, a page-table entry that is labeled as *present* contains the page frame number of the physical page frame that backs the virtual page. A page-table entry that is marked as not present contains the page's disk location. The technique of borrowing a page from a process and writing it to the disk subsystem is referred to as *paging*. A related technique is known as *swapping*—a much more aggressive form of paging that steals not only an individual page, but also a process's entire page set. Linux, as well as most other UNIX operating systems, utilizes paging but not swapping.

Replacement Policy

From an execution and stability perspective, the relevance of borrowing a certain page as memory becomes scarce is not important. On the other hand, from a performance perspective, which page to borrow and when to borrow it is paramount. The procedure that determines which page to evict from the main memory subsystem is referred to as the *replacement policy*. As an example, the least recently used (LRU) approach analyzes the past behavior and selects the page that has not been accessed for the longest period of time. Even though LRU could be implemented as a page replacement algorithm, it is not practical. This approach would require updating a data structure on *every* access to main memory, generating a rather significant overhead. In practice, most UNIX operating systems utilize variations of lower overhead replacement polices such as not recently used (NRU); Linux relies on an LRU-based approach. In a Linux environment, the page replacement mechanism is complicated by the fact that the kernel may utilize a variable amount of nonpageable memory. As an example, file data is stored in the buffer cache, which can grow and shrink in a dynamic fashion. When the kernel has to allocate a new page frame, the system is faced with two options: it can borrow a page from the kernel or steal a page from a process. In other words, the kernel has to implement not just a replacement policy, but also a *memory balancing policy* that determines how much memory is utilized for kernel buffers and how much is used to back virtual pages.

Page Replacement and Memory Balancing

The combination of page replacement and memory balancing represents a daunting task where there is no clear and perfect solution. Consequently, the Linux kernel uses a variety of procedures that tend to work well in practice. From an implementation perspective, the Linux kernel requires, from the platform-specific portion of the system, 2 extra bits in each page-table entry; they are known as the *access* and *dirty* bits. The access bit indicates whether the page has been accessed since the access bit was last cleared; the dirty bit indicates whether the page has been modified since it was last paged in. Linux utilizes the kswapd thread to periodically inspect these 2 bits. After inspection, kswapd clears the access bit. If kswapd detects that the kernel is running into a low-memory situation, it starts to proactively page out memory that has not been used recently. If a page's dirty bit is set, it is necessary to write the page to disk before the page frame can be freed. Because this represents a relatively costly exercise, kswapd prefers to free pages whose access and dirty bits are cleared (set to 0). By definition, such pages have not been accessed recently and do not have to be written back to disk before the page frame is freed; therefore, they can be reclaimed at a low performance cost.

Although systems vary as to how they manage physical pages, Linux uses the three-level page table in its architecture. These page tables can be used to convert virtual addresses to physical addresses and vice versa.

THE LINUX PAGE TABLES

The Linux system maintains a page table for each process in physical memory and accesses the actual page tables via the identity mapped kernel segment. Page tables in Linux cannot be paged out to the swap space. This implies that a process that allocates a large range of address space could potentially saturate the memory subsystem, because the page table itself would use up all the available memory. On a similar note, because hundreds of processes are active simultaneously on a system, the combined size of all the page tables could potentially use all available memory. The large memory subsystems available on contemporary systems render this scenario unusual, but it still reflects a capacity planning issue that should be addressed. Keeping the page tables in physical memory simplifies the kernel design, and there is no need to deal with nested page faults. The per-process page table layout is based on a multilayer tree consisting of three levels. The first layer consists of the global directory (pgd), the second layer consists of the middle directory (pmd), and the third layer consists of the page table entry (pte). Normally, each directory node occupies one page frame and contains a fixed number of entries. Entries in the pgd and pmd directories are either not present or they point to a directory in the next layer of the tree. The pte entries depict the leaf nodes of the tree, and they contain the actual page table entries. Because the page table layout in Linux resembles a multilayer tree, the space requirements are proportional to the actual virtual address space in use. Therefore, the space requirements are not the maximum size of the virtual address space. Further, because Linux manages memory as a set of page frames, the fixed node size-based approach does not require the large and physically contiguous region of memory that the linear page table-based implementation requires.

While processing a virtual-to-physical page translation, the virtual address is decomposed into multiple sections. The sections utilized for a page-table lookup operation relay on pgd, pmd, and pte indexes (see Figure 9-3). A lookup operation is initiated via the page-table pointer that is stored in the mm structure. The page-table pointer references the global directory that is the root directory of the page-table tree. The pgd index identifies the entry that contains the address of the middle directory. The combination of that address plus the pmd index allows the system to locate the address of the pte directory. Expanding the mechanism by one more layer lets you identify the pte of the page to which the virtual address actually maps. The pte allows the system to calculate the address of the physical page frame, and by utilizing the offset component of the virtual address, the correct location can be identified. The multilayer-based approach to implementing the page tables in Linux represents a platform-independent solution. This solution allows the collapsing of the middle directory into the global directory if the entire tree structure is not necessary to support a certain implementation. This is the approach taken in an IA-32 environment, where the size of the page middle directory is set to 1. In other words, in IA-32, the 32-bit virtual address is decomposed into 10 bits reserved for the page directory, 10 bits for the page table entry, and the remaining 12 bits are utilized by the offset section. The address translation process is considered a joint venture between hardware (the memory management unit (MMU)) and software (the kernel). The kernel communicates with the MMU to identify the virtual pages to be mapped onto physical pages for each user address space. The MMU has the capability to notify the kernel of any error conditions in the process. The most common error condition revolves around page faults, where the kernel has to retrieve the required page from secondary storage. Other possible error conditions may be related to or triggered by any potential page protection issues. From a physical address perspective, Linux differentiates among different memory zones (ZONE_DMA, ZONE_NORMAL, and ZONE_ HIGHMEM), where each zone represents different characteristics. Most of the memory allocation happens in ZONE_NORMAL, whereas ZONE_HIGHMEM represents the physical addresses greater than 896MB. (See the later section "VM Tunables" for more information on memory zones.)

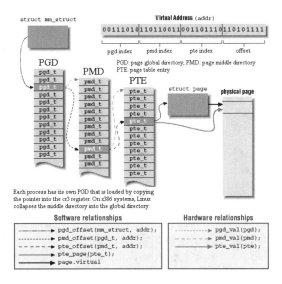

Figure 9-3   Address resolution process.

The next section introduces, from a performance perspective, some of the new features in Linux 2.6. The VM system impacts every other subcomponent in the system; this discussion extends into the CPU and the I/O subsystem components covered in a separate chapter.

NEW FEATURES IN LINUX 2.6

This study references only the new Linux 2.6 components that have a profound impact on system performance; it does not cover all the new features of Linux 2.6.

rmap and *objrmap*

One new VM feature of the Linux 2.6 kernel is referred to as reversed mapping (*rmap*). In the Linux 2.4 kernel, a single pte to (struct) page mapping exists, a technique that is sufficient for process addressing. However, this implementation presented a challenge for the page replacement algorithm because it was necessary to deal with shared pages. It was not feasible to acquire a list of ptes that map a particular (struct) page without traversing the page tables for every active process on the system. Given a physical memory page, rmap allows the VM to identify the processes that are utilizing the page. From an implementation perspective, Linux 2.6 introduces a union pte component into the page structure. As a page is shared among processes, a pte chain is created and linked to this field. The slab allocator manages the pte chain elements, and each node can locate up to NRPTE number of ptes (*NRPTE* is related to the L1 cache size of the target architecture). To summarize, the 2.4 kernel scans through all the page tables, one process at a time, invalidating entries for suitable pages. The introduction of the new data structure allows the kernel to identify the page table entries that reference a certain physical page. The problem with this implementation is that the introduced approach memory is intensive and requires a substantial amount of maintenance. Operations such as page faults, munmap, or fork encounter a slowdown in execution speed compared to Linux 2.4. The `fork()` system call slows down because it is necessary by utilizing rmap to add a new reverse mapping entry for every page in the process's address space. The introduction of object-based reversed mapping (ObjRMAP) differs from rmap. In ObjRMAP, the struct page structure utilizes the mapping file to point to an address_space structure describing the object that backs up that particular page. The address_space structure incorporates two linked lists that contain the vm_area_struct (vma) structures for each process that has a mapping into the file. The vma provides the information needed to locate a page's virtual address that can be utilized to identify the correct page table entry. The object-based approach removes the direct entry-based approach found in rmap, and the page structure points directly to the page-table entry. Identifying a page-table entry via ObjRMAP by consulting the address_space as well as the vma structures takes longer but should be accomplished with a much-reduced overhead factor compared to the rmap implementation.

Largepages Support

Most modern computer architectures support more than one page size. As an example, the IA-32 architecture supports either 4KB or 4MB pages; the Linux operating system utilized largepages only for mapping the actual kernel image. Largepage usage is primarily intended to provide performance improvements for high-performance computing (HPC) and other memory-intensive applications. Any memory-access-intensive application that utilizes large amounts of virtual memory may obtain performance improvements by using largepages. (Linux utilizes either 2MB or 4MB largepages, AIX uses 16MB largepages, and Solaris uses 4MB.) The largepage performance improvements are attributable to reduced translation lookaside buffer (TLB) misses, due to the TLB being able to map a larger virtual memory range (by increasing the reach of the TLB). Largepages also improve the process of memory prefetching by eliminating the need to restart prefetch operations on 4KB boundaries.

In Linux 2.6, the actual number of available largepages can be configured through the proc (/proc/sys/vm/nr_hugepages) interface. Because the actual allocation of largepages depends on the availability of physically contiguous memory regions, the recommendation is to launch the allocation at system startup. The core of the largepage implementation in Linux 2.6 is referred to as the hugetlbfs, a pseudo file system (implemented in fs/hugetlbfs/inode.c) based on ramfs. The idea behind the implementation is that largepages are used to back up any file that exists in the file system. The actual pseudo file system is initialized at system startup and registered as an internal file system. A process may access largepages either through the shmget() interface to set up a shared region that is backed by largepages or by utilizing the mmap() call on a file that has been opened in the huge page file system. To operate on a file that uses largepages, a hugetlbfs file system has to be mounted first. After the mount operation completes, standard file operation calls such as open() can be used to set up a file descriptor. In the case that the mmap() system call is used on an open file, the hugetlbfs registered mmap() function creates the appropriate vma structure for the process. It is recommended that you use the /proc/meminfo interface to ensure that the size, as well as the number of largepages, is set up as expected. Fragmentation may prevent the allocation process from completing successfully.

Page Allocation and Replacement

Physical page allocation in Linux 2.6 is still based on a buddy algorithm, but the mechanism itself has been extended to resemble a lazy buddy scheme that defers the coalescing part. The buffer release activity of the coalescing portion involves a two-step process, where the first step consists of pushing a buffer back onto the free list. This makes the buffer available to other requests. The second step involves referencing the buffer as free (normally in a bitmap) and combining the buffer (if feasible) with adjacent buffers. A regular buddy system implementation performs both steps on each release. The lazy buddy scheme performs the first step but defers the second step and executes it depending on the state of the buffer class. The Linux 2.6 implementation of the discussed lazy buddy concept utilizes per-CPU page lists. These pagesets contain two lists of pages (marked as hot and cold), where the hot pages have been used recently, and the expectation is that they are still present in the CPU cache. On allocation, the pageset for the running CPU is consulted first to determine if the pages are available; if so, the allocation proceeds accordingly. To determine when the pageset should be released or allocated, a low and high watermark-based approach is used. As the low watermark is reached, a batch of pages is allocated and placed on the list. As the high watermark is reached, a batch of pages is freed simultaneously. As a result of the new and improved implementation, the spinlock overhead is significantly reduced.

In the 2.4 Linux kernel, kswapd, a global daemon, acted as the page replacement activator. The kswapd was responsible for keeping a certain amount of memory available, and under memory pressure would initiate the process of freeing pages. In Linux 2.6, a kswapd daemon is available for each node in the system. The idea behind this design is to avoid situations where kswapd would have to free pages on behalf of a remote node. In Linux 2.4, a spinlock has to be acquired before removing pages from the LRU list. In Linux 2.6, operations involving the LRU list take place via pagevec structures. The pagevec structures either add or remove pages to or from the LRU lists in sets of up to PAGEVEC_SIZE pages. In the case of removing pages, the zone lru_lock lock is acquired and the pages are placed on a temporary list. After the list of pages to be removed is assembled, a call to `shrink_list()` is initiated. The actual process of freeing pages can now be performed without acquiring the zone lru_lock spinlock. In the case of adding pages, a new page vector struct is initialized via `pagevec_init()`. Pages are added to the vector through `pagevec_add()` and then are committed to being placed onto the LRU list via `pagevec_release()`.

Slab Allocator

Linux, like most other UNIX operating systems, provides a general-purpose memory allocator that provides arbitrarily sized memory allocations. The basic objective of any slab allocator is to efficiently allocate small memory buffers that are normally less than a page or not an even multiple of a page size. Another objective of a slab allocator is to effectively operate on memory objects that are frequently being allocated and freed, a process that may lead to memory fragmentation. The slab allocator allows caching these frequently used objects (such as sock, inode, or mm_struct), which minimizes the overhead of initializing and destroying these basic entities every time a new object is requested. Many of the changes in the slab allocator for Linux 2.6 are related to address lock contention scenarios. In addition, Linux 2.6 introduces a slab shrinker callback feature. In Linux 2.4, `kmem_cache_reap()` is called in low-memory situations. In Linux 2.6, the 2.4 setup has been augmented as caches register a shrinker callback via `set_shrinker()`. The `set_shrinker()` function populates a struct with a pointer to the callback and a weight that indicates the complexity of re-creating the object. During a page reclaim scenario, each shrinker is called twice. The first call passes 0 as a parameter, indicating that the callback should identify how many pages could be freed (if called properly). A basic heuristic is applied next to determine if it is worth the cost of using the callback. If so, the callback is called again with a parameter that indicates the number of objects to be freed.

VM Tunables

The following definitions summarize the VM tunables for Linux 2.6, provide some insight into the objectives of adjusting the parameters, and discuss the implications of doing so. All the parameters can be adjusted through the proc (/proc/sys/vm) file system interface. The parameters are listed in alphabetical order as listed in the proc file system.

- The *dirty_background_ratio* parameter determines the fraction of dirty memory held prior to attempting a writeback operation. In Linux 2.6, a pool of pdflush kernel threads are responsible for the VM writeback operations, as well as for periodically synchronizing file system metadata. If the background writeback percentage is exceeded, the pdflush daemon processes the writeback operations asynchronously.

- The *dirty_expire_centisecs* parameter governs the number of centiseconds that data is allowed to remain dirty, a time period determined by consulting the timestamp on all files that have dirty pages cached in memory. This parameter represents an upper bound and ensures that the data will eventually be written out to the disk subsystem. A centisecond represents a one-hundredths-of-a-second time unit.

- The *dirty_ratio* parameter indicates the fraction of memory that represents an excessive amount of dirty memory. As a task performs file write operations in an environment where there is an excessive amount of dirty memory, the system is forced to write out dirty memory pages until the percentage of dirty pages is less than the threshold specified on the system. This is significant because I/O operations are considered high-latency. A task's performance is impacted if it has to wait on writeback operations to be completed before the system can satisfy an allocation request. This is predominately considered an issue on large memory systems.

- The *dirty_writeback_sentisecs* parameter outlines the time interval between writebacks by the pdflush kernel threads (in centiseconds). As the already discussed dirty_expire_centisecs parameter governs the age of the dirty memory pages, the dirty_writeback_sentisecs parameter identifies how often the pdflush threads are being invoked. The recommendation is to specify the two parameters in a way that dirty_writeback_sentisecs is smaller than dirty_expire_centisecs (a ratio of 1:6 should be reasonable for most workloads). Larger systems that experience a kernel-intensive workload may benefit from increasing the time as well as frequency intervals (but still obeying the 1:6 ratio), because the background writeback operations may interfere with the workload's own performance behavior.

- The *lower_zone_protection* parameter identifies the weight assigned to a discouraging factor for memory zone fallbacks. The Linux operating system decomposes physical memory into three distinct zones. The ZONE_DMA section is addressable by (legacy) I/O devices, the ZONE_ NORMAL by the kernel, and the ZONE_HIGHMEM is used for user space and certain kernel (temporary) buffers. The basic philosophy behind this concept is that the ZONE_DMA section can be utilized for the same purpose as ZONE_NORMAL, and that the ZONE_NORMAL section can be used for the same purpose as ZONE_HIGHMEM, but not vice versa. As the ZONE_HIGHMEM section becomes saturated, ZONE_NORMAL can be used (through a fallback operation) for allocation purposes. ZONE_NORMAL is the only section that can be used for kernel data structures and is vital to the system. In Linux, a heuristic called the *incremental min* is used to discourage the discussed fallback to vital memory zones (at least ZONE_NORMAL). Setting lower_zone_ protection to the default 0 disables the incremental min; setting the parameter to 4 quadruples its effect. This means the parameter now governs the aggressiveness of the lower zone defense algorithm. The lower_zone_protection tunable lets you increase the amount of protection that lower zones receive against allocations that could potentially use higher zones in the system.

- The *min_free_kbytes* parameter specifies the size of the memory pool that can be used for urgent allocations such as those initiated by the interrupt handler. On larger systems, this parameter impacts the ratio of memory available to interrupt-time as opposed to runtime allocations. On smaller memory systems, the parameter is kept small to avoid allocation failures. The general consensus is that the low watermark parameter is used to determine when to reject user space allocations and to initiate page replacement scenarios. It is possible not to set the value to any large fraction of physical memory. This holds true especially if user space operations are expected to be the primary consumer of the memory subsystem.

- The *nr_pdflush_threads* parameter governs the current size of the pdflush (write-back) thread pool. The VM subsystem utilizes a dynamic algorithm to determine the number of actual threads. The focus is on reserving a certain number of pdflush threads in case of a low-memory situation, where the dynamic allocation of additional threads may fail. The lower and upper bounds, referred to in Linux as MIN_PDFLUSH_THREADS and MAX_PDFLUSH _THREADs, are set to 2 and 8, respectively. Increasing the maximum value (and recompiling the kernel) may be beneficial in an environment with many disk drives and a seek-bound workload to increase the VM I/O concurrency. Another situation where increasing the maximum value may improve performance is a writeback-related CPU-bound situation.

This is where additional processors are available in the system and could be used to process the aggregate workload.

- The *overcommit_memory* parameter represents a flag that enables memory over-commitment. When the flag is set to the default 0, the kernel initiates a check before each `malloc()` call to ensure that sufficient memory is available. If the flag is set to 1, the system pretends that there is always enough memory. When set to 0, the flag ensures that only as much user virtual memory is allocated as can be dealt with through the page replacement infrastructure, stating that every page has to have a backing store. Anonymous memory pages require swap space, whereas file pages require disk space that can be reserved. Setting the flag to 1 results in a more effective memory utilization behavior. However, it may cause scenarios based on certain workload situations, where some processes get killed. To recap, setting the flag to 0 results in the kernel performing heuristic memory overcommit handling by esti-mating the amount of memory available and failing requests that are blatantly invalid.

  Unfortunately, because memory is allocated using a heuristic rather than a precise algorithm, this setting can sometimes allow overloading the memory that is avail-able on a system. Setting the flag to 1 results in the kernel performing no memory overcommit handling. Under this setting, the potential for memory overload is increased, but so is performance for memory-intensive tasks (such as those executed by some scientific applications). An additional supported case is to set the flag to 2. In this case, the kernel fails requests for memory that add up to all of swap space plus the percentage of physical RAM specified in the overcommit_ratio para-meter, discussed next. In Linux, setting the flag to 2 allows reducing the risk of encountering a memory overcommit situation.

- The *overcommit_ratio* parameter specifies the percentage of physical memory that is considered when the overcommit_memory parameter (just discussed) is set to 2. The default value is set to 50.

- The *page-cluster* parameter represents an integer value that, when 2 is raised to the power of *x*, identifies the number of pages the kernel reads in at once (the actual swap read-ahead window). The default values of 2 for systems with less than 16MB of memory, or 3 for larger systems, are considered reasonable settings in most cir-cumstances. The parameter is used to improve the page I/O efficiency, but the sys-tem may encounter excessive I/O and memory consumption if the parameter is specified otherwise.

- The *swappiness* parameter indicates the relative preference of the VM subsystem to reclaim pages by unmapping and paging out pages as opposed to reclaiming only pages that are not mapped by any process. The actual decision depends on a binary switch that is activated when half the percentage of memory that is mapped into the processes page tables, plus the value of swappiness, exceeds 100. The system further utilizes a distress factor in the decision process that increases by a factor of 2 every time page replacement has to be retried. If the system encounters a situation where it is difficult to locate unmapped pages that can be reclaimed, the VM subsystem reverses its course and starts paging out anonymous memory. The preference of not paging out anonymous memory can be expressed by specifying a lower value for swappiness. If kswapd is utilizing significant CPU resources or the system is spending time in an iowait state, increasing the value for swappiness may increase overall system performance.

CPU Scheduler

The thread scheduler represents the subsystem responsible for decomposing the available CPU resources among the runnable threads. The scheduler's behavior and decision-making process have a direct correlation to thread fairness and scheduling latency. Fairness can be described as the capability of all threads to not only encounter forward progress but to do so in an even manner. The opposite of fairness is known as starvation, a scenario where a given thread encounters no forward progress. Fairness is frequently hard to justify because it represents an exercise in compromise between global and localized performance. Scheduling latency describes the actual delay between a thread entering the runnable state (TSRUN) and actually running on a processor (TSONPROC). An inefficient scheduling latency behavior results in a perceptible delay in application response time. An efficient and effective CPU scheduler is paramount to the operation of the computing platform; it decides which task (thread) to run at what time and for how long. Real-time and time-shared jobs are distinguished, each class revealing different objectives. Both are implemented through different scheduling disciplines embedded in the scheduler.

Linux assigns a static priority to each task that can be modified through the nice() interface. Linux has a range of priority classes, distinguishing between real time and time-sharing tasks. The lower the priority value, the higher a task's logical priority, or in other words its *general importance*. In this context, the discussion always references the logical priority when elaborating on priority increases and decreases. Real-time tasks always have higher priority than time-sharing tasks.

The Linux 2.6 scheduler, referred to as the O(1) scheduler, is a multiqueue scheduler that assigns an actual run-queue to each CPU, promoting a CPU local scheduling approach. The O(1) label describes the time complexity for retrieval; in other words, it refers to the property that no matter the workload on the system, the next task to run will be chosen in a constant amount of time.

The previous incarnation of the Linux scheduler utilized the concept of *goodness* to determine which thread to execute next. All runnable tasks were kept on a single run-queue that represented a linked list of threads in a TSRUN (TASK_RUNNABLE) state. In Linux 2.6, the single run-queue lock was replaced with a per-CPU lock, ensuring better scalability on SMP systems. The per-CPU run-queue scheme adopted by the O(1) scheduler decomposes the run-queue into a number of *buckets* (in priority order) and utilizes a bitmap to identify the buckets that hold runnable tasks. Locating the next task to execute requires a read of the bitmap to identify the first bucket with runnable tasks and choosing the first task in that run-queue of the bucket.

The per-CPU run-queue consists of two vectors of task lists, labeled as the active vector and the expired vector. Each vector index represents a list of runnable tasks, each at its respective priority level. After executing for a period of time, a task moves from the active list to the expired list to ensure that all runnable tasks get an opportunity to execute. As the active array becomes empty, the expired and active vectors are swapped by modifying the pointers.

Occasionally, a load-balancing algorithm is invoked to rebalance the run-queues to ensure that a similar number of tasks are available per CPU. As mentioned, the scheduler has to decide which task to run next and for how long. Time quanta in the Linux kernel are defined as multiples of a system tick. A tick is defined as the fixed delta (1/HZ) between two consecutive timer interrupts. In Linux 2.6, the HZ parameter is set to 1,000, indicating that the interrupt routine `scheduler_tick()` is invoked once every millisecond, at which time the currently executing task is charged with one tick. Setting the HZ parameter to 1,000 does not improve the system's responsiveness, because the actual scheduler timeslice is not affected by this setting. For systems that primarily execute in a number-crunching mode, the HZ=1,000 setting may not be appropriate. In such an environment, the aggregate system's performance could benefit from setting the HZ parameter to a lower value (around 100).

Besides the static priority (static_prio), each task maintains an effective priority (prio). The distinction is made to account for certain priority bonuses or penalties based on the recent sleep average (sleep_avg) of a given task. The sleep average accounts for the number of ticks in which a task was recently descheduled. The effective priority of a task determines its location in the priority list of the run-queue. A task is declared interactive when its effective priority exceeds its static priority by a certain level. This scenario can only be based on the task accumulating sleep average ticks. The interactive estimator framework embedded in Linux 2.6 operates automatically and transparently. In Linux, high-priority tasks reach the interactivity state with a much smaller sleep average than do lower-priority tasks. Because a task's interactivity is estimated via the sleep average,

I/O-bound tasks are potential candidates to reach the interactivity status, whereas CPU-bound tasks normally are not perceived as interactive tasks. The actual timeslice is defined as the maximum time a task can execute without yielding the CPU (voluntarily) to another task and is simply a linear function of the static priority of normal tasks. The priority itself is projected into a range of MIN_TIMESLICE to MAX_TIMESLICE, where the default values are set to 10 and 200 milliseconds, respectively. The higher the priority of a task, the greater the task's timeslice for every timer tick the task's running timeslice is decremented. If it is decremented to 0, the scheduler replenishes the timeslice, recomputes the effective priority, and re-enqueues the task either into the active vector, if the task is classified as interactive, or into the expired vector, if the task is considered noninteractive. At this point, the system dispatches another task from the active array. This scenario ensures that tasks in the active array are executed first, before any expired task has the opportunity to run again. If a task is descheduled, its timeslice is not replenished at wakeup time; however, its effective priority might have changed due to any accumulated sleep time. If all the runnable tasks have exhausted their timeslice and have been moved to the expired list, the expired and active vector are swapped. This technique ensures that the O(1) scheduler does not have to traverse a potentially large list of tasks, as is required in the Linux 2.4 scheduler. The issue with the new design is that due to any potential interactivity, scenarios may arise where the active queue continues to have runnable tasks that are not migrated to the expired list. There may be tasks starving for CPU time; to circumvent the starvation issue, the task that first migrated to the expired list is older than the STARVATION_LIMIT (which is set to 10 seconds), and the active and expired arrays are switched.

SUMMARY

In summary, although Linux is a virtual memory system, it utilizes several types of addresses. This provides a fair way for processes to access the memory and run to their completion. The data structures used by the Linux kernel to manage memory are complex. However, different kernel functions require different address types.

REFERENCES

[1] Arcangeli, A. "Evolution of Linux Towards Clustering," EFD R&D Clamart, 2003.

[2] Axboe, J. "Deadline I/O Scheduler Tunables," SUSE, 2003.

[3] Corbet, J. "A New Deadline I/O Scheduler," http://lwn.net/Articles/10874.

[4] "Anticipatory I/O Scheduling," `http://lwn.net/Articles/21274`.

[5] "The Continuing Development of I/O Scheduling," `http://lwn.net/Articles/21274`.

[6] "Porting Drivers to the 2.5 Kernel," Linux Symposium, Ottawa, Canada, 2003.

[7] Iyer, S. and P. Drushel. "Anticipatory Scheduling—A Disk Scheduling Framework to Overcome Deceptive Idleness in Synchronous I/O," SOSP, 2001.

[8] Irwin, Lee W. III. "A 2.5 Page Clustering Implementation," Linux Symposium, Ottawa, 2003.

[9] "VM Tuning," IBM Technical Document, 2003.

[10] Nagar, S., H. Franke, J. Choi, C. Seetharaman, S. Kaplan, N. Singhvi, V. Kashyap, and M. Kravetz. "Class-Based Prioritized Resource Control in Linux," 2003 Linux Symposium.

[11] McKenney, P. "Stochastic Fairness Queueing," INFOCOM, 1990.

[12] Molnar, I. "Goals, Design and Implementation of the New Ultra-scalable O(1) Scheduler," (sched-design.txt) 2003.

[13] Mosberger, D. and S. Eranian. *IA-64 Linux Kernel, Design and Implementation*, Prentice Hall, NJ, 2002.

[14] Shriver, E., A. Merchant, and J. Wilkes. "An Analytic Behavior Model with Readahead Caches and Request Reordering," Bell Labs, 1998.

[15] Wienand, I. "An Analysis of Next Generation Threads on IA64," UNSW, HP, 2003.

## CHAPTER TEN

I/O Subsystems—Performance Implications

By Dominique Heger

INTRODUCTION

In many circumstances, the perceived speed of computing is increasingly dependent on the performance of the I/O subsystem, underscoring the necessity for high-performance I/O solutions. Unfortunately, many operating systems provide inadequate support for applications, leading to poor performance and increased hardware cost of server systems.

One source of the problem is the lack of integration among the various I/O subsystems and the applications. Each I/O subsystem utilizes its own buffering or caching mechanism, and applications generally maintain their own I/O buffers. This approach leads to performance-degrading anomalies such as repeated data copying and multiple buffering scenarios of data items. Repeated data copying causes high CPU overhead and limits the throughput of a server system. Multiple buffering of data wastes memory, reducing the space available for other data items that have to be cached. This size reduction causes higher cache miss rates, increasing disk accesses and reducing I/O throughput.

Linux has multiple I/O schedulers. In the following section, we'll discuss the Linux implementation of the I/O subsystems, focusing on the various I/O schedulers available in the Linux framework.

I/O SCHEDULING AND THE BLOCK I/O (BIO) LAYER

The I/O scheduler in Linux forms the interface between the generic block layer and the low-level device drivers, respectively. The block layer provides functions that are utilized by the file systems and the virtual memory manager to submit I/O requests to block devices. These requests are transformed by the I/O scheduler and made available to the low-level device drivers. The device drivers consume the transformed requests and forward them, using device-specific protocols, to the actual device controllers that perform the I/O operations. Because prioritized resource management seeks to regulate the use of a disk subsystem by an application, the I/O scheduler is considered an important kernel component in the I/O path.

It is further possible to regulate the disk usage in the kernel layers above and below the I/O scheduler. Adjusting the I/O pattern generated by the file system or the virtual memory manager (VMM) is one option. Another option is to adjust the way specific device drivers or device controllers consume and manipulate the I/O requests.

The 2.6 Linux I/O Schedulers

The various Linux 2.6 I/O schedulers can be abstracted into a generic I/O model. The I/O requests are generated by the block layer on behalf of threads that access various file systems. These threads perform raw I/O or are generated by VMM components of the kernel, such as the kswapd or pdflush threads. The producers of I/O requests initiate a call to `__make_request()`, which invokes various I/O scheduler functions such as `elevator_merge_fn()`. The enqueuing functions in the I/O framework intend to merge the newly submitted block I/O unit with previously submitted requests. These functions sort or insert the request into one or more internal I/O queues. As a unit, the internal queues form a single logical queue that is associated with each block device.

At a later stage, the low-level device driver calls the generic kernel function `elv_next_request()` to obtain the next request from the logical queue. The `elv_next_request()` call interacts with the I/O scheduler dequeue function `elevator_next_req_fn`. The `elevator_next_req_fn` then has an opportunity to select the appropriate request from one of the internal queues. The device driver processes the request by converting the I/O submission into potential scatter-gather lists and protocol-specific commands that are submitted to the device controller.

From an I/O scheduler perspective, the block layer is considered the producer of I/O requests, and the device drivers are labeled as the actual consumers. Every read or write request launched by an application results in either utilizing the respective I/O system calls or memory mapping (mmap) the file into the address space of a process. I/O operations normally result in allocating PAGE_SIZE units of physical memory. These pages are indexed, as this enables the system to locate the page in the buffer cache. Any cache subsystem improves performance only if the data in the cache is reused. The read cache abstraction allows the system to implement file-system-dependent read-ahead functionalities, as well as to construct large contiguous (SCSI) I/O commands that can be served via a single Direct Memory Access (DMA) operation. In circumstances where the cache represents pure memory bus overhead, I/O features such as direct I/O should be explored, especially in situations where the system is CPU-bound. In a general write scenario, the system is not necessarily concerned with the previous content of a file, because a `write()` operation normally results in overwriting the contents.

The write cache emphasizes other aspects such as asynchronous updates. There is also the possibility of omitting some write requests in the case where multiple `write()` operations into the cache subsystem result in a single I/O write to a physical disk. Such a scenario may occur in an environment where updates to the same or a similar inode offset are processed within a short time span.

The block layer in Linux 2.4 is organized around the buffer_head data structure. It is a daunting task to create a truly effective and performance-enhanced block I/O subsystem if the underlying buffer_head structures force each I/O request to be decomposed into 512-byte chunks.

The new representation of the block I/O layer in Linux 2.6 encourages large I/O operations. The block I/O layer now tracks data buffers by using *struct page* pointers. Linux 2.4 systems are prone to losing sight of the logical form of the writeback cache when flushing the cache subsystem. Linux 2.6 utilizes logical pages attached to inodes to flush dirty data, which allows combining multiple pages that belong to the same inode into a single bio. The single bio can then be submitted to the I/O layer, a process that works fine if the file is not fragmented on disk.

The 2.4 Linux I/O Scheduler

The default 2.4 Linux I/O scheduler primarily manages the disk utilization. The scheduler has a single internal queue. For each new bio, the I/O scheduler determines if the bio can be merged with an existing request. If this is not the case, a new request is placed in the internal queue, and it is sorted by the starting device block number of the request. This approach focuses on minimizing disk seek times, if the actual disk device driver processes the requests in first-in first-out (FIFO) order. An aging mechanism implemented by the I/O scheduler limits the number of times an existing I/O request in the queue can be omitted and passed by a more recent request. This process prevents any potential starvation scenario. The dequeue function in the I/O framework represents a simple removal of requests from the head of the internal queue.

The 2.6 Deadline I/O Scheduler

The deadline I/O scheduler incorporates a per-request expiration-based approach and operates on five I/O queues. The basic idea behind the implementation is to aggressively reorder requests to improve I/O performance while simultaneously ensuring that no I/O request is starved. More specifically, the scheduler introduces the notion of a per-request deadline, which is used to assign a higher preference to read requests.

The scheduler maintains five I/O queues. During the *enqueue* phase, each I/O request gets associated with a deadline and is inserted into I/O queues that are organized by either the starting logical block number, a sorted list, or the deadline factor, a FIFO list. The scheduler incorporates a separate sort and FIFO lists for read and write requests, respectively. The fifth I/O queue contains the requests that are to be handed off to the device driver.

During a dequeue operation, in the case where the dispatch queue is empty, requests are moved from one of the four I/O lists (sort or FIFO) in batches. The next step consists of passing the head request on the dispatch queue to the device driver; this also holds true in the case where the dispatch queue is not empty. The logic behind moving the I/O requests from either the sort or the FIFO lists is based on the goal of the scheduler to ensure that each read request is processed by the effective deadline, without starving the queued-up write requests. In this design, the goal of economizing the disk seek time is accomplished by moving a larger batch of requests from the sort list and balancing it with a controlled number of requests from the FIFO list. Hence, the deadline I/O scheduler effectively emphasizes average read request response time over disk utilization and total average I/O request response time.

The basic idea behind the deadline scheduler is that all read requests are satisfied within a specified time period. On the other hand, write requests do not have any specific deadlines. As the block device driver is ready to launch another disk I/O request, the core algorithm of the deadline scheduler is invoked. In a simplified form, the first action taken is to identify if I/O requests are waiting in the dispatch queue; if so, no additional decision needs to be made as to what to execute next. Otherwise, it is necessary to move a new set of I/O requests to the dispatch queue. The scheduler searches for work in the following places, but it migrates requests from only the *first source* that results in a hit:

1. If there are pending write I/O requests, and the scheduler has not selected any write requests for a certain amount of time, a set of write requests is selected (see Appendix A, "Tuning Kernel Parameters").
2. If there are expired read requests in the read_fifo list, the system moves a set of these requests to the dispatch queue.
3. If there are pending read requests in the sort list, the system migrates some of these requests to the dispatch queue.
4. Last, if there are any pending write I/O operations, the dispatch queue is populated with requests from the sorted write list.

In general, the definition of a *certain amount of time* for write request starvation is normally two iterations of the scheduler algorithm. After two sets of read requests have been moved to the dispatch queue, the scheduler migrates some write requests to the dispatch queue. For example, a batch set of requests can be 64 contiguous requests, but a request that requires a disk seek operation counts the same as 16 contiguous requests.

Scheduler Tunables

The following definitions discuss the scheduler's deadline I/O tuning potential, elaborating on the exposed tunables that may have to be adjusted to optimize I/O performance. Each I/O queue discussed incorporates a set of tunables that control the actual working behavior of the deadline scheduler (see /sys/block/*device*/iosched). Although it is impossible to stipulate any generic tuning requirements for these tunables, see Chapter 19, "Case Study: Tuning the I/O Schedulers in Linux 2.6," for information on specific experiments that discuss how to tune.

- The *read_expire* parameter, which is specified in milliseconds, is part of the deadline equation. The goal of the scheduler is to guarantee a start service time for a given I/O request. Because the design focuses mainly on read requests, each read I/O that enters the scheduler is assigned a deadline factor that consists of the current time plus the read_expire value.

- The *fifo_batch* parameter governs the number of requests moved to the dispatch queue. As a read request expires, it becomes necessary to move some I/O requests from the sorted I/O scheduler list to the dispatch queue of the block device. Therefore, the fifo_batch parameter controls the batch size based on the cost of each I/O request. A request is qualified by the scheduler as either a *seek* or *stream* request. (For additional information, see the definitions of the seek_cost and stream_unit parameters, discussed in the following bullet.)

- The *seek_cost* parameter quantifies the cost of a seek operation compared to a stream_unit, which is expressed in kilobytes. The *stream_unit* parameter dictates the number of kilobytes used to describe a single stream unit. A stream unit has an associated cost of 1. If a request consists of XY kilobytes, the actual cost = (XY + stream_unit – 1) / stream_unit. The combination of the stream_unit, seek_cost, and fifo_batch parameters determines the number of requests moved as an I/O request expires.

- The *write_starved* parameter, expressed in number of dispatches, indicates the number of times the I/O scheduler assigns preference to read over write requests. When the I/O scheduler has to move requests to the dispatch queue, the preference scheme in the design favors read over write requests. However, the write requests cannot be starved indefinitely—after the read requests are favored for write_starved a number of times, write requests are dispatched.

- The *front_merges* parameter controls the request merge technique used by the scheduler. In some circumstances, a request may enter the scheduler that is contiguous to a request that is already in the I/O queue. It is feasible to assume that the new request may have a correlation to either the front or the back of the already queued request. The new request is labeled as either a front or a back merge candidate. Based on the way files are laid out, back merge operations are more common than front merges. For some workloads, it is unnecessary to even consider front merge operations; however, setting the front_merges flag to 0 disables that functionality. Despite setting the flag to 0, front merges may still occur due to the cached merge_last hint component. Because this feature represents an almost 0 cost factor, this is not considered an I/O performance issue.

The 2.6 Anticipatory I/O Scheduler

The design of the anticipatory I/O scheduler (AS) attempts to reduce the per-thread read response time. It introduces a controlled delay component into the dispatching equation. The delay is invoked on any new read request to the device driver. This allows a thread that just finished its read I/O request to submit a new read request, enhancing the chances that this scheduling behavior will result in smaller seek operations. The trade-off between reduced seeks and decreased disk utilization, due to the additional delay factor in dispatching a request, is managed by utilizing an actual cost-benefit analysis.

The next few paragraphs discuss the general design of an anticipatory I/O scheduler, outlining the different components that comprise the I/O framework. As a read I/O request completes, the I/O framework stalls for a brief amount of time, waiting for additional requests to arrive before dispatching a new request to the disk subsystem. The focus of this design is on application threads that rapidly generate another I/O request that could potentially be serviced before the scheduler chooses another task, possibly avoiding *deceptive idleness*. Deceptive idleness is defined as a condition that forces the scheduler into making a decision too early by assuming that the thread issuing the last request has no further disk requests lined up. This causes the scheduler to select an I/O request from another task.

The design discussed here argues that keeping the disk idle during the short stall period is not necessarily detrimental to I/O performance. The question of whether to wait at any given decision point and for how long is key to the effectiveness and performance of the implementation. The framework waits for the shortest possible period of time in which the scheduler expects the benefits of actively waiting to outweigh the costs of keeping the disk subsystem in an idle state. An assessment of the costs and benefits is possible only relative to a particular scheduling policy. To elaborate, a seek-reducing scheduler may want to wait for contiguous or proximal requests, whereas a proportional share scheduler may prefer weighted fairness as one of its primary criteria.

To allow for such a high degree of flexibility, while trying to minimize the burden on the development efforts for any particular disk scheduler, the anticipatory scheduling framework consists of three components:

- The original disk scheduler, which implements the scheduling policy and is unaware of any anticipatory scheduling techniques
- A scheduler-independent anticipation core
- An adaptive scheduler-specific anticipation heuristic for seek reducing, such as SPTF or C-SCAN, as well as any potential proportional share (CFQ or YFQ) scheduler

The anticipation core implements the generic logic and timing mechanisms for waiting. It relies on the anticipation heuristic to decide whether and for how long to wait. The actual heuristic is implemented separately for each disk scheduler and has access to the internal state of the scheduler. To apply anticipatory scheduling to a new scheduling policy, it is merely necessary to implement an appropriate anticipation heuristic.

Any traditional work-conserving I/O scheduler operates in two states: idle or busy. Applications may issue I/O requests at any time, and these requests are normally placed in the *pool of requests* of the scheduler. If the disk subsystem is idle at this point, or whenever another request completes, a new request is scheduled. The scheduler's select function is called, whereupon a request is chosen from the pool and is dispatched to the disk device driver. The anticipation core forms a wrapper around this traditional scheduler scheme. Whenever the disk becomes idle, it invokes the scheduler to select a candidate request. However, instead of dequeuing and dispatching a request immediately, the framework first passes the request to the anticipation heuristic for evaluation. A return value of 0 indicates that the heuristic has deemed it pointless to wait, and the core therefore proceeds to dispatch the candidate request. However, a positive integer as a return value represents the waiting period, in microseconds, that the heuristic deems suitable. The core initiates a timeout for that particular time period and enters a new wait state. Although the disk is inactive, this state is considered different from idling, having pending requests and an active timeout. If the timeout expires before the arrival of any new request, the previously chosen request is dispatched without further delay. However, new requests may arrive during the wait period; they are added to the pool of I/O requests. The anticipation core then immediately asks the scheduler to select a new candidate request from the pool and initiates communication with the heuristic to evaluate this new candidate.

This scenario may lead to an immediate dispatch of the new candidate request, or it may cause the core to remain in the wait state, depending on the scheduler's selection and the evaluation of the anticipation heuristic. In the latter case, the original timeout remains in effect, thus preventing unbounded waiting situations by repeatedly retriggering the timeout.

Because the heuristic used is disk-scheduler-dependent, the discussion here only generalizes on the actual implementation techniques that may be utilized. Therefore, the next few paragraphs discuss a shortest positioning time first (SPTF)-based implementation. This is where the disk scheduler determines the positioning time for each available request based on the current head position and chooses the request that results in the shortest seek distance.

The heuristic has to evaluate the candidate request that was chosen by the scheduling policy. If the candidate I/O request is located close to the current head position, there is no need to wait on any other requests. Assuming synchronous I/O requests initiated by a single thread, the task that issued the last request is likely to submit the next request soon. If this request is expected to be close to the current request, the heuristic decides to wait. The waiting period is chosen as the expected YZ percentile, normally around 95% think-time, within which there is an XZ probability, normally 95%, that a request will arrive. This simple approach is transformed and generalized into a succinct cost-benefit equation that is intended to cover the entire range of values for the head positioning, as well as the think-times. To simplify the discussion, the adaptive component of the heuristic consists of collecting online statistics on all the disk requests to estimate the different time variables that are used in the decision-making process. The expected positioning time for each process represents a weighted average over the time of the *positioning time* for requests from that process, as measured upon request completion. Expected median and percentile think-times are estimated by maintaining a *decayed frequency table* of request think-times for each process.

The Linux 2.6 implementation of the anticipatory I/O scheduler follows the basic idea that if the disk drive just operated on a read request, it is assumed that another read request is in the pipeline and is worth the wait. The I/O scheduler starts a timer; at this point no more I/O requests are passed to the device driver. If a close read request arrives during the wait time, it is serviced immediately. In the process, the actual distance that the kernel considers *close* grows as time passes. Eventually the close requests dry out, and the scheduler decides to submit some of the write requests.

The next few paragraphs discuss the AS I/O scheduler's tuning potential, elaborating on the exposed tunables that may have to be adjusted to optimize I/O performance. (See /sys/block/*device*/iosched.)

- The parameter `read_expire` governs the timeframe until a read quest is labeled as expired. This parameter further controls, to a certain extent, the interval in which expired requests are serviced. This approach equates to determining the timeslice that a single reader request is allowed to use in the general presence of other I/O requests. The approximation 100 * ((seek time / `read_expire`) + 1) describes the percentile of streaming read efficiency that a physical disk should receive in an environment that consists of multiple concurrent read requests.

- The parameter `read_batch_expire` governs the time assigned to a batch (or set) of read requests prior to serving any (potentially) pending write requests. A higher value increases the priority allotted to read requests. Setting the value to less than `read_expire` would reverse the scenario; at this point the write requests would be favored over the read requests. The literature suggests setting the parameter to a multiple of the `read_expire` value. The parameters `write_expire` and `write_batch_expire`, respectively, describe and govern the behavior of both read parameters for any (potential) write requests.

- The `antic_expire` parameter controls the maximum amount of time the AS scheduler will idle before moving on to another request. The literature suggests initializing the parameter slightly higher for large seek time devices.

The 2.6 CFQ Scheduler

The Completely Fair Queuing (CFQ) I/O scheduler can be considered to represent an extension to the better-known Stochastic Fair Queuing (SFQ) implementation. The focus of both implementations is on the concept of fair allocation of I/O bandwidth among all the initiators of I/O requests. An SFQ-based scheduler design was initially proposed for some network scheduling-related subsystems. The goal is to distribute the available I/O bandwidth as equally as possible among the I/O requests. The implementation utilizes n (normally 64) internal I/O queues, as well as a single I/O dispatch queue. During an enqueue operation, the process ID (PID) of the currently running process is utilized to select one of the internal queues, and the request is inserted into one of the queues in FIFO order. During dequeue, the SFQ design calls for a round-robin-based scan through the nonempty I/O queues, and it selects requests from the head of the queues. To avoid encountering too many seek operations, an entire round of requests is collected, sorted, and ultimately merged into the dispatch queue. The head request in the dispatch queue is then passed to the device driver.

Conceptually, a CFQ implementation does not utilize a hash function. Therefore, each I/O process is assigned an internal queue, which implies that the number of I/O processes determines the number of internal queues. In Linux 2.6.5, the CFQ I/O scheduler utilizes a hash function and a certain number of request queues, therefore resembling an SFQ implementation. The CFQ, as well as the SFQ, implementations strive to manage per-process I/O bandwidth and provide fairness at the level of process granularity.

The 2.6 noop I/O Scheduler

The Linux 2.6 noop I/O scheduler is a rather minimal overhead I/O scheduler that performs and provides basic merging and sorting functionalities. The main usage of the noop scheduler revolves around non-disk-based block devices. This includes memory devices as well as specialized software or hardware environments that incorporate their own I/O scheduling, and large caching functionality, which therefore requires only minimal assistance from the kernel. In large I/O subsystems that incorporate RAID controllers and a vast number of contemporary physical disk drives called TCQ drives, the noop scheduler has the potential to outperform the other three I/O schedulers as the workload increases.

I/O Scheduler–Performance Implications

The next few paragraphs augment the I/O scheduler discussion and introduce some additional performance issues that have to be taken into consideration while conducting an I/O performance analysis. The current AS implementation consists of several different heuristics and policies that determine when and how I/O requests are dispatched to the I/O controller. The elevator algorithm that is utilized in AS is similar to the one used for the deadline scheduler. The main difference is that the AS implementation allows limited backward movement and supports backward seek operations. A backward seek operation may occur while choosing between two I/O requests, where one request is located behind the current head position of the elevator and the other request is ahead of the current position of the elevator.

The AS scheduler utilizes the *lowest logical block* information as the yardstick for sorting, as well as determining the seek distance. In the case that the seek distance to the request behind the elevator is less than half the seek distance to the request in front of the elevator, the request behind the elevator is chosen. The backward seek operations are limited to a maximum of MAXBACK (1024 * 1024) blocks. This approach favors the elevator's forward movement progress while still allowing short backward seek operations. The expiration time for the requests held on the FIFO lists is tunable via read_expire and write_expire of the parameter (see Appendix A).

When a read or write operation expires, the AS I/O scheduler interrupts either the current elevator sweep or the read anticipation process to service the expired request. In the next section, we'll delve further into the world of read and write requests.

READ AND WRITE REQUEST BATCHES

The process of read anticipation solely occurs when scheduling a batch of read requests. The AS implementation allows only one read request at a time to be dispatched to the controller. This has to be compared to either the many-write-request scenario or the many-read-request case if read anticipation is deactivated.

READ ANTICIPATION HEURISTIC

In the case that read anticipation is enabled (antic_expire ≠ 0), read requests are dispatched to the disk or RAID controller one at a time. At the end of each read request, the I/O scheduler examines the next read request from the sorted read list (an actual rb-tree). If the next read request belongs to the same process as the request that just completed, or if the next request in the queue is close (data block-wise) to the just-completed request, the request is dispatched immediately. The statistics of average think-time and seek distance available for the process that just completed are examined. These statistics are associated with each process but are not associated with a specific I/O device.

To illustrate, the approach works more efficiently if there is a one-to-one correlation between a process and a disk. In the case that a process is actively working I/O requests on separate devices, the actual statistics reflect a combination of the I/O behavior across all the devices, skewing the statistics and therefore distorting the facts. If the AS scheduler guesses right, very expensive seek operations can be omitted, and hence the overall I/O throughput benefits tremendously. In the case that the AS scheduler guesses wrong, the antic_expire time is wasted. In an environment that consists of larger (hardware striped) RAID systems and tag command queuing (TCQ)-capable disk drives, it is more beneficial to dispatch an entire batch of read requests and let the controllers and disk do their magic.

From a physical disk perspective, to locate specific data, the disk drive's logic requires the cylinder, the head, and the sector information. The cylinder specifies the track on which the data resides. Based on the layering technique used, the tracks underneath each other form a cylinder. The head information identifies the specific read/write head, and therefore the exact platter. The search is then narrowed down to a single track on a single platter. Ultimately, the sector value reflects the sector on the track, and the search is completed.

Contemporary disk subsystems do not communicate in terms of cylinders, heads, and sectors. Instead, modern disk drives map a unique block number over each cylinder/head/sector construct. Therefore, that unique reference number identifies a specific cylinder/head/sector combination. Operating systems address the disk drives by utilizing these block numbers. Hence the disk drive is responsible for translating the block number into the appropriate cylinder/head/sector value. The culprit is that it is *not guaranteed* that the physical mapping is actually sequential. But the statement can be made that there is a rather high probability that a logical block n is physically adjacent to a logical block $n+1$. The existence of the discussed sequential layout is paramount to the I/O scheduler performing as advertised. Based on how the read anticipatory heuristic is implemented in AS, I/O environments that consist of RAID systems, operating in a hardware stripe setup, may experience rather erratic performance. This is due to the current AS implementation that is based on the notion that an I/O device has only one physical seek head, ignoring the fact that in a RAID environment, each physical disk has its own physical seek head construct. This is not recognized by the AS scheduler; therefore, the data used for the statistics analysis is getting skewed.

Further, disk drives that support TCQ perform best when they can operate on n, not 1, pending I/O requests. The read anticipatory heuristic disables TCQ. Therefore, environments that support TCQ or consist of RAID systems may benefit from either choosing an alternate I/O scheduler or setting the antic_expire parameter to 0. The tuning allows the AS scheduler to behave similarly to the deadline I/O scheduler, with the emphasis on *behave* and not *perform*.

In any computer system, among the disk drives, disk controllers, and actual memory subsystem is a hierarchy of additional controllers, host adapters, bus converters, and data paths that all impact I/O performance. In the following section, you will see how these components affect the I/O performance.

I/O COMPONENTS THAT AFFECT PERFORMANCE

The various I/O subsystems have to communicate with each other as efficiently and effectively as possible. In smaller systems, an I/O bus serves as the shared communication link between the I/O subsystems, utilizing a memory bus to link the CPUs to the memory subsystem. The two major advantages of a bus-based architecture are low cost and versatility. By defining a single interconnect, new devices can easily be added or even moved among computer systems that support a common I/O bus architecture.

The main drawback of a bus-based system is that the bus may create a communication bottleneck, possibly limiting the maximum I/O throughput. Larger systems bypass this potential bottleneck by incorporating multiple I/O buses. A refinement of a memory bus architecture that is designed to eliminate the potential bottleneck of the single shared path is known as a crossbar. A crossbar is a series of single buses arranged to provide multiple paths among the CPUs and the memory subsystem. The use of multiple buses in a two- or three-dimensional network implies that each CPU can have a unique access path to any part of the memory subsystem. This vastly reduces the potential for any bandwidth contention.

The two main factors that heavily impact overall system performance are the number of bus masters and the type of bus clocking mechanism, and whether the bus clocking mechanism is synchronous or asynchronous.

Bus masters are devices that can initiate a `read()` or `write()` request. A CPU is always considered a bus master. If multiple CPUs are configured, an arbitration schema is required to decide among the bus masters who get the bus next. In the case of multiple bus masters, a bus usually offers higher throughput when incorporating a split transaction technology, also referred to as a packet-switched bus technology. As an example, in a split transaction paradigm, a read() request is decomposed into a read() request transaction that contains the address and a memory reply transaction that holds the actual data. Each transaction has to be tagged so that the CPU and the memory subsystem can track the transaction.

In a split transaction design, the bus is made available to other bus masters while the memory subsystem services the request. A split transaction bus normally provides a higher throughput but also incurs a higher latency than a bus that is held throughout a transaction, referred to as a circuit-switched bus. Bus clocking implementation varies, depending on whether a bus is synchronous or asynchronous. In the synchronous case, the bus includes a clock in the control lines and utilizes a fixed protocol for addresses and data. Because little or no logic is needed to decide what to do next, synchronous buses are fast and inexpensive.

The two major disadvantages of a synchronized bus are that everything on the bus has to run at the same speed and, based on clock skew problems, the bus cannot be long. An asynchronous bus is not clocked. Instead, self-timed handshaking protocols are used between a bus sender and a bus receiver. Asynchrony provides easy accommodation of a vast variety of devices and allows for lengthening of the bus without encountering any clock skew or synchronization issues.

ADDRESSING AN I/O DEVICE

Memory-mapped I/O today is considered the de facto standard that is utilized by a CPU to address an I/O device. In such a design, portions of the virtual address space are assigned to I/O devices. Simple read() and write() operations from or to these addresses cause data to be transferred. Some portion of the virtual address space is further assigned to actually control the devices. Commands such as load and store operations to a device represent access operations to that particular range of address space. Interrupt-driven I/O allows a CPU to work on a thread that is in a runnable state, while I/O operations are serviced for other threads.

In most contemporary systems, DMA hardware enables data transfers without any CPU intervention. A DMA module is defined as a specialized processor that transfers data between the memory subsystem and an I/O device while the CPU is servicing other tasks. A DMA module is always external to a CPU and acts as a bus master.

The first step in a DMA transfer consists of a CPU setting up the DMA registers that contain a memory address and the number of bytes to be transferred. After the DMA transfer is complete, the DMA controller interrupts the CPU, increasing the intelligence of the DMA device by utilizing I/O controllers—enabling the CPU to service even more tasks. The operating system typically generates a queue of I/O control blocks that contain the data, source, and destination locations, as well as the data size. The I/O controller processes all the requests, and after the tasks are completed, it sends a single interrupt to the CPU. This scenario economizes on the number of interrupts encountered on the system; therefore, it might increase aggregate throughput performance.

The Linux file systems submit I/O requests by utilizing `submit_bio()`. This function submits requests by utilizing the request function as specified during queue creation. Technically, device drivers do not have to use the I/O scheduler; however, all SCSI devices utilize the scheduler by virtue of the SCSI midlayer. The `scsi_alloc_queue()` function calls `blk_init_queue()`, which sets the request function to `scsi_request_fn()`. The `scsi_request_fn()` function takes requests from the I/O scheduler on dequeue and passes them to the device driver.

SUMMARY

Linux has multiple I/O schedulers and tunables. Our discussions of Linux I/O scheduling and the BIO layer, and factors that affect overall system performance, will help you make important tuning decisions for your system.

REFERENCES

[1] Arcangeli, A. "Evolution of Linux Towards Clustering," EFD R&D Clamart, 2003.

[2] Axboe, J. "Deadline I/O Scheduler Tunables," SuSE, 2003.

[3] Corbet, J. "A New Deadline I/O Scheduler," http://lwn.net/Articles/10874.

[4] "Anticipatory I/O Scheduling," http://lwn.net/Articles/21274.

[5] "The Continuing Development of I/O Scheduling," http://lwn.net/Articles/21274.

[6] "Porting Drivers to the 2.5 Kernel," Linux Symposium, Ottawa, Canada, 2003.

[7] Iyer, S. and P. Drushel. "Anticipatory Scheduling—A Disk Scheduling Framework to Overcome Deceptive Idleness in Synchronous I/O," SOSP, 2001.

[8] Irwin, W. Lee III, "A 2.5 Page Clustering Implementation," Linux Symposium, Ottawa, 2003.

[9] "VM Tuning," IBM Technical Document, 2003.

[10] McKenney, P. "Stochastic Fairness Queueing," INFOCOM, 1990.

[11] Molnar, I. "Goals, Design and Implementation of the New Ultra-scalable O(1) Scheduler" (sched-design.txt), 2003.

[12] Mosberger, D. and S. Eranian. *IA-64 Linux Kernel, Design and Implementation*, Prentice Hall, NJ, 2002.

[13] Nagar, S., H. Franke, J. Choi, C. Seetharaman, S. Kaplan, N. Singhvi, V. Kashyap, and M. Kravetz. "Class-Based Prioritized Resource Control in Linux," 2003 Linux Symposium.

[14] Shriver, E., A. Merchant, and J. Wilkes. "An Analytic Behavior Model with Readahead Caches and Request Reordering," Bell Labs, 1998.

[15] Wienand, I. "An Analysis of Next Generation Threads on IA64," UNSW, HP, 2003.

## CHAPTER ELEVEN

File System Tuning

By Steve Best

INTRODUCTION

Linux supports several types of file systems, including non-journaling file systems and several journaling file systems. We will discuss the journaling and non-journaling file system types available in Linux, including their purpose, implementation, and use, and we will examine ways to tune each type of file system. We will also look at factors that affect file system performance, including how file systems are implemented and created, and how the disks on which they reside affect their performance.

FILE SYSTEM FUNDAMENTALS

This section looks at some file system basics, including factors to take into account when creating a new file system, creating optimized file systems, and basic file system terminology.

In the following sections, the term *file system* is used to indicate both a type of file system implementation and an actual hierarchical implementation of user or system data.

File System Implementation Considerations

File systems are one of the most important parts of an operating system. File systems store and manage user data on disk drives and ensure that what is read from storage is identical to what was written. In addition to storing user data in files, file systems also create and manage information about files and about themselves. Besides guaranteeing the integrity of the data, file systems need to be extremely reliable and have excellent performance.

Before creating file systems, you need a plan for their layout. The following are some general considerations to be aware of when planning your system:

- I/O workload should be distributed as evenly as possible across the disk drives.
- The number of file systems on any one disk should be kept to a minimum. All the Linux file systems are better able to manage fragmentation of a file system in a larger partition/volume than in a small, completely full partition.
- If a large set of files (in size, number, or both) has characteristics that make the files significantly different from "typical" files, create a separate file system for these files that is tuned to their requirements.

The parameters that affect file system performance are set when the file system is initially defined. When a file system is created with the mkfs command, a set of default values is applied to define the file system, unless the defaults are specifically overridden. Although it is possible to use the file system tune command to modify some of the parameters after the file system is defined, not all parameters can be changed after the file system is created. Most of the time, it is simpler to use the mkfs command to define the file system right from the beginning. Advanced planning to create the file system is essential. Later in this chapter, we examine some of the specifics that can be set when a new file system is created.

Creating Optimized File Systems

mkfs is the front end to each file system's format program and its subprograms. mkfs creates file systems on disk partitions (or volumes, if a volume manager is being used).

The mkfs command can usually run without the optional parameters that affect performance. To a large degree, this is because the default parameters are adequate in most cases. mkfs calculates the appropriate parameters to use based on the information it can ascertain about the volume or disk drive, and then it calls the file system mkfs command to actually create the file system.

Basic File System Terms

Before delving any further into file systems on Linux, it's important to learn some of the common file system terms. These terms are used throughout the remainder of this chapter.

- A *logical block* is the smallest unit of storage that can be allocated by the file system. A logical block is measured in bytes, and it may take several blocks to store a single file.

- A *logical volume* can be one or more physical disks or some subset of the physical disk space.
- *Block allocation* is a method of allocating blocks where the file system allocates one block at a time. In this method, a pointer to every block in a file is maintained and recorded. Ext2 uses block allocation.
- *Extent allocation.* Large numbers of contiguous blocks, called extents, are allocated to the file and are tracked as a unit. A pointer needs only to be maintained to the beginning of the extent. Because a single pointer is used to track a large number of blocks, the bookkeeping for large files is much more efficient.
- *Fragmentation* is the scattering of files into blocks that are not contiguous and is a problem that all file systems encounter. Fragmentation is caused when files are created and deleted. The fragmentation problem can be solved by having the file system use advanced algorithms to reduce fragmentation.
- *Internal fragmentation* occurs when a file does not a fill a block completely. For example, if a file is 10K and a block is 8K, the file system allocates two blocks to hold the file, but 6K is wasted. Notice that as blocks get bigger, so does the waste.
- *External fragmentation* occurs when the logical blocks that make up a file are scattered all over the disk. External fragmentation can cause poor performance.
- An *extent* is a large number of contiguous blocks. Each extent is described by a triple consisting of (file offset, starting block number, length), where *file offset* is the offset of the extent's first block from the beginning of the file, *starting block number* is the first block in the extent, and *length* is the number of blocks in the extent. Extents are allocated and tracked as a single unit, meaning that a single pointer tracks a group of blocks. For large files, *extent allocation* is a much more efficient technique than block allocation. Figure 11-1 shows how extents are used.
- File system *metadata* is the file system's internal data structures—everything concerning a file except the actual data in the file. Metadata includes date and timestamps, ownership information, file access permissions, other security information such as access control lists (if they exist), the file's size, and the storage location or locations on disk.
- An *inode* stores all the information *about* a file except the data itself. An inode is a bookkeeping file for a file (indeed, an inode is a file that consumes blocks, too). An inode contains file permissions, file types, and the number of links to the file. It also contains some direct pointers to file data blocks, pointers to blocks that contain pointers to file data bocks (so-called indirect pointers), and even double- and triple-indirect pointers. Every inode has a unique inode number that distinguishes it from every other inode.

- A *directory* is a special kind of file that simply contains pointers to other files. Specifically, the inode for a directory file simply contains the inode numbers of its contents, plus permissions, and so on.

- A *super* block contains partition-wide information for the file system such as the size of the partition, size of allocation groups, block size, and so on.

- *Allocation groups* divide the space in a partition into chunks and allow the file system resource allocation policies to use methods to achieve high I/O performance. First, the allocation policies cluster disk blocks and disk inodes for related data to achieve locality for the disk. Second, the allocation policies distribute unrelated data throughout the partition in order to accommodate locality.

- *Access control lists* (ACLs) allow file owners to specify extended access information about a file, granting additional rights to users/groups other than those owning the file. This form of discretionary access control allows users to manage their own collaborative projects without intervention of system administrators to maintain groups and without granting rights to all users on the system. The Samba environment is a primary user of ACL support.

- An *access control entry* (ACE) is an individual entry in an access control list (ACL). The first field of an ACL is the entry type. The second field is a group name, user-name, numeric UID, or numeric GID, depending on the value of the first field. The third field is the access permission for this ACL.

- An *extended attribute* (EA) consists of a name and a value. Applications can attach additional information to a file object in the form of an extended attribute. A file object can have more than one extended attribute. EAs associated with a file object are not part of the file object's data; they are maintained separately and managed by the file system that manages that object. Applications define and associate extended attributes with a file object through file system function calls. File systems in Linux store ACLs by using extended attributes. Figure 11-1 shows how file extents work.

If file sample.txt requires 18 blocks, and the file system can allocate one extent of length 8, a second extent of length 5, and a third extent of length 5, the file system would look something like Figure 11-1. The first extent has offset 0 (block A in the file), location 10, and length 8. The second extent has offset 8 (block I), location 20, and length 5. The last extent has offset 13 (block N), location 35, and length 5.

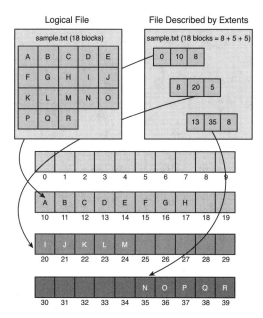

Figure 11-1   An extent is described by its block offset in the file, the location of the first block in the extent, and the length of the extent.

JOURNALED FILE SYSTEMS

Before the year 2000, Ext2 was the de facto file system for most Linux machines. Ext2 is robust, reliable, and suitable for most deployments. However, as Linux displaces UNIX and other operating systems in more and larger server and computing environments, Ext2 is being pushed to its limits. In fact, many now-common requirements—large hard-disk partitions, quick recovery from crashes, high-performance I/O, and the need to store thousands and thousands of files representing terabytes of data—exceed the capabilities of Ext2.

Fortunately, a number of other Linux file systems take up where Ext2 leaves off. Indeed, Linux now offers four alternatives to Ext2: Ext3, ReiserFS, XFS, and JFS. In addition to meeting some or all of the requirements just listed, each of these alternative file systems supports journaling, a feature demanded by enterprises and beneficial to anyone running Linux. A journaling file system can simplify restarts, reduce fragmentation, and accelerate I/O. Journaling file systems minimize the need to run file system checkers.

System administrators who maintain complex systems or those who require high availability should consider deploying one or more journaling file systems.

When Good File Systems Go Bad

The following describes the methodology for increasing the size of a file from three blocks to five blocks when it is modified:

1. Two new blocks are allocated to hold the new data.
2. The file's inode is updated to record the two new block pointers and the file's new size.
3. The actual data is written into the blocks.

Although writing data to a file appears to be a single atomic operation, the actual process involves a number of steps (even more steps than shown here, considering all the accounting required to remove free blocks from a list of free space, among other possible metadata changes).

If all the steps to write a file are completed perfectly (and this happens most of the time), the file is saved successfully. However, if the process is interrupted at any time (perhaps due to power failure or other systemic failure), a non-journaled file system can end up in an inconsistent state. Corruption occurs because the logical operation of writing (or updating) a file is actually a sequence of I/O, and the entire operation might not be totally reflected on the media at any given point in time.

If the metadata or the file data is left in an inconsistent state, the file system no longer functions properly.

Non-journaled file systems rely on fsck to examine all the file system's metadata and detect and repair structural integrity problems before restarting. If Linux shuts down smoothly, fsck typically returns a clean bill of health. However, after a power failure or crash, fsck is likely to find some kind of error in metadata.

Because file systems contain significant amounts of metadata, running fsck can be very time-consuming. fsck has to scan a file system's *entire* repository of metadata to ensure consistency and error-free operation; therefore, the speed of fsck on a disk partition is proportional to the size of the partition, the number of directories, and the number of files in each directory.

For large file systems, journaling becomes crucial. Journaled file systems provide improved structural consistency, better recovery, and faster restart times than non-journaled file systems. In most cases, journaled file systems can restart in less than a second.

Transactions Are the Solution

The magic of journaling file systems lies in *transactions*. Like database transactions, journaling file system transactions treat a sequence of changes as a single, atomic operation. However, instead of tracking updates to tables, the journaling file system tracks changes to file system metadata or user data. The transaction guarantees that either *all* or *none* of the file system updates are done.

For example, the process of creating a new file modifies several metadata structures (inodes, free lists, and directory entries). Before the file system makes those changes, it creates a transaction that describes what it is about to do. After the transaction has been recorded (on disk), the file system goes ahead and modifies the metadata. The *journal* in a journaling file system is simply a list of transactions.

In the event of a system failure, the file system is restored to a consistent state by replaying the journal. Rather than examine *all* metadata (the fsck way), the file system inspects only those portions of the metadata that have recently changed. Recovery is much faster—usually only a matter of seconds. Better yet, recovery time is not dependent on the size of the partition.

In addition to faster restart times, most journaling file systems also address another significant problem: scalability. Combining even a few large-capacity disks, it is easy to assemble some massive (certainly by early-'90s standards) file systems. Features of modern file systems include the following:

- *Faster allocation of free blocks.* Extents (as described previously) and B+ trees are used individually or together to find and allocate several free blocks quickly, either by size or location.
- *Large (or very large) numbers of files in a directory.* A directory is a special file that contains a list of files. If a directory needs to contain thousands or tens of thousands of files, something better than a linked list of (name, inode) pairs is needed. Again, advanced file systems use B+ trees to store directory entries. In some cases, a single B+ tree is used for the entire system.
- *Large files.* The old technique of storing direct, indirect, double-indirect, and even triple-indirect pointers to blocks does not scale well. For very large files, the number of disk accesses needed to retrieve a block in the data file would be prohibitively expensive.

More advanced file systems also manage sparse files, internal fragmentation, and the allocation of inodes better than Ext2.

A Wealth of Options

Although advanced file systems are tailored primarily for the high throughput and high uptime requirements of servers (from single-processor systems to clusters), these file systems can also benefit client machines where performance and reliability are wanted or needed.

Recent releases of Linux include not one, but four journaling file systems. JFS from IBM, XFS from SGI, and ReiserFS from Namesys have all been "open sourced" and subsequently included in the Linux kernel. In addition, Ext3 was developed as a journaling add-on to Ext2.

Figure 11-2 shows where file systems fit into Linux. Note that JFS, XFS, ReiserFS, and Ext3 are independent "peers." It is possible for a single Linux machine to use all these types of file systems at the same time. A system administrator can configure a system to use JFS on one partition and ReiserFS on another.

The following output from the `mount` command shows a system with all four of the journaling systems:

```
# mount

/dev/hdb6 on / type reiserfs (rw)
proc on /proc type proc (rw)
devpts on /dev/pts type devpts (rw,mode=0620,gid=5)
shmfs on /dev/shm type shm (rw)
usbdevfs on /proc/bus/usb type usbdevfs (rw)
/dev/hda1 on /xfs type xfs (rw)
/dev/hdb1 on /jfs type jfs (rw)
/dev/hda4 on /ext3 type ext3 (rw)
/dev/hda2 on /ext2 type ext2 (rw)
/dev/hda3 on /reiserfs type reiserfs (rw)
```

The `df` command shows all these file systems and their available space:

```
# df -k

Filesystem      1K-blocks      Used   Available  Use%   Mounted on
/dev/hdb6        4441800    1770448     2671352   40%    /
shmfs             192736          0      192736    0%    /dev/shm
/dev/hda1         806448        144      806304    1%    /xfs
/dev/hdb1        3999504     659320     3340184   17%    /jfs
/dev/hda4        1739324      32828     1618140    2%    /ext3
/dev/hda2         798508         20      757924    1%    /ext2
/dev/hda3         811248      32840      778408    5%    /reiserfs
```

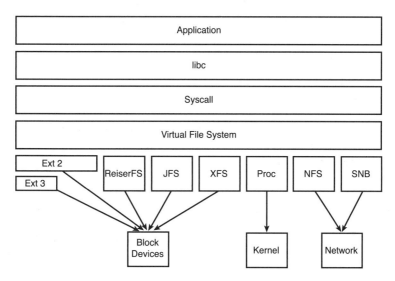

Figure 11-2 Where file systems fit in the operating system.

DISKS FACTOR INTO FILE SYSTEM PERFORMANCE

One of the factors that determine file system performance is the type and configuration of hard disks on your system. The information in this section can be used to determine the performance of the hard disks on your system and to help you choose new hard disks that meet your performance needs. Later in this chapter, the "hdparm" section discusses how to control the settings to specify Integrated Drive Electronics (IDE) hard drives.

Physical Disk Storage Considerations

The physical movement of data consumes a great amount of time relative to the processing of that data. Data movement components include the following:

- Finding data on the disk (that is, file system operations)
- Preparing to acquire the data (placing the read/write heads at the correct location on the disk and waiting for the data to appear under the heads)
- Getting the data from the disk to the disk controller
- Moving the data from the disk controller to memory
- Moving the data in memory until it resides in the location usable by an application

In this list, each operation is substantially faster than the previous one, due to the relative speeds of the technological components involved in delivering each. Because data access can require all the steps, the total elapsed time for the data movement is the sum of all of the preceding.

There are two ways to increase performance by tuning data access and movement:

1. Eliminate as many steps as possible.
2. Reduce the time required for each step.

As in all other performance tuning, changes implemented to improve data access speed can impact some other aspects of the system. In general, measure the performance before any change is made, implement each change separately, and measure the performance after the change.

Disk Anatomy

Despite the dramatic advances in the performance and price of microprocessors and memory, disks are still mechanical devices. As such, they are slow and complex. Because the physical characteristics of a disk drive impact many of the performance tuning considerations, it is important to be aware of some of the key areas involved with a disk drive.

Two significant features impact disk performance:

1. *Track-to-track seek speed.* This is a measurement of the time required for the disk heads to move from one track to the next.
2. *Rotational speed.* This is the time required to move any given sector on a track under the disk's head. The rotation rate tells how fast the disk spins under the drive head. Typical rates for mainstream desktop drives are between 4,000rpm and 5,400rpm. High-performance drives often offer 7,200rpm, and some offer 10,000rpm.

All other things being equal, the faster the rotation rate, the more data that moves under the head in a given amount of time, the more data the head reads, and the higher the sustained throughput will be. However, rotation rates don't compare as neatly as they might, because all other things are not usually equal. For example, a 5.25-inch disk platter has, on average, a larger circumference for its tracks than a 3.5-inch drive. That translates to more room for data on the tracks and more data passing under the head during each rotation.

Another variable is the density of data along the tracks. If a drive has a high-enough density, it can have more data passing under the head in a given amount of time—and therefore a faster sustained transfer rate—than another drive with a faster rotation rate but a lower density. As a rule of thumb, faster rotation translates into a faster sustained transfer rate, but the difference might not be as great as a simple comparison of the rotation rates implies.

Rotation rate also affects average access time, because one of the two components of access time—latency—is determined by the amount of time it takes the disk to rotate to the right location on a track under the drive head after the drive head has reached the right track. The faster the rotation rate, the lower the latency, and the faster the access time.

Transfer Rate

There are several kinds of transfer rates. They are not interchangeable.

- *Internal transfer rate* measures the speed at which data can move between the drive head and the drive platter. This is usually the limiting factor in transferring data to and from the drive.
- *Burst transfer rate* is the maximum speed of the interface. This is always faster than the internal transfer rate. The only time a drive transfers data at the burst rate is when it is moving data to and from the memory buffer in the drive.
- *Sustained transfer rate* measures the speed at which data can move between the drive and the computer for sustained periods of time.

The transfer rate that is seen most often is the burst transfer rate, because it is the most impressive number of the three. However, the number that matters the most is the sustained transfer rate, which essentially tells you how quickly large amounts of data can move to and from the drive. Most of the time, the drive has to read from or write to the disk platter itself, which means that the sustained transfer rate depends primarily on how quickly the drive can move data between the drive head and the disk.

Sometimes specifications give a minimum, maximum, and average sustained transfer rate. The difference comes from the fact that the outer tracks of a disk platter have more data, so more data passes under the drive head during a single rotation when reading from the outside tracks than when reading from the inside tracks. Maximum sustained transfer rate is the transfer rate for the outer tracks. The minimum is the transfer rate for the inner tracks. The average is the average over the entire disk. Other factors that affect transfer rate include the density of the data on the disk and the speed of rotation. The sustained transfer rate is equal to the internal transfer rate minus whatever overhead the drive needs for transfer operations.

hdparm

hdparm controls the settings of IDE hard drives, both in the kernel and for the drive itself. This section summarizes the various settings that are usually set to off by default, and what you can do to turn them on safely to increase the performance of your hard drive. Skip this section if you do not have IDE drives.

Read the hdparm man page, which provides detailed information on most of the options, before using hdparm.

To view information about a drive, issue `hdparm` without any options, as shown here on sample drive /dev/hdb:

```
# hdparm /dev/hdb
```

This command produces output like the following:

```
/dev/hdb:
 multcount     = 16 (on)
 IO_support    =  0 (default 16-bit)
 unmaskirq     =  0 (off)
 using_dma     =  1 (on)
 keepsettings  =  0 (off)
 readonly      =  0 (off)
 readahead     =  8 (on)
 geometry      = 1650/255/63, sectors = 26520480, start = 0
```

The following list provides a brief description of the fields:

- `multcount` is the number of sectors read at a time.
- `IO_support` indicates the operating mode of the hard disk (16/32/32sync).
- `using_dma` specifies whether the drive is using the DMA feature.
- `keepsettings` keeps the settings after a soft reset.
- `readonly` is normally set to 1 only for CD-ROMs; it tells the system whether the device is read-only.
- `readahead` shows how many sectors ahead will be read when the hard drive is accessed.

To display general information about the drive's actual capabilities, use the `-i` option:

```
# hdparm -i /dev/hdb
```

This command produces output like the following:

```
/dev/hdb:
 Model=IBM-DJNA-371350, FwRev=J76IA30K, SerialNo=GM0GMGY8991
 Config={ HardSect NotMFM HdSw>15uSec Fixed DTR>10Mbs }
 RawCHS=16383/16/63, TrkSize=0, SectSize=0, ECCbytes=34
 BuffType=DualPortCache, BuffSize=1966kB, MaxMultSect=16,
MultSect=16
 CurCHS=16383/16/63, CurSects=16514064, LBA=yes,
LBAsects=26520480
 IORDY=on/off, tPIO={min:240,w/IORDY:120}, tDMA={min:120,
rec:120}
 PIO modes:  pio0 pio1 pio2 pio3 pio4
```

```
DMA modes:   mdma0 mdma1 mdma2
UDMA modes: udma0 udma1 *udma2 udma3 udma4
AdvancedPM=no WriteCache=enabled
Drive conforms to: ATA/ATAPI-4 T13 1153D revision 17:1 2 3 4
```

One value that is worth examining is `MaxMultSect`. This field specifies the maximum number of sectors the hard disk can read at a time. The sample output shows that for drive /dev/hdb `MaxMultSect` is set to 16. Most IDE hard drives made in the past few years support 32-bit access. If your hard disk supports 32-bit access, you want this value to be 32.

The following command sets the `MaxMultSect` value to 32:

```
# hdparm -c 1 /dev/hdb
```

The number 1 turns `MaxMultSect` on; the number 0 turns `MaxMultSect` off. `MaxMultSect` is usually off by default. The default value is 16.

Test your hard drive's performance both before and after setting these various commands by typing the following:

```
# hdparm -T -t /dev/hdb
```

This command produces output like the following:

```
/dev/hdb:
Timing buffer-cache reads: 128MB in 0.97 seconds=131.96MB/sec

Timing buffered disk reads: 64MB in 3.80 seconds=16.84 MB/sec
```

The next field to look at is the drive's write caching. The command to turn on write caching is as follows:

```
# hdparm -W 1 /dev/hdb
```

The number 1 turns write caching on; the number 0 turns write caching off.

Another useful option to hdparm is `using_dma`. The command to turn dma on is the following:

```
# hdparm -d 1 /dev/hdb
```

This command produces output like the following:

```
/dev/hdb:
 setting using_dma to 1 (on)
 using_dma    =  1 (on)
```

The number 1 turns `using_dma` on; the number 0 turns `using_dma` off.

None of these settings is saved over a reboot. You have to add the appropriate commands to your /etc/rc.d/rc.sysinit file if you are using Red Hat to be sure they are run automatically on startup. If you are not running a Red Hat distribution, an easy way to find the file to change is to do a grep in the /etc directory, as shown in the following example:

```
# cd /etc
# grep -r hdparm . | more
```

After you find the configuration file that sets the options through hdparm, change that file to use the new parameters that were set with hdparm.

It is a good idea to run with the new settings for a while to ensure they are right for the system before they are permanently updated in a configuration file.

FRAGMENTING A FILE SYSTEM

Over time, the files on your file system can get broken into pieces so that they are not contiguous. This reduces file system performance when reading or writing data to the file. Defragmenting rearranges all the data on a volume so that files are written on consecutive sectors and tracks. This means that the disk heads have less moving to do in order to read from or write to a file. Thus, overall system throughput increases. To defragment a file system, see the sections describing each file system later in this chapter. Be aware that disk defragmentation can take quite a long time and it is the kind of operation that should be done when the system has a relatively small load running on it.

FILE SYNCHRONIZATION

By default, Linux systems read from and write to a buffer/page cache that is kept in memory. They avoid actually transferring data to disk until the buffer is full or until the application calls a sync function to flush the buffer/page cache. This strategy increases performance by avoiding the relatively slow mechanical process of writing to disk more often than necessary.

Input and output operations are of two types:

- *Asynchronous I/O*, which frees the application to perform other tasks while input is written or read
- *Synchronized I/O*, which performs the write or read operation and verifies its completion before returning

Synchronized I/O is useful when the integrity of data and files is critical to an application. Synchronized output assures that the data that is written to a device is actually stored there. Synchronized input assures that the data that is read from a device is a current image of data on that device.

Two levels of file synchronization are available:

- *Data integrity*

  Write operations: Data in the buffer is transferred to disk, along with file system information necessary to retrieve the data.

  Read operations: Any pending write operations relevant to the data being read complete with data integrity before the read operation is performed.

- *File integrity*

  Write operations: Data in the buffer and all file system information related to the operation are transferred to disk.

  Read operations: Any pending write operations relevant to the data being read complete with file integrity before the read operation is performed.

How to Assure Data or File Integrity

You can assure data integrity or file integrity at specific times by using function calls, or you can set file status flags to force automatic file synchronization for each `read` or `write` call associated with that file.

Note that using synchronized I/O can degrade system performance.

Using Function Calls

You can choose to write to buffer/page cache as usual and call functions explicitly when you want the program to flush the buffer to disk. For instance, you may want to use the buffer/page cache when a significant amount of I/O is occurring and call these functions when activity slows down. Two functions are available:

Function	Description
`fdatasync`	Flushes all data buffers, providing operation completion with data integrity.
`fsync`	Flushes all data and file control information from the buffers, providing operation completion with file integrity.

For a complete description of these functions, refer to the man pages for `fdatasync` and `fsync`.

Using File Descriptors

If you want to write data to disk in all cases automatically, you can set file status flags to force this behavior instead of making explicit calls to `fdatasync` or `fsync`.

To set this behavior, use these flags with the `open` function:

Flag	Description
O_DSYNC	Forces data synchronization for each write operation. For example: `fd = open("filea", O_RDWR|O_CREAT|O_DSYNC, 0666);`
O_SYNC	Forces file and data synchronization for each write operation. For example: `fd = open("filea", O_RDWR|O_CREAT|O_SYNC, 0666);`

Performance Implications of *sync/fsync*

Forced synchronization of the contents of real memory and disk takes place in several ways:

- An application program makes an `fsync()` call for a specified file. This causes all the pages that contain modified data for that file to be written to disk. The writing is complete when the `fsync()` call returns to the program.
- An application program makes a `sync()` call. This causes all the file pages in memory that contain modified data to be scheduled for writing to disk. The writing is *not necessarily* complete when the `sync()` call returns to the program.
- A user can enter the `sync` command, which in turn issues a `sync()` call. Again, some of the writes might not be complete when the user is prompted for input (or the next command in a shell script is processed).
- The sync daemon, bdflush, is called at regular intervals. This ensures that the system does not accumulate large amounts of data that exists only in volatile RAM.

BDFLUSH PARAMETERS

bdflush starts, flushes, or tunes the buffer-dirty-flush daemon. It is related to the operation of the kernel's virtual memory VM subsystem. bdflush can be tuned to improve file system performance. If you change some of the values from the default, as shown next, the system can be more responsive. The file /proc/sys/vm/bdflush controls the operation of the bdflush kernel daemon.

The default setup for the bdflush parameters under Red Hat and SUSE systems is

```
50 500   0    0    500   3000 60    20    0
```

To view the bdflush settings on a system, issue the following command:

```
# cat /proc/sys/vm/bdflush

50     500  0    0    500   3000  60    20    0
```

The first parameter (nfract), default 50, governs the maximum number of dirty buffers in the buffer cache. Setting this to a high value means that the kernel can delay writes for a longer time, but it also means that it needs to do so when memory becomes low. A low value spreads disk I/O more evenly.

The second parameter (ndirty), default 500, is the maximum number of dirty buffers that bdflush can write to the disk at one time. A high value means burst I/O, whereas a small value can lead to memory shortage when bdflush isn't started frequently.

The third and fourth parameters are not currently used.

The fifth parameter (interval), default 500, is the delay between kupdate flushes.

The sixth parameter (age_buffer), default 3000, is the time for a normal buffer to age before it is flushed.

The seventh parameter (nfract_sync), default 60, is the percentage of buffer cache that is dirty to activate bdflush synchronously.

The eighth parameter (nfract_stop_bdflush), default 20, is the percentage of buffer cache that is dirty to stop bdflush.

The ninth parameter is not currently used.

In the following example, nfract is increased from 50 to 100, and ndirty is increased from 500 to 1200:

```
# echo "100 1200 0 0 500 3000 60 20 0">/proc/sys/vm/bdflush
```

ASYNCHRONOUS INPUT AND OUTPUT

I/O operations on a file can be either synchronous or asynchronous. For synchronous I/O operations, the process calling the I/O request is blocked until the I/O operation is complete and regains control of execution only when the request is completely satisfied or fails. For asynchronous I/O operations, the process calling the I/O request immediately regains control of execution after the I/O operation is queued to the device. When the I/O operation is completed (either successfully or unsuccessfully), the calling process can be notified of the event by a signal passed through the io control block structure for the asynchronous I/O function. Alternatively, the calling process can poll the io control block structure for completion status.

Asynchronous I/O permits efficient overlap of CPU and I/O processing, which can dramatically increase the performance of demanding applications.

Using Asynchronous I/O

Asynchronous I/O is most commonly used in real-time applications requiring high-speed or high-volume data collection or low-priority journaling functions. Compute-intensive processes can use asynchronous I/O instead of blocking. For example, an application can collect intermittent data from multiple channels. Because the data arrives asynchronously—that is, when it is available rather than according to a set schedule—the receiving process must queue up the request to read data from one channel and immediately be free to receive the next data transmission from another channel. Another application might require such a high volume of reads, writes, and computations that it becomes practical to queue up a list of I/O operation requests and continue processing while the I/O requests are being serviced. Applications can perform multiple I/O operations to multiple devices while making a minimum number of function calls.

You can perform asynchronous I/O operations using any open file descriptor.

Asynchronous I/O Functions

The asynchronous I/O functions combine a number of tasks normally performed by the user during synchronous I/O operations. With synchronous I/O, the application typically calls the `lseek` function, performs the I/O operation, and then waits to receive the return status.

Asynchronous I/O functions provide the following capabilities:

- Both regular and special files can handle I/O requests.
- One file descriptor can handle multiple read and write operations.
- Multiple read and write operations can be issued to multiple open file descriptors.
- Both sequential and random access devices can handle I/O requests.
- Outstanding I/O requests can be canceled.
- The process can be suspended to wait for I/O completion.
- I/O requests can be tracked when the request is queued, in progress, and completed.

The following functions perform and manage asynchronous I/O operations:

Function	Description
aio_cancel	Cancels one or more requests pending against a file descriptor.
aio_error	Returns the error status of a specified operation.
aio_fsync	Asynchronously writes system buffers containing a file's modified data to permanent storage.
aio_read	Initiates a read request on the specified file descriptor.
aio_return	Returns the status of a completed operation.

`aio_suspend`	Suspends the calling process until at least one of the specified requests has completed.
`aio_write`	Initiates a write request to the specified file descriptor.
`lio_listio`	Initiates a list of requests.

RAW DISK I/O

Raw disk I/O is a process that interacts with a disk directly. File I/O, on the other hand, is where a process interacts with a physical device through an intermediary kernel cache. The `read()` and `write()` file I/O require the data to be copied to and from user space through kernel buffered regions. Data might exist in two memory locations simultaneously.

Some applications, such as databases, implement their own journaling. Applications that implement their own journaling can avoid duplicate logging (of their own database logs and the journaling file system logs) by performing I/O directly to the raw logical volume and bypassing the file system.

Raw disk I/O is unbuffered, and the data is not cached in a kernel buffer. One area where raw I/O is used to increase performance is in a relational database, such as IBM DB2 and Oracle. The performance can be increased in unbuffered raw I/O because these relational databases have their own I/O buffer for caching.

Setting up Raw I/O on Linux

Before setting up raw I/O on Linux, you need the following:

- One or more free IDE or SCSI disk partitions.
- A raw device controller named /dev/rawctl or /dev/raw. If you do not have such a raw device controller, create a symbolic link with the following command:

```
# ln -s /dev/your_raw_dev_ctrl/ .dev/rawctl
```

Linux has a pool of raw device nodes that must be bound to a block device before raw I/O can be performed on it. There is raw device controller that acts as the central repository of raw I/O to block device binding information. Binding is performed with a utility named raw.

Example

The following example configures raw I/O on Linux. The example uses raw partition /dev/sda5, which contains no valuable data:

1. Calculate the number of 4096-byte pages in the partition, rounding down if necessary. For example:

```
# fdisk /dev/sda

Command (m for help): p

    Device boot    Start    End    Blocks    Id    System
    /dev/sd1a      1        523    4200997   83    Linux
    /dev/sda5      524      1106   4682947   83    Linux

Disk /dev/sda: 255 heads, 63 sectors, 1106 cylinders
Units = cylinders of 16065 * 512 bytes
Command (m for help): q
#
Table 1. Linux raw I/O calculations.
        The number of pages in /dev/sda5 is
        num_pages = (((1106-524+1)*16065*512)/4096)
        num_pages = 11170736
```

2. Bind an unused raw device node to this partition. This step needs to be done every time the machine is rebooted, and it requires root access. Use `raw -a` to see which raw device nodes are already in use:

```
# raw /dev/raw/raw1 /dev/sda5

/dev/raw/raw1: bound to major 8, minor 5
```

3. Set the appropriate read permissions on the raw device controller and the disk partition. Set the appropriate read and write permissions on the raw device. The raw device is now ready to be used.

Ext2 and Ext3

As mentioned previously, Ext2 was the de facto file system for Linux. Although Ext2 lacks some of the advanced features, such as extremely large files and extent mapped files of XFS, JFS, and others, it is a reliable, stable, and still available out-of-the-box file system for all Linux distributions. The real weakness of Ext2 is fsck: the bigger the Ext2 file system, the longer it takes fsck to run. Longer fsck times translate into longer down times.

Ext2 Organization

Ext2 is divided into a number of *block groups*. Each block group holds a copy of the super block, inode, and data blocks, as shown in Figure 11-3. The block groups keep the data blocks close to the file inodes and the file inodes close to the directory inodes.

Block groups thus minimize positioning time, which reduces access time to the data. Each group contains the super block and information about the other block groups, enabling the file system to have a better chance to be covered if a block group is damaged.

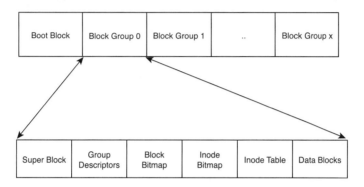

Figure 11-3   Structure of the Ext2 file system.

The inode for Ext2 is 128 bytes in size. Figure 11-4 shows the layout of the Ext2 inode structure.

File Mode	Owner (UID)	File Size	
Access Time		Creation Time	
Modification Time		Deletion Time	
Group ID (GID)	Link Count	Blocks Count	
File Flags		Reserved	
Direct Blocks		....	
Indirect Block		Indirect Block	
Indirect Block		File Version (for NFS)	
File ACL		Directory ACL	
Fragment Address		Fragment Number	Fragment Size
Reserved		Reserved	

Figure 11-4   Ext2 inode structure.

Ext2 directories are tracked with a singly linked list. Each entry in the directory has the fields that are shown in Figure 11-5.

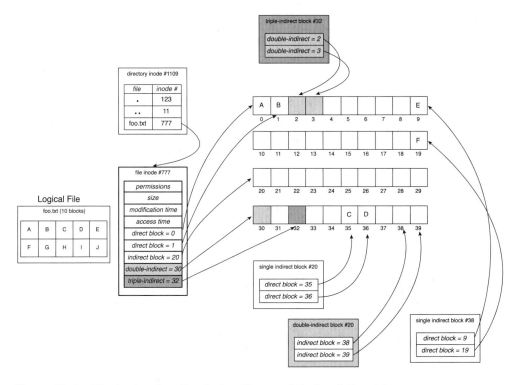

Figure 11-5   Ext2 directory structure.

Figure 11-6 illustrates blocks, inodes (with a number of metadata attributes), directories, and their relationships.

Figure 11-6   Blocks, inodes, directories, files, and their relationships.

Block Allocation in the Ext2 File System

When sequentially writing to a file, Ext2 preallocates space in units of eight contiguous blocks. Unused preallocation blocks are released when the file is closed, so space isn't wasted. This method prevents or reduces fragmentation, a condition under which many of the blocks in the file are spread throughout the disk because contiguous blocks aren't available. Contiguous blocks increase performance because when files are read sequentially there is minimal disk head movement.

Fragmentation of files—that is, the scattering of files into blocks that are not contiguous—is a problem that all file systems encounter. Fragmentation is caused when files are created and deleted. The fragmentation problem can be solved by having the file system use advanced algorithms to reduce fragmentation. The problem can also be solved by using the defrag file system utility, which moves the fragmented files so that they have contiguous blocks assigned to them. A defragmentation tool available for Ext2 is called defrag.ext2.

Creating an Ext2 File System

The program that creates Ext2 and (Ext3) file systems is called mke2fs. Two additional commands can be used to create an Ext2/Ext3 file system: `mkfs.ext2` and `mkfs -t ext2`. The rest of this section looks at some of the key options that are available with the `mkfs` command:

- The -b *block-size* option specifies the block size in bytes. Valid block size values are 1024, 2048, and 4096 bytes per block.
- The -N *number-of-inodes* option specifies the number of inodes.
- The -T *fs-type* option specifies how the file system will be used. The valid options are as follows:

  `news` creates one inode per 4KB block.
  `largefile` creates one inode per megabyte.
  `largefile4` creates one inode per 4 megabytes.

For a complete listing of the options to mkfs.ext2, see the mkfs.ext2 man page.

The following example uses the default when issuing `mkfs` on the device /dev/hdb2. The block size defaults to 4096, and the number of inodes created is 502944.

```
# mkfs.ext2 /dev/hdb2

mke2fs 1.32 (09-Nov-2002)
Filesystem label=
OS type: Linux
Block size=4096 (log=2)
Fragment size=4096 (log=2)
502944 inodes, 1004062 blocks
...
```

Next, set the block size to 1024 with the -b 1024 option, and set the file system type with the -T news option. The number of inodes created is 1005568.

```
# mkfs -t ext2 -b 1024 -T news /dev/hdb2

mke2fs 1.32 (09-Nov-2002)
Filesystem label=
OS type: Linux
Block size=1024 (log=0)
Fragment size=1024 (log=0)
1005568 inodes, 4016250 blocks
...
```

Ext3 Extensions for the Ext2 File System

The Ext3 file system provides higher availability without impacting the robustness (at least, the simplicity and reliability) of Ext2. Ext3 is a minimal extension to Ext2 to add support for journaling. Ext3 uses the same disk layout and data structures as Ext2, and it is forward- and backward-compatible with Ext2. Migrating from Ext2 to Ext3 (and vice versa) is quite easy; it can even be done in-place in the same partition. The other three journaling file systems require the partition to be formatted with their mkfs utility.

If you want to adopt a journaling file system but don't have free partitions on your system, Ext3 could be the journaling file system to use.

Kernel Configuration Support for Ext3

You can select Ext3 options from the File Systems section of the configuration menu and enable the following option:

```
Ext3 journaling file system support (CONFIG_EXT3_FS=y,m,n)
```

Click y next to the Ext3 entry if you want to build Ext3 into the kernel. Click m next to the Ext3 entry if you want to build Ext3 as a module. The n option is used if support for Ext3 is not needed.

Other options are available in the Ext3 selection for Ext3 configuration. If you need any of these options, select them here.

Working with Ext3

There are three ways to tune an Ext3 file system:

1. When the file system is created, which is the most efficient way
2. Through the tuning utility tune2fs, which can be used to tune the file system after it has been created
3. Through options that can be used when the file system is mounted

All three of these tuning options are discussed in the next sections.

Creating an Ext3 Partition

The program that creates Ext3 file systems is called mke2fs. You can also use the mkfs.ext3 and mkfs -t ext3 commands to create an Ext3 file system. The rest of this section looks at some of the key options that are available with the mkfs command:

- The -b *block-size* option specifies the block size in bytes. Valid block size values are 1024, 2048, and 4096 bytes per block.
- The -N *number-of-inodes* option specifies the number of inodes.
- The -T *fs-type* option specifies how the file system will be used. The valid options are as follows:

    news creates one inode per 4KB block.
    largefile creates one inode per megabyte.
    largefile4 creates one inode per 4 megabytes.

For a complete listing of the options to mkfs.ext3, see the mkfs.ext3 man page.

The following example uses the default when issuing mkfs on the device /dev/sdb1. The block size is 1024, and the number of inodes created is 128016.

```
# mkfs.ext3 /dev/sdb1

mke2fs 1.28 (31-Aug-2002)
Filesystem label=
OS type: Linux
Block size=1024 (log=0)
Fragment size=1024 (log=0)
128016 inodes, 511984 blocks
...
```

After the Ext3 file system is formatted, it is good practice to eliminate the automatic checking of the file system (the file system is automatically checked every 23 mounts or 180 days, whichever comes first). To eliminate the automatic checking, use the tune2fs command with the -c option to set checking to 0.

```
# tune2fs -c 0 /dev/sdb1

tune2fs 1.28(31-Aug-2002)
Setting maximal mount count to -1
```

Converting an Ext2 File System to Ext3

This section explains how to convert an Ext2 file system to Ext3:

1. Make a backup of the file system.
2. Add a journal file to the existing Ext2 file system you want to convert by running the tune2fs program with the -j option. You can run tune2fs on a mounted or unmounted Ext2 file system. For example, if /dev/hdb3 is an Ext2 file system, the following command creates the log:

```
# tune2fs -j /dev/hdb3
```

   If the file system is mounted, a journal file named .journal is placed in the root directory of the file system. If the file system is not mounted, the journal file is hidden. (When you mount an Ext3 file system, the .journal file appears. The .journal file can indicate that the file system is indeed of type Ext3.)

3. Change the entry for /dev/hdb3 in the /etc/fstab file from ext2 to ext3.
4. Reboot and verify that the /dev/hdb3 partition has type Ext3 by typing **mount** and examining the output. The output should include an entry like the following:

```
# mount

/dev/hdb3 on /test type ext3 (rw)
```

Using a Separate Journal Device on an Ext3 File System

The first thing you need to do to use an external journal for an Ext3 file system is to issue the mkfs command on the journal device. The block size of the external journal must be the same block size as the Ext3 file system. In the following example, the /dev/hda1 device is used as the external log for the Ext3 file system:

```
# mkfs.ext3 -b 4096 -O journal_dev /dev/hda1

# mkfs.ext3 -b 4096 -J device=/dev/hda1 /dev/hdb1
```

Ext2/Ext3 Utilities

The e2fsprogs package contains various utilities for use with Ext2 and Ext3 file systems. The following is a short description of each utility:

- *badblocks.* Searches for bad blocks on a device.
- *chattr.* Changes the file attributes on an Ext2 or Ext3 file system.
- *compile_et.* Converts a table, listing error-code names and associated messages into a C-source file that is suitable for use with the com_err library.

- *debugfs*. A file system debugger for examining and changing the state of an Ext2 file system.
- *dumpe2fs*. Prints the super block and blocks group information for the file system present on a specified device.
- *e2fsck* and *fsck.ext2*. Checks, and optionally repairs, an Ext2 file system.
- *e2image*. Saves critical Ext2 file system data to a file.
- *e2label*. Displays or changes the file system label on the Ext2 file system.
- *fsck.ext3*. Checks, and optionally repairs, an Ext3 file system.
- *lsattr*. Lists the file attributes on an Ext2 file system.
- *mk_cmds*. Takes a command table file as input and produces a C-source file as output, which is intended for use with the subsystem library, libss.
- *mke2fs*. Creates an Ext2 file system. mkfs.ext2 is the same as mke2fs.
- *mkfs.ext3*. Creates an Ext3 file system.
- *mklost+found*. Creates a lost+found directory in the current working directory on an Ext2 file system. mklost+found preallocates disk blocks to the directory to make it usable by e2fsck.
- *resize2fs*. Resizes Ext2 file systems.
- *tune2fs*. Adjusts tunable file system parameters on an Ext2 file system.
- *uuidgen*. Creates a new universally unique identifier (UUID) using the libuuid library.

For more information, see the man page for each utility.

ReiserFS

The ReiserFS open source journaling file system is available in most Linux distributions and supports metadata journaling. ReiserFS was merged into the 2.4.1 release of the kernel.org source tree. ReiserFS provides the following unique features that help differentiate it from the other journaling file systems:

- Stores all file system objects in a single b* balanced tree. The tree supports the following:
  - Compact, indexed directories
  - Dynamic inode allocation
  - Resizable items
  - 60-bit offsets

The tree contains the following four basic components: stat data, directory components, direct components, and indirect components. You can find components by
searching for a key (where the key has an ID), the offset in the object that is being
searched, and the item type.

Directories can increase and decrease as their contents change. A hash of the filename is used to keep an entry's offset in the directory permanent.

For files, indirect components point to data blocks, and direct components contain
packed file data.

All the components can be resized by rebalancing the tree.

- Supports *small* files—lots and lots of small files. The Reiser philosophy is simple:
  Small files encourage coding simplicity. Rather than use a database or create a file-
  caching scheme, use the file system to handle lots of small pieces of information.
  ReiserFS can be about eight times faster than Ext2 at handling files smaller than 1K.

- Stores about 6% more data than Ext2 on the same physical file system (when properly configured). Rather than allocate space in fixed 4K blocks, ReiserFS can allocate
  the exact space that's needed. A b* tree manages all file system metadata and stores
  and compresses *tails*, portions of files smaller than a block.

Tail packaging does cause a slight performance penalty when it forces ReiserFS to
rearrange the data as files are reduced or grow in size. This is one reason that this feature
can be tuned by turning off the *notail* mount option.

Kernel Configuration Support for ReiserFS

You can select ReiserFS options from the File Systems section of the configuration menu
and enable the following option:

```
Reiserfs support (CONFIG_REISERFS_FS=y,m,n)
```

Click y next to the Reiserfs entry if you want to build ReiserFS into the kernel. Click m
next to the Reiserfs entry if you want to build ReiserFS as a module.

Other options are available in the ReiserFS selection for ReiserFS configuration. If
you need any of these options, select them here.

Working with ReiserFS

There are three ways to tune a ReiserFS file system:

1. When the file system is created, which is the most efficient way
2. Through the tuning utility reiserfstune, which can be used to tune the file system
   after the file system has been created
3. Through options that can be used when the file system is mounted

All three of these tuning options are discussed in the following sections.

Creating a ReiserFS File System

ReiserFS uses the mkreiserfs utility to create a ReiserFS file system. The performance tuning options are as follows:

```
-h | --hash HASH
```

HASH specifies the name of the hash function that filenames in directories will be sorted with. (See the mount option section of the ReiserFS man page for a more complete description of each hash option.)

Choose one of the following:

- r5 (default)
- rupasov
- tea

See the subsection on the mount options for a description of these alternatives.

```
-j | --journal-device FILE
```

FILE specifies the name of the block device where the file system places the journal.

```
-o | journal-offset N
```

N specifies the offset where the journal starts when the journal is on a separate block device. The default is 0.

```
-s | journal-size N
```

N specifies the journal in blocks. When it is on a separate block device, the default size is the number of blocks on that device. When the journal is not on a separate block device, the default is 8193 and the maximum is 32749. The minimum is 513 blocks for both cases.

```
-t | --transaction-max-size N
```

N is the maximum transaction size for the journal. The default and maximum is 1024 blocks.

For a complete description of the mkreiserfs options, see the mkreiserfs man page.

To create the ReiserFS file system with the log inside the ReiserFS partition, issue the following command:

```
# mkreiserfs /dev/sdb1
```

After the file system has been created, mount it using the mount command. Determine the mount point and create a new, empty directory, such as /reiserfs, to mount the file system. The following example mounts the new file system:

```
# mount -t reiserfs /dev/sdb1 /reiserfs
```

To unmount the ReiserFS file system, use the umount command with the same mount point as the argument:

```
# umount /reiserfs
```

Increasing Speed with an External Log

An external log improves performance because the log updates are saved to a different partition than the log for the corresponding file system. This reduces the number of hard disk seeks.

To create the ReiserFS file system with the log on an external device, your system needs to have two unused partitions. In the following example, /dev/hda1 and /dev/hdb1 are spare partitions. The /dev/hda1 partition is used for the external log.

```
# mkreiserfs  -j /dev/hda1 /dev/hdb1
```

Mounting the File System

To mount the file system, use the following mount command:

```
# mount -t reiserfs /dev/hdb1 /reiserfs
```

To avoid having to mount the file system every time the system boots, add the file system to the /etc/fstab file. Make a backup of /etc/fstab and edit it with your favorite editor to add the /dev/hdb1 device. For example:

```
/dev/hdb1 /reiserfs reiserfs defaults 1 2
```

Mount Options

Three mount options can change the performance of the ReiserFS file system:

1. The hash option lets you select which hash algorithm will be used to locate and write files within directories:

   ```
   hash=rupasov|tea|r5|detect
   ```

   This specifies the hashing algorithm used to locate and write files within directories. The different hashing algorithms provided by the file system are rupasov, tea, r5, and detect.

- The `rupasov` hashing algorithm is a fast hashing method that places and pre serves locality, mapping lexicographically close filenames to the close hash values.

- The `tea` hashing algorithm is a Davis-Meyer function that creates keys by thor oughly permuting bits in the name. It gets high randomness and, therefore, low probability of hash collision, but this entails performance costs. This hashing is a good selection for large directories causing EHASHCOLLISION with `r5` hash. For example:

```
mount -t reiserfs -o hash=tea /dev/sdb2 /mnt/reiserfs
```

- The `r5` hashing algorithm is a modified version of the `rupasov` hash with a reduced probability of hashing collisions. This is the default hashing algorithm.

- The `detect` option instructs `mount` to detect the hash function in use by the instance of the file system being mounted. It writes this information into the super block. This option is useful only on the first mount of an old file system.

2. The `nolog` option disables journaling. It also provides a slight performance improvement in some situations at the cost of forcing fsck if the file system is not cleanly shut down. This is a good option to use when restoring a file system from backup. For example:

```
mount -t reiserfs -o nolog /dev/sdb2 /mnt/reiserfs
```

3. The `notail` option disables the packing of files into the tree. By default, ReiserFS stores small files and "file tails" directly into the tree. For example:

```
mount -t reiserfs -o notail /dev/sdb2 /mnt/reiserfs
```

It is possible to combine mount options by separating them with a comma. The fol lowing example uses two mount options (`noatime`, `notail`) that increase file sys tem performance:

```
# mount -t reiserfs -o noatime,notail /dev/sdc1 /fs1
```

Linux records an atime, or access time, whenever a file is read. However, this infor mation is not very useful and can be costly to track. To get a quick performance boost, simply disable access time updates with the mount option `noatime`.

Tuning ReiserFS

reiserfstune tunes the ReiserFS file system. reiserfstune changes the journal size and maximum transaction size. The journal's location can also be changed:

```
-j | --journal-device FILE
```

FILE specifies the name of the block device where the file system places the journal.

```
-o | journal-offset N
```

N specifies the offset where the journal starts when it is on a separate block device. The default is 0.

```
--no-journal-available
```

This allows the file system to continue when the current journal's block device is no longer available by having a disk that has gone bad.

```
--journal-new-device FILE
```

FILE is the name of the block device that will contain the new journal for the file system.

```
-s | journal-size N
```

N specifies the journal in blocks. When the journal is on a separate block device, the default size is the number of blocks on that device. When the journal is not on a separate block device, the default is 8193 and the maximum is 32749. The minimum is 513 blocks for both cases.

```
-t | --transaction-max-size N
```

N is the journal's maximum transaction size. The default and maximum is 1024 blocks.
  See the reiserfstune man page for information about all the options for this utility.

ReiserFS Utilities

The following ReiserFS utilities are located in the reiserfsprogs package:

- *mkreiserfs*. Creates a ReiserFS file system.
- *reiserfsck*. Checks a ReiserFS file system.
- *resize_reiserfs*. Resizes a ReiserFS file system.
- *debugreiserfs*. Debugs a ReiserFS file system.

For more information, see the man page for each of the ReiserFS utilities.

JOURNALED FILE SYSTEM (JFS)

Journaled File System (JFS) for Linux is based on the IBM JFS file system for OS/2 Warp. JFS was donated to open source in early 2000 and was ported to Linux soon after. JFS is well suited to enterprise environments. It uses many advanced techniques to boost performance, provide for very large file systems, and journal changes to the file system. Some of the features of JFS include the following:

- *Extent-based addressing structures*. JFS uses extent-based addressing structures, along with aggressive block-allocation policies to produce compact, efficient, and scalable structures for mapping logical offsets within files to physical addresses on disk. This feature yields excellent performance.

- *Dynamic inode allocation*. JFS dynamically allocates space for disk inodes as required, freeing the space when it is no longer required. This is a radical improvement over Ext2, which reserves a fixed amount of space for disk inodes at file system creation time. With dynamic inode allocation, users do not have to estimate the maximum number of files and directories that a file system will contain. Additionally, this feature decouples disk inodes from fixed-disk locations.

- *Directory organization*. Two different directory organizations are provided: one is used for small directories and the other for large directories. The contents of a small directory (up to eight entries, excluding the self (. or "dot") and parent (.. or "dot dot") entries) are stored in the directory's inode. This eliminates the need for separate directory block I/O and the need to allocate separate storage. The contents of larger directories are organized in a B+ tree keyed on name. B+ trees provide faster directory lookup, insertion, and deletion capabilities when compared to traditional unsorted directory organizations.

- *Online resizing*. This feature allows the file system to grow while it is mounted. This feature is used with a volume manager.

- *Online snapshot*. This option provides an online backup mechanism by creating a point-in-time image of the file system. It helps eliminate the need for the system to be offline to obtain a consistent backup. This feature is used with a volume manager.

- *"No integrity" mount option*. This feature of JFS disables the option to journal file system metadata changes. It can be used by a restore program to decrease the restore time.

- *64 bits*. JFS is a full 64-bit file system. All the appropriate file system structure fields are 64 bits in size. This allows JFS to support large files and partitions.

JFS has other advanced features, such as allocation groups (which speed file access times by maximizing locality) and various block sizes ranging from 512 bytes to 4096 bytes (which can be tuned to avoid internal and external fragmentation). Note that at this time 4K is the only block size currently supported.

Kernel Configuration Support for JFS

JFS was merged into the 2.4.20 release of the kernel.org source tree.

You can set JFS options from the File Systems section of the configuration menu and enable the following option:

```
JFS filesystem support (CONFIG_JFS_FS=y,m,n)
```

Click y next to the JFS entry if you want to build JFS into the kernel. Click m beside the JFS entry if you would like to build JFS as a module.

Other options are available in the JFS section for JFS configuration.

Working with JFS

There are two ways to tune a JFS file system:

1. When the file system is created, which is the most efficient way
2. Through the tuning utility jfs_tune, which can be used to tune the file system after it has been created

These tuning options are discussed in the following sections.

Creating a JFS File System

The program that creates a JFS file system is called jfs_mkfs. This program can also be invoked by using the name mkfs.jfs. For a list of all the options of the mkfs utility, see the mkfs.jfs man page.

The next example shows how to create a JFS file system using a spare partition (/dev/hdb1). (If there is unpartitioned space on your disk, you can create a partition using fdisk. After you create the partition, reboot the system to make sure that the new partition is available to create a JFS file system on it.)

To create the JFS file system with the log inside the JFS partition, issue the following command:

```
# mkfs.jfs /dev/hdb1
```

After the file system has been created, mount it by using the mount command. Determine the mount point and create a new empty directory, such as /jfs, to mount the file system with the following command:

```
# mount -t jfs /dev/hdb1 /jfs
```

After the file system is mounted, you can try out JFS.

To unmount the JFS file system, use the `umount` command with the same mount point as the argument:

```
# umount /jfs
```

Increasing Speed with an External Log for JFS

An external log improves performance because the log updates are saved to a different partition than their corresponding file system.

To create a JFS file system with the log on an external device, the system needs to have two unused partitions. In the following example, /dev/hda1 and /dev/hdb1 are spare partitions. /dev/hda1 is used as the external log.

```
# mkfs.jfs -j /dev/hda1 /dev/hdb1
```

Mounting the File System

To mount the file system, use the following `mount` command:

```
# mount -t jfs /dev/hdb1 /jfs
```

To avoid having to mount the file system every time you boot, you can add it to the /etc/fstab file. First, make a backup of /etc/fstab and then edit the file and add the /dev/hdb1 device. For example, add

```
/dev/hdb1 /jfs jfs defaults 1 2
```

Mount Options

By default, the JFS mount option `integrity` is set, which causes metadata changes to be committed to the journal. To change the performance of the JFS file system, use the `nointegrity` mount option. `nointegrity` causes the file system to not be written to the journal. The primary use of this option is to allow for higher performance when restoring a volume from backup media. However, the volume's integrity is not guaranteed if the system abnormally abends. Specify the `integrity` option to remount a volume where the `nointegrity` option was previously specified in order to restore normal behavior.

Linux records an atime, or access time, whenever a file is read. However, this information is not very useful, and it can be costly to track. To get a quick performance boost, simply disable access time updates with the mount option `noatime`.

Tuning JFS

A performance option that the jfs_tune utility provides is the capability to change the journal's location, which allows you to move the journal to an external device. Changing a journal's location involves the following steps:

1. Create a journal on an external device /dev/hda2:

   ```
   # mkfs.jfs -J journal_dev /dev/hda2
   ```

2. Attach the external journal to the file system, which is located on /dev/hdb1:

   ```
   # jfs_tune -J device=/dev/hda2 /dev/hdb1
   ```

JFS Utilities

The following JFS utilities are available in the jfsutils package:

- *jfs_fsck.* Initiates a replay of the JFS transaction log and checks and repairs a JFS formatted device.
- *jfs_mkfs.* Creates a JFS formatted partition.
- *jfs_logdump.* Dumps the journal log of a JFS formatted device.
- *jfs_tune.* Adjusts tunable file system parameters on JFS.
- *jfs_fscklog.* Extracts a JFS fsck service log into a file or format and displays the extracted file.
- *jfs_debugfs.* A shell-type JFS file system editor.

For more information, see the man pages for the JFS utilities.

NEXT-GENERATION FILE SYSTEM (XFS)

SGI has released a version of its high-end XFS file system for Linux. Based on the SGI Irix XFS file system technology, XFS supports metadata journaling and extremely large disk farms. A single XFS file system is designed to be 18,000 petabytes and a single *file* can be 9,000 petabytes.

In addition, XFS is designed to scale and have high performance. XFS uses many of the same techniques available in JFS.

XFS is a 64-bit file system. All the file system counters in the system are 64 bits in length, as are the addresses used for each disk block and the unique number assigned to each file inode number. Currently, Linux supports only 32-bit inode numbers, so this limits XFS to a 32-bit inode number. A single file system can in theory be as large as 18 million terabytes. Currently, Linux has a 2TB limit for the 2.4.x kernel and a 16TB limit for the 2.6.x kernel.

XFS partitions the file system into regions called allocation groups (AGs). Each AG manages its own free space and inodes, as shown in Figure 11-7. In addition, AGs provide scalability and parallelism for the file system. AGs range in size from 0.5GB to 4GB. Files and directories are not limited to a single AG.

Free space and inodes within each AG are managed so that multiple processes can allocate free space throughout the file system simultaneously, thus reducing the bottleneck that can occur on large, active file systems.

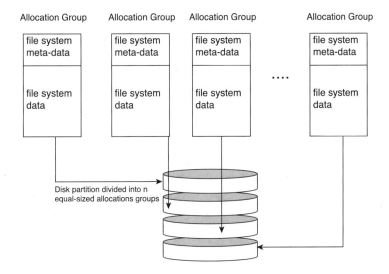

Figure 11-7   XFS file system allocation groups.

XFS was merged into the 2.4.25 release of the kernel.org source tree.

Kernel Configuration Support for XFS

You can set XFS options through the File Systems section of the configuration menu by enabling the following option:

```
XFS filesystem support (CONFIG_XFS_FS=y,m,n)
```

Click y next to the XFS entry if you want to build XFS into the kernel. Click m next to the XFS entry if you want to build XFS as a module.

Other options are available in the XFS section for XFS configuration. If you need any of these options, select them there.

Working with XFS File Systems

There are two ways to tune an XFS file system:

1. When the file system is created, which is the most efficient way
2. Through options that can be used when the file system is mounted

Both of these tuning options are discussed in the following sections.

Creating an XFS File System

The program that creates XFS file systems is called xfs_mkfs. This program can also be invoked by using the name mkfs.xfs. For a list of all the options of the mkfs utility, see the mkfs.xfs man page.

The next example shows how to create an XFS file system using a spare partition (/dev/hda1).

To create the XFS file system with the log inside the XFS partition, issue the following command:

```
# mkfs.xfs /dev/hda1
```

One option that can make a difference in the file system is the -i size=xxx option. The default inode size is 256 bytes. The inode size can be increased (up to 4KB). Doing so means that more directories keep their contents in the inode and need less disk I/O to read and write. However, inodes conversely need more I/O to read; because they are read and written in clusters, this is not a straightforward calculation. Because extents are also held in the inode if there is room, the number of files with out-of-inode metadata is reduced.

Another option that makes a difference in the file system's performance is the log size: -l size=xxx. A larger log means that when there is a large amount of metadata activity, more time elapses before modified metadata is flushed to the disk. However, a larger log also slows down recovery.

Finally, for very large file systems, keep the agcount as low as possible (specified with the -d agcount= option). An allocation group can be up to 4GB in size; more allocation groups means more of them to scan in low free-space conditions. The allocation group size also governs the maximum extent size you can have in a file.

After the file system has been created, mount it using the mount command. Determine a mount point and create a new empty directory, such as /xfs, to mount the file system:

```
# mount -t xfs /dev/hda1 /xfs
```

After the file system is mounted, you can try out XFS.

To unmount the XFS file system, use the `umount` command with the same mount point as the argument:

```
# umount /xfs
```

Full File System

An XFS file system performs allocations more slowly when the file system is very full—nearly 99%. Basically, XFS composes the file system into allocation groups (1 to 4 GB each), and free space is managed independently in each of these. The slowdown occurs when the system has to scan through a large number of allocation groups, looking for space to extend a file. An in-memory summary structure tells you if it is worth the effort to look in an allocation group, so a major slowdown does not usually occur, unless a significant number of parallel actions occur.

Increasing Speed with an External Log for XFS

An external log improves performance because the log updates are saved to a different partition than their corresponding file system.

To create an XFS file system with the log on an external device, your system needs to have two unused partitions. In the following example, /dev/hda1 and /dev/hdb1 are spare partitions. The /dev/hda1 partition is used as the external log.

```
# mkfs.xfs -l logdev=/dev/hda1 /dev/hdb1
```

Mounting the File System

To mount the file system, use the following `mount` command:

```
# mount -t xfs /dev/hdb1 /xfs
```

To avoid having to mount the file system every time the system boots, add the file system to the /etc/fstab file. Make a backup of /etc/fstab and edit it with your favorite editor to add the /dev/hdb1 device. For example:

```
/dev/hdb1 /xfs xfs defaults 1 2
```

Mount Options

At mount time, three XFS options are related to performance:

- `osyncisdsync`. Indicates that O_SYNC is treated as O_DSYNC, which is the behavior Ext2 gives you by default. Without this option, O_SYNC file I/O syncs more metadata for the file.

- `logbufsize=size`. Sets the number of log buffers that are held in memory. This means you can have more active transactions at once and can still perform metadata changes while the log is synced to disk. The flip side of this is that the number of metadata changes that might be lost due to a system crash is greater. Valid values are 2 through 8. The default value is eight buffers for file systems created with a 64KB block size, four buffers for file systems created with a 32KB block size, three buffers for file systems created with a 16KB block size, and two buffers for the other block sizes.
- `logbsize=size`. Sets the size of the log buffers held in memory.

Linux records an atime, or access time, whenever a file is read. However, this information is not very useful and can be costly to track. To get a quick performance boost, simply disable access time updates with the mount option `noatime`.

Tuning XFS

For a metadata-intensive workload, the default log size could be the limiting factor that reduces the file system's performance. Better results are achieved by creating file systems with a larger log size. The following `mkfs` command creates a log size of 32768b:

```
#  mkfs -t xfs -l size=32768b -f /dev/hdb1
```

Currently, to resize a log, you need to remake the file system.

Also, it is a good idea to mount metadata-intensive file systems with the following:

```
#  mount -t xfs -o logbufsize=8,logbsize=32768b /dev/device /mntpoint
```

XFS Utilities

The XFS utilities are available in two packages: xfsprogs and xfsdump. The xfsprogs package contains the following utilities:

- *xfs_growfs*. Expands an XFS file system.
- *xfs_admin*. Changes the parameters of an XFS file system.
- *xfs_freeze*. Suspends access to an XFS file system.
- *xfs_mkfile*. Creates an XFS file, padded with zeroes by default.
- *xfs_check*. Checks XFS file system consistency.
- *xfs_bmap*. Prints block mapping for an XFS file.
- *xfs_rtcp*. Copies a file to the real-time partition on an XFS file system.
- *xfs_repair*. Repairs corrupt or damaged XFS file systems.
- *xfs_db*. Used to debug an XFS file system.

- *xfs_logprint*. Prints the log of an XFS file system.
- *xfs_ncheck*. Generates path names from inode numbers for an XFS file system.
- *mkfs.xfs*. Constructs an XFS file system.

The xfsdump package contains the following utilities:

- *xfsdump*. Examines files in a file system, determines which ones need to be backed up, and copies those files to a specified disk, tape, or other storage medium. It uses XFS-specific directives to optimize the dump of an XFS file system. It also knows how to back up XFS extended attributes.
- *xfsrestore*. Performs the inverse function of xfsdump; it can restore a full backup of a file system. Subsequent incremental backups can then be layered on top of the full backup. Single files and directory subtrees may be restored from full or partial backups.
- *xfsdq*, *xfsrq*. XFS dump and restore quotas.
- *xfs_estimate*. Estimates the space that an XFS file system needs.
- *xfs_fsr*. Reorganizes file systems for XFS.
- *xfsinvutil*. Checks and prunes the xfsdump inventory database.

Following are descriptions of some of the key file system utilities:

- *xfs_db*. Reports overall fragmentation of the file system. The following example shows overall fragmentation of file system /dev/hda9:

```
# xfs_db -r /dev/hda9
xfs_db: frag
actual 408, ideal 408, fragmentation factor 0.00%

actual/ideal are number of extents, factor is like
(actual - ideal) / ideal
```

- *xfs_bmap*. Shows the number of extents in a file. The following example shows the number of extents in file vmlinuz:

```
# xfs_bmap vmlinuz

vmlinuz:
0: [0..2295]: 96..2391
```

SUMMARY

Although some people believe that journaling file systems provide only fast restart times, this chapter has shown that not to be the case. Journaling file systems are scalable, reliable, and fast. Whether you are running an enterprise server, a cluster supercomputer, or a small web site, Ext3, XFS, JFS, and ReiserFS add credibility and performance improvements to Linux.

One of the great things about open source is that choice is looked on favorably. Linux is the only operating system with four journaling file systems in production. All four file system types have the GPL license, and source code is available at `http://www.kernel.org` or on each project's home page. Each of the journaling file system teams follows a community model and welcomes users and contributors. In fact, the teams share their best ideas, and competitive benchmarking encourages constant improvement of all the systems.

Table 11-1 summarizes the features and limits of the four Linux journaling file systems. The first section provides some history of when the journaling file systems were accepted into the kernel.org source trees. The next section lists some of the features of the file systems.

For complete feature lists of each journaling file system, see the respective project web pages.

Table 11-1   A Comparison of Journaling File Systems

Kernel Support	Ext3	ReiserFS	XFS	JFS
In kernel.org source tree 2.4.x	2.4.15	2.4.1	2.4.25	2.4.20
In kernel.org source tree 2.6.x	2.5.0	2.5.0	2.5.36	2.5.6
License	GPL	GPL	GPL	GPL
Features				
Largest block size supported on IA32	4KB	4KB	4KB	4KB
File system size maximum	16384GB	17592GB	18,000Pb	4Pb
File size maximum	2048Gb	1Eb*	9,000Pb	4Pb
Growing the file system size	Patch	Yes	Yes	Yes

Kernel Support	Ext3	ReiserFS	XFS	JFS
Features				
Online snapshot	Yes	Yes	Yes	Yes
Access control lists	Yes	Yes	Yes	Yes
Extended attributes	Yes	Yes	Yes	Yes
Dynamic disk inode allocation	No	Yes	Yes	Yes
Data logging	Yes	Patch	No	No
Place log on an external device	Yes	Yes	Yes	Yes

Because the 2.4 kernel has a limit of 2 terabytes for a single block device, no file system larger than that can be created at this time. This restriction has been increased in the 2.6 kernel, and the limit has been raised to 16 terabytes.

REFERENCES

[1] Andrew Morton's web page has information about Ext3.
   `http://www.zipworld.com.au/~akpm/linux/ext3`.

[2] The e2fsprogs package contains the utilities for the Ext2/Ext3 file systems and the home page for e2fsprogs. `http://e2fsprogs.sourceforge.net/`.

[3] Card, R., T. Ts'o, and S. Tweedie. "Design and Implementation of the Second Extended Filesystem." `http://web.mit.edu/tytso/www/linux/ext2intro.html`.

[4] For a more in-depth discussion of ReiserFS design features and instructions on how to use and manage ReiserFS, see `http://www.namesys.com`.

[5] For a more in-depth discussion of the JFS design features and instructions on how to use and manage JFS on Linux, see `http://oss.software.ibm.com/jfs`.

[6] For a more in-depth discussion of the design features of XFS Linux and instructions on how to use and manage the XFS file system, see `http://oss.sgi.com/projects/xfs`.

CHAPTER TWELVE

Network Tuning

By Nivedita Singhvi

INTRODUCTION

The Linux kernel makes available a large set of kernel variables that can be tuned to configure the system for functionality and optimum performance. Additionally, the kernel makes a large amount of information about the system available to the user. Utilizing this information to ensure the system's health and detect problems in configuration and the network are critical performance tasks.

The predominant networking environment that applications run on is the TCP/IP (transport control protocol/Internet protocol) network protocol stack, with IP version 4 currently the standard. Linux is widely used as a platform to host network infrastructure services such as web servers, mail servers, and domain name system (DNS) servers, which makes networking performance an important consideration for system administrators.

Although this chapter covers the more important variables for network tuning, it is by no means exhaustive. Documentation available in the Documentation directory of the kernel source tree, as well as system man pages, can provide more information. The information provided here is applicable to the 2.4 through 2.6 Linux kernel versions unless otherwise noted.

Let's begin by examining the network protocol stack.

THE NETWORK PROTOCOL STACK

To understand the need for network tuning, it helps to have a picture of how the operating system takes data from the application and sends it to a remote host, and does the reverse—how it receives data from a remote host on the network and delivers it to a local application.

The parts of the operating system that handle networking operations are fairly modular in nature, with different layers handling clearly separated functions, implemented by various protocols. A collection of layers from the application interface down to the device interface is referred to as the *protocol stack*. The TCP/IP protocol family is the most widely used protocol suite. Together with the socket layer and the device driver, it makes up the typical network protocol stack.

The socket abstraction layer is the common kernel interface to the application. To open a communication channel with remote (or local) hosts, the application creates a socket, which contains, among other infrastructure, buffers used to hold the data that is read and written by the application.

The transport layer makes available two different protocols: TCP (transport control protocol) and UDP (user datagram protocol), which provide reliable, connection-oriented and unreliable, connectionless types of traffic, respectively. In the case of TCP sockets, the TCP protocol takes the data written to the socket by the application and ensures that the data is bundled into segments, sent reliably to the other end, retransmitting data that is lost, and maintaining control over the flow of data to minimize congestion on the network.

The transport layer then hands the segmented data to the IP layer, which implements typical network layer functions such as routing the data packets to the end point successfully. IP hands off the data packet to the network device driver, which ensures that the data is transferred to the hardware. Each layer encapsulates the data with its own headers containing protocol-specific information.

In the reverse direction, when a frame is received over the network, the network card generates an interrupt to the kernel, which then invokes an interrupt handler to transfer the packet from the card to kernel memory and schedules the packet to be processed by the network stack. The incoming packet is queued for delivery to the network layers in a device-specific queue. IP delivers a data packet for the application to the TCP layer, which places it in the correct socket read buffer if the packet is successfully validated at each stage.

KERNEL PARAMETER TUNING MECHANISMS

There are two primary interfaces to the kernel tunable variables: the `sysctl(8)` command-line utility and the /proc file system. For a description of how these mechanisms are used, please see Appendix A.

This chapter principally focuses on the kernel variables that are core networking variables and that are specific to TCP/IPv4. The `sysctl` parameters are in the sysctl.net.core and sysctl.net.ipv4 categories, and their associated /proc entries (following the same hierarchy) are in the /proc/sys/net/core and /proc/sys/net/ipv4 subdirectories.

The following discussion lists both the `sysctl` parameter name as well as its entry in the /proc file system. Some parameters are present in the kernel only if the kernel is compiled with certain features included. For example, if the kernel is not compiled with TCP syncookie support, the kernel parameter `tcp_syncookies` is not present.

Kernel parameters should always be tuned with care, because they usually impact the system as a whole, not just individual sockets or network connections.

KERNEL AUTO TUNING

The kernel initializes certain variables at boot up based on the resources (such as the amount of memory) in the system. Often, this initial adjustment is sufficient. Some variables are also dynamically tuned by the kernel, such as the size of the socket buffer in use. This alleviates the need for the users to track and adjust the kernel variables manually for optimum performance. However, in some cases this dynamic tuning is insufficient, and adequate or improved performance requires the manual tuning of kernel parameters.

CORE KERNEL PARAMETER DESCRIPTIONS

This section describes kernel socket buffers and covers some of the more useful core kernel parameters. Adjusting the size of the kernel socket buffers is perhaps the single most effective method for improving performance, and most of the core parameters described in this section manipulate them in some fashion.

An Introduction to Socket Buffers

Applications use the `socket()` system call to create a communication endpoint. Each socket has associated with it a read and write buffer (also known as the receive and send buffers, respectively).

The receive socket buffer holds the data that has been sent to this socket by a remote host. This data is retrieved by the application upon doing a `read()` system call (or a variant such as `recvfrom()`). If this buffer is full, any further incoming data received for this socket is dropped.

The write socket buffer holds the data written to the socket by the application before it is sent to the remote host. If there is insufficient room in the buffer, the application's `write()` system call (or a variant such as `sendto()`) blocks until the kernel makes room for all the data. If the application has chosen not to block, the kernel returns an error to the application indicating that it cannot absorb that quantity of data at this time, and to retry the write.

Default Socket Buffer Size

`net.core.wmem_default` (/proc/sys/net/core/wmem_default)
`net.core.rmem_default` (/proc/sys/net/core/rmem_default)
These two parameters are the global default size of the read and write socket buffers, respectively, associated with each socket. They are used to initialize the size of all types of sockets. In the case of TCP sockets, these values are later overwritten by the TCP protocol-specific defaults for the read and write buffer sizes (tcp_rmem and tcp_wmem, described in the forthcoming TCP/IPv4 protocol kernel parameters list).

Individual applications can adjust the size of the socket buffers by performing a `setsockopt()` call with a level of SOL_SOCKET and the options SO_SNDBUF and SO_RCVBUF for the send and receive buffers, respectively.

Systems experiencing heavy network loads benefit from increasing these variables. The kernel adjusts the initial value of these parameters at bootup based on the available memory in the system, as shown in Table 12-1.

Maximum Socket Buffer Size

`net.core.rmem_max` (/proc/sys/net/core/rmem_max)
`net.core.wmem_max` (/proc/sys/net/core/wmem_max)
These `sysctl` variables are the maximum size that the read and write socket buffers, respectively, can be set to. Their values are adjusted during system bootup to the values shown in Table 12-1 based on the memory available in the system.

All the values in Table 12-1 are in units of bytes.

Table 12-1   Core Socket Buffer Sizes

Memory	<= 4 KB	<= 128KB	> 128 KB
rmem_default	32KB	64 KB	64KB
wmem_default	32KB	64 KB	64KB
wmem_max	32KB	64 KB	128KB
rmem_max	32KB	64 KB	128KB

netdev_max_backlog

`net.core.netdev_max_backlog` (/proc/sys/net/core/netdev_max_backlog)
This parameter sets the maximum number of incoming packets that will be queued for delivery to the device queue. The default value is 300, which is typically too small for heavy network loads. Increasing this value permits a larger store of packets queued and

reduces the number of packets dropped. On long latency networks particularly, dropped packets result in a significant reduction in throughput.

somaxconn

`net.core.somaxconn` (/proc/sys/net/core/somaxconn)
This is the maximum accept queue backlog that can be specified via the `listen()` system call, or the number of pending connection requests. When the number of queued incoming connection requests reaches this value, further connection requests are dropped. Increasing this value allows a busy server to specify a larger backlog of requests. The default maximum is 128.

optmem_max

`optmem_max` (/proc/sys/net/core/optmem_max)
This variable is the maximum initialization size of socket buffers, expressed in bytes.

TCP/IPv4 PROTOCOL KERNEL PARAMETERS

This section covers some of the more useful IPv4 parameters. The IPv4 category includes the protocol-specific parameters. We pay particular attention here to the TCP protocol parameters. When a socket is created, the protocol and address families are specified. For a TCP socket, the address family is AF_INET and the type is SOCK_STREAM. For a UDP protocol socket, the address family is AF_INET but the type is SOCK_DGRAM. TCP socket buffer sizes are controlled by their own parameters rather than the core kernel buffer size parameters.

TCP Buffer and Memory Management

tcp_rmem

`net.ipv4.tcp_rmem` (/proc/sys/net/ipv4/tcp_rmem)
This variable is an array of three integers:

> net.ipv4.tcp_rmem[0] = minimum size of the read buffer
> net.ipv4.tcp_rmem[1] = default size of the read buffer
> net.ipv4.tcp_rmem[2] = maximum size of the read buffer

When a socket is created, the initial size of the read buffer, in bytes, is controlled by the core default socket sizes. If it is a TCP protocol socket, however (type = AF_INET SOCK_STREAM), the read buffer size is set to the TCP protocol-specific default, which is the second integer of this array. To increase the initial size of the TCP read buffer, this is the variable to increase. Note that the maximum value this can take is still limited by the core socket maximum size, so this value cannot be greater than `net.core.rmem_max`.

The minimum and maximum TCP read buffer size limits (the first and the third integers in the tcp_rmem array) are used by the kernel while dynamically tuning the size of the buffer. The default values of this parameter are shown in Table 12-2.

Table 12-2   Default TCP Socket Read Buffer Sizes

	Buffer Parameters		
	Minimum *net.ipv4.tcp_rmem[0]*	*Default* *net.ipv4.tcp_rmem[1]*	*Maximum* *net.ipv4.tcp_rmem[2]*
Low Memory	PAGE_SIZE	43689	43689*2
Normal	4KB	87380	87380*2

tcp_wmem

`net.ipv4.tcp_wmem` (/proc/sys/net/ipv4/tcp_wmem)
As with the read buffer, the TCP socket write buffer is also an array of three integers:

net.ipv4.tcp_wmem[0] = minimum size of the write buffer
net.ipv4.tcp_wmem[1] = default size of the write buffer
net.ipv4.tcp_wmem[2] = maximum size of the write buffer

As with the TCP read buffer, the TCP write buffer is controlled by the TCP protocol-specific parameters listed previously. Having a large write buffer is beneficial in that it allows the application to transfer a large amount of data to the write buffer without blocking. The default TCP socket write buffer sizes are shown in Table 12-3.

Table 12-3   Default TCP Socket Write Buffer Sizes

	Buffer Parameters		
	Minimum *net.ipv4.tcp_wmem[0]*	*Default* *net.ipv4.tcp_wmem[1]*	*Maximum* *net.ipv4.tcp_wmem[2]*
Low Memory	4KB	16KB	64KB
Normal	4KB	16KB	128KB

TCP is a "windowing" transmission protocol. The window that a receiver advertises—in other words, the amount of data that the receiver says it can consume—is used by the sender to determine how much data can be sent. The larger the receiver socket buffer, the larger the window advertised by TCP and the faster the sender can send data.

A significant improvement in performance can be obtained by simply increasing these values. Note that the kernel attempts to round the value provided to the nearest multiple of approximate segment size.

Table 12-4 shows some typical values these parameters are set to for large networking applications.

Table 12-4 Examples of Increased TCP Socket Buffer Sizes

	Buffer Parameters		
	Minimum *net.ipv4.tcp_wmem[0]*	*Default* *net.ipv4.tcp_wmem[1]*	*Maximum* *net.ipv4.tcp_wmem[2]*
TCP Write Buffer	8K	436600	873200
TCP Read Buffer	32K	436600	873200

tcp_mem

`net.ipv4.tcp_mem[]` (/proc/sys/net/ipv4/tcp_mem)
This kernel parameter is also an array of three integers that are used to control memory management behavior by defining the boundaries of memory management zones:

`net.ipv4.tcp_mem[0]` = pages below which TCP does not consider itself under memory pressure

`net.ipv4.tcp_mem[1]` = pages at which TCP enters memory pressure region

`net.ipv4.tcp_mem[2]` = pages at which TCP refuses further socket allocations (with some exceptions)

The term *pages* refers to the amount of memory, in pages, allocated globally to sockets in the system. The Linux kernel maintains limits on how much memory can be allocated at any given time.

Therefore, memory allocation failures while opening sockets can occur even though the system still has available memory.

For systems that need to support busy workloads, increasing the `tcp_mem[]` parameter benefits performance. For example, here are some values that it can be set to for a large networking workload:

```
net.ipv4.tcp_mem = 1000000 1001024 1002048
```

This change should be made with caution, because it comes with a trade-off.

A large amount of memory is consumed by each socket buffer, and this limits the amount of memory available for other activity in the system.

TCP Options

The following sections describe the TCP options most likely to be of use to the system administrator.

tcp_window_scaling

`net.ipv4.tcp_window_scaling` (/proc/sys/net/ipv4/tcp_window_scaling)
This kernel variable enables the TCP window scaling feature. It is on by default. Window scaling implements RFC1379.

The window scale option is required for the employment of TCP window sizes larger than 64K. Because the length field in the TCP protocol header for the advertised receive buffer is specified by 16 bits, the window size cannot be larger than 64K.

Window scaling allows buffers larger than 64K to be advertised, thereby enabling the sender to fill network pipes whose bandwidth latency is larger than 64K. Particularly for connections over satellite links and on networks with large round-trip times, employing large windows (greater than 64K) results in a significant improvement in performance.

Optimum throughput is achieved by maintaining a window at least as large as the bandwidth-delay product of the network. If that quantity is larger than 64K, window scaling can potentially provide improved throughput, with a trade-off between the overhead of creating and processing the TCP option and the much larger amount of data that can be sent in transit without delay.

It should be noted that socket buffers larger than 64K are still potentially beneficial even when window scaling is turned off.

Although the kernel does not advertise or allow windows larger than that limit, having a larger buffer enables the kernel to absorb a greater amount of data from the application one `write()` call at a time, and hence return earlier.

When applications perform a `write()` operation in normal blocking mode, they have to wait until the `write()` system call completes. Having a large-enough buffer to stage the data in the kernel allows it to return immediately. If the buffer were not large enough, the application would have to wait until the send buffer was sufficiently drained to absorb all the data from the write, which would typically include the data being sent to the destination and the sender receiving an acknowledgment in return, allowing it to free up the space. When a send buffer is set to a very small value, the throughput measured in this situation is a more accurate reflection of how fast data is actually transferred to the destination across the network.

tcp_sack

`net.ipv4.tcp_sack` (/proc/sys/net/ipv4/tcp_sack)
This variable enables the TCP Selective Acknowledgments (SACK) feature. SACK is a TCP option for congestion control that allows the receiving side to convey information to the sender regarding missing sequence numbers in the byte stream. This reduces the number of segments the sender has to retransmit in the case of a lost segment and also reduces the delays that might be suffered, thereby improving overall throughput.

SACK is expected to be beneficial when loss occurs frequently and round-trip times are long. In environments like high-speed local networks with very short round-trip times and negligible loss, performance can actually be improved by turning SACK off. This is due to avoiding the overhead of processing SACK options.

tcp_dsack

`net.ipv4.tcp_dsack` (/proc/sys/net/ipv4/tcp_dsack)
This variable enables the TCP D-SACK feature, which is an enhancement to SACK to detect unnecessary retransmits. It is enabled by default, and it should be disabled if SACK is disabled.

tcp_fack

`net.ipv4.tcp_fack` (/proc/sys/net/ipv4/tcp_fack)
This variable enables the TCP Forward Acknowledgment (FACK) feature. FACK is a refinement of the SACK protocol to improve congestion control in TCP. It should also be disabled if SACK is disabled.

TCP Connection Management

TCP is a connection-oriented protocol. The following describes some of the parameters that help the kernel manage its connections to remote hosts. Tuning these parameters can have an impact on the number of connections that it can support simultaneously, an important consideration for busy servers.

tcp_max_syn_backlog

`net.ipv4.tcp_max_syn_backlog` (/proc/sys/net/ipv4/tcp_max_syn_backlog)
This variable controls the length of the TCP Syn Queue for each port. Incoming connection requests (SYN segments) are queued until they are accepted by the local server. If there are more connection requests than specified by this variable, the connection request is dropped. If clients experience failures connecting to busy servers, this value could be increased.

tcp_synack_retries

`net.ipv4/tcp_synack_retries` (/proc/sys/net/ipv4/tcp_synack_retries)
This variable controls the number of times the kernel tries to resend a response to an incoming SYN/ACK segment. Reducing this number results in earlier detection of a failed connection attempt from the remote host.

tcp_retries2

`net.ipv4/tcp_retries2` (/proc/sys/net/ipv4/tcp_retries2)
This variable controls the number of times the kernel tries to resend data to a remote host with which it has an established connection. Reducing this number results in earlier detection of a failed connection to the remote host. This allows busy servers to quickly free up the resources tied to the failed connection and makes it easier for the server to support a larger number of simultaneous connections. The default value is 15, and, because TCP exponentially backs off with each attempt before retrying, it can normally take quite a while before it abandons an established connection. Lowering the value to 5, for example, results in five retransmission attempts being made on unacknowledged data.

TCP Keep-Alive Management

Once a connection is established, the TCP protocol does not stipulate that data be exchanged. A connection can remain idle permanently. In such a situation, if one host fails or becomes unavailable, it is not detected by the remaining host. The Keep-Alive mechanism allows a host to monitor the connection and learn of such a failure within a reasonable time. This section describes the global kernel parameters associated with the TCP Keep-Alive mechanism. Applications need to have the TCP Keep-Alive option enabled using the `setsockopt()` system call in order to make use of the kernel mechanism.

tcp_keepalive_time

`net.ipv4.tcp_keepalive_time` (/proc/sys/net/ipv4/tcp_keepalive_time)
If a connection is idle for the number of seconds specified by this parameter, the kernel initiates a probing of the connection to the remote host.

tcp_keepalive_intvl

`net.ipv4.tcp_keepalive_intvl` (/proc/sys/net/ipv4/tcp_keepalive_intvl)
This parameter specifies the time interval, in seconds, between the keepalive probes sent by the kernel to the remote host.

tcp_keepalive_probes

`net.ipv4.tcp_keepalive_probes` (/proc/sys/net/ipv4/tcp_keepalive_probes)
This parameter specifies the maximum number of keepalive probes the kernel sends to the remote host to detect if it is still alive. If it has sent this number of probes without receiving a response in return, the kernel concludes that the remote host is no longer available and closes the connection, freeing up all the local resources associated with the connection.

The default values are as follows:

```
tcp_keepalive_time = 7200 seconds (2 hours)
tcp_keepalive_probes = 9
tcp_keepalive_intvl = 75 seconds
```

These settings result in a connection getting dropped after approximately two hours and eleven minutes of idle time. Such large values are typically used to accommodate large delays and round-trip times on the Internet.

It can be desirable to lower the preceding parameters to detect remote hosts that have gone away earlier. This minimizes resources (such as memory and port space) tied up in extinct connections.

IP Port Space Range

ip_local_port_range

```
sysctl.net.ipv4.ip_local_port_range
   (/proc/sys/net/ipv4/ip_local_port_range)
```

This parameter specifies the range of ephemeral ports that are available to the system. A port is a logical abstraction that the IP protocol uses as an address of sorts to distinguish between individual sockets, and it is simply an integer sequence space. When an application connects to a remote endpoint actively, it typically asks the kernel to dynamically assign it an ephemeral, or the next available free port, as opposed to a well-known port. These are unique to each protocol (TCP and UDP). The default value is configured at boot time based on the memory in the system. For systems with more than 128KB of memory, it is set to `32768` to `61000`. Thus, a maximum of 28,232 ports can be in use simultaneously. Increasing this range allows a larger number of simultaneous connections for each protocol (TCP and UDP).

Summary

Monitoring and tuning the kernel are important tasks for networking performance. This chapter described some of the important kernel tunable variables and how they impact the system's performance. These variables are made available to the user via the `sysctl` (8) interface or the /proc interface. One of the most critical ways performance can be optimized is by setting the size of the socket buffers to be optimum for the desired workload and environment. We discussed some of the core networking variables that affect queue lengths, and also described some of the TCP protocol parameters that are commonly adjusted.

References

[1] Documentation/networking/ip_sysctls.txt

[2] man (7) tcp

[3] man (7) udp

[4] man (7) socket

[5] man (7) ip

[6] man (8) sysctl

[7] man (8) netstat

[8] man (5) proc

[9] Stevens, W. Richard, *TCP/IP Illustrated, Volume 1*, Addison-Wesley, 1994.

## CHAPTER THIRTEEN

Interprocess Communication

By Mingming Cao

INTRODUCTION

This chapter discusses interprocess communication (IPC) in Linux. Interprocess communication is a way for multiple processes in Linux to communicate with each other. First, interprocess communication and the resources it uses are defined. The chapter then discusses how to use the `ipcs` command to learn about the IPC resources on the system. Next, the various parameters available for the different IPC resources are discussed. The chapter then tells how to modify IPC parameters both statically and dynamically. Finally, the role of pipes as IPC facilities in Linux is discussed.

WHAT IS INTERPROCESS COMMUNICATION?

Interprocess communication allows processes to synchronize with each other and exchange data. In general, System V (SysV) IPC facilities provide three types of resources:

- *Semaphores.* Allow processes to synchronize with other and also prevent collisions when multiple processes are sharing resources.
- *Message queues.* Asynchronously pass small data, such as messages, between processes.
- *Shared memory segments.* Provide a fast way for processes to share relatively large amounts of data by sharing a common segment of memory among multiple processes.

In addition to these resources, IPC pipes and FIFOs are among the most commonly used IPC facilities in UNIX-based systems:

- *Pipes* are unidirectional, first-in/first-out data channels that pass unstructured data streams between related processes.
- *FIFOs* (a.k.a. named pipes) are pipes that have a persistent name associated with them.

The next section looks at interprocess communication resources and the command that returns information about those resources.

LINUX SYSV IPC RESOURCES AND THE IPCS COMMAND

Linux supports the three types of SysV IPC resources. The Linux kernel default configuration normally enables SysV IPC support. If the SysV IPC is not supported in your Linux kernel, you need to configure your kernel source with the CONFIG_SYSVIPC set to enable SysV IPC facilities. You need to rebuild your kernel after changing the configuration.

The SysV IPC facilities are widely used throughout various Linux applications. For example, some database applications create shared memory segments for data sharing. The Linux kernel dynamically allocates memory for IPC objects whenever a new IPC resource is requested. However, due to the amount of memory consumed by the kernel for these IPC resources, the kernel enforces limits on the usage of IPC resources. Some of the limits can be tuned dynamically. When tuning parameters to meet your IPC resource needs, it is important that you consider memory usage consumed by the resources.

Pipes, on the other hand, are so fundamental to UNIX system operation that they are always available in the kernel—they are not configurable into or out of the kernel. Typically, pipes are used in shell commands to direct output from one process into another process. For example:

```
bash> ls –lsR | grep linux
```

Pipes differ from the SysV IPC in that they require processes to be related. Pipes are created in pairs—the first element for reading and the second element for writing. During a fork, the pipes can then be handed off between the parent and the various child processes, and henceforth be used to communicate between these related processes.

FIFOs (named pipes) are created as special files in the file system using the mkfifo *filename* command.

The ipcs Command

Almost all Linux distributions include the ipcs command, which provides information about the IPC resources that are currently loaded on the system. ipcs lets you determine the current IPC limits that the system allows and also lets you check the status of the three IPC resources that are currently in use on the system. For example, if your application fails to start, you can check the IPC usage on your system to determine if an IPC limit has been exceeded. To determine the status of the system's IPC resources, as root, issue the ipcs command with the –u option:

```
# ipcs -u

------ Shared Memory Status --------
segments allocated 32
pages allocated 2361
pages resident  253
pages swapped   982
Swap performance: 0 attempts     0 successes

------ Semaphore Status --------
used arrays = 128
allocated semaphores = 256

------ Messages: Status --------
allocated queues = 0
used headers = 0
used space = 0 bytes
```

To determine the limits on the IPC resources reported by the ipcs -u command, use the ipcs -l command:

```
# ipcs -l

------ Shared Memory Limits --------
max number of segments = 4096
max seg size (kbytes) = 32768
max total shared memory (kbytes) = 8388608
min seg size (bytes) = 1

------ Semaphore Limits --------
max number of arrays = 128
max semaphores per array = 250
max semaphores system wide = 32000
max ops per semop call = 32
semaphore max value = 32767

------ Messages: Limits --------
max queues system wide = 16
max size of message (bytes) = 8192
default max size of queue (bytes) = 16384
```

This output shows that the system has hit the limit of the maximum number of semaphore arrays, or semaphore sets. This limit could be resolved by increasing the value of kernel parameter semmni, which defines the total number of semaphore sets a system can have. Linux supports dynamically resizing most kernel IPC parameters, as well as changing them in a static way.

IPC Identifiers and Their Limits

In the Linux kernel, each IPC resource is described as a data structure in the form of an IPC identifier or an IPC object. The IPC mechanism is implemented based on this data structure and the operations associated with it. The Linux kernel includes a set of system calls to create and manipulate the IPC identifiers and objects.

An IPC identifier is identified by a unique key for its type (either semaphores, message queues, or shared memory). Each type of the IPC resource is created by its corresponding "create" system call: `semget()` for semaphores, `msgget()` for message queues, or `shmget()` for shared memory. These `*get()` system calls return a unique IPC ID for the caller. After the application gets the ID, it can reference the IPC object via the ID and control the IPC identifier by the corresponding "control" system calls: `semctl()` for semaphores, `msgctl()` for message queues, and `shmctl()` for shared memory.

Additionally, the IPC mechanism in the Linux kernel provides system calls that allow an application to manipulate IPC resources: `semop()` increases or decreases semaphore values, `msgsnd()` and `msgrcv()` send and receive messages between processes via message queues, and `shmat()` and `shmdt()` are for shared memory operations and allow a process to attach or detach itself to or from a shared memory segment.

Each IPC identifier is of type `struct ipc_ids`, which is of size 44 bytes. Each IPC resource type contains an array to store pointers to the identifiers. The total number of entries in the global array is determined by the maximum number of identifiers of the corresponding IPC resource type (`semmni`, `msgmni`, or `shmmni`). You can resize the array by tuning the related kernel parameters. However, there is an upper limit for these parameters: IPCMNI. IPCMNI defines the maximum number of IPC identifiers system-wide for each IPC resource type. When the Linux kernel tries to resize the semaphore identifier array according to the new value of `semmni` (the maximum number of semaphore identifiers), it also checks whether the new size is over the IPCMNI limit. The default value of IPCMNI is 32767, and this parameter cannot be tuned at runtime. The IPCMNI parameter applies to all three IPC resources.

SEMAPHORE PARAMETERS

A semaphore is a counter and the operations associated with it. Semaphores provide a synchronized way for multiple processes to access a shared resource. Semaphores can be used as simple signals to synchronize processes, or as locks to prevent collisions on shared resources.

Linux includes several kernel parameters that are associated with semaphores. These parameters, based on a 32-bit Intel system, are summarized in Table 13-1.

Table 13-1   Kernel Parameters Associated with Semaphores

Name	Description	Default	Maximum
semmni	Maximum semaphore sets	128	2GB
semmsl	Maximum semaphores per semaphore set	250	65536
semmns	Maximum semaphores system-wide	32000	2GB
semopm	Maximum operations per semop system call	32	2GB
semvmx	Maximum semaphore value	32767	65536

Linux also defines other semaphore-related parameters that are not currently in use.

The following sections examine semaphore-related parameters in detail.

semmni

`semmni` sets the total number of semaphore sets that a system can have. At initialization time, the kernel creates an array of default `semmni` pointers, each of which points to a semaphore identifier structure. As a user tunes this parameter, the kernel adjusts the size of the semaphore ID array accordingly (to at most IPCMNI). Note that the hard limit of 2GB maximum value is derived from the kernel parameter's data type (`int`). Theoretically, you can have a maximum of 2GB semaphore sets in your system. In the Linux kernel, however, each semaphore identifier needs 44 bytes of kernel memory for the IPC identifier structure, plus 68 bytes for each semaphore set structure. Therefore, 2GB semaphore identifiers require at least (44+68)*2G=224GB of kernel memory. The recommended maximum is 32767.

semmns

`semmns` determines the maximum number of allowable semaphores system-wide. Because `semmni` is the maximum number of all possible semaphore sets, and `semmsl` is the maximum number of semaphores per set, the maximum total number of semaphores overall should not be greater than the product of `semmni` and `semmsl`. By default, `semmns` equals `semmni*semmsl` but is not calculated automatically.

semmsl

`semmsl` is the maximum number of semaphores allowed in a semaphore set. The default value is 250. The 65536 limit comes from the data type, `unsigned short`. In practice, `semmsl` should not be set to the upper limit in order to reduce the chance of a kernel memory allocation failure. The higher the number of semaphores in a semaphore set, the more kernel memory is required to save the undo operations. We recommend setting `semmsl` to 8000 to reduce memory pressure.

semopm

`semopm` defines how many operations a single `semop()` call can operate on a semaphore set. The `semop()` call checks the operation array size against this limit. We recommend setting `semop()` to 8000.

semvmx

`semvmx` sets the maximum value of a semaphore. The `semvmx` hard limit is 65536 because of its data type (`unsigned short`). `semvms` cannot be changed dynamically like the other four parameters; we recommend that you leave it as the default value of 32767.

Unused Semaphore Parameters in Linux

This section discusses the semaphore-related parameters defined in Linux but not currently in use in its IPC implementation. These parameters can be found in use in other UNIX-like operating systems, such as HP/UX or Solaris. It is worth mentioning that other semaphore-related parameters are defined in Linux, but are not currently in use. The /usr/include/linux/sem.h file defines the following unused parameters:

- `semume`. The maximum number of undo operations per process. The semaphore undo operation is currently implemented in the Linux kernel, but there is no per-process limit on how many undo operations it can perform. The default value for `semume` equals `semopm` (32).

- `semmnu`. The maximum number of undo operations system-wide. As with `semume`, Linux does not restrict how many semaphore undo operations can be performed in total. The default of `semmnu` is equivalent to the default of `semmns` (128).

- `semaem`. The maximum count a semaphore can be adjusted if the associated process dies. The default is `semvmx` >>1 (8192).

- `semmap`. The maximum number of entries in the semaphore map. Some operating systems preallocate memory for allocation and deallocation of the memory segments for semaphore identifiers, but this is not supported in the current Linux implementation The default value is `semmns` (32000).

- `semuse`. Defines the size of the semaphore undo structure. Its value is 20 bytes.

MESSAGE QUEUE PARAMETERS

Message queues provide an asynchronous way for processes to pass messages. After a message queue is established by calling msgget(), sending processes and receiving processes can exchange messages via the message queue. The sending process sends the messages to the specified message queue, and the receiver tries to get the messages from the specified message queue. If no message is available on the message queue, the receiver is blocked or returns with some flag, depending on whether it is willing to wait.

Table 13-2 provides brief descriptions of the three kernel parameters for message queues present in the current Linux 2.4/2.6 implementation.

Table 13-2   Kernel Parameters Associated with Message Queues

Name	Description	Default	Maximum
msgmni	Maximum of message queues	16	2GB
msgmax	Maximum message size in bytes	8192	2GB
msgmnb	Maximum bytes on a message queue	16384	2GB

Note that the maximum value listed in the fourth column is a value based on the data type. The three kernel parameters are of type int, so on a 3-bit Intel machine, the hard limit is 2GB.

Linux also defines other message queue-related parameters that are not currently in use.

The following sections examine message queue-related parameters in detail.

msgmni

msgmni defines a system-wide message queue limit. As with semaphores, message queues have an associated identifier. At system initialization time, the kernel creates an array of pointers that point to the message queue identifier structures. The number of entries in that array is determined by msgmni. For each message queue, the Linux kernel allocates 44 bytes for the identifier and 96 bytes for the message queue structure. You can dynamically increase msgmni to get more message queue resources. As with semaphores, the maximum number of message queue identifiers is limited by IPCMNI. The default limit is 16, which is probably not enough to get some of the big database applications running smoothly. We recommend the default limit be set as high as 128 if you know your system will run a database application.

msgmax

msgmax restricts the size of a message that a process can send. The msgsnd() function enforces this limit. If the message to be sent exceeds this limit, an error is returned. This parameter can be tuned at runtime.

msgmnb

msgmnb determines the capacity of a message queue. The value of msgmnb is saved in one field of the message queue identifier structure and is used to determine whether there is space to enqueue a new message. The default value is 16384. The value can be modified dynamically. Modifying the value of msgmnb affects the capacities of all new message queues. The msgctl() system call allows the user to increase the capacity of an existing message queue.

Unused Message Queue Parameters

Five additional message queue-related parameters are predefined in Linux but are not yet used:

- msgpool. The maximum size of the message pool in kilobytes. The default value is set to msgmni*msgmnb/1024.
- msgtql. The maximum count of system-wide message headers. The Linux kernel constructs a message by attaching a message header with the message body, which is obtained from the sending process, and then stores it in the corresponding message queue. Basically, this reflects the total number of messages a system allows. Currently, in the 2.4/2.6 kernel, this parameter is defined with a default value of msgmnb, but the Linux 2.6 kernel does not check this limit when a new message needs to be sent.
- msgmap. Defines the number of entries in a message queue map and is similar to the semmap parameter for semaphores. The IPC facility of other UNIX-like operating systems uses a resource allocation map to provide a convenient way of managing a small piece of kernel memory in case the resource is frequently allocated and released. This is not the method currently implemented in the Linux kernel, but the Linux kernel reserves this parameter for possible use in the future. The default value of msgmap is msgmni (16).
- msgssz. The size of message segments. The default is 16.
- msgseg. The maximum number of segments system-wide. Linux does not currently check this limit.

SHARED MEMORY SEGMENT PARAMETERS

Shared memory provides an efficient way to share large amounts of data between processes. Shared memory is one of the most important resources the IPC facility provides because it is heavily used in many database applications. A SysV shared memory segment is created by the shmget() system call. After the shared memory segment is created, a process can attach itself to the shared memory segment by issuing a shmat() system call. Then the process can perform operations (read or write) on it. The process can detach itself from the memory segment by a shmdt() system call. Because shared memory provides a common resource for multiple processes, it is often used with semaphores to prevent collisions.

Table 13-3 summarizes the shared memory segment parameters.

Table 13-3   Shared Memory Segment Parameters

Name	Description	Default	Maximum
shmmax	Maximum shared memory segment size in bytes	0x2000000	4GB
shmmin	Minimum shared memory segment size in bytes	1	2GB
shmmni	Maximum number of shared memory segments	4096	2GB
shmall	Maximum shared memory segment size in pages system-wide	0x200000	4GB

Note that some UNIX operating systems, such as Solaris, use the shmseg kernel parameter to restrict the total number of segments a process can attach itself to. Linux currently does not have this limitation but reserves this parameter in /usr/include/linux/shm.h.

The following sections describe in detail the shared memory segment parameters that are supported in Linux.

shmmni

shmmni is the total number of shared memory segments allowed in a system. Its data type is signed int on a 32-bit architecture, so theoretically its value can be increased up to 2GB. However, IPCMNI overrides this limit. You can configure IPCMNI to get more shared memory segments; however, each IPC identifier structure size is about 44 bytes. For 2GB shared memory segments, you need 2GB*44=88GB of memory.

shmmax

shmmax sets the limit of an individual shared memory segment size in bytes. The default value in the current Linux 2.4/2.6 kernel is 32MB. Some database applications might require a larger limit. shmmax is tunable dynamically but the new limit does not affect the existing shared memory segments. Increasing shmmax does not allocate additional kernel memory. The parameter itself is of type unsigned int, so theoretically you can tune it up to 4GB to fit your application needs. However, there is no point in changing this parameter to be larger than the physical memory available on your system.

shmmin

shmmin is the smallest a shared memory segment can be. We recommend that the default value be kept as is.

shmall

shmall defines the number of pages system-wide that can be used for shared memory segments. The default value is 0x200000. We recommend the value of shmall be adjusted based on the values of shmmax and shmmni .

DYNAMICALLY MODIFYING THE CONFIGURABLE IPC PARAMETERS

Beginning with the 2.4 kernel, Linux supports the dynamic modification of most of the IPC parameters through either the /proc file system interface or with the sysctl facility. The following sections discuss how to dynamically modify IPC parameters with /proc and sysctl.

Using /proc

The /proc file system contains several files that store the current IPC limit setting. You can check the limits by opening these files and modifying the limits by editing the files. The following files related to IPC resources are located in the /proc/sys/kernel directory:

```
-rw-r--r--    1 root      root        0 Jul   2 15:12 msgmax
-rw-r--r--    1 root      root        0 Jul   2 15:12 msgmnb
-rw-r--r--    1 root      root        0 Jul   2 15:12 msgmni
-rw-r--r--    1 root      root        0 Jul   2 15:12 sem
-rw-r--r--    1 root      root        0 Jul   2 15:12 shmall
-rw-r--r--    1 root      root        0 Jul   2 15:12 shmmax
-rw-r--r--    1 root      root        0 Jul   2 15:12 shmmni
```

The file sem includes all the semaphore kernel parameters (semmsl, semmns, semopm, and semmni). The other files are straightforward—the filename tells what parameter the file stores.

The following example increases the maximum number of message queues by issuing an `echo` command as root:

```
# echo 1024 > /proc/sys/kernel/msgmni
```

Alternatively, you can open the file /proc/sys/kernel/msgmni and edit the value from there.

Using sysctl

Another way to check and modify kernel parameters at runtime is with the `sysctl` command. The `sysctl` command is an interface for changing the values of kernel parameters given the kernel parameter name and the new value. For example, to increase the maximum number of message queues to 1024, issue the following `sysctl` command as root:

```
# sysctl -w kernel..msgmni= 1024
```

You can also check the current limit with the `sysctl` command:

```
# sysctl kernel.sem
kernel.sem = 250   32000 32     128
```

Note that for semaphores, the kernel defines one general kernel parameter named `kernel.sem` for all four parameters. The four limits are listed in the order of `semmsl`, `semmns`, `semopm`, and `semmni`. To modify one of the limits, provide the new value for the vector. For example, to increase the maximum number of semaphore operations per `semop()` system call from 32 to 128, issue the following:

```
# sysctl -w kernel.sem="250    32000 128    128"
```

CONFIGURING IPC PARAMETERS STATICALLY

Most IPC-related kernel parameters are tunable at runtime. However, some of the new kernel limits apply only to the resources that were created after the kernel parameter was changed. Also, some kernel parameters, such as `semvmx`, are not tunable at runtime. In both cases, you need to modify the kernel source, rebuild the kernel, and reboot the machine to have the new limit take effect globally.

PIPES

Pipes can be shared among multiple readers and writers. Hence, each pipe consists of a FIFO buffer and a list of processes that are blocked to write and read operations. Pipes are not a configurable option in Linux. They are always compiled into the Linux kernel and are implemented as a pseudo-file system. From an application's point of view, pipes are accessed through file descriptors. Hence, the number of pipes that can be created is tied to the number of file descriptors allowed for a process.

Pipes have two important parameters: the pipe buffer size and the size of bytes that can be written atomically.

The pipe buffer size determines how much data can be asynchronous buffered between the writer and the reader. If the pipe buffer is full, data must be read for the writer to continue to write. If operated in blocking mode, writers block.

The pipe buffer size is always fixed to the PAGE_SIZE of the underlying platform. The atomicity is important because pipes can be shared among multiple writers, and guarantees must exist for a writer to send chunks of data as one block. The value is currently set to 4KB or PAGE_SIZE, whichever is smaller.

SUMMARY

This chapter presented an overview of interprocess communications in Linux. We discussed the usage of the ipcs command for gathering information about the IPC resources loaded on a system and provided several examples of how to use ipcs. We described the three types of IPC facilities—semaphores, message queues, and shared memory segments—and examined the parameters associated with each type of facility. In some cases, we provided a recommended setting for a particular parameter. The chapter also discussed how to dynamically or statically modify the configurable IPC parameters, and provided examples of how to use /proc and sysctl to modify dynamic parameters. Finally, we discussed the role of pipes in interprocess communication.

## CHAPTER FOURTEEN

Code Tuning

By Edward G. Bradford and Mark Brown

INTRODUCTION

Although an understanding of the methods of tuning the operating system is needed to optimize system workload and response, an equally important aspect of performance tuning is the actual work done in the application code to maximize performance—particularly for applications that are the sole purpose of a dedicated system. Applications such as web servers, database servers, or mail servers tend to be the primary application for a system, and performance hinges just as much on the application as it does on the operating system.

This chapter addresses some of the issues of writing a program that will run efficiently. We assume performance tuning of the underlying operating system can improve performance, but we want to concentrate on those aspects of writing and assembling a program that will produce minimal tuning parameterization and maximum performance.

We will discuss general techniques for achieving high performance in programs from general considerations of performance analysis to a discussion of basic design as being a key part of application performance. The C and C++ languages will be used in describing the concepts involved, but these methods and ideas are easily applied to any of the programming facilities available to developers today. The GNU Compiler Collection (gcc) compiler will be used, but again the concepts involved can translate to other compilation tools. All the source code will be available, and it should compile in any gcc programming environment.

First, we'll discuss the general principles of performance tuning.

GENERAL PRINCIPLES

One of the primary goals of performance tuning is to find the areas of code that are used the most in an application and reduce the amount of the time it takes to process those areas. Although other areas can be considered, such as reducing memory or other resource requirements, we will concern ourselves in this section with speed as the primary measure of efficiency.

Many factors affect performance. Some of them are not under the application programmer's control, such as machine architecture. Others, such as how I/O and memory are used, are directly observable (and tunable) using the concepts described in this chapter. A few are basic to the construction of the applications and require serious consideration both before development begins and after performance analysis. These include the algorithms used as the basis of programming or the size and granularity of the tasks being performed.

To target those programs most in need of optimization, profiling tools are available. For our next discussion, we'll take a look at profiling.

PROFILING TO UNDERSTAND THE APPLICATION

It is a truism that the most time-consuming and frequently used sections of a program should be optimized first. Profiling tools should be used before performance tuning begins, both to discover these areas and to provide a baseline for measuring the effectiveness of the tuning that is being performed later. When profiling the application, use (and be consistent in using) realistic sizes of workload and datasets. Although you need to use some variety later in the fine-tuning process or else risk tuning to one model at the expense of others, early iterations using the same initial loads as the baseline can offer insight into successful tuning attacks.

The basic profiling tools in Linux are the -p (profile) and -pg (profile for gprof) options in gcc, and the prof and gprof utilities. Compiling using -p or -pg causes gcc to insert instructions necessary to obtain profiling information into the object code. Running the `prof` command with the application allows you to then obtain the following:

- Each procedure, ordered by descending processor activity
- The percentage of CPU time used by each procedure
- The execution time in seconds for all references
- The number of times each procedure was called
- The average time for a call to the procedure

Running the gprof command with the application gathers (among other information) the following:

- The percentage of CPU time used by each procedure and its calling tree
- A time breakdown for each procedure and what it calls
- The number of times a procedure was called
- What procedures were called by each procedure

Because gprof includes the descendents of a procedure in its timings, it is more useful for procedures calling library routines.

Although other profiling tools are available to the developer, prof and gprof are mentioned here because they are the most commonly available. Some of these alternative tools can be specialized for a specific purpose, such as parallel programming or massively multithreaded applications.

After successfully profiling for optimization, you are ready to begin tuning. Modern compilers offer many optional optimization features. gcc, for example, offers more than 60 options related to performance optimization. The next section discusses basic steps and compilers as tuning tools.

COMPILER OPTIONS AS TUNING TOOLS

Compilers often "know" the machine architecture and processor better than the developer, performing as a matter of course such optimizations as dead code elimination, loop unrolling, branch optimization, and function inlining. In many cases, the programmer finds that all the major and obvious bottlenecks identified via profiling are resolved by using the optimizations provided by the compiler.

In gcc, the general level of optimization is controlled by the -o flag. At its most basic level, -o1, the flag takes the most general steps to reduce code size and execution time. -o2 causes gcc to perform nearly all optimizations that do not involve a space-speed trade-off (such as loop unrolling or function inlining). -o3 turns on such additional optimizations as function inlining and register renaming. We recommend an interative process of increasing optimization/profiling cycles to determine the best level for your application. This is because it is possible, even with well-written code, for a higher level of compiler aggressiveness in optimization to hurt a piece of code's performance rather than help it. Sometimes, this is a matter of what the more aggressive optimizer is looking for as opposed to what the code is actually trying to do. A reading of the performance options section of the gcc manual reveals many additional options, most of which are more suitable for use after a particular code section has been analyzed and its problems made clear.

Basic Performance Tuning

Following are the basic steps in tuning a program:

1. Create a baseline by doing a plain compile with profiling on and analyzing it.
2. Turn on the base level of optimization for your compiler (still profiling).
3. Measure again, and identify the bottlenecks in your program.
4. Tune the bottlenecks and measure. Remove tuning that doesn't help, as measured through profiling.
5. Turn on the next level of compiler optimization.
6. Repeat from Step 3.

Tuning your application for performance is a methodical and sometimes repetitive process that nonetheless can give great rewards in program efficiency.

One Word About Compiler Optimizations

Sometimes at the higher levels of compiler optimization, you may see a *decrease* in performance instead of an increase for a given module. Compilers are not perfect, and in these cases a closer examination of the code itself is warranted to see what can be done to "help" the compiler see what needs to be optimized through making the code simpler or using a different algorithm in that section.

Following are some things to consider when developing code. Giving some consideration to your code can make all the difference.

CODE TUNING

Entire books have been written concerning good programming practices. We will simply present some highlights in the following list for the application developer to consider, especially in light of the preceding advice on "helping" the compiler "see" where optimizations can be most effective:

- Put the most common statement first when using multiple tests.
- Avoid unnecessary type conversions (implicit ones as well).
- Minimize the amount of code actually inside a loop.
- Minimize the number of expensive operations in a loop (divides, for example). In fact, it would pay to obtain texts specifically about the subject of tuning loops if this is where your bottlenecks reside. A large amount of research is available on the subject.
- Inline short subroutines.
- Keep the number of parameters low in subroutines and functions.

- Use already-tuned libraries of functions where possible instead of creating your own and reinventing the wheel.
- Eliminate unnecessary I/O and keep I/O operations out of loops where possible.
- Use parentheses in mathematical expressions to help the compiler, and break complex expressions into simpler subexpressions that can be more easily optimized. Almost always, a better solution is using already-tuned math libraries.

As a reminder, clean, straightforward approaches to a coding problem typically result in the best optimizations and good performance coding practices. Another area to consider is your choice for design.

ALGORITHM: ACHIEVING PERFORMANCE THROUGH DESIGN CHOICES

All the compiler optimizations and hand-coded tuning methods in a programmer's toolbox do not matter as much in a program's performance as the proper choice of solution for a given problem. The rest of this section examines a sample network-based program and some of the design choices that can lead to a well-performing application.

Problems and Solution Possibilities

To understand some of the choices, we will describe a sample program that will demonstrate some of the issues concerning programming and optimal performance. We will look at a typical problem to understand some performance issues.

Programmers working on network-based solutions must deal with a number of issues, some of which we will demonstrate here by focusing on a simplified multi-threaded file I/O Internet server.

We intend to demonstrate the use of threading and sockets, show reasonably high-performance programming techniques, and measure the performance of the resulting Internet page server. Note that we are spelling internet with a lowercase i here because we are not processing HTTP.

A Problem—How Fast Can We Connect, Create a File, Read It, and Disconnect?

Our program will consist of two parts: a client part and a server part. The server will initialize itself and await a command from a client. The server will have the following usage:

```
server [-t nnn] [-pooling] [ip_address]:portnum
```

where -t indicates the number of threads to use (the default is 1). The -pooling option instructs the server to use a pool of threads rather than create and destroy a thread for each incoming work item.

The client has the following usage:

```
c [-t nnn] –filesize nnn –blksize mmm –qsize jjj
 [ip_address]:portnum
```

Here, we can instruct the client to use nnn threads and create files of size nnn using a block size of mmm. Finally, we instruct the client to do this jjj times. Both client and server use the TCP/IP address [ip_address]:portnum. The meaning here is that if the ip_address is unspecified, the program (server or c) uses the local machine address.

Thus, the following command starts the server program, allows the use of up to eight worker threads, and listens on port 4001:

```
server –t 8  :4001
```

The command

```
c –t 4 –qsize 1000 –filesize 2m –blksize 8192 :4001
```

connects to the server located at port 4001 on the local machine to perform 1,000 operations, each consisting of a file create, writing 2 million (2*1024*1024) bytes, reading 2 million bytes (8192 bytes at a time), sending 2 million bytes (8K at a time) over the TCP/IP connection, and, finally, closing the file and deleting it. By specifying a complete TCP address as follows:

```
c –t 4 –qsize 1000 –filesize 2m –blksize 8192 10.0.0.4:4001
```

the client program can be run from any computer that can communicate via TCP/IP with the server program.

The server and client could be written in most of the languages listed earlier and others not listed. However, rather than digress into the reasons why one language is or is not appropriate, let me just say that the C and C++ languages give access to the system entry APIs in Linux (the system calls). These "system call" APIs provide operating system services used by high-performance programs. We will direct our attention to some the system call primitives documented in section 2 of the manual.

The Program

Our program's responsibility will be to accept the command-line parameterization, set up to accept socket connections and distribute the resulting requests across the available threads. Further, we will design the server portion and the client portion to simply be parts of the same source code. When compiled, if the resulting executable is named server, it performs the server actions; otherwise, it performs client actions.

The server portion requires several threads. The first thread initializes all other threads and then listens for incoming requests and queues them. The second thread schedules work found in the queue. The third thread cleans up threads that terminate.

Pseudocode for the first server thread would look like the code shown here:

```
Server Main

  Parse options
  Create listening socket

  Start cleanup thread
  Start threadscheduler thread

  Forever {
    Accept new socket
    If quit break
    Queue new socket
  }
  exit
```

Here, the actual socket file descriptor is the object that is queued. Two other threads must be described. The cleanup thread has pseudocode, as shown here:

```
Thread Cleanup

  While threadactive {
    Locate active thread
    "wait" for thread // cleans up
  }
  exit
```

The thread scheduler has pseudocode, as shown here:

```
Thread scheduler

  While qsize > 0 {
    Locate inactive thread
    Start inactive thread with work item
  }
  exit
```

The thread scheduler sets a thread to work on the queued socket. Surrounding the basic work to be done is the *mild* protocol, which accepts a text command from the client (over the socket), parses the command, executes the actual work, and finally sends a

"DONE" message back to the client. Code that wraps around the actual worker thread is shown here:

```
Thread wrapper

  Accept work assignment from socket
  Parse text command
    Mark myself as "active"
      Do real work
    Mark myself as "inactive"
  Reply to socket with an "DONE" message
```

We have described the server-side pseudocode that supports an almost arbitrary threaded work item. Before going into the details of what is involved in using Linux and gcc to create a program, let me also describe the client that issues the "commands" to this server and produces the timed results.

The client must be able to cause all this work to happen and report the timing of the results. If the server is multithreaded, on a multiprocessor, for a given number of threads, the results should improve as we add processors. Our server program will demonstrate that by scaling as we add processors. The client pseudocode has the following command-line behavior:

```
client -t 8 -qsize 1000 -filesize 2m -blksize 8192 :4001
```

The command-line options have the same meaning as for the server. When the client receives the last "DONE" message from a server thread, it prints a summary timing of the entire operation. The client pseudocode is shown here:

```
Client

Parse command line options
Put all work into a queue
Start each thread; each will pull something off the queue
until the queue is empty.
```

We will demonstrate some of the performance choices we must make to write a program on Linux. From this brief description, we will go into more detail on the programming aspects and how to measure the resulting performance. The client thread has the pseudocode shown here:

```
Client Thread
While there is work to be done
Get work item of work queue
Send text string describing work to server
Read and check date from server until done.
```

```
Wait for "DONE"
Send 'Q'
Close socket
```

The client performs all the timing and reports the results.

Designing the Code

The choice of C or C++ rather than other languages is due to the personal experiences of the author.

Others who have experience in other languages might use FORTRAN or Python. However, more than the individual experiences of one person should be considered. Most programs are part of a product and require multiple people to write. Programming language selection should be based on the experiences of the participants in the programming team, the supportability of the language, and the debugging tools available. C and C++ are safe choices. On Linux, the C compiler that comes with Linux is gcc, the GNU Compiler Collection.

We will go through the various issues one by one and include snapshots of code. The complete program is included in the appendix.

The Server

Our program is designed as a single source file. When invoked, it asks whether it is named server. If it is, it performs the server functions. If it is not named server, it behaves like a client. The point of including the entire source in a single program is to simplify the building of the program and copying it to other systems. It is not necessarily the best choice. The question is asked as shown here:

```
char *p;
if(strchr(av[1],"/"))
    p = strrchr(av[1],"/");
else
    p = av[1];
if(equal(p,"server"))
    ServerMain();
else
    ClientMain();
```

This coding style is a convenience. The example brings us to another simplification that really represents personalization of code. Many programmers have idiosyncratic mechanisms that are included in every program they write. There are also reasons to define shortcuts of common names for things that are different on different platforms. In multiple-person developments, the shortcuts can interfere with rapid understanding of the code if they become too plentiful. This shortcut list is reasonably small, but to have a group of people embrace it would require a discussion and consensus. Following are the shortcuts we used:

```
#    define SLASHC           '/'
#    define SLASHSTR         "/"
#    define SOCKTYPE         int
#    define SLEEP(x)         sleep(x)
#    define Errno            errno
#    define BADSOCK          -1
#    define LCK              pthread_mutex_t
#    define SEMA_T           sem_t        // (man sem_init)
#    define YIELD            Yield()
#    define SOCKET           int
#    define SOCKERR          -1
#    define EXITTHREAD()     return
#    define INT64            long long
#    define UINT64           unsigned long long

     typedef pthread_t    THREAD_T;

#    define TVAL            struct timeval

#    define equal           !strcmp
#    define equaln          !strncmp
```

It can be noted that converting these shortcuts to other platforms that support C/C++ is trivial.

Timing

The tstart(), tend(), and tval() routines provide a mechanism for recording time in the microsecond range. These routines are implemented by using the gettimeofday() routine on Linux. The documentation for gettimeofday() is accessed with the following command:

```
man getimeofday
```

Our version here is reentrant. tstart() and tend() record their values in a location specified by an input pointer. The design supports *reentrancy*, which is important when designing a multiple-thread application.

One issue with timing routines is the possibility that during a measurement session, someone or some program changes the system time. If that happens, you could get results that are not repeatable. For that reason, we make two recommendations:

1. Turn off all NTP (Network Time Protocol) servers. Using netstat -i, you can determine the list of open ports on the local machine. Make sure that port 123 is not in use. If it is, stop the service that is using it. If an NTP server is not running, there is little likelihood it will change the system time.

2. Run performance measurement tests multiple times to ensure that the results are repeatable.

With these two guidelines, it is unlikely that you will get into a lot of trouble.

The timing routines work like a stopwatch. To time something, the following sequence is used:

```
TVAL ts,te;
double t;

tstart(&ts);
do_something();
tend(&te);
t = tval(&ts, &te);
printf("do_something() took %8.5f seconds.\n",t);
```

The code for the timing routines looks like this:

```
void tstart(struct timeval *t)
{
    gettimeofday(t, NULL);
}
void tend(struct timeval *t)
{
    gettimeofday(t,NULL);
}

double tval(struct timeval *tv1, struct timeval *tv2)
{
    double t1, t2;

    t1 =    (double)tv1->tv_sec +
            (double)tv1->tv_usec/(1000*1000);
    t2 =    (double)tv2->tv_sec +
             (double)tv2->tv_usec/(1000*1000);
    return t2-t1;
}
```

Using the gettimeofday() system call allows resolution to one millionth of a second on an Intel-based Linux machine.

Sockets

Linux supports Berkeley sockets. Our program takes an input command-line parameter and converts it to an IP address and port number, suitable for use with the sockets library. For connection (client) or listening (server), both an IP address and a port number are required. The TcpParse(), ipaddress(), and portnum() routines convert an

ASCII string to an IP address or port number. All three require reasonably precise input. If any encounters an error, it prints an error message and causes the program to exit.

Our discussion won't be a tutorial on sockets. We assume you are familiar with the basics of programming sockets using the AF_INET family of protocols. We also assume our interests here are in stream-oriented sockets as opposed to datagrams (TCP versus UDP).

There are two ways to use sockets. The first is to listen for incoming connections. The second is to initiate an outgoing connection. On Linux, sockets can be used between two threads on the same machine or can be directed to a program on another machine; the distinction is only at the command-line level, where the IP address and port number of the server software are located. For our testing and demonstration purposes, we confine ourselves to a single machine. When the program is fully described, we make test runs between two different machines.

The server portion of our program creates a socket and listens for connections. It does this in a listen and accept thread, whose only responsibility is to start new thread work. Server code creates a socket, performs a `listen()` on it, and then `accepts()` new connections. The `accept` action creates a new socket that is handed off to a thread to perform work. The newly created socket is a bidirectional communication channel (a full socket). The following shows the code for the listen and accept routine:

```
void listen_and_accept(SOCKTYPE *sock)
{
    int rc;
    SOCKTYPE sock3;

    static SOCKTYPE sock1;
    static struct sockaddr_in addr1;
    struct sockaddr_in addr2;
    int addr2len;
    static int first = 1;

    if(first) {
        addr1.sin_family      = AF_INET;
        addr1.sin_addr.s_addr = naddr;   // global
        addr1.sin_port        = port;    // global

        sock1 = socket(AF_INET, SOCK_STREAM, 0);
        if(sock1 == BADSOCK) {
            printf("socket FAILED: err=%d\n",Errno);
            exit(1);
        }

        rc = bind(sock1,(const struct sockaddr *)&addr1,
```

```
                    sizeof(addr1));
        if(rc == SOCKERR) {
            printf("bind FAILED: err=%d\n", Errno);
            exit(1);
        }

        rc = listen(sock1,5);
        if(rc) {
            printf("Listen FAILED: err=%d\n", Errno);
            exit(1);
        }
        first = 0;
    }
    addr2len = sizeof(addr2);
    sock3 = accept(sock1, (struct sockaddr *)&addr2,
                (socklen_t *)&addr2len);
    if(sock3 == BADSOCK) {
        printf("Accept FAILED: err=%d\n", Errno);
        exit(1);
    }
    *sock = sock3;
}
```

In this code segment, we have decided that all unexpected results should cause a program termination. Without detailed analysis of why each error might occur, this method makes for a predictable program, notwithstanding errors. Continuing in the presence of any of the preceding errors is difficult; passing a return value back to the calling routine that a failure occurred simply compounds the problems by making the caller attempt to discover what went wrong. By printing a message and exiting the program immediately, discovering an unexpected result focuses programming efforts precisely where the problem occurred. We have found over the years that correctness and debugability are more important than performance, and our code tries to reflect this point of view.

Servers listen and accept while clients connect. The following shows another wrapper program to perform the details of establishing a connection:

```
extern int econnrefuseretries;

SOCKTYPE clientconnect(int *per_client_refusecnt)
{
    SOCKTYPE sock2;
    struct sockaddr_in addr1;
    int refusedcount;

    addr1.sin_family      = AF_INET;
    addr1.sin_addr.s_addr = naddr;
    addr1.sin_port        = port;
```

```
    sock2 = socket(AF_INET, SOCK_STREAM, 0);
    if(sock2 == BADSOCK) {
        printf("socket FAILED: err=%d\n", Errno);
        exit(1);
    }

    refusedcount = 0;
    while(connect(sock2, (struct sockaddr *)&addr1,
                  sizeof(addr1))) {
        int err;

        err = Errno;
        if(err != ECONNREFUSED) {
            printf("connect FAILED: err=%d\n",Errno);
            exit(1);
        }
        SLEEP(2); // Be polite
        *per_client_refusecnt++;
        if(refusedcount++ >= econnrefuseretries) {
            printf("connect FAILED: ");
            printf("after %d ECONNREFUSED attempts\n",
                econnrefuseretries);
            exit(1);
        }
    }
    return sock2;
}
```

These two code segments bear some discussion. The `listen_and_accept()` routine is written to be used as simply as possible; it either returns a usable socket or prints an error and exits. The `clientconnect()` routine either returns a usable socket or prints an error and exits. It processes the ECONNREFUSED error return in an attempt to deal with a server that is too busy to accept the socket request. That happens to any `listen` and `accept` loop when the queue of requests in the operating system is longer than the default of 5. For instance, if a server issues a `listen_and_accept()`, receives an incoming socket, and then simply goes to sleep, succeeding incoming requests are queued by the operating system until there are five of them. The sixth connection request is refused, and the ECONNREFUSED error is reported by the client issuing a connect request (`clientconnect()` in our case). Our code simply sleeps for 2 seconds and tries again. We have allowed, by default, four retries. The number can be changed by editing the program and recompiling. Alternatively, it would be trivial to add a new option that allows the value to be set on the command line.

We have described the actions required to create socket connections. The details of socket connections are seldom the source of performance problems. It is what happens after the socket is created that becomes interesting.

Threads

Because our program uses threads and demonstrates thread pooling, we must describe how threads work and our usage of them. We don't claim that any of the following code is the best-performing code. We do claim that the code demonstrates how threads can be used in both a pooled and nonpooled manner, and that the code is reasonably good. No doubt, improvements are possible.

Recalling from earlier, our description of the server `main` program where a scheduler and a cleanup thread were created, we will show these two modules. There is a third module we haven't yet mentioned. It is the thread that listens for new work to queue. The work is the newly created socket, and it is the socket that is queued. Our worker program reads a text string from the socket containing the file size and block size to use in doing the work. Other experimentations with this code could replace our worker thread with one written for almost any purpose whatever. To summarize, the following takes place:

1. The Listener listens for new connections and inserts work (the newly created socket) into the work queue.
2. The thread scheduler waits for work in the queue and starts a thread passing the socket file descriptor to the thread. The scheduler can be run using pooled threads or in the mode where it creates a new thread for each work item (`-pooling` command-line option).
3. The work thread does all the work and finally closes the socket.
4. The thread cleanup awaits thread deaths and cleans up after them.

Surrounding the worker thread are the fixtures to report back to the client the completion of the task.

The thread listener is coded as shown here:

```
void ServerMain()
{
    SOCKTYPE sock;

    initq(&workq);
    newThread( (void(*)(void *)) threadScheduler,0, &schedulerT);
    newThread( (void(*)(void *)) threadCleanup,0, &cleanupT);
    newThread( (void(*)(void *)) threadDbg, 0, &dbgT);

    // Server waits in a listen/accept sequence and hands off
    // request to a thread. Threads are either dynamically
    // created or there is a pool.
    //
    // listen_and_accept creates sockets
```

```
    //
    for(;;) {
        listen_and_accept(&sock);
        enqueue(&workq, sock);
        vsema(&workq.sema);
    }
}
```

The thread scheduler reads information from a queue. The queue is protected by synchronization primitives, which we discuss later in the chapter. The protections allow multiple threads to update the queue without making the queue metadata inconsistent. The thread scheduler is coded as shown here:

```
void threadScheduler()
{
    SOCKTYPE sock;
    int rc;

    //
    // threadScheduler decrements availableThreads,
    // threadCleanup   increments availableThreads.
    //
    for(;;) {

        schedulerstate = 1;
        psema(&workq.sema);

        schedulerstate = 2;
        psema(&availableThreads);

        schedulerstate = 3;
        if(dequeue(&workq, (int *)&sock)) {
            schedulerstate = 4;
            rc = threadStart(sock); // starting a thread
            if(rc == -1) {
                printf("threadStart FAILED: maxthreads=%d\n",
                    maxthreads); fflush(stdout);
                exit(1);
            }
        }
        else {
            printf("Workq Sema count wrong\n");
            exit(1);
        }
    }
}
```

Thread cleanup is coded as shown here:

```
void threadCleanup()
{
    int j = 0;

    //
    // For pooled threads, this loop will last forever.
    //
    for(;;) {
        cleanupstate = 1;
        psema(&ActiveT);
        cleanupstate = 2;

        for(j = 0; j < maxthreads; j++) {
            if(threads[j].exists) {
                threadWait(&threads[j].thrd);
                threads[j].exists = 0;
                threads[j].active = 0;
                nexists--;
                vsema(&availableThreads);
            }
        }
    }
}
```

These three modules require some background discussion. The listener module simply accepts new sockets and queues them. It is simple, and the only thing to think about is that it must queue the work consistently; therefore, it uses the enqueue() routine. The thread scheduler must create threads or allocate existing (pooled) threads. Threads are created with a pthread_create() call. Because our program wants to start a thread that is either already created (a pooled thread) or create a fresh one, we have chosen to abstract the thread-starting process with the threadStart() routine. threadStart() uses the pooling global variable to determine whether to use a pooled thread or to simply start a new thread. The pooling global defaults to no pooling and is a command-line option.

The command line tells the server and client how many threads to use. The default is one. The server runs no more than the number of threads specified on the command line at one time. This works in the same way for the client. Each server thread performs its work and *ends*. A pooled thread *ends* by marking itself as inactive and blocking on a lock. An unpooled thread simply returns, thus destroying the thread. For nonpooled threads, the cleanup routine is essential if the system is not to run out of resources. It is the cleanup routine that returns the resources used by nonpooled threads to the system.

We add one further observation about our thread code. Writing threaded code that schedules work using pooled threads is not exactly trivial. Determining why things are not working properly can be time-consuming. We demonstrate here one method of making the debugging task simpler. Our thread management routines (scheduler and cleanup) each have a global state variable. The state variables represent the current state of the routine and are accessible from all threads in the program. The variables are changed just prior to any function call that could block. By printing these two state variables, we can determine exactly where in the code the scheduler and cleanup threads are currently blocked. We wrote a trivial debug thread that can print the values of these state variables, and together with the state variables the debugging task was significantly accelerated.

Synchronization

The scheduler uses synchronization primitives (semaphores) to block when there is nothing to do. Semaphores are used as a synchronized counting mechanism where, if there are things to do, the number of things to do is reflected in the value of the semaphore. If the count is greater than zero, the `psema()` routine decrements the count by one and returns to the calling program. If the value of the semaphore is zero, the `psema()` routine blocks. The `vsema()` operation increments the semaphore and never blocks. Our `psema()` and `vsema()` routines are based on the `semaphores(3)` interfaces defined in section 3 of the manual (`man 3 semaphores`). Our interfaces take a name that enables us to debug them with more clarity—we can print the name of the semaphore we are examining by inserting appropriate print statements. We use one semaphore to count the number of available threads (either pooled or nonpooled), one to count the number of tasks (jobs, work items, or whatever we want to call them), and one to count the number of active threads.

The semaphore interfaces are defined as shown here:

```
void initsema(PVSEMA *s, int initvalue, int hi, char *name)
{
  if(sem_init(&s->pv,0,initvalue) == -1) {
    printf("sem_init() FAILED: sema=<%s> err=%d\n",name,Errno);
      exit(1);
  }
  s->name = name;
}
void psema(PVSEMA *s)    // decrements or blocks if s==0
{
  sem_wait(&s->pv);
}
void vsema(PVSEMA *s)    // increments
{
```

```
   int rc;

   rc = sem_post(&s->pv);
   if(rc == -1) {
     printf("sem_post(<%s>) FAILED: err=%d\n",Errno);
     exit(1);
   }
}
```

Finally, there are the queuing operations. Their job is to protect the data structures describing the queue of jobs coming in. The queue is operated with `enqueue()` and `dequeue()` operations. To support the queuing and dequeuing of data, `lck` and `unlck` implement locks on specified objects (the work queue in this case). We will show the `enqueue` routine and the associated `dequeue` routine.

You might ask why there are two counting mechanisms. The semaphore counting mechanism is specifically for counting. Because the numbers of threads (active and available) are strictly numbers, the only mechanism we need is counting. The queuing routines were written for more general queuing where objects could be queued. In this case, they require more than a simple count. For our particular demonstration here, they have been detuned to queue only integers (socket file descriptors); thus, they are similar in function to the semaphore operations.

That said, the following shows the queue initialization and the enqueuing routines:

```
void initq(queue_t *q)
{
    initsema(&q->sema, 0, workqsize, qsema);
    q->val = (int *)Malloc(workqsize*sizeof(int));
    memset(q->val,'\0',workqsize*sizeof(int));
    q->qmax = workqsize;
    initlck(&q->lck, workqname);
    q->head = q->tail = 0;
}


//
// This version stops queuing when it bumps
// into its own tail.
//
int enqueue(queue_t *q, int val)
{
    int ret = 1;
    int h;

    lck(&q->lck);
    h = q->head + 1;
    if(h == q->qmax)
```

```
            h = 0;
    if(h != q->tail) {
        q->val[h] = val;
        q->head = h;
        q->qcnt++;
    }
    else
        ret = 0;
    unlck(&q->lck);
    return ret;
}
```

The `dequeue` routine is similar.

The locking (`lck` and `unlck`) routines are built from Posix thread *mutexes*. Mutexes are efficient thread synchronization primitives defined in the Posix thread library. They support mutual exclusion between threads, but not between processes. A Posix mutex supports three kinds of mutex:

- PTHREAD_MUTEX_FAST_NP
- PTHREAD_MUTEX_RECURSIVE_NP
- PTHREAD_MUTEX_ERRORCHECK_NP

The FAST variant does not allow reentry into the mutex by the calling thread. Thus, if thread A locks using a `pthread_mutex_lock` and it attempts to lock the same mutex a second time, it blocks. Depending on the program's design, this might produce a deadlock. The RECURSIVE kind allows multiple `pthread_mutex_lock()` calls within a thread. However, for each `pthread_mutex_lock()` call, there must be a corresponding `pthread_mutex_unlock()` call. Finally, the ERRORCHECK kind returns an error if thread A attempts to lock a mutex more than once.

Our lock and unlock calls use the FAST kind because our design is such that if a thread calls a mutex lock more than once, it is an error in our logic. Debugging such a design is more easily accomplished if the ERRORCHECK kind is substituted during development. The following shows the lock and unlock primitives:

```
void initlck(LCK *l, char *name)
{
    //
    // Linux default is a "fast" mutex. A "fast" mutex
    // locks when the same thread calls it twice.
    //
    pthread_mutex_init(l,NULL);
}
void lck(LCK *l)
{
```

```
    int err;

    err = pthread_mutex_lock(1);
    if(err != 0) {
        printf("pthread_mutex_lck FAILED: err=%d\n",err);
        exit(1);
    }
}
void unlck(LCK *1)
{
    pthread_mutex_unlock(1);
}
int islocked(LCK *1)
{
    return (pthread_mutex_trylock(1) != EBUSY) ;
}
```

Of these primitives, only the mutexes from the thread library are based on the mutual exclusion instructions of the native processor. They should be significantly faster than interprocess synchronization primitives, because frequently no system call is required to execute. Contrast that with a semaphore operation that must maintain a counter that is visible to all processes. To either increment the counter or decrement it, the interface must issue a system call necessitating a transition into the operating system proper. For this overhead reason, mutexes are generally recognized as delivering high performance—or, to put it another way, to take less time to execute.

Using the timing primitives described previously, it is trivial to make a program that executes millions of calls to the interface and prints the time it takes to do it. One of the authors has done this and published the results for Red Hat 7.0. The results are reproduced here:

Interface	Linux 2.4.2 (microseconds per call)
SRV5_Semaphores	1.828
Posix Semaphores	0.487
Pthread_mutex	0.262

This measurement was done in a ThinkPad 600X (650MHz, 512MB memory). (SVR5 semaphores are a second variety of semaphores, older in design, and, obviously, as shown in the table, a bit slower.) Documentation for SVR5 semaphores can be seen with the man semop command. Documentation for the Posix semaphores can be found with man sem_init, and documentation for the Posix thread mutexes can be seen using the man pthread_mutex_init command.

FILE I/O

Our file I/O is quite simple. We want to create a file of arbitrary length, write data into it, read it back, and check the data. As we read the data from the file, it is sent over the internet to the client who requested it. We invent data on the fly. Basically, we write blocks of data into a file until it reaches the requisite size. We also write the page number or the block number into each block. Thus, each block is self-identifying to some extent. The following shows the code within the worker thread that creates, writes, reads, closes, and removes the file:

```
int fd;

fd = open(namebuf, O_RDWR|O_CREAT, S_IRWXU);
if(fd == -1) {
  printf("open <%s> FAILED: err=%d\n",namebuf,Errno);
  exit(1);
}

//writeFile();

pageno = 0;
bytesleft = fsz;

while(bytesleft > 0) {
  cnt = (bytesleft < bsz) ? bytesleft : bsz;
  if(cnt > 4)
    memcpy(buf, &pageno, sizeof(pageno));
  if(write(fd, buf, cnt) != cnt) {
    printf("write %d bytes FAILED: err=%d\n",Errno);
    exit(1);
  }
  pageno++;
  bytesleft -= cnt;
}

//readFile();

lseek(fd, 0L, SEEK_SET);

bytesleft = fsz;
rpageno = 0;

while(bytesleft > 0) {
  cnt = (bytesleft < bsz) ? bytesleft : bsz;
  if(read(fd, buf, cnt) != cnt) {
    printf("read %d bytes FAILED: err=%d\n",Errno);
    exit(1);
  }
```

```
if(cnt > 4) {
  if(0 != memcmp(buf, &rpageno, sizeof(rpageno))) {
    printf("Read Compare ERROR: rpageno=%d",rpageno);
    printf(" buf[0] = %x %x %x %x\n",
      buf[0]&0xFF,
      buf[1]&0xFF,
      buf[2]&0xFF,
      buf[3]&0xFF);
    exit(1);
  }
}
rc = Send(sock, buf, cnt, 0);
if(rc != cnt) {
  printf("th[%d]: SERVER: Send FAILED: rc=%d err=%d\n",
      th, rc,Errno);
  exit(1);
}
rpageno++;
bytesleft -= cnt;
}

//closeFile();

if(close(fd) == -1) {
  printf("close FAILED: err=%d\n",Errno);
  exit(1);
}
//deleteFile();

if(unlink(namebuf) == -1) {
  printf("unlink <%s> FAILED: err=%d\n",namebuf,Errno);
  exit(1);
}
```

As you can see from this example, the code is straightforward. After writing all the data to the file, the program uses `lseek()` to return to the beginning of the file, where it begins reading the file. Each block of the file is checked for correctness (trivial check, admittedly) and then is transmitted to the client program (the client program also checks the data). There is nothing complex about this code, other than the fact that the file size and the block size can be parameterized.

The Client

The client portion of the code uses some of the facilities previously discussed. Whether or not the server configures itself to use pooled threads, the client simply starts the number of threads specified on the command line and waits until all the work is completed.

Each client thread continues in a loop, taking a single item of the work queue, sending it to the server, receiving all the data the server transmits back, checking the data as it arrives, and finally closing the socket. The client then proceeds to get another item of the work queue, starting the same process all over again. Each client thread continues these operations until the work queue is empty. As each client determines that the queue is empty, it exits.

This particular design methodology represents an asynchronous approach to problem solving. A thread is dedicated to each work item. If any particular work item takes a longer amount of time, the remaining threads continue emptying the queue. Using this methodology, computing fractal pictures could easily be optimized where some pixels take millions of iterations to complete and some take less than 100. The difficult pixels would occupy a thread, while many trivial pixels (fractal points with a small number of iterations) would be completed by the remaining threads.

The client code loops look like this:

```
while(workqcnt > 0) {
  lck(&workqcntL);
    if(workqcnt == 0) {
      unlck(&workqcntL);
      break;
    }
    workqcnt--;
  unlck(&workqcntL);
  sock = clientconnect(&tp->refusecnt);
  rpageno = 0;

// Send command to server.
  sprintf(tp->cbuf, "F,%d,%d", filesize,fileblksz);
  rc = Send(sock, (char *)tp->cbuf, CBUFSIZE, 0);
  if(rc != CBUFSIZE) {
    printf("\tCLIENT[%d]: CBUF Send FAILED: err=%d\n",
      th,Errno);
    exit(1);
  }
  tp->sndbytes += CBUFSIZE;

// set buffer size using thread safe reMalloc()
  if(fileblksz > threads[th].bufmax) {
    threads[th].buf = (char *)reMalloc(threads[th].buf,
                                       fileblksz);
    threads[th].bufmax = fileblksz;
  }
  threads[th].bufsiz = fileblksz;
  buf = threads[th].buf;
```

```
// Receive filesize bytes from Server and check contents.
  bytesleft = filesize;
  while(bytesleft > 0) {
    cnt = (bytesleft < fileblksz) ? byteslett : fileblksz;
    rc = Recv(sock, buf, cnt, 0);
    if(rc == SOCKERR) {
      printf("CLIENT: th[%d]: Recv failed: rc=%d err=%d\n",
          th, rc,Errno);
      exit(1);
    }
    else if(rc == 0)
      break;
    if(rc > 4) {
      if(0 != memcmp(&rpageno, buf, 4)) {
        printf("CLIENT: compare error on pageno %d",rpageno);
        printf(" buf[0] = %x %x %x %x\n",
          buf[0]&0xFF,
          buf[1]&0xFF,
          buf[2]&0xFF,
          buf[3]&0xFF);
        exit(1);
      }
    }
    tp->rcvbytes += rc;
    rpageno++;
    bytesleft -= rc;
  }

// Wait for "DONE" from Server
  rc = Recv(sock, (char *)tp->cbuf, 4, 0);
  if(rc != 4 || !equaln(tp->cbuf, "DONE", 4)) {
    printf("\tCLIENT[%d]: Recv 'DONE' FAILED: rc=%d err=%d\n",
      th,rc,Errno);
    fflush(stdout);
    exit(1);
  }
  tp->rcvbytes += 4;

// Send 'Q'
  tp->cbuf[0] = 'Q';
  rc = Send(sock, (char *)tp->cbuf, 1, 0);
  if(rc != 1) {
    printf("\tCLIENT[%d]: Send 'Q' FAILED: rc=%d err=%d\n",
        th,rc,Errno);
    fflush(stdout);
    exit(1);
  }
```

```
  tp->sndbytes += 1;
  rc = CLOSESOCK(sock);
  if(rc != 0) {
    printf("\tCLIENT[%d]: close socket %d FAILED: Errno=%d\n",
           th,sock,Errno);
    exit(1);
  }
}
```

Code Discussion

A number of different synchronization mechanisms have been used here. Counting semaphores are used to simply count available resources. The counter blocks when none is available. Both the thread scheduler and cleanup thread use a semaphore to know when something needs to be done. An earlier cleanup design simply looked for active threads every 2 seconds. Although the performance difference is probably negligible, the resulting design using semaphores leaves the system completely idle when there is nothing to do. (psema, vsema, and initsema are based on Posix semaphores.)

Locking primitives are used to count the number of work items in the client. They are based on a memory variable and a critical section lock. This design was devolved from the queuing primitives described in the next paragraph. The desire to queue millions of items suggested that each should take no memory. Therefore, this interface was derived to support decrementing a counter as the mechanism for dequeuing an object. (initlck, lck, and unlck are based on Posix thread mutexes.)

Finally, the third version of synchronization used is to queue objects. A Posix pthread mutex is used to guard an actual memory queue, each element of which can contain a single integer. The integer in our case is a socket file descriptor received from the listen_and_connect() routine in the server's main thread. (initq, enqueue, and dequeue are based on the previously described locking primitives, which in turn are based on Posix pthread mutexes.)

Our design is asynchronous. The server consumes no CPU cycles if there is nothing to do. The client either has something to do or it exits. The client's responsibility is to pass all the work to be done to the server, wait until the server completes all the work, and finally print timing and performance results.

Compilation Options

After we have written our program, we want to compile it and run it. Our program is called srv3.cpp. To compile it, the following command line is used:

```
g++ -O2 -Wall srv3.cpp -lpthread -o server && cp server c
```

The g++ command is used to assure we are compiling using the strong typing of C++. This particular program uses almost no C++ features, but the strong typing of C++ is used. The command line above the -Wall option instructs the compiler to print all warnings. Demanding the strictest possible conformance to excellent programming standards is guaranteed to produce code that requires less debugging and less support. One of the authors has seen software projects remove unknown bugs from programs simply by changing the compilation option to more emit warnings and changing the code to remove the warnings. If a program of any size compiles and executes properly and has never endured the removal of all warnings, we challenge you to go through the effort once. If after the effort you aren't convinced that bugs were removed, we would be quite surprised.

The -Wall command line is intended to produce two executables. The first is a program called server, and the second is a program called c. The first is our server program, and the other is our client program. (We didn't name it client for fear of colliding with an existing program that might be called client.)

A useful option to the GNU C compiler is the -v option, which causes g++ to print all the intermediate steps it takes to produce the executables. When using the verbose option to g++, g++ does not instruct the linker to also produce verbose output. To do that, the following addition is required:

```
-Xlinker -verbose
```

Thus, the following produces the most output (into a file called xx). From it you can see what the compiler and linker are doing:

```
g++ -O2 -Wall -v -Xlinker -verbose srv3.cpp -lpthread -o server 2>xx
```

Libraries

We compiled our program using the Posix thread dynamic link library by specifying -lpthread on the command line. We could have used statically linked libraries. As installed, we could not compile our program using static libraries. That said, why would we want to?

Static versus dynamic libraries is a question whose answer is surprising. Dynamic link libraries have the following benefits:

- *GPL independence.* If your programs are linked to dynamic link libraries, they are not encumbered with GPL (GNU Public Library) provisions. The GPL license requires all who embed GPL code in a program to make available the source code. The current understanding is that statically linking a program is a form of embedding GPL code in a program. Therefore, development teams that produce programs statically linked with GPL could also be required to publish the source code of the entire program. This reason alone is generally enough to eliminate the thought of statically linking programs.

- *Dynamic linking allows bugs to be fixed independent of the program.* If a bug shows up in a dynamic link library, simply shipping a new library can fix your program. Due to the heightened awareness of security issues, updated dynamic link libraries are quite likely to happen.

- *Dynamic linking produces smaller programs.* Programs dynamically linked contain only stubs of APIs needed to execute the program. Clearly, stubs are much smaller than the actual code to implement an API or even an entire suite of functions.

- *An increase in portability.* The emerging Linux Standards Base specification for Linux operating systems requires applications to be dynamically linked to ensure proper use of local system services. A static version of a system library may no longer work properly on future revisions of the OS.

The reasons seem compelling, but the other side of the picture leaves the issue open to design. Here are some counterpoints:

- GPL independence can also be achieved by simply buying the appropriate libraries to use with your product. That becomes difficult with system libraries and may not be possible. The Posix threading library is a case in point where obtaining a GPL free version might be exceedingly difficult.

- Static libraries mean that when a bug is fixed, your program is unaffected. When your program uses a single API in a library containing possibly thousands of APIs, the likelihood of the library's being updated is high. Each update to the library is a risk to your program over which you have no control. Such risks are worth investigating.

- Because the size of disk drives has increased much faster than program size, on-disk footprint is less of an issue.

The general recommendation is to use dynamic link libraries where possible, using static linking for libraries that may not be found on the destination platform and that cannot be distributed with your application.

Summary

Tuning code for performance is a combination of efforts, beginning with choosing the proper ways to solve a problem and using the proper tools (the appropriate system resources) for the job. After writing the code, a cycle of analysis (profiling) and tuning, in combination with proper compilation, can help you can achieve even greater performance.

## PART IV

Performance Characterization of Linux Server Applications

CHAPTER FIFTEEN

Web Servers

By Erich Nahum

INTRODUCTION

One of the most popular ways Linux is used is as a platform for running a web server. These days, most people are familiar with the World Wide Web (WWW). Much like many other distributed systems described in this book, the WWW is built on the client/ server model. In the web, clients are the people who "surf," using browsers such as Internet Explorer or Mozilla, generating web requests that are sent to web servers, which respond to these requests. The server is responsible for receiving the request, taking the appropriate actions to find and process the request, and then sending the proper response to the client. Thus, web servers implement the server-side functionality in the WWW and communicate with clients using HyperText Transfer Protocol (HTTP). HTTP is the standard by which clients and servers communicate, allowing interoperability between different vendors and different software. This chapter provides an overview of the following:

- What web servers do
- How web servers use the network
- What steps web servers take to service requests
- What concurrency models are used
- Common tuning options for web servers
- How web server performance is evaluated

We'll focus on how web servers deal with static content, such as HTML files and GIF images. By static content, we mean that the HTTP *responses* that are provided by the server change relatively infrequently—for example, through human intervention. In this context, web servers are similar to file servers in that their main function is to distribute files, albeit files that have special meaning and interpretation to HTTP clients. Web servers also can produce content that is generated more *dynamically*—namely, through a parameter-driven program such as CGI or PHP. However, dynamic content generation has evolved considerably beyond simple HTTP. This chapter sticks to relatively simple HTTP requests.

HTTP REQUESTS AND RESPONSES

HTTP requests and responses are unusual compared to other client/server exchanges in that they are ASCII text-based rather than binary encoded, as in NFS. This is an artifact of how the web was developed, yet it is convenient in that it allows humans to easily read the generated requests and responses. The following is an example of a web request generated by a browser (in this case, Mozilla):

```
GET /index.html HTTP/1.1Host: www.kernel.org
User-Agent: Mozilla/5.0 (X11; U; Linux i686; en-US;
rv:1.0.2)
Accept:text/xml,application/xml,application/xhtml+xml,
text/html;
q=0.9,text/plain;q=0.8,video/x-mng,image/png,image/jpeg,
image/gif;q=0.2,text/css,*/*;q=0.1
Accept-Language: en-us, en;q=0.50
Accept-Encoding: identity;q=1.0, *;q=0
Accept-Charset: ISO-8859-1, utf-8;q=0.66, *;q=0.66
Cache-Control: max-age=0
Connection: close
<cr><lf>
```

Note that the first line contains the request for the file desired and that each following line contains headers with appropriate values. The GET request specifies both the file requested and the protocol version used by the client. The headers communicate information to the server about what kinds of features this particular client supports. In this case, the client is Mozilla, which accepts various formats such as HTML text, GIF, JPEG, and XML, and uses the English language. This negotiation allows clients and servers to dynamically learn each others' capabilities so that they can communicate most effectively. We continue the example with the server's ASCII HTTP response:

```
HTTP/1.1 200 OK
Date: Wed, 17 Mar 2004 21:38:55 GMT
Server: Apache/2.0.40 (Red Hat Linux)
Accept-Ranges: bytes
Connection: close
Transfer-Encoding: chunked
Content-Type: text/html
<cr><lf>
50c
<!DOCTYPE HTML PUBLIC "-//W3C//DTD HTML 3.2 Final//EN">
<!-- $Id: index.shtml,v 1.222 2004/02/24 02:05:15
```

```
hpa Exp $ -->
<HTML>
<HEAD>
   <META HTTP-EQUIV="Content-Type" CONTENT="text/html;
   charset=utf-8">
   <TITLE>The Linux Kernel Archives</TITLE>
   <LINK REL="icon" TYPE="image/png"
   HREF="images/tux16-16.png">
</HEAD>
<BODY TEXT="#000000" BGCOLOR="#FFFFFF" LINK="#0000E0"
VLINK="#8A1A49" ALINK="#ff0000" BACKGROUND="images/splash.png">

<CENTER><P><H1>The Linux Kernel Archives</H1></CENTER>
<P>
<CENTER>
Welcome to the Linux Kernel Archives.  This is the primary site for
   the Linux kernel source, but it has much more than just kernels.
</CENTER>
```

This response shows that the server understood the client request and is providing the response (indicated by the 200 OK message). In addition, the server uses the headers to tell the client that it is using a feature to send messages in chunks rather than all at once (called *chunked encoding*) and is capable of sending subsets of the response rather than the entire response (called *byte range requests*). Finally, the HTML content is returned, which is parsed and displayed by the browser. This exchange is just an example of *one* of the ways in which HTTP works, albeit perhaps the most common example. HTTP is a large, complex protocol, and elaborating on its many intricacies is beyond the scope of this book. We refer you to Krishnamurthy and Rexford 2001 for an excellent overview of HTTP.

NETWORK BEHAVIOR OF A WEB SERVER

Like other protocols, HTTP is layered above the TCP/IP stack. The following shows this layering, using the same ISO model from Chapter 16, "File and Print Servers."

ISO Layering Model

Application	HTTP
Presentation	
Session	
Transport	TCP
Network	IP
Data link	IEEE 802.3
Physical	Ethernet

Using the Ethereal packet-capture tool discussed in Chapter 16, we can see the individual requests and responses from the "Protocol Layering" section of Chapter 16. Figure 15-1 shows the packet exchange used in that example.

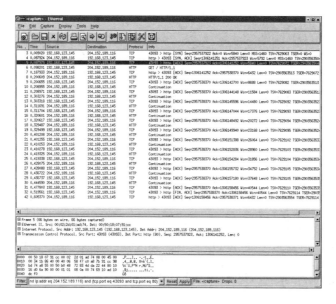

Figure 15-1   Sample packet exchanges captured by the Ethereal tool.

The first three packets illustrate the TCP three-way handshake used to establish a connection to the web server. The fourth packet contains the HTTP request from the client, and the sixth contains the response header with the 200 OK message. The remaining packets are mostly either data packets containing the body of the HTTP response (packets from the server to the client) or the TCP acknowledgments for that data (packets from the client to the server). The final four packets are the four-way handshake used to shut down the connection (the first FIN from the server is packet number 30; the FIN bit is not visible in the figure but it is there if you expand the view of the packet).

Figure 15-2 illustrates one packet in detail.

Zooming in on packet 8, which contains the HTTP response headers from the server, we see that this is an HTTP packet encapsulated on top of TCP, which in turn is embedded in an IP packet, which itself is the payload of an Ethernet packet.

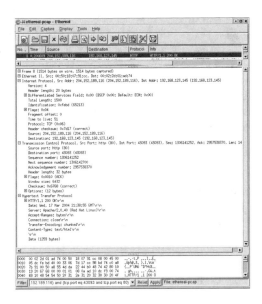

Figure 15-2   Detail of one packet exchange captured by the Ethereal tool.

ANATOMY OF A WEB SERVER TRANSACTION

Next, we'll show the steps a web server takes in response to a client request. For this purpose, we provide the following pseudocode:

```
s = socket(); /* allocate listen socket */
bind(s, 80);  /* bind to TCP port 80     */
listen(s);    /* indicate willingness to accept */
while (1) {
newconn = accept(s);          /* accept new connection */
remoteIP = getsockname(newconn);   /* get remote IP addr */
remoteHost = gethostbyname(remoteIP);
/* get remote IP DNS name */
gettimeofday(currentTime);
/* determine time of day */
read(newconn, reqBuffer, sizeof(reqBuffer));
 /* read client request */
reqInfo = serverParse(reqBuffer);
/* parse client request */
fileName = parseOutFileName(requestBuffer);
/* determine file name */
fileAttr = stat(fileName);  /* get file attributes */
serverCheckFileStuff(fileName, fileAttr);
/* check permissions */
```

```
open(fileName);          /* open file */
read(fileName, fileBuffer);     /* read file into buffer */
headerBuffer = serverFigureHeaders(fileName,
/* determine headers */
reqInfo);
write(newSock, headerBuffer);  /* write headers to socket */
write(newSock, fileBuffer);    /* write file to socket */
close(newSock);                /* close socket */
close(fileName);               /* close file */
write(logFile, requestInfo);   /* write log info to disk */
}
```

This pseudocode is a relatively simple implementation of a server that does not employ any possible optimizations and can handle only one request at a time. This example only hints at the more complex functionality that is required by the server, such as how to parse the HTTP request and determine whether the client has the appropriate permissions to view the file. In addition, it has no error handling—for example, if the client requests a file that does not exist. However, this example gives a good idea of what steps are required by a server.

DIFFERENT MODELS OF WEB SERVERS

Like many other servers, web servers have certain performance requirements that affect how the server is implemented. Several possibilities are available for the architectural model that the server is implemented with. One of the major issues is how the server handles *concurrency*. Web servers are required to handle many clients simultaneously, sometimes up to tens of thousands of clients. In the previous example, the server deals with only one client at a time. For example, if the file that the client requests is not in the server's file cache, the server *blocks* waiting for the file to be loaded from disk. During this time, the server could be handling other requests that may be less expensive to serve, but the previous example instead waits, wasting cycles. In addition, because the previous example uses a single process, if the server is an SMP, other processors are completely underutilized. The typical approach to dealing with this problem is through some form of concurrency mechanism; we describe several approaches in this section.

The most common form of concurrency is using processes. The most popular web server, Apache, was originally implemented using processes. Each process has a separate address space and is fully protected and isolated from other processes through a virtual machine abstraction. By assigning each request to a separate process, one process can make forward progress while another is blocked on another activity (such as waiting for a client or disk). In addition, on an SMP, multiple processes can run in parallel. The disadvantage of processes is that they are relatively expensive abstractions to use, requiring resources such as memory to be allocated to them. If a server has thousands of clients, it may have thousands of processes, which can tax a system's resources. Typically, any system is limited in the number of processes it can have active.

The next most common approach is using threads. Apache 2.0 provides the option of using threads rather than processes. Threads are similar to processes but are lighter-weight—namely, they require fewer system resources. Threads typically share address spaces but have separate program counters and stacks. Threads are cheaper than processes but trade protection for speed. In addition, systems can run low on resources even using threads, given a large enough number of clients.

Many research web servers, such as the Flash web server from Rice University (not to be confused with MacroMedia's Flash browser plug-in), use something called the event-driven model. In this model, a single process is used, without threads, and connections are managed using a multiplexing system call such as `select()` or `poll()`. The server queries the readiness of all connections using the system call and determines which connections require service (and, conversely, which are idle). The server then reads requests or writes responses as appropriate for that particular connection. The advantage of the event-driven model is that it is typically faster than process- or thread-based servers, because it maximizes locality and has many performance optimizations not available to these other models. The disadvantage is that it is more difficult to program, because the developer must explicitly manage state for many requests, each of which can be in a different stage of progress. In addition, operating system support for interacting with the disk in this model (namely, asynchronously) has been historically absent in Linux. However, with the introduction of asynchronous I/O in Linux 2.6, this limitation is being remedied.

The final architectural model we consider here is the in-kernel model. Examples include Red Hat's Tux server and IBM's AFPA server. In this approach, the entire web server is run as a set of kernel threads, rather than in user space. The advantages of this approach are that performance is maximized (because sharing is easy), data copies are avoided, and no expensive user-kernel crossings are incurred. The disadvantages are that kernel programming is more difficult, less portable, and more dangerous than user-space programming. For example, if the server has a programming error and crashes, an in-kernel server could take down the whole machine with it.

TUNING WEB SERVERS

Many of the approaches to tuning other servers given in other chapters are appropriate for web servers as well. For example, increasing the size of the send and receive socket buffers via `sysctl` or `setsockopt`, as described in Chapter 12, "Network Tuning," is useful. Similarly, increasing the size of the accept queue helps prevent requests from being dropped by the operating system before the web server even sees them. In this section, we focus on tuning that is done for web servers in particular. This is in addition to tuning that is done on the operating system.

Tuning for All Web Servers

These changes are useful for all web servers, regardless of the architectural model.

The following parameter increases the number of TCP SYN packets that the server can queue before SYNs are dropped:

```
echo 30000 > /proc/sys/net/ipv4/tcp_max_syn_backlog
```

Web servers typically have a large number of TCP connections in the TIME-WAIT state. The following parameter increases the number connections that are allowed in that state:

```
echo 2000000 > /proc/sys/net/ipv4/tcp_max_tw_buckets
```

The following parameter sets the length for the number of packets that can be queued in the network core (below the IP layer). This allows more memory to be used for incoming packets, which would otherwise be dropped.

```
echo 50000 > /proc/sys/net/core/netdev_max_backlog
```

Apache

Apache's main configuration file is httpd.conf. Several parameters can be modified in that file to improve performance:

The following parameter sets the upper bound on the number of processes that Apache can have running concurrently:

```
MaxClients 150
```

Larger values allow larger numbers of clients to be served simultaneously. Very large values may require Apache to be recompiled. This change should be used with care, because large numbers of processes can cause excessive overhead.

The following parameter indicates the number of requests that a single Apache process will perform on a connection for a client before it closes the connection:

```
MaxKeepAliveRequests 100
```

Opening and closing connections consumes CPU cycles, so it is better for the server to provide as many responses on a single connection as possible. Therefore, larger numbers are better. In fact, setting this value to 0 indicates that the server should never close the connection if possible.

The following parameter determines the number of requests an individual Apache process will serve before it dies (and is reforked). 0 implies that the number is unlimited, but on some systems with memory leaks in the operating system, setting this to a nonzero value keeps the memory leak under control.

```
MaxRequestsPerChild 0
```

The following parameters determine the minimum and maximum number of idle processes that Apache keeps in anticipation of new requests coming in:

```
MinSpareServers 5
MaxSpareServers 10
```

The idea is that it is cheaper to keep a live process idle than to fork a new process in response to a new request arrival. For highly loaded sites, you might want to increase these values.

Flash and Other Event-Driven Servers

A common problem event-driven servers have is that they use a large number of file descriptors and thus can run out of these descriptors if the maximum is not increased.

The following is an `sh` (shell) command that increases the number of open files a process may have:

```
ulimit -n 16384
```

The process (in this case, the web server) must also be modified to take advantage of large numbers of descriptors:

```
#include <bits/types.h>
#undef  _ _FD_SETSIZE
#define _ _FD_SETSIZE 16384
```

The default `FD_SETSIZE` on Linux 2.4 is only 1024.

Tux

The following parameter determines the number of active simultaneous connections:

```
echo 20000 > /proc/sys/net/tux/max_connect
```

The following parameter sets the maximum number of connections waiting in Tux's accept queue:

```
echo 8192 > /proc/sys/net/tux/max_backlog
```

The following parameter disables logging of requests to disk:

```
echo 0 > /proc/sys/net/tux/logging
```

Performance Tools for Evaluating Web Servers

Many tools are available for evaluating the performance of web servers, also known as *workload generators*. These are programs that run on client machines, emulating a client's behavior, constructing HTTP requests, and sending them to the server. The workload generator can typically vary the volume of requests it generates, called *load*, and measures how the server behaves in response to that load. Performance metrics include items such as request latency (how long it took an individual response to come back from the server) and throughput (how many responses a server can generate per second).

Perhaps the most commonly used tool is SPECWeb99. This tool is distributed by the Standard Performance Evaluation Corporation (SPEC) nonprofit organization, whose web site is www.spec.org. This tool is probably the most-cited benchmark, and it is used for marketing purposes by server vendors such as IBM, Sun, and Microsoft. Unfortunately, the tool costs money, although it is available freely to member institutions such as IBM. The benchmark is intended to capture the main performance characteristics that have been observed in web servers, such as the size distribution and popularity of files requested. The tool is considered a macro-benchmark in that it is meant to measure whole system performance.

Another tool frequently used is httperf from HP Labs, which is available freely under an open-source license. This tool is highly configurable, allowing you to stress isolated components of a web server—for example, how well a server handles many idle connections. Thus, it is used more as a microbenchmark.

Many other tools exist for evaluating web server performance, including SURGE, WebBench, and WaspClient. However, describing them all is outside the scope of this chapter. Nevertheless, many options are available for stressing, testing, and measuring servers, and many of these are freely available.

Also useful to web site operators are *log analysis tools*. These tools look through the logs generated by the server and report information such as how many visits a site received over a period of time and where the visitors came from. Performance can be optimized when the operator understands how visitors are using a site. Logs are typically kept in a standard format called the Apache Common Log format. Many commercial tools are available; however, two freely available open-source tools are analog and webalizer.

SUMMARY

We've presented a brief overview of web servers in Linux and discussed what web servers are, what they do, and how they use the network. We also described how web servers need to handle many simultaneous clients, and we outlined the possible architectures used to implement concurrency. These include the process-based, thread-based, event-based, and kernel-based approaches; the advantages and disadvantages of each were discussed. We presented the most common tuning options for web servers on Linux, both for the operating system and for the server itself. Finally, we discussed how web server performance is evaluated and gave examples of some of the software tools used for that purpose.

REFERENCES

[1] Krishnamurthy, Balachander and Jennifer Rexford, *Web Protocols and Practice HTTP/1.1, Networking Protocols, Caching and Traffic Measurement*, Addison-Wesley, 2001.

## CHAPTER SIXTEEN

File and Print Servers

By Steven French

INTRODUCTION

As the need for more network storage continues to increase, file and print servers continue to quietly fill a key role in business, school, and even home networks. However, they are often taken for granted. Since the introduction of the first Network Operating Systems (NOSs) by Novell, 3Com, IBM, and others in the 1980s, file and print servers have increased in importance in the enterprise as their ease of use, security, performance, and reliability have improved. Although primitive UNIX file and print servers based on Network File System (NFS) were available as early as 1985 (at roughly the same time that the IBM PC LAN Program was introduced for DOS/Windows), Windows 2000 was a significant improvement over existing servers, bringing to the mass market an easy-to-manage, integrated suite of services, including the following:

- Distributed file services
- Advanced print server
- Centralized directory and integrated management
- Rich security framework and single sign-on

These services were tied together tightly and were better than earlier broad attempts at integrated services such as OSF DCE, helping Windows 2000 become popular. Businesses that stored data centrally in file servers often could better utilize resources by amortizing server storage cost among many employees and efficiently managing these server systems with consistent, easy-to-use tools. However, this quiet revolution in integrated file servers created an opportunity for the Linux community. Windows 2000 (and even its successor, Windows 2003) did not offer the configuration flexibility of Linux, was harder to integrate into heterogeneous environments (for example, with mixed UNIX and Windows systems), and often was at a performance disadvantage when compared to Linux. Also, its implementation complexity and lack of openness made the actual security of the network hard to predict and nearly impossible to assess. The open-source community responded. With dramatic improvements to the Linux kernel,

Samba, and the NFS subsystem, Linux has become an appealing file and print server choice with impressive performance.

In the sections ahead, we describe the major types of network file servers, their performance tuning and measurement, and print server performance.

TYPES OF DEDICATED NETWORK STORAGE SERVERS

Dedicated network storage servers are often classified into two types based on whether data is accessed across the network by filename (offsets in a file) or by location on disk (raw disk block numbers). The former is often called network attached storage (NAS), whereas the latter is usually referred to as storage area network (SAN), although hybrid approaches have been proposed. Examples of NAS include SMB/CIFS, AFS, and NFS servers. Examples of SAN include GPFS (IBM's General Parallel File System) and various iSCSI implementations.

File servers, in effect, are NAS servers running on a more general-purpose server operating system. NAS can be considered a specialized device that provides network file services.

OPTIMIZING THE PERFORMANCE OF NETWORK STORAGE

The remaining sections in this chapter discuss various configuration and implementation issues to consider when determining how to best optimize the performance of your network storage. Specifically, these sections discuss the following:

- Storing data remotely or locally
- Using SAN versus the Network File System
- Choosing the system protocol
- Choosing the client and server to implement
- Optimally tuning the client for the workload
- Optimally tuning the server for the workload
- Validating the performance and identifying bottlenecks
- Measuring load and improving capacity planning
- Print server performance

Determining What Data to Store Remotely

The performance of local file I/O is usually better than when the same files are accessed through a network file system. Local I/O does not overload network resources such as routers and Ethernet segments. When the server has a large amount of RAM available, sufficient for caching the commonly accessed files, there are cases in which network file system speeds can exceed local noncached file access. Storage is easier to manage centrally, and keeping a few copies of large, infrequently accessed files can avoid the problem of duplicate copies of the same files being kept on each enterprise desktop filling them to overflowing.

SAN Versus Network File Systems/NAS

As a general rule, storage area networks can transfer data faster than network file systems over networks of similar speed, because less processing is involved in parsing the network requests at the block (rather than the file) level. In addition, storage area networks often use specialized high-speed Fibre Channel switches and network hardware. Network file systems, however, provide additional security as well as the capability to back up and manage files more intuitively, advantages that often outweigh the performance advantages of SAN. Additionally, SAN cabling restrictions (and concerns about security when accessing data over corporate networks) can limit the appeal of SANs to large server rooms.

The Network File System Protocol

Network file system protocols come in all shapes and sizes. Some require complex clients to manage complex state information (such as AFS), whereas others are idempotent (stateless), such as NFS version 3. They vary from OS/2-centric (such as SMB) to Windows-centric (such as CIFS) and UNIX-centric (such as NFS). They vary in their security models, performance, and, of course, complexity. SANs move data as if it were blocks on disk, whereas most network file systems move data based on the filename or file identifier.

Making sense of this maze of protocols requires looking back and categorizing the protocols into families. The following list groups related network file system protocols into families to make it easier to understand their characteristics:

Major Network File System Families

HTTP → WebDAV

SMB → CIFS

NCP (Netware Core Protocol)

NFSv2 → NFSv3 → WebNFS → NFSv4 → DAFS

AFS → DCE/DFS, AFS → Coda → Intermezzo

AFP

GFS, GPFS, and hybrid network file systems

A more detailed description of the more popular network file systems follows. The file systems are listed in order of the approximate size of their installed base:

- *SMB/CIFS*. This network file system was invented by Dr. Barry Feigenbaum of IBM in the early 1980s, was extended heavily by Microsoft, and then was renamed CIFS in the late 1990s by Microsoft. This protocol is the default network file system on most versions of Windows (and even OS/2 and DOS), and most modern operating systems support it. The 2.6 Linux kernel includes two client implementations: the legacy smbfs and the newer CIFS VFS client, which will eventually replace smbfs. There are also user space SMB file system tools, which are commonly used on Linux (although, not part of the kernel itself), including the popular smbclient utility program, which includes an FTP-like option for retrieving files via the SMB protocol.

  The Linux 2.6 kernel also has been helpful for SMB servers. The popular open-source Samba SMB server performs up to 50% faster on the Linux 2.6 kernel than on Linux 2.4. Samba also has been ported to many other UNIX and UNIX-like operating systems. The CIFS protocol, which the Samba server and the CIFS client implement, can be used reasonably securely, and it is very rich in function due to many optional extensions. However, CIFS itself is not considered a formal standard in the sense that NFS version 4 (IETF RFC 3010) and HTTP (IETF RFC 2616) are. The Storage Network Industry Association (SNIA) does document the core CIFS protocol, and Linux/UNIX extensions to the CIFS network protocol are also standardized by SNIA. Standards proposals on additional "CIFS POSIX extensions" are in progress.

  Network protocols are often described in terms of an abstract layered model called the ISO/OSI model. This model, when applied to CIFS, can be used to represent the implementation in the layers, as shown in Figure 16-1.

- *NFS*. Since 2003, NFS version 4 (NFSv4) has become the official Internet Engineering Task Force (IETF) network file system standard. However, more widely deployed are systems based on the much more primitive NFS versions 2 and 3, which are commonly used for UNIX-to-UNIX network file system access. NFS version 3, although it performs reasonably well in Linux-to-Linux (and UNIX-to-UNIX) environments, does not handle distributed caching as safely as some other protocols. It is also prone to security problems because of its primitive design. NFSv4, which includes many CIFS-like features, addresses many of the functional and security deficiencies of version 3, but it often shows worse performance than CIFS.

  The ISO/OSI model, when applied to NFS, divides the implementation into the layers shown in Figure 16-1.

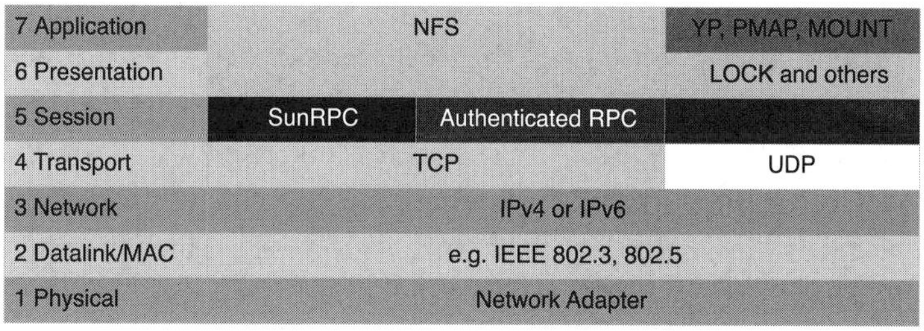

7 Application	NFS		YP, PMAP, MOUNT
6 Presentation			LOCK and others
5 Session	SunRPC	Authenticated RPC	
4 Transport	TCP		UDP
3 Network	IPv4 or IPv6		
2 Datalink/MAC	e.g. IEEE 802.3, 802.5		
1 Physical	Network Adapter		

Figure 16-1   The ISO/OSI model applied to NFS.

- *WebDAV (HTTP extensions)*. The WebDAV extensions to HTTP can be used to mount (NET USE) from newer Windows clients to many popular web servers when DAV extensions are enabled on the server. WebDAV, sometimes described as Web Folders, also has been included in applications such as web browsers. The Internet Explorer (IE) browser has included WebDAV support since IE version 5.5. WebDAV is not optimized for performance, and Linux does not include a client file system for it in the kernel at this time (although some distributions include a user-space implementation of a Linux WebDAV client). Various popular Linux applications are WebDAV-enabled.

- *AFS/DFS*. During the mid-1990s, these were the most sophisticated of the commonly deployed network file systems and commonly were used on mid- to high-end UNIX systems. AFS (and the loosely related DCE/DFS) is gradually fading in importance as IBM and others have announced plans to eventually discontinue support for them. An open full function implementation of AFS client and server, OpenAFS exists for Linux, as well as a second, more primitive AFS client, which has been accepted into the 2.6 kernel.

- *AFP*. Older Apple Macintosh operating systems (prior to OS X) used a filing protocol called AFP by default, instead of CIFS or NFS, although third-party CIFS clients for these systems were available from companies such as Thursby. Some Linux distributions include the open-source Netatalk server for handling requests from AFP clients, and at least one commercial AFP server is available (from Helios). AFP is quickly fading in importance as these clients become less common. No AFP file system client is included in the Linux kernel.

- *Specialized network file system protocols*, such as Coda and Intermezzo, and also various hybrid (some proprietary) SAN/NAS protocols, are less widely deployed. The most popular protocol from the early days of network file systems, Novell's NCP, is fading in popularity. NCP's current installed base is hard to measure, and NCP servers are rarely deployed on Linux.

- *Cluster file systems.* A battle is looming over the best Linux cluster file system. Lustre and GFS (from Red Hat/Sistina) are the early leaders in this race to get accepted into the 2.6 kernel. Cluster file systems can be thought of as network file systems that support strict POSIX file system semantics (just like local file systems) designed for use by groups of homogeneous systems coupled by high-speed networks. In addition, some of the SAN file systems, such as IBM's StorageTank and GPFS, have similar characteristics and goals. None of these have been accepted into the Linux kernel as yet, but pressure is mounting to include at least one, and they are likely to become important for supercomputer clusters in particular.

We have discussed multiple popular network file systems (including NFSv3, NFSv4, CIFS, HTTP/WebDAV, and AFS). Because network file systems have been around for almost 20 years, as can be seen from the history mentioned here, why haven't we converged on one dominant network file system (as we have converged on TCP/IP for the lower layers)? Because network and SAN file systems present unique design problems that are not perfectly addressed by any one network file system. Why are network file systems so hard to design? The following are some reasons:

- Network file systems, unlike local file systems, have to manage two views of the same data/metadata (local and server).
- They should implement distributed cache coherence over multiple machines in order to guarantee POSIX file API semantics and preserve the integrity of the following:

    File data
    File metadata (date/timestamps, ACLs)
    Directory data

- Network file systems have to work around the potential for "redundant" locks being enforced in conflicting ways on client and server.
- Network file systems have to adjust to transient identifiers for files and differing inode numbering on client and server.
- Network file systems cannot assume that the file namespace is the same on server and client, or even that the code page (the character set used for converting language characters and displaying filenames) is the same on client and server.
- Network file systems must compensate for holes, omissions, and errors in the network protocol design and/or server operating system. The NFS network file system when running on Windows, for example, has to be able to translate to UNIX-like NFS protocol frames (which were designed to map to Solaris, Linux, and similar operating system functions) from Windows file requests. This is difficult because

the Windows file API is so much bigger than the POSIX file API and includes flags that have no POSIX counterpart.

- Most network file systems implement various network security features, such as those in the following list, to provide safer transfer of data across potentially hostile routers:

  Distributed authorization
  Access control
  PDU integrity

- Network file systems deal with much more exotic, multiple-machine, network-failure scenarios, which are complex to analyze. Network file systems also have a harder time than local file systems in implementing file and server "migration" (movement/replication of data from one volume to another) and transparent recovery.

NFS version 4 and CIFS/Samba (CIFS kernel client and Samba server) on Linux address most of the issues listed here and are commonly used. But is one clearly better? Is NFS better than CIFS? Not always. The trade-offs to consider are as follows:

- NFS version 3, although quite fast, is less secure than SMB/CIFS.
- NFS maps slightly better than SMB/CIFS maps to the internal Linux VFS file system kernel API, although the CIFS VFS provides excellent POSIX semantics when mounted to a Samba server, which has enabled the optional CIFS UNIX Extensions (available in Samba version 3 or later).
- The Linux NFS client lacks support for Linux xattrs (which the CIFS client does provide) but the NFS client can handle direct I/O (which the Linux CIFS implementation currently does not).
- The CIFS mount protocol (SMB SessionSetupAndX and SMB TreeConnectAndX) does not require use of a UNIX UID, which is helpful in heterogeneous networks. UID mapping in networks that include Windows and Linux servers can be difficult. Therefore, having consistent UID mapping among servers and clients is helpful when using NFS versions 2 and 3.

Note that NFS is not popular on Windows, because most Windows versions do not include an NFS server or client in the operating system itself, and the NFS protocol maps better to the simpler UNIX VFS interface than to the complex, functionally rich Windows IFS. Microsoft does offer a simple NFS (version 2 and 3) server as a free download as part of its Services for UNIX.

NFS version 4, due to new security and caching features, will be appealing in the future, especially for Linux-to-Linux network file system access, but because it is not well supported on most Windows clients and servers, its adoption has been slow. Its Linux implementation in the 2.6 kernel is as yet unproven and is missing some optional features. NFSv3 performance from Linux clients over Gigabit Ethernet can be spectacular, especially to NFS servers based on the 2.6 kernel. NFS version 3 (over UDP, at least) receives the most testing and is most likely the most stable choice for network file systems when mounting from Linux clients to Linux servers.

Client and Server Implementation Choices

For NFS, the implementation choice is simple: The most popular client and server implementation is the one available in the kernel itself. However, there are choices for the RPC (SunRPC) daemon. The choices available when building the Linux 2.6 kernel are whether to enable support for the following:

- NFS version 3 (highly recommended) client or server
- NFS over TCP on the server (recommended); it is always on in the client
- NFS version 4 (experimental)
- NFS direct I/O (experimental)

For SMB/CIFS, there is a choice of two clients: the legacy smbfs and the newer CIFS VFS. For the server, by far the most popular choice is the Samba network file server, which provides not just SMB/CIFS network file serving but also the following:

- A logon server for Windows and winbind Linux clients
- A network print server
- Administration tools and DCE/RPC-based management services
- An RFC 1001/1002 NetBIOS name server

Tuning the Linux Client—Some Key Concepts

This section covers some of the key concepts you need to consider when tuning the Linux client. These concepts include the following:

- Protocol layering
- Opportunistic locking
- Metadata
- File change notification
- Read-only volumes and read-only files

Protocol Layering

The following trace, taken from the Ethereal network analyzer, shows the typical 20 network frames (requests and responses) that occur at mount time (see Figure 16-2). The trace was taken from the `mount` command using CIFS VFS version 1.0.3 running on a Linux kernel 2.4.23 based client.

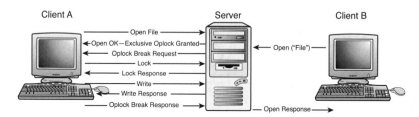

Figure 16-2 The typical 20 network frames that occur at mount time.

Figure 16-3 shows a more detailed view of a particular frame—in this case, the Tree Connect request clearly shows the layering of an SMB request (the mount data, with the SMB header) inside an RFC 1001 (NetBIOS session service) frame, inside a TCP/IP frame, inside an Ethernet frame.

Figure 16-3 A detailed view of the Tree Connect request.

In this example, the SMB request is 86 bytes (including 32 bytes of SMB header), preceded by a 4-byte RFC 1001 header (length), preceded by 32 bytes of TCP header, 20 bytes of IP header, and 14 bytes of Ethernet header. This layering is much like nesting envelopes—that is, enclosing an envelope with a letter for a child inside a larger envelope addressed to the child's parent.

Opportunistic Locking

Figure 16-4 shows the protocol flow involved in opportunistic locking (oplock) handling for CIFS. CIFS has two types of opportunistic locks that are used to control distributed access to files. By contrast, AFS and DFS have much more complex but heavyweight token-management mechanisms. NFS versions 2 and 3 have no locking mechanisms and therefore have relaxed UNIX file semantics at the risk of data integrity.

The first type of opportunistic lock is the whole file lock (exclusive oplock), which allows the client to do aggressive write-behind and read-ahead caching on the file, often greatly improving performance.

Figure 16-4   Protocol flow in opportunistic locking.
(Source: www.microsoft.com/Mind/1196/CIFS.htm)

The second type of oplock is a read oplock. A read oplock allows multiple clients to read, but not update, a file. Attempts to update such a file by one client cause all clients with that file open to lose their caching privileges for that file. Distributed caching encounters a problem with Linux because files that are closed cannot be safely cached with the oplock mechanism alone. (Although not particularly common, the standard POSIX file semantics allow a memory mapped file to have no open file instances, but the data associated with the inode can still be read.)

A third type of oplock, the batch oplock, is more rare. It is used to address certain performance problems associated with the line-by-line interpretation of DOS batch files (scripts) by allowing limited read-ahead caching of batch files by the client. These distributed caching mechanisms in the Linux client are in addition to and unrelated to caching being done in the server file system's page manager, and again in the server disk controllers.

Metadata

File and directory timestamps reflect the time of the last update to a file or directory. The CIFS network file system client uses timestamps to determine whether data in its page cache needs to be discarded when reopening a file that has been closed, but this caching is transparent to the user. AFS and DFS clients have a much more complex token-management approach to achieving cache consistency, which can safely cache network files on disk on the client for long periods. NFS versions 2 and 3 generally have looser data consistency and read-ahead and write-behind cache data based on timers.

File Change Notification

File change notification is available in NFS version 4 and CIFS as a way of allowing a client application to be notified of changes to certain files and directories. File change notification can be used to augment the client file system's distributed caching facility, although this has not been proven to be efficient and is not currently implemented for this purpose in the Linux clients.

Read-only Volumes and Read-Only Files

Read-only clients can cache aggressively if the mounted volume is known to contain read-only data (such as a mount to a server that is exporting a read-only CD-ROM or DVD). However, read-only clients provide little benefit over oplock, which in effect allows the same thing.

The legacy smbfs client does not do safe distributed caching (oplock). Instead, it relies on timers to determine the invalidation frequency for client-cached network file data and has limited performance adjustments. A significant improvement in smbfs performance was obtained midway through the 2.4 kernel development when the smbfs network request buffer size was increased from 512 bytes to approximately one page (4096 bytes).

The Linux CIFS client implements oplock, which is enabled by default (oplock can be disabled by setting /proc/fs/cifs/OplockEnabled to 1 on the client). The Linux CIFS client attempts to negotiate a buffer size of about 16K. If the server supports this buffer size, more efficient read and write transfers with fewer network round trips can be achieved. By reducing the rsize and wsize (configurable by specifying the size as an option on `mount`), as with the NFS client, the default read and write size can be reduced in an attempt to minimize TCP packet fragmentation, but this usually slows performance. The lookup caching mechanism in the CIFS VFS, as in smbfs, is done based on a timer rather than with the CIFS FindNotify API. This caching of inode metadata, even for short periods, improves performance over the alternative—that is, revalidating inode metadata on every lookup, but with the risk that the client's view of stat information (such as file size and timestamps) on a file will be out of date more often. CIFS lookup caching can be disabled by setting /proc/fs/cifs/LookupCacheEnabled. A limited set of statistics is kept by the CIFS client in /proc/fs/cifs/Stats. Enabling debugging or tracing (setting /proc/fs/cifs/cifsFYI to 1, or setting /proc/fs/cifs/traceSMB to 1) can slow the client performance slightly.

Unlike the current 2.6 smbfs and cifs client file system modules, the NFS client does a good job of dispatching multiple read-ahead requests in parallel to a single server from a single client. This parallelism helps keep the server disk busy. The difference is even more significant when writing large files from a single process on the client to the server. A Linux client can copy files using NFS version 3 much faster to a lightly loaded Linux server on Gigabit Ethernet than using CIFS copying to a Linux/Samba server. This is due to the efficient implementation of multipage asynchronous write-behind in the NFS client. The differences in read performance between NFS and CIFS are not as dramatic because both implement multipage read-ahead (readpages). The CIFS client is in turn faster than the smbfs client for file copy from the same Samba server because CIFS can use a larger read size (16K versus 4K) of the CIFS VFS and can read more than one page at a time (via the new readpages function, which is now an optional feature that 2.6 kernel file systems may implement). Future versions of the CIFS VFS client should be able to narrow the performance gap against NFS. However, exceeding NFS performance for large file copy will require a redesign of the SMB dispatching mechanism of the Samba server, as is being done for Samba version 4. When multiple processes copy different files to the same server, CIFS benefits from the capability to queue as many as 50 simultaneous read or write requests to the server.

Linux File Server Tuning

Network file system tuning is complex. Bottlenecks can be caused by high CPU usage, disk usage, or network usage, and network latency can dramatically influence throughput. The following list summarizes some general principles to use when evaluating performance improvements:

- Maximize parallelism from each client
- Maximize server parallelism in adapter interrupt dispatching
- Maximize server CPU parallelism
- Maximize client caching opportunities
- Minimize data sent

- Minimize round trips from client to server

   Maximize command chaining
   Piggybacked ACKs

- Minimize protocol overhead (frame headers)
- Limit latency when lightly loaded (such as timers and TCP ACK settings)
- Examine session establishment and authentication overhead

A common approach for evaluating potential performance improvements due to altered configuration settings is the following:

1. Select a file copy workload or benchmark test.
2. Perform the tests more than once to warm the cache and smooth out variations; perform the test on lightly loaded networks.
3. Evaluate interim results against a baseline (such as performing the same test locally or over another network file system or FTP) to sanity-check your goals.
4. Steadily increase the benchmark load until maximum overall throughput is achieved.
5. Alter server or client configuration settings and retest, measuring changes to performance and to network traffic (such as number of frames and average response time).
6. Analyze the side effects of the configuration changes by careful examination of network trace data (such as by using the Ethereal network analyzer).
7. Divide and conquer. Simulate the test using two smaller tests—one of local file calls and one for the network socket calls—to focus on performance optimizations of a narrower subsystem (such as is done by running dbench and tbench locally on the server instead of running the larger NetBench simulator across the network).

NFS

For the NFS client, the default rsize and wsize can be specified on `mount`. Typical values are 4K to 32K. For NFS versions they are constrained by the server and were changed with the implementation of NFS server over TCP to support 32K. The Linux client supports up to a 32K rsize/wsize. Setting an rsize larger than the MTU (typically 1500 bytes) results in fragmentation and reassembly of the higher-level SunRPC frames across multiple TCP frames, which in some cases slows performance. You can experiment with IOzone and Bonnie to determine optimal values. The netstat and nfsstat tools can be used to get useful TCP and NFS statistics, respectively, to correlate with benchmark throughput and timing results, and tracepath can be used to determine network frame sizes (which can be changed via the ifconfig MTU option). 2.6 adds the capability to configure NFS/SunRPC for TCP, which is somewhat slower than the default

(NFS/SunRPC over TCP). NFS over UDP is often used on local area networks, but if timeouts reported by the `nfsstat` command are excessive, consider increasing the values of the NFS `mount` options retrans and timeo. The number of server instances of nfsd can greatly affect performance and can be adjusted in the Linux server system's startup script. Linux NFS servers can export data using the "sync" or "async" flag, with the latter yielding better performance due to write-behind at the server at the risk of data integrity problems if the server fails.

Samba

Three configuration settings significantly impact Samba performance and should be examined in the server's smb.conf file:

- *Sendfile.* Sendfile is a mechanism that reduces the number of copy operations performed on outgoing file data. Samba can be configured with the option `-with-sendfile` that enables it to send data directly from the file system on the server to the network adapter, improving throughput and reducing server utilization.

- *Case-sensitive file matching for partial wildcard searches.* Caching directory entries is complicated in Samba by the differences between CIFS (Windows/DOS/OS2), which typically requests case-insensitive file matching, and the POSIX file API on the Linux server, which provides only case-sensitive file searches. As an example, a CIFS search for file `\\server\share\file*.exe` to a case-insensitive file system would result in a relatively small number of server operations to perform. However, Samba on Linux requires checking for matches with all forms of "file" and "exe," including "File1.Exe," "FILE2.EXE," "file3.EXE," and "FILE4.exe." The Samba version 3 server matches paths against a buffer containing a list of the equivalent lowercase filenames (the "stat cache") to improve the performance of these operations, but this approach does not work well for large directories (although it has been much improved in Samba version 3.0.12 and later). By using Linux xattrs to store the case-preserved filenames, Samba 4 can handle search operations on large directories much more efficiently. Even on Samba version 3, performance can be greatly improved on partial wildcard searches (giving more than a 5% gain on some benchmarks) by enabling case-sensitive searches in Samba's configuration file, smb.conf. Setting `case sensitive = on` in smb.conf can affect the behavior of Windows applications (because they expect case-insensitive file matching behavior) unless the exported share is on a partition that has been formatted as case-sensitive (such as VFAT). Case-insensitive JFS partitions can be created by passing the `-o` format option to the mkfs.jfs tool.

- *SMB logging.* SMB logging can be a significant performance drain at higher log levels. Setting the log level in smb.conf down to 0 or 1 can result in a measurable performance improvement.

In addition to the preceding, Samba performance can be reduced by enabling kernel oplocks (rather than letting the Samba server manage oplocks internally) and by enabling ACLs and ACL inheritance in the file system (which puts additional load on the server's local file system to retrieve xattrs). Samba performance is also sensitive to changes in TCP socket options (such as TCP_NODELAY, which can be specified in the smb.conf parameter `socket_options`).

Performance Measurement

Many tools for performance measurement exist and can be used in conjunction with server utilization information. Some tools are now conveniently viewable as text via pseudo files in the /proc directory, in order to help you evaluate performance trade-offs. The most commonly used tools to measure file I/O performance are as follows:

- *iozone.* A great benchmark for measuring network file I/O performance in various categories such as reads versus writes, different sizes, and random versus sequential.
- *Bonnie*
- *NetBench.* The classic CIFS benchmark developed by Ziff Davis labs is showing its age. It requires a prohibitively large number of clients to adequately load a modern Linux Samba server.
- *dbench, tbench, smbtorture.* These offer more efficient simulation of the file activity generated by a NetBench run, the corresponding network socket activity, and the SMB activity, respectively.
- *spec cifs.* Work is under way with SNIA and SPEC to develop a next-generation CIFS benchmark.
- *specsfs.* The most common benchmark used to report NFS version 3 performance.
- *The Connectathon NFS suite.* When run with `runtests -a -t` it generates useful and granular timing information on common operations.

These tools are discussed in detail in Chapter 6, "Benchmarks as an Aid to Understanding Workload Performance."

Load Measurement for Improved Capacity Planning

The CIFS client can measure the number of common requests by enabling CIFS statistics in the kernel configuration and by examining /proc/fs/cifs/Stats. This can be useful for determining when a server is responding slowly. An example of the statistics follows:

```
Resources in use
CIFS Session: 2
Share (unique mount targets): 2
SMB Request/Response Buffer: 2
Operations (MIDs): 0

0 session 0 share reconnects
Total vfs operations: 550378 maximum at one time: 6

1) \\localhost\stevef
SMBs: 11956 Oplock Breaks: 0
Reads: 89 Bytes 1145705
Writes: 3962 Bytes: 1888452
Opens: 868 Deletes: 934
Mkdirs: 118 Rmdirs: 118
Renames: 263 T2 Renames 0
2) \\192.168.0.4\c$
SMBs: 365570 Oplock Breaks: 0
Reads: 124712 Bytes 456637519
Writes: 152198 Bytes: 613673810
Opens: 3 Deletes: 0
Mkdirs: 0 Rmdirs: 0
Renames: 0 T2 Renames 0
```

Print Server Performance

Print server performance is affected by four major factors:

- Where the job is rendered
- How large the job is when sent across the network and stored on the server disk
- How many layers of software the print job passes through on the server
- How efficient the server driver for the print device is

In the case of Windows systems printing to Linux servers due to the breadth of Windows print driver support, it is common for the print job to be processed mostly on the client (rather than partially on the client and partially on the server, as is often the case on Windows clients printing to Windows servers). When a print job is rendered on the client and sent as a raw print file to the server, the amount of network traffic required to print the network print job is much larger, and the file may use significant disk space on the server, but the amount of server CPU required for printing the job is less. When Samba in particular is used as a print server, print jobs usually pass through multiple additional layers on the server—the CUPS subsystem, then Ghostscript, and then a print driver that can slow performance. Print drivers on Linux vary widely in quality of implementation, but the OMNI and CUPS projects are bringing more consistency to the Linux print architecture, which should be reflected in improved Linux print driver performance over time.

REFERENCES

[1] Shepler, S. et al. "Network File System (NFS) version 4 Protocol," RFC 2530, April 2003.

[2] SNIA Common Internet File System (CIFS) Technical Reference. Storage Networking Industry Association CIFS Work Group, March 2002.

[3] Hertel, C. *Implementing CIFS: The Common Internet File System*, Prentice Hall PTR, August 2003.

[4] Satran, J. et al. "Internet Small Computer Systems Inferface (iSCSI)," RFC 3720, May 2004.

[5] Web resource: http://www.snia.org, Storage Networking Industry Association.

[6] Web resource: http://www.samba.org, Samba SMB/CIFS server project page.

[7] Web resource: http://linux-cifs.samba.org, Linux SMB/CIFS client project page.

[8] Web resource: http://www.nfsv4.org, NFS version 4 information.

## CHAPTER SEVENTEEN

Database Servers

By Ruth Forester and John Tran

INTRODUCTION

More and more businesses are looking to Linux as a possible platform for their database servers. The low cost of maintaining a Linux server makes it appealing to small- and medium-sized businesses, and even to enterprise businesses that want to reduce operational costs. Improvements in the kernel's reliability and performance, better hardware and device driver support, and an abundance of third-party tools to help businesses maintain their servers make Linux a viable and effective solution for database systems. (A distinction is made here between a database server, which is vendor-specific software that maintains a database, and a database system, which is the incorporation of the operating environment—hardware, operating system, libraries, and so on).

The enterprise database server requires a tremendous amount of system resources. Because a database must be capable of handling thousands of concurrent user connects and processing terabytes of data, it requires a high level of parallel processing power, a large amount of memory, and very large I/O bandwidth and throughput. As such, its performance is highly dependent on how effectively the kernel manages these resources. Inefficiencies in this area can lead to excessive time spent in kernel space. Also, certain inefficiencies can cause lock contentions, which can lead to poor scalability and serialization problems. Both of these behaviors can severely impact database performance because they either consume processor cycles that would normally be used by the database or force the database applications to serialize on a kernel resource.

We'll discuss various aspects of database server performance and tuning, including the following:

- An overview of database architectures
- Tunable areas of databases that have an impact on performance
- Tunable areas of the Linux kernel that have an impact on database performance

OVERVIEW OF DATABASE ARCHITECTURES

There are several approaches to database architecture, but all of them have at least some of the following characteristics:

- Organized tables/views, recorded, and contained typically on raw character devices or file systems
- Global memory area
- Transaction logging mechanism

These characteristics are the crux of database performance. Simple tuning of small databases can be as simple as the following:

- Load-balancing the disk I/O
- Ensuring that the device chosen for logging is not interfered with by average user processes
- Ensuring that adequate memory is available so that the transactions are cached rather than all disk-based.

(Note: Database clustering interconnect technology is a recent innovation; however, this chapter is concerned with less exotic and more conventional database implementations.)

Modern commercial databases are either shared storage or shared nothing. Depending on the primary applications to be run, one type might perform better than the other. In particular, shared-storage database types tend to perform online transaction processing (OLTP) workloads better, whereas shared-nothing databases are better for decision support query workloads, because they can be configured in advance. Also, process- and thread-based implementations are a consideration, particularly for decision support system (DSS) workloads, where maximizing memory is critical. Modern leading commercial databases implement either processes, fat threads, or thread hybrids.

DATABASE TUNING AREAS TO CONSIDER

Consider the following areas within a database that can be tuned for improved performance:

- I/O
- Queue length and response times
- Load balancing
- Global memory
- Logging device

Each of these sections gives an in-depth look at things to consider.

I/O Tuning

You must make many decisions when it comes to I/O tuning. Will you use raw devices or file systems? What about direct I/O? What blocksizes should you choose for your database? If you are running strictly an OLTP (online transaction processing, characterized by small, random reads/writes) workload, you want to choose a smaller blocksize—for example, 2K. For DSS long running queries, a database that implements a sophisticated query optimizer and complex memory (sort/hash area) parameter controls, a larger blocksize improves database scans—8K (or larger if the database provides). What if your workload entails both OLTP and DSS? Careful database parameter tuning needs to be considered; in some instances, compromise is the way to go, perhaps settling with a 4K blocksize.

Queue Length and Response Times

On Linux, vmstat is a good tool for measuring I/O bandwidth. Two columns under the I/O section are labeled bi and bo. These columns are supposed to be blocks in and blocks out from a block device, as described in the man pages for vmstat. However, in various Linux distributions these columns actually report transfer rate in KBps from character devices (raw) or a block device (file system) during the measurement interval. For both workloads, if queue length is greater than 1, there is likely some contention. For OLTP, response times over 50ms are a concern.

Load Balancing

In Linux, several tools can help you determine whether your database system is in need of load balancing. A simple way to do this is to use iostat (for descriptions of iostat, see Chapter 4, "System Performance Monitoring," under the "I/O Utilization" section).

Following is an example of the `iostat -x` output:

```
Device:   rrqm/s wrqm/s    r/s     w/s    rsec/s    wsec/s \
rkB/s     wkB/s  avgrq-sz avgqu-sz   await  svctm  %util

sda       0.00    0.00     272.86 97.37 2489.63   842.95\
1244.81   421.47 9.00      2.61       7.05   2.10    77.59

sdb       0.00    0.00     0.00   0.00  0.00      0.00\
0.00      0.00   0.00      0.00       0.00   0.00    0.00

sdc       0.00    0.00     272.22 102.00 2495.50 878.43\
1247.75   439.21 9.02      2.64       7.05   2.04    76.42
```

```
sdd      0.00   0.00     0.00  0.00   0.00    0.00\
0.00     0.00   0.00     0.00       0.00   0.00    0.00

sde      0.00   0.00   277.96 99.77 2532.04 865.89\
1266.02  432.94 9.00     2.59       6.87   2.05    77.29

sdf      0.00   0.00     0.00  0.00   0.00    0.00\
0.00     0.00   0.00     0.00       0.00   0.00    0.00

sdg      0.00   0.00   272.29 102.00 2483.49 878.69\
1241.75  439.35 8.98     2.62       7.01   2.06    77.20

sdh      0.00   0.00     0.00  0.00   0.00    0.00\
0.00     0.00   0.00     0.00       0.00   0.00    0.00

sdi      0.00   0.00     0.00  693.03 0.00   6326.38\
0.00     3163.19 9.13    0.63       0.91   0.91    63.00

sdj      0.00   0.00     0.00  0.00   0.00    0.00\
0.00     0.00   0.00     0.00       0.00   0.00    0.00

sdk      0.00   0.03   276.03 98.80  2542.71 855.49\
1271.36  427.74 9.07     2.60       6.94   2.05    76.67

sdl      0.00   0.00     0.00  0.00   0.00    0.00\
0.00     0.00   0.00     0.00       0.00   0.00    0.00

sdm      0.00   0.00   272.92 96.73  2480.03 836.28\
1240.01  418.14 8.97     2.55       6.89   2.06    76.30

sdn      0.00   0.00     0.00  0.00   0.00    0.00\
0.00     0.00   0.00     0.00       0.00   0.00    0.00

sdo      0.00   0.00   272.19 100.47 2486.96 866.16\
1243.48  433.08 9.00     2.64       7.10   2.07    77.21

sdp      0.00   0.00     0.00  0.00   0.00    0.00\
0.00     0.00   0.00     0.00       0.00   0.00    0.00

sdq      0.00   0.00   268.09 96.57  2445.08 838.95\
1222.54  419.47 9.01     2.53       6.93   2.09    76.18

sdr      0.00   0.00     0.00  0.00   0.00    0.00\
0.00     0.00   0.00     0.00       0.00   0.00    0.00

avg-cpu:  %user   %nice   %sys %iowait   %idle
          90.63    0.00   8.90    0.47    0.00
```

Notice that some disks are not being accessed at all. You should make sure that all tables are evenly laid out across all disks if a software striping capability is not used. Note that disk sdi is actually performing writes during this read-only piece of the benchmark. This is because the logs are apparently located there. Logs should be on a separate stripe volume, or a separate disk where possible, so that disk sdi is not slowed down by other aspects of the benchmark.

Global Memory

In general, for OLTP workloads, as much of the I/O as possible should be moved to memory using the global cache area of the database. Most databases provide tools that allow you to see whether user transactions are being cached, including statistics on dirty buffers and buffers used. To properly size the memory under Oracle, the database_block_buffers need to be set. This is done simply by determining how much free memory is available to be dedicated to the database and then dividing that by the database_block_size, as follows:

4GB = 2.5GB for the database, so 2684354560 / 4096 = 655360

Following is an example of a db_block_buffers formula:

```
Database heap (4KB)                        (DBHEAP) = 6654
 Size of database shared memory (4KB)(DATABASE_MEMORY)\
     = AUTOMATIC
Catalog cache size (4KB)              (CATALOGCACHE_SZ) = 386
Log buffer size (4KB)                      (LOGBUFSZ) = 2048
Utilities heap size (4KB)            (UTIL_HEAP_SZ) = 10000
Buffer pool size (pages)                  (BUFFPAGE) = 40000
Extended storage segments size (4KB)  (ESTORE_SEG_SZ) = 16000
Number of extended storage segments (NUM_ESTORE_SEGS) = 0
Max storage for lock list (4KB)           (LOCKLIST) = 16384
```

OLTP/WEB workloads that tend to rely on primary key index lookups can benefit from large bufferpools to cache results and reduce a bottleneck on I/O throughput (I/O per second) of your I/O subsystem. DSS workloads that tend to have large table scans returning many rows can benefit by configuring memory for large sorts and joins, to avoid overflows or spills to temporary disk space that can hamper large I/O bandwidth/throughput (MBps). This is done by configuring the hash and sort size database parameters. For these workloads, the global cache size does not need to be large—it can be an order of magnitude smaller than the global cache area required for an OLTP workload.

Here is an example of using vmstat to determine free and used memory, followed by a description of various relevant columns. Note that several columns of data that are normally returned by vmstat are not included in this example.

```
[root@raleigh root]# vmstat 4
```

procs				memory				swap	
r	b	w	swpd	free	buff	cache		si	so
1	0	0	0	199328	56792	123040	0	0	4

- The `free` column is the first column to look at. This column is reported in kilobytes. If you have free memory available, it is probably not the limiting resource.
- The `swpd` column is looked at next. Reported in kilobytes, this column tells you how much virtual memory is used or how much of your memory was pushed out to disk.
- The `si` column reports how much memory was swapped in from disk during the reporting interval.
- The `so` column reports how much memory was swapped out to disk (virtual memory) during the reporting interval.

If you have a large `swpd` and you see heavy swapping activity in the `si` and `so` columns, you may want to add more memory or reduce the amount of memory that is allocated to your database, leaving more memory for the applications. Be sure memory is available to allocate to the database. Additionally, this assumes care has been taken to lock down the global cache area of the database in Linux.

You can also use the Linux `top` command to get more detailed information on your large memory consumers. If you press **h** while the `top` command is running, you can get a list of options. Press **m** to sort by resident memory usage to determine which processes are the largest consumers. The Linux tool /usr/bin/top is more intrusive than vmstat, using more CPU. Begin with vmstat and continue with top if you need additional information.

It is important to remember that on 32-bit Linux systems, it is possible to have more memory than the database software can address. In this situation, you should look for creative ways to use spare memory if you have an I/O problem. Use memory whenever possible to reduce I/O; in some cases, the databases' tempspace areas can be taken advantage of, particularly for individual processes using sort or hash areas (typical in DSS workloads). Be sure that the database parameters controlling these are set to the highest possible maximum (divided by the number of database agents) but still are under the system memory (including the kernel).

Logging Device

Most often, when all other bottlenecks are resolved, the optimization of the logging device ultimately determines OLTP database performance. It is important to separate the logfile from all other database files as much as possible.

Your next step is deciding whether to run logfile using raw devices or file system devices. Historically, raw devices are the preferred logging device for databases that support it. Some databases use direct I/O file systems, which can provide performance within 5% of raw device performance. Other (typically noncommercial) databases choose to utilize file system buffering, taking advantage of buffering as provided by Linux. A direct comparison in the individual proposed environment is advised.

Typical Database Workloads

It is important to distinguish between OLTP and DSS workloads, because these workloads are diametrically opposed in their resource utilization; your environment may contain some combination of these workloads. Tuning for one may cause performance degradation in the other.

OLTP workloads are database workloads composed of many (hundreds or more) users and heavy transaction processing. These workloads are characterized by small random reads/writes and a high number of iops (I/Os per second). A decision support system workload refers to a workload requiring intensive query processing, typically fewer users but significant query processing that fully utilizes total system resources. Note that the TPC's (Transaction Processing Council) TPC-C is an example of an intensive (steady state) OLTP database benchmark, whereas TPC-H is an example of a DSS workload benchmark, not a steady-state workload. In other words, barring logging or database checkpoints that are performed during or as part of the TPCC/OLTP benchmark, the workload remains at a steady state. That is, all system resources remain in a steady state of system utilization. However, the TPC-H workload does not maintain a steady-state workload, particularly during the power test. Rather, the workload exhibits wildly inconsistent resource utilization as it moves from queries that require memory, to memory that requires intensive I/O scanning, to queries that demand intensive CPU utilization. During the throughput phase of this test, the workload may at times appear to be in more of a steady state, but only if it is perfectly tuned. Otherwise, it may appear to be "stuck" on a certain query, causing inconsistent, not steady, performance. Particular care and attention to any optimization of a long-running query are critical, and different databases have varying query optimization technology. So, it is important to examine databases that emphasize their query optimization techniques if this is a priority in your individual workload.

Both these TPC benchmarks are mentioned here as examples of particular workloads. But for these benchmarks to run in a way that is meaningful to anyone, they need sophisticated tuning techniques that are beyond the scope of this book. Moreover, all TPC benchmarks require a paid certified auditor, and there are strict rules regarding the use of TPC benchmark metrics. These rules are not intended to prevent practical running of the workloads, but rather to protect existing published benchmark numbers and other proprietary TPC property. In general, these workloads are far too complex for desktop environments to attempt anyway; however, the existing published TPC metrics are very useful to any administrator considering a particular hardware or software platform, regardless of size. The complexity of these benchmarks lends itself well to a large enterprise system selection. Other benchmarks that might be of interest to both a desktop environment and an enterprise system are the SpecJappServer, Trade2, SAP, and Baan benchmarks, which incorporate simultaneous web/Java and accounting and database activity. Published numbers are readily available on a variety of hardware and software platforms and can be extremely helpful in database, disk subsystem, or overall system selections for desktop to enterprise environments.

PROCESS MANAGEMENT

An enterprise database server can have thousands of users accessing the database concurrently. Some users might perform simple transactions that require little processing power, whereas others might perform complex transactions that require much more system resources. Database performance is often discussed in terms of metrics such as transactions per hour or minimum response time with X number of current connections. These performance constraints are imposed by businesses to ensure a level of quality assurance for the customer. With such a high demand on concurrent processing, an enterprise database server needs to run on large SMP servers.

Early Linux kernels were not well suited for use as database servers requiring a high degree of concurrency. These kernels did not scale well as the number of processors on the system increased because early kernel developments were driven by single-processor machines. Migration to a multiprocessor platform exposed many global kernel locks, which can cause serialization problems. The largest of these global locks is a spin lock protecting a single unordered run queue. In a single-processor environment, a single queue is sufficient to handle the scheduling of all runnable tasks. However, in an SMP environment, a single run queue is inadequate and can become a bottleneck. As the number of processors increases, the potential for lock contention on the run queue also increases. Furthermore, because the queue is unordered, the scheduler has to examine every task in the queue while the lock is held to determine the goodness of the tasks.

(Each task is assigned a goodness value, which is used to determine which task is the best candidate to be scheduled to run on a processor.) This increases the lock hold time, which increases the chances of lock contentions or exacerbates current contention conditions. In the 2.5 kernel, the single run queue is removed and replaced with per-CPU run queues. Having multiple run queues removes the single global lock and improves overall scalability. In addition, each run queue maintains a priority list, which helps the scheduler pick the best task to run. This prioritization reduces the lock hold time on the queue and further reduces lock contentions.

MEMORY MANAGEMENT

As mentioned earlier, a database managing an enterprise business needs to run on a large Symmetrical Multiprocessing (SMP) server. Such a server is often equipped with a large amount of physical memory. Most of a system's memory is allocated to the database buffer cache area (referred to as the database buffers). Database buffers are used to cache table and index data pages read from disk into memory. Because disk access is slow compared to memory access, having more memory allocated for database buffers greatly improves database performance. A well-tuned database utilizes most of the available memory, leaving just enough for other running applications and the operating system. Allocating too much memory for a database deprives other applications of memory. Also, overallocating memory can result in excessive swapping, which is extremely detrimental to database performance.

How the Linux kernel manages physical memory is also important to the performance of a database server. On the IA-32 architecture, the kernel manages memory in 4KB pages. On the other hand, most modern processors can work with larger pages (up to multiple megabytes). For many applications, using 4KB pages is ideal. Small pages reduce internal fragmentation, incur a smaller overhead when swapping data in and out of memory, and ensure that the virtual memory that is in use is resident in physical memory. Most database servers use large shared-memory segments for their database buffers. The result is that a lot of page table entries (PTEs) are required. This adds a considerable maintenance overhead for the memory manager. For example, take a database server that allocates 1GB of shared memory for its buffers using 4MB shared memory segments. A kernel using a 4KB page size would require 262,144 PTEs—a significant number of page tables, which adds considerable maintenance overhead for the memory manager. This calculation is, of course, oversimplified. The actual number of PTEs would be much larger because Linux is unable to share page tables for shared memory.

The capability of using larger pages is available in the 2.6 kernel. A process can explicitly request large pages from a memory pool. Using large pages reduces the number of PTEs required when an application requests large memory blocks. Consequently, the computational costs of maintaining the PTEs are also reduced. Going back to the previous example, if the page size is 4MB instead of 4KB, only 1,024 PTEs would be required for the 1GB database buffers (again, this calculation is oversimplified). Another advantage of large-page support is that large pages also increase the range of memory covered by the translation lookaside buffer (TLB), thus decreasing the possibility of TLB misses. TLB access is extremely fast compared to accessing a page table because the TLB is a CPU cache area.

I/O MANAGEMENT

Database performance depends heavily on fast, efficient I/O operations. With potentially terabytes of data to process, any I/O bottleneck can render a database server ineffective to meet business demands. A database administrator (DBA) typically spends a lot of time and money optimizing an I/O subsystem to reduce I/O latencies and maximize I/O throughput.

Early Linux kernels had many deficiencies that hindered I/O performance. Lack of features such as raw I/O, vectored I/O, asynchronous I/O, and direct I/O limited a DBA's ability to leverage technologies that are available on other platforms and that are known to help database performance. Also, functional deficiencies, such as bounce buffering and single I/O request-queue lock, added unnecessary system costs and introduced serialization problems. Fortunately, all of these problems have been eliminated in the 2.6 kernels or via patches to the 2.4 kernels.

Bounce Buffers

In early Linux kernels (early 2.4 and prior kernel versions), device drivers could not directly access virtual addresses in high memory. In other words, these device drivers could not perform direct memory access I/O to high memory. Instead, the kernel allocates buffers in low memory, and data is transferred between high memory and the device drivers via the kernel buffer. This kernel buffer is commonly referred to as a bounce buffer, and the process is referred to as bouncing, or bounce buffering. Because of the intensive I/O characteristics of a database server, bouncing severely degrades the performance of the database server. First, bounce buffers consume low memory, which can lead to memory shortage problems. Second, excessive bouncing leads to high system time, which can cause a database system to become completely CPU-bound. The elimination of bounce buffering in recent kernels is a major achievement in database server performance.

Raw I/O

Introduced in the 2.4 kernel, the raw I/O interface for block devices provided the capability to perform I/O directly from the user-space buffer without additional copying through a file system interface. Using the raw interface can dramatically improve the I/O performance of a database server because the file system layer is avoided. However, it should be noted that not all database workloads benefit from using raw I/O. If the same data is referenced frequently, raw I/O cannot take advantage of the file system buffer cache. The raw I/O interface gives a DBA more flexibility to design a database for performance. Depending on the I/O characteristic of the database server, a DBA can choose to use the raw interface for faster I/O operation, or use the file system leverage caching and reduce disk access, or a combination of both, depending on how database tables are accessed.

Vectored I/O

The 2.6 Linux kernel provides a full implementation of vectored I/O (also referred to as scattered I/O) through the readv and writev interfaces. The vectored read interface, readv, reads contiguous pages on disk into noncontiguous pages in memory. Conversely, the vectored write interface, writev, writes noncontiguous pages in memory onto disk in a single function call. This I/O mechanism is advantageous for database servers that frequently perform large sequential I/Os. Without a proper vectored read and write implementation, an application performing sequential I/Os does one of the following:

- Issues database page size I/Os
- Issues large block I/Os and uses the memcpy function to copy data pages between the read/write buffers and the database buffers

Both of these approaches incur expensive computational overhead when scanning terabytes of data, which is a common database size in today's data warehouses.

Asynchronous I/O

The asynchronous I/O mechanism gives an application the capability to issue an I/O request without having to block until the I/O is complete. This mechanism is ideal for database servers. Other platforms have provided asynchronous I/O interfaces for quite some time, but this feature is relatively new to Linux. To drive I/O throughput without an asynchronous I/O mechanism, database servers usually create many processes or threads that are dedicated to performing I/O. With many processes/threads doing the I/O activity, the database application is no longer blocked on a single I/O request. The downside of using so many processes/threads is the extra overhead costs associated with creating, managing, and scheduling these processes/threads.

The GNU C Library (GLIBC) asynchronous I/O interface utilizes user-level threads to perform blocking I/O operations. This approach simply makes the request appear asynchronous to the application. However, it is no different from the approach previously described and suffers from the same performance drawbacks. To eliminate the problem, the 2.6 kernel introduced a kernel asynchronous I/O (KAIO) interface. KAIO implements asynchronous I/O in the kernel rather than in user space via threads and guarantees true asynchrony.

Direct I/O

Direct I/O provides performance comparable to raw I/O, but with the added flexibility of a file system. As such, it is attractive to database administrators who want to leverage the flexibility of maintaining their databases when using file systems as the storage medium.

The main attraction of using file systems as a storage medium over raw devices is that resizing the database storage can be done easily; increasing the size of a file system can be done by simply adding more disks. Another advantage of file systems is the available tools, such as fsck, that the DBA can use to help maintain the data integrity.

There are some disadvantages to using file systems as a storage medium without the direct I/O interface. One is the added cost of the buffer cache daemon, which actively flushes dirty pages to disk. This activity consumes CPU cycles, which are a valuable resource for CPU-intensive database workloads. Another disadvantage relates to buffer-cache misses, which can be expensive if data is not frequently reused.

For large database systems, memory is allocated to the database buffers. Large database buffers reduce the frequency with which the database applications have to read or write to disks. They also reduce the amount of available memory for the file system buffer cache. This scenario has a twofold effect on server performance. First, the buffer-cache daemon is more active flushing dirty pages to disk (pages become dirty more quickly). Second, with a smaller buffer cache size, the likelihood that data resides in the buffer cache is much lower, which increases the likelihood of a buffer cache miss.

Block Size I/O

Device drivers transfer data in a group of bytes called a block. The block size is set to the sector size of the device and is normally 512 bytes (although many hardware devices and their associated drivers can handle larger transfer files). Associated with each block is a buffer head structure in memory. When a read request arrives from the application via a read call, the device driver breaks up the read buffer sector-size blocks, fills the buffer heads associated with each block with the data from the physical device, and then coalesces the blocks back into the original read buffer. Similarly, when a write request arrives from an application, the device driver divides the write buffer into sector-sized blocks and updates the physical data on disk with the values of the associated buffer heads. With the 2.6 kernel, the block size for raw I/O is set to 4096 bytes instead of 512 bytes. This simple change improves overall I/O throughput and CPU utilization by reducing the number of buffer heads required by raw I/O operations. The advent of fewer buffer heads reduces the kernel overhead required to maintain them, and the use of large blocks reduces the number of divide-and-coalesce operations a device driver has to perform for an I/O request.

I/O Request Lock

The Linux kernel maintains an I/O request queue for each block device. The queue is used to order I/O requests in such a way as to maximize system performance. In the 2.2 and early 2.4 kernels, all request queues were protected by a global spin lock called io_request_lock. This I/O request lock can cause serious serialization problems for database servers running on SMP machines with many disks.

In more recent kernel levels, this single global lock (io_request_lock) has been removed from the SCSI subsystem. In its place, each I/O request queue is protected by its own lock, request_queue_lock. Serialization of I/O requests still occurs, but on only a single request queue and not at the SCSI subsystem for all request queues.

SUMMARY

The transition from Linux version 2.4 to version 2.6 has seen an abundance of kernel changes that have improved database server performance. Some of the changes, such as multiple run queues, enhance SMP scalability by removing serialization points. Other changes, such as vectored I/O, asynchronous I/O, and direct I/O, provide kernel services that, on other platforms, have been known to help database performance. The good news is that most of these changes are available in the 2.4 kernel release through the SUSE or RHEL distributions. As Linux continues its shift into the database server domain, more performance bottlenecks will be exposed, driving kernel development to improve performance, and in the process making Linux more attractive as a solution for all types of database application workloads.

## CHAPTER EIGHTEEN

Application Servers

By Wilfred C. Jamison

INTRODUCTION

Application servers are one of the most popular types of middleware in the IT industry today. Application servers have become the cornerstone of many electronic businesses on the Internet. In the following pages, we'll introduce you to application servers, and also discuss their performance characteristics, cover methods for improving the performance and high availability of an application, and provide Linux-specific information for managing application servers.

We assume you have a good understanding of web servers, including some of the key technologies surrounding web servers such as HTTP, HTML, and CGI. Knowledge of Java and J2EE is also helpful but not necessary.

THE APPLICATION SERVER DEFINED

Web servers alone are not enough to put a business online. Applications need to be written that encapsulate both the user interactions and the logic of the business enterprise. First, applications have to be deployed into the application server and then loaded for execution. All resources needed by the application—data sources and resource adaptors—are also loaded. In the world of application servers, data sources can mean many things. In most situations, the main data sources can be disparate databases, such as Oracle, Informix, Sybase, DB2, or Microsoft. Accessing data from data sources can be done via native database drivers or other back-end data sources like ERP systems—for example, BEA Tuxedo or SAP R/3—and transaction managers. For security services, application servers might communicate with authentication tools such as RADIUS or LDAP servers.

Java, J2EE, and Application Servers

Web servers, by extending and delegating their functionality, paved the way for the development of application servers. (Web servers are discussed in Chapter 19, "Case Study: Tuning the I/O Schedulers in Linux 2.6.") When we talk about application servers, we are talking about servers in the context of web sites and the Internet, and of enterprise applications.

Toward the middle of the 1990s, when object-oriented programming was gaining acceptance in the community, a new programming language, Java, was developed by Sun Microsystems, Inc. Developers quickly embraced Java mainly for its simplicity, ease of use, readability, portability, and automatic memory management. Both the academic community and the IT industry quickly adopted Java.

In addition to the preceding qualities, Java's success can also be attributed to its network readiness. Java was designed to work easily in a distributed system and was even dubbed the language of the Internet. But what made Java very popular on the Internet are its *applets*. Applets are Java programs that reside on the web server but can be requested by a user through HTML so that they are executed in the Java Virtual Machine (JVM) that comes with the web browser. This is done by including the applet tag in an HTML page. The idea is similar to including an image file in an HTML page. When the page is requested, the image file is also fetched. Hence, instead of running an application on the server side, applets move the computation to the client side. Applets can also be used to communicate back to the server without having to send another HTTP request.

This new paradigm of computing became very popular. Previous to Java, the Common Gateway Interface (CGI) scripting technology was widely used as a dynamic HTML generator. CGI, however, has a number of shortcomings, including platform dependence and scalability problems. To address these limitations, Sun Microsystems, Inc. introduced the Java servlet technology as a portable way to provide dynamic and user-oriented contents. Servlets are pieces of Java source code that add functionality to a web server similar to the way applets added functionality to a browser. Servlets were designed to be another dynamic HTML generator that could be used as an alternative to the CGI technology. Early servlet implementations were extensions of the web server. Later, we will see that servlets were the predecessors of modern-day application servers.

The Java 2 Enterprise Edition (J2EE) was introduced near the end of the 1990s as a Java platform for enterprise applications. J2EE defines a programming model based on Enterprise Java Beans (EJB) technology and was developed in response to the growing interest in Java as an enterprise computing language. As J2EE evolved, many other developments in the Java space took place. These developments include standardizing database programming interfaces using Java through the Java Database Connections (JDBC) framework, developing a transaction model through the Java Transaction Architecture (JTA), and messaging in Java through the Java Messaging Service (JMS). Ultimately, J2EE has become a suite of specifications that describe the different elements included in the framework.

The J2EE specification provides a blueprint for implementing application servers that support servlets and EJBs, and it has become the ideal model for enterprise applications that implement business decisions and generate dynamic HTML. Most application servers are now based on the J2EE blueprint.

Although this chapter addresses J2EE-based application servers, it is important to note that not all application servers are fully compliant with the J2EE specification. In fact, some application servers serve only servlets and JavaServer Pages (JSPs)—for example, Tomcat. Also, some application servers might not be restricted to Java at all—for example, the Microsoft .NET Framework is designed to support various programming languages, including $C^{\#}$, Forth, Pascal, Perl, Python, SmallTalk, and so on. Thus, theoretically, any programming language or scripting language can be implemented on an application server. The fact remains, however, that Java is currently the most successful platform for enterprise computing on the Internet and, therefore, the majority of application servers are based on Java technologies, particularly EJBs.

Another major concern of businesses is integrating their legacy systems to the new programming model. A successful application server vendor will include facilities to connect and integrate seamlessly with legacy systems as part of the whole migration process.

The J2EE specification is an extensive topic and is not the main subject of this book. Many application servers are available. Some of them are open-source—for example, JBoss, Zope, and Tomcat. Examples of commercial application servers include Orion, BEA WebLogic, IBM WebSphere, Oracle, and Sun ONE.

PERFORMANCE CHARACTERIZATION OF APPLICATION SERVERS

Businesses that adapt and use the J2EE programming model to write their enterprise applications have specific requirements from the application server. The following are some of the most common requirements:

- *Performance.* An application server should have the power to process a very large workload and be able to manifest an acceptable level of response time and throughput.

- *Scalability.* An application server should be able to meet performance requirements by adding more computing power to the overall system. The cost ratio of additional computing power and performance gain should be within the expected vicinity.

- *High availability.* An application server should be able to serve requests without interruption. If for any reason the system has to be offline, that time should be very minimal. The rule of thumb is that the system should be up and working 99.999% of the time.

- *Fault tolerance/failover.* If a user has already launched a request, an application server failure should be transparent to the user. With both server- and session-level failover, if a server becomes unavailable in a cluster, an application can be rerouted to another server in the cluster. The new server then restores information about the session and presents the user with the next page in the application. If all goes well, the user won't know that the (initial) server failed.

- *Full compliance with the standards.* Business owners expect that the applications they write will run in any application server they choose without having to rewrite their applications. This promotes vendor server portability.

- *Support for different database systems.* Databases are central to business operations. Different companies use different database systems. Thus, an application server is likely to succeed if it provides support for different database systems by providing their corresponding JDBC drivers.

- *Security.* The Internet, being a public domain, is open to malicious attacks. Therefore, companies are very concerned about the security of their data and their system. They are also concerned about making customers confident that whatever sensitive data they submit will be protected from sniffers. An application server is therefore expected to either provide security mechanisms that authenticate and authorize users, handle encryption protocols such as SSL, or be able to work with third-party security applications.

- *Data integrity.* An application server should be able to ensure transactional operations so that the integrity of information is maintained. Transactions are just one of the major services that J2EE provides.

Generally, customers give very high importance to the first four items in the list—performance, scalability, high availability, and fault tolerance. There is very high expectation that application servers perform well and stay operational 24/7.

Performance is the capability to sustain "good" or "acceptable" response time to user requests. In some cases, this expectation is driven by the nature of the business. Some businesses just cannot afford to be unresponsive, not even for a minute or so. This is true of time-critical systems. Good examples of these businesses are stock trading, online auctions, banking, and airline reservations.

Some people consider good performance to include the capability to withstand catastrophic situations, which can be categorized under fault tolerance and high availability.

In some cases, businesses are motivated by the quality of service they can give to customers. Response time and user experience are very important to businesses such as merchandisers and retailers. A useful performance metric that shows how well an enterprise is doing is the system's overall throughput (the amount of work done over a period of time). Of course, the higher the throughput, the better for the company's bottom line. The quality of service is also important to ensure that there are repeat customers (users who come back to the web site after a successful transaction). A simple yet useful metric for determining the popularity or success of a web site is the average number of hits to the site every day. The more users who visit the site, the higher the likelihood that serious transactions from customers occur. The business motivation, therefore, is to be able to accommodate as many visitors as possible without sacrificing excellent user experience.

Before analyzing the performance characteristics of an application server, it is helpful to first identify some of the application server's characteristics with regard to its usage and environment.

Characteristics of the Application Server

The following eight characteristics define the typical application server:

- *Interactive.* First and foremost, an application server should be interactive because it has to respond to incoming requests the moment they arrive. The server should be prompt and able to complete transactions within a reasonable amount of time. Also, the application server should be able to maintain sessions so that users can send a series of requests based on what transpired during the session.

- *Concurrent.* This characteristic is not inherent to application servers. However, for an application server to service requests in a timely manner, it should have enough capacity to accommodate concurrent users. Also, the application server should be able to maintain data integrity when doing transactions and serialize actions where necessary.

- *Distributable.* A number of application servers must be able to be created and grouped in a cluster.

- *Heterogeneous.* Application servers running on different platforms should be able to interoperate.

- *Multiple services in one.* Although the application server's main function is to execute web and Enterprise Java Beans applications, many services are componentized within the server itself. These services include transaction services, security services, web services, and naming services. Thus, the application server is much more complicated than it first appears.

- *Multiple applications in one.* An application server must be able to serve many applications. In other words, business owners should be able to deploy as many applications as they deem necessary. The direct effect of this is a greater workload for the application server itself, especially when these applications are made available at the same time to their respective target users.

- *Non-uniform, unpredictable requests.* The incoming flow of requests to the application server can fluctuate. Because of the nature of the web, there are often high and low volume times that can vary from day to day and from hour to hour within a day. The application server must be able to handle situations where there is a sudden avalanche of requests.

- *High volume.* The high volume of transactions that need to be processed is what really separates application servers from other servers. The exposure to the world via the Internet is what made transaction processing transcend to a different level. Transactions can be on the order of thousands or even millions each day.

Application Servers on Linux

Commercial application servers that run in Linux exist today and have become undeniably popular. Vendors of application server products, including those known to support only the powerhouse servers, now have Linux in their platform portfolio. Table 18-1 is just a short list of these vendors. Notice that even the major application server vendors, such as IBM, BEA, and Oracle, are major supporters of Linux.

Enterprise businesses are investing seriously on Linux-based applications. Future predictions from Giga and Gartner are all in favor of Linux. For example, the Gartner group thinks that by 2006, Linux will be a key foundation for a strategic cross-development platform environment creating a powerful alternative to Microsoft's .NET on Windows. Reports like these are just one of the strong reasons why people migrate to Linux, not to mention the attractive cost-effectiveness of the platform. The good thing is that although application servers are not lightweight servers, they are small enough to run in small and less-expensive machines. Thus, a network of Linux servers can provide the necessary horsepower.

Table 18-1 Application Server Vendors with Linux Support.

Vendor	Product	JDK Version	EJB Version	JSP Version	Linux Distribution
BEA	WebLogic	1.4	2.0	1.2	RH AS 2.1
Borland	Enterprise Server	1.3, 1.4	2.0	1.2	Linux
Bull	JonAS	1.2, 1.3, 1.4	1.1, 2.0		Linux
Caucho	Resin	1.1, 1.2, 1.3		1.2	Linux
Fujitsu Software Corp.	Interstage	1.3	2.0	1.2	Linux
IBM	WebSphere	1.3	2.0	1.2	RH Linux, SUSE, Turbo Linux, Linux/390
IONA	Orbix ASP	1.3, 1.4	2.0	1.2	RH 7.2
Ironflare	Orion	1.4	2.0	1.2	Linux
JBoss.org	JBoss	1.3, 1.4	2.0	1.2	Linux
Macromedia	JRun	1.3	2.0	1.2	SUSE Linux, RH Linux
Novell	extend Application Server	1.3	2.0	1.2	Linux
Oracle	Oracle9i AS	1.3, 1.4	2.0	1.1, 1.2	Linux
Persistence	Power Tier for J2EE	1.2, 1.3	1.1	1.1	Linux
Pramati Technologies	Pramati Server	1.3	2.0	1.1	Linux
SAP AG	Web Application Server	1.3	1.1	1.1	Linux
Sun Microsystems	Sun ONE	1.4	2.0	1.2	RH 7.2, Sun Linux 5.0
Sybase	EAServer	1.2, 1.3	1.1, 2.0	1.1, 1.2	Linux
Trifork	Enterprise Application Server	1.4	2.0	1.2	RH Linux 6.2

Data was taken from TheServerSide.com web site at `http://theserverside.com`.

The Software Performance Stack

This section focuses on the performance needs of application servers and is centered on three major topics:

- Major contributors to the overall performance
- Ways to improve performance
- The influence of Linux on performance

Unlike the performance characterization of other systems, such as network servers and file server, the performance characterization of application servers is much more involved because of the complex nature of application servers. Network and file servers are easier to understand and control because they are stand-alone and very lightweight, and the interactions involved with them are very minimal or limited only to the operating system. The J2EE specification continues to evolve to include more services and functional requirements and enhancements. For example, the latest specification, J2EE 1.4, includes web services, among other things, which necessitates more computations and processing (for example, SOAP protocol processing, XML parsing, and JAX-RPC, to name a few). For more information on J2EE specifications, visit the J2EE web site at `http://java.sun.com/j2ee`.

Application servers are also very high-level applications whose scope encompasses many, if not all, of the subsystems discussed in this book. For that matter, application servers can serve as excellent end-to-end benchmark applications for Linux servers.

The Complexity of the J2EE Framework

Under the hood, the J2EE-based application server is a complex aggregate of components that correspond to numerous services. To characterize the application server's overall performance, the individual performance of these components and their underlying infrastructure must be taken into account. Because this is not an easy task, the most common and accepted approach is to benchmark the application server with a representative J2EE application. Different benchmark applications can be written, with each focusing on a certain aspect of the application server. For example, one application can exercise HTTP session performance, while another can exercise persistence performance of entity beans. An industry-standard benchmark application by the Standard Performance Evaluation Corporation (SPEC; `http://www.spec.org`), called SPECjAppServer, is frequently used to benchmark application servers.

What happens beneath the application is transparent when benchmarking an application server. Figure 18-1 shows the layers of components that are involved in a J2EE environment where the performance of one layer affects that of the next layer. We call this layered model the *software performance stack*.

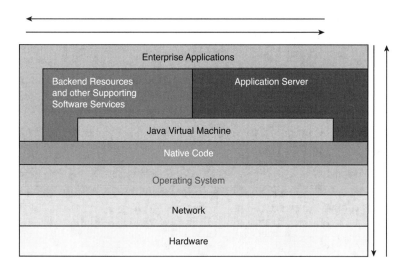

Figure 18-1 Software performance stack. The stack is intended to show which components affect the performance of another component.

At the very top of the stack are the J2EE enterprise applications that are executed by the application server. The application server strictly provides the runtime and threads of execution for the applications as defined by the J2EE specifications. Notice that applications can interact with other back-end resources either through the application server or directly—the application can call special libraries that provide a wrapper for accessing databases, or the application can use data sources via JDBC. Nothing prohibits application developers from writing some parts of their applications in native code. The same is true with back-end resources and other software services.

The application server itself is a Java application (although some parts of it can be written in native code), which means that the JVM's performance plays a major part. The enterprise applications coexist with the application server in the JVM's runtime environment. From the JVM's perspective, the enterprise applications are just part of the application server because the latter executes the former.

The remaining layers, of course, are typical in many other systems. Note that as the method or function calls go down the stack, some overhead is accrued and the overall performance of the application is affected by how good or bad the underlying layers performed.

The Enterprise Application

Many performance analysts say that at least 75% of the time the leading cause of bad performance is the enterprise application itself. If the problem in the performance stack is at the uppermost layer, the lower layer cannot do much to help improve it. In our experience with many customers in the field, many of the problems uncovered can be fixed by making changes in the application alone.

The two main reasons for a badly performing application are as follows:

- *Bad application design.* Not even the smartest application server can help if the design of the enterprise application is very bad to begin with. Architectural designs and design patterns are one of the leading areas of expertise today. Software architects should be sure to consider performance early in the design of an application.

- *Poor programming practices.* Bad programming habits can easily lead to poor performance. Programmers should be educated and understand well the programming model and language they are using. Many papers and presentations cover best practices for J2EE application development and Java programming.

The Application Server

The application server can be written in native code, but J2EE is essentially a Java framework. For easier interaction and integration with other Java-based frameworks, such as JMX, JDBC, and JNDI, most application servers are written in Java. This is also favorable for application server vendors because they can easily port their product to different platforms.

As a Java application, the application server is subjected to the same assessments as enterprise applications. A badly designed application server will very likely exhibit poor performance. In this market, vendors compete as to who has the best-performing application server. Thus, every ounce of improvement in the design and implementation of an application server can go a long way. A good design is one that is performance-oriented from the start.

Figure 18-2 shows the generic architecture of a J2EE application server. Note that the diagram is not a software architecture; instead, it simply shows what components are included and the interactions of those components.

Requests can be channeled to the application server from two possible types of clients: the HTTP client and the thick Java client. The HTTP client is usually done through a web browser that transmits an HTTP request to a web server that is a front end to the application server. A plug-in is typically installed into the web server to enable communication with the application server. This installation can be done during the installation of the application server. When an application server receives an HTTP request from the web server, it determines which web application must handle the request by examining the Uniform Resource Identifier (URI). For dynamic HTML pages, the request is served by a servlet (Java Server Pages are converted to servlets after compilation). Per the J2EE specification, web requests are processed in a web container inside the application server. Meanwhile, servlets can also call an EJB, which resides in the EJB container of the application server. Depending on the business logic, the request may involve accessing resources, such as a data source, through a JDBC provider or a message queue through JMS.

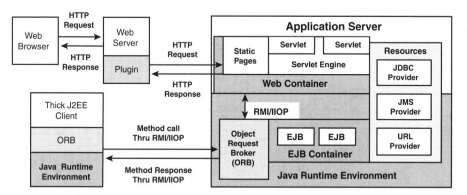

Figure 18-2 The application server that is shown here is based mainly on the J2EE specifications, which require two containers: the web and EJB containers.

A thick client is a complete Java application running somewhere in its own Java runtime environment. EJB lookups, creations, and calls to EJB methods are coded in the application. This is similar to Remote Procedure Calls (RPC), a mechanism used in distributed systems prior to the creation of Java. The protocol used to execute the remote method is typically the Remote Method Interface over Internet Inter-Orb Protocol (RMI/IIOP), which allows the capabilities of the Common Object Request Broker Architecture (CORBA) for distributed systems to be implemented on the Java 2 platform. CORBA is a specification by the Object Management Group (OMG). Some vendors, such as BEA, use a proprietary protocol, but RMI/IIOP is the expected protocol by most J2EE application servers. Java clients communicate directly with EJBs; requests are routed through the EJB container of the application server.

The dominant type of client remains the HTTP client (or web client). Most J2EE enterprise applications have a web module and EJB modules. The Java-based clients are catching up, but the web clients are likely to remain the dominant interface in the coming years. This is especially true now that web services are the cutting-edge technology. Most web services use the SOAP protocol with HTTP as the transport mechanism.

In summary, the critical, major components in an application server for performance are the web container, the web server plug-in, the EJB container, the ORB, and the interfaces within the various resources.

The Java Virtual Machine

From a performance perspective, the Java Virtual Machine (JVM) is one of the most critical components of the application server because most, if not all, of the application server's code is executed by the JVM. The application server must be written in such a way that it leverages the best features of the JVM.

Some vendors offer several JVMs to run the application server and allow the user to select his preference and others ship and prepackage their JVM. Ideally, however, users should be able to manually change their JVM (possibly with extra steps that are specific to the application server configuration). The ability to change the JVM is advantageous because it lets you use the best-performing JVM there is currently.

The SPEC organization provides a standard benchmark application called SPECjbb2000 that can be used to evaluate the performance of servers running typical Java business applications. The evaluation takes into consideration both hardware and software aspects of JVM servers. SPECjbb2000 represents an order-processing application for a wholesale supplier. For more information, visit SPEC at `http://www.spec.org/jbb2000`.

The specific components of the JVM that are critical to application servers include the networking libraries, the garbage-collection mechanism, the memory management subsystem, and the JIT compiler. Extensions to JVM, such as RMI/IIOP and Java security, are also important components.

Another important area to consider is the set of flags that are available for the JVM. You can use these flags to tune the JVM based on the characteristics of the J2EE application and the application server itself.

Native Code

In the performance stack, some native code has to be executed one way or another. Native code is closest to the operating system. In the case of the application server, the JVM is written in a third-generation language such as C or C++ and is directly compiled to produce the native code that is then executed by the host machine. Other components, such as back-end resources and enterprise applications, might contain some native code as well.

We believe that native application performance also depends heavily on how the application is written. The JVM itself is an application program that has been architected, designed, and implemented. A critical component of the JVM is the JIT (*just-in-time*) compiler, in which some methods of a Java application might be compiled to native code at runtime. In general, compilers (the JIT compiler and C++ compiler, for example) contain code optimization features so that the code they produce performs as well as possible. To achieve high performance, compiler writers need to have a deep understanding of the host machine's architecture as well as the underlying operating system. They also need to understand the resources and system calls available from the operating system, as well as its policies. In this case, understanding how the Linux kernel works and the major features and fixes that come with every release of the kernel is very important.

The Hardware and the Operating System

The choice of hardware platform on which to run your application server is a big factor to consider because it is the hardware that executes all instructions. It is almost superfluous to discuss hardware in this section, but some things need to be emphasized.

First, choosing a hardware platform is a task that every business owner must do at an early stage. This task may or may not be easy, depending on many factors and their impact, such as the existing hardware the business currently has and the legacy applications on these assets.

Second, business owners are constantly faced with the many challenges of rapid advances in hardware performance. For example, processor speeds continue to go up, and performance techniques, such as hyperthreading, are on the rise. Computer architecture continues to evolve toward better performance and higher capacity. 64-bit machines are on their way, Non-Uniform Memory Access (NUMA) is getting a lot of attention, and blade servers are currently very popular because they have the advantage of being small and yet are very powerful and scalable.

The third and probably most important issue is the choice of operating system on these machines. The purpose of the operating system is to manage the hardware resources and the processes that run on the machines. Bad and inefficient operating systems can waste a lot of what the hardware has to offer. Thus, the operating system is a key contributor to the performance stack.

An operating system is essentially a software application, and its performance depends heavily on its overall design and implementation. The Linux operating system started as a UNIX-like operating system for the personal computer. It has now matured to the operating system for many enterprise-level systems, such as IBM's eServers that span the Intel, PowerPC, and 390 architectures; the Sun Fire systems from Sun; the SGI Altix systems; the HP ProLiant Servers; and the HP Integrity Superdome (based on Itanium processors).

One of the advantages of application servers using Java is portability. Portability is ideal for a heterogeneous environment. Portability lets you write applications without worrying about the target platform ahead of time. Heterogeneity gives you the flexibility to mix and match available hardware and operating system platforms that you may already have or are planning to requisition.

Because the application server is just one component of a bigger enterprise system, you need to plan which platform and operating system each component should run on. For example, most systems use Intel servers for their web servers and big UNIX systems for their application servers. The back-end data sources are typically mainframe systems or legacy systems.

The following sections examine the Linux operating system as the platform of choice for application servers. The growing popularity of Linux in the open-source community has helped improve its performance and reliability. With the support of big companies like IBM, Red Hat, HP, and Sun, the Linux operating system has evolved from an inexpensive UNIX-like desktop operating system into a powerful enterprise server. Many Linux boxes are now used as web servers, mail servers, network gateways, and DNS servers. In the application server space, big companies have already begun migrating their J2EE applications to Linux. At the same time, more and more application server vendors are supporting different versions of Linux.

Application Server Hot Spots

This section discusses some of the performance "hot spots" common across most application servers.

JVM

The Java Virtual Machine that comes with the application server interprets and executes both the application server and the enterprise applications. A poorly performing JVM can cause the whole system to degrade. A JVM can perform well on a different operating system than Linux on the same hardware. A possible reason for this is that the Linux implementation might not have used the right system calls for a given function. The JIT compiler is a critical piece of the JVM because it translates Java byte code to the native code. Again, if the JIT compiler does not use or misuses the services available in Linux, performance can be affected significantly. Performance differences can also be seen even for the same JVM on Linux from the same vendor but on two different platforms. A classic example is the use of the system call `usleep()` emitted by the JIT compiler for the PowerPC platform using Linux kernel 2.4. It turns out that on the IA32 platform, the JIT compiler emits `sched_yield()` instead of `usleep()`. The semantics of `usleep(n)` are to make the calling thread sleep for n microseconds, but `usleep()` calls `nanosleep()`, which has a minimum granularity of 10 milliseconds (longer than 100 microseconds). Thus, the thread sleeps longer than intended. As an effect, this has caused tremendous scalability problems on the PowerPC platform. The JIT compiler must be fixed to use the `sched_yield()` system call instead.

It is important not only to choose a high-performing JVM, but also to tune the JVM properly. Performance tuning is discussed later in this chapter in the "Performance Tuning" section.

Networking
Application servers, because they are servers, imply network communication. However, application servers are not just plain files or timer servers. Application servers are highly complex, and consequently, high network traffic is an inherent characteristic of application servers.

Threads
Another important aspect of the application server is thread management. As stipulated in the J2EE specifications, both the web and EJB containers are responsible for providing threads of execution for every request that comes in. Threads are hot spots because the application server gets to manage the thread in its own way. Some application servers may have some user parameters available pertaining to threads, and you should pay close attention to what these parameters mean. Moreover, the thread management characteristics of the underlying operating system are very critical to performance.

Memory Usage
Application servers tend to use a lot of memory. Most implementations cache objects, sessions, connections, results, and many other artifacts to expedite executions. The typical virtual memory used for data by commercial application servers ranges from 300MB to 400MB. The Linux process size in real memory ranges from 50MB to 125MB. Memory usage is critical in Java because of garbage collection. Garbage collection affects performance because it freezes the application server for a while; thus, no real work is done during this time. The amount of memory allocated to the JVM must be carefully measured, and the right balance must be determined for your applications, depending on their usage patterns.

Synchronization
Another hot spot is the handling of synchronization. Although application servers process requests concurrently, each request is not entirely independent or exclusive from other requests. Some requests are processed by the same application code or might share the same resources. Thus, synchronization is necessary for proper functioning. Points of synchronization are normally found with data and resource sharing. Pools are also places of synchronization because there are limited objects in the pool. Some threads (a running thread is always associated with a particular request) are forced to wait until some objects are placed back in the pool.

String Manipulation
An application server is a huge string manipulation program. The profile of an application server typically shows that the majority of the objects being created are String objects. This is not surprising, considering that most inputs to the program are HTTP requests and the outputs are HMTL, which is also String extensive. With XML coming into the picture, application servers spend a significant amount of time parsing XML files, constructing trees, and the like. Protocols for communication with resource providers are also mostly done with string objects, such as SQL queries, messages, and URLs.

Web Server
Because an application server is a back-end server for the web server, the first point of potential bottleneck is the web server. The function of the application server depends on the number of requests channeled by the web server. Properly tuning the web server is therefore a critical step in the entire process.

File Systems
The Linux file system is another hot spot because an application server performs a lot of reading and writing to the local file system. Commercial application servers typically log their activities. For the JVM, classes or jar files are loaded from the file system. When class garbage collection is enabled, the same class or jar file can be loaded several times, depending on whether it was garbage-collected.

IMPROVING PERFORMANCE AND HIGH AVAILABILITY

This section discusses three major approaches that enterprise businesses use to improve the performance of their J2EE enterprise applications as well as their high availability. These approaches are SMP scaling, clustering, and topology.

SMP Scaling

Systems with multiple processors are very common nowadays, even for low-end systems. For example, the IBM xSeries systems for desktops can easily be equipped with two to eight Intel Xeon processors. Adding extra processors to an existing system has become an attractive option for business owners. Adding more processors to a system basically adds more horsepower, or computing power. Theoretically, when more computing power is added to the system, the application server should be able to process more requests in the same amount of time as it did previously with fewer requests

SMP systems are called symmetric because the processors added are identical and connected to the same bus. The processors also share a common memory store. Ideally, when n processors are added to a system, an n times boost in performance is the result.

However, to achieve this, a balance must be maintained between the additional processors and the other resources that are being shared, such as the system bus, memory, and network interfaces. By adding more processors, it is likely that more contentions will occur in accessing the shared resources. When this occurs, synchronization needs to be imposed; thus, some of the computing power cannot be used.

SMP systems are definitely a good way to boost an application server's overall performance. As more processors are added, however, the application server might not yield the expected performance boost. If this occurs, the system is experiencing scalability problems.

The cause of scalability problems can come from all layers in the software performance stack shown in Figure 18-1. It is possible that the enterprise application itself is not scalable, or the problem could be the application server, or even the JVM. Do not discount the fact that Linux might not be scaling very well. The hardware itself has limitations on the maximum number of processors it can handle to get good scalability. Thus, it is important to become familiar with the performance specifications of your hardware platform.

Because Linux was originally designed as a UNIX-like operating system for the desktop, its internal design did not originally consider SMP scaling. Today, the Linux kernel has undergone major improvements to address SMP scaling issues. If you are using an SMP system, make sure that your kernel supports SMP. You can verify that your kernel supports SMP by issuing the `uname -a` command and looking for the `-smp` extension following the kernel version and the SMP before the date, as shown in the following sample output:

```
Linux vivaldi 2.4.21-17-smp #1 SMP Wed Jul 30 17:18:41\
 UTC 2003 i686 unknown
```

SMP systems are a common configuration choice of many business enterprises for their application servers running on non-Linux systems. So far, the most likely cause of scaling problems is either the enterprise application or the operating system.

Clustering

Clustering is another approach to improve the overall performance of enterprise applications. Clustering can also be used to ensure high availability. Clustering has nothing to do with adding more processors, but instead with adding more instances of the application server. These instances serve exactly the same applications. In other words, imagine these application servers to be clones of each other. In so doing, incoming HTTP requests can be processed by any of these application server instances.

There are two types of clustering: vertical and horizontal. *Vertical clustering* refers to the creation of two or more instances of the same application server on the same Linux server, as shown in Figure 18-3. Because these application servers are independent processes, it is important in vertical clustering that there is enough memory to share among the instances. Requests that come in through the web server are still channeled to the same host machine. However, so that these requests are sprayed to the different instances, these application servers must be identical and deploy the same enterprise applications. Any assignment policy, normally round-robin, can be used when spraying the requests. Vertical clustering is typically used when the machine's CPU utilization is better consumed with more application servers. Also, vertical clustering can be used for fault tolerance for the server machine so that when one application server dies, requests can be rerouted to a different application server.

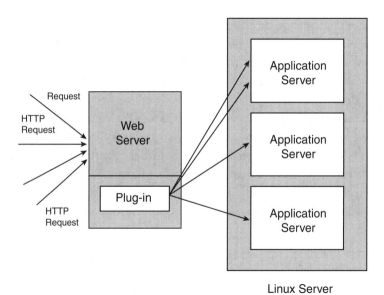

Figure 18-3   Vertical clustering. Two or more instances of the same application server are co-located in the same host machine.

Horizontal clustering is the creation of two or more instances of the same application server across different Linux servers. Thus, strictly more CPU power is added in this approach because more Linux servers are actually added. Note that these servers do not have to be identical but the application servers do, as shown in Figure 18-4. The idea is the same as vertical clustering when requests come in through the web server. The only difference is that requests are sprayed across different Linux servers. Horizontal clustering shows more performance gains because there are physically more machines. Unlike with vertical clustering, where the application servers still have to contend for the available CPUs, application servers in horizontal clustering have their own set of CPUs. Also, the fault tolerance provided by horizontal clustering is at the Linux server level. When a Linux server fails, incoming requests can be rerouted to a different Linux server, thus increasing high availability. In vertical clustering, when the Linux server itself fails, all the application servers fail as well. Of course, horizontal clustering might require more investment because it involves more than one Linux server.

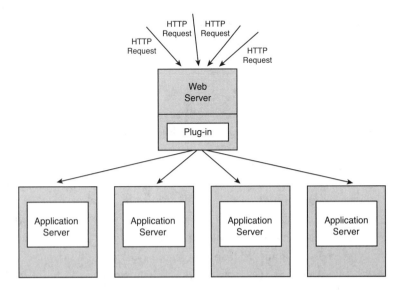

Figure 18-4   Horizontal clustering. Two or more instances of the same application server are created in different Linux servers.

Of course, it is also possible to combine the two approaches to have a cluster of several Linux servers, where each Linux server hosts more than one application server. Some business owners do this combined approach to implement two or more sets of horizontal clusters. In other words, the application servers in a Linux server are not really identical in the strict sense of vertical clustering, in that they do not have the same applications. They were created in the same server just to make use more of the available CPU power. In some application servers, the plug-in can spray the requests across the different servers. In some other application servers, a third-party sprayer program—for example, the IBM Network Dispatcher or BigIP by f5 Networks—is placed between the web server and the Linux servers.

Scalability is also a concern in clustering. In the case of vertical clustering, only so many instances of the application server can be added. Beyond that limit, additional instances of the application server are not helpful and can lead to poorer performance.

The most likely causes of scalability problems in a cluster are the hardware resources—the CPU, system bus, and memory. Another possible cause of scalability problems is the scheduler system of the operating system, because a cluster has more processes to schedule for the same amount of resources. In the case of horizontal clustering, scalability can be hampered by the networking subsystem, because as more and more requests come in, the traffic in the network connecting the cluster becomes heavier. Additionally, the plug-in or sprayer might not be scalable. Also, some application servers might include a workload manager that routes the requests based on the load of each node in the cluster. The workload manager can also be a potential cause of bottlenecks.

Topology

Another approach that enterprise businesses use to improve the performance of their J2EE enterprise applications is the type of topology they use to set up the application server infrastructure. Each business system can come up with its own topology based on its needs and, possibly, the nature of the applications that need to be deployed. Remember, however, that the goal of a topology should always be that of addressing the fundamental requirements of high performance and high availability.

Generally, how an application server is used covers a wide spectrum, which is also why the performance characterization of application servers is not a straightforward process. On the one hand, an application server can be used only to serve static pages, like a web server. On the other hand, a cluster of application servers can be configured to communicate with back-end database servers and gateways to external services. In addition, the cluster can be protected by a firewall and replicated in a geographically different location. The application servers can be running hundreds of applications. The choice of a topology mostly depends on the system's complexity and the requirements, such as security, performance, fail-over, and high availability. Figure 18-5 shows the basic three-tier topology in which the web server and the application server are hosted in the same server machine.

Most businesses use a database to store their persistent data. In this topology, the database server is hosted on a separate server box, possibly a mainframe. The J2EE application makes some JDBC calls to retrieve and update data from the database. In a typical scenario, a web user sends an HTTP request to the web server that is hosted on Server A. By examining the request, the web server determines that it should be processed by the application server and therefore passes the request to the application server. The application server processes the request by giving it to the appropriate application deployed on the server. That application processes the request and returns a response to the web server. The web server in turn returns the response to the original sender of the request. This type of topology might suffice for small businesses. Small businesses typically use

Secure Sockets Layer (SSL) to protect customer information and make use of the security features provided by the application server.

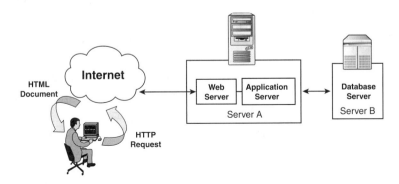

Figure 18-5   Basic three-tier topology.

Figure 18-6 is a more sophisticated topology for a medium- to large-scale enterprise that requires more stringent security. In this topology, firewalls are set up to put the web server in a demilitarized zone (DMZ) while the application servers and back-end databases or legacy systems are completely protected from the Internet. The DMZ is a location where a computer or a small subnetwork sits between a trusted internal network, such as a corporate private local area network (LAN), and an untrusted external network, such as the public Internet.

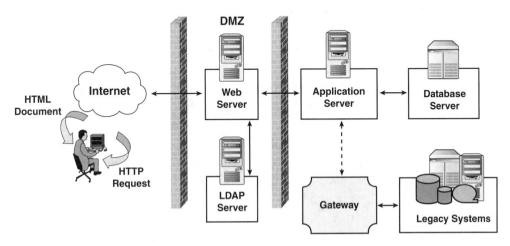

Figure 18-6   DMZ topology.

Typically, a security mechanism such as basic user ID and password is used to authenticate the web user. LDAP servers are commonly used to store users and their respective authorization information. The web server queries the LDAP server to authenticate and authorize a user who just logged in. In the case of an authorized user, the request is passed to the application server through a firewall, and the latter processes the request. For example, the request might be processed by a servlet, which requires data that exists on two different data sources, an Oracle database and a SQL Server database. When the request is made, an application requests the data by summoning either a native database driver or a generic (JDBC or ODBC) driver, which formats the resulting data in a way the web browser can understand using HTML, Java, or XML, and then places the data into a template. The web browser then receives the data and renders it for the user.

This example is a simplified view that hides a lot of the things that happen "under the hood." For example, the application server must be able to authenticate the user in some fashion, the server must have the processing power to run an applet and deal with the importing of data, and it must work in conjunction with an efficient web server (such as the Apache web server) to make sure that data is sent back to the user properly.

The next topology, shown in Figure 18-7, extends the previous topology by adding more application servers. The idea behind this topology is to increase the enterprise's processing capability, and thus the overall throughput by increasing the number of processors. In this case, one or more machines are added. Each additional box has the same configuration as the original—the same application server and the same applications are deployed. When the number of simultaneous requests coming in to the web server is high, so that the performance of only one application server reaches its saturation point, the additional application servers can help by taking in some of the load. The web server, therefore, must be able to spray the requests across the available application servers using a load-balancing algorithm. The most straightforward algorithm is round-robin, where requests are distributed to each application server in a fixed sequence one after the other and repeating the same sequence over and over. Theoretically, the round-robin algorithm distributes the load uniformly among all the application servers. With load balancing, requests are spread among all running application servers in a cluster, rather than risking having one or two servers overworked and on the edge of failure. This type of load balancing is a staple in the overall web server world. Typically, application servers take one or two approaches: they either employ a simple round-robin method that sends an incoming request to a less-busy server, or they institute an algorithm-based system in which usage on the entire network is analyzed and a request is sent to the server that can best handle the request based on parameters set up by the system administrator.

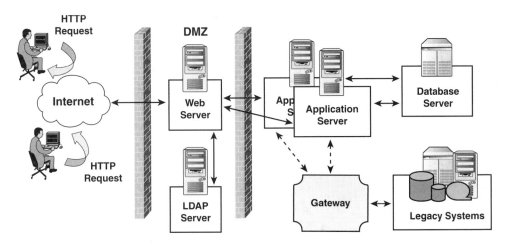

Figure 18-7   Load balancing.

The next topology, shown in Figure 18-8, is a further extension of the previous topology. The main distinction is that the same topology is now being replicated into several instances. Figure 18-8 shows only two instances. Each instance is called a domain, so this topology is called the multidomain topology. This topology essentially achieves another layer of high availability and load balancing. Domains can be spread geographically in many places. Notice that a new server, called the Request Sprayer, becomes the front end (and thus a single point of entry), which accepts requests and distributes them to the available web servers. A web server performs the necessary security checks and the distribution of requests to the application servers, as described in the previous topology. Note that the web servers typically share the same LDAP repository because the splitting of the application servers into several domains is transparent to users. In some architectures, there could be a pool of LDAP servers so that the web servers can access any of them. It is important in this situation, however, that the repositories of these LDAP servers are synchronized for consistency.

This multiple LDAP servers approach is excellent for fail-over. The multidomain topology shown in Figure 18-8 shows that the back-end is shared by all domains. Again, this is not necessarily true, as in the case of the multiple-LDAP servers.

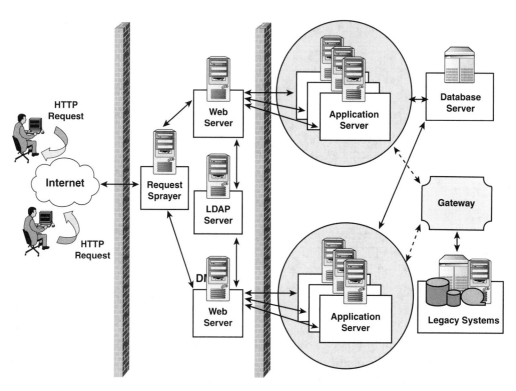

Figure 18-8   Multidomain topology.

Although it's costly, the advantage of the multidomain topology is high availability. A domain can be down for a while due to different reasons—for example, a power outage, application deployment, version upgrade, or system crash. However, this outage will not shut down the entire operation of the enterprise because requests can be routed to the other domain that is still online. The multidomain topology also provides scalability to the system as the workload increases.

Performance Tuning

Performance tuning is a fundamental way to improve the performance of any server. Key to performance tuning is finding the performance bottlenecks in the system under investigation. After they are identified, the bottlenecks should be fixed and/or tuned. Performance tuning can be performed at any layer in our software performance stack where parameters can be set. Performance tuning is about finding the right values for these parameters. Performance tuning is also the art of putting the system in harmony by making sure that the combinations of all parameter values create a balanced system.

Tuning the performance of an application server is broader in scope than general performance tuning. The system under test must be analyzed from end to end, including all the external components that communicate with the application server. This can be done in a top-down fashion, where the whole system is treated as a blackbox at first. As performance data is gathered, an analysis is made, and possible suspects are identified, you can go one step lower to get more information related to the suspects. This is done repeatedly until the cause of the bottleneck is discovered.

Performance analysis tools are very important in this undertaking. The golden rule is to use the right tool for the right problem. Hundreds of tools are available for analyzing the performance of J2EE applications, and some of them are commercial tools. Tools for Linux servers are discussed in this book in Part III, "System Tuning." These tools are very handy for analyzing performance at the operating system level.

Performance analysis of application servers can be divided into three levels: J2EE-related, JVM-related, and Linux operating system- and hardware-related. These areas are shown in Figure 18-9.

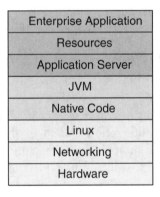

Figure 18-9   Three levels of performance tuning. Level 3 is typically independent of the operating system, whereas Levels 1 and 2 may involve closer investigation of the OS.

Level 3 represents J2EE-specific areas, including the application server itself. These areas can be tuned independent of the underlying operating system. For example, certain parameters in the application servers can be tuned without regard to Linux-specific parameters, including prepared statement cache size, connection pools, and transaction timeouts. Literature on performance analysis and tuning of J2EE applications is abundant; a good reference is.

Level 2 represents areas very specific to the JVM, the native code that implements the JVM, and the native code emitted by the JIT compiler. Specific parameters in the JVM are also independent of the operating system, such as the maximum and minimum heap size and garbage collection policies. But other parameters are tightly coupled with the operating system—for example, the maximum heap size. Most literature on J2EE performance tuning includes JVM performance tuning as well.

Level 1 represents areas that are more specific to the Linux operating system and the hardware platform it is running on.

When looking for the cause of a performance problem, the recommended approach is to go from Level 3 to Level 1. This means that before delving into tuning Linux, make sure as much as possible that all the other layers above it have been exhausted. *Give Linux the benefit of the doubt by making it the last suspect* except when it is rather obvious and undeniable that the problem is Linux-related. Your system administrator should have configured Linux to be at its optimal configuration. However, not all global configurations of Linux may work well with all applications in your system.

When tuning an application server, the best approach is to use CPU utilization as your goal for optimization. This is true in both single-server and clustered configurations. Here is a rough outline of the steps involved in this approach:

1. Choose an application to run on the application server.
2. Set up your environment for testing.
3. Perform a user ramp-up test.

    Run a test with one user and gather the necessary statistics, such as the throughput, average response time, CPU utilization, and so on. If other systems are involved in the environment, such as a remote database machine or a web server, also gather OS-level statistics such as CPU utilization and I/O statistics.

    Perform the previous step, but double the number of users.

    Stop when the CPU utilization is either maxed out (100% used) or tends to stay approximately the same as the previous runs.

4. If the CPU was maxed out, the system has no bottleneck. Otherwise, you need to investigate what is causing the idle time.
5. After you have determined a possible cause of the bottleneck and have fixed/tuned it, perform another user ramp-up test.
6. Repeat this process until you can max out the application server's CPU.

In the case of a clustered configuration, investigate the CPU utilization of all application server boxes. Test a clustered configuration only after you have done a single-server test.

A clustered configuration is good for testing scalability problems. Also, it is recommended that you assign a box exclusively to an application server and move all other servers (database server, JMS server, and so on) to remote boxes. A later chapter illustrates this approach by using a real life example.

When you have determined that a bottleneck exists, the next step is to look for it. It takes experience and exposure to a number of problem cases to be able to hunt down the culprit quickly. Some guidelines that we can offer include the following:

- *Enterprise application.* Make sure that the enterprise application is not causing the problem. Profile the application using tools to detect problems with path length, method time, memory usage, and thread waits. Some commercial tools for J2EE performance profiling that are now available on the Linux platform are JProbe from Quest Software, OptimizeIt from Borland, and Rational Purify/Quantify from IBM. Eclipse is an open-source profiler available on Linux.

  To be an expert performance analyst, you have to be familiar with J2EE programming concepts and the best programming practices for good performance.

- *Java Virtual Machine.* The JVM is crucial for the application server. Make sure that it is properly tuned based on the behavior of the enterprise applications. More specifically, check if the heap size is set properly. Examine the behavior of the garbage collector. Does using the parallel garbage collector help? If the JVM is based on hot-spot technology, is it enabled? Is large page support available, and does your Linux kernel support it as well? Is JIT enabled? These are just some of the things you can check.

  The best thing you can do is check the JVM implementor's help guide or web site to find what parameters are available for tuning. If you intend to be an expert performance analyst for application servers, you must understand intimately the underpinnings of the Java Virtual Machine and some of its implementation details.

- *Security.* If the web server uses security, verify that it is tuned properly to handle SSL requests. Also, the application server might have some performance tuning knobs that are available for SSL or J2EE security. Security itself is an overhead. It is estimated that security can slow down an application server by 20% to 25%. Test your system by turning off security, and check if you are getting a lot more than this percentage.

- *Networking.* Because the application server is very intensive with network communications to the web server, database server, JMS server, LDAP server, and other remote servers, verify that the TCP/IP stack is properly tuned. It is also important to check the performance of the servers that the application server is talking to. For example, check if the database server is properly tuned and if it can process the amount of data being passed to it by the application server in a timely manner. Another critical server to look at is the web server. In these situations, you might need the help of other people with the necessary skills to examine those servers.

- *File system.* Take note of the file system activity by using tools such as sar and iostat. Also check to see if a lot of file swapping is occurring.

- *Concurrency.* If you are using kernel 2.4, examine the context switches that are taking place by running vmstat. If the context switches are a bit too high, make sure that the application server's thread pool is not too high. Typically, a thread pool of 10 to 20 threads is sufficient. Beyond that, performance can degrade. With NPTL supported in the Linux 2.6 kernel, this limitation might be alleviated.

- *Memory.* Check the system memory usage—specifically, the memory that is allocated to the application server. Determine if the system needs to be upgraded with more memory.

- *Scaling.* Verify that the system is scaling well. In SMP systems, if the number of processors is a detriment rather than a help, it might be wise to disable some of the processors. If vertical clustering is configured, make sure that there are not too many instances of the application server. Determine whether adding more application servers increases CPU utilization. If it does, kill some of your application servers.

Depending on the type of environment you have (for example, hyperthreading or NUMA), there might be other things you can look into. Verify that your Linux kernel supports these additional features on your system.

Tuning an application server is a system-wide activity. All the pieces of the system need to have a performance story, and you should be able to work on all the layers in the software performance stack. The application server is a complex piece of middleware and so is the tuning process.

Summary

Application servers are complex pieces of middleware that have become some of the most useful tools in the IT industry today. Application servers are typically used by business enterprises to put their business on the Internet. The specific type of application server discussed in this chapter is the J2EE-based application server, which is currently the most widely used type of application server.

Characterizing the performance of an application server is not straightforward because doing so involves many external components. Those components need to be considered because their own performance affects the overall performance of the application server. We provided a software performance stack to illustrate the different layers of software that contribute to the performance of the application server. Each of these layers must be addressed individually to diagnose performance problems and improve performance.

We also provided some key concepts pertaining to the different ways of improving performance and high availability. The important thing to remember is that you have to determine the performance requirements of your enterprise—the anticipated volume of requests and the expected response time. From there, you can determine what the capacity of the system should be to meet those requirements. There are many topologies to choose from, but your decision depends largely on your requirements.

REFERENCES

[1] Brown, K., G. Craig, G. Hester, et. al. *Enterprise Java Programming with IBM WebSphere*, 2nd Edition. Addison-Wesley, 2003.

[2] Joines, S., R. Willenborg, and K. Hygh. *Performance Analysis for Java Web Sites*. Addison-Wesley, 2003. ISBN 0-20-184454-0.

[3] Menasce, D. A. and V. A. F. Almeida. *Capacity Planning for Web Performance: Metrics, Models, & Methods*. Prentice Hall PTR, Upper Saddle River, New Jersey, 1998. ISBN 0-13-693822-1.

## PART V

Tuning Case Studies

## CHAPTER NINETEEN

Case Study: Tuning the I/O Schedulers in Linux 2.6

By Dominique Heger and Steven Pratt

INTRODUCTION

The goal of this chapter is to quantify I/O performance in Linux 2.6 under varying workload conditions. These workload conditions are in environments ranging from single-CPU, single-disk setups to SMP systems that utilize large, sophisticated RAID systems. Incorporating different I/O workload patterns, the focus is on quantifying the baseline, as well as the optimized performance behavior under different Linux 2.6 I/O scheduler and file system configurations. The analysis results in the establishment of performance metrics that outline the I/O performance behavior and guide the configuration, setup, and fine-tuning process.

The point of convergence in the analysis is the entire I/O stack, incorporating the major software and hardware I/O optimization features that are present in the I/O path. The I/O stack in general has become considerably more complex over the last few years. Contemporary I/O solutions include hardware, firmware, and software support for features such as request coalescing, adaptive prefetching, automated invocation of direct I/O, or asynchronous write-behind polices. From a hardware perspective, incorporating large cache subsystems on a memory, RAID controller, and physical disk layer allows for a very aggressive utilization of these I/O optimization techniques. The interaction of the different optimization methods that are incorporated in the different layers of the I/O stack is neither well understood nor quantified to an extent necessary to make a rational statement on I/O performance. A rather interesting feature of the Linux operating system is the I/O scheduler. Unlike the CPU scheduler, an I/O scheduler is not a necessary component of any operating system per se. Therefore, it is not an actual building block in some of the commercial UNIX systems.

Before looking at the Linux 2.6 I/O schedulers and their performance, we first discuss the benchmark environment and workload profiles used throughout this chapter.

BENCHMARK ENVIRONMENT AND WORKLOAD PROFILES

All of the benchmarks used to gather results for this chapter were run in a Linux 2.6.4 environment. For this study, the CFQ I/O scheduler was backported from Linux 2.6.5 to 2.6.4. The benchmarks were run on the following systems:

- 16-way 1.7GHz Power4+ IBM p690 SMP system configured with GB memory. 28 15,000-RPM SCSI disk drives configured in a single RAID-0 setup that uses Emulex LP9802-2G Fiber controllers (one in use for the actual testing). The system is configured with the Linux 2.6.4 operating system.

- 8-way NUMA system. IBM x440 with Pentium IV Xeon 2.0GHz processors and 512KB L2 cache subsystem. Configured with four qla2300 fiber cards (only one is used in this study). The I/O subsystem consists of two FAST700 I/O controllers and utilized 15,000-RPM SCSI 18GB disk drives. The system is configured with GB of memory, set up as a RAID-5 (five disk) configuration, and uses the Linux 2.6.4 operating system.

- Single CPU system. IBM x440 (8-way; only one CPU is used in this study) with Pentium IV Xeon 1.5GHz processor, and a 512k L2 cache subsystem. The system is configured with an Adaptec aic7899 Ultra160 SCSI adapter and a single 10,000-RPM 18GB disk. The system uses the Linux 2.6.4 operating system and is configured with 1GB of memory.

The benchmarks we used for this study are the following:

- *Web Server Benchmark*. This benchmark utilizes four worker threads per available CPU. In the first phase, the benchmark creates several hundred thousand files ranging from 4KB to 64KB. The files are distributed across 100 directories. The goal of the create phase is to exceed the size of the memory subsystem by creating more files than what can be cached by the system in RAM. Each worker thread executes 1,000 random read operations on randomly chosen files. The workload distribution in this benchmark is derived from Intel's Iometer benchmark.

- *File Server Benchmark*. This benchmark utilizes four worker threads per available CPU. In the first phase, the benchmark creates several hundred thousand files ranging from 4KB to 64KB. The files are distributed across 100 directories. The goal of the create phase is to exceed the size of the memory subsystem by creating more files than what can be cached by the system in RAM. Each worker thread executes 1,000 random read or write operations on randomly chosen files. The ratio of read to write operations on a per-thread basis is specified as 80% to 20%, respectively. The workload distribution in this benchmark is derived from Intel's Iometer benchmark.

- *Mail Server Benchmark*. This benchmark utilizes four worker threads per available CPU. In the first phase, the benchmark creates several hundred thousand files ranging from 4KB to 64KB. The files are distributed across 100 directories. The goal of the create phase is to exceed the size of the memory subsystem by creating more files than what can be cached by the system in RAM. Each worker thread executes 1,000 random read, create, or delete operations on randomly chosen files. The ratio of read to create to delete operations on a per-thread basis is specified as 40% to 40% to 20%, respectively. The workload distribution in this benchmark is (loosely) derived from the SPECmail2001 benchmark.

- *Metadata Benchmark*. This benchmark utilizes four worker threads per available CPU. In the first phase, the benchmark creates several hundred thousand files ranging from 4KB to 64KB. The files are distributed across 100 directories. The goal of the create phase is to exceed the size of the memory subsystem by creating more files than what can be cached by the system in RAM. Each worker thread executes 1,000 random create, write (append), or delete operations on randomly chosen files. The ratio of create to write to delete operations on a per-thread basis is specified as 40% to 40% to 20%.

- *Sequential Read Benchmark*. This benchmark utilizes four worker threads per available CPU. In the first phase, the benchmark creates several hundred 50MB files in a single directory structure. The goal of the create phase is to exceed the size of the memory subsystem by creating more files than what can be cached by the system in RAM. Each worker thread executes 64KB sequential read operations, starting at offset 0 reading the entire file up to offset 5GB. This process is repeated on a per-worker thread basis 20 times on randomly chosen files.

- *Sequential Write (Create) Benchmark*. This benchmark utilizes four worker threads per available CPU. Each worker thread executes 64KB sequential write operations up to a target file size of 50MB. This process is repeated on a per-worker thread basis 20 times on newly created files.

I/O SCHEDULERS AND PERFORMANCE

As a workload generator, this case study utilizes the flexible file system benchmark (FFSB) infrastructure. FFSB represents a benchmarking environment that facilitates I/O performance analysis by simulating a diverse set of I/O patterns. The benchmarks are executed on multiple individual file systems, utilizing an adjustable number of worker threads, where each thread may operate either out of a combined or a thread-based I/O profile. Aging the file systems, as well as collecting system utilization and throughput statistics, is part of the benchmarking framework. In addition to the more traditional sequential read and sequential write benchmarks, this case study uses a file server, a web server, a mail server, and a metadata-intensive I/O profile (discussed in the preceding section).

The file and mail server workloads are based on the Iometer benchmark from Intel, whereas the mail server transaction mix is loosely derived from the SPECmail2001 I/O profile. The I/O analysis in this case study is composed of two distinct focal points. One emphasis of the study is on aggregate I/O performance achieved across the four benchmarked workload profiles, whereas a second emphasis is on the sequential read and write performance behavior. The emphasis on aggregate performance across the four distinct workload profiles is based on the claim made that an I/O scheduler has to provide adequate performance in a variety of workload scenarios and hardware configurations. All the conducted benchmarks are executed with the default tuning values, if not otherwise specified, in an Ext3 and XFS file system environment. In this chapter, the term *response time* represents the total runtime of the actual FFSB benchmark, incorporating all the I/O operations that are executed by the worker threads.

The following section discusses the benchmark conducted on the single-CPU single-disk system.

SINGLE-CPU SINGLE-DISK SETUP

The normalized results across the four workload profiles reveal that the deadline, the noop, and the CFQ schedulers perform within 2% and 1% percent on *Ext3* and *XFS* (see Figure 19-1). On *Ext3*, the CFQ scheduler has a slight advantage, whereas on *XFS* the deadline scheduler provides the best aggregate (normalized) response time. On both file systems, the AS scheduler represents the least-efficient solution, trailing the other I/O schedulers by 4.6% and 13% on *Ext3* and *XFS*, respectively. Not surprisingly, among the four workloads benchmarked in a single-disk system, AS trailed the other three I/O schedulers by a significant margin in the web server scenario, which reflects 100% random read operations. On sequential read operations, the AS scheduler outperformed the other three implementations by an average of 130% and 127% on *Ext3* and *XFS*, respectively. The sequential read results clearly support the discussion in this chapter of where the design focus for AS is directed. In the case of sequential write operations, AS reveals the most efficient solution on *Ext3*, whereas the noop scheduler provides the best throughput on *XFS*. The performance delta for the sequential write scenarios among the I/O schedulers is 8% on *Ext3* and 2% on *XFS*.

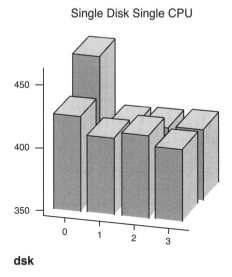

Single Disk Single CPU

dsk

Figure 19-1 Aggregate response time (normalized).

In Figure 19-1, the x-axis depicts the I/O schedulers; 0 = AS, 1 = deadline, 2 = noop, and 3 = CFQ. The front row reflects the Ext3 setup, whereas the back row shows XFS. The y-axis discloses the aggregate (normalized) response time over the four bench-marked profiles per I/O scheduler.

Table 19-1 shows data from a single disk, single CPU.

Table 19-1 Single Disk Single CPU—Mean Response Time in Seconds (AS, Deadline, Noop, CFQ)

	AS - Ext3	DL - Ext3	NO - Ext3	CFQ - Ext3	AS - XFS	DL - XFS	NO - XFS	CFQ - XFS
File Server	610.9	574.6	567.7	579.1	613.5	572.9	571.3	569.9
Metadata	621	634.1	623.6	597.5	883.8	781.8	773.3	771.7
Web Server	531.4	502.1	498.3	486.8	559	462.7	461.6	462.9
Mail Server	508.9	485.3	522.5	505.5	709.3	633	648.5	650.4
Seq. Read	405	953.2	939.4	945.4	385.2	872.8	881.3	872.4
Seq. Write	261.3	276.5	269.1	282.6	225.7	222.6	220.9	222.4

Next, we will describe a benchmark on a midrange 8-way NUMA RAID-5 system.

8-Way RAID-5 Setup

In the RAID-5 environment, the normalized response time values, across all four profiles, disclose that the deadline scheduler provides the most efficient solution on Ext3 as well as XFS (see Figures 19-2 and 19-3). While executing in an Ext3 environment, all four I/O schedulers are within 4.5%, with the AS I/O scheduler trailing noop and CFQ by approximately 2.5%. On XFS, the study clearly discloses a profound AS I/O inefficiency while executing the metadata benchmark. The deltas among the schedulers on XFS are much larger than on Ext3, as the CFQ, noop, and AS implementations trail the deadline scheduler by 1%, 6%, and 145%, respectively. As seen in the single-disk setup, the AS scheduler provides the most efficient sequential read performance. The gap between AS and the other three implementations is reduced significantly compared to the single-disk scenarios. The average sequential read throughput for the other three schedulers is approximately 20% less on both Ext3 and XFS, respectively. The sequential write performance is dominated by the response time of the CFQ scheduler that outperformed the other three solutions. The delta between the most- (CFQ) and least-efficient implementation is 22% (AS) and 15% (noop) on Ext3 and XFS, respectively.

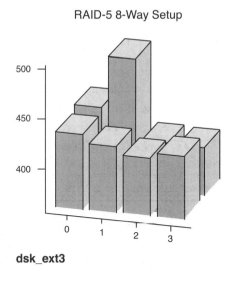

RAID-5 8-Way Setup

dsk_ext3

Figure 19-2   Ext3—aggregate response time (normalized).

In Figure 19-2, the x-axis depicts the I/O schedulers; 0 = AS, 1 = noop, 2 = deadline, and 3 = CFQ (for Ext3). The front row reflects the nontuned environments, and the back row reflects the tuned environments. The y-axis discloses the normalized response time (over the four profiles) per I/O scheduler.

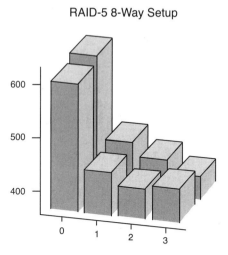

Figure 19-3 XFS–aggregate response time (normalized).

In Figure 19-3, the x-axis depicts the I/O schedulers; 0 = AS, 1 = noop, 2 = deadline, and 3 = CFQ (for XFS). The front row reflects the nontuned environments, and the back row reflects the tuned environments. The y-axis discloses the normalized response time (over the four profiles) per I/O scheduler.

Table 19-2 shows data from a RAID-5 8-way setup with no tuning.

Table 19-2 RAID-5 8-Way Setup–No Tuning–Mean Response Time in Seconds (AS, Deadline, Noop, CFQ)

	AS - Ext3	*DL - Ext3*	*NO - Ext3*	*CFQ - Ext3*	*AS - XFS*	*DL - XFS*	*NO - XFS*	*CFQ - XFS*
File Server	77.2	81.2	86.5	82.7	83.8	90.3	96.6	90.7
Metadata	147.8	148.4	133	145.3	205.8	90.8	101.6	100.8
Web Server	70.2	58.4	66.2	59.2	82.1	81.3	78.8	75.2
Mail Server	119.2	114.8	115.3	119.3	153.9	92.1	100.7	92.2
Seq. Read	517.5	631.1	654.1	583.5	515.8	624.4	628.7	604.5
Seq. Write	1033.2	843.7	969.5	840.5	426.6	422.3	462.6	400.4

In the second phase, all the I/O scheduler setups are tuned by adjusting the tunable *nr_requests* from its default value of 128 to 2,560. The results reveal that the CFQ scheduler reacts in a positive way to the adjustment and can provide an efficient solution on

Ext3 as well as on *XFS*. The tuning results in decreasing the response time for CFQ in all the conducted benchmarks on both file systems. Although CFQ benefits from the tuning, the results for the other three implementations are inconclusive. Based on the profile, the tuning results in either a gain or loss in performance. Because CFQ is designed to operate on larger sets of I/O requests, the results reflect the scheduler's design goals. This is in contrast to the AS implementation, where by design, any read intensive workload cannot directly benefit from the change. On the other hand, for sequential write operations, AS can take advantage of the tuning as the response time decreases by 7% and 8% on Ext3 and XFS, respectively. The conducted benchmarks reveal another significant inefficiency behavior in the I/O subsystem, because the write performance for all the schedulers on Ext3 is significantly lower (by a factor of approximately 2.1) than on XFS. The issue here is the Ext3 reservation code. The Ext3 patches to resolve the issue are available at `http://www.kernel.org`.

Table 19-3 shows data from a RAID-5 8-way setup with `nr_requests`.

Table 19-3   RAID-5 8-Way Setup—nr_requests = 2,560—Mean Response Time in Seconds (AS, Deadline, Noop, CFQ)

	AS - Ext3	*DL - Ext3*	*NO - Ext3*	*CFQ - Ext3*	*AS - XFS*	*DL - XFS*	*NO - XFS*	*CFQ - XFS*
File Server	78.3	72.1	87.1	70.7	94.1	75	89.2	76
Metadata	127.1	133	137.3	124.9	189.1	101.1	104.6	99.3
Web Server	62.4	58.8	75.3	57.5	79.4	72.83	80.6	71.7
Mail Server	110.2	92.9	118.8	99.6	152.5	100.2	95.1	81
Seq. Read	523.8	586.2	585.3	618.7	518.5	594.8	580.7	594.4
Seq. Write	968.2	782.9	1757.8	813.2	394.3	395.6	549.9	436.4

Finally, a benchmark was performed on a 16-way SMP system that utilizes a 28-disk RAID-0 configuration.

16-WAY RAID-0 SETUP

Utilizing the 28-disk RAID-0 configuration as the benchmark environment reveals that across the four workload profiles, the deadline implementation can outperform the other three schedulers. However, the CFQ, as well as the noop scheduler, slightly outperforms the deadline implementation in three out of the four benchmarks. Overall, the deadline scheduler gains a substantial lead processing the web server profile, outperforming the other three implementations by up to 62%. On Ext3, the noop scheduler reflects the most efficient solution while operating on sequential read and write requests, whereas on XFS, CFQ and deadline dominate the sequential read and write benchmarks. The performance delta among the schedulers for the four profiles is much more noticeable on XFS (38%) than on Ext3 (6%), which reflects a similar behavior as encountered on the RAID-5 setup. Increasing `nr_requests` to 2,560 on the RAID-0 system leads to inconclusive results for all the I/O schedulers on Ext3 as well as XFS.

Table 19-4 shows data from a RAID 0 16-way setup.

Table 19-4   RAID-0 16–Default I/O Schedulers, No Tuning, Mean Response Time (in Seconds)

	AS - Ext3	DL - Ext3	NO - Ext3	CFQ - Ext3	AS - XFS	DL - XFS	NO - XFS	CFQ - XFS
File Server	44.5	40	41.9	40.8	42.5	43	45.9	42.5
Metadata	66.7	64.6	66.2	64	101.8	71.7	72.4	66.7
Web Server	43.4	38.2	37.9	42.9	68.3	42.8	69.3	64.5
Mail Server	60.3	58.5	58.7	58.1	100.3	66.2	65.8	65.1
Seq. Read	2582.1	470.4	460.2	510.9	2601.2	541	576.1	511.2
Seq. Write	1313.8	1439.3	1171.1	1433.5	508.5	506.2	508.5	509.8

As we continue to the next section, we further illustrate the performance behavior of the AS scheduler design that views the I/O subsystem based on a notion that an I/O device has only one physical (seek) head; this study analyzes the sequential read performance in different hardware setups. The results are compared to the CFQ scheduler.

AS SEQUENTIAL READ PERFORMANCE

In the single disk setup, the AS implementation can approach the capacity of the hardware and therefore provides optimal throughput performance. Under the same workload conditions, the CFQ scheduler substantially hampers throughput performance and does not allow the system to fully utilize the capacity of the I/O subsystem. The described behavior holds true for the Ext3 and the XFS file systems. Hence, in the case of sequential read operations and CFQ, the I/O scheduler, not the file system per se, reflects the actual I/O bottleneck. This picture is reversed as the capacity of the I/O subsystem is increased.

As depicted in Table 19-5, the CFQ scheduler approaches the throughput of the AS implementation in the benchmarked RAID-5 environment, and can approach the capacity of the hardware in the large RAID-0 setup; the AS scheduler approaches only approximately 17% of the hardware capacity (180 MBps) in the RAID-0 environment. To reiterate, the discussed I/O behavior is reflected in the Ext3 and XFS benchmark results. From any file system perspective, performance should not degrade if the size of the file system, the number of files stored in the file system, or the size of the individual files stored in the file system increases. Further, the performance of a file system is supposed to approach the capacity of the hardware. This study clearly outlines that in the discussed workload scenario, the two benchmarked file systems can achieve these goals, but only in the case where the I/O schedulers are exchanged depending on the physical hardware setup. The read-ahead code in Linux 2.6 has to operate as efficiently as possible in conjunction with the I/O scheduler, and the file system has to be considered as well.

Table 19-5   AS Versus CFQ Sequential Read Performance

Hardware Setup	AS Throughput	CFQ Throughput
Single Disk	52 MBps	23 MBps
RAID-5	46 MBps	39.2 MBps
RAID-0	31 MBps	158 MBps

Based on the benchmarked profiles and hardware setups, the AS scheduler provides, in most circumstances, the least-efficient I/O solution. Because the AS framework represents an extension to the deadline implementation, the next section explores the possibility of tuning AS to approach deadline behavior.

AS VERSUS DEADLINE PERFORMANCE

In the case of tuning AS to approach deadline behavior, the tuning consists of setting `nr_requests` to 2,560, `antic_expire` to 0, `read_batch_expire` to 1,000, `read_expire` to 500, `write_batch_expire` to 250, and `write_expire` to 5,000. Setting the `antic_expire` value to 0 (by design) disables the anticipatory portion of the scheduler. The benchmarks are executed utilizing the RAID-5 environment, and the results are compared to the deadline performance results reported in this study. On Ext3, the non-tuned AS version trails the nontuned deadline setup by approximately 4.5% across the four profiles. Tuning the AS scheduler results in a substantial performance boost, because the benchmark results reveal that the tuned AS implementation outperforms the default deadline setup by approximately 6.5%. The performance advantage is offset, though, while comparing the tuned AS solution against the deadline environment with `nr_requests` set to 2,560. Across the four workload profiles, deadline again outperforms the AS implementation by approximately 17%. As anticipated, setting `antic_expire` to 0 results in lower sequential read performance, stabilizing the response time at deadline performance. On XFS, the results are based on the erratic metadata performance behavior of AS, which is inconclusive. One of the conclusions is based on the current implementation of the AS code that collects the statistical data; the implemented heuristic is not flexible enough to detect any prolonged random I/O behavior. This is a scenario where it is necessary to *deactivate* the *active wait* behavior. Further, setting `antic_expire` to 0 should force the scheduler into deadline behavior, a claim that is not backed up by the empirical data collected for this study. One explanation for the discrepancy is that the short backward seek operations supported in AS are not part of the deadline framework. Therefore, depending on the actual physical disk scheduling policy, the AS backward seek operations may be counterproductive from a performance perspective.

Table 19-6 shows data from a RAID-5 8-way with default AS, default deadline, and tuned AS comparison.

Table 19-6   RAID-5 8-Way—Default AS, Default Deadline, and Tuned AS Comparison—Mean Response Time in Seconds

	AS – Ext3	*DL – Ext3*	*AS Tuned – Ext3*	*AS - XFS*	*DL - XFS*	*AS Tuned - XFS*
File Server	77.2	81.2	72.1	83.8	90.3	84.5
Metadata	147.8	148.4	133.7	205.8	90.8	187.4
Web Server	70.2	58.4	62	82.1	81.3	75.9
Mail Server	119.2	114.8	103.5	153.9	92.1	140.2
Seq. Read	517.5	631.1	634.5	515.8	624.4	614.1
Seq. Write	1033.2	843.7	923.4	426.6	422.3	389.1

This benchmark study has revealed that the tuned CFQ setup is the proven remedy for the RAID-5 environment.

CFQ PERFORMANCE

The studied benchmarks reveal that the tuned CFQ setup provides the most efficient solution for the RAID-5 environment. Therefore, this case study further explores various ways to improve the performance of the CFQ framework. The CFQ I/O scheduler in Linux 2.6.5 resembles an SFQ implementation, which operates on a certain number of internal I/O queues and hashes on a per-process granularity to determine where to place an I/O request. The CFQ scheduler in Linux 2.6.5 hashes on the thread group ID (tgid), which represents the process ID (PID), as in POSIX.1. The approach chosen is to alter the CFQ code to hash on the Linux PID. This code change introduces fairness on a per thread granularity and therefore alters the distribution of the I/O requests in the internal queues. In addition, the `cfq_quantum` and `cfq_queued` parameters of the CFQ framework are exported into user space. In the first step, the default tgid-based CFQ version with `cfq_quantum` set to 32 (the default equals 8) is compared to the PID-based implementation that used the same tuning configuration. Across the four profiles, the PID-based implementation reflects the more efficient solution, processing the I/O workloads approximately 4.5% and 2% faster on Ext3 and XFS, respectively. To further quantify the performance impact of the different hash methods (tgid- versus PID-based), in the second step, the study compares the default Linux 2.6.5 CFQ setup to the PID-based code that is configured with `cfq_quantum` adjusted to 32. Across the four profiles benchmarked on Ext3, the new CFQ scheduler that hashed on a PID granularity outperformed the status quo by approximately 10%. With the new method, the sequential read and write performance improves by 3% and 4%, respectively. On XFS, across the four profiles, the tgid-based CFQ implementation proves to be the more efficient solution, outperforming the PID-based setup by approximately 9%. On the other hand, the PID-based solution is slightly more efficient while operating on the sequential read (2%) and write (1%) profiles. The ramification is that based on the conducted benchmarks and file system configurations, certain workload scenarios can be processed more efficiently in a tuned, PID hash-based configuration setup.

In Figure 19-4, the x-axis depicts the I/O schedulers; 0 = default CFQ, 1 = CFQ with PID, 2 = AS, 3 = deadline, and 4 = noop. The front row reflects the XFS, whereas the back row depicts the Ext3-based environment. The y-axis discloses the *actual* response time for the mixed workload profile.

RAID-5 8-Way Setup

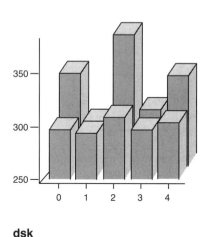

dsk

Figure 19-4 Mixed workload behavior.

Table 19-7 shows data from a RAID-5 8-way with various CFQ and PID settings.

Table 19-7 RAID-5 8-Way—Default CFQ, PID Hashed CFQ, and cfq_quantum=32, Default CFQ, and cfq_quantum=32—Mean RT

	CFQ	*PID and Tuned*	*CFQ Tuned*	*CFQ*	*PID and Tuned*	*CFQ Tuned*
File Server	70.7	71.1	70.6	76	75.9	74.3
Metadata	124.9	122	125.1	99.3	92.9	97.4
Web Server	57.5	55.8	58	71.7	73	72.5
Mail Server	99.6	94.5	93.3	81	93.6	93.3
Seq. Read	618.7	599.5	595.4	594.4	583.7	604.1
Seq. Write	813.2	781.1	758.4	436.4	432.1	414.6

To further substantiate the potential of the proposed PID-based hashing approach, a mixed I/O workload consisting of 32 concurrent threads is benchmarked. The environment used reflects the RAID-5 setup. The I/O profile is decomposed into four subsets of eight worker threads, with each subset executing either 64KB sequential read, 4KB random read, 4KB random write, or 256KB sequential write operations (see Figure 19-4).

The benchmark results reveal that in this mixed I/O scenario the PID-based CFQ solution (tuned with `cfq_quantum` = 32) outperforms the other I/O schedulers by at least 5% and 2% on Ext3 and XFS, respectively. The performance delta among the schedulers is greater on Ext3 (15%) than on XFS (6%).

Table 19-8 shows data from a RAID-5 8-way with mixed workload behavior.

Table 19-8 RAID-5 8-Way—Mixed Workload Behavior (CFQ-T = PID and cfq_quantum = 32), Response Time (in Seconds)

	CFQ	CFQ-T	AS	DL	NO
Mixed Ext3	334.1	288.1	371.2	301.2	333.5
Mixed XFS	295	291	308.4	296	302.8

SUMMARY

The benchmarks conducted on varying hardware configurations reveal a strong, setup-based correlation among the I/O scheduler, the workload profile, the file system, and ultimately I/O performance. The empirical data discloses that most tuning efforts result in reshuffling the scheduler's *performance ranking*. The ramification is that the choice of an I/O scheduler has to be based on the workload pattern, the hardware setup, and the file system used. To reemphasize the importance of the discussed approach, an additional benchmark is executed utilizing a Linux 2.6 SMP system, the JFS file system, and a large RAID-0 configuration, consisting of 84 RAID-0 systems (five disks each). The SPECsfs benchmark is used as the workload generator. The focus is on determining the highest throughput achievable in the RAID-0 setup by substituting the I/O scheduler only between SPECsfs runs. The results reveal that the noop scheduler can outperform the CFQ, as well as the AS scheduler. The result reverses the order and contradicts the ranking established for the RAID-5 and RAID-0 environments benchmarked in this study. On the smaller RAID systems, the noop scheduler cannot outperform the CFQ implementation in any random I/O test. In the large RAID-0 environment, the 84 rb-tree data structures that have to be maintained (from a memory as well as a CPU perspective) in CFQ represent a substantial, noticeable overhead factor.

The results show that no I/O scheduler consistently provides the best possible I/O performance. Although the AS scheduler excels on small configurations in a sequential read scenario, the nontuned deadline solution provides acceptable performance on smaller RAID systems. The CFQ scheduler exhibits the most potential from a tuning perspective on smaller RAID-5 systems, because increasing the `nr_requests` parameter provides the lowest response time. Because the noop scheduler represents a rather lightweight solution, large RAID systems that consist of many individual logical devices may benefit from the reduced memory, as well as CPU overhead encountered by this solution. On large RAID systems that consist of many logical devices, the other three implementations have to maintain complex data structures as part of the operating framework. Further, the study reveals that the proposed PID-based and tunable CFQ implementation reflects a valuable alternative to the standard CFQ implementation. The empirical data collected on a RAID-5 system supports that claim, because true fairness on a per-thread basis is introduced. Future work items include analyzing the erratic performance behavior encountered by the AS scheduler on XFS while processing a metadata-intensive workload profile. Another focal point is an in-depth analysis of the inconsistent `nr_requests` behavior observed on large RAID-0 systems. Different hardware setups will be used to aid this study. The anticipatory heuristics of the AS code used in Linux 2.6.5 are the target of another study, aiming at enhancing the *adaptiveness* of the (status quo) implementation based on certain workload conditions. Additional research in the area of the proposed PID-based CFQ implementation, as well as extending the I/O performance study into larger I/O subsystems, represents other work items that will be addressed in the near future.

REFERENCES

[1] The Linux Source Code.

[2] Arcangeli, A. "Evolution of Linux Towards Clustering," EFD R&D Clamart, 2003.

[3] Axboe, J. "Deadline I/O Scheduler Tunables," SuSE, EDF R&D, 2003.

[4] Corbet, J. "A New Deadline I/O Scheduler," `http://lwn.net/Articles/10874`.

[5] "Anticipatory I/O Scheduling," `http://lwn.net/Articles/21274`.

[6] "The Continuing Development of I/O Scheduling," `http://lwn.net/Articles/21274`.

[7] "Porting Drivers to the 2.5 Kernel," Linux Symposium, Ottawa, Canada, 2003.

[8] Heger, D., J. Jacobs, B. McCloskey, and J. Stultz. "Evaluating Systems Performance in the Context of Performance Paths," IBM Technical White Paper, Austin, 2000.

[9] Iyer, S. and P. Drushel. "Anticipatory Scheduling—A Disk Scheduling Framework to Overcome Deceptive Idleness in Synchronous I/O," SOSP 2001.

[10] Irwin, Lee W. III, "A 2.5 Page Clustering Implementation," Linux Symposium, Ottawa, 2003.

[11] Nagar, S., H. Franke, J. Choi, C. Seetharaman, S. Kaplan, N. Singhvi, V. Kashyap, and M. Kravetz. "Class-Based Prioritized Resource Control in Linux," 2003 Linux Symposium.

[12] McKenney, P. "Stochastic Fairness Queueing," INFOCOM, 1990.

[13] Molnar, I. "Goals, Design and Implementation of the New Ultra-scalable O(1) Scheduler" (sched-design.txt).

[14] Mosberger, D. and S. Eranian. *IA-64 Linux Kernel, Design and Implementation*, Prentice Hall, NJ, 2002.

[15] Shriver, E., A. Merchant, and J. Wilkes. "An Analytic Behavior Model with Readahead Caches and Request Reordering," Bell Labs, 1998.

[16] Wienand, I. "An Analysis of Next Generation Threads on IA64," HP, 2003.

[17] Zimmermann, R. and S. Ghandeharizadeh. "Continuous Display Using Heterogeneous Disk-Subsystems," ACM Multimedia, 1997.

[18] Web resource: `http://www.iometer.org/`.

[19] Web resource: `http://www.specbench.org/osg/mail2001`.

[20] Web resource: `http://www.specbench.org/sfs97r1/docs/chapter1.html`.

## CHAPTER TWENTY

Case Study: File System Tuning

By Steve Best

INTRODUCTION

Linux provides several utilities for each type of file system for looking at file system metadata and analyzing on-disk structures. With these tools, you can view a file system's structures. Generally, these tools are intended for use by developers of a file system to analyze structures; however, they can also be used to find performance problems.

In this case study, we'll provide examples of viewing an inode on Ext2, JFS, ReiserFS, and XFS file systems. Next, we'll show how to tune each type of file system by using an external log. An external log improves performance because the log updates are saved to a different partition than the corresponding file system. This reduces the number of hard disk seeks. We'll show the results of using file system test programs on a file system that uses an external log. We'll also discuss mount options that some file systems have to increase file system performance. We'll then show how you can identify bottlenecks on physical disks by using the sar and iostat tools.

ANALYZING FILE LAYOUT

Each file system has a unique layout that features the structures that files need to manage the metadata of the file system. The following four sections provide examples of how to look at structures of Ext2/Ext3, JFS, ReiserFS, and XFS file systems. Although the utilities that come with the file systems for looking at the on-disk structures are used mainly by developers to view the different structures of file systems, they can also be used to find and resolve performance issues with each file system.

Ext2/Ext3 Layout

The following example shows some of the structures of an Ext2 file system. In the example, an Ext2 file system is used to format a floppy disk with the mkfs command.

```
# mkfs /dev/fd0

mke2fs 1.32 (09-Nov-2002)
Filesystem label=
OS type: Linux
Block size=1024 (log=0)
Fragment size=1024 (log=0)
184 inodes, 1440 blocks
72 blocks (5.00%) reserved for the super user
First data block=1
1 block group
8192 blocks per group, 8192 fragments per group
184 inodes per group

Writing inode tables: 0/1 done
Writing superblocks and filesystem accounting information: done
```

The debugfs command produces output that is useful for analyzing a file system's on-disk structures. For example, the show_super_stats option displays the super block and disk group structures.

```
# debugfs /dev/fd0

debugfs 1.32 (09-Nov-2002)
debugfs: show_super_stats

debugfs 1.32 (09-Nov-2002)
debugfs:  Filesystem volume name:    <none>
Last mounted on:  <not available>
Filesystem UUID:   cb45e547-1618-4b70-bd91-22e651e19583
Filesystem magic number:   0xEF53
Filesystem revision #:    1 (dynamic)
Filesystem features:     filetype sparse_super
Default mount options:    (none)
Filesystem state:       clean
Errors behavior:       Continue
Filesystem OS type:     Linux
Inode count:         184
Block count:         1440
Reserved block count:    72
Free blocks:         1399
Free inodes:         173
First block:         1
```

```
Block size:            1024
Fragment size:         1024
Blocks per group:      8192
Fragments per group:   8192
Inodes per group:      184
Inode blocks per group: 23
Filesystem created:    Mon Jun  9 19:06:00 2003
Last mount time:       n/a
Last write time:       Mon Jun  9 19:06:01 2003
Mount count:           0
Maximum mount count:   29
Last checked:          Mon Jun  9 19:06:00 2003
Check interval:        15552000 (6 months)
Next check after:      Sat Dec  6 19:06:00 2003
Reserved blocks uid:   0 (user root)
Reserved blocks gid:   0 (group root)
First inode:           11
Inode size:            128
Directories:           2
 Group  0: block bitmap at 3, inode bitmap at 4,
           inode table at 5
           1399 free blocks, 173 free inodes,
           2 used directories
debugfs: quit
```

The block group information is displayed after the super block. The block group information shows the block numbers where various structures are located, such as block bitmap, inode bitmap, inode table, and free blocks. For example, the inode bitmap for block group 0 is at block 4. Use the dump2efs command to display further information about the block group.

```
# dumpe2fs /dev/fd0

dumpe2fs 1.32 (09-Nov-2002)
Filesystem volume name:    <none>
Last mounted on: <not available>
Filesystem UUID: cb45e547-1618-4b70-bd91-22e651e19583
Filesystem magic number:   0xEF53
Filesystem revision #:     1 (dynamic)
Filesystem features:       filetype sparse_super
Default mount options:     (none)
Filesystem state:          clean
Errors behavior:           Continue
Filesystem OS type:        Linux
Inode count:               184
Block count:               1440
Reserved block count:      72
```

```
Free blocks:              1399
Free inodes:              173
First block:              1
Block size:               1024
Fragment size:            1024
Blocks per group:         8192
Fragments per group:      8192
Inodes per group:         184
Inode blocks per group:   23
Filesystem created:       Mon Jun  9 19:06:00 2003
Last mount time:          n/a
Last write time:          Mon Jun  9 19:06:01 2003
Mount count:              0
Maximum mount count:      29
Last checked:             Mon Jun  9 19:06:00 2003
Check interval:           15552000 (6 months)
Next check after:         Sat Dec  6 19:06:00 2003
Reserved blocks uid:      0 (user root)
Reserved blocks gid:      0 (group root)
First inode:              11
Inode size:               128


Group 0: (Blocks 1-1439)
  Primary superblock at 1, Group descriptors at 2-2
  Block bitmap at 3 (+2), Inode bitmap at 4 (+3)
  Inode table at 5-27 (+4)
  1399 free blocks, 173 free inodes, 2 directories
  Free blocks: 41-1439
  Free inodes: 12-184
```

One of the limits of the Ext2 file system is the static allocation of inodes. There are 184 inodes available on this Ext2 file system, which means that it can contain a total of only 184 files or directories. In the example, the file system runs out of inodes before it runs out of free space.

First, the mount point of /mnt/floppy mounts the floppy device /dev/fd0. Next, the create.sh script is run. create.sh creates one directory called "a" and then up to 300 files in that directory. When the script runs, it shows that the limit of the number of inodes is hit before the available free space is exhausted.

```
# mount /dev/fd0 /mnt/floppy
```

The create.sh script creates 300 files and returns an error after it has run out of inodes.

```
#!/bin/sh

for count in 'seq 1 1';
do
  echo Count: $count
  mkdir a
  for i in 'seq 1 300';
  do
    echo  abcdefghijklmnopqrstuvwxyz > a/$i
  done

  done
```

Use the `df -k` command to determine the amount of free space available for each mounted file system. This command produces output similar to the following:

```
# df -k

Filesystem    1K-blocks     Used Available Use% Mounted on
/dev/hda2      3265260  1581308   1518084  52% /
/dev/hda1       101089     9324     86546  10% /boot
none            192292        0    192292   0% /dev/shm
/dev/fd0          1412       14      1326   2% /mnt/floppy
/dev/hdb1      3999504   659260   3340244  17% /jfs
```

The output shows that the /dev/fd0 device, which is the floppy, has 2% of its space used. Output from the `ls -all` command shows that there is now one file called create.sh and the file system's lost+found directory.

```
# ls -all

lost+found
create.sh
```

The `df` command with the `-i` option displays the number of free inodes, which is 172 in our example.

```
# df -i

Filesystem    Inodes   IUsed    IFree IUse% Mounted on
/dev/hda2     415168   96813   318355  24% /
/dev/hda1      26104      41    26063   1% /boot
none           48073       1    48072   1% /dev/shm
/dev/fd0         184      12      172   7% /mnt/floppy
/dev/hdb1    6726720   44242  6682478   1% /jfs
```

If create.sh is run on the floppy, the Ext2 file system runs out of inodes before it runs out of file system space. Note that although the following error message makes it look like the file system is out of space, it is really out of free inodes to create files or directories.

```
# ./create.sh

Count: 1
./create.sh: line 9: a/172: No space left on device
./create.sh: line 9: a/173: No space left on device
./create.sh: line 9: a/174: No space left on device
./create.sh: line 9: a/175: No space left on device
...
```

The df -k command shows that the space used on the file system is only 15%.

```
# df -k

Filesystem  1K-blocks     Used Available Use% Mounted on
/dev/hda2    3265260  1581308   1518084  52% /
/dev/hda1     101089     9324     86546  10% /boot
none          192292        0    192292   0% /dev/shm
/dev/fd0        1412      188      1152  15% /mnt/floppy
/dev/hdb1    3999504   659280   3340224  17% /jfs
```

The ls -R command shows that 171 files and one directory called "a" were created that used up the 172 free inodes.

```
# ls -R

.:
a
lost+found
create.sh

./a:
1 10 100 101 102 103 104 105 106 107 108 109 11 110 111
112 113 114 115 116 117 118 119 12 120 121 122 123 124
125 126 127 128 129 13 130 131 132 133 134 135 136 137
138 139 14 140 141 142 143 144 145 146 147 148 149 15
150 151 152 153 154 155 156 157 158 159 16 160 161 162
163 164 165 166 167 168 169 17 170 171 18 19 2 20 21 22
23 24 25 26 27 28 29 3 30 31 32 33 34 35 36 37 38 39 4
40 41 42 43 44 45 46 47 48 49 5 50 51 52 53 54 55 56 57
58 59 6 60 61 62 63 64 65 66 67 68 69 7 70 71 72 73 74
75 76 77 78 79 8 80 81 82 83 84 85 86 87 88 89 9 90 91
92 93 94 95 96 97 98 99

./lost+found:
```

The df command with the -i option displays the number of free inodes, as shown here; we see the floppy device /dev/fd0 currently has the value 0.

```
# df -i
Filesystem    Inodes    IUsed    IFree IUse% Mounted on
/dev/hda2     415168    96814   318354   24% /
/dev/hda1      26104       41    26063    1% /boot
none           48073        1    48072    1% /dev/shm
/dev/fd0         184      184        0  100% /mnt/floppy
/dev/hdb1    6726720    44242  6682478    1% /jfs
```

These examples show that when using the Ext2/Ext3 file systems, there is a need to create enough inodes when using mkfs to create the file system because there is no way to increase the number of inodes after the file system has been formatted.

> The other journaling file systems provide the dynamic inode creation feature that allows the file system to create inodes as needed.

The next step is to unmount the floppy device and format it again by using mkfs; then remount the floppy device.

```
# umount /mnt/floppy
# mkfs /dev/fd0
# mount /dev/fd0 /mnt/floppy
```

Next, copy a file to the floppy device and then use the debugfs utility to view file system information about the file. In the following example, the file is named fstab. The inode for fstab is 12. In the example, the ls -l option in debugfs gathers file system information, and the stat option in debugfs displays the inode for file fstab.

```
# cp /etc/fstab /mnt/floppy/fstab
# umount /mnt/floppy
# debugfs /dev/fd0

debugfs : ls -l
1.32 (09-Nov-2002)
debugfs:
  2  40755 (2) 0 0  1024  9-Jun-2003 19:43 .
  2  40755 (2) 0 0  1024  9-Jun-2003 19:43 ..
 11  40700 (2) 0 0 12288  9-Jun-2003 19:06 lost+found
 12 100644 (1) 0 0   697  9-Jun-2003 19:43 fstab

debugfs:  stat <12>
debugfs: Inode: 12   Type: regular    Mode:   0644
Flags: 0x0   Generation: 295695
```

```
User:     0   Group:     0   Size: 697
File ACL: 0     Directory ACL: 0
Links: 1   Blockcount: 2
Fragment:  Address: 0     Number: 0     Size: 0
ctime: 0x3ee537a8 — Mon Jun  9 19:43:04 2003
atime: 0x3ee537a8 — Mon Jun  9 19:43:04 2003
mtime: 0x3ee537a8 — Mon Jun  9 19:43:04 2003
BLOCKS:
(0):41
TOTAL: 1
```

The Fragment information shown in the output is used to determine whether the file is contiguous. Fragmented files do not provide the best performance. However, the fstab file in the example is not fragmented.

The final step is to umount the floppy device.

```
# umount /mnt/floppy
```

Journaled File System (JFS) File Layout

The jfs_debugfs utility provides an examination of the structures of the Journaled File System (JFS) file system. The jfs_debugfs utility takes the device as the only parameter. The jfs_debugfs man page contains information on how to display the data structures for JFS. This section shows how to collect information on some of the key structures that are part of the file system.

In the examples, the /dev/hda1 device contains the JFS file system for which structures will be displayed.

```
# jfs_debugfs /dev/hda1
```

The su option of jfs_debugfs can be used to display the super block. The following example is sample output from a system:

```
>su
[1] s_magic:  'JFS1'        [15] s_ait2.addr1:      0x00
[2] s_version:  1           [16] s_ait2.addr2:      0x00000097
[3] s_size: 0x00000000007fa970 s_ait2.address:    151
[4] s_bsize: 4096           [17] s_logdev:          0x00000000
[5] s_l2bsize: 12           [18] s_logserial:       0x00000000
[6] s_l2bfactor:3           [19] s_logpxd.len:      4352
[7] s_pbsize: 512           [20] s_logpxd.addr1:    0x00
[8] s_l2pbsize: 9           [21] s_logpxd.addr2:    0x000ff581
[9] pad: Not Displayed          s_logpxd.address:  1045889
[10] s_agsize:0x00002000    [22] s_fsckpxd.len:     83
[11] s_flag:  0x10200900    [23] s_fsckpxd.addr1:   0x00
JFS_LINUX                   [24] s_fsckpxd.addr2:   0x000ff52e
```

```
JFS_COMMIT  JFS_GROUPCOMMIT    s_fsckpxd.address: 1045806
JFS_INLINELOG              [25] s_time.tv_sec:    0x3f002d2d
                           [26] s_time.tv_nsec:   0x00000000
                           [27] s_fpack:              `       `
[12] s_state: 0x00000000
            FM_CLEAN
[13] s_compress:        0
[14] s_ait2.len:        4

display_super: [m]odify or e[x]it: ✗
```

The following example uses /jfs as the mount point, mounts the file system, and copies over the fstab file, resulting in a file that is available to view on the JFS file system:

```
# mount -t jfs /dev/hda1 /jfs
# cd /jfs
# cp /etc/fstab .
```

To look at the inode of a file, its inode number is required. Use the ls command with the -i option to determine the file's inode number.

```
# ls -i
```

```
2 . 2.. 4 fstab
```

In this example, the one file that is in this subdirectory is named fstab, and its inode number is 4.

```
#cd ..
# umount /jfs
# jfs_debug /dev/hda1
```

The i option in jfs_debugfs displays the inode information for the *fstab* file.

```
>i 4
Inode 4 at block 155, offset 0x800:
```

```
[1] di_inostamp:    0x3f002d2d       [19] di_mtime.tv_nsec:
0x00000000
[2] di_fileset:     16               [20] di_otime.tv_sec:
0x3f002f06
[3] di_number:      4                [21] di_otime.tv_nsec:
0x00000000
[4] di_gen:         1                [22] di_acl.flag:
0x00
[5] di_ixpxd.len:   4                [23] di_acl.rsrvd:
Not Displayed
[6] di_ixpxd.addr1: 0x00             [24] di_acl.size:
0x00000000
```

```
[7]  di_ixpxd.addr2: 0x0000009b        [25] di_acl.len:         0
     di_ixpxd.address:   155           [26] di_acl.addr1:
0x00                                   [27] di_acl.addr2:
[8]  di_size:0x00000000000003b4
0x00000000                                  di_acl.address:     0
[9]  di_nblocks: 0x0000000000000001    [28] di_ea.flag:
[10] di_nlink:       1
0x00                                   [29] di_ea.rsrvd:
[11] di_uid:         0
Not Displayed                          [30] di_ea.size:
[12] di_gid:         0
0x00000000                             [31] di_ea.len:          0
[13] di_mode:        0x000681a4        [32] di_ea.addr1:
              0100644      -rw-        [33] di_ea.addr2:
0x00
[14] di_atime.tv_sec: 0x3f002f06            di_ea.address:      0
0x00000000                             [34] di_next_index:      0
[15] di_atime.tv_nsec: 0x00000000      [35] di_acltype:
[16] di_ctime.tv_sec:  0x3f002f06
[17] di_ctime.tv_nsec: 0x00000000
0x00000000
[18] di_mtime.tv_sec:    0x3f002f06
change_inode: [m]odify or e[x]it > x
```

ReiserFS File Layout

This section starts by looking at the layout of the ReiserFS file system. The utility to view the structures of the ReiserFS file system is debugreiserfs. It takes the device as one of the parameters; additional parameters can be used to display the file system structures. The following example formats the file system and copies one file named fstab to the ReiserFS file system. The -d option of debugreiserfs prints formatted nodes of the internal tree of the file system.

```
# mkreiserfs /dev/hdb1
```

The following example uses /reiserfs as the mount point, mounts the file system, and copies over the fstab file, resulting in a file that is available to view on the ReiserFS file system.

```
# mount -t reiserfs /dev/hdb1 /reiserfs
# cd /reiserfs
# cp /etc/fstab .
# ls -all
total 6
drwxr-xr-x    4 root    root    104 Dec 19 06:26 .
drwxr-xr-x   30 root    root   1824 Dec 20 12:10 ..
-rw-r--r--    1 root    root    948 Dec 19 06:26 fstab
```

```
# cd ..
# umount /reiserfs
# debugreiserfs -d /dev/hdb1
debugreiserfs 3.6.4

Filesystem state: consistent

Reiserfs super block in block 16 on 0x341 of format 3.6
with standard journal
Count of blocks on the device: 1004054
Number of bitmaps: 31
Blocksize: 4096
Free blocks (count of blocks - used [journal, bitmaps,
data, reserved] blocks): 995812
Root block: 8211
Filesystem is clean
Tree height: 2
Hash function used to sort names: "r5"
Objectid map size 2, max 972
Journal parameters:
        Device [0x0]
        Magic [0x431098f2]
        Size 8193 blocks (including 1 for journal header)
(first block 18)
        Max transaction length 1024 blocks
        Max batch size 900 blocks
        Max commit age 30
Blocks reserved by journal: 0
Fs state field: 0x0
sb_version: 2
inode generation number: 0
UUID: 1f0d2fd3-6fd6-412c-982d-4a16f0a37de9
LABEL:
Set flags in SB:
        ATTRIBUTES CLEAN

====================================================================
LEAF NODE (8211) contains level=1, nr_items=6,
free_space=2692 rdkey (real items 6)
-------------------------------------------------
|###|type|ilen|f/sp| loc|fmt|fsck|                    key
  |
|   |    |    |e/cn|    |   |need|
  |
-------------------------------------------------
|  0|1 2 0x0 SD (0), len 44, location 4052 entry count 0,
```

```
fsck need 0, format new|
(NEW SD), mode drwxr-xr-x, size 104, nlink 4, mtime 12/19/2003
06:26:51 blocks 1, uid 0
```

```
|  1|1 2 0x1 DIR (3), len 104, location 3948 entry count 4,
fsck need 0, format old|
###: Name            length  Object key      Hash     Gen number
  0: ".              "(  1)  [1 2]            0        1, loc 96
  1: "..             "(  2)  [0 1]            0        2, loc 88
  2: "fstab          "(  5)  [2 4]       293528832     0, loc 80
  3: ".reiserfs_priv "( 14)  [2 3]      1105744768     0, loc 64
```

```
|  2|2 3 0x0 SD (0), len 44, location 3904 entry count 65535,
fsck need 0, format new|
(NEW SD), mode drwx------, size 48, nlink 2, mtime 12/19/2003
06:26:18 blocks 1, uid 0
```

```
|  3|2 3 0x1 DIR (3), len 48, location 3856 entry count 2,
fsck need 0, format old|
###: Name     length   Object key     Hash    Gen number
  0: ".      "(  1)    [2 3]          0       1, loc 40
  1: "..     "(  2)    [1 2]          0       2, loc 32
```

```
|  4|2 4 0x0 SD (0), len 44, location 3812 entry count 65535,
fsck need 0, format new|
(NEW SD), mode -rw-r--r--, size 948, nlink 1, mtime 12/19/2003
06:26:51 blocks 8, uid 0
```

```
|  5|2 4 0x1 DRCT (2), len 952, location 2860 entry count
65535, fsck need 0, format new|
======================================================================
File system uses 0 internal + 1 leaves + 0 unformatted

nodes = 1 blocks
```

First the super block information is displayed for the file system, and then the leaf node 8211 is displayed. The highlighted information for the file fstab shows some common inode information for the file. The permissions are -rw-r-r--, the size is 948, and the mtime is 12/19/2003 06:26:51.

The debugreiserfs man page contains information about how to display the key structures for ReiserFS. To display the debugreiserfs man page, type the following command:

```
# man debugreiserfs
```

XFS File Layout

The xfs_db enables the examination of XFS file system structures. The xfs_db utility takes the device as the parameter. The xfs_db man page contains information about how to display the data structures for XFS.

This section shows how to display an inode on an XFS system.

The XFS file system is on the device /dev/hda5.

```
# mount -t xfs /dev/hda5 /xfs
# cd /xfs
```

Copy the fstab file located in the /etc directory onto the XFS file system.

```
# cp /etc/fstab .
# ls -all

total 12
drwxr-xr-x    2 root     root           18 Dec  8 10:57 .
drwxr-xr-x   24 root     root         4096 Dec  8 10:54 ..
-rw-r--r--    1 root     root          948 Dec  8 10:57 fstab
```

To look at a file's inode, its inode number is required. Use the ls command with the -i option to determine this number. In the following example, the inode number for the fstab file is 131.

```
# ls -i

  128 .          2 ..       131 fstab

# cd ..
# umount /xfs
```

The xfs_db option to look at an inode is the inode command. The inode command uses the inode number as the parameter. To print the file system information about the inode, use the p command.

```
# xfs_db /dev/hda5

xfs_db> inode 131
xfs_db> p
core.magic = 0x494e
core.mode = 0100644
core.version = 1
core.format = 2 (extents)
core.nlinkv1 = 1
core.uid = 0
core.gid = 0
core.flushiter = 2
```

```
core.atime.sec = Mon Dec  8 10:57:53 2003
core.atime.nsec = 123719000
core.mtime.sec = Mon Dec  8 10:57:53 2003
core.mtime.nsec = 123943000
core.ctime.sec = Mon Dec  8 10:57:53 2003
core.ctime.nsec = 123943000
core.size = 948
core.nblocks = 1
core.extsize = 0
core.nextents = 1
core.naextents = 0
core.forkoff = 0
core.aformat = 2 (extents)
core.dmevmask = 0
core.dmstate = 0
core.newrtbm = 0
core.prealloc = 0
core.realtime = 0
core.gen = 0
next_unlinked = null
u.bmx[0] = [startoff,startblock,blockcount,extentflag]
0:[0,12,1,0]
xfs_db> q
```

TUNING FILE SYSTEMS

Now that you're familiar with the layout of the various types of file systems supported in Linux, let's examine how to tune the Ext3, ReiserFS, JFS, and XFS file systems. We'll show how to tune each of the file systems by using an external log and using some of the mount options that are available on each file system.

Tuning Options for Ext3: Using a Separate Journal Device

External logs improve file system performance because the log updates are saved to a different partition than the corresponding file system, thereby reducing the number of hard disk seeks.

To use an external journal for the Ext3 file system, first run `mkfs` on the journal device. The block size of the external journal must be the same block size at the Ext3 file system. The example in this section uses the /dev/hdb1 device as the external log for the Ext3 file system.

There are two steps to creating an external log. The first is to format the journal; the second is to format the partition and tell `mkfs` that the log will be external. In the

following example, the Ext3 partition will be on device /dev/hda1, and the external log
will be on device /dev/hdb1. The `mkfs -b` option sets the block size for the file system.

```
# mkfs.ext3 -b 4096 -O journal_dev /dev/hdb1
# mkfs.ext3 -b 4096 -J device=/dev/hdb1 /dev/hda1
```

The next few examples use the tiobench program to see if an external log helps the performance of this benchmark on an Ext3 file system. The tiobench benchmark is a multithreaded I/O benchmark. It is used to measure file system performance in four basic
operations: sequential read, random read, sequential write, and random write.

First, the device /dev/hda1 is formatted as ext3.

```
# mkfs.ext3 /dev/hda1
# mount -t ext3 /dev/hda1 /ext3
# cd /ext3

# tar zxvf tiobench-0.3.3.tar.gz
# cd tiobench-0.3.3
# make
# date && ./tiobench.pl --size 500 --numruns 5 -threads\
32 && date
```

The following is sample tiobench output with the log inside the partition.

```
Fri Jun 27 10:17:14 PDT 2003
Run #1: ./tiotest -t 32 -f 15 -r 125 -b 4096 -d . -T
Run #2: ./tiotest -t 32 -f 15 -r 125 -b 4096 -d . -T
Run #3: ./tiotest -t 32 -f 15 -r 125 -b 4096 -d . -T
Run #4: ./tiotest -t 32 -f 15 -r 125 -b 4096 -d . -T
Run #5: ./tiotest -t 32 -f 15 -r 125 -b 4096 -d . -T


Unit information
================
File size = megabytes
Blk Size  = bytes
Rate      = megabytes per second
CPU%      = percentage of CPU used during the test
Latency   = milliseconds
Lat%      = percent of requests that took longer than
X seconds
CPU Eff   = Rate divided by CPU% - throughput per cpu load


Sequential Reads
                        File  Blk   Num                 Avg       Maximum    Lat%    Lat%    CPU
Identifier              Size  Size  Thr   Rate  (CPU%)  Latency   Latency    >2s     >10s    Eff
----------------------- ----  ----  ---   ----  ------  -------   -------    ----    ----    ---
2.4.20-4GB              500   4096  32    6.93  3.555%  72.342    39522.87   1.56413 0.00000 195

Random Reads
                        File  Blk   Num                 Avg       Maximum    Lat%    Lat%    CPU
Identifier              Size  Size  Thr   Rate  (CPU%)  Latency   Latency    >2s     >10s    Eff
```

Identifier	File Size	Blk Size	Num Thr	Rate	(CPU%)	Avg Latency	Maximum Latency	Lat% >2s	Lat% >10s	CPU Eff
2.4.20-4GB	500	4096	32	0.89	1.011%	514.676	2536.44	0.00000	0.00000	88

Sequential Writes

Identifier	File Size	Blk Size	Num Thr	Rate	(CPU%)	Avg Latency	Maximum Latency	Lat% >2s	Lat% >10s	CPU Eff
2.4.20-4GB	500	4096	32	4.69	6.986%	49.635	23386.91	1.28907	0.00000	67

Random Writes

Identifier	File Size	Blk Size	Num Thr	Rate	(CPU%)	Avg Latency	Maximum Latency	Lat% >2s	Lat% >10s	CPU Eff
2.4.20-4GB	500	4096	32	0.53	0.434%	0.302	573.19	0.00000	0.00000	122

```
Fri Jun 27 10:37:14 PDT 2003

# umount /ext3
```

Next, to determine whether an external log increases the performance of the file system under this file system benchmark, change the configuration to have an external log. In the example, the external log is located on /dev/hdb1.

```
# mkfs.ext3 -b 4096 -O journal_dev /dev/hdb1
# mkfs.ext3 -b 4096 -J device=/dev/hdb1 /dev/hda1
# mount -t ext3 /dev/hda1 /ext3
# cd /ext3

# tar zxvf tiobench-0.3.3.tar.gz
# cd tiobench-0.3.3
# make
# date && ./tiobench.pl --size 500 --numruns 5 -threads\
32 && date


tiobench output with log external.

Fri Jun 27 11:10:17 PDT 2003
Run #1: ./tiotest -t 32 -f 15 -r 125 -b 4096 -d . -T
Run #2: ./tiotest -t 32 -f 15 -r 125 -b 4096 -d . -T
Run #3: ./tiotest -t 32 -f 15 -r 125 -b 4096 -d . -T
Run #4: ./tiotest -t 32 -f 15 -r 125 -b 4096 -d . -T
Run #5: ./tiotest -t 32 -f 15 -r 125 -b 4096 -d . -T

Unit information
================
File size = megabytes
Blk Size  = bytes
Rate      = megabytes per second
CPU%      = percentage of CPU used during the test
Latency   = milliseconds
Lat%      = percent of requests that took longer than
X seconds
```

```
CPU Eff   = Rate divided by CPU% - throughput per cpu load

Sequential Reads
            File  Blk   Num                     Avg      Maximum       Lat%      Lat%     CPU
Identifier  Size  Size  Thr   Rate  (CPU%)  Latency      Latency        >2s      >10s     Eff
_____ ____  ____  __    ____  _____   _____     _____      _____    _____      ___

2.4.20-4GB   500  4096   32   6.54 3.496%    83.189     40436.07    2.41211  0.00081      187

Random Reads
            File  Blk   Num                     Avg      Maximum       Lat%      Lat%     CPU
Identifier  Size  Size  Thr   Rate  (CPU%)  Latency      Latency        >2s      >10s     Eff
_____ ____  ____  __    ____  _____   _____     _____      _____    _____      ___

2.4.20-4GB   500  4096   32   0.89 0.890%   540.200      2620.12    0.00000  0.00000      100

Sequential Writes
            File  Blk   Num                     Avg      Maximum       Lat%      Lat%     CPU
Identifier  Size  Size  Thr   Rate  (CPU%)  Latency      Latency        >2s      >10s     Eff
_____ ____  ____  __    ____  _____   _____     _____      _____    _____      ___

2.4.20-4GB   500  4096   32   4.71 6.682%    53.069     23588.61    1.31673  0.00000       71

Random Writes
            File  Blk   Num                     Avg      Maximum       Lat%      Lat%     CPU
Identifier  Size  Size  Thr   Rate  (CPU%)  Latency      Latency        >2s      >10s     Eff
_____ ____  ____  __    ____  _____   _____     _____      _____    _____      ___

2.4.20-4GB   500  4096   32   0.53 0.432%     0.278       404.22    0.00000  0.00000      122
Fri Jun 27 11:30:35 PDT 2003
```

Because tiobench does not create a large amount of metadata activity, there is no benefit to having an external log. In terms of time, the tiobench program took an additional 18 seconds to complete when the log was on an external device.

With the dbench benchmark, which creates a very large amount of metadata activity, the results show a decrease in the amount of time needed to run the benchmark and an increase in throughput for what the benchmark measures. Therefore, determining the metadata activity for your system helps determine the type of tuning that will be most useful.

In the next few examples, dbench is run first with the log inside the partition and then with the log external to the partition.

```
# mkfs.ext3 /dev/hda1
# mount -t ext3 /dev/hda1 /ext3


# tar zxvf dbench-1.2.tar.gz
# cd dbench
# make
# date && ./dbench 20 && date

output for dbench
```

```
Fri Jun 27 14:36:39 PDT 2003
......................+.................+..+..
+20 clients started

Throughput 15.443 MB/sec (NB=19.3037 MB/sec  154.43 MBit/sec)
Fri Jun 27 14:39:30 PDT 2003
```

In the next example, the log is changed to use /dev/hdb1 as the external log device. When dbench is run again, the throughput increases from 15.443 MBps to 17.2484 MBps. The time taken to run the program was reduced from 2 minutes and 51 seconds to 2 minutes and 33 seconds.

```
# mkfs.ext3 -b 4096 -O journal_dev /dev/hdb1
# mkfs.ext3 - b 4096 -J device=/dev/hdb1 /dev/hda1

# tar zxvf dbench-1.2.tar.gz
# cd dbench
# make
# date && ./dbench 20  && date

output for dbench

Fri Jun 27 14:52:13 PDT 2003
.................................+...........+.+
+20 clients started

Throughput 17.2484 MB/sec (NB=21.5605 MB/sec
172.484 MBit/sec)
Fri Jun 27 14:54:46 PDT 2003

# umount /ext3
```

Tuning Options for ReiserFS: Go Faster with an External Log

External logs improve file system performance because the log updates are saved to a different partition than the corresponding file system, thereby reducing the number of hard disk seeks.

To create a ReiserFS file system with the log on an external device, your system must have at least two unused partitions. The test system used in the following examples has spare partitions /dev/hda1 and /dev/hdb1. In the examples, the /dev/hdb1 partition is used for the external log.

```
# mkreiserfs  -j /dev/hdb1 /dev/hda1
```

In the following example, the dbench program creates file system activity. The default mount option is used with an external log on device /dev/hdb1.

```
# mount -t reiserfs /dev/hda1 /reiserfs
# cd /reiserfs
# tar zxvf dbench-1.2.tar.gz
# cd dbench
# make
# date && ./dbench 15 && date

output from dbench

Sat Jun 28 10:23:06 PDT 2003
....................................+...........+.+
+15 clients started
Throughput 21.7191 MB/sec (NB=27.189 MB/sec
217.191 MBit/sec)
Sat Jun 28 10:24:37 PDT 2003
```

The next example uses the `notail` mount option to increase the performance of the file system. The `notail` option disables the storage of small files and file tails directly into the directory tree.

```
# mount -t reiserfs -o notail /dev/hda1 /reiserfs
# cd /reiserfs
# tar zxvf dbench-1.2.tar.gz
# cd dbench
# make
# date && ./dbench 15 && date

output from dbench

Sat Jun 28 10:28:42 PDT 2003
....................................+...........+.+
+15 clients started
Throughput 25.8765 MB/sec (NB=32.3456 MB/sec
258.765 MBit/sec)
Sat Jun 28 10:29:59 PDT 2003

# cd /
# umount /reiserfs
```

By adding the `notail mount` option, the throughput of the ReiserFS file system running the dbench program with 15 clients increased from 21.7191 MBps to 25.8765 MBps. The time to run the program went from 1 minute and 31 seconds to 1 minute and 17 seconds.

Tuning Options for JFS: Go Faster with an External Log

External logs improve file system performance because the log updates are saved to a different partition than the corresponding file system, thereby reducing the number of hard disk seeks.

The following examples create a baseline for the file system by using the default option of having the log of the file system inside the volume. The test program is executed again with the log on external device /dev/hdb1.

```
# mkfs.jfs /dev/hda1

# mount -t jfs /dev/hda1 /jfs
```

The stress.sh script, which creates a high number of metadata changes, shows the benefit of using an external log.

```
#!/bin/sh

for count in `seq 1 30`;
do
  echo Count: $count
  mkdir a
  for i in `seq 1 10000`;
  do
    echo  0123456789ABCDEFGHIJKLMNOPQRSTUVWXYZabcdefghijklmnopqrstuvw\
xyz > a/$i
  done

  mkdir b
  for j in `seq 1 10000`;
  do
    ln -s `pwd`/a/$j b/$j
  done

  rm -fr b
  rm -fr a
done


# cd /jfs
# mkdir test
```

If you want to try this example on your own machine, place the stress.sh script in the /jfs/test subdirectory.

```
# date && ./stress.sh && date
```

```
Output from stress.sh script

Sat Jun 28 10:47:27 PDT 2003

Count: 1
Count: 2
...
Count: 30

Sat Jun 28 12:48:35 PDT 2003

# umount /jfs
```

Tuning JFS with jfs_tune

The jfs_tune can change the location of the journal. One way to increase the file system performance is by moving the journal to an external device.

The first step is to create a journal on an external device /dev/hdb1 by using mkfs.jfs.

```
# mkfs.jfs -J journal_dev /dev/hdb1
```

The next step is to attach that external journal to the file system that is located on /dev/hda1.

```
# jfs_tune -J device=/dev/hdb1 /dev/hda1
# mount -t jfs /dev/hda1 /jfs
# date && ./stress.sh && date

output from stress.sh script

Mon Jun 30 02:42:08 PDT 2003

Count: 1
Count: 2
...
Count: 30

Mon Jun 30 04:39:08 PDT 2003
```

With an external log, the test program execution time was reduced by 4 minutes and 8 seconds.

Tuning Options for XFS

The examples in this section show three ways of tuning the XFS file system for running the dbench utility. The first example uses the defaults to format an XFS partition, with the log inside the partition. The second example uses the mount options `logbufsize` and `logbsize`. The third example uses an external log and the two mount options.

Using the Defaults

In the following example, an XFS partition is formatted with the log inside the partition.

```
# mkfs.xfs -f /dev/hda1

# mount -t xfs /dev/hda1 /xfs
# cd /xfs

# tar zxvf dbench-1.2.tar.gz
# cd dbench
# make
# date && ./dbench 30 && date
Output from dbench is as follows:
Fri Jun 27 15:48:52 PDT 2003

.+++++30 clients started

Throughput 1.45512 MB/sec (NB=1.8189 MB/sec  14.5512 MBit/sec)
Fri Jun 27 16:34:13 PDT 2003
```

Using logbufsize and logbsize

The example in this section shows how to tune an XFS file system using the mount options `logbufsize` and `logbsize`.

The `logbufsize` option sets the number of log buffers held in memory. The value of `logbufsize` can be 2 to 8. Eight is the default for file systems created with a 64KB block size, 4 for file systems created with a 32KB block size, 3 for file systems created with a 16KB block size, and 2 for other block sizes. When `logbufsize` is set to the maximum, more active transactions can occur at once, and metadata changes can still be performed while the log is being synced to the disk. However, should a crash occur, a higher number of metadata changes is likely to be lost, relative to setting `logbufsize` to a smaller value. The `logbsize` size option sets the size of the log buffers held in memory.

```
# mkfs.xfs -f /dev/hda1
# mount -t xfs -o logbufsize=8,logbsize=32768b\
 /dev/hda1 /xfs
# cd dbench
# date && ./dbench 30 && date

Output from dbench

Sat Jun 28 02:01:36 PDT 2003
```

```
+..............++.++......++.++++++.++++++++++30 clients
started ****************************
Throughput 1.97025 MB/sec (NB=2.46281 MB/sec
19.7025 MBit/sec)
Sat Jun 28 02:35:05 PDT 2003
```

Placing the Log on an External Device

External logs improve file system performance because the log updates are saved to a different partition than the corresponding file system, thereby reducing the number of hard disk seeks.

The example in this section runs dbench with the same parameters as in the previous examples, but the log is placed on external device /dev/hdb1.

```
# mkfs.xfs -l logdev=/dev/hdb1,size=32768b -f /dev/hda1
# mount -t xfs -o logbufsize=8,logbsize=32768b,\

logdev=/dev/hdb1 /dev/hda1 /xfs
```

The `mount` command can be used to check the mount options for each file system, as shown in the following example.

```
# mount

/dev/hdb6 on / type reiserfs (rw)
proc on /proc type proc (rw)
devpts on /dev/pts type devpts (rw,mode=0620,gid=5)
shmfs on /dev/shm type shm (rw)
usbdevfs on /proc/bus/usb type usbdevfs (rw)
/dev/hda1 on /xfs type xfs
   (rw,logbufs=8,logbsize=32768,logdev=/dev/hdb1)

# cd dbench
# date && ./dbench 30 && date

Output from dbench

Sat Jun 28 02:57:08 PDT 2003
.....+..........+........+.....+..+..+++....
+30 clients started
Throughput 18.9072 MB/sec (NB=23.634 MB/sec
189.072 MBit/sec)
Sat Jun 28 03:00:38 PDT 2003
```

When the `logbufsize` and `logbsize` mount options are added, the throughput increases from 1.45512 MBps to 1.97025 MBps. When the log is moved to an external device, the throughput increases to 18.9072 MBps. Clearly, the external log increases file system performance under a test program that has a large amount of metadata activity.

MEASURING I/O

The sysstat package contains the `sar` and `iostat` commands. The `sar` command collects and reports system activity information. The `iostat` command reports CPU utilization and I/O statistics for disks.

The following subsections discuss the `iostat` command in detail and describe how to use `iostat` and `sar` to analyze and report I/O and CPU utilization and allocation.

iostat

The `iostat` command monitors system input and output device loading by observing the time the devices are active in relation to their average transfer rates. The command generates reports that can be used to change the system configuration to better balance the input and output load between the physical disks.

As with most monitoring commands, the first line of `iostat output` reflects a summary of statistics since boot time. To look at meaningful real-time data, run `iostat` with a timestamp and look at the lines that report summaries over the time step intervals. `iostat` can provide a way to balance the load among the physical hard drives by viewing statistics from bytes read or written to the drive.

When bytes are either read or written, `iostat` reports the following information:

- *tps*. Number of transfers per second.
- *device*. Disk device name.
- *Blk_read/s*. Amount of data read from the device, expressed in number of blocks per second.
- *Blk_wrtn/s*. Amount of data written to the device, expressed in number of blocks per second.
- *Blk_read*. Total number of blocks read.
- *Blk_wrtn*. Total number of blocks written.
- *kB_read/s*. Amount of data read from the device, expressed in kilobytes per second.
- *kB_wrtn/s*. Amount of data written from the device, expressed in kilobytes per second.
- *kB_read*. Total number of kilobytes read.
- *kB_wrtn*. Total number of kilobytes written.
- *rrqm/s*. Number of read requests merged per second that were issued to the device.
- *wrqm/s*. Number of write requests merged per second that were issued to the device.
- *r/s*. Number of read requests that were issued to the device per second.
- *w/s*. Number of write requests that were issued to the device per second.

- *rsec/s*. Number of sectors read from the device per second.
- *wsec/s*. Number of sectors written from the device per second.
- *rkB/s*. Number of kilobytes read from the device per second.
- *wkB/s*. Number of kilobytes written to the device per second.
- *avgrp-sz*. Average size (in sectors) of requests that were issued to the device.
- *avgqu-sz*. Average queue length.

Using the iostat and sar Utilities

The Linux iostat and sar utilities analyze and report on I/O and CPU utilization and allocation by providing a simultaneous interval-by-interval profile of disk and CPU usage. These utilities can indicate which system resource might be limiting overall system performance if used during heavy workloads or periods of inadequate system performance. After the system bottleneck is identified, directed actions can be taken to improve system performance.

The following example walks through the execution of iostat on the /dev/hda1 device and presents the output.

```
# iostat -x /dev/hda1

Linux 2.4.20-4GB

avg-cpu:  %user   %nice   %sys    %idle
          0.67    0.00    0.18    99.15

Device:    rrqm/s wrqm/s  r/s   w/s  rsec/s  wsec/s   rkB/s    wkB/s
   avgrq-sz avgqu-sz   await  svctm  %util
/dev/hda1   0.00   0.00  0.00  0.00    0.03    0.01    0.01     0.00
   8.71     0.01  199.71 199.41   0.08
```

This example illustrates the execution of tiobench to produce file system activity on the /dev/hda1 device.

```
# date && ./tiobench.pl --size 500 --numruns 5\

 -threads 32 && date

Fri Jun 27 05:41:03 PDT 2003
Run #1: ./tiotest -t 32 -f 15 -r 125 -b 4096 -d . -T
Run #2: ./tiotest -t 32 -f 15 -r 125 -b 4096 -d . -T
Run #3: ./tiotest -t 32 -f 15 -r 125 -b 4096 -d . -T
Run #4: ./tiotest -t 32 -f 15 -r 125 -b 4096 -d . -T
Run #5: ./tiotest -t 32 -f 15 -r 125 -b 4096 -d . -T
```

```
Unit information
================
File size = megabytes
Blk Size  = bytes
Rate      = megabytes per second
CPU%      = percentage of CPU used during the test
Latency   = milliseconds
Lat%      = percent of requests that took longer than
X seconds
CPU Eff   = Rate divided by CPU% - throughput per cpu load
Sequential Reads
```

Identifier	File Size	Blk Size	Num Thr	Rate	(CPU%)	Avg Latency	Maximum Latency	Lat% >2s	Lat% >10s	CPU Eff
2.4.20-4GB	500	4096	32	10.46	4.810%	22.227	20407.44	0.11800	0.00000	217

Random Reads

Identifier	File Size	Blk Size	Num Thr	Rate	(CPU%)	Avg Latency	Maximum Latency	Lat% >2s	Lat% >10s	CPU Eff
2.4.20-4GB	500	4096	32	0.75	0.715%	438.919	1926.01	0.00000	0.00000	104

Sequential Writes

Identifier	File Size	Blk Size	Num Thr	Rate	(CPU%)	Avg Latency	Maximum Latency	Lat% >2s	Lat% >10s	CPU Eff
2.4.20-4GB	500	4096	32	2.94	3.460%	1.798	9288.13	0.02279	0.00000	85

Random Writes

Identifier	File Size	Blk Size	Num Thr	Rate	(CPU%)	Avg Latency	Maximum Latency	Lat% >2s	Lat% >10s	CPU Eff
2.4.20-4GB	500	4096	32	0.50	1.081%	0.198	206.05	0.00000	0.00000	46

After tiobench is finished, run iostat again to look at the disk activity produced by this program. A sample of iostat output is shown here:

```
# iostat -x /dev/hda1

Linux 2.4.20-4GB

avg-cpu:  %user   %nice   %sys   %idle
          1.73    0.00    0.62   97.65

Device:    rrqm/s wrqm/s   r/s   w/s  rsec/s  wsec/s    rkB/s     wkB/s
   avgrq-sz avgqu-sz   await  svctm  %util
/dev/hda1   28.38  58.58  2.99  6.19  251.00  518.18   125.50    259.09
   83.76    11.50   125.25  14.61  13.42
```

```
Linux 2.4.20-4GB (steveb)      12/15/2003
Device:          tps    Blk_read/s   Blk_wrtn/s   Blk_read    Blk_wrtn
dev3-0          0.00         0.00         0.00         40            0
dev3-1          0.15         0.10         2.61       459576    12354928
dev22-2         0.00         0.00         0.00       2852            0

Device:          tps    Blk_read/s   Blk_wrtn/s   Blk_read    Blk_wrtn
dev3-0          0.00         0.00         0.00          0            0
dev3-1          0.10         1.20         0.00         24            0
dev22-2         0.00         0.00         0.00          0            0

Device:          tps    Blk_read/s   Blk_wrtn/s   Blk_read    Blk_wrtn
dev3-0          0.00         0.00         0.00          0            0
dev3-1         37.75         0.00       568.80          0        11376
dev22-2         0.00         0.00         0.00          0            0
```

The statistics that iostat captured after tiobench was run show that the r/s (number of read requests issued to the device per second) went from 0.00 to 2.99, and the w/s (the number of write requests issued to the device per second) went from 0.0 to 6.19. By using other statistics from iostat, such as rkb/s and wkb/s, you can conclude that the test workload is writing more than it is reading.

A useful way to use iostat is to use the interval option, which provides information that might help balance the load among physical hard drives. The -d option repeats the display for count times. If no wait interval is specified, the default is 1 second.

The next example shows what happens when the -d option is run with an interval set to 20 seconds.

```
# iostat -d 20
Linux 2.4.20-4GB (steveb)      12/15/2003
Device:     tps   Blk_read/s   Blk_wrtn/s   Blk_read    Blk_wrtn
dev3-0     0.00         0.00         0.00        40            0
dev3-1     0.15         0.10         2.61      459576    12354928
dev22-2    0.00         0.00         0.00      2852            0

Device:     tps   Blk_read/s   Blk_wrtn/s   Blk_read    Blk_wrtn
dev3-0     0.00         0.00         0.00         0            0
dev3-1     0.10         1.20         0.00        24            0
dev22-2    0.00         0.00         0.00         0            0

Device:     tps   Blk_read/s   Blk_wrtn/s   Blk_read    Blk_wrtn
dev3-0     0.00         0.00         0.00         0            0
dev3-1    37.75         0.00       568.80         0        11376
dev22-2    0.00         0.00         0.00         0            0
```

The output shows three samplings of data collected by iostat. The third sample illustrates that 11,376 blocks were written (Blk_wrtn) during the 20-second interval.

iostat can be used to measure the results of tuning a system by load balancing between disks on a system. The example that follows shows that dev8-1 starts out with 0 blk_wrtn. After the workload has finished, blk_wrtn has increased to 6129208. It also shows that device dev8-0 has a very small amount of activity.

```
iostat before workload
Linux 2.4.21-1.1931.2.349.2.2.entsmp 02/09/2004

Device:      tps   Blk_read/s   Blk_wrtn/s   Blk_read   Blk_wrtn
dev8-0   164.69      1312.58       361.87     150002      41354
dev8-1     2.81         5.71         0.00        652          0

iostat after workload
Linux 2.4.21-1.1931.2.349.2.2.entsmp 02/09/2004

Device:      tps   Blk_read/s   Blk_wrtn/s   Blk_read   Blk_wrtn
dev8-0    55.12       410.41       146.44     152426      54386
dev8-1   341.88      2828.43     16502.98    1050478    6129208
```

Now we tune this system to balance the reads and writes from dev8-0 and dev8-1 and then rerun iostat to determine the effectiveness of the balancing. After the system balancing, dev8-0 has blk_read as 1253186 and dev8-1 has blk_read as 1051798. For blk_wrtn, dev8-0 has 6209198 and dev8-1 has 6138576. The workload balancing was very effective in that roughly the same number of reads and writes occurred for each device.

```
iostat after the workload balancing
Linux 2.4.21-1.1931.2.349.2.2.entsmp 02/09/2004

Device:      tps  Blk_read/s  Blk_wrtn/s  Blk_read  Blk_wrtn
dev8-0   121.60      612.59     3035.21   1253186   6209198
dev8-1   110.10      514.15     3000.69   1051798   6138576
```

For a complete list of iostat options, see the iostat man page.

The following rpm command displays the version of the iostat utility.

```
# rpm -qf /usr/bin/iostat

sysstat-4.0.17-12
```

iostat uses /proc/stat to get its information. The following output shows information that is available on a typical system.

```
# cat /proc/stat
```

```
cpu  51736 468 97549 1554177
cpu0 51736 468 97549 1554177
page 118861 2298217
swap 752 1654
intr 2663947 1703930 3850 0 0 0 2920 2 0 2 0 0 16035 18696 0
918510 2 0 0 0 0 0 0 0 0 0 0 0 0 0 0 0 0 0 0 0 0 0 0 0 0 0 0 0
0 0 0 0 0 0 0 0 0 0 0 0 0 0 0 0 0 0 0 0 0 0 0 0 0 0 0 0 0 0 0 0
0 0 0 0 0 0 0 0 0 0 0 0 0 0 0 0 0 0 0 0 0 0 0 0 0 0 0 0 0 0 0 0
0 0 0 0 0 0 0 0 0 0 0 0 0 0 0 0 0 0 0 0 0 0 0 0 0 0 0 0 0 0 0 0
0 0 0 0 0 0 0 0 0 0 0 0 0 0 0 0 0 0 0 0 0 0 0 0 0 0 0 0 0 0 0 0
0 0 0 0 0 0 0 0 0 0 0 0 0 0 0 0 0 0 0 0 0 0 0 0 0 0 0 0 0 0 0 0
0 0 0 0 0 0 0 0 0 0 0 0 0 0 0 0 0 0 0 0 0 0 0 0 0 0 0 0 0 0 0 0
0 0
disk_io: (3,0):(902005,1069,9164,900936,8177312)
   (3,1):(16317,9670,227616,6647,356816)
ctxt 5243949
btime 1056965685
processes 602555
```

The sar utility with the –b option reports the I/O and transfer rate. sar –b reports the following I/O rates:

- *tps*. Number of transfers per second issued to device.
- *rtps*. Total number of read requests per second to the device.
- *wtps*. Total number of write requests per second to the device.
- *bread/s*. Total amount of data read from the device in blocks per second.
- *bwrtn/s*. Total amount of data written to the device in blocks per second.

```
# sar -b

Linux 2.4.20-4GB
```

02:40:00	tps	rtps	wtps	bread/s	bwrtn/s
02:50:00	89.04	4.91	84.13	82.38	1240.69
03:00:00	125.44	0.03	125.41	0.21	1121.14
03:10:00	118.48	0.03	118.45	0.23	1066.31
03:20:00	114.50	0.03	114.47	0.24	1036.06
03:30:00	135.21	0.03	135.19	0.23	1206.21
03:40:00	135.15	0.03	135.12	0.25	1211.16
03:50:00	127.35	0.03	127.31	0.28	1156.07
04:00:00	145.69	0.04	145.65	0.31	1302.00
04:10:02	152.42	0.21	152.21	1.98	1375.69
04:20:01	148.50	0.60	147.90	6.12	1331.70
04:30:00	113.48	0.36	113.12	3.03	1017.97
04:40:00	108.75	0.50	108.25	4.49	968.44
04:50:00	1.09	0.71	0.38	22.71	24.78

05:00:00	0.51	0.26	0.25	3.11	3.90
05:10:00	0.55	0.18	0.37	2.55	11.66
05:20:00	0.13	0.00	0.13	0.00	2.07
05:30:01	0.60	0.02	0.58	0.61	61.96
05:40:00	2.31	1.84	0.47	39.99	8.30
05:50:00	0.32	0.00	0.32	0.05	5.32
06:00:00	0.44	0.10	0.35	2.94	19.77
06:10:00	0.18	0.04	0.14	0.60	2.72
06:20:00	0.25	0.01	0.24	0.16	3.87
06:30:00	0.10	0.00	0.10	0.00	1.51
06:40:00	0.11	0.00	0.11	0.00	1.64
06:50:00	0.13	0.00	0.13	0.00	2.00
07:00:00	0.09	0.00	0.09	0.00	1.51
07:10:00	0.11	0.00	0.11	0.00	1.68
07:20:00	0.36	0.12	0.23	3.78	4.10
07:30:01	0.38	0.04	0.34	0.77	5.65
07:40:00	0.19	0.00	0.19	0.11	3.12
07:50:00	0.13	0.00	0.13	0.00	2.01
08:00:00	0.10	0.00	0.10	0.00	1.57
08:10:00	0.11	0.00	0.11	0.00	1.68
08:20:00	0.14	0.00	0.14	0.00	2.12
08:30:00	0.09	0.00	0.09	0.00	1.41
08:40:00	0.11	0.00	0.11	0.00	1.71
08:50:00	0.13	0.00	0.13	0.00	2.03
09:00:01	0.09	0.00	0.09	0.00	1.56
09:10:00	0.11	0.00	0.11	0.00	1.68
09:20:00	0.15	0.00	0.15	0.00	2.27
09:30:00	0.09	0.00	0.09	0.00	1.40
09:40:00	0.11	0.00	0.11	0.00	1.72
09:50:00	0.20	0.01	0.19	0.20	3.40
10:00:00	100.04	100.06	100.04	100.06	99.86
10:10:00	4.06	3.27	0.79	92.14	16.17
Average:	1.00	0.28	0.72	5.93	9.92

The sar output shows that the peek of 1375.59 bwrtn/s (the total amount of data written to the device in blocks per second) occurred on the system at 04:10:02.

SUMMARY

Most file system tuning is built directly into the file system. Depending on the workload on the file system, the file system performance can be increased by placing the log on an external device. Some file systems also provide `mkfs` and `mount` options for tuning the file system.

In the next case study, we'll examine another performance aspect of the system: the network.

REFERENCES

[1] dbench can be downloaded from `http://freshmeat.net/projects/dbench/`.

[2] tiobench can be downloaded from `http://sourceforge.net/projects/tiobench`.

## CHAPTER TWENTY-ONE

Case Study: Network Performance on Linux

By Vijayanthimala Anand

INTRODUCTION

Network performance of computer systems is important to many organizations, especially in this era of the Internet. Therefore, Linux network developers have been working hard to improve the network stack performance of the Linux kernel. Because network performance also plays an important role in making Linux ready for the enterprise market segment, it is important to evaluate the performance progress of the Linux network stack to determine how well Linux handles various network workloads.

This chapter presents a case study that evaluates network performance on Linux through the use of various industry-standard benchmarks. Also included in this chapter is a discussion of network features whose performance was enhanced in the Linux 2.4, 2.5, and 2.6 kernels, and a discussion of the performance gain achieved by each feature, individually and cumulatively throughout the operating system.

The SUSE and Red Hat Linux distributors introduced the 2.6 Linux kernel in the SLES 9 and RHEL 4 releases. They have also both backported most of the 2.5 and 2.6 kernel features to their 2.4 kernel-based releases. Although the study presented in this chapter looks at both the 2.4 and 2.5 kernels, it also reflects the performance of the 2.6 distribution kernel as the 2.5 development kernel morphed into the 2.6 release level kernel.

Chapter 12, "Network Tuning," discusses the network parameters that can be tuned to increase the network's efficiency and performance. This chapter shows how network tuning was done in a case study to establish the baseline from which performance gains were measured.

Because TCP/IP is the most commonly used Internet protocol, this chapter concentrates only on the TCP/IP stack and Ethernet network. The terms *Linux TCP/IP stack* and *Linux network stack* are used interchangeably because the TCP/IP stack is part of the Linux kernel and is also considered the default Linux network stack.

We'll begin by briefly looking at each of the benchmarks used in the case study.

BENCHMARKS USED IN THIS CASE STUDY

The information collected in this case study was obtained by running the following benchmarks.

NetBench

NetBench is a Ziff-Davis benchmark that measures how well a file server handles remote file I/O requests from the clients that pelt the server with requests for network file operations. NetBench reports throughput and client response time measurements. This benchmark is mainly useful for measuring the performance of the Linux TCP/IP send side (NetBench server) throughput because the receiving clients are 32-bit Windows clients for this benchmark.

Netperf3

Netperf3 is a microbenchmark that tests the Linux network throughput and network scalability. Netperf3, available at `http://www.netperf.org`, is an experimental version. This version has multithread support and IBM enhanced Netperf3 to include multiple network interface cards (NICs) and multiclient support. These two features are added to measure the Linux network SMP and network card scalability. IBM also added another interface to test just the network drivers, bypassing the TCP/IP stack. The metric measured is throughput in megabits per second. The extended Netperf3 is available at `http://www-124.ibm.com/developerworks/opensource/linuxperf/netperf/netperf3_patch`.

VolanoMark

VolanoMark is a Java Server benchmark that implements a chat room server to measure the performance of different implementations of Java and operating systems. Because VolanoMark is a chat room server benchmark servicing client requests, it uses the TCP/IP network for communication. Although VolanoMark also measures the performance of the scheduler and signal subsystem, the main value of this benchmark is to measure the send and receive side of the TCP/IP stack in loopback mode. The metric measured by this benchmark is messages per second.

SPECWeb99

The SPECWeb99 benchmark measures a system's capability to act as a web server servicing both static and dynamic web page requests (no SSL content). SPECWeb99 is relevant because web serving, especially with Apache, is one of the most common uses of Linux servers and their network stack. Apache is rich in functionality and is not designed for high performance. Apache was chosen as the web server for this benchmark because it currently hosts more web sites than any other web server on the Internet. SPECWeb99 is the accepted standard benchmark for web serving. SPECWeb99 stresses the following kernel components: TCP/IP, network device driver, various threading models, and the scheduler. The following is the disclaimer for the SPECWeb99 results discussed in this chapter:

SPEC and the benchmark name SPECWeb are registered trademarks of the Standard Performance Evaluation Corporation. This benchmarking was performed for research purposes only and is noncompliant with the following deviations from the rules:

- It was run on hardware that does not meet the SPEC availability-to-the-public criteria. The machine is an engineering sample.
- Access_log wasn't kept for full accounting. It was being written, but it was deleted every 200 seconds.

ENHANCEMENTS IN THE LINUX 2.4 AND 2.6 KERNELS

Linux network stack performance depends on many factors, such as the system where the kernel is running, the network stack implementation, and the network stack's interaction with other parts of the Linux kernel components. Although this chapter does not deal with all the other subsystem enhancements in the kernel and their effect on network performance, this section does look at a few of the kernel features that are new in 2.4 and 2.6, such as the O(1) scheduler and read copy update (RCU), as well as the effects of these changes on some of the network benchmarks.

In the current evolution of computer systems, interconnect bus speed and memory access latency are not increasing proportionally to processor speed (GHz) and network bandwidth capacity (gigabit networks). Reducing the number of accesses to these relatively slower components, such as the interconnect bus and memory, improves the system's performance in general, including the network. In the TCP/IP stack, the data is copied many times as part of transmit and receive processes, generating heavy traffic in the interconnect buses. This traffic leads to increased memory accesses, which can result in poor network performance and scalability issues. The scalability issues are exacerbated in SMP and NUMA systems by additional high-speed CPUs and relatively slower interconnect buses.

The bus speed, its throughput rate, and how much bus traffic is generated by the workload are crucial for improving the performance of the Linux network stack. Any improvement to the Linux network stack that eliminates or reduces the number of times data flows through these buses and reduces the memory accesses improves the Linux stack performance. The following sections look at some of the enhancements that were made to both the 2.4 and 2.6 kernels that reduce the number of copies made in the

TCP/IP stack and thereby boost the network stack performance. Specifically, these enhancements are in the following areas:

- SendFile support
- TCP Segmentation Offloading (TSO) support
- Process and IRQ affinity
- Network device driver API (NAPI)
- TCP Offload Engine (TOE)

We'll start by looking at SendFile support.

SendFile Support

The Linux 2.4 network stack supports the SendFile API, which allows application data to be sent directly from the file system buffer cache to the network card's buffer through direct memory access (DMA). Through the use of Zerocopy support in the network stack and network interface card (NIC), the SendFile API lets the application data be sent via DMA directly to the network for transfer, without having to do the usual user space-to-kernel space copying. In the typical non-SendFile case, the application follows these steps to send a file:

1. Allocates a buffer.
2. Copies the file data into its buffer (the file data is first copied from disk to kernel buffer cache and then to the application buffer).
3. Issues a send with the data that gets copied to the kernel socket buffer.
4. Gets the DMA to the NIC.

The SendFile API and Zerocopy bypass the extra copies and thereby reduce the context-switch procedure that involves many complex and CPU-intensive operations. Moreover, multiple copies of the same data, if processed in multiple CPUs, adversely affect performance by increasing memory latency, cache miss rate, and translation lookaside buffer (TLB) cache miss rate. The extra copies have direct and indirect consequences that can lead to poor network performance.

As the name implies, the SendFile API can only transfer file system data. Therefore, applications such as WebServer, Telnet, and so on that deal with dynamic and interactive data cannot use the SendFile API. Because a major part of the data that travels the Internet is static (file) data and file transfer is a major part of that traffic, the SendFile API and Zerocopy are important for improving the performance of network applications. Applications that use the SendFile API and Zerocopy, where applicable, can significantly improve network performance.

SendFile API support in Linux and Zerocopy support in both the Linux TCP/IP stack and the network driver achieve this single copy during TCP/IP data processing. SendFile is not transparent to the applications, because the applications need to implement the SendFile API to take advantage of this feature.

Two of the benchmarks that are used in this study—NetBench and SPECWeb99— use the SendFile API. Table 21-1 shows the SendFile throughput performance improvement using NetBench. The Baseline columns show results using a Linux kernel without SendFile API/Zerocopy support; the Samba application uses the SendFile API. The Zerocopy in the table refers to the SendFile /Zerocopy support in the Linux TCP/IP stack and the Intel Gigabit Ethernet NIC driver. Samba 2.3.0 is patched to include SendFile support. The Linux kernel used for this study was Linux 2.4.4 and Samba 2.2.0 with the SendFile patch.

Server: 8×700 MHz PIII, 1MB L2 (four CPUs used), Intel Profusion chipset

4 GB memory, 4×1 Gbps Ethernet, 18 GB SCSI

Linux 2.4.4, Samba 2.2.0

Clients: 866 MHz PIII, 256k L2

Windows 2000, NetBench 7.0.1

Table 21-1   NetBench Results Showing SendFile+Zerocopy Benefits

Number of Clients	Linux 2.4.4 Baseline+Samba SendFile (Mbps)	Linux 2.4.4 Baseline +Samba SendFile+ Zerocopy (Mbps)	% Improvement
24	516.8	571.0	10
28	540.0	609.2	12
32	551.9	635.1	15
36	556.6	647.2	16
40	560.6	655.4	17
44	562.5	661.8	18

The Baseline+Samba SendFile without the SendFile API+Zerocopy support in the Linux kernel used the regular send path of the TCP/IP stack. This is the baseline in this case, and when the SendFile+Zerocopy support was applied to the TCP/IP stack and to the Intel Gigabit driver, the results improved, as shown in Table 21-1 .The SendFile feature is clearly a winner in this case. As the number of clients increases, the amount of data that is processed also increases, as does the network performance when the SendFile feature is used. SendFile is enabled in the kernel by default, and some network device drivers support Zerocopy. Therefore, if an application supports the SendFile API, and if the system where the application runs has the NIC that has Zerocopy support, the SendFile feature is used; otherwise, even though the application has implemented the SendFile API, it just falls through the normal send path of the network stack. The network stack learns the capabilities of the NIC during initialization.

TCP Segmentation Offloading Support

For every TCP/IP transmit or receive of a network packet, multiple PCI bus accesses occur as the data gets transmitted to and received from the NIC. With the TCP Segmentation Offloading (TSO) feature in the NIC and the Linux TCP/IP stack, the number of PCI bus accesses is reduced on the send side to one per 64KB buffer size instead of one per network packet (1518 bytes) for an Ethernet network. If the application issues a buffer size greater than the frame size, the TCP/IP stack splits it into multiple frames, each with a TCP/IP header, and maps it via DMA to the NIC.

When TSO is enabled, 64KB data is sent via DMA to the NIC with one pseudo header. The network adapter's controller parses the 64KB block into standard Ethernet packets, reducing the host processor utilization and access to the PCI bus. TSO increases efficiency by reducing CPU utilization and increasing the network throughput. The network silicon is designed specifically for this task. Enabling TSO in Linux and the Gigabit Ethernet silicon designed for TSO enhances system performance. Figure 21-1 explains TSO operation versus non-TSO operation in the Linux kernel.

Server applications that use the large message size (and a large socket buffer size), such as SPECWeb99, benefit the most from TSO. A gain in the performance of microbenchmarks, such as Netperf3, is seen when the large message size is used. Unlike SendFile, TSO can be used for both static and dynamic content to improve the network performance of a SPECWeb99 workload. In 2.5.33 and later Linux kernels, TSO is enabled by default. TSO is transparent to the application, so no application change is needed to use TSO.

The SPECWeb99 results on Linux kernel 2.5.33 using the TSO feature on an Intel e1000 gigabit driver showed a 10% improvement in simultaneous connections (such as 2,906 versus 2,656 simultaneous connections). For this test, the Apache 2.0.36 web server was used, which uses the SendFile API for anything other than dynamic content over 8k in size. Because SendFile is not used for dynamic content, the benefits of TSO are realized only for dynamic content. The system configuration for this workload includes an 8-way 900MHz Pentium III and four Intel e1000 gigabit NICs. Pentium III desktops were used for clients.

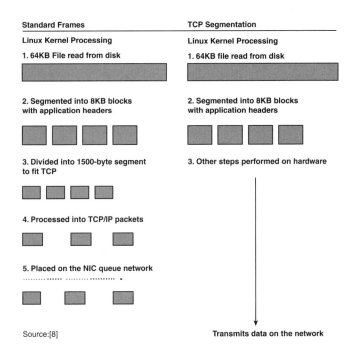

Figure 21-1   Standard frames compared to TSO segmentation.

Figure 21-2 depicts a study that was conducted at Intel, which shows the benefits of TSO in an environment using Intel PRO network connections and Dell PowerEdge servers running Linux.

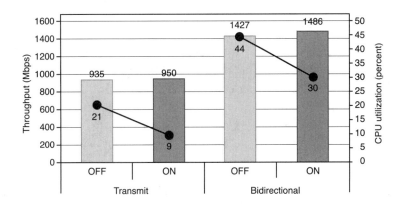

Figure 21-2   NetIQ Chariot network testing software results: TCP segmentation on servers running Linux, on versus off.
Source: Intel Labs, September 2002.

From the experiments shown in Figure 21-2, it is obvious that TCP segmentation offloading provides a significant boost to Linux network performance. TSO support is available in the 2.5.x and 2.6 mainline kernels. The Linux distributor SUSE AG has this support in the SUSE Linux Enterprise Server 9 (SLES 9) kernel through a configuration option.

Process and IRQ Affinity in Network Load

Affinity, or binding, refers to the process of forcing process interrupts to execute only on one or multiple chosen CPUs. In a multiprocessor system, the processes are migrated to other processors under certain conditions based on the policies used by the scheduler in the operating system. By keeping a process on the same processor—forcing the scheduler to schedule a particular task on a specified CPU—the likelihood of the required data being in the cache is highly improved, which reduces the memory latency. There are cases where even if the process is bound to schedule on the same CPU, factors such as large working set and multiple processes sharing the same CPU tend to flush the cache, so the process affinity may not work in all situations. The case study shown in this chapter is perfectly suited to take advantage of process affinity.

The Linux kernel implements the following two system calls to facilitate binding processes with processors:

```
asmlinkage int sys_sched_set_affinity(pid_t pid, unsigned
    int mask_len, unsigned long *new_mask_ptr);

 asmlinkage int sys_sched_get_affinity(pid_t pid, unsigned
    int *user_mask_len_ptr, unsigned long *user_mask_ptr);
```

The `sched_set_affinity()` syscall also ensures that the target process will run on the right CPU (or CPUs). The `sched_get_affinity(pid, &mask_len, NULL)` can be used to query the kernel's supported CPU bitmask length.

Process affinity refers to binding the process or thread to a CPU. IRQ affinity refers to forcing the interrupt processing of an individual IRQ to execute on a particular CPU. In Linux, the /proc interface can be used to set IRQ affinity. You can set the IRQ affinity by finding the IRQ used for an I/O interface and then changing the mask for this selected IRQ. For example, the following command sets the IRQ 63 to CPU 0 and routes the interrupts generated by IRQ 63 to CPU 1:

```
echo "1" > /proc/irq/63/smp_affinity
```

Process and IRQ affinity are common practices for performance optimization to improve the throughput and scalability of applications and systems. These methods require that the processes of an application need to be identified and isolated and the interrupts need to be identified to map to the application processes and the processor where it is running. Therefore, this n-to-n mapping is not always feasible in complex environments.

Our Netperf3 case study clearly indicates that the Linux network SMP scalability and network throughput performance improved when IRQ and process affinity were used. Netperf3 multiadapter support measured the network scalability in this case. For each NIC, one process was created, which was bound to one of four CPUs and one NIC. The NIC was intended to be used by the process and was bound to the same CPU. The processing of one Netperf3 process was isolated and the execution of the interrupts generated by one NIC to a single processor. This was done on the Netperf3 server using the TCP_STREAM test.

On the server, the receipt of data was processed heavily in this workload, which results in multiple data copies (copy from NIC to kernel memory and from kernel memory to application memory). The binding boosted the performance because these copies were done on a single processor, which eliminated the need to load the data into two different processor caches. Binding reduces the memory latency when both the affinities are applied. Although the IRQ and process affinities can be applied separately, applying them together can boost performance further, as shown in Figure 21-3. Figure 21-3 shows the data collected using the Linux 2.4.17 kernel (from `www.kernel.org`) with IRQ, process affinities, and the O(1) scheduler patch. The reason why the O(1) scheduler patch was selected to compare with process affinity is because the O(1) scheduler enforces affinity in scheduling the process/task. The O(1) scheduler tries to schedule the task to the same processor as much as it can, which seems to improve Netperf3 TCP_STREAM performance similar to the run with process affinity.

The best performer in Figure 21-3 is the case where both IRQ and process affinities are applied. It achieved almost three-out-of-four scalability for most of the message sizes, whereas the base kernel achieved only two out of four for two messages and less than two for the rest of the message sizes. The results of the cases where these affinities were applied individually and the O(1) scheduler patch hover around 2 and 2.5 out of four scalability.

In Figure 21-3, the legend 2.4.17+irq/proc aff means that there are four Netperf3 processes, each bound to one processor, and four IRQs resulting from four network interface cards that are bound to each of the four processors. Therefore, Netperf3 process 1 is bound to processor0, and the first NIC's IRQ is bound to processor 0. The connections established by Netperf3 process 1 go through NIC 1 on processor 0.

The 2.4.17+irq aff label means that four IRQs are bound to four CPUs.

The 2.4.17+proc aff means that the Netperf 3 processors are bound to four of the processors in the system.

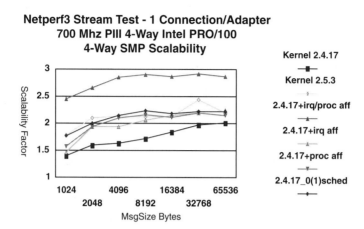

Figure 21-3   Netperf3 TCP stream—4-way scalability.

NAPI Support

The network device driver API (NAPI) was developed to improve Linux network performance under a heavy interrupt load. The system's load is used to determine if polling or interrupts are used to process incoming data to improve the performance. Polling improves performance when the interrupt load is heavy but wastes CPU cycles when the interrupt load is light. Interrupts improve latency under a low interrupt load but make the system vulnerable to live lock when the interrupt load exceeds the Maximum Loss Free Forwarding Rate (MLFFR). NAPI works only with NICs that implement a "ring" of DMA buffers. When a network packet is received, it is placed in the next buffer in the ring. Normally, the processor is interrupted for each packet and the system is expected to empty the packet from the ring. When NAPI is enabled, it responds to the first interrupt by telling the NIC to stop interrupting. NAPI then polls the ring. As it processes the packets, NAPI pulls new packets without the need for further interrupts, leading to a dramatic reduction in receive interrupts that helps the system function normally under heavy network load.

The implementation of NAPI in the Linux 2.5 kernel saves network device driver developers from manually implementing polling in each driver, manages the flood of interrupts, and protects the system from denial of service (DoS) attacks. The flood ceiling is much lower without NAPI because of the CPU overhead of interrupt handlers. NAPI also eliminates the need for lots of code to implement NIC hardware interrupt mitigation variants. To make use of NAPI advantages, the network device drivers have to use the new network API (NAPI). Currently, many network device drivers have NAPI support. Some network drivers, such as Intel Gigabit Ethernet, support NAPI as an option that can be built into the driver, whereas others, such as the BroadCom Tg3 driver, support NAPI by default. If a network driver does not use NAPI, the NAPI code in the kernel is not used either. For more information on NAPI, see the networking/ NAPI_HOWTO.txt file in the Documentation section under the Linux source directory on your system.

For our NAPI test, we used the Intel Gigabit Ethernet driver built with NAPI support. The Intel Gigabit NIC also provides another option to mitigate transmit and receive interrupts. This receive interrupt or receive interrupt delay basically enables the driver to interrupt the processor when the configurable time delay has elapsed. As a result, the processor is not interrupted for every packet. With the advent of high-bandwidth network cards, the interrupt rate has increased tremendously. Without techniques like NAPI or interrupt delay, the processor ends up spinning most of its cycles in interrupt processing. Interrupt delay is discussed in more detail in the section "Netperf3 (Gigabit Ethernet Tuning Case Study)."

NAPI has helped improve network throughput performance in Internet packet forwarding services such as routers. NAPI test results are shown in Tables 21-2, 21-3, and 21-4. Netperf TCP single stream, UDP stream, and packet forwarding were used to obtain these results. The hardware and software configurations used for these tests include the following:

- Two uniprocessor Pentium III @ 933MHz with Intel Gigabit Ethernet (e1000) NIC
- Linux 2.4.20-pre4 kernel with e1000 driver version 4.3.2-k1
- NAPI patch

The Receive Interrupt Delay (RxIntDelay) was set to 1 in the case of NAPI because RxIntDelay=0 caused a problem, and RxIntDelay was set to 64 in the case of base e1000 driver without NAPI support. The receive and transmit descriptors were set to 256 on both systems for the e1000 driver. For the TCP Stream test, the TCP socket size was set to 131070. The test duration for both the TCP Stream and the UDP Stream was 30 seconds. One million packets at 970 kpackets per second were injected into the packet-forwarding experiments.

The packet-forwarding results in Table 21-4 clearly show that NAPI is a winner for routing packets. TCP and UDP stream tests using Netperf, as shown in Tables 21-2 and 21-3, indicate that NAPI does not improve network throughput. In fact, network throughput caused performance to moderately regress.

Table 21-2   Netperf TCP Single Stream with and Without NAPI

Message Size (Bytes)	e1000 Baseline in Mbps	e1000 NAPI in Mbps
4	20.74	20.69
128	458.14	465.26
512	836.40	846.71
1024	936.11	937.93
2048	940.65	939.92
4096	940.86	937.59
8192	940.87	939.95
16384	940.88	937.61
32768	940.89	939.92
65536	940.90	939.48
131070	940.84	939.74

Table 21-3   Netperf, UDP_STREAM, with and Without NAPI

Intel e1000 Driver Baseline Throughput in Mbps	Intel e1000 Driver with NAPI Support Throughput in Mbps
955.7	955.7

Table 21-4   Packet Forwarding (Routing) with and Without NAPI

Intel e1000 Driver Baseline Throughput in Packets Forwarded	Intel e1000 Driver with NAPI Support Throughput in Packets Forwarded
305	298580

The results of TCP stream, UDP stream, and packet forwarding in Tables 21-2, 21-3, and 21-4 show that NAPI helped improve performance significantly in routing tests. Because NAPI is optionally available in many network drivers, you can choose to use NAPI depending on your environment.

TCP Offload Engine Support

Server applications that do not use some of the unique features of the Linux TCP/IP protocol, such as IP filtering or quality of service (QoS), can instead use network interface cards that support TCP/IP offloading to improve network performance. TCP Offload Engine (TOE) technology consists of software extensions to existing TCP/IP stacks that enable the use of hardware planes implemented on specialized TOE network interface cards (TNICs). This hardware/software combination lets operating systems offload all TCP/IP traffic to the specialized hardware on the TNIC. As a result, the server resources are no longer needed to process TCP/IP frames and are used instead for application and other system needs, bolstering overall system performance. This sounds like a great solution for improving network performance; however, general-purpose TCP offload solutions have repeatedly failed, and TOE is suitable for some specific application environments. One of the contexts where TCP Offload is suitable is the storage-specific interconnect via commoditized network hardware, and another context is high-performance clustering solutions.

Analysis of Gigabit Ethernet workloads indicates that for every gigabit of network traffic a system processes, a GHz of CPU processing power is needed to perform the work. With the advent of higher-speed processor systems, high-performance serial PCI-Express system buses, Ethernet controllers with built-in checksum operations logic, and interrupt mitigation, users will be able to use multiple Gigabit Ethernet connections in servers without performance degradation. However, the improvement in network bandwidth also keeps pace with the improvements in other system components that necessitate a solution like TOE to improve network performance. But TCP Offload as a general-purpose solution has failed due to fundamental performance issues and the difficulties resulting in the complexities of deploying TCP Offload in practice. TOE has both proponents and opponents in the academic and commercial worlds. However, many vendors develop TNICs that are used for various workloads in addition to clustering and network storage solutions.

The TOE solutions are proprietary and vary in functionality when compared to Linux TCP/IP software stack code; unique features such IPCHAINS, IPTABLES, and general-purpose packet handling capability may not be available in these proprietary TOE solutions. Many vendors that build TNICs and drivers support different operating systems. Although our early results showed a 17% improvement in NetBench performance on Linux, the drivers used were not stable at the time they were tested, so further investigation is needed for this feature. More stable drivers and NICs should yield higher performance results.

Note that TOE is different from TCP Segmentation Offloading (TSO). TSO offloads only the segmenting of data. In the case of TSO, the TCP/IP stack hands the whole message that the application passed it to the NIC in one frame. The NIC splits the data (message) into multiple frames, building headers to each frame for transmission. This offload is done only for the send side (outbound traffic); it does not handle the inbound traffic. On the other hand, TOE offloads the whole TCP/IP stack processing to the NIC, which includes both inbound and outbound processing.

Although the TOE solution is a much-needed technology for improving network performance, how it will be adopted by the Linux open source community is yet to be seen. The contention of some in the open source community is that because the Linux TCP/IP stack already supports Zerocopy, the number of copies is already reduced. The checksum, segmentation offloading, and interrupt mitigation support in the NIC would get most of the benefit from TOE adoption, so there is no need for TOE because these remaining functions handle basic socket management and process wakeup. If the TOE solution evolves and can show a tremendous advantage over the software network stack, adoption of the TOE technology might increase.

For now, only commercial companies are developing TOE engines. As a result, the implementation of this solution varies from vendor to vendor. Perhaps the vendors will be able to mitigate or resolve the difficulties in the implementation and deployment of TOE and change the minds of skeptics who are unwilling to accept the TOE solution as a viable alternative for improving network performance.

CASE STUDY

This section presents the results of the benchmarks used for the case study and shows the cumulative improvements of all the performance enhancement features discussed so far. Some of the benchmarks captured the cumulative gain of all the features, whereas others captured selected gains for specific workloads.

NetBench

Figure 21-4 summarizes the performance improvements made to the NetBench benchmark throughput through various Linux kernel and Samba enhancements and tuning. These tests were conducted on a Pentium 4 system with four 1.5GHz P4 processors, four gigabit Ethernet adapters, 2GB memory, and fourteen 15k rpm SCSI disks. SUSE version 8.0 was used for all tests. Each subsequent test included one new kernel, tuning, or Samba change. The NetBench Enterprise Disk Suite by Ziff-Davis was used for all tests.

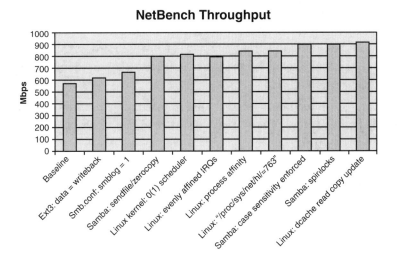

Figure 21-4 NetBench case study.

The following list describes the column names in Figure 21-4:

- *Baseline.* Represents a clean installation of SUSE Enterprise Linux Server 8.0 (SUSE SLES 8) with no performance configuration changes.
- *data=writeback.* A configuration change was made to the default Ext3 mount option from `ordered` to `writeback` for the /data file system (where the Samba shares reside). This improved file system performance greatly on metadata-intensive workloads such as this one.
- *smblog=1.* The Samba logging level was changed from 2 to 1 to reduce disk I/O to the Samba log files. A level of 1 is verbose enough to log critical errors.
- *SendFile/Zerocopy.* A patch that makes Samba use SendFile for client read requests. This, combined with Linux Zerocopy support (first available in 2.4.4), eliminates two very costly memory copies.
- *O(1) scheduler.* A small improvement that will facilitate other performance improvements in the future. The O(1) scheduler is the multiqueue scheduler that improves the performance of symmetrical multiprocessors. This is the default scheduler in the Linux 2.5 and 2.6 kernels.
- *evenly affined IRQs.* Each of the four network adapters' interrupts was handled by a unique processor. SUSE SLES 8, for P4 architecture, defaults to a round-robin assignment (`destination = irq_num % num_cpus`) for IRQ-to-CPU mappings. In this particular case, all of the network adapters' IRQs are routed to CPU0. This can be very good for performance because cache warmth on this code is improved, but

one CPU may not be able to handle the entire network load as more NICs are added to the system. The ideal solution is to evenly affine these IRQs so that each processor handles interrupts from one NIC. Along with process affinity, this should keep the process that is assigned to a particular NIC also assigned to one CPU for maximum performance.

- *process affinity.* This technique ensures that for each network interrupt that is processed, the corresponding smbd process is scheduled on the same CPU to further improve cache warmth.

> This is primarily a benchmark technique and is not commonly used elsewhere. If a workload can logically be divided evenly across many CPUs, this can be a big gain. Most workloads in practice are dynamic, and affinity cannot be predetermined.

- */proc/sys/net/hl=763.* Increases the number of buffers held in the network stack code so that the network stack code does not have to call the memory system to get or free a buffer from and to the memory system. This tuning is not available in the 2.6 kernel.

- *case sensitivity enforced.* When case sensitivity is not enforced, Samba might have to search for different versions of a filename before it can start that file, because many combinations of filenames can exist for the same file. Enforcing case sensitivity eliminates those guesses.

- *spinlocks.* Samba uses fcntl() for its database, which can be costly. Using spinlocks avoids a fcntl() call. The use of the Big Kernel Lock found in posix_lock_file() reduces contention and wait times for Big Kernel Lock. To use this feature, configure Samba with --use-spin-locks, as shown in the following example:

```
Smbd  --use-spin-locks  -p <port_number> -O<socket option>
-s <configuration file>
```

- *dcache read copy update.* Directory entry lookup times are reduced with a new implementation of dlookup(), using the read copy update technique. Read copy update is a two-phase update method for mutual exclusion in Linux that allows avoiding of the overheads of spin-waiting locks. For more information, see the locking section of the Linux Scalability Effort project.

Netperf3 (Gigabit Ethernet Tuning Case Study)

Gigabit Ethernet NICs are becoming cheaper and are quickly replacing 100Mb Ethernet cards. The system manufacturers are including Gigabit Ethernet on motherboards, and system suppliers and integrators are choosing Gigabit Ethernet network cards and switches for connecting disk servers, PC computer farms, and departmental backbones. This section looks at gigabit network performance in the Linux operating system and how tuning the Gigabit Ethernet improves network performance.

The Gigabit Ethernet network cards (Intel Gigabit Ethernet and Acenic Gigabit Ethernet) have a few additional features that facilitate handling high throughput. These features include support for jumbo frame (MTU) size, interrupt-delay, and TX/RX descriptors:

- *Jumbo frame size.* With Gigabit Ethernet NICs, the MTU size can be greater than 1500 bytes. The limitation of 1500 MTU for 100Mb Ethernet does not exist anymore. Increasing the size of the MTU usually improves the network throughput, but make sure that the network routers support the jumbo frame size. Otherwise, when the system is connected to a 100Mb Ethernet network, the Gigabit Ethernet NICs will drop to 100Mb capacity.

- *Interrupt-delay/interrupt coalescence.* The interrupt coalescence can be set for receive and transmit interrupts that let the NIC delay generating interrupts for the set time period. For example, when RxInt is set to 1.024us (which is the default value on Intel Gigabit Ethernet), the NIC places the received frames in memory and generates an interrupt only when 1.024us has elapsed. This can improve CPU efficiency as it reduces the context switches, but at the same time, it also has the effect of increasing receive packet latency. If properly tuned for the network traffic, interrupt coalescence can improve CPU efficiency and network throughput performance.

- *Transmit and receive descriptors.* This value is used by the Gigabit Ethernet driver to allocate buffers for sending and receiving data. Increasing this value allows the driver to buffer more incoming packets. Each descriptor includes a transmit and receive descriptor buffer along with a data buffer. This data buffer size depends on the MTU size; the maximum MTU size is 16110 for this driver.

Other Gigabit Ethernet studies also indicate that for every Gigabit of network traffic a system processes, approximately 1GHz of CPU processing power is needed to perform the work. Our experiment also proved that this is true, but adding more GHz processors and more Gigabit Ethernet network cards did not scale the network throughput even when the number of GHz processors equaled the number of Gigabit Ethernet NICs. Other bottlenecks, such as system buses, affect the scalability of the Gigabit Ethernet

NICs on SMP processors. The NIC test shows that in only three out of four NICs media speed was achieved.

These tests were run between a Pentium 4 1.6GHz 4-way machine and four client machines (Pentium 3 1.0GHz) capable of running 1 gigabit NIC at media limit. All machines had the Linux 2.4.17 SMP vanilla kernel. The e1000 driver was version 4.1.7. These are Netperf3 PACKET_STREAM and PACKET_MAERTS runs, all with an MTU of 1500 bytes. The Pentium 4 machine had 16GB RAM with four CPUs. The four NICs were distributed equally between 100MHz and 133MHz PCI-X slots. The hyperthreading was disabled on the Pentium 4 system.

The PACKET_STREAM test transfers raw data without any TCP/IP headers. None of the packets transmitted or received go through the TCP/IP layers. This is a test that only exercises the CPU, memory, PCI bus, and the NIC's driver to look for bottlenecks in these areas. The interrupt delay and transmit and receive descriptors for the Gigabit driver were tuned with different values to determine what works best for the environment. Another element of tuning was added using different socket buffer sizes.

Table 21-5 shows that the maximum throughput achieved is 2808 Mbps out of four NICs, and the tuning that helped achieve this throughput are 4096 transmit and receive descriptors and interrupt delay set to 64 for both the receive and send sides with a 132k socket buffer size.

Table 21-5   Intel Gigabit NICs Tuning Case Study

Receive / Four Adapters / Four Processors / 2.4.17 Kernel

Descriptors, Interrupt Delay	Socket Size	Total Throughput (Mbps)	Dropped Packets %		% CPU (vmstat)
			Driver	Upper Layers	
256,16	131072	2472	35	72	41.0
256,16	65536	2496	35	72	39.2
256,16	32768	2544	33	71	38.2
256,64	131072	2628	37	68	46.6
256,64	65536	2640	35	69	43.2
256,64	32768	2700	24	68	39.6
256,96	131072	2628	25	64	45.2
256,96	65536	2664	23	64	45.6

Receive / Four Adapters / Four Processors / 2.4.17 Kernel

Descriptors, Interrupt Delay	Socket Size	Total Throughput (Mbps)	Dropped Packets %		% CPU (vmstat)
			Driver	Upper Layers	
256,96	32768	2724	19	61	41.2
4096,16	131072	2628	28	98	27.8
4096,16	65536	2664	29	98	28.0
4096,16	32768	2640	28	98	27.8
4096,64	131072	2808	19	97	28.6
4096,64	65536	2784	20	97	28.4
4096,64	32768	2664	25	97	30.4
4096,96	131072	2772	18	97	28.2
4096,96	65536	2748	19	97	28.6
4096,96	32768	2616	21	97	28.6

VolanoMark

The VolanoMark benchmark creates 10 chat rooms of 20 clients. Each room echoes the messages from one client to the other 19 clients in the room. This benchmark, not yet an open source benchmark, consists of the VolanoChat server and a second program that simulates the clients in the chat room. It is used to measure the raw server performance and network scalability performance. VolanoMark can be run in two modes: loopback and network. The loopback mode tests the raw server performance, and the network mode tests the network scalability performance. VolanoMark uses two parameters to control the size and number of chat rooms.

The VolanoMark benchmark creates client connections in groups of 20 and measures how long it takes the server to take turns broadcasting all the clients' messages to the group. At the end of the loopback test, it reports a score of the average number of messages transferred per second. In network mode, the metric is the number of connections between the clients and the server. The Linux kernel components stressed with this benchmark include TCP/IP, the scheduler, and signals.

Figure 21-5 shows the results of the VolanoMark benchmark run in loopback mode. The improvements shown resulted from various factors such as tuning the network, kernel enhancements, and two prototype patches. The Performance team at the IBM Linux

Technology Center created the prototype patches, but they have not been submitted to the upstream kernel. The first patch is the priority preemption patch, which enables a process to run longer without being preempted by a higher-priority process. Because this policy of turning off the priority preemption is not acceptable for all workloads, the patch is enabled through a new scheduler tuning parameter. The other patch, the TCP soft affinity patch, is related to TCP/IP, so a detailed discussion of this patch is not appropriate for this chapter.

The loopback code path in the TCP/IP stack is inefficient. The send and receive threads of this benchmark always execute on different CPUs in an SMP system. This results in extra loading of data in two different L2 caches. To make the sender and the receiver threads of a connection execute on the same CPU, the code is changed to wake the receiver thread on the sender's CPU. Because the O(1) scheduler tries to keep the thread on the same processor, after the receiver thread is moved to the sender CPU, the receiver thread stays on the sender CPU, eliminating the loading of the same data on two different CPUs.

Patch1 in Figure 21-5 is the SMP Scalable Timer patch. Patch2 is the Scheduler Priority Preemption patch. Patch3 is the TCP Soft Affinity patch. The SMP Scalable Timer patch is already included in the 2.5 Linux kernel. The two prototype patches are done to exemplify the problems unique to this benchmark. These patches are enabled in the kernel through the configuration option and can be made available through tuning to suit appropriate workloads. The Priority Preemption patch was submitted to the open source community, but the TCP soft affinity is not disclosed except in this book.

Additional enhancements that are part of the 2.5 and 2.6 kernels and that improved the performance of VolanoMark include the O(1) scheduler and the SMP scalable timer.

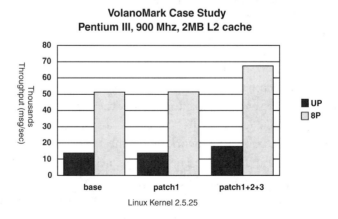

Figure 21-5   VolanoMark case study.

SPECWeb99

The SPECWeb99 benchmark presents a demanding workload to a web server. This workload requests 70% static pages and 30% simple dynamic pages. Sizes of the web pages range from 102 bytes to 921,000 bytes. The dynamic content models GIF advertisement rotation; there is no SSL content. SPECWeb99 is relevant because web serving, especially with Apache, is one of the most common uses of Linux servers. Apache is rich in functionality but is not designed for high performance. Apache was chosen as the web server for this benchmark because it currently hosts more web sites than any other web server on the Internet. SPECWeb99 is the accepted standard benchmark for web serving. SPECWeb99 stresses the following kernel components:

- Scheduler
- TCP/IP
- Various threading models
- SendFile
- Zerocopy
- Network drivers

Figures 21-6 and 21-7 show the results of SPECWeb99 using web static content and web dynamic content, respectively. Also included is a description of the hardware and software configurations used for each test.

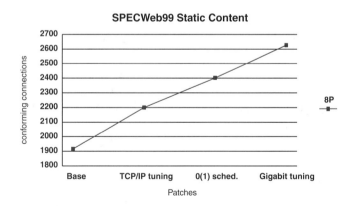

Intel 8-way 900 MHz Pentium III with 2MB L2 cache, 32GB RAM (4) GB Ethernet
Red Hat 7.1 Linux 2.4.17 kernel Apache 2.0.36, SPECWeb99 1.02

Figure 21-6   SPECWeb99 static content case study.

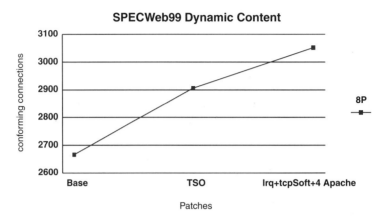

Figure 21-7   SPECWeb99 dynamic content case study.

Some of the issues we have addressed that have resulted in the improvements shown include adding O(1) and RCU dcache kernel patches and adding a new dynamic API mod_specweb module to Apache.

SUMMARY

This case study clearly shows that network performance in the Linux 2.4, 2.5, and 2.6 kernels has been improving because of new feature enhancements. The TCP/IP Offload Engine is a controversial piece of work that is likely to become an important performance enhancement for the Linux storage network workload. The TCP Segment Offload, process and IRQ affinity, SendFile, and Zerocopy are all important network features likely to be widely exploited by network applications. SPECWeb99 SSL is an examination of the benchmark results from SPECWeb99. On Linux, SPECWeb99 SSL is an indication that Linux network performance is comparable to that of other commercial operating systems.

In this chapter, only the performance of some of the network features was discussed. Asynchronous network I/O, which improves the number of simultaneous connections a server can sustain, is not discussed. Features such as Stream Control Transmission Protocol (SCTP) and IPV6 that are being added to the 2.5 and 2.6 kernels were not explored here. The Linux 2.5 and 2.6 kernels also support 10 Gigabit Ethernet NICs, whose performance evaluation will be another interesting topic for future work. Determining whether multiple Gigabit Ethernet NICs scale on newer processors and on higher-speed buses is another challenge that needs evaluation to improve Gigabit Ethernet NIC scalability.

Network SMP scalability and NIC scalability were discussed to some extent, but as network bandwidth increases, the system bus, processor, and other system components need to improve to keep up with the higher-bandwidth network data. Therefore, the performance of high-bandwidth networks, such as Gigabit, is likely to improve as the systems improve.

Another technological development that is being introduced to overcome the Gigabit Ethernet bottleneck is remote direct memory access (RDMA). RDMA is a network interface card feature that lets one computer directly place information in the memory of another computer. RDMA justifies offloading the TCP/IP protocol more than any other application.

The Linux network performance study is a vibrant subject relevant to the entire computing community. How the emerging technologies in networking are being adopted by Linux and evaluated for performance are ongoing areas of interest for the Linux and networking communities.

REFERENCES

[1] Netbench benchmark. `http://www.veritest.com/benchmarks/netbench/default.asp`.

[2] Netperf. `http://www.netperf.org`.

[3] Netperf3 patch. `http://www-124.ibm.com/developerworks/opensource/linuxperf/netperf/netperf3_patch`.

[4] VolanoMark benchmark. `http://www.volano.com/benchmarks.html`.

[5] SPECWeb99. `http://www.spec.org/web99`.

[6] Molnar, Ingo. `http://people.redhat.com/mingo/O(1)-scheduler`.

[7] McKenney, Paul. "Using RCU in the Linux 2.5 Kernel," Kernel Korner, Issue 114, *Linux Journal*.

[8] McKenney, Paul E., et al. "Read-Copy Update," Ottawa Linux Symposium 2001.

[9] TSO study. `http://www.dell.com/us/en/biz/topics/power_ps1q03-intel.htm`.

[10] A sample program to set the process affinity in Linux. `http://www-124.ibm.com/developerworks/opensource/linuxperf/netperf/patches/Affinity_program`.

[11] Open Source kernel locking project. http://lse.sourceforge.net/locking/.

[12] Kelly, T. "Improving the Performance of a Gigabit Ethernet Driver under Linux," DataTAG project meeting, February 2003, University College London. http://www-lce.eng.cam.ac.uk/~ctk21/papers/.

[13] Hughes-Jones, R., et al. "Performance Measurements on Gigabit Ethernet NICs and Server Quality Motherboards." http://datatag.web.cern.ch/datatag/pfldnet2003/papers/hughes-jones.pdf.

[14] Priority Preemption patch. http://www-124.ibm.com/developerworks/opensource/linuxperf/volanomark/15Oct02/pri_preempt-2.5.38.patch.

[15] TCP Soft Affinity patch created by Linux Technology Center, IBM. http://www-124.ibm.com/developerworks/opensource/linuxperf/netperf/patches/tcp_softaffinity_patch.

[16] SMP Scalable Timer patch. http://www.uwsg.iu.edu/hypermail/linux/kernel/0101.3/0930.html.

[17] SCTP. http://www.sctp.org/.

[18] IPV6. http://www.ipv6.org/.

[19] RDMA Over TCP. Breaking the Gigabit Ethernet bottleneck. http://www.nwfusion.com/columnists/2004/080204tolly.html.

[20] RDMA. http://www.rdmaconsortium.org/home.

[21] SendFile patch created by Linux Technology Center, IBM. http://www-124.ibm.com/developerworks/opensource/linuxperf/netperf/patches/sendfile_patch.

[22] Mogul, J.C. "TCP Offload Is a Dumb Idea Whose Time Has Come." http://www.usenix.org/events/hotos03/tech/full_papers/mogul/mogul_html/.

## CHAPTER TWENTY-TWO

Case Study: Commercial Workload Tuning

By Wilfred C. Jamison

INTRODUCTION

This chapter is a case study of application servers with an emphasis on performance analysis and tuning. In this chapter, you'll learn about the following:

- What is involved in commercial workload tuning
- The standard workload benchmark for J2EE application servers
- The principles and guidelines for performance analysis and tuning
- The step-by-step process of tuning a real performance problem presented through a specific example

We'll begin by examining what is involved in commercial workload tuning.

OVERVIEW OF COMMERCIAL WORKLOAD TUNING

Using a commercial workload to benchmark a Linux server is the best way to fully cover most, if not all, subsystems in the server. The application server, which is the typical mode for servicing commercial applications, involves many layers of the software performance stack described in Chapter 21, "Case Study: Network Performance on Linux."

Performance analysis of an application server is a system-wide process that involves analyzing the network configuration, the file system, the JVM, the kernel scheduler, memory usage, and CPU utilization. Performance analysis might also require analyzing the operating system and obtaining kernel traces and kernel profiling information, as well as obtaining information from the JVM itself using the JVM's debugging and tracing utilities. Last, performance analysis might include gathering performance data on the application itself with an application-level profiler.

Instead of presenting an actual commercial workload of a specific enterprise, this chapter works with commercial workload models, which are typically used in performance benchmarks and analysis. Commercial workload models are also often used in reference implementations of new programming model specifications. For example, when J2EE was introduced, a sample application called PetStore was used to illustrate some of the best practices for J2EE application development. PetStore was also intended for customers to use when building their own enterprise web applications. PetStore is a commercial workload model for online retail applications. Sun maintains a blueprint of the Java PetStore at `http://java.sun.com/blueprints/`.

Commercial workloads are typically simulated using a representative application for a given application domain. The performance of an application server can then be determined by tuning the application server and the system platform. Most performance testing of commercial workloads is done by gradually increasing the load against the server until a saturation point is reached.

One of the hardest parts of performance tuning is making sense of the performance data that has been collected and determining the problem that needs analysis.

STANDARD COMMERCIAL WORKLOAD MODEL FOR J2EE

Currently, there is only one accepted industry-wide standard benchmark application for J2EE-compliant application servers. The benchmark, SPECjAppServer, is from the SPEC organization and is the successor to ECPerf, which was the premier benchmark application in 2000. The SPECjAppServer application emulates a heavyweight manufacturing, supply chain management, and order/inventory system. Because the goal of SPECjAppServer is to benchmark the EJB container, it uses a thin Java client to send requests via RMI/IIOP instead of HTTP requests to the web server.

In 2001, SPECjAppServer2001 was developed in a concerted effort by companies such as IBM, BEA, and Oracle. SPECjAppServer2001 is based on the J2EE 1.2 specifications. Currently, a new benchmark application called SPECappPlatform is being developed that is designed to measure the scalability and performance of enterprise platforms that are based on J2EE and .NET with web services. SPECappPlatform is a superset of SPECjAppServer. SPECjAppServer2002, which was released in September 2002, is similar to SPECjAppServer2001 except that the SPECjAppServer2002 is based on the J2EE 1.3 specification. More specifically, SPECjAppServer2002 uses EJB 2.0 instead of EJB 1.1, which was used in J2EE 1.2.

The SPECjAppServer2002 benchmark consists of order and manufacturing applications. The throughput of this benchmark is directly related to the load (injection rate) used by these applications. Hence, the injection rate needs to be increased to scale up the throughput. The metric Total Operations Per Second (TOPS) is the average number of successful total operations per second completed during the measurement interval.

TOPS is composed of the total number of business transactions completed in the customer domain added to the total number of work orders completed in the manufacturing domain, normalized per second. The benchmark also requires a number of rows to be populated in the various tables. The cardinality of the customer orders and supplier tables scale based on the load (which is influenced by the injection rate). Therefore, as the injection rate is increased, the database grows larger.

A number of submissions from different vendors showcase the performance of their application servers using the SPECjAppServer standard workload. There are several categories, depending on how the system was configured (for example, dual node and distributed). Information about SPECjAppServer and submission results is available publicly at `http://www.spec.org/jAppServer2002`.

OUR COMMERCIAL WORKLOAD MODEL: STOCK TRADING

The representative application domain discussed in this chapter is stock trading. Not only is the domain widely known, but it is also representative of many electronic businesses online that use the "buy and sell" model, which is rudimentary to commerce. The application, called Trade3, is a benchmarking application developed by IBM for measuring the performance of its own application server, the IBM WebSphere Application Server. Trade3 is publicly available from IBM at `http://www-306.ibm.com/software/webservers/appserv/benchmark3.html`.

Trade3 models an electronic stock brokerage providing web-based online securities trading. Trade3 uses many features of J2EE 1.3, which is the supported J2EE version by IBM WebSphere Application Server Version 5.1. Some of the items included in J2EE 1.3 are local interfaces, message-driven beans, and Container-Managed Relationships (CMRs). Trade3 also incorporates web services as one of its major enhancements. For more information about J2EE 1.3, visit the Sun web site at `http://java.sun.com/j2ee/1.3/index.jsp`.

Before jumping into the performance analysis exercise, the remainder of this section discusses the following three areas:

- The configuration of the system in which the application is deployed. In performance analysis, it is highly important to fully understand the system-wide configuration. All future analyses will be based on this understanding. In a real customer environment, this configuration can be very complicated. For example, firewalls and DMZ might be in place, a number of geographically dispersed subnetworks hosting the same application could exist, database replication might occur on different hosts, and gateways to legacy systems or web services might be available to external systems. You also need to know the hardware specifications used across the entire system to account for their performance contribution.

- Background information on the Trade3 application from the user's perspective without discussing how the application was implemented or how many J2EE features it uses. Performance tuning requires that you have some background information on the enterprise application itself because some performance problems can be traced back to the enterprise application.

- The performance analysis methodology. When fixing a performance problem, it is important to have a good methodology in place. Not only does it allow you to solve the problem in a very systematic way, it also makes the whole experience less painful.

The next section details the configuration of the system where the application used for our performance exercise was run.

System Configuration

The case study involves a four-tier, nonclustered configuration, as shown in Figure 22-1. There are four machines, one for each tier, that are connected via a 100mbps Ethernet network. As indicated, all four machines have exactly the same specifications. The first tier is the client tier with a workload driver that sends HTTP requests to the web server. The driver, a homegrown tool called the Web Performance Tool (WPT), simulates concurrent users by creating a thread for each virtual user. WPT lets you specify the URL requests to send to the web server and the number of concurrent users who will send those requests. For the length of the test run, you can specify either the total number of requests that need to be sent or an absolute period of time—for example, 15 minutes. At the end of each run, the tool outputs statistics such as throughput, average response time, total requests sent, and number of failed responses.

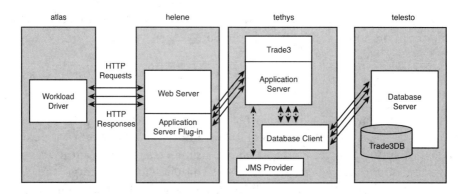

Machine Specs: UnitedLinux 1.0, Kernel 2.4.21-17-smp, 2-Way Intel Xeon 2.8GHz, Cache size 512KB, 4GB RAM 30GB Disk, 2GB swap

Note: All four machines are identical.

Figure 22-1   Four-tier configuration for the Trade3 performance benchmark.

The second tier contains an Apache-based web server along with a plug-in that allows the web server to route requests to the application server. Putting the web server in a separate machine is a common configuration in big enterprises. For security purposes, the web server might be placed in a DMZ (demilitarized zone) where it is protected by two firewalls.

The third tier contains the application server with the Trade3 application. The application server used is the IBM WebSphere Application Server 5.1. The Trade3 application uses two resources—one for messaging through the JMS framework and the other for data source. The messaging is used for notification that a transaction, such as buying stock, has been completed. The data source contains user account information as well as stocks and their prices. The JMS provider is IBM WebSphere MQ v5.1, which ships with the application server. The database provider, which is located in the fourth tier, is IBM DB2 v8.1 SP3. The JDBC driver uses type 2, which requires a DB2 database client module running on the application server box to communicate with the database server. The arrows in the diagram indicate the flow of data. Arrows with dotted lines indicate data flow within the same box.

After Trade3 was installed on the application server, the database, Trade3DB, was populated with 500 users and 1,000 stocks using the application itself as a configuration option. The queues for JMS were also created, and IBM WebSphere MQ processes were started.

A Little More About Trade3

About 75% of the time performance problems can be attributed to the application. Thus, it is important to profile the application to find potential performance problems. Ideally, the development team should practice *software performance engineering*, which advocates the early consideration of performance from the beginning of the development cycle. For some, this may be a revolutionary idea—quite different from what most of us were taught in school.

In this exercise, we assume that Trade3 has been carefully analyzed and optimized. Our focus is on the system itself—the application server, database server, and Linux. This section shows what the application looks like from a user's perspective and how it flows.

Use any browser to get to the application by entering the URL `http://helene/trade`, where *helene* is the hostname of the web server. The Trade3 welcome page is shown in Figure 22-2. The welcome page itself shows the high-level architecture of the Trade3 application. It shows that requests can be handled by either a servlet or a web service. This chapter does not use any of Trade3's web services features.

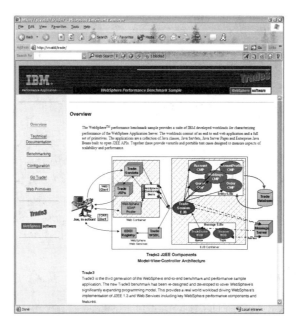

Figure 22-2   Trade3's welcome page.

Trade3 uses servlets to process requests and then passes the requests to WebSphere's Command Bean framework. From there, the requests are wrapped in a command bean and passed to a session bean in the EJB container. From the EJB container, the session bean decides which entity beans the request must be handled by as well as any message-driven beans (MDBs). The entity beans actually access the database, while the MDBs talk to the JMS provider. Response back to the user is implemented through JSPs.

To use the application, click Go Trade! Trade3 prompts you for a username and password. After validation, the home screen opens for the user who logged on, as shown in Figure 22-3.

Figure 22-3   The Trade3 home screen after a successful login.

After you are inside the home screen, you can view your account and edit your account information. To sell some of your stocks, click the Portfolio link. A screen similar to what is shown in Figure 22-4 opens. You can sell a stock by clicking the Sell link of the corresponding stock or "holding" what you want to sell. Similarly, click the Quotes/Trade link if you want to buy a stock. The screen for buying stocks is shown in Figure 22-5.

To check the current price of a stock, check its ticker symbols. To buy the stock, specify in the corresponding box the number of shares to buy, and then click Buy. The transaction is processed, and you are notified when the transaction has been completed.

Figure 22-4 The Portfolio screen, where you can sell a stock.

When we run our performance tests, the workload driver sends HTTP requests corresponding to logging in to an account, viewing an account, buying and selling a stock, and logging out.

Figure 22-5 The screen for buying stocks.

Performance Analysis and Methodology

Before attempting to analyze and tune the performance of any system, you need a well-defined methodology for carrying out the analysis. Table 22-1 lists several points to consider when developing a methodology for performance analysis and tuning.

For the performance exercise discussed in this chapter, the main goal is to determine the maximum capacity of the 2-way 2.8GHz System on IBM WebSphere Application Server 5.1 running Trade3 on Linux (kernel 2.4.21-17smp). *Capacity* refers to the number of concurrent users. The requirements are as follows:

- The throughput is maximized.
- The average response time is no more than two seconds.

Some Key Points to Remember When Tuning for Performance

- Know what the performance requirements/goals are, and determine which performance metrics really matter.

- Perform the right test for the right purpose.

- Define how the test will be performed—what data to use, how long is a test run, when do you start getting numbers during the run, what tools to use, and so on.

- Stick to the performance goals. Do not attempt to change them unless there are good reasons to do so—for example, the goals are unrealistic given the environment.

- It is important that the tests be done consistently and that results are repeatable if exactly the same set of data and procedures were used.

- Change only one variable at a time when running a series of tests for problem analysis or diagnosis.

- Record all results in a methodical manner with very good documentation. Your records are good if someone can understand the historical results, visualize the tests without having seen them, and draw some conclusions.

- Automate the procedures whenever possible to reduce human error. However, it is important that the correctness of the automation be verifiable and that 100% confidence in the test results can be claimed.

- Minimize sharing of resources whenever possible to avoid contamination. If sharing is inevitable, back up your system before giving up resources for the next person. It is also a good practice to maintain an audit trail of what changes were made to the system.

- Perform the same test run at least three times to make sure that the numbers are right.

The next step is to determine which performance tests need to be run. We need to do a User Ramp Up test to determine the performance of the system while the workload is increased. The workload is influenced by the number of concurrent users sending requests to the server. We will stop increasing the workload when the average response time goes above 2 seconds. To maximize throughput, the CPU utilization can be near 100% on the application server as long as there are no major bottlenecks. Thus, important metrics to gather for each test run are CPU utilizations on the web, application and database servers, the throughput, and the average response time.

A performance test run consists of a warmup run followed by the actual run. For each actual run, the number of concurrent users should be defined in the workload driver. Our test starts with one user, then two, then five, and continues to double the number of users from then on. The warmup run consists of sending 1,000 requests by one user, then by two users, five users, 10 users, 20 users, and so on up to 100 users. An actual test run is 5 minutes long. The actual test run (for a given number of concurrent users) should be repeated three times. No warmup is needed between these runs, but the database needs to be reset. The final results should be the average of the three runs. Make sure that the results produced by these three runs are not very different from each other. Use the sar or iostat tools to get the CPU utilization of each box. You should be able to differentiate between the CPU used by the user processes and the CPU used by the system (kernel).

In the case study, the tests were run with no *think time*. When a user submits an HTTP request, he waits until he gets the response in his browser. Typically, a user spends some time (for example, reading the page) before sending another HTTP request. That time interval is called think time (or pause time). So by not specifying any think time (think time=0) to the workload driver, a user immediately submits the next request upon receiving the response to the previous request. Eliminating think time works the application server really hard. In the real world, however, users do pause for some time. One hundred concurrent users with no think time is actually equivalent to a higher number of users in the real world. There is no exact formula for computing for the actual "higher number of users," but the most simplistic approximation is to multiply the number of users by the estimated think time divided by the average response time plus 1. While a user is thinking for, say, 8 seconds, other users are submitting their requests and waiting for the response to come back. If the average response time is 2 seconds, that means that while the user was thinking, four other users were able to submit a request and get a response. Four other users plus the thinking user equals five. Multiplying five by 100 gives us 500 users, which is the estimated number of real-world users.

THE PERFORMANCE ANALYSIS EXERCISE

The remainder of this chapter is devoted to the actual tuning exercise of the Trade3 application on our four-tier system configuration. Because the goal is to make sure that Trade3 can utilize the most precious resource, the CPU, in the three boxes (especially the application server box), the first thing we did was capture the initial performance data by performing a User Ramp Up test run.

The goal of User Ramp Up tests is to determine the maximum amount of CPU that will be utilized by the three boxes (web server, application server, and database server), and at what amount of workload. The amount of workload corresponds to the number of users submitting requests at the same time (the users are called concurrent users). As we increase the workload by adding more users, the CPU utilization is expected to go up as well, as are the throughput (requests processed per second) and the average response time. At some point, no matter how many more users are added, the throughput no longer increases significantly and the CPU utilization of the application server remains almost the same. The only thing that changes significantly is the response time, which is expected because more users are contending for resources. When this point is reached, the system has reached its saturation point.

We can be confident that good performance is achieved if the application server box achieves close to 100% CPU utilization, because that means the bottleneck is the CPU. To get more throughput, either the system needs to be tuned further or more CPUs need to be added to the box to create a cluster. In the performance world, it is best for the bottleneck source to be the CPU because the workload at which the system maxes out is the system's capacity. So, if 1,000 users max out the system with two CPUs, that means that the system's capacity is 1,000 concurrent users (with zero think time) with a throughput of X.

Initially, the web and application servers are set up with the out-of-the-box configuration (that is, not tuned). The database server, on the other hand, is tuned the best we can in an application-independent way. It is not the purpose of this chapter to show how to tune the database server, because it depends on which database product you are using. The same is true for the JMS provider.

Table 22-1 shows our initial performance data. A corresponding graph for throughput and response time is shown in Figure 22-6. CPU utilization has two numbers (separated by a slash). The first number is the portion for the user and the second is the portion for the system. We used the sar tool to get this information. A heuristic that we commonly use is that the system usage should not be more than 20% of the total CPU utilization. We want to minimize system calls so that user code can do more work and thus increase the throughput. Too much time spent on the system can indicate inefficiencies or problems in the kernel. The Little's Law column is a convenient way to verify the validity of our response time and throughput on each run. The law says that the product of the throughput and response time is equal to the number of concurrent users. The numbers are rounded off to the nearest whole number. In some instances, when the number of concurrent users is large, Little's Law might not give the exact number, but it should be very close.

Table 22-1   Initial Performance Data for the User Ramp Up Test of Trade3

Number of Concurrent Users	Throughput (Req/Sec)	Avg Response Time (Seconds)	Application Server CPU %	Database Server CPU %	Little's Law
1	15.92	0.062	10.7/1.16	1.83/0.47	1
2	30.72	0.064	20.84/2.25	3.87/0.82	2
5	54.82	0.09	41.16/4.89	9.05/1.74	5
10	67.69	0.147	51.96/5.35	12.48/2.31	10
20	67.7	0.294	53.22/6.38	14.29/2.32	20
40	67.03	0.597	52.98/5.73	16.84/2.56	40
80	66.7	1.2	49.99/5.93	16.41/2.19	80
160	62.1	2.562	51.81/6.34	18.19/2.57	159

These numbers show that there is a serious performance problem. The numbers show that the throughput started to stay almost the same at 10 concurrent users (which also gave the highest throughput) at a response time of about 0.3 seconds. The CPU utilization of the application server started to maintain at that time. Thus, the highest CPU utilization was about 28% to 29%, which is a horrible number by anyone's standard. At 80 users, although the throughput is on par with the previous ones, the response time already went above the requirement of no more than 2 seconds response time. Thus, the acceptable number of concurrent users that this application server can handle is between 40 and 80—more likely between 65 and 70.

Figure 22-6 is a visual representation of the performance data. The figure shows where the saturation point is and at what number of users the performance remains acceptable. The immediate goal now is to find out why the system's saturation point is at a very low CPU utilization of the application server.

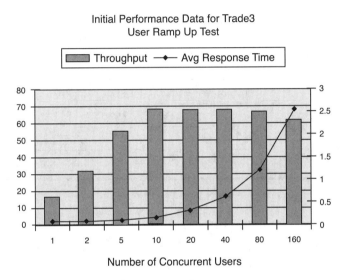

Figure 22-6   Initial User Ramp Up Graph

The Web Server

Although not shown in our table, we noticed that the CPU utilization on the web server tier is very low—about 3%. There are times when the system usage is even higher than the user usage, but this is really not much of an issue because the numbers are very low to begin with. So, we are hypothesizing that the web server itself is the bottleneck and that it goes on a wait state too long or too many times (which explains the low CPU utilization). Thus, this could cause a lower rate of requests being passed on to the application server.

This assumption is easy to verify. The plug-in passes the original HTTP request "as-is" to the application server. The application server has an HTTP transport layer that can accept full-fledged HTTP requests through port 9080. This means that we could skip the web server altogether and make the workload driver send the request to tethys:9080.

The test was performed starting with 10 users to see if we could see some improvements. The second set of performance data is shown in Table 22-2. Unfortunately, there is no significant difference from the original results. The throughput and response time are still within the range. The same is true with the application server CPU utilization. Thus, we can eliminate the web server as the source of the problem.

Table 22-2   Performance Data for Trade3 User Ramp Up Test Without the Web Server

Number of Concurrent Users	Throughput (Req/sec)	Avg Response Time (seconds)	Application Server CPU%	Database Server CPU%	Little's Law
10	68.17	0.145	52.34/7.11	12.62/2.22	10
20	69.75	0.285	52.87/7.29	14.51/2.45	20
40	69.23	0.576	54.75/7.92	15.85/2.29	40
80	68.52	1.167	54.15/6.45	18.64/2.5	80

The Database Back End: A Bottleneck?

One way to view this problem is to investigate what causes the application server to "wait." From our knowledge of the application, there is a significant portion of the code that calls the database back end. The application uses container-managed entity beans extensively. It is possible that the application server is being blocked somehow due to some contentions in the database, physical disk, or buffers, which then cause the application server to spend too much time waiting on the database.

There are two approaches to determine if this is the case. The first is to get to the database server and collect some traces, either through the database debugging facilities or with Linux tools. We recommend the database debugging tools because they immediately provide information about locks and waits on the database. Linux tools require the correlation of system-level information to the database, which might not be that straightforward. The second, and easier, approach is to look into the application server to check if many or some of its threads are waiting on the database to respond back. If so, we know that the database is the bottleneck.

Thread Dump

Examining the thread dump from the Java Virtual Machine is a useful way to detect where possible bottlenecks might be. The dump provides a snapshot of information on the current state of each thread in the JVM and the history of the threads' execution through stack traces. Possible states are as follows:

- *R* for running, which means that the thread is actively executing (it does not necessarily mean that it is actually running, but at least it is in the runqueue of the kernel scheduler).
- *CW* for conditional wait, which means that the Java thread has explicitly invoked the `wait()` method on an object and that it is waiting to be notified. Thus, if the notification does not arrive soon, the thread will wait a long time and might cause a bottleneck if other threads are depending on this thread to run before they can proceed. Otherwise, it is not that harmful.
- *MW* for monitor wait, which means that the thread is queued in a monitor of a Java object. Remember that all Java objects have their own monitor. A thread would get in this state if it enters a *synchronized* method or block and another thread has already gotten the "right" to execute the synchronized method or block. Unless that executing thread leaves the synchronized method or block, no other thread waiting on it can proceed. Thus, this is the highest possible cause of bottlenecks.

We will perform one test run with 10 concurrent users. During that time, we will take note of the process ID of the Java process (which corresponds to the application server). During the run, we will issue the following command:

```
# kill -3 process id
```

You can check the process ID of the application server by looking for Java processes using the `ps` command. Some application servers log their process ID when they are started. Although the command says "kill," it does not terminate the process. Instead, it produces a thread dump and saves it on a file of the form *javacorexxxxxxx.txt*. Note that thread dumps are not part of the JVM or Java Specifications, so different JVM implementations might use different filenaming schemes. We typically issue this command in succession (three to five times) to get more than one thread dump and to monitor the progress of the threads by checking to see if they ever change their state at all.

> Never take a thread dump if you are running a test run and getting performance data. Thread dumps slow down the JVM and thus affect its performance.

We took a thread dump of the application server while running a test with 10 concurrent users. Thread dumps can be huge files, depending on the number of threads in the JVM. Thread dump output also provides information about the system and the JVM.

Although this chapter does not cover how to interpret thread dump output, for the purposes of this case study, we are only interested in finding out if any threads are in the MW state—specifically, on the database routines.

Figure 22-7 shows a snippet of thread information from the thread dump that we took. Note that we show only the topmost part of the stack trace because the stack traces are really deep. The thread in Figure 22-7 is just one of the Servlet.Engine. Transports threads (threads are pooled in this application server). This thread is basically a worker thread that receives the request from the plug-in and executes it. As you can see, the state of the thread is R. The top of the stack trace tells us that this thread is in the JDBC code, which communicates with the local database client. The database client communicates with the remote database server.

```
3XMTHREADINFO      "Servlet.Engine.Transports : 360" (TID:0x105389C0, sys_thread_t:0x941D0B8, state:R, native
ID:0x6EC38) prio=5
4XESTACKTRACE           at COM.ibm.db2.jdbc.app.DB2XAResource.xaCommit(Native Method)
4XESTACKTRACE           at COM.ibm.db2.jdbc.app.DB2XAResource.commit(DB2XAResource.java(Compiled Code))
4XESTACKTRACE           at com.ibm.ws.rsadapter.spi.WSRdbXaResourceImpl.commit(WSRdbXaResourceImpl.java(Compiled
Code))
4XESTACKTRACE           at com.ibm.ejs.j2c.XATransactionWrapper.commit(XATransactionWrapper.java(Compiled Code))
4XESTACKTRACE           at
com.ibm.ws.Transaction.JTA.JTAXAResourceImpl.commit_one_phase(JTAXAResourceImpl.java(Compiled Code))
4XESTACKTRACE           at
com.ibm.ws.Transaction.JTA.RegisteredResources.flowCommitOnePhase(RegisteredResources.java(Compiled Code))
4XESTACKTRACE           at
com.ibm.ws.Transaction.JTA.RegisteredResources.distributePrepare(RegisteredResources.java(Compiled Code))
4XESTACKTRACE           at com.ibm.ws.Transaction.JTA.TransactionImpl.internalPrepare(TransactionImpl.java(Compiled Code))
4XESTACKTRACE           at com.ibm.ws.Transaction.JTA.TransactionImpl.commit(TransactionImpl.java(Compiled Code))
4XESTACKTRACE           at com.ibm.ws.Transaction.JTA.TranManagerImpl.commit(TranManagerImpl.java(Compiled Code))
4XESTACKTRACE           at com.ibm.ws.Transaction.JTA.TranManagerSet.commit(TranManagerSet.java(Compiled Code))
4XESTACKTRACE           at com.ibm.ejs.csi.TranStrategy.commit(TranStrategy.java(Compiled Code))
4XESTACKTRACE           at com.ibm.ejs.csi.TranStrategy.postInvoke(TranStrategy.java(Compiled Code))
4XESTACKTRACE           at com.ibm.ejs.csi.TransactionControlImpl.postInvoke(TransactionControlImpl.java(Compiled Code))
4XESTACKTRACE           at com.ibm.ejs.container.EJSContainer.postInvoke(EJSContainer.java(Compiled Code))
4XESTACKTRACE           at com.ibm.ejs.container.EJSContainer.postInvoke(EJSContainer.java(Compiled Code))
4XESTACKTRACE           at com.ibm.websphere.samples.trade.ejb.EJSRemoteStatelessTradeEJB_90439d68.getQuote(Unknown
Source)
4XESTACKTRACE           at com.ibm.websphere.samples.trade.ejb._Trade_Stub.getQuote(_Trade_Stub.java(Compiled Code))
4XESTACKTRACE           at com.ibm.websphere.samples.trade.command.QuoteCommand.performExecute(Unknown Source)
4XESTACKTRACE           at com.ibm.websphere.command.LocalTarget.executeCommand(LocalTarget.java(Compiled Code))
4XESTACKTRACE           at com.ibm.ws.cache.command.CommandCache.executeCommand(CommandCache.java(Compiled
4XESTACKTRACE           at
com.ibm.ws.webcontainer.webapp.WebAppRequestDispatcher.handleWebAppDispatch(WebAppRequestDispatcher.java(Compiled
Code))
```

Figure 22-7   A snippet of a thread stack trace taken from a thread dump.

We examined all of the threads, and none of them are in the MW state. In fact, all threads that are in the JDBC code are in the R state. We can conclude that the database server is not a bottleneck because none of the threads is blocked by it.

Database I/O Activity

The next step is to check the I/O activity at the database server. We ran the same test and used `iostat` on the database server:

```
iostat -d 2
```

This command monitors the disk activity every 2 seconds. Following is a segment of the trace:

Device:	tps	Blk_read/s	Blk_wrtn/s	Blk_read	Blk_wrtn
dev3-0	39.00	0.00	400.00	0	800

Device:	tps	Blk_read/s	Blk_wrtn/s	Blk_read	Blk_wrtn
dev3-0	32.50	0.00	480.00	0	960

Device:	tps	Blk_read/s	Blk_wrtn/s	Blk_read	Blk_wrtn
dev3-0	49.00	0.00	504.00	0	1008

Device:	tps	Blk_read/s	Blk_wrtn/s	Blk_read	Blk_wrtn
dev3-0	33.00	0.00	356.00	0	712

Device:	tps	Blk_read/s	Blk_wrtn/s	Blk_read	Blk_wrtn
dev3-0	33.50	0.00	380.00	0	760

Device:	tps	Blk_read/s	Blk_wrtn/s	Blk_read	Blk_wrtn
dev3-0	34.50	0.00	364.00	0	728

Device:	tps	Blk_read/s	Blk_wrtn/s	Blk_read	Blk_wrtn
dev3-0	32.00	0.00	464.00	0	928

Device:	tps	Blk_read/s	Blk_wrtn/s	Blk_read	Blk_wrtn
dev3-0	39.50	0.00	400.00	0	800

Device:	tps	Blk_read/s	Blk_wrtn/s	Blk_read	Blk_wrtn
dev3-0	25.50	0.00	280.00	0	560

Device:	tps	Blk_read/s	Blk_wrtn/s	Blk_read	Blk_wrtn
dev3-0	20.00	0.00	216.00	0	432

We removed the other devices from this trace because there were no activities on them. The trace shows not a lot of I/O activity (write operations) is going on, which leads to one possibility. Because the database is actually doing some work, and none of the application server threads is blocked on the database, it is apparent that communication or transfer of data is occurring. Even when the workload is increased, the I/O activity remains the same, and yet none of the threads is blocked. This might mean that the communication between the application server and the database server is the bottleneck. The rate of data transfer over the wire is the same regardless of the load. The threads are taking a long time to receive and send data. Note that sending and receiving data is a task and that is why the threads are in the R state.

Network Activity Between the Application Server and Database Server

We suspect that the network speed between the application server and the database server is slow. The quickest way we can tell this is to use the `ping` command. When we ping the workload driver, which is the host atlas, the following is returned:

```
PING atlas.raleigh.ibm.com (9.27.175.20) from 9.27.175.25 : 56(84)
  bytes of data.
64 bytes from atlas.raleigh.ibm.com (9.27.175.20):icmp_seq=1
ttl=128 time=0.220 ms
64 bytes from atlas.raleigh.ibm.com (9.27.175.20):icmp_seq=2
ttl=128 time=0.127 ms
64 bytes from atlas.raleigh.ibm.com (9.27.175.20):icmp_seq=3
ttl=128 time=0.127 ms
64 bytes from atlas.raleigh.ibm.com (9.27.175.20):icmp_seq=4
ttl=128 time=0.125 ms
64 bytes from atlas.raleigh.ibm.com (9.27.175.20):icmp_seq=5
ttl=128 time=0.121 ms
64 bytes from atlas.raleigh.ibm.com (9.27.175.20):icmp_seq=6
ttl=128 time=0.124 ms
64 bytes from atlas.raleigh.ibm.com (9.27.175.20):icmp_seq=7
ttl=128 time=0.127 ms
64 bytes from atlas.raleigh.ibm.com (9.27.175.20):icmp_seq=8
ttl=128 time=0.119 ms
64 bytes from atlas.raleigh.ibm.com (9.27.175.20):icmp_seq=9
ttl=128 time=0.128 ms
64 bytes from atlas.raleigh.ibm.com (9.27.175.20):icmp_seq=10

ttl=128 time=0.126 ms
```

When we ping the database server, which is the host telesto, we get the following output:

```
PING telesto.raleigh.ibm.com (9.27.175.24) from 9.27.175.25 : 56(84)
  bytes of data.
64 bytes from telesto.raleigh.ibm.com (9.27.175.24):icmp_seq=1
ttl=64 time=1.96 ms
64 bytes from telesto.raleigh.ibm.com (9.27.175.24):icmp_seq=2
ttl=64 time=0.384 ms
64 bytes from telesto.raleigh.ibm.com (9.27.175.24):icmp_seq=3
ttl=64 time=0.448 ms
```

```
64 bytes from telesto.raleigh.ibm.com (9.27.175.24):icmp_seq=4
ttl=64 time=5.61 ms
64 bytes from telesto.raleigh.ibm.com (9.27.175.24):icmp_seq=5
ttl=64 time=0.382 ms
64 bytes from telesto.raleigh.ibm.com (9.27.175.24):icmp_seq=6
ttl=64 time=0.389 ms
64 bytes from telesto.raleigh.ibm.com (9.27.175.24):icmp_seq=7
ttl=64 time=0.677 ms
64 bytes from telesto.raleigh.ibm.com (9.27.175.24):icmp_seq=8
ttl=64 time=0.356 ms
64 bytes from telesto.raleigh.ibm.com (9.27.175.24):icmp_seq=9
ttl=64 time=1.99 ms
64 bytes from telesto.raleigh.ibm.com (9.27.175.24):icmp_seq=10
ttl=64 time=1.19 ms
```

Comparing the turnaround time for both outputs, it is clear that something is not right with the connection to the database server. To investigate the cause of this problem, the recommended approach is to try first from the lowest level—hardware, connections, NIC, and network drivers—before even going into tuning the TCP/IP stack. An important question to ask is "What speed and duplex are being used by the database server's network card?"

To determine the speed and duplex of the database server's network card, we log on to the database server and issue the command `mii-tool`. Unfortunately, the mii-tool on the database server fails with the following message:

```
SIOCGMIIPHY on 'eth0' failed: Operation not supported
```

A tool that is useful when the mii-tool does not work is ethtool. We issue `ethtool` on the database server (we know that eth0 is the interface that we are using on this server) as follows:

```
# ethtool eth0
```

Output from ethtool follows:

```
Settings for eth0:
     Supported ports: [ TP ]
     Supported link modes:   10baseT/Half 10baseT/Full
                             100baseT/Half 100baseT/Full
                             1000baseT/Full
     Supports auto-negotiation: Yes
     Advertised link modes:  10baseT/Half 10baseT/Full
                             100baseT/Half 100baseT/Full
                             1000baseT/Full
     Advertised auto-negotiation: Yes
     Speed: 10Mb/s
     Duplex: Half
```

```
Port: Twisted Pair
PHYAD: 0
Transceiver: internal
Auto-negotiation: on
Supports Wake-on: umbg
Wake-on: d
Link detected: yes
```

The output indicates that the current setting for eth0 is 10Mbps using half-duplex. This is a very big discovery that could help improve performance. To change the setting, issue the following command:

```
# ethtool -s eth0 speed 100 duplex full
```

Note that you could also set the speed to "auto" instead of 100. We ran the same tests again after fixing the network card settings. Table 22-3 summarizes the new results. The improvements gained were phenomenal. We raised the maximum CPU utilization on the application server from ~59% to ~94%. Also, we added 56% more to the maximum throughput. More importantly, we now can support up to 200 users and still get a response time of less than 2 seconds.

Table 22-3   Resulting Performance Data After Fixing the Network Problem

Number of Concurrent Users	Throughput (Req/Sec)	Avg Response Time (Seconds)	Application Server CPU%	Database Server CPU%	Little's Law
1	25.48	0.038	16.19/1.7	1.87/0.85	1
2	46.04	0.042	33.72/3.52	4.19/1.79	2
5	77.38	0.063	61.06/6.72	9.18/3.15	5
10	89.43	0.110	81.45/8.27	11.2/3.46	10
20	106.12	0.187	89.25/9.94	14.09/3.94	20
40	104.76	0.380	86.47/10.77	14.27/4.46	40
80	102.15	0.782	85.48/10.02	14.55/4.38	80
160	101.86	1.564	83.74/10.23	14.28/4.20	159
200	101.17	1.971	84.77/10.01	14.03/4.07	199
220	102.02	2.15	84.25/10.10	14.47/4.03	219

We challenged ourselves to do better because 6% of CPU is not being used.

The Java Virtual Machine

The next step is to tune the application server and the JVM. Because IBM WebSphere Application Server does not use the hotspot technology in its JVM, there is only one thing that we need to investigate—the heap size settings. The default values used are a minimum of 50MB and a maximum of 256MB. To determine if the defaults are the right values or if we have enough heap, we need to examine the garbage collection (GC) activities in the JVM. We know that garbage collection is an overhead that must be minimized to get more throughput from the application. So we ran one test with 20 concurrent users and enabled the -verbosegc flag in the JVM parameters. The garbage collection outputs are emitted on the standard error, so we need to redirect them to a file.

Analyzing the raw output of verbosegc from the file is very tedious and time consuming. We developed a tool called *GCAnalyzer* to capture this information and summarize the results. The tool graphs each garbage collection event and shows how much memory was collected and how much is still live. We used the tool with gc.output as the name of the file where the raw GC outputs were saved using the following command:

```
GCAnalyzer -mb –chartdata gc.txt gc.output
```

This command specifies that all units be expressed in megabytes and that, in addition to the summary, a text file, gc.txt, be produced that can be imported from Microsoft Excel to create a graph. The results of the summary are shown here:

```
Total  number of GC: 222
Total runtime=464541 ms.
Total number of GC: 222
Total time in GC: 21997 ms.
 % of time spent on GC: 4%
Avg GC time: 99 ms.
Longest GC time: 146 ms.
Shortest GC time: 14 ms.
Avg. time between GC: 1993 ms.
Avg. GC/Work ratio: 0.047361907
Avg. bytes needed per GC: 1380 bytes
Total garbage collected: 7,400.87 MB
Avg garbage collected per GC: 33.34 MB
Total live memory: 12,559.26 MB
Avg live memory per GC: 56.57 MB
Avg. % heap of free bytes before GC: 0.9 %
Avg. % heap of free bytes after GC: 38.12 %
Avg. % heap as garbage per GC: 37.03 %
```

```
Avg. marking time: 83 ms.
Avg. sweeping time: 12 ms.
Number of compaction(s): 6 (2.7%)
Avg. compaction time: 1 ms.
Number of heap expansion(s): 4 (1.8%)
Avg. expansion time:  34 ms.
Avg  size of additional bytes per expansion: 11632 KB.
Avg. garbage created per second (global): 16.74  MB per second
```

Looking at these numbers, we cannot see a major problem with garbage collection. In fact, the amount of time spent on garbage collection is only 4% of the 5-minute test run. In our experience, 5% is the upper limit that can be imposed for a good garbage collection time. Performing garbage collection is very quick—83ms for marking and 12ms for sweeping, and the compaction time is 1ms! We believe that there was a great improvement with the garbage collector in JVM 1.4.1, which is the version that comes with IBM WebSphere Application Server 5.1. Figure 22-8 further shows there is no problem with garbage collection.

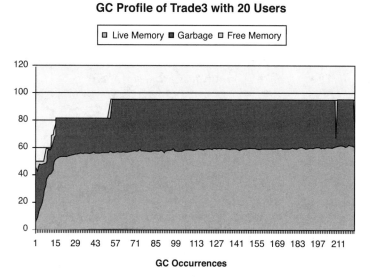

Figure 22-8   The resulting graph taken from the GCAnalyzer output.

We can infer from the graph that the heap size settled at around 98MB, which is a lot less than the 256MB maximum that was set. In other words, there is no need to increase the heap size. Note that the first few garbage collections took place during the startup of the application server.

However, another JVM flag, `Xnoclassgc`, might help improve performance. `Xnoclassgc` causes GCAnalyzer to avoid collecting class objects that are not used when the garbage collection occurs. Given the good garbage collection profile, we do not foresee a major improvement. However, it is worth testing the flag because if it gives us more throughput, it is still worth it. We tested with that flag, and as expected, the results showed miniscule improvement, but we decided to retain the flag anyway.

The Application Server

A layer in the software performance stack that might need tuning is the application server itself. Different application servers might have different tuning knobs to offer, but they are very similar in many respects. This is partly due to the fact that they are all J2EE-based.

Thread Pools

The first thing to address within the application server is the thread pool. Pooling threads is typical in all application servers. This is a good approach because providing threads is the responsibility of the application server—enterprise applications are not supposed to create threads. Thread pooling is a performance-enhancing mechanism for avoiding the cost of creating and destroying threads whenever they are needed.

Linux kernels 2.4 and earlier are very sensitive to threads, especially where a large number of active threads are in the system. This is because these kernels are still using the original threading model and scheduler. Linux was initially designed for small desktops with one processor, so the original design of the scheduler was not very concerned with scaling issues. Linux uses a single runqueue for all threads. Thus, a number of processors that are ready to take a queued runnable process must synchronize their access to the queue. Worse, the scheduler evaluates each process in the queue to choose which of them must be scheduled next. The time complexity is a function of the number of threads in the queue. This explains why a larger thread pool may perform worse. Somehow, it is faster to make some other requests wait for an available thread than to assign a thread to it and contribute to the cost of scheduling. Linux kernel 2.6, however, introduced the $O(1)$ scheduler and a new threading model that conforms to Native POSIX. In the $O(1)$ scheduler, each processor has its own runqueue instead of the single-queue model.

For now, we need to look at our thread pool size because we are using kernel 2.4. The default thread pool size of the web container is 50. By setting it at 20, we get the results shown in Table 22-4.

Table 22-4   Results of Setting the Web Container Thread Pool Size to 20

Number of Concurrent Users	Throughput (Req/Sec)	Avg Response Time (Seconds)	Application Server CPU %	Database Server CPU %	Little's Law
10	96.04	0.103	79.33/8.68	13.91/4.18	10
20	106.81	0.186	87.92/11.15	14.05/3.95	20
40	109.01	0.336	89.23/9.72	14.03/4.42	40
80	107.19	0.745	88.56/10.59	13.88/4.33	80

Compared to the results shown in Table 22-3, we see considerable improvement. We also figured that the benefit will be manifested more with users 20 and up because that is where we can see the benefits of fewer threads and more incoming requests.

Pass-by-Reference

The next parameter to set is the pass-by-reference in the ORB component of the application server. The J2EE specification mandates that all EJB method calls have to pass parameters by value, not by reference. This is needed because for remote method calls, references cannot be maintained in two remote machines. Therefore, the actual values must be passed.

Here is when a knowledge of the application helps. We know that all requests to Trade3 come through the HTTP transport and all EJB calls are done locally in the same JVM. It happens that Trade3 does not change the values of the parameters being passed to EJB method calls. Pass-by-reference is a performance enhancement mechanism where, instead of deeply copying objects, only the references to the objects are passed.

Data Source Prepared Statements and Connection Pool

The prepared statement size and connection pool size of the data source are two knobs that you can tune if you are having database bottlenecks. However, based on our thread dump analysis, we are not experiencing a performance problem on the database side. Thus, it appears that the default value of 60 prepared statements and 50 connection pools works well for the Trade3 workload.

Finally, we reran our tests with pass-by-reference enabled and set the ORB Thread Pool size down to 10. The results are shown in Table 22-5. The performance graph is also shown in Figure 22-9. Compare these results with the initial performance data, and you will see that a big difference has been made. At this point, we have used ~99% of the application server's CPU and raised the number of users to 250.

Table 22-5   Final Results of a Tuned System for the Trade3 Workload

Number of Concurrent Users	Throughput (Req/Sec)	Avg Response Time (Seconds)	Application Server CPU %	Database Server CPU %	Little's Law
1	27.96	0.036	14.65/2.0	2.25/1.12	1
2	50.99	0.038	29.63/3.78	4.61/1.73	2
5	87.61	0.056	53.69/6.54	9.66/3.18	5
10	112.71	0.088	76.40/10.21	14.11/4.17	10
20	124.36	0.159	86.86/11.97	15.94/4.58	20
40	125.89	0.317	87.28/11.78	16.67/4.38	40
80	126.02	0.633	86.94/12.25	17.12/4.94	80
160	126.15	1.263	86.81/12.35	16.85/4.53	159
250	128.49	1.929	87.37/11.94	16.71/4.85	250

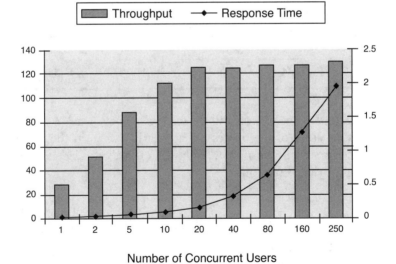

Performance of a Tuned System for Trade3

Figure 22-9   Performance graph of a tuned system running Trade3.

Hyperthreading

Our final attempt to improve performance was to take advantage of the hyperthreading feature of the Intel Xeon processor. Fortunately, our Linux kernel supports hyperthreading. Using the same system in its tuned state, we enabled hyperthreading through the hardware system configuration and recycled the application server box. The results of rerunning the tests are shown in Table 22-6.

Table 22-6   Performance Graph with Hyperthreading

Number of Concurrent Users	Throughput (Req/Sec)	Avg Response Time (Seconds)	Web Server CPU%	Application Server CPU %	Database Server CPU %	Little's Law
1	29.82	0.033	0.44/0.64	8.46/1.53	2.34/1.11	1
2	53.46	0.037	0.82/1.48	17.64/3.27	5.05/1.99	2
5	90.46	0.055	1.26/1.87	41.58/7.47	10.28/3.26	5
10	112.07	0.089	1.67/2.40	67.83/11.20	14.10/4.04	10
20	119.18	0.167	1.92/2.58	81.28/14.08	16.36/4.62	20
40	117.71	0.339	1.53/2.52	79.71/14.44	15.63/4.42	40
80	117.34	0.679	1.54/2.65	79.36/14.06	15.59/4.86	80
160	117.10	1.357	1.51/2.81	79.84/14.21	15.71/4.70	159
250	116.10	2.134	1.60/2.52	81.11/12.66	15.54/4.64	250

It appears that the Trade3 application and the settings we have used so far do not lend to the hyperthreading feature of the processors as clearly shown in the results. This just goes to show that the promise of hyperthreading should be studied carefully and must be applied only in the right situations.

SUMMARY

The main focus of this chapter was performance analysis and tuning of a commercial workload. We provided some background information on this discipline as well as some guidelines for performing this type of task. We also briefly mentioned the effort that is taking place in the industry as far as standardized performance measurement of application servers is concerned.

The majority of this chapter was spent on an example that illustrated step-by-step the process of tuning a commercial workload. The following are some of the key points of this chapter:

- Performance tuning is a skill that is acquired through constant exposure to different problem situations.
- Performance tuning should be executed with a well-defined methodology.
- If there is no obvious suspect, make the problem scope smaller through an elimination process.
- Always choose the easier and faster way to get what you need.
- Always pay attention to the kernel level of your Linux installation. In this way, you will know if you are missing patches, for example.
- Do not expect a patch, a kernel-level parameter, or a tuning parameter to work for you in all cases.
- Always be aware of the changes and improvements being made by the open source community to the Linux operating system.
- Not all new hardware features can be helpful—for example, hyperthreading. A lot of it still depends on the nature and usage pattern of your application and the middleware.

REFERENCES

[1] Gunther, Harvey. "WebSphere Application Server: Best practices for developing high performance Web and enterprise applications," `http://www-306.ibm.com/software/webservers/appserv/ws_bestpractices.pdf`, Sept. 7, 2000.

[2] Comer, Douglas E. *Internetworking with TCP/IP Volume I: Principles, Protocols, and Architecture*, Second Edition, Prentice Hall, New Jersey, 1991.

[3] Jamison, Wilfred C. "Improving Performance of J2EE Applications," *WebSphere Journal*, May 20, 2003.

Tuning Kernel Parameters

By Badari Pulavarti and Narasimha Sharoff

INTRODUCTION

This appendix lists and describes many of the kernel tunable parameters available through the sysctl, /proc, and sysfs interfaces. It provides an overview of how to use the various interfaces to tune the Linux kernel and other key components of the system. Topics covered in this appendix include the following:

- An overview and description of how to use sysctl
- An overview and description of how to use /proc
- An overview and description of how to use sysfs
- A discussion of each type of tunable parameter, including the following:

  General kernel parameters
  Virtual memory parameters
  File system parameters
  Network parameters

THE SYSCTL INTERFACE

The sysctl interface lets you configure kernel parameters at runtime. sysctl lists kernel parameters, modifies the parameters temporarily through the command-line interface, loads the settings from a file, or modifies the kernel parameters permanently by adding in a configuration file for loading at boot time.

The parameters are organized in a hierarchical, or tree, structure. For example, all the parameters related to devices start with *dev*. The parameters for a specific device, such as cdrom, are under dev.cdrom.

By default, kernel support for sysctl is enabled. To enable sysctl support when building a new kernel, use menuconfig, choose General Setup from the main menu, and select sysctl support. Alternatively, you can edit the configuration file to set the CONFIG_SYSCTL option.

Using *sysctl*

The `sysctl` command usually resides in the /sbin directory. You can view the complete list of tunable parameters and their settings by executing the `sysctl -a` command. To set a specific parameter, use the `-w` option. For example, the following command sets the message queue identifiers to 32:

```
$ sysctl -w kernel.shmmax=32
```

Note that this change is temporary and does not persist across system reboots.

To make a change that will persist across reboots, use the `-p` option to load a set of values from a configuration file. In the following example, the values from the configuration file /etc/sysctl.conf are loaded:

```
$ sysctl -p /etc/sysctl.conf
```

For more information on different usage options, refer to the sysctl(8) man page.

The procfs Interface

Another way to modify kernel parameters is to use the file system interface through procfs. The /proc file system (`procfs`) is a special file system. It is a virtual file system; it is not associated with a block device, but exists only in memory. The /proc/ directory shows a hierarchical view of the parameters. You can view the parameters by looking at the file's contents. The parameters can be modified by echoing the value in the file. However, changes made this way do not persist across machine reboots.

/proc is organized into the following directories:

/proc/bus	Bus-specific information
/proc/driver	Driver-specific information
/proc/fs	File system parameters
/proc/irq	Masks for IRQ-to-CPU affinity
/proc/net	Networking information
/proc/scsi	SCSI-related information
/proc/sys	Kernel parameters
/proc/sys/fs	Generic file system data
/proc/sys/kernel	General kernel parameters

/proc/sys/vm	Memory management parameters
/proc/sys/dev	Device-specific information
/proc/sys/sunrpc	RPC information
/proc/sys/net	Networking information
/proc/sysvipc	System V IPC information
/proc/tty	TTY driver information
/proc/*pid*	Per-process information

Using procfs

The parameters can be viewed or changed by writing to the appropriate file in the /proc/ directory.

For example, to view the current value of shmmax, enter the following:

```
$ cat  /proc/sys/kernel/shmmax
```

Similarly, you can change the value of shmmax by entering this command:

```
$ echo "32" > /proc/sys/kernel/shmmax
```

Note that this change is temporary and does not persist across reboots.

SYSFS (LINUX KERNEL 2.6 ONLY)

sysfs is another virtual file system that provides an easy interface to the kernel parameters. Currently, all nonprocess information in the procfs is ported to sysfs. The plan is to combine the sysctl and /proc interfaces into one. sysfs is also designed to replace devfs because drivers are expected to be ported to the new interfaces. This file system is automatically generated by the kernel and updated whenever devices are added or removed.

Using sysfs

The parameters can be viewed or changed by writing to the appropriate file in the sysfs file system.

GENERAL KERNEL PARAMETERS

This section discusses general kernel parameters, including those for the following:

- Shared memory
- Processes
- Signals

- Profiling/debugging
- System

Shared Memory

Sysctl Prefix: kernel
/proc Prefix: /proc/sys/kernel/

Parameter	Description
sem	Semaphore values
msgmnb	Maximum message queue in bytes
msgmni	Maximum allowed message queue identifiers
msgmax	Maximum message size in bytes
shmmni	Number of shared segments system-wide
shmall	Shared memory system-wide in pages
shmmax	Shared segment size in bytes

Processes

Sysctl Prefix: kernel
/proc Prefix: /proc/sys/kernel/

Parameter	Description
thread_max	Maximum threads allowed in the system

Signals

Sysctl Prefix: kernel
/proc Prefix: /proc/sys/kernel/

Parameter	Description
rtsig-max	Maximum real-time signals
rtsig-nr	Number of currently queued real-time signals

Profiling/Debugging

Sysctl Prefix: kernel
/proc Prefix: /proc/sys/kernel/

Parameter	Description
sysrq	System trace request
printk	Printk values

The `printk` parameter has four fields: `console_loglevel`, `default_message_loglevel`, `minimum_console_level`, and `default_console_level`. Messages with a higher priority than `console_loglevel` are printed to the console. Messages without an explicit priority are printed with `default_message_loglevel` priority. The minimum (highest) value to which `console_loglevel` can be set is determined by the `minimum_console_level` parameter. The `default_console_loglevel` is the default value for `console_loglevel`.

System

Sysctl Prefix: kernel
/proc Prefix: /proc/sys/kernel/

Parameter	Description
domainname	Domain name
hostname	Host name
ostype	Operating system type
osrelease	Operating system release
version	Kernel version
real-root-dev	Real root device partition

VIRTUAL MEMORY

Sysctl Prefix: vm
/proc Prefix: /proc/sys/vm/

Parameter	Description
max_map_count	Maximum number of memory map areas per process
max-readahead	Maximum I/O read-ahead size
min-readahead	Minimum I/O read-ahead size
vm.heap-stack-gap	Enforces a gap between heap and stack

The `vm.heap-stack-gap` parameter allows a gap to be enforced between the heap and the stack. Any access to memory in the gap area causes a segmentation fault. This action avoids silent corruption that could occur when allocating on stack runs over the heap. The gap enforced is in number of pages.

Parameter	Description
`pagetable_cache`	Cache size per processor for page tables

The `pagetable_cache` parameter specifies low and high cache size per processor to be used for page tables. On SMP systems, this parameter allows the system to do fast pagetable allocations without having to acquire the kernel memory lock. On a single-CPU system, these values can be set to 0 to avoid wasting memory.

Parameter	Description
`page_cluster`	Pages to read on a page fault

The `page_cluster` parameter is used to determine the number of pages the kernel can read at once on a page fault. The number of pages is 2 ^ `page_cluster`. This VM subsystem tries to reduce excessive seeks by reading multiple pages on a page fault.

Parameter	Description
`kswapd`	Swaps out memory pages to disk

The kernel swapout daemon, kswapd, swaps out pages to disk when memory gets fragmented or full. This is a three-field value that corresponds to `tries_base`, `tries_min`, and `swap_cluster`.

The maximum number of pages kswapd tries to free at once is determined by the `tries_base` field. This number is divided by 4 or 8 to determine the number of pages (mm/vmscan.c).

The `tries_min` field specifies the minimum number of pages kswapd tries to free each time it is called.

The `swap_cluster` field is the number of pages kswapd writes in one turn. Keeping this value large ensures that kswapd does its I/O in large chunks and that the disk doesn't have to seek often. If it is too large, it may cause request queue flooding.

Parameter	Description
`bdflush`	Dirty page handling

The first field, `nfract`, determines the percentage of dirty buffer cache to activate `bdflush`. A higher value can delay disk writes for a longer time but will have to do a lot of I/O when memory becomes short. A lower value spreads I/O more evenly at the cost of frequent I/O operations. The default value is 50%.

The second field, `ndirty`, is the maximum number of dirty blocks that `bdflush` can write to disk at once. A higher value can delay I/O and can lead to I/O burst, whereas a lower value can lead to a memory shortage as `bdflush` isn't awakened frequently enough.

The third field, `nrefill`, is the number of buffers that `bdflush` tries to obtain and add to the list of free buffers when refill is called.

The fourth field, `nref_dirt`, is the dirty buffer threshold for activating `bdflush`.

The sixth field, `age_buffer`, is the maximum time before writing out a dirty normal buffer to disk. The value is in jiffies.

The seventh field, `age_super`, is the maximum time before writing out a dirty super block buffer to disk.

Parameter	Description
`vm_passes`	Memory balancing
`vm_lru_balance_ratio`	Active and inactive cache ratio
`vm_mapped_ratio`	Pageout rate
`vm_cache_scan_ratio`	LRU queue to scan in one go
`vm_vfs_scan_ratio`	VFS queues to scan in one go
`vm_gfp_debug`	Enable to send debug messages to log

The `vm_passes` parameter is the number of vm passes before failing the memory balancing.

The `vm_lru_balance_ratio` parameter determines the balance between active and inactive cache. A bigger value means active cache grows as active cache is rotated slowly.

The `vm_mapped_ratio` parameter determines the pageout rate. A smaller value indicates an early start to pageout.

The `vm_cache_scan_ratio` parameter specifies how much of inactive LRU queue is scanned in one go. A value of 6 implies that a scan of 1/6 of the inactive list is done.

The `vm_vfs_scan_ratio` parameter specifies how much of VFS queues is scanned in one go. A value of 6 implies that 1/6 of the unused inode, dentry, and dquot caches will be freed.

FILE SYSTEM

Sysctl Prefix: fs
/proc Prefix: /proc/sys/fs/

Parameter	Description
`file-max`	Maximum number of file descriptors
`file-nr`	Number of file handles

The system `file_descriptor` limit is set using `file-max`. The descriptor limit is the maximum number of file descriptors that any one process may open at once. The `file-nr` has three fields: the number of allocated file handles, the number of used file handles, and the maximum number of file handles.

Parameter	Description
inode-state	Inode status
inode-nr	Free and used inodes

The first field of `inode-state`, `nr_inodes`, denotes the number of inodes the system has allocated. The second field, `nr_free_inodes`, specifies the number of free inodes. The `inode-nr` parameter contains the first two fields of the `inode-state` parameter.

Parameter	Description
super-max	Maximum number of file systems
super-nr	Number of mounted file systems

The `super-max` parameter controls the maximum number of super blocks and thus determines the maximum number of mounted file systems the kernel can have. This value needs to be increased if there is a need to mount more file systems than the current value in `super-max`.

Parameter	Description
dentry-state	Status of directory cache

The directory entries are dynamically allocated and deleted. These parameter values show the current status. The first field, `nr_dentry`, specifies the number of directory entries. The second field, `nr_unused`, specifies the number of unused directory entries.

Parameter	Description
dquot-nr	Number of allocated and free disk quota entries
dquot-max	Maximum number of cached disk quota entries

Parameter	Description
dir-notify-enable	Enables dnotify

The `dir-notify-enable` field enables or disables the dnotify interface on a system-wide basis.

Parameter	Description
aio-max-nr	Maximum number of AIO requests
aio-nr	Number of AIO requests

NETWORK

This section discusses network kernel parameters, including those for the following:

- Net core
- ICMP
- NEIGHBOR
- CONFIG
- Routing
- TCP
- IP fragmentation

Net Core

Sysctl Prefix: net.core
/proc Prefix: /proc/sys/net/core

Parameter	Description
hot_list_length	Maximum number of skb-heads to be cached
optmem_max	Maximum ancillary buffer size per socket
message_burst	Limits warning messages
message_cost	Limits warning messages
netdev_max_backlog	Maximum number of packets queued
rmem_default	Socket receive buffer size
wmem_default	Socket send buffer size
rmem_max	Maximum receive socket buffer size
wmem_max	Maximum send socket buffer size

The message_cost and message_burst parameters are used to limit the warning messages written to the kernel log. The default setting limits warning messages to one every 5 seconds. The higher the error_cost is, the fewer messages are written. The error_bust parameter controls when messages are dropped.

ICMP

Sysctl Prefix: net.ipv4
/proc Prefix: /proc/sys/net/ipv4

Parameter	Description
icmp_ratemask	Mask value for ICMP types
icmp_ratelimit	Rate for sending ICMP packets

`icmp_ignore_bogus_error_responses`	Warning messages from router
`icmp_echo_ignore_broadcasts`	ICMP echo requests to broadcast addresses
`icmp_echo_ignore_all`	ICMP echo requests
`igmp_max_membership`	Maximum number of multicast groups

The `icmp_ratemask` parameter contains ICMP types for which rates are limited.

The `icmp_ratelimit` parameter limits the maximum rates for sending ICMP packets whose type matches the `icmp_ratemask` parameter to specific targets. A value of 0 disables any limit. The value is in jiffies.

If `icmp_ignore_bogus_error_responses` is enabled, the kernel does not issue any log warnings when routers send bogus responses to broadcast frames.

If the `icmp_echo_ignore_all` parameter is enabled, the kernel ignores all the ICMP echo requests sent to it. If `icmp_echo_ignore_broadcasts` is enabled, the kernel ignores all the ICMP echo requests sent to broadcast/multicast addresses.

The `igmp_max_membership` parameter is the maximum number of multicast groups we can subscribe to.

NEIGHBOR

Sysctl Prefix: net.ipv4.neigh.*interface*
/proc Prefix: /proc/sys/net/neigh/*interface*/

Parameter	Description
`locktime`	Time before replacing an old ARP entry
`proxy_delay`	Maximum time before answering an ARP request
`anycast_delay`	Maximum delay for neighbor solicitation messages
`proxy_qlen`	Maximum queue length of delayed proxy ARP
`unres_qlen`	Maximum queue length for pending ARP request
`gc_stale_time`	Time before a check for stale ARP entries
`delay_first_probe_time`	Delay for first probe if neighbor is reachable
`base_reachable_time`	Validity period of an entry once a neighbor has been found. Default is 30 seconds.
`retrans_time`	Time between neighbor solicitation retransmits
`app_solicit`	Number of requests to send to user-level ARP daemon
`ucast_solicit`	Maximum number of retries for unicast solicitation
`mcast_solicit`	Maximum number of retries for multicast solicitation

CONFIG

Sysctl Prefix: net.ipv4.conf.*interface*
/proc Prefix: /proc/sys/net/conf/*interface*/

Parameter	Description
proxy_arp	Responds to ARP requests if enabled
rp_filter	Source validation is required if enabled
bootp_relay	Accepts packets with 0.x.y.z addresses
accept_source_route	Accepts set of IP addresses to visit on way
send_redirects	Sends ICMP redirects
shared_media	Different subnet communication
secure_redirects	Packet resend using secure interface
accept_redirects	Packet resend on same interface on an ICMP redirect
mc_forwarding	Multicast forwarding
forwarding	IP forwarding

The secure_redirects parameter accepts ICMP redirect messages only for a gateway listed in the default gateway list. The send_redirects parameter determines whether such redirects are sent.

Turning on the accept_source_route parameter gives a packet a list of IP addresses it should go through on its way.

The bootp_relay parameter accepts packets with source addresses of 0.x.y.z with destinations not to this host as local ones. The BOOTP daemon is expected to catch and forward such packets.

The mc_forwarding parameter enables or disables multicast forwarding on this interface.

The shared_media parameter allows the kernel to assume that different subnets on this device can communicate directly.

Routing

Sysctl Prefix: net.ipv4.route
/proc Prefix: /proc/sys/net/route/

Parameter	Description
error_burst	Time before logging a warning message
error_cost	Cost factor for logging a warning message
max_size	Maximum size of routing cache
max_delay	Maximum delay in seconds for flushing routing cache
min_delay	Minimum delay in seconds for flushing routing cache

The `error_cost` and `error_bust` parameters limit the warning messages written to the kernel log. The default setting limits warning messages to one every 5 seconds. The higher `error_cost` is, the fewer messages are written. The `error_bust` parameter controls when messages are dropped.

TCP

Sysctl Prefix: net.ipv4
/proc Prefix: /proc/sys/net/ipv4/

Parameter	Description
`tcp_app_win`	Maximum window for application buffer
`tcp_reordering`	Maximum reordering of packets in a TCP stream
`tcp_max_syn_backlog`	Length of per-socket backlog queue
`tcp_rfc1337`	Sets TCP stack confirming to RFC1337
`tcp_stdurg`	Enables strict RFC793 interpretation of the TCP urgent pointer field
`tcp_fin_timeout`	Time in seconds it takes to receive a final FIN before the socket closes
`tcp_tw_reuse`	Reuse of timewait sockets
`tcp_max_orphans`	Maximum number of orphaned connections
`tcp_max_tw_buckets`	Maximum number of timewait sockets
`tcp_window_scaling`	Enables window scaling as defined in RFC1323
`tcp_timestamps`	Enables timestamps as defined in RFC1323
`tcp_rmem`	Receive buffers for TCP socket
`tcp_wmem`	Send buffers for TCP socket
`tcp_mem`	Memory pages for TCP usage

The `tcp_wmem` parameter has three fields. The first field, `min`, specifies the amount of memory reserved for send buffers for a TCP socket. The second field is the default amount of memory allowed for send buffers for a TCP socket. The last field, `max`, is the maximum amount of memory allowed for automatically selected send buffers for a TCP socket.

The `tcp_rmem` parameter has three fields. The first field, `min`, is the minimum size of receive buffer used by TCP sockets. The second is the default amount of memory allowed for receive buffers used by TCP sockets. The last field, `max`, is the maximum size of the receive buffer allowed for automatically selected receive buffers for TCP sockets.

The `tcp_mem` parameter has three fields. The first field, `low`, specifies the low limit on the number of pages below which TCP is not bothered about its usage of memory pages. The second field is `high`; when the amount of memory allocated by TCP exceeds this, TCP takes corrective actions until memory consumption falls below the low value. The last field, `max`, is the maximum number of pages allowed for queuing by all TCP sockets.

Parameter	Description
tcp_sack	Enables sack to acknowledge when a packet is received
tcp_fack	Enables forward acknowledgment
tcp_dsack	Enables extension to sack for duplicate packet detection
ecn	Enables explicit congestion notification

Parameter	Description
tcp_keepalive_intvl	Frequency of keepalive probes
tcp_keepalive_probes	Number of keepalive probes
tcp_keepalive_time	Keepalive message interval
tcp_syn_retries	Number of initial SYNs for outgoing connection
tcp_retries1	Number of retries for incoming connections
tcp_retries2	Number of retries before terminating

The `tcp_keepalive_probes` parameter is the number of times the probes are sent before killing the nonresponding connections.

The `tcp_syn_retries` parameter is the number of times initial SYNs for a TCP connection are transmitted. This timeout is for outgoing connections. For incoming connections, the number of retransmits is defined by the `tcp_retries1` parameter.

IP Fragmentation

Sysctl Prefix: net.ipv4
/proc Prefix: /proc/sys/net/ipv4

Parameter	Description
ip_nonlocal_bind	Binds to nonlocal IP address
ip_no_pmtu_disc	Disables MTU path discovery
ip_autoconfig	How host got IP configuration
ip_default_ttl	Maximum number of hops a packet may travel
ip_forward	Forward packets between interfaces
ipfrag_time	Time in seconds to keep IP fragment in memory

`ip_dynaddr`	Enables dynamic socket address rewriting on interface address change
`ipfrag_low_thresh`	Low-memory watermark for fragment handler
`ipfrag_high_thresh`	Maximum amount of memory used to reassemble IP fragments
`ip_local_port_range`	Range of ports used by TCP and UDP to choose the local port

INDEX

Symbols

3Com, 343
16-way RAID-0 setup,
    414-415
8-way NUMA RAID setup,
    412-414

A

Above Idle tool (Performance
    Inspector), 102, 104-105
accept_redirects parameter
    (kernel), 517
accept_source_route
    parameter (kernel), 517
access bits, 203
ACEs (access control entries),
    file systems, 236
ACLs (access control lists), 236
active balancing, 191
address spaces, 21
    kernel address space, 21
    Moore's Law, 200
    user address space, 21
    virtual address spaces,
        196-197
        area structures, 198-199
        highmem interface, 201
        kernel address
            spaces, 199
        kernel image
            section, 200

kernel module
    section, 199
paging, 201-203
swapping, 201-203
user address spaces,
    197-198
virtual memory generic
    view, 196
address translation process,
    204-205
addressing, I/O devices,
    229-230
affinity, IRQ, 462-464
AFP file system, 347
AFS/DFS, 347
agebuffer parameter
    (bdflush), 249
AIM7 benchmarks, 142
AIM9 benchmarks, 143, 147
aio-max-nr parameter
    (kernel), 514
aio-nr parameter (kernel), 514
algorithms, code tuning,
    305-328
allocation, pages, 207
allocation groups
    file systems, 236
    XFS (Next-Generation File
        System), 269
analysis methodologies
    (benchmarks), 175-176
    exit strategies, 179

measurements, 177-179
run rules, 176
target setting, 177
tuning, 177-179
anticipatory I/O elevators, 9
anticipatory I/O scheduler
    (AS), 222-225
    decayed frequency
        tables, 224
    lowest logical block
        information, 226
    positioning time, 224
    read anticipation process,
        227-228
    tuning, 224-225
antic_expire parameter
    (AS I/O scheduler), 225
anycast_delay parameter
    (kernel), 516
Apache web servers, tuning,
    338-339
APIs (application programming
    interfaces), 21
    NAPI (network device
        driver API), 464-466
    SendFile, 458-460
applets (Java), 376
application benchmarks,
    133, 161
    database benchmarks,
        164-166
    Java benchmarks, 161-163

521